Mastering Delphi Programming: A Complete Reference Guide

Learn all about building fast, scalable, and high performing applications with Delphi

Primož Gabrijelčič

Packt

BIRMINGHAM - MUMBAI

Mastering Delphi Programming: A Complete Reference Guide

First published: November 2019

Production reference: 1251119

Published by Packt Publishing Ltd.
Livery Place
35 Livery Street
Birmingham
B3 2PB, UK.

ISBN 978-1-83898-911-8

www.packtpub.com

Contributors

About the author

Primož Gabrijelčič started coding in Pascal on 8-bit micros in the 1980s and he never looked back. In the last 20 years, he was mostly programming high-availability server applications used in the broadcasting industry. A result of this focus was the open sourced parallel programming library for Delphi—OmniThreadLibrary. He's also an avid writer and has written several hundred articles, and he is a frequent speaker at Delphi conferences where he likes to talk about complicated topics, ranging from memory management to creating custom compilers.

Packt is searching for authors like you

If you're interested in becoming an author for Packt, please visit `authors.packtpub.com` and apply today. We have worked with thousands of developers and tech professionals, just like you, to help them share their insight with the global tech community. You can make a general application, apply for a specific hot topic that we are recruiting an author for, or submit your own idea.

Table of Contents

Preface

Delphi is a cross-platform Integrated Development Environment (IDE) that supports rapid application development for most operating systems, including Microsoft Windows, iOS, and now Linux with RAD Studio 10.2. If you already know how to use Delphi features, you can easily create scalable applications quickly and confidently with this comprehensive book.

This Learning Path begins by helping you learn how to find performance bottlenecks and apply the correct algorithm to fix them. You'll even brush up on tricks, techniques, and best practices to solve common design and architectural challenges. Next, you'll get up to speed with using external libraries to write better-performing programs. The book will also guide you through the eight most important patterns that'll help you develop and improve the interface between items and harmonize shared memories within threads. Finally, you'll delve into improving the performance of your code and mastering cross-platform RTL improvements.

By the end of this Learning Path, you'll have the expertise you need to address common design problems and efficiently build scalable projects.

This Learning Path includes content from the following Packt products:

- Delphi High Performance by Primož Gabrijelčič
- Hands-On Design Patterns with Delphi by Primož Gabrijelčič

Who this book is for

This Learning Path is for intermediate-level Delphi programmers who want to build robust applications using Delphi features. Prior knowledge of Delphi is assumed.

So, whoever you are, dear reader, I'm pretty sure you'll find something new in this book. Enjoy!

What this book covers

`Chapter 1`, *About Performance,* talks about performance. We'll dissect the term itself and try to find out what users actually mean when they say that a program is performing (or not performing) well. Then, we will move into the area of algorithm complexity. We'll skip all the boring mathematics and just mention the parts relevant to programming. We will also look at different ways of finding the slow (non-performant) parts of the program, from pure guesswork to measuring tools of a different sophistication, homemade and commercial.

`Chapter 2`, *Fixing the Algorithm,* examines a few practical examples where changing an algorithm can speed up a program dramatically. In the first part, we'll look at graphical user interfaces and what we can do when a simple update to `TListBox` takes too long. The second part of the chapter explores the idea of caching and presents a reusable caching class with very fast implementation. In the last part, we'll revisit some code from `Chapter 1`, *About Performance,* and make it faster, again, by changing an algorithm.

`Chapter 3`, *Fine-Tuning the Code,* deals with lots of small things. Sometimes, performance lies in many small details, and this chapter shows how to use them to your advantage. We'll check the Delphi compiler settings and see which ones affect the code speed. We'll look at the implementation details for built-in data types and method calls. Using the correct type in the right way can mean a lot. Of course, we won't forget about the practical side. This chapter will give examples of different optimization techniques, such as extracting common expressions, using pointers to manipulate data, and implementing parts of the solution in assembler. In the end, we'll revisit the code from `Chapter 1`, *About Performance,* and make it even faster.

`Chapter 4`, *Memory Management,* is all about memory. It starts with a discussion on strings, arrays, and how their memory is managed. After that, we will move to the memory functions exposed by Delphi. We'll see how we can use them to manage memory. Next, we'll cover records—how to allocate them, how to initialize them, and how to create useful dynamically-allocated generic records. We'll then move into the murky waters of memory manager implementation. I'll sketch a very rough overview of FastMM, the default memory manager in Delphi. First, I'll explain why FastMM is excellent and then I'll show when and why it may slow you down. We'll see how to analyze memory performance problems and how to switch the memory manager for a different one. In the last part, we'll revisit the `SlowCode` program and reduce the number of memory allocations it makes.

`Chapter 5`, *Getting Started with the Parallel World,* moves the topic to parallel programming. In the introduction, I'll talk about processes and threads, and multithreading and multitasking to establish some common ground for discussion. After that, you'll start learning what not to do when writing parallel code. I'll explain how the user interface must be handled from background threads and what problems are caused by sharing data between threads. Then, I'll start fixing those problems by implementing various kinds of synchronization mechanisms and interlocked operations. We'll also deal with the biggest problem synchronization brings to the code—deadlocking. As synchronization inevitably slows the program down, I'll explain how to achieve the highest possible speed using data duplication, aggregation, and communication. At the end, I'll introduce two third-party libraries that contain helpful parallel functions and data structures.

`Chapter 6`, *Working with Parallel Tools,* focuses on a single topic, Delphi's `TThread` class. In the introduction, I'll explain why I believe that `TThread` is still important even in this modern age. I will explore different ways in which `TThread` based threads can be managed in your code. After that, I'll go through the most important `TThread` methods and properties and explain what they're good for. In the second part of the chapter, I'll extend `TThread` into something more modern and easier to use. Firstly, I'll add a communication channel so that you'll be able to send messages to the thread. After that, I'll implement a derived class designed to handle one specific usage pattern and show how this approach simplifies writing parallel code to the extreme.

`Chapter 7`, *Exploring Parallel Practices,* moves the multithreaded programming to more abstract terms. In this chapter, I'll discuss modern multithreading concepts: tasks and patterns. I'll look into Delphi's own implementation, Parallel Programming Library, and demonstrate the use of `TTask/ITask`. We'll look at topics such as task management, exception handling, and thread pooling. After that, I'll move on to patterns and talk about all Parallel Programming Library patterns: Join, Future, and Parallel For. I will also introduce two custom patterns—Async/Await and Join/Await—and finish the chapter with a discussion on the Pipeline pattern from OmniThreadLibrary.

`Chapter 8`, *Using External Libraries,* admits that sometimes Delphi is not enough. Sometimes the problem is too complicated to be efficiently solved by a human. Sometimes Pascal is just lacking the speed. In such cases, we can try finding an existing library that solves our problem. In most cases, it will not support Delphi directly but will provide some kind of C or C++ interface. This chapter looks into linking with C object files and describes typical problems that you'll encounter on the way. In the second half, I'll present a complete example of linking to a C++ library, from writing a proxy DLL to using it in Delphi.

`Chapter 9`, Introduction to patterns, introduces the concept of patterns. We'll see why patterns are useful and how they should be used in programming. The book will explore the difference between design principles, patterns, and idioms. It will present a hierarchical overview of design patterns, talk a bit about anti-patterns, and finish with a description of some important design principles.

`Chapter 10`, *Singleton, Dependency Injection, Lazy Initialization, and Object Pool,* covers four patterns from the creational group. The chapter will first look into the singleton pattern, which makes sure that a class has only one instance. Next in line, the dependency injection pattern makes program architecture more flexible and appropriate for unit testing. In the second half, the chapter explores two optimization patterns. The lazy initialization pattern saves time and resources, while the object pool pattern speeds up the creation of objects.

`Chapter 11`, *Factory Method, Abstract Factory, Prototype, and Builder,* examines four more creational patterns. The factory method pattern simplifies the creation of dependent objects. The concept can be extended into the abstract factory pattern, which functions as a factory of factories. The prototype pattern is used to create copies of objects. Last, in this group, the builder pattern separates instructions for creating an object from its representation.

`Chapter 12`, *Composite, Flyweight, Marker Interface, and Bridge,* covers four patterns from the structural group. The composite pattern allows client code to treat simple and complex objects the same. The flyweight pattern can be used to minimize memory usage by introducing data sharing between objects. The marker interface allows us to unleash a new level of programming power by introducing metaprogramming. The bridge pattern helps us separate an abstract interface from its implementation.

`Chapter 13`, *Adapter, Proxy, Decorator, and Facade,* explores four more structural patterns. The adapter pattern helps in adapting old code to new use cases. The proxy pattern wraps an object and exposes an identical interface to facilitate caching, remoting, and access control, among other things. The decorator pattern specifies how the functionality of existing objects can be expanded, while the facade pattern shows us how to create a simplified view of a complex system.

`Chapter 14`, *Nullable Value, Template Method, Command, and State,* covers four patterns from the behavioral group. The null object pattern can reduce the need for frequent `if` statements in the code. The template method pattern helps with creating adaptable algorithms. The command pattern shows how we can treat actions as objects. It is a basis for Delphi *actions.* The state pattern allows an object to change its behavior on demand and is useful when we are writing state machines.

`Chapter 15`, *Iterator, Visitor, Observer, and Memento,* examines four more behavioral patterns. The iterator pattern allows us to effectively access data structures in a structure-independent way. This pattern is the basis of Delphi's `for..in` construct. The visitor pattern allows us to extend classes in accordance with the Open/Closed design principle. To write loosely coupled programs that react to changes in the business model, we can use the observer pattern. When we need to store the state of a complex object, the memento pattern comes to help.

`Chapter 16`, *Lock Patterns,* is entirely dedicated to data protection in a multithreaded world and covers five concurrency patterns. The lock pattern enables the code to share data between threads and is the basis for other patterns from this chapter. The lock striping pattern specifies how we can optimize locking when accessing a granular structure, such as an array. The double-checked locking pattern optimizes the creation of shared resources, while the optimistic locking pattern speeds up this process even more. The readers-writer lock is a special version of the locking mechanism designed for situations where a shared resource is mostly read from, and only rarely written to.

`Chapter 17`, *Thread Pool, Messaging, Future, and Pipeline,* finish the overview of design patterns by exploring four more concurrency patterns. As a specialized version of the object pool pattern, the thread pool pattern speeds up thread creation. The messaging pattern can be used to remove shared data access completely, and by doing so, can simplify and speed up the program. The future pattern specifies how we can integrate parallel execution of calculations into existing code. This chapter ends with a discussion of the pipeline pattern, which is a practical application of messaging designed to speed up tasks that are hard to parallelize with other approaches.

Download the example code files

You can download the example code files for this book from your account at `www.packtpub.com`. If you purchased this book elsewhere, you can visit `www.packtpub.com/support` and register to have the files emailed directly to you.

You can download the code files by following these steps:

1. Log in or register at `www.packtpub.com`.
2. Select the **SUPPORT** tab.
3. Click on **Code Downloads & Errata**.
4. Enter the name of the book in the **Search** box and follow the onscreen instructions.

Once the file is downloaded, please make sure that you unzip or extract the folder using the latest version of:

- WinRAR/7-Zip for Windows
- Zipeg/iZip/UnRarX for Mac
- 7-Zip/PeaZip for Linux

The code bundle for the book is also hosted on GitHub at `https://github.com/PacktPublishing/Mastering-Delphi-Programming-A-Complete-Reference-Guide`. In case there's an update to the code, it will be updated on the existing GitHub repository.

We also have other code bundles from our rich catalog of books and videos available at `https://github.com/PacktPublishing/`. Check them out!

Conventions used

There are a number of text conventions used throughout this book.

`CodeInText`: Indicates code words in the text, database table names, folder names, filenames, file extensions, pathnames, dummy URLs, user input, and Twitter handles. Here is an example: "A string parameter `value` is present in a string list."

A block of code is set as follows:

```
function IsPresentInList(strings: TStrings; const value: string): Boolean;
var
  i: Integer;
begin
  Result := False;
  for i := 0 to strings.Count - 1 do
    if SameText(strings[i], value) then
      Exit(True);
end;
```

Bold: Indicates a new term, an important word, or words that you see onscreen. For example, words in menus or dialog boxes appear in the text like this. Here is an example: "Go to **Options** | **Options**, then select **General** | **Search directory**."

Warnings or important notes appear like this.

Tips and tricks appear like this.

Get in touch

Feedback from our readers is always welcome.

General feedback: Email `feedback@packtpub.com` and mention the book title in the subject of your message. If you have questions about any aspect of this book, please email us at `questions@packtpub.com`.

Errata: Although we have taken every care to ensure the accuracy of our content, mistakes do happen. If you have found a mistake in this book, we would be grateful if you would report this to us. Please visit `www.packtpub.com/submit-errata`, selecting your book, clicking on the Errata Submission Form link, and entering the details.

Piracy: If you come across any illegal copies of our works in any form on the Internet, we would be grateful if you would provide us with the location address or website name. Please contact us at `copyright@packtpub.com` with a link to the material.

If you are interested in becoming an author: If there is a topic that you have expertise in and you are interested in either writing or contributing to a book, please visit `authors.packtpub.com`.

Reviews

Please leave a review. Once you have read and used this book, why not leave a review on the site that you purchased it from? Potential readers can then see and use your unbiased opinion to make purchase decisions, we at Packt can understand what you think about our products, and our authors can see your feedback on their book. Thank you!

For more information about Packt, please visit `packtpub.com`.

1
About Performance

"My program is not fast enough. Users are saying that it is not performing well. What can I do?"

These are the words I hear a lot when consulting on different programming projects. Sometimes the answer is simple, sometimes hard, but almost always the critical part of the answer lies in the question. More specifically, in one word - **performing**.

What do we mean when we say that a program is performing well? Actually, nobody cares. What we have to know is what **users** mean when they say that the program is **not** performing well. And users, you'll probably admit, look at the world in a very different way than we programmers.

Before starting to measure and improve the performance of a program, we have to find out what users really mean by the word **performance**. Only then can we do something productive about it.

We will cover the following topics in this chapter:

- What is performance?
- What do we mean when we say that a program performs well?
- What can we tell about the code speed by looking at the algorithm?
- How does the knowledge of compiler internals help us write fast programs?
- Why is it better to measure than to guess?
- What tools can we use to find the slow parts of a program?

What is performance?

To better understand what we mean when we say that a program is *performing* well, let's take a look at a user story. In this book, we will use a fictitious person, namely Mr. Smith, Chief of Antarctica Department of Forestry. Mr. Smith is stationed in McMurdo Base, Antarctica, and he doesn't have much real work to do. He has already mapped all the forests in the vicinity of the station and half of the year it is too dark to be walking around and counting trees, anyway. That's why he spends most of his time behind a computer. And that's also why he is very grumpy when his programs are not performing well.

Some days he writes long documents analyzing the state of forests in Antarctica. When he is doing that, he wants the document editor to *perform* well. By that he actually means that the editor should work *fast enough* so that he doesn't feel any delay (or *lag*, as we call the delay when dealing with user input) while typing, preparing graphs, formatting tables, and so on.

In this scenario, performance simply means *working fast enough* and nothing else. If we speed up the operation of the document editor by a factor of two, or even by a factor of ten, that would make no noticeable improvement for our Mr. Smith. The document editor would simply stay *fast enough* as far as he is concerned.

The situation completely changes when he is querying a large database of all of the forests on Earth and comparing the situation across the world to the local specifics of Antarctica. He doesn't like to wait and he wants each database query to complete in as short a time as possible. In this case, performance translates to **speed**. We will make Mr. Smith a happier person if we find a way to speed up his database searches by a factor a ten. Or even a factor of five; or two. He will be happy with any speedup and he'd praise us up to the heavens.

After all this hard work, Mr. Smith likes to play a game. While the computer is thinking about a next move, a video call comes in. Mr. Smith knows he's in for a long chat and he starts resizing the game window so that it will share the screen with a video call application. But the game is thinking hard and is not processing user input and poor Mr. Smith is unable to resize it, which makes him unhappy.

In this example, Mr. Smith simply expects that the application's user interface will **respond** to his commands. He doesn't care if the application takes some time to find the next move, as long as he can do with the application what he wants to. In other words, he wants a user interface that doesn't **block**.

Different types of speed

It is obvious from the previous example that we don't always mean the same thing when we talk about a program's speed. There is a **real speed**, as in the database example, and there is a **perceived speed**, hinted at in the document editor and game scenario. Sometimes we don't need to improve the program speed at all. We just have to make it not stutter while working (by making the user interface responsive at all times) and users will be happy.

We will deal with two types of performance in this book:

- Programs that react quickly to user input
- Programs that perform computations quickly

As you'll see, the techniques to achieve the former and the latter are somehow different. To make a program react quickly, we can sometimes just put a long operation (as was the calculation of the next move in the fictitious game) into a background thread. The code will still run as long as in the original version but the user interface won't be blocked and everybody will be happy.

To speed up a program (which can also help with a slowly-reacting user interface), we can use different techniques, from changing the algorithm to changing the code so that it will use more than one CPU at once to using a hand-optimized version, either written by us or imported from an external library.

To do anything, we have to know which part of the code is causing a problem. If we are dealing with a big legacy program, problematic part may be hard to find. In the rest of this chapter, we will look at different ways to locate such code. We'll start by taking an educated **guess** and then we'll improve that by **measuring** the code speed, first by using home-grown tools and then with a few different open source and commercial programs.

Algorithm complexity

Before we start with the dirty (and fun) job of improving program speed, I'd like to present a bit of computer science theory, namely the **Big O** notation.

You don't have to worry, I will not use pages of mathematical formulas and talk about *infinitesimal asymptotics*. Instead, I will just present the essence of the Big O notation, the parts that are important to every programmer.

In the literature and, of course, on the web, you will see expressions such as *O(n)*, *O(n^2)*, *O(1)* and similar. This fancy-looking notation hides a really simple story. It tells us how much slower the algorithm will become if we increase the data size by a factor of **n**.

The *n^2* notation means "*n* to the power of two", or n^2. This notation is frequently used on the internet because it can be written with the standard ASCII characters. This book uses the more readable variant $O(n^2)$.

Let's say we have an algorithm with complexity of **O(*n*)**, which on average takes T seconds to process input data of size *N*. If we increase the size of the data by a factor of 10 (to *10*N*), then the algorithm will (on average) also use 10 times more time (that is, *10*T*) to process the data. If we process 1,000 times more data, the program will also run 1,000 times slower.

If the algorithm complexity is $\mathbf{O(n^2)}$, increasing the size of the data by a factor of 10 will cause the algorithm to run 10^2 or 100 times longer. If we want to process 1,000 times more data, then the algorithm will take $1{,}000^2$ or a million times longer, which is quite a hit. Such algorithms are typically not very useful if we have to process large amounts of data.

Most of the time, we use the Big O notation to describe how the computation **time** relates to the input data size. When this is the case, we call the Big O notation **time complexity.** Nevertheless, sometimes the same notation is used to describe how much **storage** (memory) the algorithm is using. In that case, we are talking about a **space complexity**.

You may have noticed that I was using the word **average** a lot in the last few paragraphs. When talking about the algorithm complexity, we are mostly interested in the average behavior, but sometimes we will also need to know about the worst behavior. We rarely talk about best behavior because users don't really care much if the program is sometimes faster than average.

Let's look at an example. The following function checks whether a string parameter `value` is present in a string list:

```
function IsPresentInList(strings: TStrings; const value: string): Boolean;
var
  i: Integer;
begin
  Result := False;
  for i := 0 to strings.Count - 1 do
    if SameText(strings[i], value) then
      Exit(True);
end;
```

What can we tell about this function? The best case is really simple—it will find that the `value` is equal to `strings[0]` and it will exit. Great! The best behavior for our function is *O(1)*. That, sadly, doesn't tell us much as that won't happen frequently in practice.

The worst behavior is also easy to find. If the `value` is not present in the list, the code will have to scan all of the `strings` list before deciding that it should return `False`. In other words, the worst behavior is *O(n)*, if the *n* represents the number of elements in the list. Incidentally (and without proof), the average behavior for this kind of search is also *O(n)*.

The Big O limits don't care about constant factors. If an algorithm would use *n/2* steps on average, or even just *0.0001 * n* steps, we would still write this down as *O(n)*. Of course, a *O(10 * n)* algorithm is slower than a *O(n)* algorithm and that is absolutely important when we fine-tune the code, but no constant factor C will make *O(C * n)* faster than *O(log n)* if *n* gets sufficiently large.

There are better ways to check whether an element is present in some data than searching the list sequentially. We will explore one of them in the next section, *Big O and Delphi data structures.*

While the function of *n* inside the *O()* notation can be anything, there are some *O* functions that appear constantly in standard programming problems. The following table shows those Big O limits and the most common examples of problems that belong to each class:

Time complexity	**Common examples of problems with that time complexity**
O(1)	Accessing array elements
O(log n)	Search in an ordered list
O(n)	Linear search
O(n log n)	Quick sort (average behavior)
$O(n^2)$	Quick sort (worst behavior), naive sort (bubblesort, insertion sort, selection sort)
$O(c^n)$	Recursive Fibonacci, travelling salesman problem using dynamic programming (*c* is some numeric constant)

If we care about program performance, then *O(1)* algorithms are of special interest to us as they present algorithms which don't get slower (at least not noticeably) when we increase the problem size. We'll see an example of such *O(1)* algorithms in the next section.

When we deal with algorithms that search in some datasets, we usually try to make them behave as *O(log n)*, not *O(n)*, as the former slows down much, much slower than the latter.

Another big class of problems deals with sorting the data. While the naive approaches sort in $O(n^2)$, better algorithms (such as mergesort and quicksort) need on average just *O(n log n)* steps.

The following image shows how the time complexity for these typical limits (we have used 2^n as an example of a more generic c^n) grows when we increase the problem size up to 20-fold:

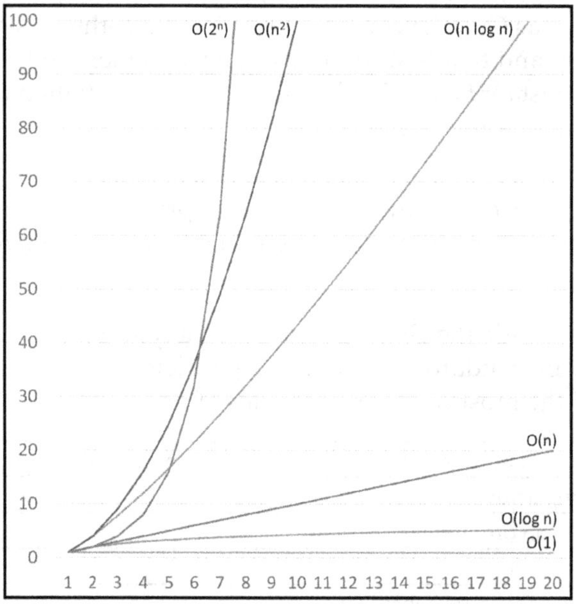

Most frequently encountered Big-O limits

We can see that *O(1)* and *O(log n)* grow very slowly. While *O(n log n)* grows faster than *O(n)*, it also grows much slower than $O(n^2)$, which we had to stop plotting when data was increased nine-fold.

The $O(2^n)$ starts slowly and looks like a great solution for small data sizes (small *n*), but then it starts rising terribly fast, much faster than $O(n^2)$.

The following table shows how fast *O(n log n)* and $O(n^2)$ are growing if we compare them with *O(n)* and how quickly $O(2^n)$ explodes.

The **data** column shows the data size increase factor. The number 10 in this column, for example, represents input with 10 times more elements than in the original data:

Data size	O(1)	O(log n)	O(n)	O(n log n)	$O(n^2)$	$O(2^n)$
1	1	1	1	1	1	1
2	1	2	2	4	4	2
10	1	4	10	43	100	512
20	1	5	20	106	400	524,288
100	1	8	100	764	10,000	10^{29}
300	1	9	300	2,769	90,000	10^{90}

We can see from this table that *O(log n)* algorithms present a big improvement over *O(n)* algorithms (8 versus 100 times increase in time when data increases 100-fold). We can also see that the $O(2^n)$ quickly becomes completely unmanageable.

The last cell in this table is particularly interesting. There are different estimates for the number of elementary particles (electrons, protons, neutrons, and so on) in the visible universe, but they all lie somewhere around 10^{90}. Suppose we have a computer which can solve an $O(2^n)$ in a reasonable time. If we would increase the input data by a factor of just 300, then we would need 10^{90} computers to solve the new problem in the same time. That is as much as the number of particles in the visible universe!

TIP

Don't use algorithms which have time complexity $O(2^n)$. It won't end well.

Big O and Delphi data structures

Delphi's **Run-Time Library (RTL)** contains many **data structures** (classes that are specifically designed to store and retrieve data), mostly stored in `System.Classes` and `System.Generics.Collection` units that greatly simplify everyday work. We should, however, be aware of their good and bad sides.

Every data structure in the world is seeking a balance between four different types of data access: accessing the data, inserting the data, searching for data, and deleting data. Some data structures are good in some areas, others in different ones, but no data structure in this world can make all four operations independent of data size.

When designing a program, we should therefore know what our needs are. That will help us select the appropriate data structure for the job.

The most popular data structure in Delphi is undoubtedly `TStringList`. It can store a large amount of strings and assign an object to each of them. It can—and this is important—work in two modes, **unsorted** and **sorted.** The former, which is a default, keeps strings in the same order as they were added while the latter keeps them alphabetically ordered.

This directly affects the speed of some operations. While accessing any element in a string list can always be done in a constant time (*O(1)*), adding to a list can take *O(1)* when the list is not sorted and *O(log n)* when the list is sorted.

Why that big difference? When the list is unsorted, `Add` just adds a string at its end. If the list is, however, sorted, `Add` must first find a correct insertion place. It does this by executing a *bisection search*, which needs *O(log n)* steps to find the correct place.

The reverse holds true for searching in a string list. If it is not sorted, `IndexOf` needs to search (potentially) the whole list to find an element. In a sorted list, it can do it much faster (again by using a bisection) in *O(log n)* steps.

We can see that `TStringList` offers us two options - either a fast addition of elements or a fast lookup, but not both. In a practical situation, we must look at our algorithm and think wisely about what we really need and what will behave better.

To sort a string list, you can call its `Sort` method or you can set its `Sorted` property to `True`. There is, however, a subtle difference that you should be aware of. While calling `Sort` sorts the list, it doesn't set its internal *is sorted* flag and all operations on the list will proceed as if the list is unsorted. Setting `Sorted := True`, on the other hand, does both - it sets the internal flag and calls the `Sort` method to sort the data.

To store any (non-string) data, we can use traditional `TList` and `TObjectList` classes or their more modern generic counterparts, `TList<T>` and `TObjectList<T>`. They all always work in an **unsorted** mode and so adding an element takes *O(1)* while finding and removing an element takes *O(n)* steps.

All provide a `Sort` function which sorts the data with a quicksort algorithm (*O(n log n)* on average) but only generic versions have a `BinarySearch` method, which searches for an element with a bisection search taking *O(log n)* steps. Be aware that `BinarySearch` requires the list to be sorted but doesn't make any checks to assert that. It is your responsibility to sort the list before you use this function.

If you need a very quick element lookup, paired with a fast addition and removal, then `TDictionary` is the solution. It has methods for adding (`Add`), removing (`Remove`) and finding a key (`ContainsKey` and `TryGetValue`) that, on average, function in a constant time, *O(1)*. Their worst behavior is actually quite bad, *O(n)*, but that will only occur on specially crafted sets of data that you will never see in practical applications.

I've told you before that there's no free lunch and so we can't expect that `TDictionary` is perfect. The big limitation is that we can't access the elements it is holding in a direct way. In other words, there is no `TDictionary[i]`. We can walk over all elements in a dictionary by using a `for` statement, but we can't access any of its elements directly. Another limitation of `TDictionary` is that it does not preserve the order in which elements were added.

Delphi also offers two simple data structures that mimic standard queue—`TQueue<T>`—and stack—`TStack<T>`. Both have very fast *O(1)* methods for adding and removing the data, but they don't offer any bells and whistles—there is no direct data access, we cannot search for data, and so on. We can only insert (`Enqueue` in queue or `Push` in stack) and remove (`Dequeue` and `Pop`) data.

To help you select the right tool for the job, I have put together a table showing the most important data structures and their most important methods, together with average and (when they differ from the average) worst-case time complexities:

Data structure	**Operation**	**Average**	**Worst**
TStringList	Direct access	O(1)	
	Add	O(1) / O(*log n*)	
	Insert	O(1)	
	Delete	O(1)	
	IndexOf	O(*n*) / O(*log n*)	
	Sort	O(*n log n*)	O(n^2)

TList, TObjectList	Direct access	O(1)	
	Add	O(1)	
	Insert	O(1)	
	Delete	O(1)	
	Remove	O(n)	
	IndexOf	O(n)	
	Sort	$O(n \log n)$	$O(n^2)$
TList<T>, TObjectList<T>	Direct access	O(1)	
	Add	O(1)	
	Insert	O(1)	
	Delete	O(1)	
	Remove	$O(n)$	
	IndexOf	$O(n)$	
	BinarySearch	$O(\log n)$	
	Sort	$O(n \log n)$	$O(n^2)$
TDictionary	Direct access	Not possible	
	Add	O(1)	$O(n)$
	Remove	O(1)	$O(n)$
	TryGetValue	O(1)	$O(n)$
	ContainsKey	O(1)	$O(n)$
	ContainsValue	O(n)	
TQueue<T>	Direct access	Not possible	
	Enqueue	O(1)	
	Dequeue	O(1)	
TStack<T>	Direct access	Not possible	
	Push	O(1)	
	Pop	O(1)	

The table shows the time complexity of the most important operations on built-in Delphi data structures. Complexity for the worst case is only listed if it differs from the average complexity.

Data structures in practice

Enough with the theory already! I know that you, like me, prefer to talk through the code. As one program explains more than a thousand words could, I have prepared a simple demo project: `RandomWordSearch`.

This program functions as a very convoluted random word generator. When started, it will load a list of 370,101 English words from a file. It will also prepare three internal data structures preloaded with these words:

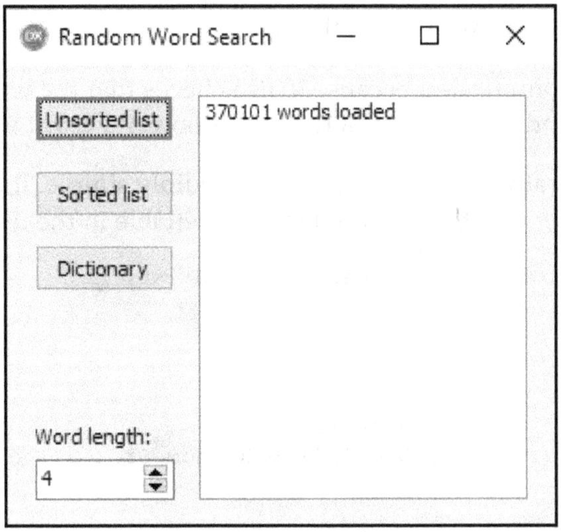

Random word generator

The program shows three buttons to the user. All three run basically the same code. The only difference is the test function which is passed to the centralized word generator as a parameter:

```
procedure TfrmRandomWordSearch.FindGoodWord(const wordTest:
TWordCheckDelegate);
var
  word: string;
  isWordOK: boolean;
  time: TStopwatch;
begin
  time := TStopwatch.StartNew;
  repeat
    word := GenerateWord;
    isWordOK := wordTest(word);
  until isWordOK or (time.ElapsedMilliseconds > 10000);
```

```
    if isWordOK then
      lbWords.ItemIndex := lbWords.Items.Add(Format('%s (%d ms)', [word,
  time.ElapsedMilliseconds]))
    else
      lbWords.ItemIndex := lbWords.Items.Add('timeout');
  end;
```

The core of the `FindGoodWord` method can be easily described:

1. Generate a random word by calling `GenerateWord`.
2. Call the test function `wordTest` on that word. If this function returns `False`, repeat *Step 1*. Otherwise show the word.

The code is a bit more complicated because it also checks that the word generation part runs for at most 10 seconds and reports a timeout if no valid word was found in that time.

The random word generator `GenerateWord` is incredibly simple. It just appends together lowercase English letters until the specified length (settable in the user interface) is reached:

```
function TfrmRandomWordSearch.GenerateWord: string;
var
  pos: integer;
begin
  Result := '';
  for pos := 1 to inpWordLength.Value do
    Result := Result + Chr(Ord('a') + Random(Ord('z') - Ord('a') + 1));
end;
```

Let's now check the data preparation phase. The not very interesting (and not shown here) `OnCreate` handler loads data from a file into a `TStringList` and calls the `LoadWords` method:

```
procedure TfrmRandomWordSearch.LoadWords(wordList: TStringList);
var
  word: string;
begin
  FWordsUnsorted := TStringList.Create;
  FWordsUnsorted.Assign(wordList);

  FWordsSorted := TStringList.Create;
  FWordsSorted.Assign(wordList);
  FWordsSorted.Sorted := True;

  FWordsDictionary := TDictionary<string,boolean>.Create(wordList.Count);
  for word in wordList do
    FWordsDictionary.Add(word, True);
end;
```

The first data structure is an unsorted `TStringList`, `FWordsUnsorted`. Data is just copied from the list of all words by calling the `Assign` method.

The second data structure is a sorted `TStringList`, `FWordsSorted`. Data is firstly copied from the list of all words. The list is then sorted by setting `FWordsSorted.Sorted := True`.

The last data structure is a `TDictionary`, `FWordsDictionary`. A `TDictionary` always stores **pairs** of keys and values. In our case, we only need the **keys** part as there is no data associated with any specific word, but Delphi doesn't allow us to ignore the **values** part and so the code defines the value as a `boolean` and always sets it to `True`.

Although the dictionaries can grow, they work faster if we can initially set the number of elements that will be stored inside. In this case that is simple—we can just use the length of the `wordList` as a parameter to `TDictionary.Create`.

The only interesting part of the code left is `OnClick` handlers for all three buttons. All three call the `FindGoodWord` method, but each passes in a different test function.

When you click on the **Unsorted list** button, the test function checks whether the word can be found in the `FWordsUnsorted` list by calling the `IndexOf` function. As we will mostly be checking non-English words (remember, they are just random strings of letters), this `IndexOf` will typically have to compare all 307,101 words before returning `-1`:

```
procedure TfrmRandomWordSearch.btnUnsortedListClick(Sender: TObject);
begin
  FindGoodWord(
    function (const word: string): boolean
    begin
      Result := FWordsUnsorted.IndexOf(word) >= 0;
    end);
end;
```

When you click on the **Sorted list** button, the test function calls `FWordsSorted.IndexOf`. As this `TStringList` is sorted, `IndexOf` will use a binary search that will need at most *log(307101) = 19* (rounded up) comparisons to find out that a word is not found in the list. As this is much less than 307.101, we can expect that finding words with this approach will be much faster:

```
procedure TfrmRandomWordSearch.btnSortedListClick(Sender: TObject);
begin
  FindGoodWord(
    function (const word: string): boolean
    begin
      Result := FWordsSorted.IndexOf(word) >= 0;
    end);
end;
```

A click on the last button, **Dictionary**, calls `FWordsDictionary.ContainsKey` to check if the word can be found in the dictionary, and that can usually be done in just one step. Admittedly, this is a bit of a slower operation than comparing two strings, but still the `TDictionary` approach should be faster than any of the `TStringList` methods:

```
procedure TfrmRandomWordSearch.btnDictionaryClick(Sender: TObject);
begin
  FindGoodWord(
    function (const word: string): boolean
    begin
      Result := FWordsDictionary.ContainsKey(word);
    end);
end;
```

If we use the terminology from the last section, we can say that the *O(n)* algorithm (unsorted list) will run much slower than the *O(log n)* algorithm (sorted list), and that the *O(1)* algorithm (dictionary) will be the fastest of them all. Let's check this in practice.

Start the program and click on the **Unsorted list** button a few times. You'll see that it typically needs few hundred milliseconds to a few seconds to generate a new word. As the process is random and dependent on CPU speed, your numbers may differ quite a lot from mine. If you are only getting *timeout* messages, you are running on a slow machine and you should decrease the **Word length** to `3`.

If you increment the **Word length** to `5` and click the button again, you'll notice that the average calculation time will grow up to a few seconds. You may even get an occasional *timeout*. Increase it to `6` and you'll mostly be getting timeouts. We are clearly hitting the limits of this approach.

Prepare now to be dazed! Click on the **Sorted list** button (while keeping the **Word length** at `6`) and words will again be calculated blazingly fast. On my computer, the code only needs 10 to 100 milliseconds to find a new word:

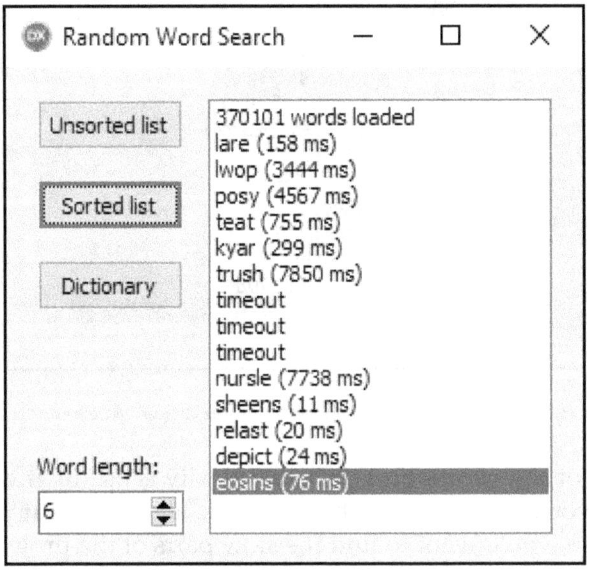

Testing with different word length and with first two algorithms

To better see the difference between a sorted list and a dictionary, we have to crank up the word length again. Setting it to `7` worked well for me. The sorted list needed from a few 100 milliseconds to a few seconds to find a new word while the dictionary approach mostly found a new word in under 100 milliseconds.

Increase the **Word length** to `8` and the sorted list will start to time out while the dictionary will still work. Our O(*1*) approach is indeed faster than the O(*log n*) code:

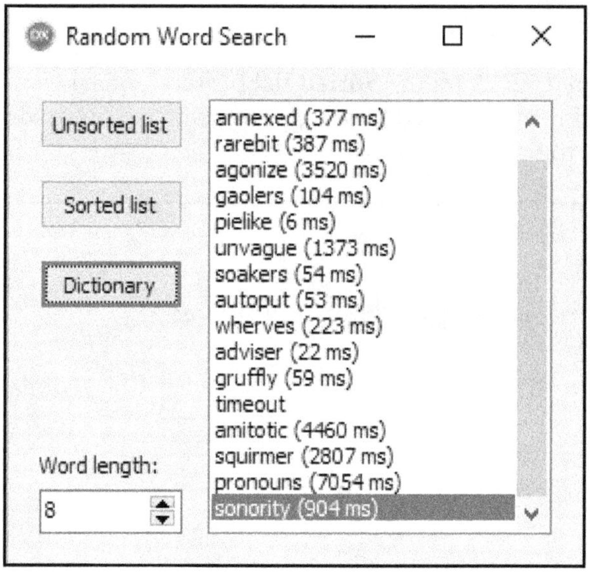

Comparing sorted list (first six words and the two after "timeout") with the dictionary approach (next five and last two).

While the knowledge of algorithms and their complexity is useful, it will not help in every occasion. Sometimes you already use the best possible algorithm but your program is still too slow. At such times, you'll want to find the slow parts of the program and speed them up with whatever trick possible. To do that, you have to find them first, which is the topic of the rest of this chapter.

Mr. Smith's first program

While I was talking about theory and data structures and best practices, our friend Mr. Smith read everything about polar forests on the internet and then got really bored. In a moment of sheer panic—when he was thinking about watching videos of cute kittens for the whole polar night—he turned to programming. He checked various internet sources and decided that Delphi is the way to go. After all, he could use it to put together a new game for iOS *and* Android and make lots of money while waiting for the sun to show up!

As he didn't have any programming literature on the Antarctic base, he learned programming from internet resources. Sadly, he found most of his knowledge on Experts Exchange and Yahoo Answers and his programs sometimes reflect that.

As of this moment, he has written one working program (and by working I mean that it compiles), but he is not really sure what the program actually does. He only knows that the program is a bit slow and because of that he named it `SlowCode`.

His program is a console mode program which upon startup calls the `Test` method:

```
procedure Test;
var
  data: TArray<Integer>;
  highBound: Integer;
begin
  repeat
    Writeln('How many numbers (0 to exit)?');
    Write('> ');
    Readln(highBound);
    if highBound = 0 then
      Exit;

    data := SlowMethod(highBound);
    ShowElements(data);
   until false;
end;
```

That one, at least, is easy to grasp. It reads some number, passes it to something called `SlowMethod` (hmm, Mr. Smith really should work on naming techniques), and then passes the result (which is of type `TArray<Integer>`) to a method called `ShowElements`. When the user types in `0`, the program exits.

Let's check the `ShowElements` function:

```
function SlowMethod(highBound: Integer): TArray<Integer>;
var
  i: Integer;
  temp: TList<Integer>;
begin
  temp := TList<Integer>.Create;
  try
    for i := 2 to highBound do
      if not ElementInDataDivides(temp, i) then
        temp.Add(i);
    Result := Filter(temp);
  finally
    FreeAndNil(temp);
  end;
end;
```

The code creates a list of integers. Then it iterates from a value 2 to the value that was entered by the user and for each value calls `ElementInDataDivides`, passing in the list and the current value. If that function returns `True`, the current value is entered into the list.

After that, `SlowMethod` calls the `Filter` method which does something with the list and converts it into an array of integers which is then returned as a function result:

```
function ElementInDataDivides(data: TList<Integer>; value: Integer):
boolean;
var
  i: Integer;
begin
  Result := True;
  for i in data do
    if (value <> i) and ((value mod i) = 0) then
      Exit;
  Result := False;
end;
```

The `ElementInDataDivides` function iterates over all the numbers in the list and checks if any element in the list divides the `value` (with the additional constraint that this element in the list must not be equal to the `value`).

Let's check the last part of the puzzle—the `Filter` function:

```
function Reverse(s: string): string;
var
  ch: char;
begin
  Result := '';
  for ch in s do
    Result := ch + Result;
end;
function Filter(list: TList<Integer>): TArray<Integer>;
var
  i: Integer;
  reversed: Integer;
begin
  SetLength(Result, 0);
  for i in list do
  begin
    reversed := StrToInt(Reverse(IntToStr(i)));
    if not ElementInDataDivides(list, reversed) then
    begin
      SetLength(Result, Length(Result) + 1);
      Result[High(Result)] := i;
```

```
      end;
    end;
  end;
```

This one again iterates over the list, reverses the numbers in each element (changes 123 to 321, 3341 to 1433, and so on) and calls `ElementInDataDivides` on the new number. If it returns `True`, the element is added to the returned result in a fairly inefficient way.

I agree with Mr. Smith—it is hard to tell what the program does. Maybe it is easiest to run it and look at the output:

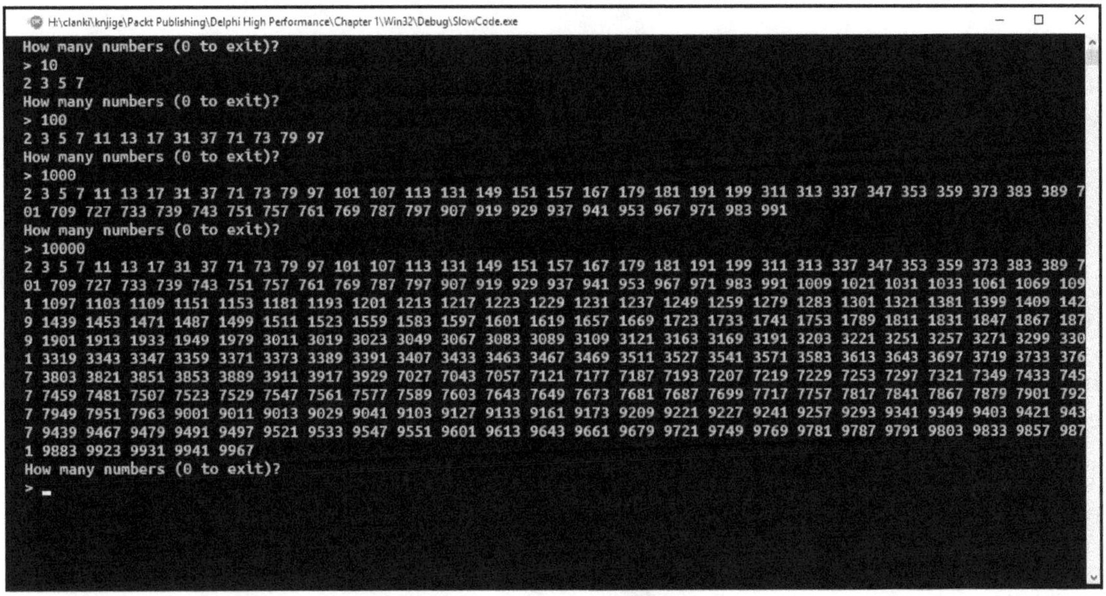

It looks like the program is outputting prime numbers. Not all prime numbers, just some of them. (For example, 19 is missing from the list, and so is 23.) Let's leave it at that for the moment.

Looking at code through the Big O eyes

We can tell more about the program, about its good and bad parts, if we look at it through the eyes of time complexity, in terms of the Big O notation.

We'll start where the code starts—in the `SlowMethod` method. It has a loop iterating from `2` to the user-specified upper bound, `for i := 2 to highBound do`. The size of our data, or *n*, is therefore equal to `highBound` and this `for` loop has time complexity of *O(n)*:

```
for i := 2 to highBound do
  if not ElementInDataDivides(temp, i) then
    temp.Add(i);
```

Inside this loop, the code calls `ElementInDataDivides` followed by an occasional `temp.Add`. The latter will execute in O(1), but we can't say anything about the `ElementInDataDivides` before we examine it.

This method also has a loop iterating over the `data` list. We can't guess how many elements are in this list, but in the short test that we just performed, we know that the program writes out 13 elements when processing values from 2 to 100:

```
for i in data do
  if (value <> i) and ((value mod i) = 0) then
    Exit;
```

For the purpose of this very rough estimation I'll just guess that the `for i in data do` loop also has a time complexity of O(*n*).

In `SlowMethod` we therefore have an O(*n*) loop executing another O(*n*) loop for each element, which gives us a O(n^2) performance.

The `SlowMethod` then calls the `Filter` method which also contains O(*n*) for loop calling `ElementInDataDivides`, which gives us O(n^2) complexity for this part:

```
for i in list do
begin
  reversed := StrToInt(Reverse(IntToStr(i)));
  if not ElementInDataDivides(list, reversed) then
  begin
    SetLength(Result, Length(Result) + 1);
    Result[High(Result)] := i;
  end;
end;
```

There's also a conversion to string, some operation on that string, and conversion back to the integer `StrToInt(Reverse(IntToStr(i)))`. It works on all elements of the list (O(n)) but in each iteration it processes all characters in the string representation of a number. As a length of the number is proportional to *log n*, we can say that this part has complexity of O($n \log n$), which can be ignored as it is much less than the O(n^2) complexity of the whole method.

There are also some operations hidden inside `SetLength`, but at this moment we don't know yet what they are and how much they contribute to the whole program. We'll cover that area in `Chapter 4`, *Memory Management*.

The `SlowMethod` therefore consists of two parts, both with complexity O(n^2). Added together, that would give us $2*n^2$, but as we ignore constant factors (that is, 2) in the Big O notation, we can only say that the time complexity of `SlowMethod` is O(n^2).

So what can we say simply by looking at the code?

- The program probably runs in O(n^2) time. It will take around 100 times longer to process 10,000 elements than 1,000 elements.
- There is a conversion from the integer to the string and back (`Filter`), which has complexity of only O($n \log n$) but it would still be interesting to know how fast this code really is.
- There's a time complexity hidden behind the `SetLength` call which we know nothing about.
- We can guess that most probably the `ElementInDataDivides` is the most time-consuming part of the code and any improvements in this method would probably help.
- Fixing the terrible idea of appending elements to an array with `SetLength` could probably speed up a program, too.

As the code performance is not everything, I would also like to inform Mr. Smith about a few places where his code is less than satisfactory:

- The prompt *How many numbers* is misleading. A user would probably expect it to represent the number of numbers outputted, while the program actually wants to know how many numbers to test.
- Appending to `TArray<T>` in that way is not a good idea. Use `TList<T>` for temporary storage and call its `ToArray` method at the end. If you need `TArray<T>`, that is. You can also do all processing using `TList<T>`.

- `SlowMethod` has two distinctive parts - data generation, which is coded as a part of `SlowMethod`, and data filtering, which is extracted in its own method, `Filter`. It would be better if the first part is extracted into its own method, too.
- Console program, really? Console programs are good for simple tests, but that is it. Learn VCL or FireMonkey, Mr. Smith!

We can now try and optimize parts of the code (`ElementInDataDivides` seems to be a good target for that) or, better, we can do some measuring to confirm our suspicions with hard numbers.

In a more complicated program (what we call a *real life*), it would usually be much simpler to measure the program performance than to do such analysis. This approach, however, proves to be a powerful tool if you are using it while designing the code. Once you hear a little voice nagging about the time complexities all the time while you're writing a code, you'll be on the way to becoming an excellent programmer.

Don't guess, measure!

There is only one way to get a good picture about the fast and slow parts of a program—by measuring it. We can do it manually, by inserting time-measuring calls in the code, or we can use specialized tools. We have a name for measuring—**profiling**—and we call specialized tools for measuring **profilers**.

In the rest of this chapter, we'll look at different techniques of measuring the execution speed. First we will measure the now familiar program, `SlowCode`, with a simple software stopwatch and then we'll look at a few open source and commercial profilers.

Before we start, I'd like to point out a few basic rules that apply to all profiling techniques:

- Always profile **without** the debugger. The debugger will slow the execution in unexpected places and that will skew the results. If you are starting your program from the Delphi IDE, just press *Ctrl+Shift+F9* instead of *F9*.
- Try not to do anything else on the computer while profiling. Other programs will take the CPU away from the measured program which will make it run slower.
- Take care that the program doesn't wait for user action (data entry, button click) while profiling. This will completely skew the report.

- Repeat the tests a few times. Execution times will differ because Windows (and any other OS that Delphi supports) will always execute other tasks besides running your program.
- All the above especially holds for multithreaded programs, which is an area explored in Chapters 5 to 7.

Profiling with TStopwatch

Delphi includes a helpful unit called `System.Diagnostics`, which implements a `TStopwatch` record. It allows us to measure time events with a better precision than 1 millisecond and has a pretty exhaustive public interface, as shown in the code fragment below:

```
type
  TStopwatch = record
  public
    class function Create: TStopwatch; static;
    class function GetTimeStamp: Int64; static;
    procedure Reset;
    procedure Start;
    class function StartNew: TStopwatch; static;
    procedure Stop;
    property Elapsed: TTimeSpan read GetElapsed;
    property ElapsedMilliseconds: Int64 read GetElapsedMilliseconds;
    property ElapsedTicks: Int64 read GetElapsedTicks;
    class property Frequency: Int64 read FFrequency;
    class property IsHighResolution: Boolean read FIsHighResolution;
    property IsRunning: Boolean read FRunning;
  end;
```

To use a stopwatch, you first have to create it. You can call `TStopwatch.Create` to create a new **stopped** stopwatch or `TStopwatch.StartNew` to create a new **started** stopwatch. As `TStopwatch` is implemented as a `record`, there's no need to destroy a stopwatch object.

When a stopwatch is started, it is measuring time. To start a stopwatch, call the `Start` method and to stop it, call the `Stop` method. The `IsRunning` property will tell you if the stopwatch is currently started. Call the `Reset` method to reset the stopwatch to zero.

The `TStopwatch` contains a few functions that return the currently measured time. The most precise of them is `ElapsedTicks`, but as there is no built-in (public) function to convert this into standard time units, this function is hard to use. My recommendation is to just use the `ElapsedMilliseconds` property which will give you elapsed (measured) time in milliseconds.

For a simple demo, this code will return 1,000 or a bit more:

```
function Measure1sec: int64;
var
  sw: TStopwatch;
begin
  sw := TStopwatch.StartNew;
  Sleep(1000);
  Result := sw.ElapsedMilliseconds;
end;
```

Let's now use this function to measure the `SlowMethod` method.

First, you have to add the `System.Diagnostics` unit to the `uses` list:

```
uses
  System.SysUtils,
  System.Generics.Collections,
  System.Classes,
  System.Diagnostics;
```

Next, you have to create this stopwatch inside `SlowMethod`, stop it at the end, and write out the elapsed time:

```
function SlowMethod(highBound: Integer): TArray<Integer>;
var
 // existing variables
 sw: TStopwatch;
begin
  sw := TStopwatch.StartNew;

  // existing code

  sw.Stop;
  Writeln('SlowMethod: ', sw.ElapsedMilliseconds, ' ms');
end;
```

We can use this code to verify the theory that `SlowCode` has time complexity O(n^2). To do this, we have to measure the execution times for different counts of processed numbers (different values entered at the *How many numbers* prompt).

I did some testing for selected values from 10,000 to 1,000,000 and got the following numbers:

Highest number	**Execution time [ms]**
10,000	15
25,000	79
50,000	250
75000	506
100,000	837
250,000	4,515
500.000	15564
750,000	30,806
1,000,000	54,219

If you repeat the tests, you will of course measure different values, but the growth rate should be the same.

For a quick confirmation, I have plotted a **Scatter Chart** of this data in Excel and the result surely looks like a square function. To be more sure, I have added a **power trendline** which created a function in the form of n^c, where *c* was a constant that Excel has calculated from the data.

In the case of my specific measurements, this *fitting* function was $y = 10^{-6} * x^{1.7751}$, which is not that far from x^2:

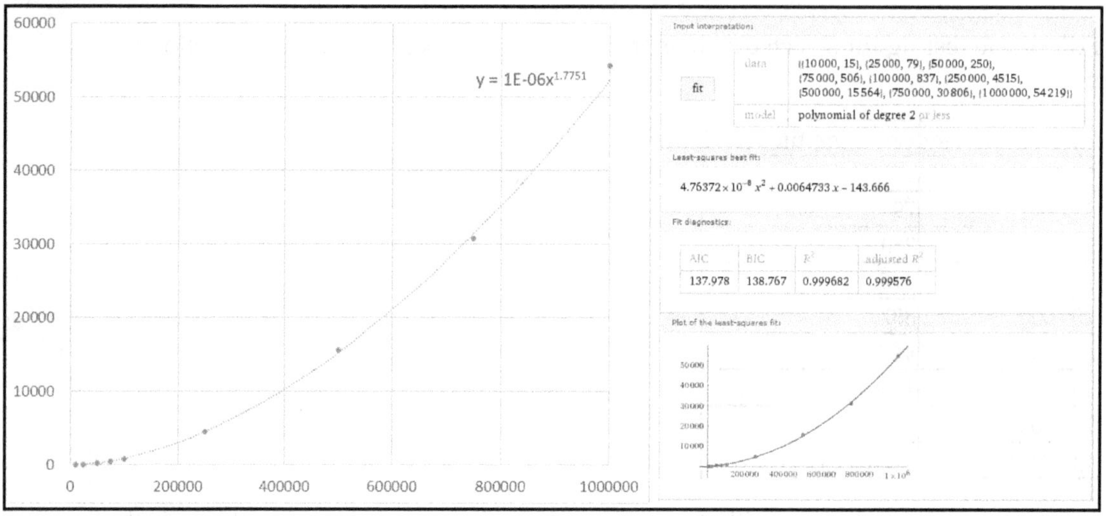

Curve fitting in Excel (left) and Wolfram Alpha (right)

Next, I repeated this *curve fitting* process on the wonderful Wolfram Alpha (`www.wolframalpha.com`) where you can find a *Regression Calculator Widget,* a tool designed specifically for this task. I entered measurements into the widget and it calculated a fitting function of 4.76372×10^-8 * **x^2** + 0.0064733 * x - 143.666. If we ignore all unimportant factors and constants, the only part left is x^2. Another confirmation for our analysis!

Now we know how the program behaves in global terms, but we still have no idea of which part of the code is the slowest. To find that out, we also have to measure execution times of the `ElementInDataDivides` and `Filter` methods.

These two methods are called multiple times during the execution of the program so we can't just create and destroy a stopwatch each time `Filter` (for example) is executed. We have to create a global stopwatch, which is a bit inconvenient in this program because we have to introduce a global variable.

If you check the `SlowCode_Stopwatch` program, you'll see that it actually creates three global stopwatches, one for each of the functions that we want to measure:

```
var
  Timing_ElementInData: TStopwatch;
  Timing_Filter: TStopwatch;
  Timing_SlowMethod: TStopwatch;
```

All three stopwatches are created (but not started!) when the program starts:

```
Timing_ElementInData := TStopwatch.Create;
Timing_Filter := TStopwatch.Create;
Timing_SlowMethod := TStopwatch.Create;
```

When the program ends, the code logs elapsed time for all three stopwatches:

```
Writeln('Total time spent in SlowMethod: ',
  Timing_SlowMethod.ElapsedMilliseconds, ' ms');
Writeln('Total time spent in ElementInDataDivides: ',
  Timing_ElementInData.ElapsedMilliseconds, ' ms');
Writeln('Total time spent in Filter: ',
  Timing_Filter.ElapsedMilliseconds, ' ms');
```

In each of the three methods, we only have to *Start* the stopwatch at the beginning and *Stop* it at the end:

```
function Filter(list: TList<Integer>): TArray<Integer>;
  // existing variables
begin
 Timing_Filter.Start;

 // existing code

 Timing_Filter.Stop;
end;
```

The only tricky part is the `ElementInDataDivides` function which calls `Exit` as soon as one element divides the `value` parameter. The simplest way to fix that is to wrap the existing code in a `try .. finally` handler and to stop the stopwatch in the `finally` part:

```
function ElementInDataDivides(data: TList<Integer>; value: Integer):
boolean;
var
  i: Integer;
begin
  Timing_ElementInData.Start;
  try
    Result := True;
    for i in data do
      if (value <> i) and ((value mod i) = 0) then
        Exit;
    Result := False;
  finally
    Timing_ElementInData.Stop;
  end;
end;
```

If you run the program and play with it for a while and then exit, you'll get a performance report. In my case, I got the following result:

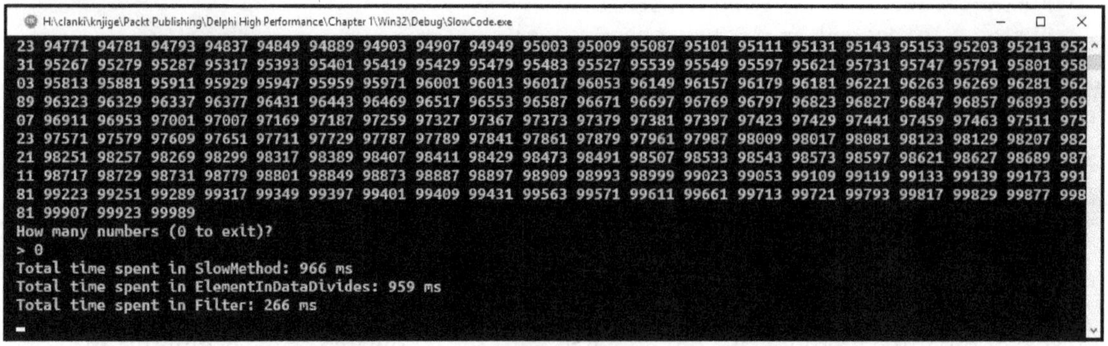

H:\clanki\knjige\Packt Publishing\Delphi High Performance\Chapter 1\Win32\Debug\SlowCode.exe
23 94771 94781 94793 94837 94849 94889 94903 94907 94949 95003 95009 95087 95101 95111 95131 95143 95153 95203 95213 952
31 95267 95279 95287 95317 95393 95401 95419 95429 95479 95483 95527 95539 95549 95597 95621 95731 95747 95791 95801 958
03 95813 95881 95911 95929 95947 95959 95971 96001 96013 96017 96053 96149 96157 96179 96181 96221 96263 96269 96281 962
89 96323 96329 96337 96377 96431 96443 96469 96517 96553 96587 96671 96697 96769 96797 96823 96827 96847 96857 96893 969
07 96911 96953 97001 97007 97169 97187 97259 97327 97367 97373 97379 97381 97397 97423 97429 97441 97459 97463 97511 975
23 97571 97579 97609 97651 97711 97729 97787 97789 97841 97861 97879 97961 97987 98009 98017 98081 98123 98129 98207 982
21 98251 98257 98269 98299 98317 98389 98407 98411 98429 98473 98491 98507 98533 98543 98573 98597 98621 98627 98689 987
11 98717 98729 98731 98779 98801 98849 98873 98887 98897 98909 98993 98999 99023 99053 99109 99119 99133 99139 99173 991
81 99223 99251 99289 99317 99349 99397 99401 99409 99431 99563 99571 99611 99661 99713 99721 99793 99817 99829 99877 998
81 99907 99923 99989
How many numbers (0 to exit)?
> 0
Total time spent in SlowMethod: 966 ms
Total time spent in ElementInDataDivides: 959 ms
Total time spent in Filter: 266 ms

We now know that most of the time is spent in `ElementInDataDivides`, but we don't know how many calls to it were made directly from `SlowMethod` and how many from the `Filter` method. To find that out, we have to add two new global variables and some more code:

```
var
  Generate_ElementInData_ms: int64;
  Filter_ElementInData_ms: int64;

function SlowMethod(highBound: Integer): TArray<Integer>;
var
  i: Integer;
  temp: TList<Integer>;
begin
  Timing_SlowMethod.Start;
  temp := TList<Integer>.Create;
  try

    Timing_ElementInData.Reset;
    for i := 2 to highBound do
      if not ElementInDataDivides(temp, i) then
        temp.Add(i);
    Generate_ElementInData_ms := Generate_ElementInData_ms +
      Timing_ElementInData.ElapsedMilliseconds;

    Timing_ElementInData.Reset;
    Result := Filter(temp);
    Filter_ElementInData_ms := Filter_ElementInData_ms +
      Timing_ElementInData.ElapsedMilliseconds;

  finally
```

```
        FreeAndNil(temp);
      end;
      Timing_SlowMethod.Stop;
    end;
```

The code (which can be found in the `SlowCode_Stopwatch2` program) now resets the `Timing_ElementInData` stopwatch before the data generation phase and adds the value of the stopwatch to `Generate_ElementInData_ms` afterwards. Then it resets the stopwatch again for the `Filter` phase and adds the value of the stopwatch to `Filter_ElementInData_ms` afterwards.

At the end that will give us the cumulative execution time for `ElementInDataDivides` called directly from `SlowMethod` in `Generate_ElementInData_ms` and the cumulative execution time for `ElementInDataDivides` called from `Filter` in `Filter_ElementInData_ms`.

A test run with an upper bound of 100,000 produced the following output:

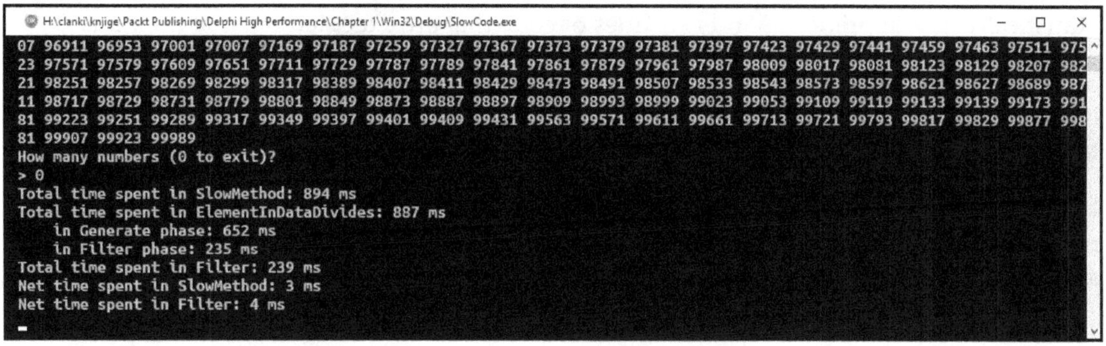

Now we can be really sure that almost all the time is spent in `ElementInDataDivides`. We also know that approximately 75% of the time it is called directly from `SlowMethod` and 25% of the time from the `Filter` method.

We are now ready to optimize the program. We can either improve the implementation to make it faster, or replace it with a faster algorithm, or both.

But first, let's see what *profilers* can tell us about our program.

Profilers

Measuring the speed of a program by inserting special code into the program by hand is perfect if you want to measure a very specific part of the code, but becomes cumbersome if you don't know exactly which part of the program you should focus on. In such cases, it is best to use specialized software - profilers.

Profilers can measure all kinds of parameters. Sure, they are mostly used for measuring execution speed, at a method or even on a line level, but they can do much more. They can display the *call tree* - a graph showing how methods call one another. They can show memory usage in a program so you can quickly find the one method which is constantly eating the memory. They can show you the *coverage* of your tests so you can see which code was tested and which not. And much more.

They do that magic in two ways, by *sampling* or *instrumentation.*

Sampling profiling looks at the state of your program at regular intervals (for example, 100 times per second) and each time checks which line of the code is currently being executed. Statistically, it will predominantly *see* lines of code that are executed most of the time.

Sampling profiling will give us only a rough overview of behavior inside the program but it will do that without affecting the program speed, and because of that is excellent for taking a first look at some code.

Instrumenting profiles do their magic by changing—*instrumenting*—the code. They are, in fact, doing almost exactly the same kind of changing the code as we did by inserting the stopwatch calls.

There are two ways to do instrumentation. The profiler can change the source code or it can change the program binary. Source instrumenting profilers are rare because they are less safe to use (there's always the possibility that a compiler will mess up the source) and because you have to recompile the code after it is instrumented (modified by the profiler).

Most of the instrumenting profilers on the market modify the binary code, which is a bit more tricky to implement but doesn't require a recompilation and cannot destroy the source code.

The advantage of instrumentation over sampling is that the former can collect everything that is going on inside the program and not just a few samples here and there. The disadvantage is that instrumentation reduces the speed of the program. Although instrumenting profilers take extra care to optimize the code that is inserted into your program, executing this code in many instrumented methods can still take a long time.

The other problem is the amount of collected data. A short and fast method which is called 100,000 times in 1 second will generate 100,000 data samples in an instrumenting profiler and only 100 samples in a sampling profiler (provided that it samples the code 100 times a second).

Because of all that, instrumenting profilers are best used once we already know on which part(s) of the program we want to focus.

I'll end this chapter with an overview of four profilers, two open source and free (AsmProfiler and Sampling Profiler) and two commercial (AQTime and Nexus Quality Suite), to make it easier for you to choose the best fit for your situation. These four profilers are, of course, not your only options. If you need a very precise profiling of short methods, check out ProDelphi (`www.prodelphi.de`). And if you need a high-end tool that will not only profile your application but help it optimize to its fullest potential, take a look at Intel's VTune Amplifier (`software.intel.com/en-us/intel-vtune-amplifier-xe`).

AsmProfiler

AsmProfiler is a 32-bit instrumenting and sampling profiler written by André Mussche. Its source, along with Windows exe, can be found at `https://github.com/andremussche/asmprofiler`. Although the latest version was released in 2016, it works well with the newest Delphi at the time of writing this book, 10.2 Tokyo.

The sampling and instrumenting profilers are used in a different way, so I'll cover them separately.

To use AsmProfiler you first have to unpack the release ZIP into some folder on your disk. That will create two subfolders—`Sampling` and `Instrumenting`. To start the sampling profiler, start `AsmProfiling_Sampling` from the `Sampling` folder and then click **Start profiling**.

AsmProfiler has two ways of starting a profiling session. You can start the program manually, click **Select process** in AsmProfiler, and select your program from the list of running processes. Alternatively, you can click **Select exe**, browse to the compiled EXE of your program, and then click **Start process now**, which will start the program or click **Start sampling** which will start the program and also start sampling the code.

The reasoning behind the two different ways of starting the program is that mostly you want to profile a specific part of the program, so you would load it into the profiler, navigate to the specific part, click **Start sampling**, do the required steps in your program, click **Stop sampling**, and analyze the results. Sometimes, however, you would want to profile the very startup of the program so you would want sampling to start immediately after your program is launched. The following screenshot shows the initial AsmProfiler screen:

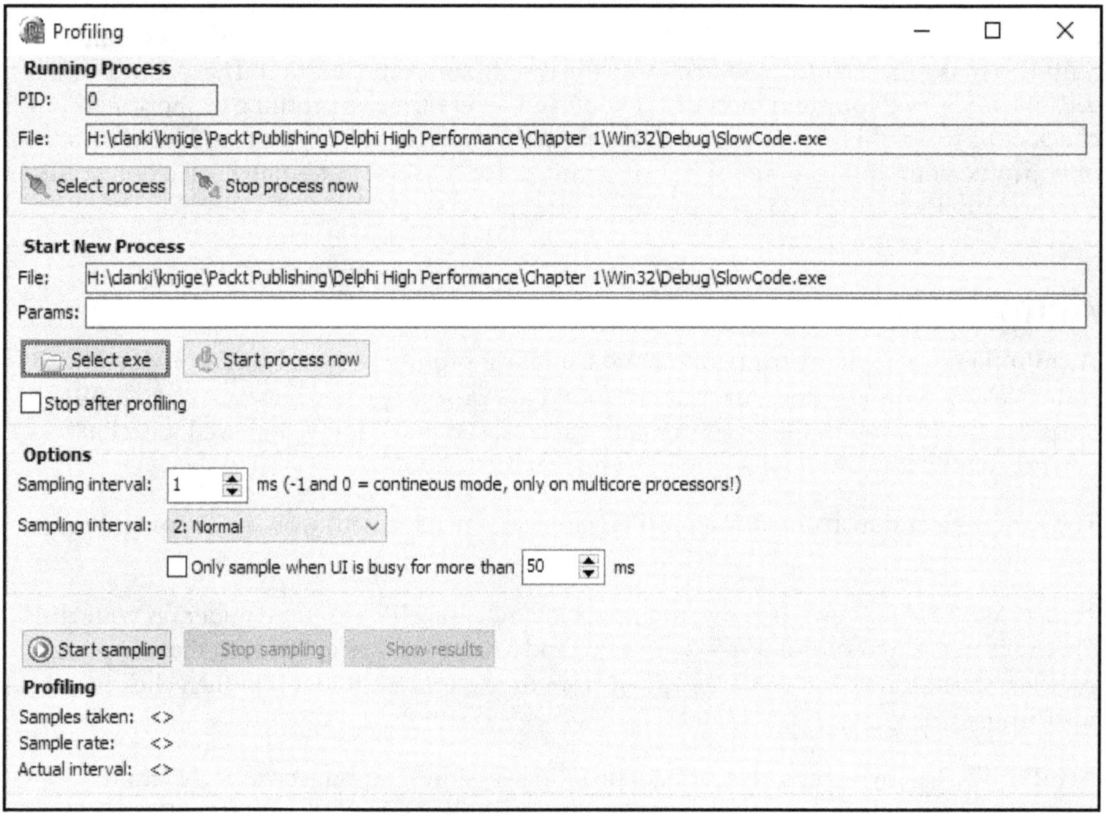

Starting profiling session in AsmProfiler

Sampling options can be configured in the **Options** group. You can set the sampling interval—how many milliseconds will pass between two samples. Setting this value to `4`, for example, will generate 250 (1000/4) samples per second.

Setting the sampling interval to 0 enables a continuous sampling mode which still leaves some time to threads running on the same CPU. (The sampling code calls `Sleep(0)` between taking two samples.) Setting it to `-1` causes the samples to be taken as fast as possible. In effect, AsmProfiler will use one CPU core for itself.

You can also set the priority of sample-taking threads from the default, **Normal**. I will discuss threads and priorities in `Chapter 5`, *Getting Started with the Parallel World.*

After you have taken the samples and clicked **Stop sampling**, click the **Show results** button to analyze the results.

If you want to compare your results with mine, here are steps to produce the results (as shown in the following screenshot):

1. Start AsmProfiler.
2. Click **Select exe** and select the `SlowCode.exe`.
3. Click **Start process now**.
4. Click **Start sampling**.
5. Enter `100,000` into the program.
6. Click **Stop sampling**.
7. Enter `0` into the program to exit.
8. Click **Show results**.

9. Click **Results** on the **Sampling Results** form.

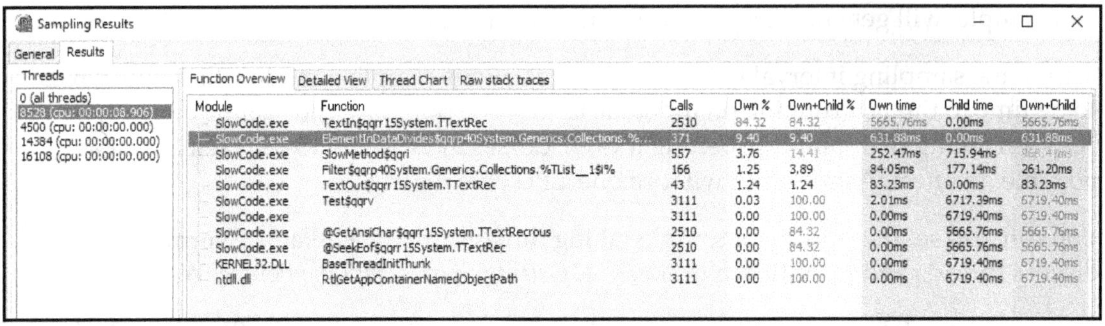

Result of a test run profiled with AsmProfiler's Sampling profiler

AsmProfiler displays results organized by threads, but it automatically highlights the main thread so you don't have to care about that detail if your program doesn't use multithreading.

In the result grid, it shows the module (main EXE or DLL), name of the function, how many times the code was found to be in this function, and times (absolute and percentage) the code spent in that function (**Own**), in all functions called from it (**Child**), and both in that function and in all functions called from it (**Own+Child**).

If we sort results by the time spent only in the function (**Own time**), we'll see that function `TextIn$qqrr15System.TTextRec` comes to the top. This a function that reads console input (in the `Readln` statement) and we can safely ignore it.

The next one on the list, `ElementInDataDivides$qqrp40...`, is the one that interests us. We can see that it was sampled 371 times (*Calls*) and that it needed 0.6 seconds to execute. If you switch to the **Detailed view** tab and select this function, you'll see in the **Parent calls (called by...)** panel that it was called 258 times from `SlowMethod` and 113 times from the `Filter` method. In reality, of course, it was called many more times, but most of them were not *seen* by the sampling profiler.

In this view, we can also see how many times each line of some method was hit, which will give us a good idea about where the program spends most of the time. Unfortunately, we cannot sort the data on different criteria:

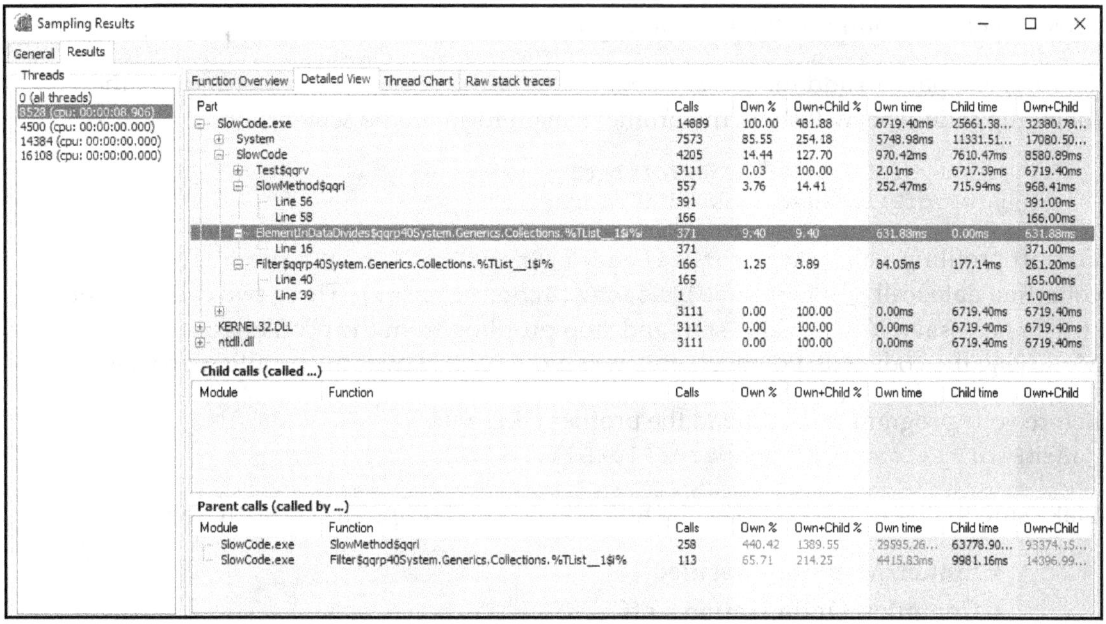

Detailed view showing information for each line of the program

The names of the methods in these outputs are very weird, but that is how the Delphi compiler calls these methods internally. The part after the **$** encodes the parameter types. This process is called **name mangling** (and the part after **$** is sometimes referred to as a **decoration**) and it enables us to use overloaded methods with the same name and different parameters—internally they all have different names.

For example, the function `SlowMethod(highBound: Integer)` is internally known as `SlowMethod$qqri`. The `qqr` part specifies the *fastcall* calling convention (it describes how parameters are passed to the function in registers and on stack) and `i` identifies one `integer` parameter.

AsmProfiler's instrumenting profiler requires a bit more work. Firstly, you have to copy `AsmProfiler.dll` from the `Instrumenting` subfolder into a folder on the Windows environment path or into the `exe` folder. Secondly, you have to copy `Instrumenting\API\_uAsmProfDllLoader.pas` into Delphi's library path, into your project's folder or add this folder to your project's search path.

Thirdly, you have to add the *_uAsmProfDllLoader* unit to your project and call the following code. This will show the profiler's main form on the screen:

```
if _uAsmProfDllLoader.LoadProfilerDll then
  _uAsmProfDllLoader.ShowProfileForm;
```

To start profiling, call `_uAsmProfDllLoader.StartProfiler(False);`. To stop collecting data, call `_uAsmProfDllLoader.StopProfiler;`. These two calls are not strictly necessary. You can also start and stop profiling from the profiler's user interface. Modifying the code will, however, give you more control over the profiling process.

Before your program exits, unload the profiler DLL with `_uAsmProfDllLoader.UnLoadProfilerDll;`.

Make sure that your program has the following compiler options correctly set:

- **Linker, Map file = detailed**
- **Compiler, Optimization = off**
- **Compiler, Stack frames = on**

The instrumenting profiler requires your program to process messages which makes it mostly useless when used in Mr. Smith's program, as it is spending most of the time inside a `Readln` call (and is not processing messages). As I still wanted to show you how this profiler works, I have converted `SlowCode` into a more modern VCL version, `SlowCode_VCL`.

At first I wanted to start/stop profiling right in `SlowMethod`:

```
function TfrmSlowCode.SlowMethod(highBound: Integer): TArray<Integer>;
var
  i: Integer;
  temp: TList<Integer>;
begin
  _uAsmProfDllLoader.StartProfiler(False);

  // existing code

  _uAsmProfDllLoader.StopProfiler;
end;
```

That attempt, however, misfired, as AsmProfiler didn't want to show profiling results for `SlowCode`. It turned out to be better to move the start/stop calls out of this method and into the method which calls `SlowCode`:

```
procedure TfrmSlowCode.btnTestClick(Sender: TObject);
var
  data: TArray<Integer>;
begin
  outResults.Text := '';
  outResults.Update;

  _uAsmProfDllLoader.StartProfiler(False);
  data := SlowMethod(inpHowMany.Value);
  _uAsmProfDllLoader.StopProfiler;

  ShowElements(data);
end;
```

A version of the program, ready for profiling with the AsmProfiler, is stored in the `SlowCode_VCL_Instrumented` project. You will still have to download AsmProfiler and store `AsmProfiler.dll` and `_uAsmProfDllLoader.pas` into appropriate places.

When you start the program, a small form will appear alongside the program's main form. From here you can start and stop profiling, select items (methods) that should be profiled (**Select items**), and open results of the profiling session (**Show results**):

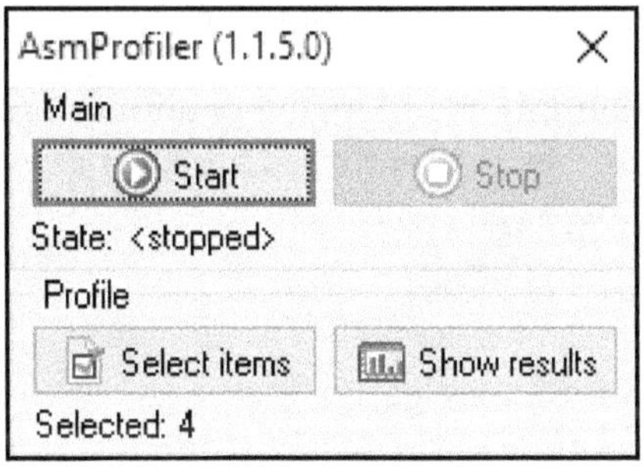

AsmProfiler's instrumenting profiler

We are interested only in three methods, so click the **Select items** button, select the `ElementInDataDivides`, `Filter` and `SlowMethod` methods, and click **OK**:

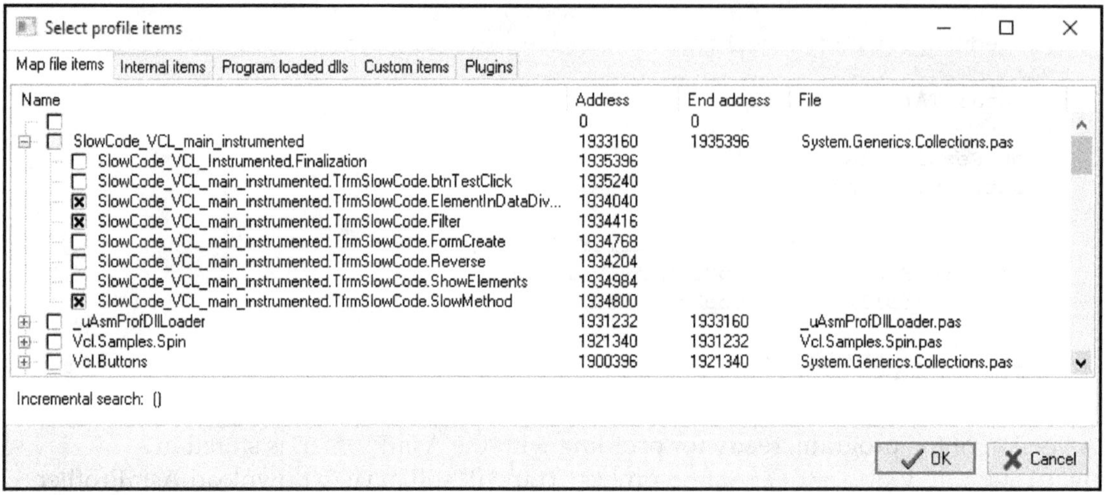

Selecting methods to be profiled

Next, enter `100000` into the **How many numbers** field and click the **Test** button. You don't have to start and stop the profiler, as the program will do that. When the values are calculated and displayed on the screen, click the **Show results** button. Don't close the profiled program as that would close the profiler form, too.

The result form of the instrumenting profiler is very similar to the equivalent form of the sampling profiler. The most interesting feature is the **Unit overview** tab, which combines detailed timing information and a call tree:

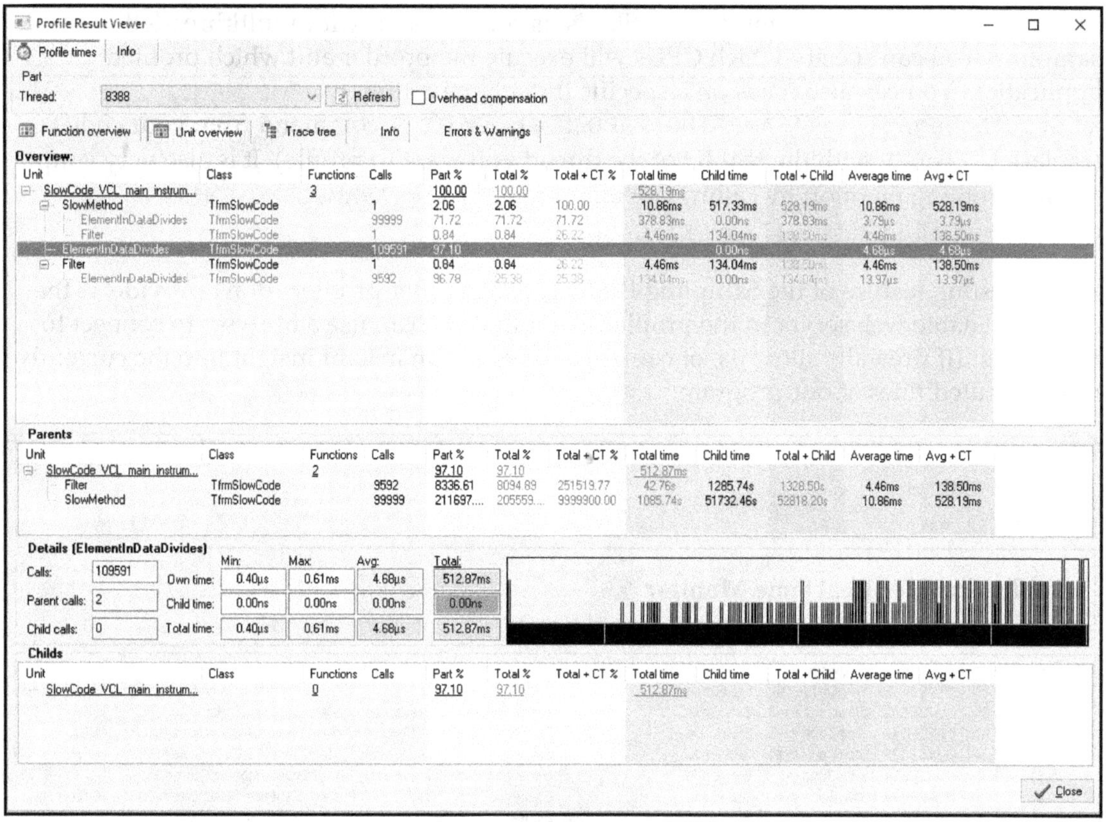

Unit overview display

We can see that `ElementInDataDivides` is in fact called 99,999 times directly from the `SlowMethod` and only 9,592 times from the `Filter` method, not 258 and 113 times, as shown by the sampling profiler.

AsmProfiler gives a good combination of a global overview and detailed analysis, although it is rough around the edges and requires more effort on your part than more polished commercial profilers.

Sampling Profiler

The Sampling Profiler is, as its name suggests, a sampling profiler for Delphi, written by Eric Grange. You can find it at `www.delphitools.info`. Although it officially supports only Delphi 5 to XE4, it will function well with applications written in modern Delphis.

The strongest part of the Sampling Profiler is its configurability for multithreaded sampling. You can specify which CPUs will execute the profiler and which profiled application. You can also focus on a specific thread by issuing a `OutputDebugString('SAMPLING THREAD threadID')` command from your code (replace `threadID` with the real ID of the thread you want to profile). It is also very simple to turn profiling on or off by calling `OutputDebugString('SAMPLING ON')` and `OutputDebugString('SAMPLING OFF')`.

An interesting feature of the Sampling Profiler, which other profilers don't provide, is the ability to enable web server in the profiler. After that, we can use a browser to connect to the profiler (if firewalls allow us, of course) and we get an instant insight into the currently most executed lines of our program:

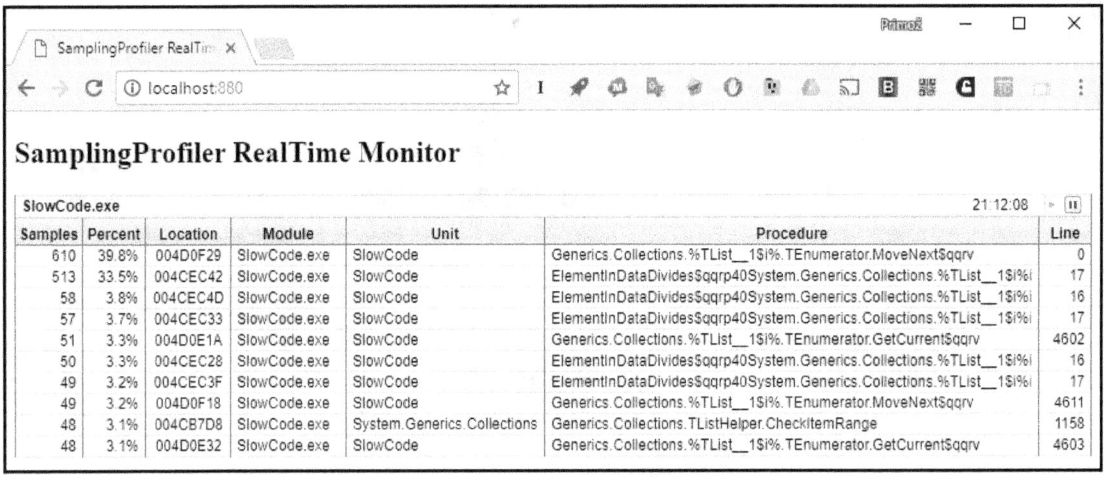

Samples	Percent	Location	Module	Unit	Procedure	Line
610	39.8%	004D0F29	SlowCode.exe	SlowCode	Generics.Collections.%TList__1$i%.TEnumerator.MoveNext$qqrv	0
513	33.5%	004CEC42	SlowCode.exe	SlowCode	ElementInDataDivides$qqrp40System.Generics.Collections.%TList__1$i%i	17
58	3.8%	004CEC4D	SlowCode.exe	SlowCode	ElementInDataDivides$qqrp40System.Generics.Collections.%TList__1$i%i	16
57	3.7%	004CEC33	SlowCode.exe	SlowCode	ElementInDataDivides$qqrp40System.Generics.Collections.%TList__1$i%i	17
51	3.3%	004D0E1A	SlowCode.exe	SlowCode	Generics.Collections.%TList__1$i%.TEnumerator.GetCurrent$qqrv	4602
50	3.3%	004CEC28	SlowCode.exe	SlowCode	ElementInDataDivides$qqrp40System.Generics.Collections.%TList__1$i%i	16
49	3.2%	004CEC3F	SlowCode.exe	SlowCode	ElementInDataDivides$qqrp40System.Generics.Collections.%TList__1$i%i	17
49	3.2%	004D0F18	SlowCode.exe	SlowCode	Generics.Collections.%TList__1$i%.TEnumerator.MoveNext$qqrv	4611
48	3.1%	004CB7D8	SlowCode.exe	System.Generics.Collections	Generics.Collections.TListHelper.CheckItemRange	1158
48	3.1%	004D0E32	SlowCode.exe	SlowCode	Generics.Collections.%TList__1$i%.TEnumerator.GetCurrent$qqrv	4603

Live status view from remote location

The weakest point of the Sampling Profiler is its complete inability to select methods that are of interest to us. As we can see in the following screenshot, we get some methods from `Generics.Collections` mixed between methods from `SlowCode`. This only distracts us from our task—trying to find the slow parts of `SlowCode`.

Saying all that, I must admit that the display of profiling results is really neatly implemented. The results view is simple, clean, and easy to use:

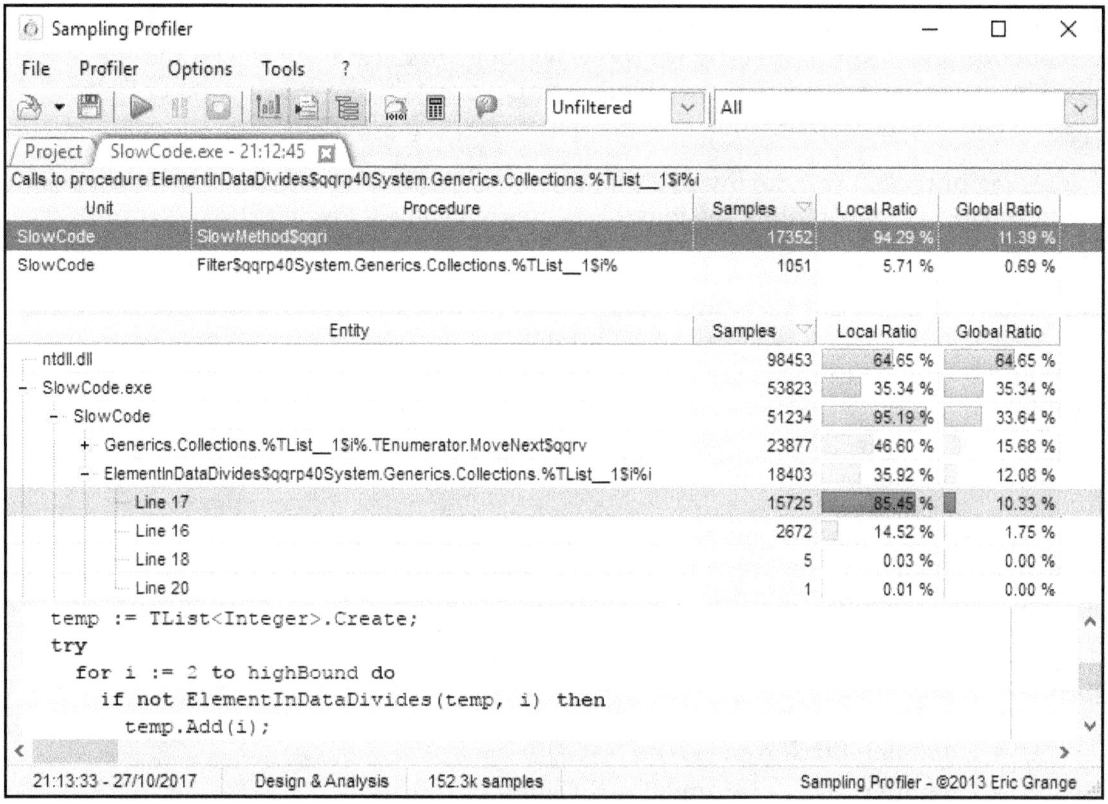

Simple and effective result view

The Sampling Profiler would be a perfect solution for occasional profiling if it would only allow us to select topics of interest.

AQTime

AQTime is a performance and memory profiler for C/C++, Delphi, .NET, Java, and Silverlight, produced by SmartBear Software. It supports 32- and 64-bit applications and can be found at `www.smartbear.com`.

Previously, a special Standard version of AQTime was included with RAD Studio, C++Builder, and Delphi. This offer was only available for releases XE to XE8 and the licensing was not renewed after that. If you want to use AQTime with any other Delphi release, you have to buy AQTime Professional.

For testing purposes, you can install a trial version of AQTime Professional, which will only allow you to run five profiling sessions. Dedicate some time to testing and use your five sessions wisely!

AQTime Professional supports all Delphi version from 2006 to Tokyo and you can even use it in Visual Studio, which is a great plus for multiplatform developers. It contains a variety of profilers—from the *performance profiler* (binary instrumentating profiler) and the *sampling profiler*, to the *coverage profiler* (to see which parts of the program were executed) and more specific tools such as *BDE SQL profiler*, *static analysis* (a code analysis tool which is not really a profiler), and more.

It integrates nicely into the Delphi IDE but you can also use it as a standalone application. That gives you more flexibility during the profiling and result analysis and that's why I also used the standalone AQTime Professional for the examples.

To prepare your program for profiling, make sure that the following compiler options are set:

- **Compiler, Stack frames = on**
- **Compiler, Debug information = Debug information**
- **Compiler, Local symbols = true**
- **Linker, Debug information = true**

In order for AQTime to be able to find the source file for your project, you have to specify a search path. Go to **Options | Options**, then select **General | Search directory**, and add all the folders with your source files.

Next you can choose to profile all units, but unless you are using a sampling profiler this will slow down the execution in a typical program a lot. It is better to select just a few units or, as in our example, just a few methods.

The easiest way to do that is to create a new *profiling area* and the easiest way to do that is to select one or more methods in the left tree (use *Shift+click* and *Ctrl+click*), then right-click and select **Add selected to | New profiling area**. After that you can add additional methods to that profiling area by right-clicking and selecting **Add selected to | Existing profiling area**, or simply with drag-and-drop.

When creating a new profiling area, you also have to choose whether to profile on a method or on a line level by checking or unchecking the **Collect info about lines** checkbox:

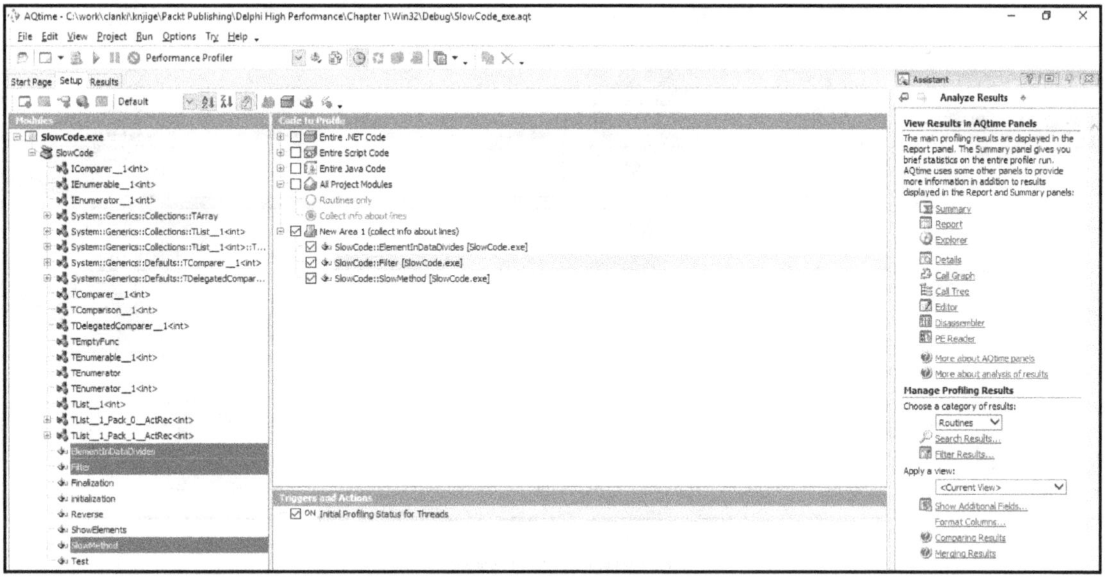

Creating new profiling area

Then start the program from AQTime—or select the **AQTime | Run with profiling** menu from Delphi, do the necessary steps you want to profile, and exit. AQTime will show the profiling results. Similarly to all other profilers, it will show a grid with measured methods, net time spent in each, time with children, and a **hit count**—an indicator showing how many times the method executed.

More interesting info is hiding in the lower panel. There is a very detailed *Call Graph*, which displays a call tree for the selected method, and a very useful *Editor* panel, which shows the source together with the *hit count* information for each line:

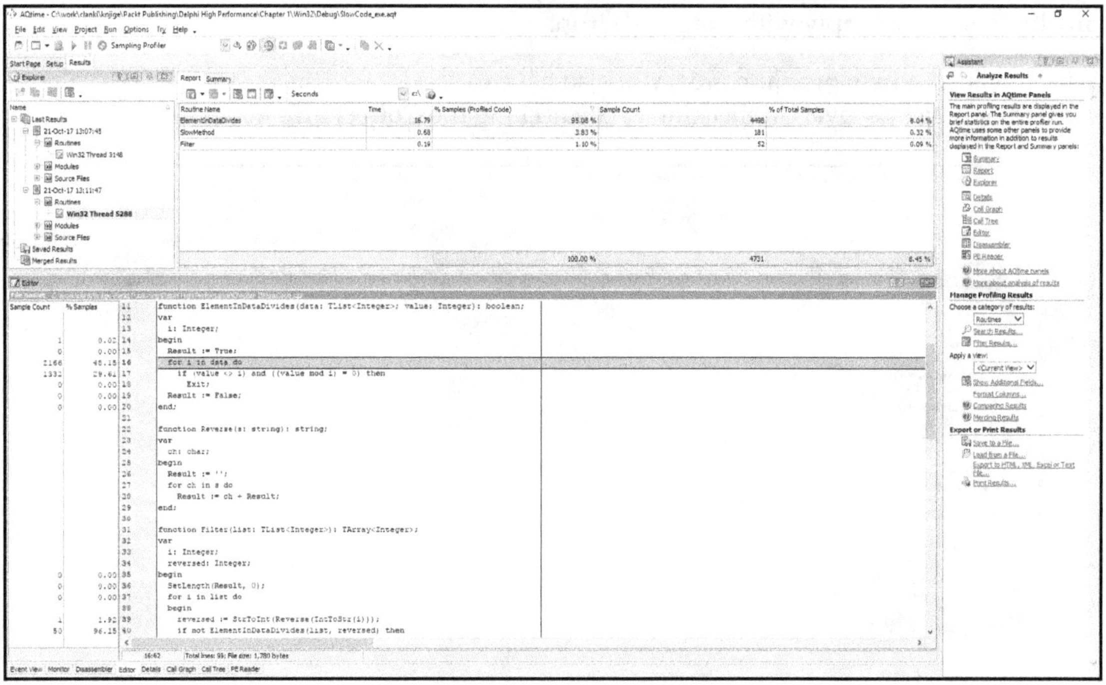

Editor view showing hit count for instrumented methods

AQTime is a great tool provided that you stay away from the very limited Standard edition and go directly for the Professional.

Nexus Quality Suite

Nexus Quality Suite (**NQS**) is a successor to the long-defunct TurboPower's SleuthQA, published by NexusQA Pty Ltd. It supports 32- and 64-bit applications written in Delphi from 5 to 10.2 Tokyo. You can find it at `www.nexusdb.com`.

The trial version has fewer limitations than AQTime's. Some functions are disabled and some are limited in the quantity of collected data. Still, the program is not so limited that you wouldn't be able to test it out.

NQS integrates into Delphi's *Tools* menu and extends it with all the profilers it brings to Delphi. Of the most interest to us are **Method Timer**, an instrumenting profiler working at a method level, and **Line Timer**, an instrumenting profiler working at a line level. There is also a **Block Timer**, an instrumenting profiler working on a block level (a `for` loop, for example), which was not working correctly at the time of writing this book and so I wasn't able to test it. That's really bad luck, as there are no other profilers working on a block level and it would be really interesting to compare it with more standard approaches.

A few other tools are also interesting from the profiling viewpoint. **Coverage Analyst** will help you analyze code coverage, which is an important part of unit testing. After all, you definitely want to know whether your unit tests test all of the methods in a unit or not.

Also interesting is **CodeWatch**, which hunts for bugs in the code by looking for memory and resource leaks.

All these profilers, with the exception of CodeWatch, are available in 32-bit and 64-bit versions, although the 64-bit operation is not as stable as in the 32-bit counterparts. I was only able to use Line Timer in 32-bit mode, for example, while Method Timer worked flawlessly in 32-bit and 64-bit modes.

Both Method Timer and Line Timer require no special preparation. You just have to have debug information turned on in the linker options.

When you start the Method Timer, a profiler window opens. Click on the **Routines** button to select methods to profile. To change the profiling status of a method, double-click its name or right-click and select **Profile Status** | **Enable Profile Status For Selected**.

When you are done, press *F9* to start the program, go through the steps that you want to profile, and exit the program.

The program will then display basic timing information including net time per method and *gross time* (what other programs call "time with children"). If you click on a method, the lower two panes will display information about methods that called the current method and methods that were called from the current method.

If you double-click on a method, another window will appear showing the source code for the selected method but without any information about the profiling results:

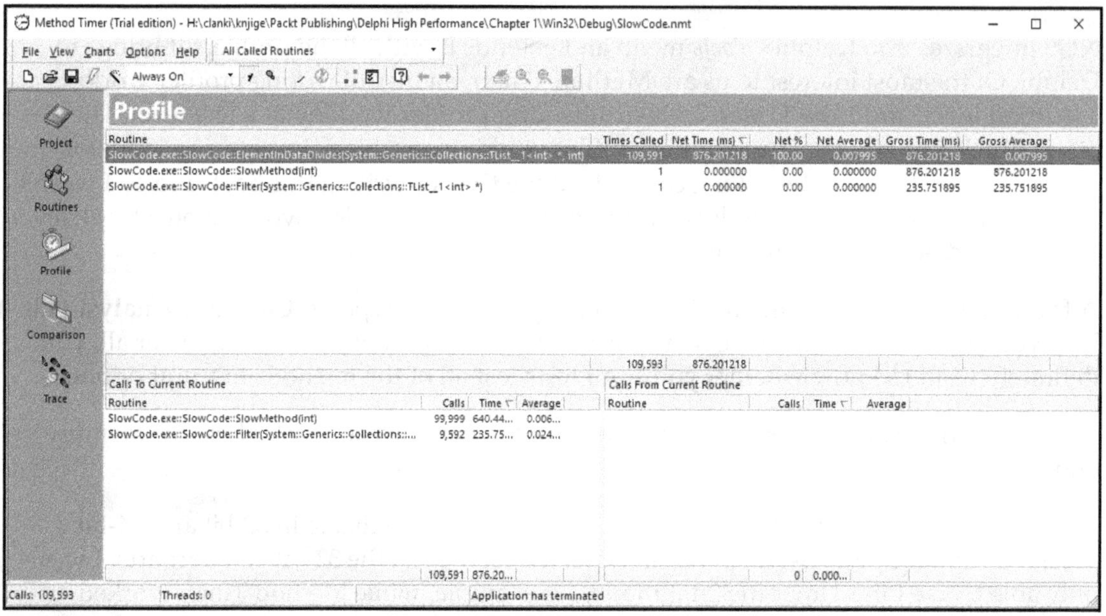

Method Timer result window

Line Timer has a similar user interface. First you select the methods to be profiled in the *Routines* view, then you run the program, and at the end examine the results in the **Line Times** window.

This profiler has a display that is a bit different from other profilers that support line-level profiling. It is not grouped by methods, but by line numbers. This gives us an immediate overview of the most critical part of the code, but is hard to integrate into a bigger picture.

As in the Method Timer, a double-click on a line in the results grid opens up an editor window which displays the source code, together with the time spent in each profiled line and the number of times this line was executed:

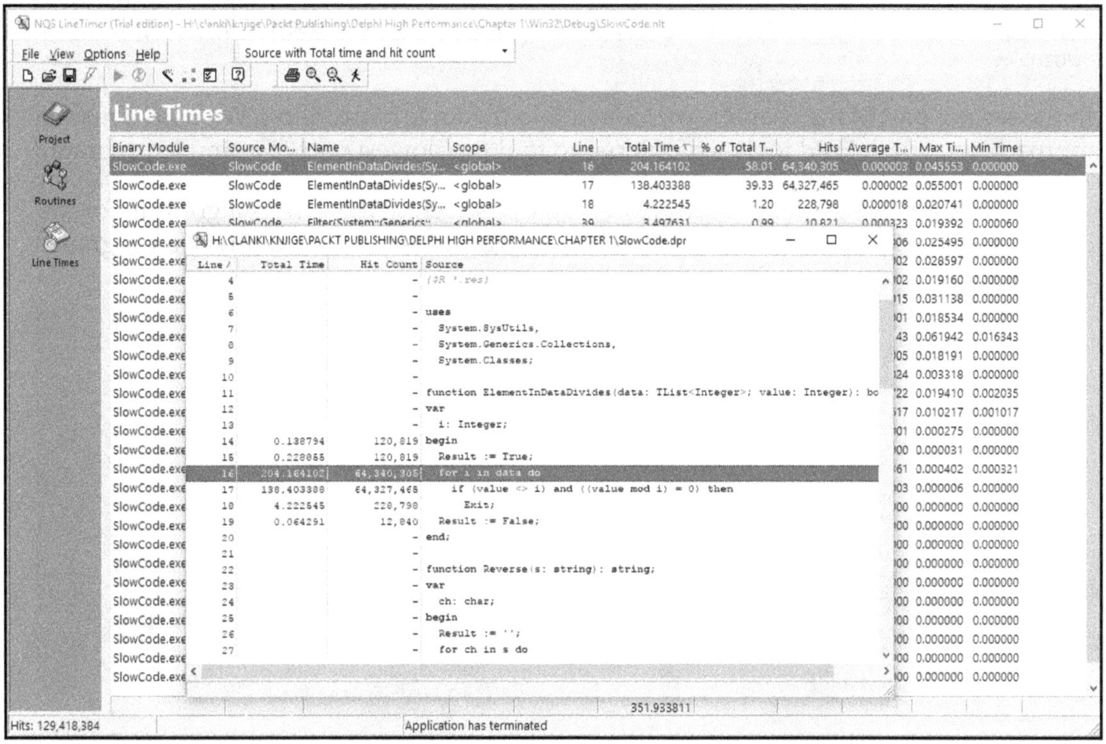

Line Timer with built-in code display

Nexus Quality Suite is a nice set of tools and we can only hope that its stability will improve with future releases.

Summary

This chapter provided a broad overview of the topics we'll be dealing with in this book. We took a look at the very definition of performance. Next we spent some time describing the Big O notation for describing time and space complexity and we used it in a simple example.

In the second part of the chapter, we looked into the topic of profiling. We used a manual approach and specialized tools—profilers—to find the slowest part of a simple program.

In the next chapter, I'll briefly return to the topic of selecting the correct algorithm for the job. With a few examples, I'll show you how an algorithm can make or break a program's performance.

2
Fixing the Algorithm

In the previous chapter, we explored the concept of *performance* and looked at different scenarios where we would like to make the program faster. The previous chapter was largely theoretical, but now is the time to look at it in a more practical way.

There are two main approaches to speeding up a program:

- Replace the algorithm with a better one.
- Fine-tune the code so that it runs faster.

I spent lots of time in the previous chapter discussing the *time complexity* simply to make it clear that a difference between two algorithms can result in impressive speed-up. It can be much more than a simple constant factor (such as a 10-times speed-up). If we go from an algorithm with bad time complexity (say, $O(n^2)$) to an algorithm with a better behavior ($O(n \log n)$, for example), then the difference in speed becomes more and more noticeable when we increase the size of the data.

Saying all that, it should not be surprising that I prefer the first approach (fixing the algorithm) to the second one (fine-tuning the code). To continue this point, this chapter will deal with several practical examples of speeding up the code by changing the algorithm.

Firstly, we will look at user interfaces. As we can't speed up VCL or Windows by fine-tuning the code (simply because we cannot modify that code), any speed-up in user interface responsiveness can only be a result of a better algorithm.

After that, I'll introduce the concept of *caching*. This approach can help you when everything else fails. Maybe it is not possible to change an algorithm, but introducing a cache of frequently-calculated values can still improve the code speed drastically.

As implementing a fast cache is quite a tricky business, I'll also present a generic cache class that you can use freely in your own code.

Before concluding the chapter, I'll look at Mr. Smith's `SlowCode` example and try to speed it up by implementing a better algorithm.

We will cover the following topics in this chapter:

- Writing responsive user interfaces
- How to update VCL and FMX controls without waiting
- Speeding up functions by introducing caching
- How to implement a reusable generic caching class
- How to analyze and improve an unknown algorithm

Responsive user interfaces

A user's first contact with any program is always the user interface. A good UI can make or break a program. Leaving the user interface design aside (as I am not qualified to speak about that), I will focus on just one fact.

Users hate user interfaces that are not **responsive**.

In other words, every good user interface must react quickly to a user's input, be that a keyboard, mouse, touchpad, or anything else.

What are the tasks that can make a user interface unresponsive? Basically, they all fall into one of two categories:

1. A program is running a slow piece of code. While it is running, the UI is not responding.
2. Updating the user interface itself takes a long time.

The problems from the first category fall into two subsets—functions that have non-blocking (asynchronous) alternatives and functions that don't.

Sometimes we can replace the slow function with another one that runs *asynchronously*. For example, instead of using a standard function for reading from a file, we can use the Windows Asynchronous File I/O API. File reading will then occur in parallel with our program and we will be notified of successful or unsuccessful reads via some other mechanism.

Often, however, this is not possible (there is no alternative for the slow function) or the asynchronous version is too complicated to implement. In that case, we can execute the slow code in a thread. This will be covered in chapters 5 to 7.

An excellent candidate for the multithreaded approach is the file reading example. True, Windows offers an asynchronous API for that, but it is quite complicated and tricky to implement correctly. Pushing a read operation into a thread is simpler **and** cross-platform compatible if that is important for your application.

The second category (updating the UI takes a long time) is typically solved with a simple solution: *Do less updating!* Delphi/Windows controls are typically very fast and they only fail when we want them to do too many operations in a short time.

We will now focus on that category. I'll show a few examples of overabundant updates and give solutions for faster code.

Updating a progress bar

Almost any change to VCL controls can cause one or more Windows messages to be sent to the operating system. That takes time, especially as the program waits for the operating system to process the message and return an answer. This can happen even if nothing has changed in the user interface.

The next demonstration will show how an abundance of messages can slow down the execution speed. I must admit that the code in the `ProgressBar` demo is a bit contrived. Still, I assure you that I have seen a similar code running in production.

This demo simulates reading a large file block by block. (The code doesn't really open and read the file; it just runs a loop which would do the reading.) For each read block, a progress bar is updated.

For speed comparison, this progress bar update is done in two ways. In the first, slow approach, the `Max` property of the progress bar is set to the size of the file we are reading. After each block, the progress bar's `Position` is set to the number of bytes read so far:

```
function TfrmProgressBar.Test0To2G: Integer;
var
  total: Integer;
  block: Integer;
  sw: TStopwatch;
begin
  sw := TStopwatch.StartNew;
  ProgressBar1.Max := CFileSize;
  ProgressBar1.Position := 0;

  total := 0;
  while total < CFileSize do begin
    block := CFileSize - total;
```

```
    if block > 1024 then
      block := 1024;
    // reading 'block' bytes
    Inc(total, block);

    ProgressBar1.Position := total;
    ProgressBar1.Update;
  end;
  Result := sw.ElapsedMilliseconds;
end;
```

This code runs slow for two reasons. Firstly, setting the `Position` property sends a message `PBM_SETPOS` to Windows and that is a relatively slow operation when compared with non-graphical program code. Secondly, when we call `Update`, Windows API function `UpdateWindow` gets called. This function repaints the progress bar even if its position didn't change and that takes even more time. As all this is called 1,953,125 times it adds up to a considerable overhead.

The second, faster approach, sets `Max` to 100. After each block, the progress is calculated in *percentage* with `currPct := Round(total / CFileSize * 100);`.
The `Position` property is updated only if this percentage differs from the current progress bar's position.

As reading the `Position` property also sends one message to the system, the current position is stored in a local variable, `lastPct`, and a new value is compared to it:

```
function TfrmProgressBar.Test0To100: Integer;
var
  total: Integer;
  block: Integer;
  sw: TStopwatch;
  lastPct: Integer;
  currPct: Integer;
begin
  sw := TStopwatch.StartNew;
  ProgressBar1.Max := 100;
  ProgressBar1.Position := 0;
  lastPct := 0;

  total := 0;
  while total < CFileSize do begin
    block := CFileSize - total;
    if block > 1024 then
      block := 1024;
    // reading 'block' bytes
    Inc(total, block);
```

```
      currPct := Round(total / CFileSize * 100);
      if currPct > lastPct then
      begin
        lastPct := currPct;
        ProgressBar1.Position := currPct;
        ProgressBar1.Update;
      end;
    end;
    Result := sw.ElapsedMilliseconds;
  end;
```

File size is set to **2,000,000,000** bytes, or 1.86 GB. That is a lot, but completely reasonable for a video file or database storage. The block is set to 1024 to amplify the problem. With a more reasonable size of 65536 bytes, the difference is less noticeable.

As you can see, the second example contains more code and is a bit more complex. The result of those few additional lines is, however, more than impressive.

When you start the test program and click on a button, it will first run the slow code followed by the fast code. You will see a noticeable difference in display speed. This is also confirmed by the measurements:

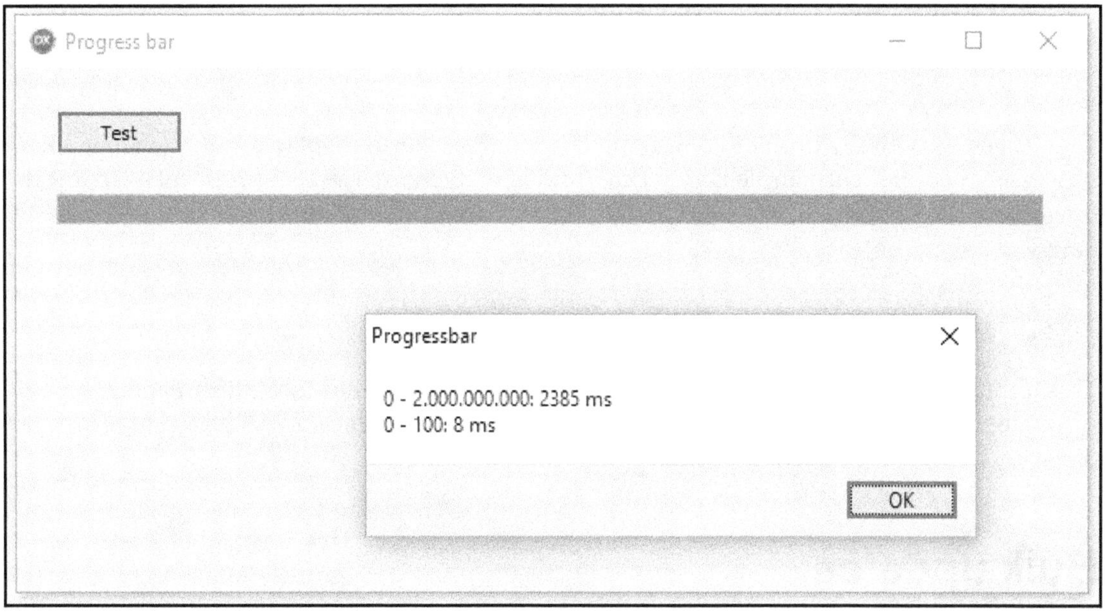

If you ran the demo code, you have probably noticed that the message showing the timing results is displayed *before* the progress bar finishes its crawl towards the full line. This is caused by a feature introduced in Windows Vista.

In Windows XP and before, updates to the progress bar were immediate. If you set `Max` to 100, `Position` to 0 and then a bit later updated `Position` to 50, the progress bar display would jump immediately to the middle. Since Vista, every change to the progress bar is animated. Changing `Position` from 0 to 50 results in an animation of the progress bar going from the left side to the middle of the control.

This makes for a nicer display but sometimes—as in our example—causes weird program behavior. As far as I know, there is only one way to work around the problem.

When I said that *every* change results in animation, I lied a bit. In reality, the animation is only triggered if you *increase* the position. If you *decrease* it, the change is displayed immediately.

We can, therefore, use the following trick. Instead of setting the `Position` to the desired value—`ProgressBar1.Position := currPct;`—we do that in two steps. Firstly we set it a bit too high (this causes the animation to start) and then we correctly position it to the correct value (this causes an immediate update):

```
ProgressBar1.Position := currPct+1;
ProgressBar1.Position := currPct;
```

This leaves us with the problem of forcing the progress bar to display a full line when all processing is done. The simplest way I can find is to decrease the `Max` property so that it is lower than the current `Position`. That also causes an immediate update to the progress bar:

```
ProgressBar1.Position := ProgressBar1.Max;
ProgressBar1.Max := ProgressBar1.Max - 1;
```

This technique of minimizing the number of changes also applies to multithreaded programs, especially when they want to update the user interface. I will return to it in `Chapter 7`, *Exploring Parallel Practices.*

Bulk updates

Another aspect of the same problem of overabundance of messages occurs when you want to add or modify multiple lines in a `TListBox` or `TMemo`. The demonstration program, `BeginUpdate`, demonstrates the problem and shows possible solutions.

Let's say we have a listbox and we want to populate it with lots of lines. The demo program displays 10,000 lines, which is enough to show the problem.

A naive program would solve the problem in two lines:

```
for i := 1 to CNumLines do
  ListBox1.Items.Add('Line ' + IntToStr(i));
```

This, of course, works. It is also unexpectedly slow. 10,000 lines is really not much for modern computers so we would expect this code to execute very quickly. In reality, it takes 1.4 seconds on my test machine!

We could do the same with a `TMemo`. The result, however, is a lot more terrible:

```
for i := 1 to CNumLines do
  Memo1.Lines.Add('Line ' + IntToStr(i));
```

With the memo we can see lines appear one by one. The total execution time on my computer is a whopping 12 seconds!

This would make both listbox and memo unusable for displaying a large amount of information. Luckily, this is something that the original VCL designers anticipated, so they provided a solution.

If you look into the code, you'll see that both `TListBox.Items` and `TMemo.Lines` are of the same type, `TStrings`. This class is used as a base class for `TStringList` and also for all graphical controls that display multiple lines of text.

The `TStrings` class also provides a solution. It implements methods `BeginUpdate` and `EndUpdate`, which turn visual updating of a control on and off. While we are in *update* mode (after `BeginUpdate` was called), visual control is not updated. Only when we call `EndUpdate` will Windows redraw the control to the new state.

`BeginUpdate` and `EndUpdate` calls can be nested. Control will only be updated when every `BeginUpdate` is paired with an `EndUpdate`:

```
ListBox1.Items.Add('1');   // immediate redraw
ListBox1.BeginUpdate;      // disables updating visual control
ListBox1.Items.Add('2');   // display is not updated
ListBox1.BeginUpdate;      // does nothing, we are already in *update* mode
ListBox1.Items.Add('3;);   // display is not updated
ListBox1.EndUpdate;        // does nothing, BeginUpdate was called twice
ListBox1.Items.Add('4');   // display is not updated
ListBox1.EndUpdate;        // exits update mode, changes to ListBox1 are
                           // displayed on the screen
```

Adding `BeginUpdate/EndUpdate` to existing code is very simple. We just have to wrap them around existing operations:

```
ListBox1.Items.BeginUpdate;
for i := 1 to CNumLines do
  ListBox1.Items.Add('Line ' + IntToStr(i));
ListBox1.Items.EndUpdate;

Memo1.Lines.BeginUpdate;
for i := 1 to CNumLines do
  Memo1.Lines.Add('Line ' + IntToStr(i));
Memo1.Lines.EndUpdate;
```

If you click on the second button in the demo program you'll see that the program reacts much faster. Execution times on my computer were 48 ms for `TListBox` and 671 ms for `TMemo`. This second number still seems suspicious. Why does `TMemo` need 0.7 seconds to add 10,000 lines if changes are not painted on the screen?

To find an answer to that we have to dig into VCL code, into the `TStrings.Add` method:

```
function TStrings.Add(const S: string): Integer;
begin
  Result := GetCount;
  Insert(Result, S);
end;
```

Firstly, this method calls `GetCount` so that it can return the proper index of appended elements. Concrete implementation in `TMemoStrings.GetCount` sends two Windows messages even when the control is in the *updating* mode:

```
Result := SendMessage(Memo.Handle, EM_GETLINECOUNT, 0, 0);
if SendMessage(Memo.Handle, EM_LINELENGTH, SendMessage(Memo.Handle,
  EM_LINEINDEX, Result - 1, 0), 0) = 0 then Dec(Result);
```

After that, `TMemoStrings.Insert` sends three messages to update the current selection:

```
if Index >= 0 then
begin
  SelStart := SendMessage(Memo.Handle, EM_LINEINDEX, Index, 0);
  // some code skipped ... it is not executed in our case
  SendMessage(Memo.Handle, EM_SETSEL, SelStart, SelStart);
  SendTextMessage(Memo.Handle, EM_REPLACESEL, 0, Line);
end;
```

All that causes five Windows messages to be sent for each appended line and that slows the program down. Can we do it better? Sure!

To speed up TMemo, you have to collect all updates in some secondary storage, for example in a TStringList. At the end, just assign the new memo state to its Text property and it will be updated in one massive operation.

The third button in the demo program does just that:

```
sl := TStringList.Create;
for i := 1 to CNumLines do
  sl.Add('Line ' + IntToStr(i));
Memo1.Text := sl.Text;
FreeAndNil(sl);
```

This change brings execution speed closer to the listbox. My computer needed only 75 ms to display 10,000 lines in a memo with this code.

An interesting comparison can be made by executing the same code in the FireMonkey framework. Graphical controls in FireMonkey are not based directly on Windows controls, so effects of BeginUpdate/EndUpdate may be different.

The program BeginUpdateFMX in the code archive does just that. I will not go through the whole process again, but just present the measurements. All times are in milliseconds:

framework	**update method**	**TListBox**	**TMemo**
VCL	direct update	1444	12231
	BeginUpdate	48	671
	Text	N/A	75
FireMonkey	direct update	8760	406
	BeginUpdate	44	137
	Text	N/A	131

We can see that BeginUpdate/EndUpdate are also useful in the FireMonkey framework.

TIP

If a class implements BeginUpdate/EndUpdate, use it when doing bulk updates.

In the next part, we'll see how we can replace a TListBox with an even faster solution if we are programming with the VCL framework.

Virtual display

A long time ago Mike Lischke wrote a great Delphi component—Virtual TreeView. He stopped supporting it a long time ago, but the component found a new sponsor and a place on GitHub: `https://github.com/Virtual-TreeView`.

Virtual TreeView supports the VCL framework in Delphi XE3 and later. There are also versions of code that support older Delphis, but you'll have to look around for them. To use it, you have to download the source and recompile two included packages. That will add three new components to Delphi. This example will use the most useful of them, `TVirtualStringTree`.

> Alternatively, you can install Virtual TreeView with the Delphi's GetIt Package Manager if you are using Delphi XE8 or newer.

The `VirtualTree` demo compares `TListBox` with `TVirtualStringTree` where the latter is used in different ways. Although `TVirtualStringTree` is very flexible and designed to display tree structures, we can also use it as a very fast listbox, as I will do in this example. To use it as a listbox, you should **remove** options `toShowRoot` and `toShowTreeLines` from the component's `TreeOptions.PaintOptions` property.

> Before you start using Virtual TreeView, go through the included demos. They show all the power of this component.

This demo compares two different modes of operation. One is adding lots of lines in one operation. We already know that we should use `BeginUpdate`/`EndUpdate` in this case.

The other mode is adding just one line to the list. As this is hard to measure precisely, the operation is repeated 100 times.

Virtual TreeView is different from other components included with Delphi. It operates on a *view/model* principle. The component itself just displays the data (presents a *view* on the data) but doesn't store it internally. Data itself is stored in a storage that we have to maintain (a *model*). Virtual TreeView only stores a short reference that helps us access the data.

The first thing that we must do before we can use the component is to decide how large this *reference to data* is and set the `NodeDataSize` property accordingly.

Typically, we'll use an integer index (4 bytes), or an object or interface (4 bytes on Win32 and 8 bytes on Win64). We can also store larger quantities of data in this area, but that kind of defeats the view/model separation principle. In this example, I'll use a simple `integer` so `NodeDataSize` is set to 4.

The simplest way to use `TVirtualStringTree` is to use the `AddChild` method to add a new *node* (display line) and pass a *user data* (reference to model) as a parameter:

```
VirtualStringTree1.BeginUpdate;
for i := 1 to 10000 do begin
  idx := FModel1.Add('Line ' + IntToStr(i));
  VirtualStringTree1.AddChild(nil, pointer(idx));
end;
VirtualStringTree1.EndUpdate;
```

The code uses global `FModel1: TStringList` for data storage. It firstly adds the data to the model `FModel1.Add` and sets the index of this data (`idx`) as user data for the newly-created node (`AddChild`).

The first parameter to `AddChild` is a reference to the node's parent. As we are not displaying a tree structure but a list, we simply set it to `nil` (meaning that there is no parent). The second parameter represents user data. `AddChild` supports only `pointer` user data so we have to cast our parameter accordingly.

We also have to take care of retrieving the data from the model so it can be displayed on the screen. For that, we have to write `OnGetText` event handler. This event is called once for each column of each **visible** line. It is not called for lines that are not visible on the screen.

The code must firstly call `Node.GetData` to get the *user data* associated with the node. To be more precise, `GetData` returns a **pointer** to user data. As we know that our user data is just an integer, we can cast this pointer to `PInteger` to access the value (index into the `FModel1` string list):

```
procedure TfrmVTV.VirtualStringTree1GetText(Sender: TBaseVirtualTree;
  Node: PVirtualNode; Column: TColumnIndex; TextType: TVSTTextType;
  var CellText: string);
begin
  CellText := FModel1[PInteger(Node.GetData)^];
end;
```

If you run the demonstration program and click the **Add 10.000 lines** button, you'll see that the listbox needs more time for the operation (68 ms in my case) than Virtual TreeView (16 ms). Quite nice!

Clicking the second button, **Add 1 line 100 times**, shows something completely different. In this case, the listbox is a lot faster (17 ms) than the Virtual TreeView (184 ms).

I must admit that I didn't expect that so I did some digging around. As it turns out, `TVirtualStringTree` **sorts** its data on each call to `AddChild` (unless we called `BeginUpdate` before that!) This may be useful if you are using a multi-column view where data can be sorted on the selected column, but in our case, it only destroys the performance.

The fix for that is very simple. Just remove the `toAutoSort` option from the component's `TreeOptions.AutoOptions` property.

I cleared this flag in the second `TVirtualStringTree` and the result is obvious. Adding 100 lines now takes 17 ms instead of 184 ms and is on par with the listbox.

The third `TVirtualStringTree` pushes the whole virtual aspect to the max. Instead of initializing nodes in code (by calling `AddChild`), we just tell the component how many nodes it must display by setting the `RootNodeCount` property and the component will call the `OnInitNode` event handler for each node that is currently **visible on the screen**. In this mode, not only painting but the initialization is executed on demand!

```
for i := 1 to 10000 do
  FModel3.Add('Line ' + IntToStr(i));
VirtualStringTree3.RootNodeCount := VirtualStringTree3.RootNodeCount +
10000;
```

This approach is only feasible if we can somehow determine the part of the model that is associated with the given node in the `OnInitNode` handler. The only information we have at that moment is the node's index in the list (the `Node.Index` property). The first node gets index 0, second index 1, and so on. Luckily, that is exactly the same as the index into the `TStringList` so we can just use the `SetData` method to set the user data:

```
procedure TfrmVTV.VirtualStringTree3InitNode(Sender: TBaseVirtualTree;
  ParentNode, Node: PVirtualNode;
  var InitialStates: TVirtualNodeInitStates);
begin
  Node.SetData(pointer(Node.Index));
end;
```

TIP

In addition to `SetData` and `GetData` there are also generic versions of those functions, `GetData<T>` and `SetData<T>`, which are of tremendous use if we want to use user data as a storage for an object or an interface. The code implements all necessary reference counting so that interfaces are correctly managed.

This on-demand initialization approach speeds the program up even more. The addition of 10,000 lines now takes only 3 ms. The speed when adding lines one by one is not affected, though:

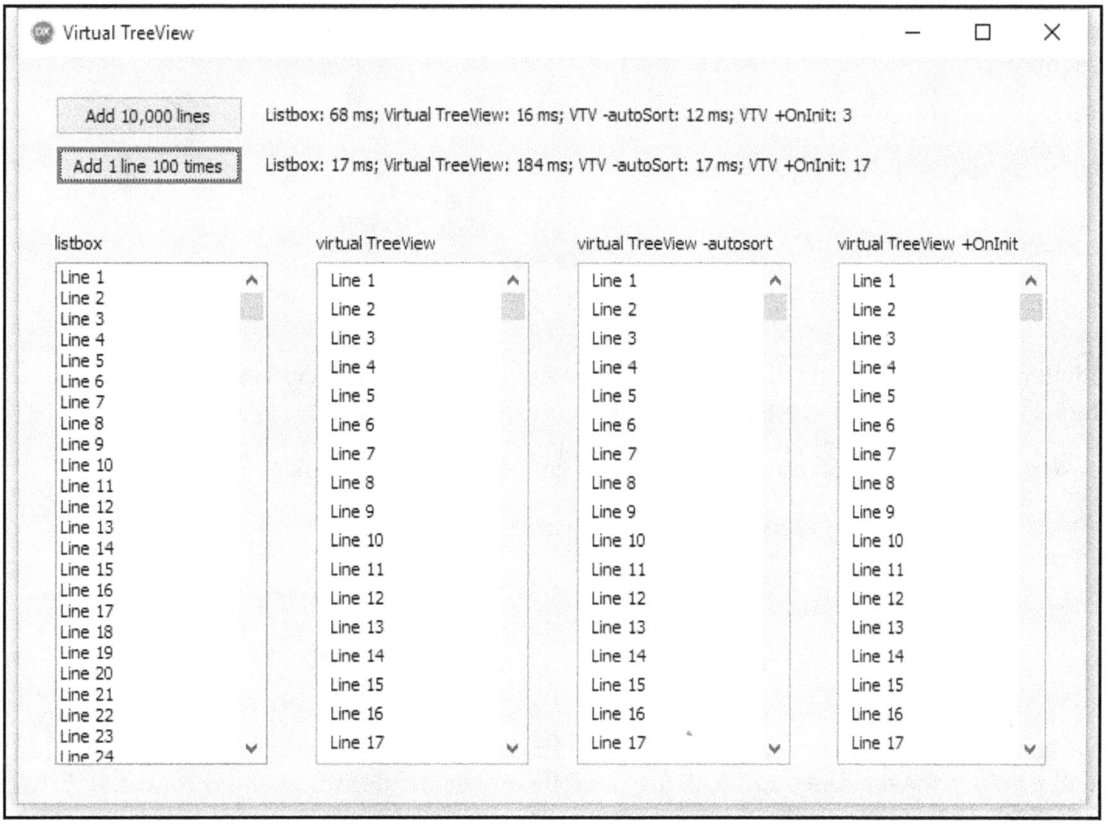

VirtualTree demo showing different approaches to managing the TVirtualStringTree component

This concludes my foray into user interface land. The second part of this chapter will deal with an aspect of algorithmic improvement which we usually ignore—caching. And at the very end I will return to Mr. Smith's code from `Chapter 1`, *About Performance*, and make it run much faster.

Caching

Our good friend Mr. Smith has improved his programming skills considerably. Currently, he is learning about recursive functions and he programmed his first recursive piece of code. He wrote a simple seven-liner which calculates the nth element in the *Fibonacci* sequence:

```
function TfrmFibonacci.FibonacciRecursive(element: int64): int64;
begin
  if element < 3 then
    Result := 1
  else
    Result := FibonacciRecursive(element - 1) +
              FibonacciRecursive(element - 2);
end;
```

I will not argue with him—if you look up the definition of a Fibonacci sequence it really looks like it could be perfectly solved with a recursive function.

A sequence of Fibonacci numbers, *F*, is defined with two simple rules:

- First two numbers in the sequence are both 1 ($F_1 = 1$, $F_2 = 1$),
- Every other number in the sequence is the sum of the preceding two ($F_n = F_{n-1} + F_{n-2}$).

You will also find a different definition of the Fibonacci sequence in the literature, starting with values 0 and 1, but it only differs from our definition in the initial zero. Our definition will produce the sequence 1, 1, 2, 3, 5, 8 ... while the second definition will produce 0, 1, 1, 2, 3, 5, 8.

As I've said, a naive approach to writing a Fibonacci function is to write a recursive function, as Mr. Smith did. This way, however, leads to an exceedingly slow program.

Try it yourself. A program, *Fibonacci*, from the code archive for this book implements Mr. Smith's functions in the `FibonacciRecursive` method. Enter a number up to `30` in the **Element number** edit field, click **Recursive** and you'll get your answer in a few milliseconds. Increase this value to `40` and you'll have to wait about a second!

The numbers show that if you increase the element number just by one, the calculation time goes up about 50%. That accumulates quickly. My computer needs more than 13 seconds to calculate element number 46, and 96 seconds—a minute and a half!—for element number 50. What is going on?

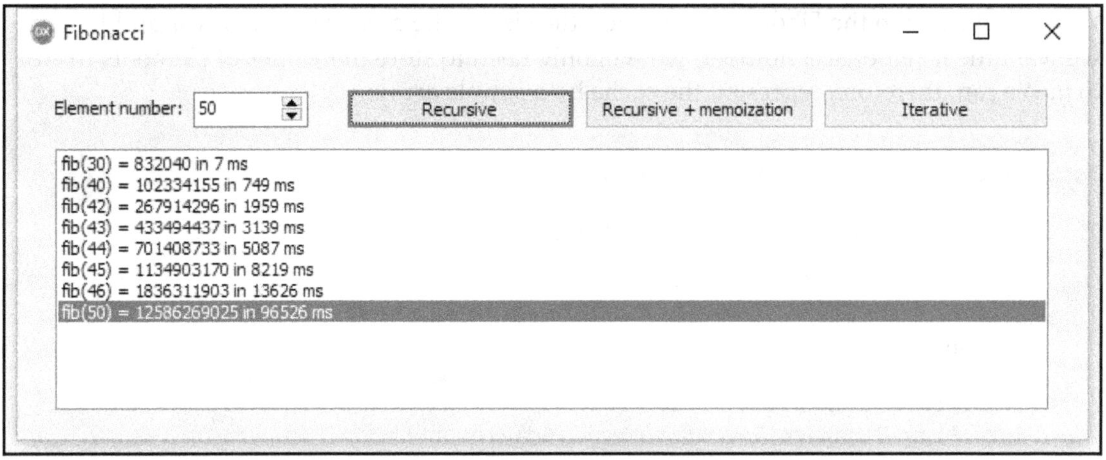

Calculating Fibonacci numbers the recursive way

The problem with the naive implementation is that it has $O(2^n)$ complexity. When you calculate a value of the function, the first call to `FibonacciRecursive` causes two new calls. These cause two more calls each (2*2 = 4) and these four causes two more calls each (2*4 = 8) and so on. We have, therefore, 2^0 (= 1) calls initially, $2^1 = 2$ on the first level of recursion, $2^2 = 4$ on the second level, $2^3 = 8$ on the third, and that goes on and on until we need to calculate elements 1 or 2.

A careful examination of these recursive calls shows us something interesting. Let's say we want to calculate the 10th element in the sequence, F_{10}. That causes recursive calls to calculate F_9 and F_8. F_9 causes recursive calls for F_8 and F_7, while F_8 causes recursive calls for F_7 and F_6. In the next level of recursion we have to calculate F_7 an F_6, F_6 and F_5, F_6 and F_5 again, and F_5 and F_4. We see that we are calculating the same values over and over again, and that definitely doesn't help the execution speed.

A solution to this type of problem is *caching* (sometimes also called *memoization*). Simply put, whenever we calculate a result corresponding to some inputs, we put it into storage—a *cache*. When we have to calculate a value corresponding to the *same* inputs, we just pull it from the cache.

This is a very powerful technique that brings in its own collection of problems. We have to decide the size of the cache. Maybe we could cache every already-calculated value, but they will often be too abundant to store. We also have to create and destroy this cache somewhere.

When dealing with the Fibonacci sequence, the size of the cache is not really a problem. If we want the nth Fibonacci number, we will only need to store the values of elements from 1 to n. We can, therefore, represent the cache by a simple array:

```
var
  FFibonacciTable: TArray<int64>;

function TfrmFibonacci.FibonacciMemoized(element: int64): int64;
var
  i: Integer;
begin
  SetLength(FFibonacciTable, element+1);
  for i := Low(FFibonacciTable) to High(FFibonacciTable) do
    FFibonacciTable[i] := -1;
  Result := FibonacciRecursiveMemoized(element);
end;
```

The main function, `FibonacciMemoized`, firstly creates the cache `FFibonacciTable`. As dynamic arrays start counting elements with 0, the code allocates one element more than needed, simply to be able to address this array with index `[element]` instead of `[element-1]`. One `int64` more for better code clarity; not a bad compromise!

Secondly, the code initializes all cache elements to -1. As the elements of the Fibonacci sequence are always a positive number, we can use -1 to represent an uninitialized cache slot.

In the end, the code calls the memoized version of the recursive function.

As dynamic arrays are managed by the compiler, we don't have to destroy the cache after the calculation.

The recursive method, `FibonacciRecursiveMemoized`, is very similar to Mr. Smith's code, except that it adds the cache management. At the beginning, it will check the cache to see if the value for the current element was already calculated. If it was, the result is simply taken from the cache. Otherwise, the value is calculated recursively and the result is added to the cache:

```
function TfrmFibonacci.FibonacciRecursiveMemoized(element: int64): int64;
begin
  if FFibonacciTable[element] >= 0 then
    Result := FFibonacciTable[element]
  else
  begin
    if element < 3 then
      Result := 1
    else
```

```
      Result := FibonacciRecursiveMemoized(element - 1) +
                FibonacciRecursiveMemoized(element - 2);
    FFibonacciTable[element] := Result;
  end;
end;
```

In the *Fibonacci* program, you can use the *Recursive + memoization* button to test this version. You'll see that it will need very little time to calculate Fibonacci sequence elements up to number 92. On my computer, it always needs less than 1 millisecond.

Why 92, actually? Well, because the 93rd Fibonacci number exceeds the highest `int64` value and the result turns negative. Indeed, F_{92} is larger than 2^{63}, which is a really big number by itself!

So, is this memoized solution a good way of calculating Fibonacci numbers? No, it is not! A much better way is just to start with the first two values (1 and 1), then add them to get F_3 (1 + 1 = 2), add F_2 and F_3 to get F_4 (1 + 2 = 3), and so on. This *iterative* solution is much faster than the cached recursive solution although our timing doesn't show that. The precision is simply not good enough and both versions will show a running time of 0 milliseconds:

```
function TfrmFibonacci.FibonacciIterative(element: int64): int64;
var
  a,b: int64;
begin
  a := 1;
  b := 0;
  repeat
    if element = 1 then
      Exit(a);
    b := b + a;
    if element = 2 then
      Exit(b);
    a := a + b;
    Dec(element, 2);
  until false;
end;
```

Dynamic cache

A static cache that can only grow has only limited use. We could, for example, use it to store RTTI properties of types, as access to the RTTI is relatively slow. In most cases, however, a limited-size cache that stores only N most recently used values is more appropriate.

Writing such a cache is quite a tricky operation. First and foremost, we need quick access to a value associated with a specific input (let's call that input a **key**). In `Chapter 1`, *About Performance*, we found out that the best way to do that is a hash table (or, in Delphi terms, `TDictionary`), which has $O(1)$ lookup time.

So that's solved, our cache will store data in a dictionary. But we also have to remove the values from the dictionary (as this cache has a limited size) and there lies the big problem!

When a cache is full (when it reaches some pre-set size) we would like to remove the **oldest** element from the cache. We could, for example, replace the value part of the dictionary with a pair (date/time, value) where *date/time* would contain the last modification time of this key, but finding the oldest key in the cache then becomes an $O(n)$ operation (in the worst case we have to scan all (date/time, value) pairs) which is something that we would like to avoid.

> Removing the *oldest* elements from the cache is an implementation detail, not a requirement. We could also remove the element which was not *accessed* for the longest time or which was least recently *updated*.

Another alternative would be a sorted list of all keys. When we need to update a key, we can find it with $O(\log n)$ steps and insert it at the beginning in $O(1)$ steps (but this is an expensive step as it needs to move other elements around in memory). To get the oldest element, we can just check the last element in the list (very fast $O(1)$). However, we can do even better than that.

Let's look again at the requirements. We need a data structure that satisfies the following criteria:

- Data is kept in the *modification* order. In other words, when you insert an item into the structure, that item becomes the first element in the structure.
- When you update an item, it moves to the front (it becomes the first element).

Whenever you need a data structure with these conditions, the answer is always a *doubly-linked list*. This is a list of items where each item contains some value, plus two pointers - one pointing to the previous element and one to the next one. The first element doesn't have a predecessor and the last element doesn't have a successor. These two links point to a special value (for example, `nil`).

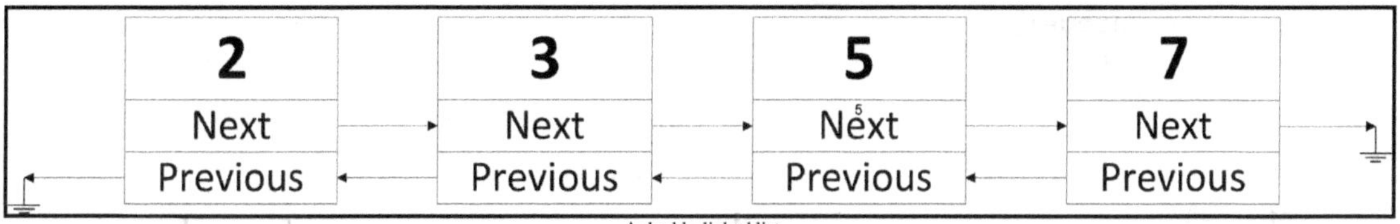

A doubly-linked list

Removing an element from such a list is very fast. You just have to change a few pointers. The same goes for insertion into such a list.

> Keep in mind that *pointers* in this context don't necessarily mean Delphi pointers. One can also build a list in an array and a *pointer* would then simply be an integer index into this array.

I have implemented a very fast cache, `TDHPCache<K,V>`, based around a hash table and doubly-linked list. You can find it in the `DHPCache` unit, together with a simple test app, `CacheDemo`.

`TDHPCache` is a generic cache class with two type parameters—the key `K` and value `V`. Its public interface implement only a few functions:

```
TDHPCache<K,V> = class
public
  constructor Create(ANumElements: Integer; AOwnsValues: boolean = false);
  destructor Destroy; override;
  function TryGetValue(const key: K; var value: V): boolean;
  procedure Update(const key: K; const value: V);
end;
```

The `Create` constructor creates a cache with the specified maximum size. The cache can optionally own values that you insert into the cache, which allows you to cache objects.

The `TryGetValue` function tries to retrieve a value associated with the specified key. Success or failure is indicated through the Boolean result.

The `Update` procedure stores the value in the cache and associates it with the specified key. It also makes sure that the key is now first in the list of most recently used keys.

Internally, all keys and values are stored in a doubly-linked list. As we know the maximum size of this list (`ANumElements` parameter passed to the constructor), we can create it as a simple array of elements of (internal) type `TListElement`:

```
strict private type
  TListElement = record
```

```
      Next : Integer;
      Prev : Integer;
      Key : K;
      Value: V;
    end;
  var
    FCache : TDictionary<K,Integer>;
    FKeys : TArray<TListElement>;
    FFreeList : Integer;
    FHead : Integer;
    FTail : Integer;
```

This list is not using Delphi pointers to link elements. Instead, each `Next` and `Prev` field simply contains an index into the `FKeys` array or -1 if there is no next/previous item. (-1, in this case, corresponds to a `nil` pointer.)

Two lists are actually stored in this array. One element is always in exactly one of those two lists, so parallel storage is not a problem.

The first list contains all unused items. The `FFreeList` field points to the first element in this list. When a `TDHPCache` class is created, the `BuildLinkedList` method (not shown here) adds all elements of `FKeys` to this list.

The second list contains all used (cached) items. The `FHead` field points to the first (most recently modified) element in this list and the `FTail` field points to the last (oldest) element in this list. In the beginning, this list is empty and both `FHead` and `FTail` contain -1.

The cache also uses a `FCache` dictionary, which maps keys into array indexes.

To retrieve a value, `TryGetValue` calls `FCache.TryGetValue` to get the array index associated with the key. If that function returns `True`, the associated value is read from the `FKeys` array. Both operations execute in *O(1)* time, which makes the whole function *O(1)*:

```
function TDHPCache<K, V>.TryGetValue(const key: K; var value: V): boolean;
var
  element: Integer;
begin
  Result := FCache.TryGetValue(key, element);
  if Result then
    value := FKeys[element].Value;
end;
```

Updating a value is a bit more complicated. The function first tries to find the key in the cache. If found, the value in the `FKeys` is updated. Both operations are *O(1)*.

The code looks a bit more complicated because it must handle the destruction of the old value when the cache owns its values:

```
procedure TDHPCache<K, V>.UpdateElement(element: Integer; const key: K;
const value: V);
var
  oldValue: V;
begin
  if not FOwnsValues then
    FKeys[element].Value := value
  else
  begin
    oldValue := FKeys[element].Value;
    if PObject(@value)^ <> PObject(@oldValue)^ then
    begin
      FKeys[element].Value := value;
      PObject(@oldValue)^.DisposeOf;
    end;
  end;
  MoveToFront(element);
end;

procedure TDHPCache<K, V>.Update(const key: K; const value: V);
var
  element: Integer;
begin
  if FCache.TryGetValue(key, element) then
    UpdateElement(element, key, value)
  else
    AddElement(key, value);
end;
```

The `AddElement` gets executed when a new (key, value) pair is added to the cache. First, it checks whether the list is full. This can be done simply by checking the `FFreeList` pointer—if it points to an array element, the list is not yet full. Then the code either removes the oldest element from the list (discussed in the following) or allocates a new element from the free list. The latter is done by moving a few pointers around in *O(1)* time.

Next, a new element is inserted at the beginning of the list. Again, just a few pointers are moved and the code runs in *O(1)*.

Finally, key and value are updated and (key, index) mapping is inserted into the dictionary, which is again an *O(1)* operation:

```
procedure TDHPCache<K, V>.AddElement(const key: K; const value: V);
var
  element: integer;
begin
  if IsFull then
    element := RemoveOldest
  else
    element := GetFree;
  InsertInFront(element);
  FKeys[element].Key := key;
  FKeys[element].Value := value;
  FCache.Add(key, element);
end;
```

The only unsolved part is the `RemoveOldest` function. It will first remove the last element from the list (`Unlink(FTail)`), which is a simple *O(1)* operation. Then it will remove the (key, index) mapping from the cache (*O(1)*) and destroy the old value if the cache owns its values:

```
function TDHPCache<K, V>.RemoveOldest: Integer;
var
  element: Integer;
begin
  if FTail < 0 then
    raise Exception.Create('TDHPCache<K, V>.RemoveOldest: List is empty!');
  Result := FTail;
  Unlink(FTail);
  FCache.Remove(FKeys[Result].Key);
  if FOwnsValues then
    PObject(@FKeys[Result].Value)^.DisposeOf;
end;
```

As you can see, we have created a data structure that can insert, update, delete (when it is full), and retrieve elements all in *O(1)*. In `Chapter 1`, *About Performance,* however, I stated that there is always a trade-off and that not all operations can be fast in one data structure. What is going on here?

The answer is that we are gaining speed by duplicating the data, namely the keys. Each key is stored twice—once in the doubly—linked list and once in the dictionary. If you remove one copy of this key, some operations will slow down.

Speeding up SlowCode

For the last practical example, we can try speeding up Mr. Smith's `SlowCode` from `Chapter 1`, *About Performance*. Here, we immediately ran into a problem. To fix or change an algorithm we must understand what the code does. This happens a lot in practice, especially when you inherit some code. Reading and understanding code that you didn't write is an important skill.

Let's try to understand the first part of `SlowCode`. The `for` loop in `SlowMethod` starts counting with 2. Then it calls `ElementInDataDivides`, which does nothing as the `data` list is empty. Next, `SlowMethod` adds 2 to the list.

Next, `i` takes the value of 3. `ElementInDataDivides` checks if 3 is divisible by 2. It is not, so `SlowMethod` adds 3 to the list.

In the next step, *i = 4*, it is divisible by 2, and 4 is **not** added to the list. 5 is then added to the list (it is not divisible by 2 or 3), 6 is not (divisible by 2), 7 is added (not divisible by 2, 3, or 5), 8 is not (divisible by 2), 9 is not (divisible by 3), and so on:

```
function ElementInDataDivides(data: TList<Integer>; value: Integer):
boolean;
var
  i: Integer;
begin
  Result := True;
  for i in data do
    if (value <> i) and ((value mod i) = 0) then
      Exit;
  Result := False;
end;

function SlowMethod(highBound: Integer): TArray<Integer>;
var
  i: Integer;
  temp: TList<Integer>;
begin
  temp := TList<Integer>.Create;
  try
    for i := 2 to highBound do
      if not ElementInDataDivides(temp, i) then
        temp.Add(i);
    Result := Filter(temp);
  finally
    FreeAndNil(temp);
  end;
end;
```

We now understand what the first part (before calling the `Filter` method) does. It calculates prime numbers with a very simple test. It tries to divide each candidate by every already-generated prime. If the candidate number is not divisible by any known prime number, it is also a prime number and we can add it to the list.

Can we improve this algorithm? With a bit of mathematical knowledge, we can do exactly that! As it turns out (the proof is in the next information box and you can safely skip it), we don't have to test divisibility with every generated prime number. If we are testing number *value*, we only have to test divisibility with a prime number smaller or equal to *Sqrt(value)* (square root of *value*).

> My assumption is this: If we have number n, which is not divisible by any number smaller than or equal to *Sqrt(n)*, then it is also not divisible by any number larger than *Sqrt(n)*. The simplest way to prove that is by establishing a contradiction.
>
> Let's say that we can divide n by p. We can, therefore, write $n = p * k$. As n is not divisible by numbers smaller than or equal to *Sqrt(n)*, both p and k must be strictly larger than *Sqrt(n)*. If that is true, $p * k$ must be strictly larger than *Sqrt(n) * Sqrt(n)*, or n.
>
> On one side we have $n = p * k$, and on the other $p * k > n$. These cannot both be true at the same time so we have run into a contradiction. Therefore, the initial assumption is correct.

We can, therefore, rewrite `ElementInDataDivides` so that it will stop the loop when the first prime number larger than `Sqrt(value)` is encountered. You can find the following code in the `SlowCode_v2` program:

```
function ElementInDataDivides(data: TList<Integer>; value: Integer):
boolean;
var
  i: Integer;
  highBound: integer;
begin
  Result := True;
  highBound := Trunc(Sqrt(value));
  for i in data do begin
    if i > highBound then
      break;
    if (value <> i) and ((value mod i) = 0) then
      Exit;
```

```
    end;
    Result := False;
  end;
```

If we compare the original version with time complexity *O(n^2)* with this improved version with time complexity *O(n * sqrt n)*, we can see a definite improvement. Still, we can do even better!

Try to search *prime number generation* on the internet and you'll quickly find a very simple algorithm which was invented way before computers. It is called the *sieve of Eratosthenes* and was invented by the Greek scholar who lived in the third century BC.

I will not go into detail here. For the theory, you can check Wikipedia and for a practical example, see the `SlowCode_Sieve` program in the code archive. Let me just say that the sieve of Eratosthenes has a time complexity of *O(n log log n)*, which is very close to *O(n)*. It should, therefore, be quite a bit faster than our *Sqrt(n)* improvement.

The following table compares `SlowCode`, `SlowCode_v2`, and `SlowCode_Sieve` for different inputs. The highest input was not tested with the original program as it would run for more than an hour. All times are in milliseconds:

highest number tested	**SlowCode**	**SlowCode_v2**	**SlowCode_Sieve**
10,000	19	2	0
100,000	861	29	7
1,000,000	54.527	352	77
10,000,000	not tested	5769	1072

Summary

In this chapter, I touched on two very different topics. First, I looked at responsive user interfaces and how to make them faster and then I continued with the concept of *caching*. That topic was introduced with a simple example, followed by a fully-featured cache implementation that you can use in your programs.

In the end, I returned to the example `SlowCode` program from `Chapter 1`, *About Performance*. First, I used some detective work to find out what it really does, which allowed me to improve it a lot. The code now processes a million numbers in mere milliseconds and not **minutes** as the original program did.

In the next chapter, I'll focus on optimizing the code on a smaller level. We will look at various Delphi language and RTL elements and you'll learn which parts of the language and system libraries can behave slower than one would expect and what you can do to improve that.

3
Fine-Tuning the Code

I have stated repeatedly that the best way to improve code speed is to change the algorithm. Sometimes, however, this is just not possible because you are already using the best possible algorithm. It may also be completely impractical as changing the algorithm may require rewriting a large part of the program.

If this is the case and the code is still not running fast enough, we have multiple available options. We can start *optimizing* the program, by which I mean that we can start changing small parts of the program and replacing them with faster code. This is the topic of the chapter that you are currently reading.

Another option would be to rewrite a part of the program in *assembler*. Delphi offers quite decent support for that and we'll look into that possibility near the end of this chapter. We can also find a *library* that solves our problem. It could be written in an assembler or created by a compiler that produces faster code than Delphi—typically we don't care. We only have to know how to *link* it into our program and that will be the topic of `Chapter 8`, *Using External Libraries.*

The last option is to somehow split our problem into multiple parts and solve them in parallel. We'll dig into this approach in Chapters 5 to 7.

But first, fine-tuning the code, or how to make the program run faster with small changes. In this chapter, you'll find:

- How Delphi compiler settings can affect the program speed
- Why it is good to use local variables to store intermediate results
- How to work with the CPU window
- What happens behind the scenes when you work with different data types

- How to speed up the code by using RTL functions
- How to use an assembler to speed up the code
- How we can make `SlowCode` run even faster

Delphi compiler settings

First things first—before you start meddling with the code, you should check the Delphi compiler settings for your project. In some situations, they can affect the code speed quite a lot.

To check and possibly change compiler settings, open your project, then select **Project | Options** from the menu or press *Ctrl* + *Shift* + *F11*. Relevant options can be found in the branch **Delphi Compiler | Compiling**, as shown in the following screenshot here:

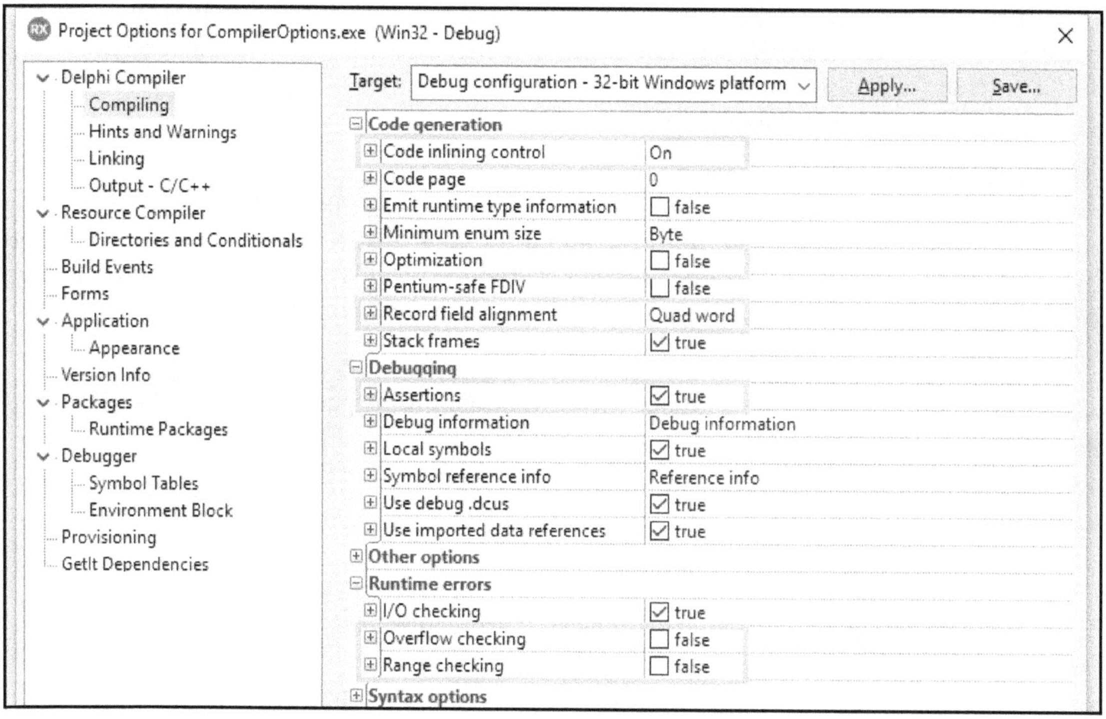

Compiler settings that influence program speed

We will look into the following options:

- Code inlining control
- Optimization
- Record field alignment
- Assertions
- Overflow checking
- Range checking

All of these settings can be enabled/disabled for the complete project and they can also be turned on/off in the code by using *compiler directives* (comments that start with `{$`).

Code inlining control

We will look into the concept of **code inlining** later in this chapter, in the section, *Optimizing method calls*, so this text will serve just as an introduction.

By setting the value of **Code inlining control**, you define the default behavior for the complete project. The possible values for that setting are `On`, `Off`, and `Auto`. This default value can be changed in the code by inserting `{$INLINE ON}`, `{$INLINE OFF}`, or `{$INLINE AUTO}` into the source.

The `INLINE` state can be set to a different value at a place where the inlined method is defined and a place where it is used (called). This creates six possible combinations.

When we look at the method definition, INLINE has the following meaning:

- `INLINE ON`: If the method is marked with the `inline` directive (more on that later), it will be marked as *inlineable*
- `INLINE AUTO`: Same as `INLINE ON`, with the addition that any routine not marked with `inline` will still be marked *inlineable* if its code size is less than or equal to 32 bytes
- `INLINE OFF`: The routine will not be marked as *inlineable* even if it is marked with `inline`

At the place of use, `INLINE` has a different meaning:

- `INLINE ON`: If a called method is marked as *inlineable*, it will be expanded inline (at the place of call) if possible

- `INLINE AUTO`: Same as `INLINE ON`
- `INLINE OFF`: The routine will not be expanded inline, even if it is marked *inlineable*

Optimization

The **Optimization** option controls code optimization. The possible values are `On` and `Off`. This setting can also be controlled with compiler directives `{$OPTIMIZATION ON}` and `{$OPTIMIZATION OFF}` or with equivalent `{$O+}` and `{$O-}`.

When optimization is enabled, the compiler optimizes generated code for speed. Optimizations are guaranteed not to change the behavior of the program. The only reason you may want to turn optimization off is to improve debugging. When optimization is turned on, debugging—especially stepping through the code and evaluating variables—may not be working correctly in all cases.

TIP: My approach is to turn optimization off during development, and on when building the release version.

The `$O` (or `$OPTIMIZATION`) directive can only turn optimization on or off for an entire method. You cannot turn optimization on or off for selected lines within a method.

To show the effect of different compiler options, I have written a `CompilerOptions` demo. When you click the **Optimization** button, the following code will be run twice—once with optimization turned on and once off.

The code initializes an array and then does some calculations on all of its elements. All of this is repeated 1,000 times because otherwise it is hard to measure differences. Modern CPUs are fast!

```
function NonOptimized: int64;
var
  arr1: array [1..50000] of Integer;
  i,j: Integer;
begin
  for j := 1 to 1000 do
  begin
    for i := Low(arr1) to High(arr1) do
      arr1[i] := i;
    for i := Low(arr1) to High(arr1)-1 do
      arr1[i] := arr1[i] + arr1[i+1];
```

```
  end;
end;
```

The results will be different depending on the CPU speed and model, but on all computers the optimized version should be significantly faster. On my test machine, the optimized version runs approximately six times faster than the non-optimized! Here are the results:

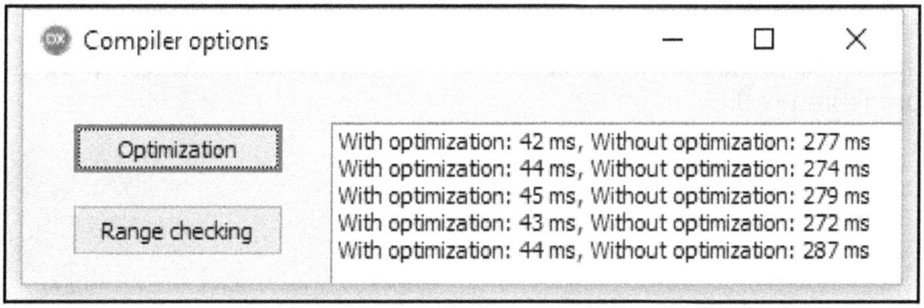

Although you can turn compilation options on and off with compiler directives, Delphi provides no direct support for switching back to the previous state. You can, however, check whether a compilation option is currently turned on or off by using the `{$IFOPT}` compiler directive.

Then you can define or undefine some conditional compilation symbol that will tell you later what the original state of the compilation option was:

```
{$IFOPT O+}{$DEFINE OPTIMIZATION}{$ELSE}{$UNDEF OPTIMIZATION}{$ENDIF}
 {$OPTIMIZATION ON}
```

When you want to restore the original state, use this conditional to turn the compilation option on or off:

```
{$IFDEF OPTIMIZATION}{$OPTIMIZATION ON}{$ELSE}{$OPTIMIZATION OFF}{$ENDIF}
```

This technique is used throughout the `CompilerOptions` demo with different compilation options.

Record field alignment

The third compiler option I'd like to discuss regulates the alignment of fields in Delphi record and class types. It can be set to the following values: `Off`, `Byte`, `Word`, `Double Word`, and `Quad Word`. Settings are a bit misleading, as the first two values actually result in the same behavior.

You can use compiler directives `{$ALIGN 1}`, `{$ALIGN 2}`, `{$ALIGN 4}`, and `{$ALIGN 8}` to change record field alignment in code, or equivalent short forms `{$A1}`, `{$A2}`, `{$A4}`, and `{$A8}`. There are also two directives which exist only for backward compatibility. `{$A+}` means the same as `{$A8}` (which is also a default for new programs) and `{$A-}` is the same as `{$A1}`.

Field alignment controls exactly how fields in records and classes are laid out in memory.

Let's say that we have the following record. And let's say that the address of the first field in the record is simply 0:

```
type
  TRecord = record
    Field1: byte;
    Field2: int64;
    Field3: word;
    Field4: double;
  end;
```

With the `{$A1}` alignment, each field will simply follow the next one. In other words, `Field2` will start at address 1, `Field3` at 9, and `Field4` at 11. As the size of `double` is 8 (as we'll see later in this chapter), the total size of the record is 19 bytes.

> **TIP:** The Pascal language has a syntax that enforces this behavior without the use of compiler directives. You can declare a record as a `packed record` and its fields will be packed together as with the `{$A1}` alignment, regardless of the current setting of this directive. This is very useful when you have to interface with libraries written in other languages.

With the `{$A2}` alignment, each field will start on a word boundary. In layman's terms, the address of the field (offset from the start of the record) will be divisible by 2. `Field2` will start at address 2, `Field3` at 10, and `Field4` at 12. The total size of the record will be 20 bytes.

With the `{$A4}` alignment, each field will start on a double word boundary so its address will be divisible by 4. (You can probably see where this is going.) `Field2` will start at address 4, `Field3` at 12, and `Field4` at 16. The total size of the record will be 24 bytes.

Finally, with the `{$A8}` alignment, each field will start on a quad word boundary so its address will be divisible by 8. `Field2` will start at address 8, `Field3` at 16, and `Field4` at 24. The total size of the record will be 32 bytes.

Saying all that, I have to add that $A directive doesn't function exactly as I described it. Delphi knows how simple data types should be aligned (for example, it knows that an integer should be aligned on a double word boundary) and will not move them to higher alignment, even if it is explicitly specified by a directive. For example, the following record will use only 8 bytes even though we explicitly stated that fields should be quad word aligned:

```
{$A8}
TIntegerPair = record
  a: integer;
  b: integer:
end;
```

If you need to exactly specify size and alignment of all fields (for example if you pass records to some API call), it is best to use the packed record directive and insert unused padding fields into the definition. The next example specifies a record containing two quad word aligned integers:

```
TIntegerPair = packed record
  a: integer;
  filler: integer;
  b: integer:
end;
```

The following image shows how this record is laid out in memory with different record field alignment settings. Fields are renamed `F1` to `F4` so that their names would fit in the available space. `X` marks unused memory:

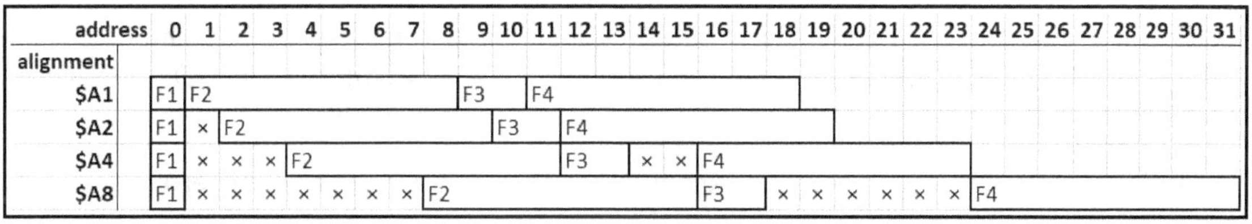

Why is all this useful? Why don't we always just pack fields together so that the total size of a record or class is as small as possible? Well, that is an excellent question!

As traditional wisdom says, CPUs work faster when the data is correctly aligned. Accessing a four-byte data (an `integer`, for example) is faster if its address is double word aligned (is divisible by four). Similarly, two-byte data (`word`) should be word aligned (address divisible by two) and eight-byte data (`int64`) should be quad word aligned (address divisible by eight). This will significantly improve performance in your program.

Will it really? Does this traditional wisdom make any sense in the modern world?

The `CompilerOptions` demo contains sets of measurements done on differently aligned records. It is triggered with the **Record field align** button.

Running the test shows something surprising—all four tests (for A1, A2, A4, and A8) run at almost the same speed. Actually, the code operating on the best-aligned record (A8) is the slowest! I must admit that I didn't expect this while preparing the test.

A little detective work has shown that somewhere around year 2010, Intel did a great job optimizing the data access on its CPUs. If you manage to find an older machine, it will show a big difference between unaligned and aligned data. However, all Intel CPUs produced after that time will run on unaligned and aligned data at the same speed. Working on unaligned (packed) data may actually be faster as more data will fit into the processor cache.

What is the moral lesson of all that? **Guessing is nothing, hard numbers are all!** Always measure. There is no guarantee that your changes will actually speed up the program.

Assertions

The **Assertions** compiler options enables or disables code generation for `Assert` statements. You can use compiler directives `{$ASSERTIONS ON}` and `{$ASSERTIONS OFF}` to turn this option on or off in the code. Short forms of this directive are rather cryptic `{$C+}` and `{$C-}`.

Delphi allows us to use runtime checks in the code in a form of `Assert` statements. `Assert` will check whether the first parameter evaluates to `false` and will raise an exception with the (optional) second parameter in an exception message, if that is true.

The following statement will raise an exception if variable `i` is smaller than zero:

```
Assert(i >= 0, 'Expecting a positive value here');
```

If you turn code generation for assertions off, the compiler will just skip such statements and they will not generate any code. You can for example use this to remove assertions from the release code. Even if any argument to `Assert` contains a function call, this function will not be called when assertions are turned off.

Overflow checking

The **Overflow checking** option regulates whether the compiler checks if certain arithmetic operations (+, -, *, Abs, Sqr, Inc, Dec, Succ, and Pred) produce a number that is too large or too small to fit into the data type. You can use compiler options, `{$OVERFLOWCHECKS ON}` and `{$OVERFLOWCHECKS OFF}` (or short forms `{$Q+}` and `{$Q-}`), to turn this option on and off in a specific part of a program.

For example, the following program will silently increment `$FFFFFFFF` to `0` in the first `Inc` statement but will raise `EIntOverflow` exception in the second `Inc` statement:

```
procedure TfrmCompilerOptions.btnOverflowErrorClick(Sender: TObject);
var
  i: cardinal;
begin
  {$Q-}
  i := $FFFFFFFF;
  // Without overflow checks, Inc will work and i will be 0
  Inc(i);

  {$Q+}
  i := $FFFFFFFF;
  // With overflow checks, Inc will raise an exception
  Inc(i);
end;
```

Enabling overflow checking doesn't make a big change in the program speed, so you can freely use it whenever it is needed. I would suggest turning it on at least in debug configuration as that will help with finding errors in the code.

Range checking

The last compiler option I want to discuss, **Range checking**, tells the compiler whether to check indexes to arrays and strings. In other words, it will check if in expression such as `s[idx+1]`, `idx+1` represents a valid index.

You can turn range checking on and off with compiler directives `{$RANGECHECKS ON}` and `{RANGECHECKS OFF}` (or `{$R+}` and `{$R-}`).

Let's take a look at an example. In the method shown here, the second `for` loop accesses element `arr[101]` without any error, although the maximum array element is `arr[100]`. The third `for` loop, however, will raise an `ERangeCheck` exception when accessing `arr[101]`:

```
procedure TfrmCompilerOptions.btnRangeErrorClick(Sender: TObject);
var
  arr: array [1..100] of Integer;
  i: Integer;
begin
  for i := Low(arr) to High(arr) do
    arr[i] := i;
  {$R-}
  for i := Low(arr) to High(arr) do
    arr[i] := arr[i] + arr[i+1];

  {$R+}
  for i := Low(arr) to High(arr) do
    arr[i] := arr[i] + arr[i+1];
end;
```

This kind of checking is so important that I always leave it in my code, even in the release version. Accessing a nonexistent array or string element may not seem so dangerous, but what if you are writing into that element? If this is not caught, your code just overwrites some other data with nonsense values. This leads to extremely hard to find problems! By default, range checking is turned off even in debug build and you really should turn it on in every program.

What about the "cost" of this checking? As the `CompilerOptions` program shows, it can be significant. In this example, turning range checking on slows down the code by a whole 50%:

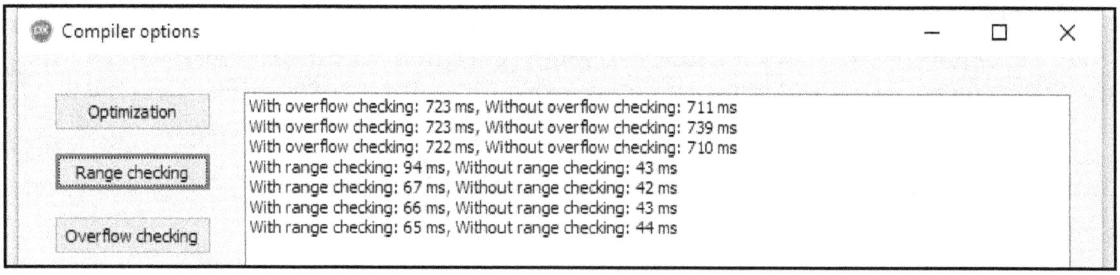

Comparing the code running with or without overflow checking and range checking

In such cases, turning range checking off can speed up the program. I would still recommend that you do that just for critical parts of code, not for the whole program.

This brings us to the end of this very long, but necessary, section as understanding the developer tools is always a good thing. Let us now—finally!—switch to something more interesting, to real programming.

Extracting common expressions

This next tip will sound obvious, but it will nicely introduce us to the next topic. Plus, it is a real problem frequently found in production code.

The `ExtractCommonExpression` demo creates a list box with a mere 1,000 entries, all in the form Author–Title. A click on the **Complicated expression** button runs a short code which reverts the order of Author and Title in the list box so that it shows entries in the form Title–Author:

```
procedure TfrmCommonExpression.Button1Click(Sender: TObject);
var
  i: Integer;
  sw: TStopwatch;
begin
  ListBox1.Items.BeginUpdate;
  try
    sw := TStopwatch.StartNew;
    for i := 0 to ListBox1.Count - 1 do
      ListBox1.Items[i] :=
        Copy(ListBox1.Items[i], Pos('-', ListBox1.Items[i]) + 1,
          Length(ListBox1.Items[i]))
        + '-'
        + Copy(ListBox1.Items[i], 1, Pos('-', ListBox1.Items[i]) - 1);
    sw.Stop;
    Button1.Caption := IntToStr(sw.ElapsedMilliseconds);
  finally ListBox1.Items.EndUpdate; end;
end;
```

The code goes over the list and for each entry finds the `'-'` character, extracts the first and second part of the entry and combines them back together, reversed. It does that, however, in a terrible copy-and-paste way. The code refers to `ListBox1.Items[i]` five times while calculating the result. It also calls `Pos('-', ListBox1.Items[i])` twice.

In a language with a really good compiler, you could expect that both subexpressions mentioned in the previous paragraph would be calculated only once. Not with Delphi's compiler, though. It has some optimization built in, but Delphi's optimization is far from the level required for such tricks to work. That leaves a burden of optimization on us, the programmers.

The second button in this demo executes the code shown next. This implementation of the same algorithm is not only more readable, but accesses `ListBox1.Items[i]` only once. It also calculates the position of `'-'` inside the string only once:

```
procedure TfrmCommonExpression.Button2Click(Sender: TObject);
var
  i: Integer;
  s: string;
  p: Integer;
  sw: TStopwatch;
begin
  ListBox1.Items.BeginUpdate;
  try
    sw := TStopwatch.StartNew;
    for i := 0 to ListBox1.Count - 1 do begin
      s := ListBox1.Items[i];
      p := Pos('-', s);
      ListBox1.Items[i] := Copy(s, p + 1, Length(s)) + '-' +
        Copy(s, 1, p - 1);
    end;
    sw.Stop;
    Button2.Caption := IntToStr(sw.ElapsedMilliseconds);
  finally ListBox1.Items.EndUpdate; end;
end;
```

Comparing both approaches shows a definite improvement in the second case. The first method uses around 40 ms and the second one around 30 ms, which is 25% faster. The code only times the inner `for` loop, not the updating of the list box itself, which takes the same time in both cases.

I can recap all this with a simple statement—*Calculate every subexpression only once.* Good advice but, still, don't exaggerate. Simple expressions, such as `i+1` or `2*i` are so *cheap* (in computing time) that extracting them in a subexpression won't speed up the code.

The helpful CPU window

In situations similar to the previous example, it doesn't hurt if you can look at the generated assembler code to check what is going on behind the scenes. Luckily, Delphi IDE provides a great way to do just that.

I will be the first to admit that examining assembler code is not for everyone. You can be a great Delphi programmer and still have no idea how to read assembler instructions.

If you found yourself in the previous words, don't worry. This section is included just for people who want to know everything. You can safely skip it knowing that you'll still be able to understand everything else in the book. However, if you're still interested then, by all means, read on!

The Delphi IDE gives us a few different tools for viewing the low-level state of the code and computer. They are stowed away in the not-so-obvious submenu **View, Debug Windows, CPU Windows**. The most useful view is called **Entire CPU** and encompasses all other views in that submenu. It is displayed as an editor tab named **CPU**.

Be aware, though, that it is only useful while you are debugging the program. The best way to use it is to pause the program (either by inserting a breakpoint or clicking the *pause* icon or selecting the **Run, Program Pause** menu) and then switch to the **CPU** view.

> TIP: You can quickly access the **Entire CPU** view with the key combination *Ctrl* + *Alt* + *C*. If that doesn't work, check whether you have installed some add-on expert that overrides this key combination. For example, GExperts assigns this combination to the `Copy Raw Strings` command.

This view is composed of five parts. The **Disassembly** panel (top left) shows your code as assembler instructions intermixed with Pascal source lines for easier orientation. If you don't see Pascal lines, right-click into that view and verify if the menu item, **Mixed source** is checked.

On the right of that (top right corner) are two small panels showing **processor registers** and **flags**. Below them (bottom right corner) is the current thread's **stack**. To finish it up, a panel in the bottom left corner shows the process' **memory** at some address.

If you use the *F8* key to step to the next command while the **Entire CPU** view is active, Delphi will not step to the next Pascal instruction but to the next assembler instruction. If you want to go to the next Pascal instruction, use the *Shift* + *F7* combination or menu **Run, Trace to Next Source Line.**

We can use the **CPU** view to verify that the first code example from the previous section really compiles to much worse code than the second example.

The image here shows part of the code from the original (on the left) and hand-optimized method (on the right). Green rectangles mark the code that accesses `ListBox1.Items[i]`. We can clearly see that the original code does that three times before calling the `Pos` function (at the very bottom of the image) while the hand-optimized method executes the same sequence of instructions only once:

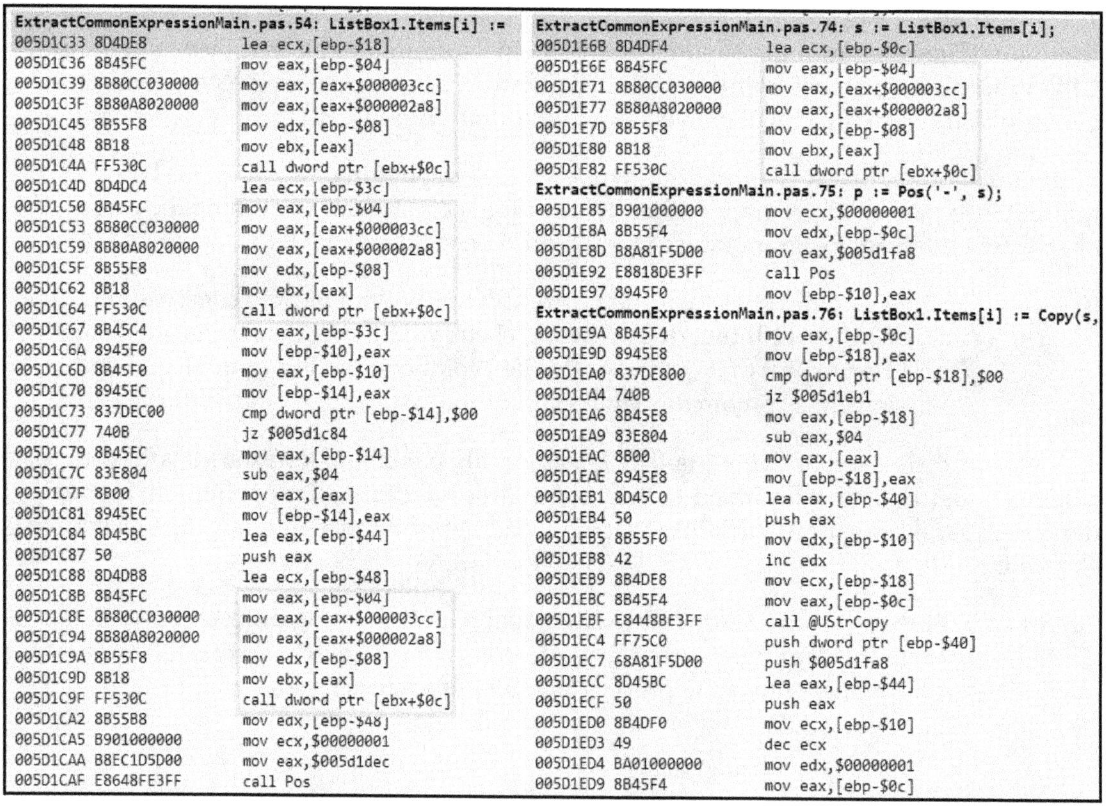

```
ExtractCommonExpressionMain.pas.54: ListBox1.Items[i] :=
005D1C33 8D4DE8          lea ecx,[ebp-$18]
005D1C36 8B45FC          mov eax,[ebp-$04]
005D1C39 8B80CC030000    mov eax,[eax+$000003cc]
005D1C3F 8B80A8020000    mov eax,[eax+$000002a8]
005D1C45 8B55F8          mov edx,[ebp-$08]
005D1C48 8B18            mov ebx,[eax]
005D1C4A FF530C          call dword ptr [ebx+$0c]
005D1C4D 8D4DC4          lea ecx,[ebp-$3c]
005D1C50 8B45FC          mov eax,[ebp-$04]
005D1C53 8B80CC030000    mov eax,[eax+$000003cc]
005D1C59 8B80A8020000    mov eax,[eax+$000002a8]
005D1C5F 8B55F8          mov edx,[ebp-$08]
005D1C62 8B18            mov ebx,[eax]
005D1C64 FF530C          call dword ptr [ebx+$0c]
005D1C67 8B45C4          mov eax,[ebp-$3c]
005D1C6A 8945F0          mov [ebp-$10],eax
005D1C6D 8B45F0          mov eax,[ebp-$10]
005D1C70 8945EC          mov [ebp-$14],eax
005D1C73 837DEC00        cmp dword ptr [ebp-$14],$00
005D1C77 740B            jz $005d1c84
005D1C79 8B45EC          mov eax,[ebp-$14]
005D1C7C 83E804          sub eax,$04
005D1C7F 8B00            mov eax,[eax]
005D1C81 8945EC          mov [ebp-$14],eax
005D1C84 8D45BC          lea eax,[ebp-$44]
005D1C87 50              push eax
005D1C88 8D4DB8          lea ecx,[ebp-$48]
005D1C8B 8B45FC          mov eax,[ebp-$04]
005D1C8E 8B80CC030000    mov eax,[eax+$000003cc]
005D1C94 8B80A8020000    mov eax,[eax+$000002a8]
005D1C9A 8B55F8          mov edx,[ebp-$08]
005D1C9D 8B18            mov ebx,[eax]
005D1C9F FF530C          call dword ptr [ebx+$0c]
005D1CA2 8B55B8          mov edx,[ebp-$48]
005D1CA5 B901000000      mov ecx,$00000001
005D1CAA B8EC1D5D00      mov eax,$005d1dec
005D1CAF E8648FE3FF      call Pos
```

```
ExtractCommonExpressionMain.pas.74: s := ListBox1.Items[i];
005D1E6B 8D4DF4          lea ecx,[ebp-$0c]
005D1E6E 8B45FC          mov eax,[ebp-$04]
005D1E71 8B80CC030000    mov eax,[eax+$000003cc]
005D1E77 8B80A8020000    mov eax,[eax+$000002a8]
005D1E7D 8B55F8          mov edx,[ebp-$08]
005D1E80 8B18            mov ebx,[eax]
005D1E82 FF530C          call dword ptr [ebx+$0c]
ExtractCommonExpressionMain.pas.75: p := Pos('-', s);
005D1E85 B901000000      mov ecx,$00000001
005D1E8A 8B55F4          mov edx,[ebp-$0c]
005D1E8D B8A81F5D00      mov eax,$005d1fa8
005D1E92 E8818DE3FF      call Pos
005D1E97 8945F0          mov [ebp-$10],eax
ExtractCommonExpressionMain.pas.76: ListBox1.Items[i] := Copy(s,
005D1E9A 8B45F4          mov eax,[ebp-$0c]
005D1E9D 8945E8          mov [ebp-$18],eax
005D1EA0 837DE800        cmp dword ptr [ebp-$18],$00
005D1EA4 740B            jz $005d1eb1
005D1EA6 8B45E8          mov eax,[ebp-$18]
005D1EA9 83E804          sub eax,$04
005D1EAC 8B00            mov eax,[eax]
005D1EAE 8945E8          mov [ebp-$18],eax
005D1EB1 8D45C0          lea eax,[ebp-$40]
005D1EB4 50              push eax
005D1EB5 8B55F0          mov edx,[ebp-$10]
005D1EB8 42              inc edx
005D1EB9 8B4DE8          mov ecx,[ebp-$18]
005D1EBC 8B45F4          mov eax,[ebp-$0c]
005D1EBF E8448BE3FF      call @UStrCopy
005D1EC4 FF75C0          push dword ptr [ebp-$40]
005D1EC7 68A81F5D00      push $005d1fa8
005D1ECC 8D45BC          lea eax,[ebp-$44]
005D1ECF 50              push eax
005D1ED0 8B4DF0          mov ecx,[ebp-$10]
005D1ED3 49              dec ecx
005D1ED4 BA01000000      mov edx,$00000001
005D1ED9 8B45F4          mov eax,[ebp-$0c]
```

Behind the scenes

A critical part of writing fast code is to understand what happens behind the scenes. Are you appending strings? You should know how that is implemented in a compiler. Passing a dynamic array into a function? Ditto. Wondering whether you should create 10,000 instances of a class or just create a large array of records? Knowing the implementation details will give you the answer.

In this section, I'll dig down into some frequently used data types and show how using them will bring in unexpected complexity. I will discuss memory and memory allocation, but I will treat them as very abstract entities. I'll say words like "A new string gets allocated" with which I'll mean that a secret part of code, called **memory manager**, gets memory from the Windows and tells the program: "You can store your string here." We'll dig deep into the bowels of memory manager in `Chapter 4`, *Memory Management*.

A plethora of types

The Delphi language contains an immense number of built-in types. There's no chance to cover them one by one, so let us firstly establish some classification that will simplify the rest of the discussion.

The most basic of all built-in types are **simple types**. In this group belong **integer types** (Byte, ShortInt, Word, SmallInt, Integer, Cardinal, Int64, UInt64, NativeInt, NativeUInt, LongInt, and LongWord), **character types** (Char, AnsiChar, WideChar, UCS2Char, and UCS4Char), **boolean types** (Boolean, ByteBool, WordBool, LongBool), **enumerated types** (such as TScrollBarStyle = (ssRegular, ssFlat, ssHotTrack)), and **real types** (Real48, Single, Real, Double, Extended, Comp, and Currency).

Similar to them are **pointer types**, such as pointer, `PByte`, `^TObject` etc. They are, after all, just memory addresses, so we can always treat a pointer as a NativeUInt and vice versa.

Following them are **strings**, a very interesting family hiding intriguing implementation details. It contains **short strings** (such a string[42]), *ansi strings* (AnsiString, RawByteString, UTF8String), and **unicode strings** (string, UnicodeString, and WideString).

The last group is **structured types**. This group, which will be of great interest in this chapter, is composed of **sets** (such as TAlignSet = set of TAlign), **arrays** (static arrays and dynamic arrays), **records** (traditional and advanced—records with methods), **classes**, and **interfaces**. Anonymous methods can also be treated as interfaces as they are implemented in the same way.

A different classification, which I'll also occasionally use, splits all types into two groups—unmanaged and managed. Managed types are types for which the compiler automatically generates life cycle management code and unmanaged types are all the rest.

When a type's life cycle is managed, the compiler automatically initializes variables and fields of that type. The compiler also inserts the code that automatically releases the memory associated with data of such type when it is no longer used anywhere in the program (goes *out of scope* are the words often used).

Managed types include strings, dynamic arrays, and interfaces. Records are managed only when they contain at least one field of these types. On platforms that support ARC (iOS, Android, and Linux), classes are also managed.

Different types (more specifically, different classes of types) are implemented differently by the Delphi compiler and as such, present a different challenge for a developer. In the rest of this section, I'll describe the internal implementation of the most interesting data types.

TIP

The best resource to really understand how all data types are implemented in Delphi is available in Embarcadero's *Docwiki* under the title *Internal Data Formats (Delphi).* `http://docwiki.embarcadero.com/RADStudio/en/Internal_Data_Formats_(Delphi)`.

Simple types

Let's start with simple types, as their implementation is indeed simple. Simple types don't allocate any memory. They are either stored as part of structured types (classes, records and so on), on the stack (local variables of such types) or in the part of a process memory (global variables of such types). Because of that, all operations with them are very fast.

To initialize the variable of a simple type, the compiler just has to move a few bytes around. The same goes for modifying the variable or copying one variable into another. (Fields behave just the same as variables for all Delphi data types so in the future I'll just talk about variables.)

Strings

String is probably the most used data type in Delphi. They also have a very interesting implementation, optimized for fast execution. To be exact, AnsiString (with all its variations) and UnicodeString (also known as string) are optimized. The WideString type is implemented in a different manner. As short strings (declarations like `string[17]`) are only used for backward compatibility, I won't discuss them in this book.

Let's deal with the more widely used AnsiString and UnicodeString first. A data of such type is represented with a pointer to a block, allocated from the memory manager. If a string is empty, this pointer will be `nil` (which is at the CPU level represented with number zero) and if a string is not empty, it will point to some memory.

Strings are managed types and as such are always initialized to the default value, `nil`. When you set a string to a value (when you assign a constant to it, for example, `s := 'Delphi'`), the compiler allocates a memory block to store the string and copies a new value into that block.

Something similar happens when you extend a string (`s := s + '!'`). In such cases, the compiler will reallocate the memory holding the string (more on that in the next chapter), and copy new characters to that memory.

Initializing a string and appending to a string are therefore relatively expensive operations as both allocate memory. (Memory manager performs some interesting optimizations to make string modification much cheaper—in terms of CPU cycles—than one would expect. Read more about that in the next chapter.)

Modifying part of the string without changing its length is, however, a pretty simple operation. Code just has to move the appropriate number of bytes from one place in memory to another and that's that.

Interesting things happen when you assign one non-empty string to another (`s := '42'; s1 := s;`). To make such operations fast and efficient, the compiler just points both variables to the same memory and increments an integer-sized counter (called *reference count*) in that same memory. A reference count represents the number of variables that are currently sharing the same string data.

A reference count is initialized to 1 when a string is initialized (meaning that only one variable is using this string). After the `s1 := s`, both `s` and `s1` are pointing to the same memory and the reference count is set to 2.

If one of these two variables is no longer accessible (for example, it was a local variable in a method which is no longer executing), the compiler will generate a life cycle management code which decrements the reference count. If the new reference count is zero, nobody is using the string data anymore and that memory block is released back to the system.

After `s := s1` we, therefore, have two strings pointing to the same memory. But what happens if one of these strings is modified? What happens, for example, if we do `s1[1] := 'a'`? It would be very bad if that would also modify the original string, `s`.

Again, the compiler comes to the rescue. Before any modification of a string, the code will check whether the string's reference count is larger than one. If so, this string is shared with another variable. To prevent any mess, the code will at that point allocate new memory for the modified string, copy the current contents into this memory, and decrement the original reference count. After that, it will change the string so it will point to the new memory and modify the content of that memory. This mechanism is called **copy-on-write**.

You can also force this behavior without actually modifying the string by calling the `UniqueString` function. After `s1 := s; UniqueString(s1);` both variables will point to separate parts of memory and both will have a reference count of 1.

> TIP: Calling the `SetLength` method on a string also makes the string unique.

The following code, taken from the `DataTypes` demo, demonstrates a part of that behavior. Firstly, the code initializes `s1` and `s2` so that they point to the same string. It will then log two items for each string—a pointer to the string memory and the contents of the string. After that, the code will modify one of the strings and log the same information again:

```
procedure TfrmDataTypes.btnCopyOnWriteClick(Sender: TObject);
var
  s1, s2: string;
begin
  s1 := 'Delphi';
  s2 := s1;
  ListBox1.Items.Add(Format('s1 = %p [%s], s2 = %p [%s]',
    [PPointer(@s1)^, s1, PPointer(@s2)^, s2]));

  s2[1] := 'd';
  ListBox1.Items.Add(Format('s1 = %p [%s], s2 = %p [%s]',
    [PPointer(@s1)^, s1, PPointer(@s2)^, s2]));
end;
```

If you run this program and click on the **string copy-on-write** button, you'll see that in the first log line, both pointers will be the same and in the second, the pointers will be different:

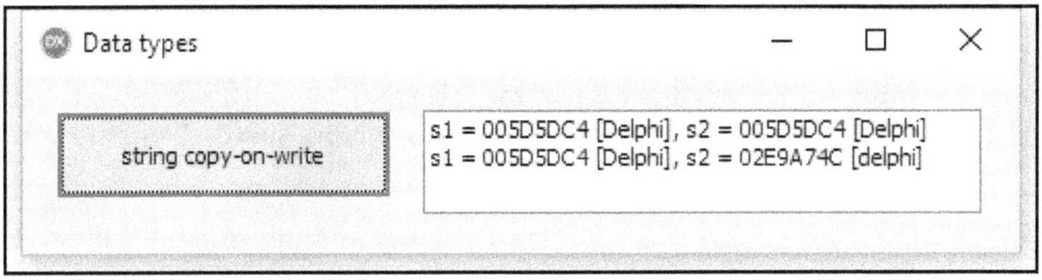

Demonstration of a copy-on-write mechanism

This wraps up the implementation behind Ansi and Unicode strings. The `WideString` type is, however, implemented completely differently. It was designed to be used in OLE applications where strings can be sent from one application to another. Because of that, all `WideStrings` are allocated with Windows' OLE memory allocator, not with standard Delphi's memory management mechanism.

There is also no copy-on-write implemented for `WideStrings`. When you assign one `WideString` to another, new memory is allocated and data is copied. Because of that, `WideStrings` are slower than Ansi and Unicode strings, and as such, should not be used needlessly.

Arrays

Delphi supports two kinds of arrays. One is of a fixed size and has settable lower and upper bounds. We call them **static arrays**. Others have a lower bound fixed at zero, while the upper bound is variable. In other words, they can grow and shrink. Because of that, they are called **dynamic arrays.**

The following code fragment shows how static and dynamic arrays are declared in Delphi:

```
var
  sarr1: array [2..22] of integer; // static array
  sarr2: array [byte] of string;   // static array
  darr1: array of TDateTime;       // dynamic array
  darr2: TArray<string>;           // dynamic array
```

Every array stores elements of some type. The compiler will treat these elements just the same as variables of that type. In the second declaration above, for example, the element type is `string`. This is a managed type and all 256 elements of the array will be initialized to `nil` automatically.

Static arrays are pretty dull. They have a constant size and as such are created exactly the same way as simple types (except that they typically use more space). Dynamic arrays, on the other hand, are similar to strings, but with a twist.

When you declare a dynamic array, it will start as empty and the variable will contain a `nil` pointer. Only when you change an array size (by using `SetLength` or a `TArray` constructor), memory will be allocated and a pointer to that memory will be stored in the dynamic array variable. Any change to array size will reallocate this storage memory—just like with the strings.

Modifying elements of an array is simple—again just like with the strings. An address of the element that is being modified is calculated and then item data is copied from one location to another. Of course, if array elements are not of a simple type, appropriate rules for that type will apply. Setting an element of `array of string` brings in the rules for the `string` type and so on.

When you assign one array to another, Delphi again treats them just the same as strings. It simply copies one pointer (to the array data) into another variable. At the end both variables contain the same address. A reference count in the array memory is also incremented. Again, just as strings.

The similarities with string types end here. If you now modify one element in one of the arrays, the same change will apply to the second array! There is no copy-on-write mechanism for dynamic arrays and both array variables will still point to the same array memory.

This is great from the efficiency viewpoint, but may not be exactly what you wanted. There's, luckily, a workaround that will split both arrays into two separate copies. Any time you call a `SetLength` on a shared array, the code will make this array unique, just like `UniqueString` does to strings. Even if the new length is the same as the old one, a unique copy of an array will still be made.

The following code from the `DataTypes` demo demonstrates this. Firstly, it allocates the `arr1` array by using a handy syntax introduced in Delphi XE7. Then it assigns `arr1` to `arr2`. This operation merely copies the pointers and increments the reference count. Both pointers and contents of the arrays are then shown in the log.

After that, the code modifies one element of `arr1` and logs again. To complete the test, the code calls `SetArray` to make `arr2` unique and modifies `arr1` again:

```
procedure TfrmDataTypes.btnSharedDynArraysClick(Sender: TObject);
var
  arr1, arr2: TArray<Integer>;
begin
  arr1 := [1, 2, 3, 4, 5];
  arr2 := arr1;
  ListBox1.Items.Add(Format('arr1 = %p [%s], arr2 = %p [%s]',
    [PPointer(@arr1)^, ToStringArr(arr1),
      PPointer(@arr2)^, ToStringArr(arr2)]));

  arr1[2] := 42;
  ListBox1.Items.Add(Format('arr1 = %p [%s], arr2 = %p [%s]',
    [PPointer(@arr1)^, ToStringArr(arr1),
      PPointer(@arr2)^, ToStringArr(arr2)]));

  SetLength(arr2, Length(arr2));
  arr1[2] := 17;
  ListBox1.Items.Add(Format('arr1 = %p [%s], arr2 = %p [%s]',
    [PPointer(@arr1)^, ToStringArr(arr1),
      PPointer(@arr2)^, ToStringArr(arr2)]));
end;
```

The output of the program shows that after the assignment both arrays point to the same memory and contain the same data. This doesn't change after `arr1[2] := 42`. Both arrays still point to the same memory and contain the same (changed) data.

After `SetLength`, however, arrays point to a separate memory address and changing `arr1` only changes that array:

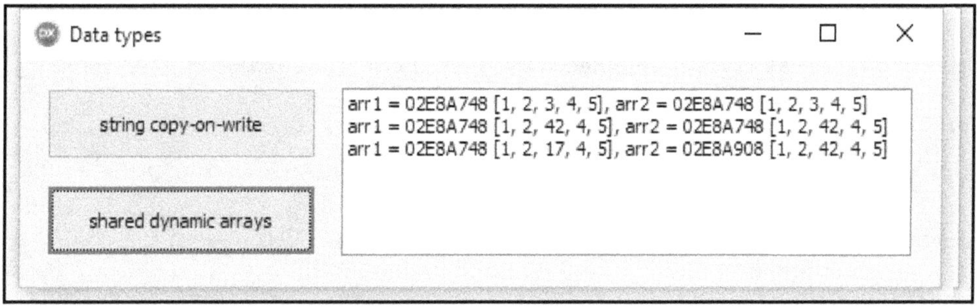

Records

To wrap up the analysis of built-in data types, we have to discuss structured types that can store elements of different types—namely records, classes, and interfaces.

The simplest of them are records. They are actually quite similar to simple types and static arrays. As simple types, records are, as we say, statically allocated. Local variables of record type are part of a thread's stack, global variables are part of the global process memory, and records that are parts of other structured types are stored as part of the owner's memory.

The important thing that you have to remember when using records is that the compiler manages the life cycle for their fields that are themselves managed. In other words, if you declare a local variable of a record type, all its managed fields will be automatically initialized, while unmanaged types will be left at random values (at whatever value the stack at that position contains at that moment).

The following code from the `DataTypes` demo demonstrates this behavior. When you run it, it will show some random values for fields `a` and `c` while the `b` field will always be initialized to an empty string.

The code also shows the simplest way to initialize a record to default values (zero for integer and real types, empty string for strings, `nil` for classes and so on). The built-in (but mostly undocumented) function `Default` creates a record in which all fields are set to default values and you can then assign it to a variable:

```
type
  TRecord = record
    a: integer;
    b: string;
    c: integer;
  end;

procedure TfrmDataTypes.ShowRecord(const rec: TRecord);
begin
  ListBox1.Items.Add(Format('a = %d, b = ''%s'', c = %d',
    [rec.a, rec.b, rec.c]));
end;

procedure TfrmDataTypes.btnRecordInitClick(Sender: TObject);
var
  rec: TRecord;
```

```
begin
  ShowRecord(rec);
  rec := Default(TRecord);
  ShowRecord(rec);
end;
```

When you run this code, you'll get some random numbers for `a` and `c` in the first log, but they will always be zero in the second log:

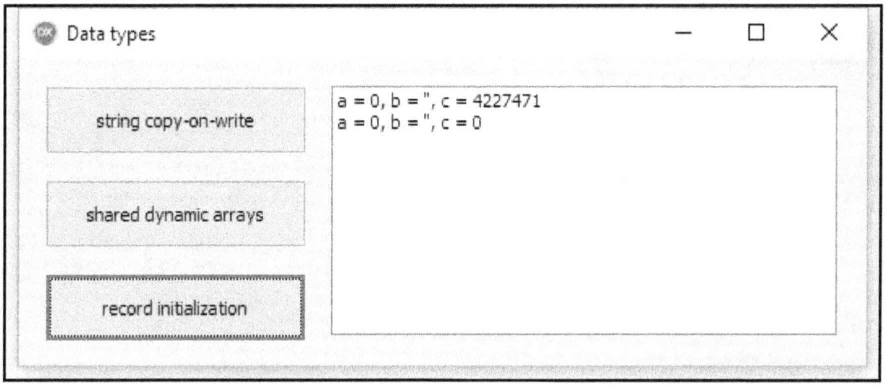

The initialization of managed fields affects the execution speed. The compiler doesn't create an optimized initialization code for each record type but does the initialization by calling generic and relatively slow code.

This also happens when you assign one record to another. If all fields are unmanaged, the code can just copy data from one memory location to another. However, when at least one of the fields is of a managed type, the compiler will again call a generic copying method which is not optimized for the specific record.

The following example from the `DataTypes` demo shows the difference. It copies two different records a million times. Both records are of the same size, except that `TUnmanaged` contains only fields of unmanaged type `NativeUInt` and `TManaged` contains only fields of managed type `IInterface`:

```
type
  TUnmanaged = record
    a, b, c, d: NativeUInt;
  end;

  TManaged = record
    a, b, c, d: IInterface;
  end;
```

```
procedure TfrmDataTypes.btnCopyRecClick(Sender: TObject);
var
  u1, u2: TUnmanaged;
  m1, m2: TManaged;
  i: Integer;
  sw: TStopwatch;
begin
  u1 := Default(TUnmanaged);
  sw := TStopwatch.StartNew;
  for i := 1 to 1000000 do
    u2 := u1;
  sw.Stop;
  ListBox1.Items.Add(Format('TUnmanaged: %d ms',
[sw.ElapsedMilliseconds]));

  m1 := Default(TManaged);
  sw := TStopwatch.StartNew;
  for i := 1 to 1000000 do
    m2 := m1;
  sw.Stop;
  ListBox1.Items.Add(Format('TManaged: %d ms', [sw.ElapsedMilliseconds]));
end;
```

The following image shows the measured difference in execution time. Granted, 31 ms to copy a million records is not a lot, but still the *unmanaged* version is five times faster. In some situations, that can mean a lot:

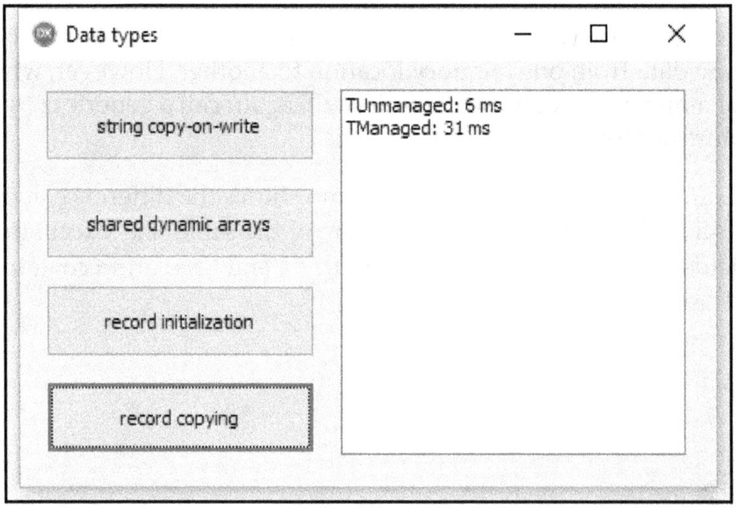

Classes

While classes look superficially similar to records, they are in fact implemented in a completely different manner.

When you create an object of a class by calling the constructor for that class, the code allocates memory from the memory manager and fills it with zeroes. That, in effect, initializes all fields, managed and unmanaged, to default values. A pointer to this memory is stored in the variable which receives the result of a constructor.

When an object is destroyed, its memory is returned to the system (again, through the memory manager).

The rest of this section applies only to *standard* compilers (Window 32- and 64-bit and OS/X). If you are using an ARC-enabled compiler (Android, iOS, and Linux) then classes behave the same as interfaces. See the next section for more details.

Copying one variable of a class type to another just copies the pointer. In effect, you then have two variables pointing to the same object. There is no reference counting associating with objects and if you now destroy one variable (by calling the `Free` method), the other will still point to the same part of memory. Actually, both variables will point to that unused memory and if it gets allocated later (and it will), both variables will point to memory belonging to another object:

```
var
  o1, o2: TObject;
begin
  o1 := TObject.Create;
  o2 := o1;
  // o1 and o2 now point to the same object
  o1.Free;
  // o1 and o2 now point to unowned memory
  o1 := nil;
  // o2 still points to unowned memory
end;
```

If you have a long-living variable or field containing an object of some class and you destroy the object, make sure that you also set the value/field to `nil`.

Interfaces

From the viewpoint of memory management, interfaces in Delphi are implemented as classes with added reference counting. To create an interface, you actually have to create an object of a class, which will get a reference count of 1. If you then assign this interface to another variable, both will point to the same memory and the reference count will be incremented to 2.

There is no equivalent to `SetLength` or `UniqueString` that would make a unique copy of an interface. That would require duplicating the underlying object and Delphi has no built-in support for that.

The object implementing the interface is destroyed when its reference count falls to 0:

```
var
  i1, i2: IInterface;
begin
  i1 := TInterfacedObject.Create;
  // i1 points to an object with reference count 1
  i2 := i1;
  // both i1 and i2 point to a same object with reference count 2
  i1 := nil;
  // i2 now points to an object with reference count 1
  i2 := nil;
  // reference count dropped to 0 and object is destroyed
end;
```

Although interfaces are very similar to classes, all this reference count management takes its cost. It is implemented with something called *interlocked* instructions which are a bit slower than normal increment/decrement instructions. I'll discuss this in more detail in `Chapter 5`, *Getting Started with the Parallel World*.

This only makes a measurable difference when you are assigning interfaces a lot, but sometimes this is exactly what happens. I'll show an example in the next section.

Optimizing method calls

I know you are eagerly waiting to optimize some real code, but please let me stay for a little bit more on the theoretical side of the equation. I spent all that time talking about the behavior of built-in data types but I didn't say anything about how data is passed to methods. This, much shorter and more surprising section (you'll see!) will fix this. As I'll be talking about speeding up method calls, I'll also throw in a short discussion of method inlining, just for a good measure. But first, parameters!

Parameter passing

In essence, Delphi knows two ways of passing parameters to a method (or procedure, or function, or anonymous method, it's all the same). Parameters can be passed by value or by reference.

The former makes a copy of the original value and passes that copy to a method. The code inside the method can then modify its copy however it wants and this won't change the original value.

The latter approach doesn't pass the value to the method but just an address of that value (a pointer to it). This can be faster than passing by value as a pointer will generally be smaller than an array or a record. In this case, the method can then use this address to access (and modify) the original value; something that is not possible if we pass a parameter by value.

Passing by reference is indicated by prefixing a parameter name with `var`, `out`, or `const`. A parameter is passed by value when no such prefix is used.

The difference between `var` and `out` is mostly semantic (although small changes in generated code are possible). Prefixing a parameter by `out` tells the compiler that we are not passing anything into the method (it may even be an uninitialized value) and we are only interested in the result. The `var` prefix, on the other hand, declares that we will be passing some value in and that we expect to get something out.

> In practice, `var` is usually used even when a parameter is not used to provide any data to the method; just to return something.

The `const` prefix is a bit different. When it is used, the compiler will prevent us from making any changes to the parameter. (With some exceptions, as we'll soon see.) In essence, `const` is an optimization prefix used when we want to pass a larger amount of data (a record, for example). It will ensure that the parameter is passed by reference while the compiler will make sure that the data is not changed.

The `const` prefix is also useful when the parameter is a managed type (for example a string or interface). When you pass such type by value, the code increments the reference count at the beginning of the method and decrements it at the end. If the parameter is marked as `const`, the reference count is not incremented/decremented and this can make a difference in the long run.

The ParameterPassing demo passes an array, string, record, and interface parameters to a method multiple times and measures the time. I will skip most of the code here as it is fairly dull and looks all the same. I'll just focus on a few interesting details first and then give an overview of the measured results.

The most uninteresting of all are static arrays and records. Passing by value makes a copy while passing by reference just passes a pointer to the data. That is all.

When you pass a string by using const, just an address is passed to the method and a reference count is not touched. That makes such calls very fast.

Passing by value, however, uses the copy-on-write mechanism. When a string is passed by value, a reference count is incremented and a pointer to string data is passed to the method. Only when the method modifies the string parameter, is a real copy of the string data made.

As an example, the following code in the demo is called 10 million times when you click the **string** button:

```
procedure TfrmParamPassing.ProcString(s: string);
begin
  // Enable next line and code will suddenly become much slower!
  // s[1] := 'a';
end;
```

This executes in a few hundred milliseconds. Uncomment the assignment and the code will suddenly run for 20 seconds (give or take) as a copy of quite large string will be made each time the method is called.

Interfaces behave similarly to strings, except that there is no copy-on-write mechanism. The only difference in execution speed comes from incrementing and decrementing the reference count.

At the beginning of this section, I promised some interesting results, so here they are! When a parameter is a dynamic array, strange things happen. But let's start with the code.

To measure parameter passing, the code creates an array of 100,000 elements, sets the element [1] to 1 and calls ScanDynArray 10,000 times. ScanDynArray sets arr[1] to 42 and exits.

Another method, `btnConstDynArrayClick` (not shown) works exactly the same except that it calls `ScanDynArrayConst` instead of `ScanDynArray`:

```
const
  CArraySize = 100000;

procedure TfrmParamPassing.ScanDynArray(arr: TArray<Integer>);
begin
  arr[1] := 42;
end;

procedure TfrmParamPassing.ScanDynArrayConst(const arr: TArray<Integer>);
begin
  // strangely, compiler allows that
  arr[1] := 42;
end;

procedure TfrmParamPassing.btnDynArrayClick(Sender: TObject);
var
  arr: TArray<Integer>;
  sw: TStopwatch;
  i: Integer;
begin
  SetLength(arr, CArraySize);
  arr[1] := 1;
  sw := TStopwatch.StartNew;
  for i := 1 to 10000 do
    ScanDynArray(arr);
  sw.Stop;
  ListBox1.Items.Add(Format('TArray<Integer>: %d ms, arr[1] = %d',
    [sw.ElapsedMilliseconds, arr[1]]));
end;
```

Can you spot the weird code in this example? It is the assignment in the `ScanDynArrayConst` method. I said that the `const` prefix will prevent such modifications of parameters, and in most cases it does. Dynamic array are, however different.

When you pass a dynamic array to a method, Delphi treats it just like a pointer. If you mark it as `const`, nothing changes as only this pointer is treated as a constant, not the data it points to. That's why you can modify the original array even through the `const` parameter.

That's the first level of weirdness. Let's crank it up!

If you check the System unit, you'll see that `TArray<T>` is defined like this:

```
type
  TArray<T> = array of T;
```

So, in theory, the code will work the same if we replace `TArray<Integer>` with `array of Integer`? Not at all!

```
procedure TfrmParamPassing.ScanDynArray2(arr: array of integer);
begin
  arr[1] := 42;
end;

procedure TfrmParamPassing.ScanDynArrayConst2(const arr: array of integer);
begin
  // in this case following line doesn't compile
  // arr[1] := 42;
end;
```

In this case, the compiler won't allow us to modify `arr[1]` when the parameter is marked `const`! Even more, in the `ScanDynArray2` method, the code makes a full copy of the array, just as if we were passing a normal static array!

This is a legacy from the versions before Delphi 2009 when we didn't have generics yet but we already got dynamic arrays through the `array of T` syntax. The compiler has special handling for this syntax built-in and this handling is still in effect in the modern-day.

Is this weird enough for you? No? No problem, I can go one better.

If we declare `type TIntArray = array of Integer` and then rewrite the code to use this array, we get the original `TArray<T>` behavior back. The array is always passed by reference and the code can modify the original array through the `const` parameter:

```
type
  TIntArray = array of Integer;

procedure TfrmParamPassing.ScanDynArray3(arr: TIntArray);
begin
  arr[1] := 42;
end;

procedure TfrmParamPassing.ScanDynArrayConst3(const arr: TIntArray);
begin
  // it compiles!
  arr[1] := 42;
end;
```

Let's now analyze the results of the `ParameterPassing` demo program.

Static arrays are passed as a copy (by value) or as a pointer (by reference). The difference in speed clearly proves that (174 vs. 0 ms). In both cases, the original value of the array element is not modified (it is 1).

The same happens when the array is declared as `array of Integer` (lines starting with `array of Integer` and `const array of Integer`) in the image.

TArray<Integer> and `TIntArray` behave exactly the same. An array is always passed by reference and the original value can be modified (it shows as `42` in the log).

Records are either copied (by value) or passed as a pointer (by reference) which brings the difference of 157 vs. 51 ms.

Strings are always passed as a pointer. When they are passed as a normal parameter, the reference count is incremented/decremented. When they are passed as a `const` parameter, the reference count is not modified. This brings a difference of 257 vs. 47 ms. A similar effect shows with the interface type parameters:

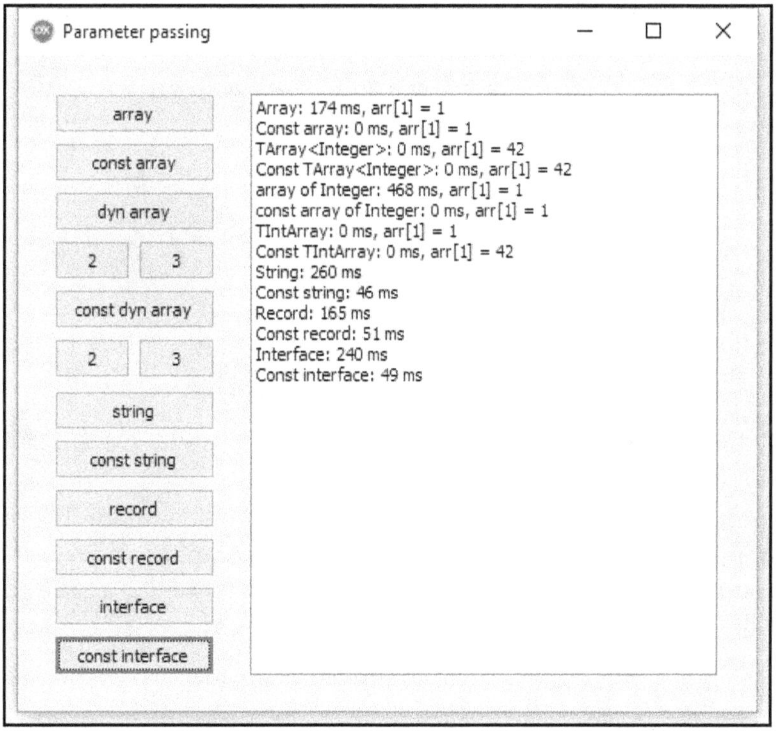

I have to point out that demos for different types cannot be compared directly with one another. For example, the loop for testing array types repeats 10,000 times while the loop for testing strings and interfaces repeats 10,000,000 times.

Method inlining

Previously in this chapter, I spent quite some time describing the mechanics of enabling and disabling method inlining, but I never said what that actually means. To put it simply, method inlining allows one method to be compiled as if its code would be a part of another.

When you call a method that is not marked as inlineable (doesn't have the `inline` suffix), the compiler prepares method parameters in an appropriate way (in registers and on the stack, but I'm not going there) and then executes a `CALL` assembler instruction.

If the called method is marked as inlineable, then the compiler basically just inserts the body of the inlineable method inside the code of the caller. This speeds up the code but also makes it larger as this happens in every place that calls the inlineable method.

Let me give you an example. The following code from the `Inlining` demo increments a value 10 million times:

```
function IncrementInline(value: integer): integer; inline;
begin
  Result := value + 1;
end;

procedure TfrmInlining.Button2Click(Sender: TObject);
var
  value: Integer;
  i: Integer;
begin
  value := 0;
  for i := 1 to 10000000 do
    value := IncrementInline(value);
end;
```

As the `IncrementInline` is marked as `inline` (and is therefore inlineable if the compiler settings are not preventing it), the code generated by the compiler doesn't actually `CALL` into that method 10 million times. The code actually looks more like a code generated by the next example:

```
procedure TfrmInlining.Button2Click(Sender: TObject);
var
  value: Integer;
```

```
  i: Integer;
begin
  value := 0;
  for i := 1 to 10000000 do
    value := value + 1;
end;
```

If you run the demo, you'll see that the inlined version executes much faster than the non-inlined code. On my test computer, the non-inlined version needed 53 ms while the inline version executed in 26 ms.

When you call the `inline` method from the same unit, make sure that the `inline` method is implemented **before** it is called. Otherwise, the compiler will just silently use the method as if it was a normal method and won't generate even a hint. In the next example, the method is actually not inlined, although we may expect it to be:

```
type
  TfrmInlining = class(TForm)
    // some unimportant stuff ...
    procedure Button3Click(Sender: TObject);
  private
    function IncrementShouldBeInline(value: integer): integer; inline;
  public
  end;

procedure TfrmInlining.Button3Click(Sender: TObject);
var
  value: Integer;
  i: Integer;
begin
  value := 0;
  for i := 1 to 10000000 do
    value := IncrementShouldBeInline(value);
end;

function TfrmInlining.IncrementShouldBeInline(value: integer): integer;
begin
  Result := value + 1;
end;
```

Another problem that inline code can cause, is that in some situations the result may even be slower than the non-inlined version. Sometimes the compiler just doesn't do a good enough job. Remember, always measure!

For a long time, the compiler had another problem. When the inlined function returned an interface, it made another, hidden copy of the returned value which was only released at the end of the method that called the inlined function. That could cause the interface to not be destroyed as the programmer expected.

This problem, for example, caused threads in Delphi's `TThreadPool` object not to be released at the correct time. It was only fixed in the 10.2 Tokyo release where Embarcadero introduced an improved compiler which generates better code.

And now I'm really finished with theory. Let's do some code!

The magic of pointers

Our friend, Mr. Smith, has progressed a lot from his first steps in Delphi. Now he is playing with graphics. He wants to build a virtual reality app that would allow you to walk through the Antarctica forests. While he's getting some success, he has problems displaying the correct colors on the screen.

A part of his code is producing textures in **Blue-Green-Red** (**BGR**) byte order, while the graphics driver needs them in the more standard **Red-Green-Blue** (**RGB**) order. He already wrote some code to fix this problem, but his solution is a bit too slow. He'd like to push a frame or two more from the system and so I promised that I'd help him optimize the converter. I'd be glad to do it, as his problem neatly fits into the story of *pointers*.

A pointer is a variable that stores an *address* of some data (other variables, dynamically allocated memory, specific character in the string ...). It is always of the same size, 4 bytes on 32-bit systems and 8 bytes on 64-bit systems—just the same as `NativeInt` and `NativeUInt`. This is not a coincidence as converting a pointer into an integer or back is sometimes quite practical.

Let's say, for example, that we have a `TPoint3` record containing a three-dimensional point. We can then declare a pointer to this type with the syntax `^TPoint3` and we can give this type a name, `PPoint3`. While the size of `TPoint3` is 24 bytes, the size of `PPoint3` is 4 or 8 bytes, depending on the compiler target (32- or 64-bit):

```
type
  TPoint3 = record
    X,Y,Z: double;
  end;
  PPoint3 = ^TPoint3;
```

If we now declare a variable P3 of type TPoint3 and variable PP3 of type PPoint3, we can then change the contents of PP3 to the address of P3 by executing `PP3 := @P3`. After that, we can use the `PP3^` notation to refer to the data that PP3 is *pointing to* (that is P3).

Delphi also allows a shorter form to access fields via a pointer variable. We don't have to write `PP3^.X`; a simpler `PP3.X` is enough:

```
var
  P3: TPoint3;
  PP3: PPoint3;
begin
  PP3 := @P3;
  PP3^.X := 1;
  // P3.X is now 1
  PP3.Y := 2;
  // P3.Y is now 2
  P3.Z := 3;
  // PP3^.Z is now 3
end;
```

Unlike the original Pascal, Delphi allows some arithmetical operations on the pointer. For example, you can always do `Inc(ptr)` and that will increment the address stored in `ptr`. It will not increment it by 1, though, but by the size of the type that the `ptr` is pointing to.

Some types, such as `PChar`, `PAnsiChar`, and `PByte`, will also allow you to use them in some basic arithmetic expressions. In reality, all pointer types support that, but only pointer types that were defined when the compiler directive `{$POINTERMATH ON}` was in effect will allow you to do that by default. For other types, you have to enable `{$POINTERMATH ON}` in the place where you do the calculation.

In the following example, the code `pi := pi + 1` wouldn't compile without explicit `{$POINTERMATH ON}` as this directive is not present in the System unit where `PInteger` is defined:

```
procedure TfrmPointers.btnPointerMathClick(Sender: TObject);
var
  pb: PByte;
  pi: PInteger;
  pa: PAnsiChar;
  pc: PChar;
begin
  pb := pointer(0);
  pb := pb + 1;
  ListBox1.Items.Add(Format('PByte increment = %d', [NativeUInt(pb)]));

  pi := pointer(0);
```

```
    {$POINTERMATH ON}
    pi := pi + 1;
    {$POINTERMATH OFF}
    ListBox1.Items.Add(Format('PInteger increment = %d', [NativeUInt(pi)]));

    pa := pointer(0);
    pa := pa + 1;
    ListBox1.Items.Add(Format('PAnsiChar increment = %d', [NativeUInt(pa)]));

    pc := pointer(0);
    pc := pc + 1;
    ListBox1.Items.Add(Format('PChar increment = %d', [NativeUInt(pc)]));
  end;
```

Pointers are very useful when you are creating dynamic data structures, such as trees and linked lists, but that is a bit beyond the scope of this book. They are also important when you want to dynamically allocate records. We'll cover that in the next chapter. And they are very handy—as you'll see immediately—when we are processing data buffers.

Let us return to Mr. Smith's problem. He has a graphic texture, organized as an array of pixels. Each pixel is stored as a cardinal value. The highest byte of a pixel contains the Transparency component (also known as **Alpha**), the next byte contains the Blue component, the byte after that the Green component, and the lowest byte contains the Red component:

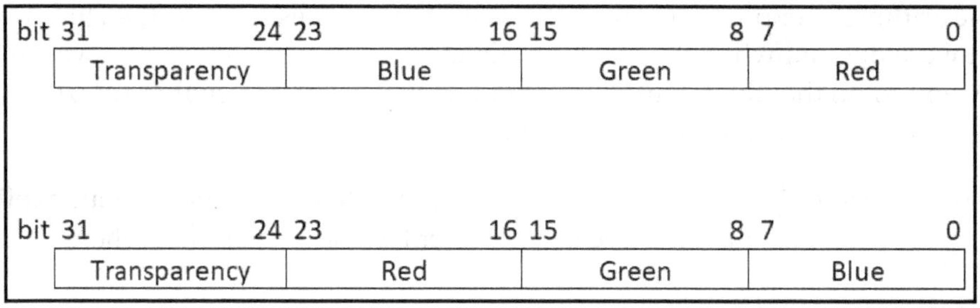

Pixel storage. Above—original format. Below—desired format.

Mr. Smith has already created a small test code which you can find in the demo `Pointers`. The code creates an array with 10 million elements and fills it with the value `$0055AACC`. The Blue color is set to `$55`, Green to `$AA`, and Red to `$CC` for all pixels.

The code then walks over the array and processes each element. Firstly, it extracts the Blue component by masking only one byte (`AND $00FF0000`) and moving it 16 bits to the right (`SHR 16`). Then it extracts the Red component (`AND $000000FF`). At the end, it clears both Blue and Red out of the original data (`AND $FF00FF00`) and `OR`s the Red and Blue components back in. Red is now shifted left by 16 places (`SHL 16`) so that it will be stored in the second-highest byte:

```
function TfrmPointers.PrepareData: TArray<Cardinal>;
var
  i: Integer;
begin
  SetLength(Result, 100000000);
  for i := Low(Result) to High(Result) do
    Result[i] := $0055AACC;
end;

procedure TfrmPointers.btnArrayClick(Sender: TObject);
var
  rgbData: TArray<Cardinal>;
  i: Integer;
  r,b: Byte;
begin
  rgbData := PrepareData;

  for i := Low(rgbData) to High(rgbData) do
  begin
    b := rgbData[i] AND $00FF0000 SHR 16;
    r := rgbData[i] AND $000000FF;
    rgbData[i] := rgbData[i] AND $FF00FF00 OR (r SHL 16) OR b;
  end;
end;
```

This code runs quite fast, but all that bit operations take some time. How can we speed it up?

The best approach is just to ignore the concept that *a pixel is a Cardinal* and treat each color component as an individual byte. We can then point one pointer to the Red component of the first pixel and another to the Blue component and just swap the values. Then we can advance each pointer to the next pixel and repeat the process.

To do that, we have to know at least a few things about how Delphi stores integer values in memory. The simple answer to that is—as the CPU expects them. Intel processors are using a *little-endian* format (yes, that is a technical term) which defines that the least important byte is stored in memory first (*little end* first).

If we put three pixels into memory so that the first starts at address 0, they would look just as in the image here:

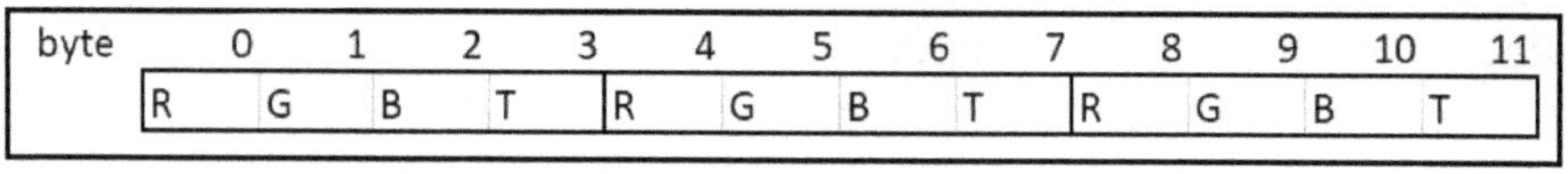

Memory layout of three consecutive pixels

Our improved code uses that knowledge. It uses two pointers, both of type `PByte` (a pointer to a `byte` value). The `pBlue` pointer points to the current Blue byte and the `pRed` pointer points to the current Red byte. To initialize them, the code sets both to the address of the first pixel (which is the same as the address of its lowest byte) and then increments `pBlue` by 2 bytes.

In the loop, the code simply stores current the Red pixel into a temporary value (`r := pRed^`), copies the Blue pixel into the Red pixel (`pRed^ := pBlue^`) and stores the temporary Red pixel into the Blue location (`pBlue^ := r`). It then increments both pointers to the next pixel:

```
procedure TfrmPointers.btnPointerClick(Sender: TObject);
var
  rgbData: TArray<cardinal>;
  i: Integer;
  r: Byte;
  pRed: PByte;
  pBlue: PByte;
begin
  rgbData := PrepareData;

  pRed := @rgbData[0];
  pBlue := pRed;
  Inc(pBlue,2);
  for i := Low(rgbData) to High(rgbData) do
  begin
    r := pRed^;
    pRed^ := pBlue^;
    pBlue^ := r;
    Inc(pRed, SizeOf(rgbData[0]));
    Inc(pBlue, SizeOf(rgbData[0]));
  end;
end;
```

The code is a bit more convoluted but not that harder to understand, as all that pixel operations (AND, SHR ...) in the original code weren't easy to read either. It is also much faster. On my test computer, the original code needs 159 ms, while the new code finishes in 72 ms, which is more than twice the speed!

To make a long story short—pointers are incredibly useful. They also make the code harder to understand, so use them sparingly and document the code.

Going the assembler way

Sometimes, when you definitely have to squeeze everything from the code, there is only one solution—rewrite it in assembler. My response to any such idea is always the same—don't do it! Rewriting code in an assembler is almost always much more trouble than it is worth.

I do admit that there are legitimate reasons for writing assembler code. I looked around and quickly found five areas where an assembler is still significantly present. They are memory managers, graphical code, cryptography routines (encryption, hashing), compression, and interfacing with hardware.

Even in these areas, situations change quickly. I tested some small assembler routines from the graphical library, *GraphicEx*, and was quite surprised to find out that they are not significantly faster than the equivalent Delphi code.

The biggest gain that you'll get from using an assembler is when you want to process a large buffer of data (such as a bitmap) and then do the same operation on all elements. In such cases, you can maybe use the SSE2 instructions which run circles around the slow 386 instruction set that Delphi compiler uses.

As assembler is not my game, (I can read it but I can't write good optimized assembler code), my example is extremely simple. The code in the demo program, AsmCode implements a four-dimensional vector (a record with four floating-point fields) and a method that multiplies two such fields:

```
type
  TVec4 = packed record
    X, Y, Z, W: Single;
  end;

function Multiply_PAS(const A, B: TVec4): TVec4;
begin
  Result.X := A.X * B.X;
  Result.Y := A.Y * B.Y;
```

```
  Result.Z := A.Z * B.Z;
  Result.W := A.W * B.W;
end;
```

As it turns out, this is exactly an operation that can be implemented using SSE2 instructions. In the code shown next, first `movups` moves vector *A* into register `xmm0`. Next, `movups` does the same for the other vector. Then, the magical instruction `mulps` multiplies four single-precision values in register `xmm0` with four single-precision values in register `xmm1`. At the end, `movups` is used to copy the result of the multiplication into the function result:

```
function Multiply_ASM(const A, B: TVec4): TVec4;
asm
  movups xmm0, [A]
  movups xmm1, [B]
  mulps xmm0, xmm1
  movups [Result], xmm0
end;
```

Running the test shows a clear winner. While `Multiply_PAS` needs 53 ms to multiply 10 million vectors, `Multiply_ASM` does that in half the time—24 ms.

As you can see in the previous example, assembler instructions are introduced with the `asm` statement and ended with `end`. In the Win32 compiler, you can mix Pascal and assembler code inside one method. This is not allowed with the Win64 compiler. In 64-bit mode, a method can only be written in pure Pascal or in pure assembler.

The `asm` instruction is only supported by Windows and OS/X compilers. In older sources, you'll also find an `assembler` instruction which is only supported for backwards compatibility and does nothing.

I'll end this short excursion into the assembler world with some advice. Whenever you are implementing a part of your program in assembler, please also create a Pascal version. The best practice is to use a conditional symbol, `PUREPASCAL` as a switch. With this approach, we could rewrite the multiplication code as follows:

```
function Multiply(const A, B: TVec4): TVec4;
{$IFDEF PUREPASCAL}
begin
  Result.X := A.X * B.X;
  Result.Y := A.Y * B.Y;
  Result.Z := A.Z * B.Z;
  Result.W := A.W * B.W;
end;
{$ELSE}
```

```
asm
  movups xmm0, [A]
  movups xmm1, [B]
  mulps xmm0, xmm1
  movups [Result], xmm0
end;
{$ENDIF}
```

Returning to SlowCode

At the end of this chapter, I'll return to the now well-known `SlowCode` example. At the end of the previous chapter, we significantly adapted the code and ended with a version that calculates prime numbers with the Sieve of Eratosthenes (`SlowCode_Sieve`). That version processed 10 million numbers in 1,072 milliseconds. Let's see if we can improve that.

The obvious target for optimization is the `Reverse` function which creates the result by appending characters one at a time. We've seen in this chapter that modifying a string can cause frequent memory allocations:

```
function Reverse(s: string): string;
var
  ch: char;
begin
  Result := '';
  for ch in s do
    Result := ch + Result;
end;
```

Instead of optimizing this function, let's look at how it is used. The `Filter` method uses it to reverse a number:

```
reversed := StrToInt(Reverse(IntToStr(i)));
```

This statement brings in another memory allocation (in function `IntToStr` which creates a new string), and executes some code that has to parse a string and return a number (`StrToInt`). Quite some work for an operation that doesn't really need strings at all.

It turns out that it is very simple to reverse a decimal number without using strings. You just have to repeatedly divide it by 10 and multiply remainders back into a new number:

```
function ReverseInt(value: Integer): Integer;
begin
  Result := 0;
  while value <> 0 do
  begin
```

```
      Result := Result * 10 + (value mod 10);
      value := value div 10;
    end;
  end;
```

The new `Filter` method can then use this method to reverse a number:

```
function Filter(list: TList<Integer>): TArray<Integer>;
var
  i: Integer;
  reversed: Integer;
begin
  SetLength(Result, 0);
  for i in list do
  begin
    reversed := ReverseInt(i);
    if not ElementInDataDivides(list, reversed) then
    begin
      SetLength(Result, Length(Result) + 1);
      Result[High(Result)] := i;
    end;
  end;
end;
```

The new code in the demo program, `SlowCode_Sieve_v2` indeed runs a bit faster. It processes 10 million elements in 851 milliseconds, which is roughly a 20% improvement.

Is there something more that we learned in this chapter and can be applied to that program? Sure—turn on the optimization! Just add one line—`{$OPTIMIZATION ON}`—and you'll get a significantly faster version. `SlowCode_Sieve_v2_opt` processes 10 million elements in a mere 529 ms!

There is still room for improvement in that program. It will, however, have to wait until the next chapter.

Summary

The topic of this chapter was fine-tuning the code. We started with Delphi compiler settings which can, in some cases, significantly change the code execution speed, and we learned what those situations are.

Then I introduced a simple but effective optimization—extracting common expressions. This optimization served as an introduction to the *CPU Window*, which can help us analyze compiled Delphi code.

After that, I returned to basics. Creating a fast program means knowing how Delphi works and so I looked into built-in data types. We saw what is fast and what is not.

As a logical follow-up to data types, we looked into methods—what happens when you pass parameters to a method and how to speed that up. We also reviewed a few surprising implementation details which can create problems in your code.

I ended the chapter with three practical examples. Firstly, we used pointers to speed up bitmap processing. Next, a short section on assembler code has shown how to write a fast assembler replacement for Pascal code. In the end, we revisited the `SlowCode` program (which isn't so slow anymore) and made it even faster.

In the next chapter, we'll go even deeper. I'll explore the topic of *memory managers*—what and how they are and why it is important to know how the built-in memory manager in Delphi is implemented. As usual, we'll also optimize some code. So stay tuned!

4
Memory Management

In the previous chapter, I explained a few things with a lot of hand-waving. I was talking about memory being *allocated* but I never told what that actually means. Now is the time to fill in the missing pieces.

Memory management is part of practically every computing system. Multiple programs must coexist inside a limited memory space, and that can only be possible if the operating system is taking care of it. When a program needs some memory, for example, to create an object, it can ask the operating system and it will give it a slice of shared memory. When an object is not needed anymore, that memory can be returned to the loving care of the operating system.

Slicing and dicing memory straight from the operating system is a relatively slow operation. In lots of cases, a memory system also doesn't know how to return small chunks of memory. For example, if you call Windows' `VirtualAlloc` function to get 20 bytes of memory, it will actually reserve 4 KB (or 4,096 bytes) for you. In other words, 4,076 bytes would be wasted.

To fix these and other problems, programming languages typically implement their own internal memory management algorithms. When you request 20 bytes of memory, the request goes to that internal memory manager. It still requests memory from the operating system but then splits it internally into multiple parts.

In a hypothetical scenario, the internal memory manager would request 4,096 bytes from the operating system and give 20 bytes of that to the application. The next time the application would request some memory (30 bytes for example), the internal memory manager would get that memory from the same 4,096-byte block.

To move from hypothetical to specific, Delphi also includes such a memory manager. From Delphi 2006, this memory manager is called *FastMM*. It was written as an open source memory manager by Pierre LeRiche with help from other Delphi programmers, and was later licensed by Borland. FastMM was a great improvement over the previous Delphi memory manager and, although it does not perform perfectly in the parallel programming world, it still functions very well after more than ten years.

Delphi exposes a public interface to replace the internal memory manager, so you can easily replace FastMM with a different memory manager. As we'll see later in this chapter, this can sometimes be helpful.

We will cover the following topics in this chapter:

- What happens when strings and arrays are reallocated and how can we speed this up?
- Which functions can an application use to allocate memory?
- How can we use memory manager to dynamically create a record?
- How is FastMM internally implemented and why does it matter to a programmer?
- How can we replace FastMM with a different memory manager?
- What can we do to improve SlowCode even more?

Optimizing strings and array allocations

When you create a string, the code allocates memory for its content, copies the content into that memory, and stores the address of this memory in the string variable. Of course, you all know that by now as this was the topic of the previous chapter.

If you append a character to this string, it must be stored somewhere in that memory. However, there is no place to store the string. The original memory block was just big enough to store the original content. The code must therefore enlarge that memory block, and only then can the appended character be stored in the newly acquired space.

As we'll see further on in the chapter, FastMM tries to make sure that the memory can be expanded *in place*, that is, without copying the original data into a new, larger block of memory. Still, this is not always possible and sometimes data must be copied around.

A very similar scenario plays out when you extend a dynamic array. Memory that contains the array data can sometimes be extended in place (without moving), but often this cannot be done.

If you do a lot of appending, these constant reallocations will start to slow down the code. The `Reallocation` demo shows a few examples of such behavior and possible workarounds.

The first example, activated by the **Append String** button, simply appends the `'*'` character to a string 10 million times. The code looks simple, but the `s := s + '*'` assignment hides a potentially slow string reallocation:

```
procedure TfrmReallocation.btnAppendStringClick(Sender: TObject);
var
  s: String;
  i: Integer;
begin
  s := '';
  for i := 1 to CNumChars do
    s := s + '*';
end;
```

By now, you probably know that I don't like to present problems that I don't have solutions for and this is not an exception. In this case, the solution is called `SetLength`. This function sets a string to a specified size. You can make it shorter, or you can make it longer. You can even set it to the same length as before.

In case you are enlarging the string, you have to keep in mind that `SetLength` will allocate enough memory to store the new string, but it will not initialize it. In other words, the newly allocated string space will contain random data.

A click on the **SetLength String** button activates the optimized version of the string appending code. As we know that the resulting string will be `CNumChars` long, the code can call `SetLength(s, CNumChars)` to preallocate all the memory in one step. After that, we should not *append* characters to the string as that would add new characters at the end of the preallocated string. Rather, we have to store characters directly into the string by writing to `s[i]`:

```
procedure TfrmReallocation.btnSetLengthClick(Sender: TObject);
var
  s: String;
  i: Integer;
begin
  SetLength(s, CNumChars);
  for i := 1 to CNumChars do
```

```
    s[i] := '*';
end;
```

Comparing the speed shows that the second approach is significantly faster. It runs in 33 ms instead of the original 142 ms.

This code still calls some string management functions internally, namely `UniqueString`. It returns fairly quickly, but still represents some overhead. If you are pushing for the fastest possible execution, you can initialize the string by using a *sliding pointer*, just as in the example from the previous chapter.

A similar situation happens when you are extending a dynamic array. The code triggered by the **Append array** button shows how an array may be extended by one element at a time in a loop. Admittedly, the code looks very weird as nobody in their right mind would write a loop like this. In reality, however, similar code would be split into multiple longer functions and may be hard to spot:

```
procedure TfrmReallocation.btnAppendArrayClick(Sender: TObject);
var
  arr: TArray<char>;
  i: Integer;
begin
  SetLength(arr, 0);
  for i := 1 to CNumChars do begin
    SetLength(arr, Length(arr) + 1);
    arr[High(arr)] := '*';
  end;
end;
```

The solution is similar to the string case. We can preallocate the whole array by calling the `SetLength` function and then write the data into the array elements. We just have to keep in mind that the first array element always has index 0:

```
procedure TfrmReallocation.btnSetLengthArrayClick(Sender: TObject);
var
  arr: TArray<char>;
  i: Integer;
begin
  SetLength(arr, CNumChars);
  for i := 1 to CNumChars do
    arr[i-1] := '*';
end;
```

Improvements in speed are similar to the string demo. The original code needs 230 ms to append ten million elements, while the improved code executes in 26 ms.

The third case when you may want to preallocate storage space is when you are appending to a list. As an example, I'll look into a `TList<T>` class. Internally, it stores the data in a `TArray<T>`, so it again suffers from constant memory reallocation when you are adding data to the list.

The short demo code appends 10 million elements to a list. As opposed to the previous array demo, this is a completely normal looking code, found many times in many applications:

```
procedure TfrmReallocation.btnAppendTListClick(Sender: TObject);
var
  list: TList<Char>;
  i: Integer;
begin
  list := TList<Char>.Create;
  try
    for i := 1 to CNumChars do
      list.Add('*');
  finally
    FreeAndNil(list);
  end;
end;
```

To preallocate memory inside a list, you can set the `Capacity` property to an expected number of elements in the list. This doesn't prevent the list from growing at a later time; it just creates an initial estimate. You can also use `Capacity` to reduce memory space used for the list after deleting lots of elements from it.

The difference between a list and a string or an array is that, after setting `Capacity`, you still cannot access `list[i]` elements directly. Firstly you have to `Add` them, just as if `Capacity` was not assigned:

```
procedure TfrmReallocation.btnSetCapacityTListClick(Sender: TObject);
var
  list: TList<Char>;
  i: Integer;
begin
  list := TList<Char>.Create;
  try
    list.Capacity := CNumChars;
    for i := 1 to CNumChars do
      list.Add('*');
  finally
```

```
    FreeAndNil(list);
  end;
end;
```

Comparing the execution speed shows only a small improvement. The original code executed in 167 ms, while the new version needed 145 ms. The reason for that relatively small change is that `TList<T>` already manages its storage array. When it runs out of space, it will always at least double the previous size. Internal storage therefore grows from 1 to 2, 4, 8, 16, 32, 64, ... elements.

This can, however, waste a lot of memory. In our example, the final size of the internal array is 16,777,216 elements, which is about 60% elements too many. By setting the capacity to the exact required size, we have therefore saved 6,777,216 * *SizeOf(Char)* bytes or almost 13 megabytes.

Other data structures also support the `Capacity` property. We can find it in `TList`, `TObjectList`, `TInterfaceList`, `TStrings`, `TStringList`, `TDictionary`, `TObjectDictionary` and others.

Memory management functions

Besides the various internal functions that the Delphi runtime library (RTL) uses to manage strings, arrays and other built-in data types, RTL also implements various functions that you can use in your program to allocate and release memory blocks. In the next few paragraphs, I'll tell you a little bit about them.

Memory management functions can be best described if we split them into a few groups, each including functions that were designed to work together.

The first group includes `GetMem`, `AllocMem`, `ReallocMem`, and `FreeMem`.

The procedure `GetMem(var P: Pointer; Size: Integer)` allocates a memory block of size `Size` and stores an address of this block in a pointer variable `P`. This pointer variable is not limited to `pointer` type, but can be of any pointer type (for example `PByte`).

The new memory block is not initialized and will contain whatever is stored in the memory at that time. Alternatively, you can allocate a memory block with a call to the function `AllocMem(Size: Integer): Pointer` which allocates a memory block, fills it with zeroes, and then returns its address.

To change the size of a memory block, call the procedure `ReallocMem(var P: Pointer; Size: Integer)`. Variable `P` must contain a pointer to a memory block and `Size` can be either smaller or larger than the original block size. FastMM will try to resize the block in place. If that fails, it will allocate a new memory block, copy the original data into the new block and return an address of the new block in the `P`. Just as with the `GetMem`, newly allocated bytes will not be initialized.

To release memory allocated in this way, you should call the `FreeMem(var P: Pointer)` procedure.

The second group includes `GetMemory`, `ReallocMemory`, and `FreeMemory`. These three work just the same as functions from the first group, except that they can be used from C++ Builder.

The third group contains just two functions, `New` and `Dispose`.

These two functions can be used to dynamically create and destroy variables of any type. To allocate such a variable, call `New(var X: Pointer)` where `P` is again of any pointer type. The compiler will automatically provide the correct size for the memory block and it will also initialize all *managed* fields to zero. Unmanaged fields will not be initialized.

To release such variables, don't use `FreeMem` but `Dispose(var X: Pointer)`. In the next section, I'll give a short example of using `New` and `Dispose` to dynamically create and destroy variables of a record type.

> You must **never** use `Dispose` to release memory allocated with `GetMem` or `AllocateMem`. You must also **never** use `FreeMem` to release memory allocated with `New`.

The fourth and last group also contains just two functions, `Initialize` and `Finalize`. Strictly speaking, they are not memory management functions. Still, they are used almost exclusively when dynamically allocating memory and that's why they belong in this chapter.

If you create a variable containing managed fields (for example, a record) with a function other than `New` or `AllocMem`, it will not be correctly initialized. Managed fields will contain random data and that will completely break the execution of the program. To fix that, you should call `Initialize(var V)` passing in the variable (and not the pointer to this variable!). An example in the next section will clarify that.

Before you return such a variable to the memory manager, you should clean up all references to managed fields by calling `Finalize(var V)`. It is better to use `Dispose`, which will do that automatically, but sometimes that is not an option and you have to do it manually.

Both functions also exist in a form that accepts a number of variables to initialize. This form can be used to initialize or finalize an array of data:

```
procedure Initialize(var V; Count: NativeUInt);
procedure Finalize(var V; Count: NativeUInt);
```

In the next section, I'll dig deeper into the dynamic allocation of record variables. I'll also show how most of the memory allocation functions are used in practice.

Dynamic record allocation

While it is very simple to dynamically create new objects—you just call the `Create` constructor—dynamic allocation of records and other data types (arrays, strings ...) is a bit more complicated.

In the previous section, we saw that the preferred way of allocating such variables is with the `New` method. The `InitializeFinalize` demo shows how this is done in practice.

The code will dynamically allocate a variable of type `TRecord`. To do that, we need a pointer variable, pointing to `TRecord`. The cleanest way to do that is to declare a new type `PRecord = ^TRecord`:

```
type
  TRecord = record
    s1, s2, s3, s4: string;
  end;
  PRecord = ^TRecord;
```

Now, we can just declare a variable of type `PRecord` and call `New` on that variable. After that, we can use the `rec` variable as if it was a normal record and not a pointer. Technically, we would have to always write `rec^.s1`, `rec^.s4` and so on, but the Delphi compiler is friendly enough and allows us to drop the ^ character:

```
procedure TfrmInitFin.btnNewDispClick(Sender: TObject);
var
  rec: PRecord;
begin
  New(rec);
```

```
  try
    rec.s1 := '4';
    rec.s2 := '2';
    rec.s4 := rec.s1 + rec.s2 + rec.s4;
    ListBox1.Items.Add('New: ' + rec.s4);
  finally
    Dispose(rec);
  end;
end;
```

Technically, you could just use `rec: ^TRecord` instead of `rec: PRecord`, but it is customary to use explicitly declared pointer types, such as `PRecord`.

Another option is to use `GetMem` instead of `New`, and `FreeMem` instead of `Dispose`. In this case, however, we have to manually prepare allocated memory for use with a call to `Initialize`. We must also prepare it to be released with a call to `Finalize` before we call `FreeMem`.

If we use `GetMem` for initialization, we must manually provide the correct size of allocated block. In this case, we can simply use `SizeOf(TRecord)`.

We must also be careful with parameters passed to `GetMem` and `Initialize`. You pass a pointer (`rec`) to `GetMem` and `FreeMem` and the actual record data (`rec^`) to `Initialize` and `Finalize`:

```
procedure TfrmInitFin.btnInitFinClick(Sender: TObject);
var
  rec: PRecord;
begin
  GetMem(rec, SizeOf(TRecord));
  try
    Initialize(rec^);
    rec.s1 := '4';
    rec.s2 := '2';
    rec.s4 := rec.s1 + rec.s2 + rec.s4;
    ListBox1.Items.Add('GetMem+Initialize: ' + rec.s4);
  finally
    Finalize(rec^);
    FreeMem (rec);
  end;
end;
```

This demo also shows how the code doesn't work correctly if you allocate a record with `GetMem`, but then don't call `Initialize`. To test this, click the third button (**GetMem**). While in actual code the program may sometimes work and sometimes not, I have taken some care so that `GetMem` will always return a memory block which will not be initialized to zero and the program will certainly fail:

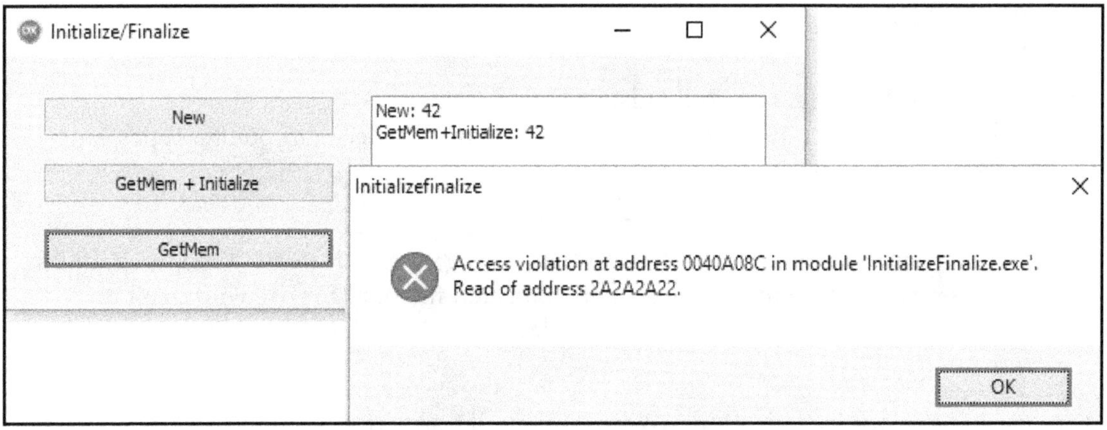

It is certainly possible to create records dynamically and use them instead of classes, but one question still remains—why? Why would we want to use records instead of objects when working with objects is simpler? The answer, in one word, is **speed**.

The demo program, `Allocate`, shows the difference in execution speed. A click on the **Allocate objects** button will create ten million objects of type `TNodeObj`, which is a typical object that you would find in an implementation of a *binary tree*. Of course, the code then cleans up after itself by destroying all those objects:

```
type
  TNodeObj = class
    Left, Right: TNodeObj;
    Data: NativeUInt;
  end;

procedure TfrmAllocate.btnAllocClassClick(Sender: TObject);
var
  i: Integer;
  nodes: TArray<TNodeObj>;
begin
  SetLength(nodes, CNumNodes);
  for i := 0 to CNumNodes-1 do
    nodes[i] := TNodeObj.Create;
  for i := 0 to CNumNodes-1 do
```

```
    nodes[i].Free;
end;
```

A similar code, activated by the **Allocate records** button creates ten million records of type `TNodeRec`, which contains the same fields as `TNodeObj`:

```
type
  PNodeRec = ^TNodeRec;
  TNodeRec = record
    Left, Right: PNodeRec;
    Data: NativeUInt;
  end;

procedure TfrmAllocate.btnAllocRecordClick(Sender: TObject);
var
  i: Integer;
  nodes: TArray<PNodeRec>;
begin
  SetLength(nodes, CNumNodes);
  for i := 0 to CNumNodes-1 do
    New(nodes[i]);
  for i := 0 to CNumNodes-1 do
    Dispose(nodes[i]);
end;
```

Running both methods shows a big difference. While the class-based approach needs 366 ms to initialize objects and 76 ms to free them, the record-based approach needs only 76 ms to initialize records and 56 to free them. Where does that big difference come from?

When you create an object of a class, lots of things happen. Firstly, `TObject.NewInstance` is called to allocate an object. That method calls `TObject.InstanceSize` to get the size of the object, then `GetMem` to allocate the memory and in the end, `InitInstance` which fills the allocated memory with zeros. Secondly, a chain of constructors is called. After all that, a chain of `AfterConstruction` methods is called (if such methods exist). All in all, that is quite a process which takes some time.

Much less is going on when you create a record. If it contains only unmanaged fields, as in our example, a `GetMem` is called and that's all. If the record contains managed fields, this `GetMem` is followed by a call to the `_Initialize` method in the *System* unit which initializes managed fields.

The problem with records is that we cannot declare generic pointers. When we are building trees, for example, we would like to store some data of type `T` in each node. The initial attempt at that, however, fails. The following code does not compile with the current Delphi compiler:

```
type
  PNodeRec<T> = ^TNodeRec<T>;
  TNodeRec<T> = record
    Left, Right: PNodeRec<T>;
    Data: T;
  end;
```

We can circumvent this by moving the `TNodeRec<T>` declaration inside the generic class that implements a tree. The following code from the `Allocate` demo shows how we could declare such internal type as a generic object and as a generic record:

```
type
  TTree<T> = class
  strict private type
    TNodeObj<T1> = class
      Left, Right: TNodeObj<T1>;
      Data: T1;
    end;

    PNodeRec = ^TNodeRec;
    TNodeRec<T1> = record
      Left, Right: PNodeRec;
      Data: T1;
    end;
    TNodeRec = TNodeRec<T>;
  end;
```

If you click the **Allocate node<string>** button, the code will create a `TTree<string>` object and then create 10 million class-based nodes and the same amount of record-based nodes. This time, `New` must initialize the managed field `Data: string` but the difference in speed is still big. The code needs 669 ms to create and destroy class-based nodes and 133 ms to create and destroy record-based nodes.

Another big difference between classes and records is that each object contains two hidden pointer-sized fields. Because of that, each object is 8 bytes larger than you would expect (16 bytes in 64-bit mode). That amounts to 8 * 10,000,000 bytes or a bit over 76 megabytes. Records are therefore not only faster but also save space!

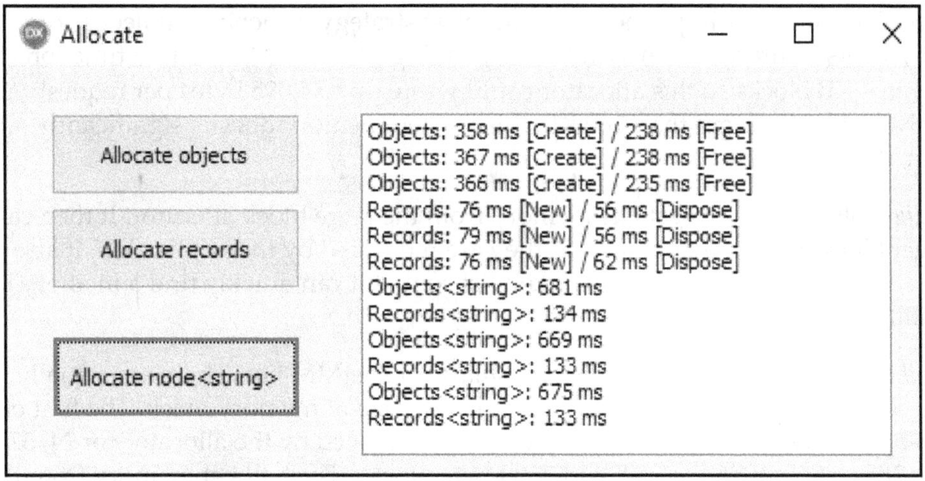

FastMM internals

To get a full speed out of anything, you have to understand how it works and memory managers are no exception to this rule. To write very fast Delphi applications, you should therefore understand how Delphi's default memory manager works.

FastMM is not just a memory manager—it is three memory managers in one! It contains three significantly different subsystems—*small block allocator*, *medium block allocator*, and *large block allocator*.

The first one, the allocator for *small blocks*, handles all memory blocks smaller than 2,5 KB. This boundary was determined by observing existing applications. As it turned out, in most Delphi applications, this covers 99% of all memory allocations. This is not surprising, as in most Delphi applications most memory is allocated when an application creates and destroys objects and works with arrays and strings, and those are rarely larger than a few hundred characters.

Next comes the allocator for *medium blocks*, which are memory blocks with a size between 2,5 KB and 160 KB. The last one, allocator for *large blocks*, handles all other requests.

The difference between allocators lies not just in the size of memory that they serve, but in the strategy they use to manage memory.

The *large* block allocator implements the simplest strategy. Whenever it needs some memory, it gets it directly from Windows by calling `VirtualAlloc`. This function allocates memory in 4 KB blocks so this allocator could waste up to 4,095 bytes per request. As it is used only for blocks larger than 160 KB, this wasted memory doesn't significantly affect the program, though.

The *medium* block allocator gets its memory from the large block allocator. It then carves this larger block into smaller blocks, as they are requested by the application. It also keeps all unused parts of the memory in a linked list so that it can quickly find a memory block that is still free.

The *small* block allocator is where the real smarts of FastMM lies. There are actually 56 small memory allocators, each serving only one size of memory block. The first one serves 8-byte blocks, the next one 16-byte blocks, followed by the allocator for 24, 32, 40, ... 256, 272, 288, ... 960, 1056, ... 2384, and 2608-byte blocks. They all get memory from the medium block allocator.

If you want to see block sizes for all 56 allocators, open `FastMM4.pas` and search for `SmallBlockTypes`.

What that actually means is that each memory allocation request will waste some memory. If you allocate 28 bytes, they'll be allocated from the 32-byte allocator, so 4 bytes will be wasted. If you allocate 250 bytes, they'll come from the 256-byte allocator and so on. The sizes of memory allocators were carefully chosen so that the amount of wasted memory is typically below 10%, so this doesn't represent a big problem in most applications.

Each allocator is basically just an array of equally sized elements (memory blocks). When you allocate a small amount of memory, you'll get back one element of an array. All unused elements are connected into a linked list so that the memory manager can quickly find a free element of an array when it needs one.

The following image shows a very simplified representation of FastMM allocators. Only two small block allocators are shown. Boxes with thick borders represent allocated memory. Boxes with thin borders represent unused (free) memory. Free memory blocks are connected into linked lists. Block sizes in different allocators are not to scale:

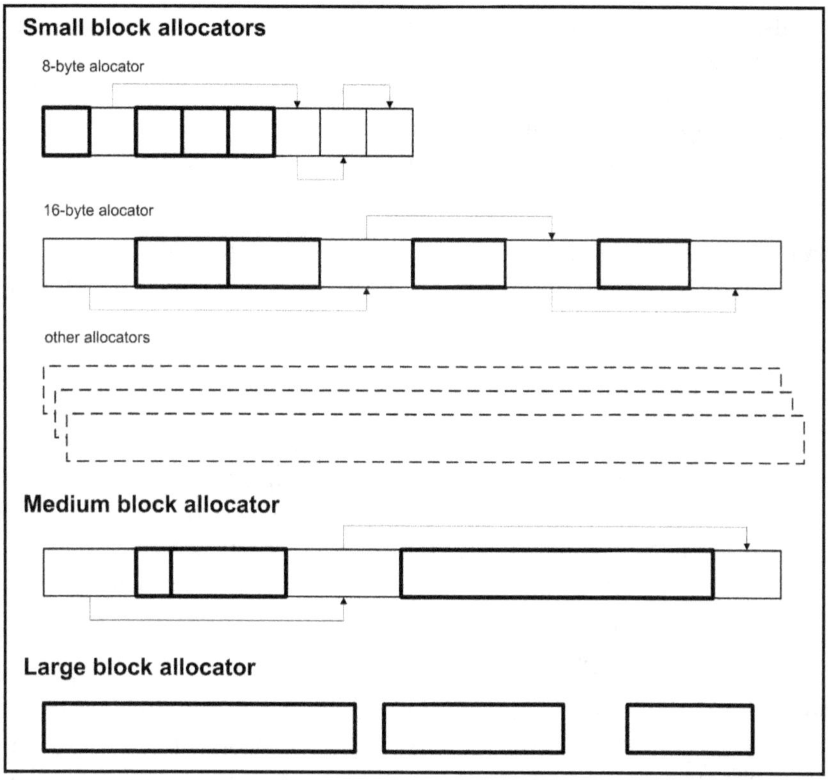

Simplified representation of FastMM memory manager

FastMM implements a neat trick which helps a lot when you resize strings or arrays by a small amount. In the beginning of this chapter, I talked about that (*Optimizing strings and array allocations*), and have shown a small program that demonstrated how appending characters one by one works much slower than preallocating a whole string. There was a 4x speed difference (142 vs 33 ms) between these approaches.

Well, the truth be told, I had to append lots and lots of characters—ten million of them—for this difference to show. If I were appending only a few characters, both versions would run at nearly the same speed. If you can, on the other hand, get your hands on a pre-2006 Delphi and run the demo program there, you'll see that the *one-by-one* approach runs terribly slow. The difference in speed will be of a few more orders of magnitude larger than in my example.

The trick I'm talking about assumes that if you had resized memory once, you'll probably want to do it again, soon. If you are enlarging the memory, it will limit the smallest size of the new memory block to be at least twice the size of the original block plus 32 bytes. Next time you'll want to resize, FastMM will (hopefully) just update the internal information about the allocated memory and return the same block, knowing that there's enough space at the end.

All that trickery is hard to understand without an example, so here's one. Let's say we have a string of 5 characters which neatly fits into a 24-byte block. Sorry, what am I hearing? "What? Why!? 5 unicode characters need only 10 bytes!" Oh, yes, strings are more complicated than I told you before.

In reality, each Delphi `UnicodeString` and `AnsiString` contains some additional data besides the actual characters that make up the string. Parts of the string are also: 4-byte length of string, 4-byte reference count, 2-byte field storing the size of each string character (either 1 for `AnsiString` or 2 for `UnicodeString`), and 2-byte field storing the character code page. In addition to that, each string includes a terminating `Chr(0)` character. For a 5-character `string` this gives us *4 (length) + 4 (reference count) + 2 (character size) + 2 (codepage) + 5 (characters) * 2 (size of a character) + 2 (terminating Chr(0)) = 24* bytes.

When you add one character to this string, the code will ask the memory manager to enlarge a 24-byte block to 26 bytes. Instead of returning a 26-byte block, FastMM will round that up to *2 * 24 + 32 = 80* bytes. Then it will look for an appropriate allocator, find one that serves 80-byte blocks (great, no memory loss!) and return a block from that allocator. It will, of course, also have to copy data from the original block to the new block.

This formula, *2 * size + 32*, is used only in small block allocators. A medium block allocator only overallocates by 25%, and a large block allocator doesn't implement this behavior at all.

Next time you add one character to this string, FastMM will just look at the memory block, determine that there's still enough space inside this 80-byte memory block and return the same memory. This will continue for quite some time while the block grows to 80 bytes in two-byte increments. After that, the block will be resized to *2 * 80 + 32 = 192* bytes (yes, there **is** an allocator for this size), data will be copied and the game will continue.

This behavior indeed wastes some memory but, under most circumstances, significantly boosts the speed of code that was not written with speed in mind.

Memory allocation in a parallel world

We've seen how FastMM boosts the reallocation speed. Let's take a look at another optimization which helps a lot when you write a multithreaded code—as we will in the next three chapters.

The life of a memory manager is simple when there is only one thread of execution inside a program. When the memory manager is dealing out the memory, it can be perfectly safe in the knowledge that nothing can interrupt it in this work.

When we deal with parallel processing, however, multiple paths of execution simultaneously execute the same program and work on the same data. (We call them *threads* and I'll explain them in the next chapter.) Because of that, life from the memory manager's perspective suddenly becomes very dangerous.

For example, let's assume that one thread wants some memory. The memory manager finds a free memory block on a free list and prepares to return it. At that moment, however, another thread also needs some memory from the same allocator. This second execution thread (running in parallel with the first one) would also find a free memory block on the free list. If the first thread didn't yet update the free list, that may even be the same memory block! That can only result in one thing—complete confusion and crashing programs.

It is extremely hard to write a code that manipulates some data structures (such as a free list) in a manner that functions correctly in a multithreaded world. So hard that FastMM doesn't even try it. Instead of that, it regulates access to each allocator with a lock. Each of the 56 small block allocators get their own lock, as do medium and large block allocators.

When a program needs some memory from, say, a 16-byte allocator, FastMM will lock this allocator until the memory is returned to the program. If, during this time, another thread requests a memory from the same 16-byte allocator, it will have to wait until the first thread finishes.

This indeed fixes all problems but introduces a *bottleneck*—a part of the code where threads must wait to be processed in a serial fashion. If threads do lots of memory allocation, this serialization will completely negate the speed-up that we expected to get from the parallel approach. Such a memory manager would be useless in a parallel world.

To fix that, FastMM introduces memory allocation optimization which only affects small blocks.

When accessing a small block allocator, FastMM will try to lock it. If that fails, it will not wait for the allocator to become unlocked, but will try to lock the allocator for the next block size. If that succeeds, it will return memory from the second allocator. That will indeed waste more memory, but will help with the execution speed. If the second allocator also cannot be locked, FastMM will try to lock the allocator for yet the next block size. If the third allocator can be locked, you'll get back memory from it. Otherwise, FastMM will repeat the process from the beginning.

This process can be somehow described with the following pseudo-code:

```
allocIdx := find best allocator for the memory block
repeat
  if can lock allocIdx then
    break;
  Inc(allocIdx);
  if can lock allocIdx then
    break;
  Inc(allocIdx);
  if can lock allocIdx then
    break;
  Dec(allocIdx, 2)
until false

allocate memory from allocIdx allocator

unlock allocIdx
```

A careful reader would notice that this code fails when the first line finds the last allocator in the table, or the one before that. Instead of adding some conditional code to work around the problem, FastMM rather repeats the last allocator in the list three times. The table of small allocators actually ends with the following sizes: 1,984; 2,176; 2,384; 2,608; 2,608; 2,608. When requesting a block size above 2,384 the first line in the pseudo-code above will always find the first 2,608 allocator, so there will always be two more after it.

This approach works great when memory is allocated but hides another problem. And how can I better explain a problem than with a demonstration ...?

An example of this problem can be found in the program, `ParallelAllocations`. If you run it and click the **Run** button, the code will compare the serial version of some algorithm with a parallel one. I'm aware that I did not explain parallel programming at all, but the code is so simple that even somebody without any understanding of the topic will guess what it does.

The core of a test runs a loop with the `Execute` method on all objects in a list. If a `parallelTest` flag is set, the loop is executed in parallel, otherwise it is executed serially. The only mystery part in the code, `TParallel.For` does exactly what it says—executes a `for` loop in parallel.

```
if parallelTest then
  TParallel.For(0, fList.Count - 1,
    procedure(i: integer)
    begin
      fList[i].Execute;
    end)
else
  for i := 0 to fList.Count - 1 do
    fList[i].Execute;
```

If you'll be running the program, make sure that you execute it without the debugger (*Ctrl* + *Shift* + *F9* will do that). Running with the debugger slows down parallel execution and can skew the measurements.

On my test machine I got the following results:

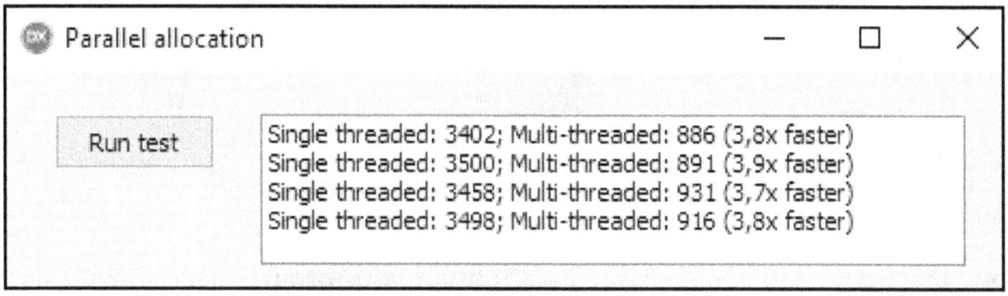

In essence, parallelizing the program made it almost 4 times faster. Great result!

Well, no. Not a great result. You see, the machine I was testing on has 12 cores. If all would be running in parallel, I would expect an almost 12x speed-up, not a mere 4-times improvement!

If you take a look at the code, you'll see that each `Execute` allocates a ton of objects. It is obvious (even more given the topic of the current chapter) that a problem lies in the memory manager. The question remains though, where exactly lies this problem and how can we find it?

I ran into exactly the same problem a few years ago. A highly parallel application which processes gigabytes and gigabytes of data was not running fast enough. There were no obvious problematic points and I suspected that the culprit was FastMM. I tried swapping the memory manager for a more multithreading-friendly one and, indeed, the problem was somehow reduced but I still wanted to know where the original sin lied in my code. I also wanted to continue using FastMM as it offers great debugging tools.

In the end, I found no other solution than to dig in the FastMM internals, find out how it works, and add some logging there. More specifically, I wanted to know when a thread is waiting for a memory manager to become unlocked. I also wanted to know at which locations in my program this happens the most.

To cut a (very) long story short, I extended FastMM with support for this kind of logging. This extension was later integrated into the main FastMM branch. As these changes are not included in Delphi, you have to take some steps to use this code.

Firstly, you have to download FastMM from the official repository at `https://github.com/pleriche/FastMM4`. Then you have to unpack it somewhere on the disk and add `FastMM4` as a first unit in the project file (`.dpr`). For example, the `ParallelAllocation` program starts like this:

```
program ParallelAllocation;
uses
  FastMM4 in 'FastMM\FastMM4.pas',
  Vcl.Forms,
  ParallelAllocationMain in 'ParallelAllocationMain.pas'
{frmParallelAllocation};
```

When you have done that, you should firstly rebuild your program and test if everything is still working. (It should but you never know ...)

To enable the memory manager logging, you have to define a conditional symbol `LogLockContention`, rebuild (as `FastMM4` has to be recompiled) and, of course, run the program without the debugger.

If you do that, you'll see that the program runs quite a bit slower than before. On my test machine, the parallel version was only 1.6x faster than the serial one. The logging takes its toll, but that is not important. The important part will appear when you close the program.

At that point, the logger will collect all results and sort them by frequency. The 10 most frequent sources of locking in the program will be saved to a file called `<programname>_MemoryManager_EventLog.txt`. You will find it in the folder with the `<programname>.exe`. The three most frequent sources of locking will also be displayed on the screen.

The following screenshot shows a cropped version of this log. Some important parts are marked out:

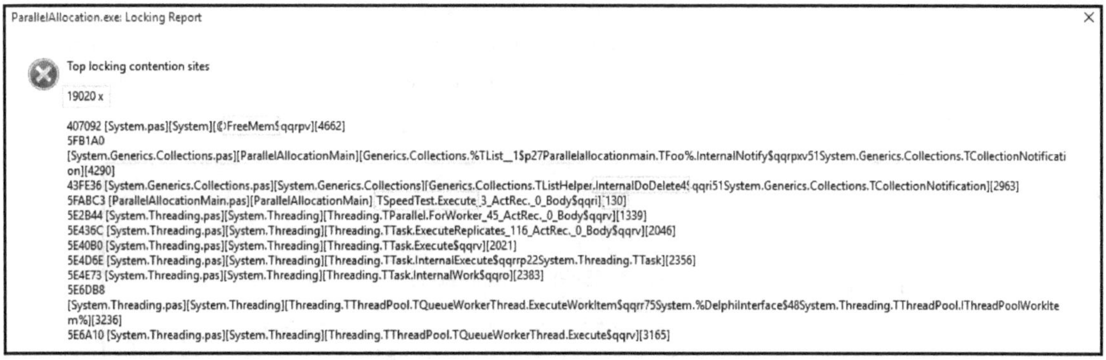

For starters, we can see that at this location the program waited **19,020** times for a memory manager to become unlocked. Next, we can see that the memory function that caused the problem was `FreeMem`. Furthermore, we can see that somebody tried to delete from a list (`InternalDoDelete`) and that this deletion was called from `TSpeedTest.Execute`, line 130. `FreeMem` was called because the list in question is actually a `TObjectList` and deleting elements from the list caused it to be destroyed.

The most important part here is the memory function causing the problem—`FreeMem`. Of course! Allocations are optimized. If an allocator is locked, the next one will be used and so on. Releasing memory, however, is not optimized! When we release a memory block, it **must** be returned to the same allocator that it came from. If two threads want to release memory to the same allocator at the same time, one will have to wait.

I had an idea on how to improve this situation by adding a small stack (called **release stack**) to each allocator. When `FreeMem` is called and it cannot lock the allocator, the address of the memory block that is to be released will be stored on that stack. `FreeMem` will then quickly exit.

When a `FreeMem` successfully locks an allocator, it firstly releases its own memory block. Then it checks if anything is waiting on the release stack and releases these memory blocks too (if there are any).

This change is also included in the main FastMM branch, but it is not activated by default as it increases the overall memory consumption of the program. However, in some situations it can do miracles and if you are developing multithreaded programs you certainly should test it out.

To enable release stacks, open the project settings for the program, remove the conditional define `LogLockContention` (as that slows the program down) and add the conditional define `UseReleaseStack`. Rebuild, as `FastMM4.pas` has to be recompiled.

On my test machine, I got much better results with this option enabled. Instead of a 3,9x speed-up, the parallel version was 6,3x faster than the serial one. The factor is not even close to 12x, as the threads do too much fighting for the memory, but the improvement is still significant:

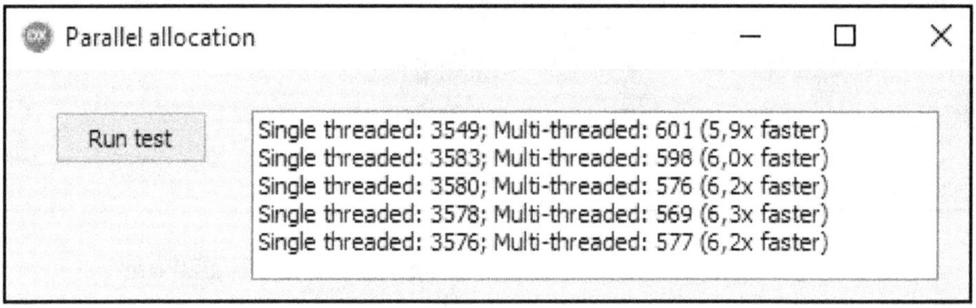

That is as far as FastMM will take us. For a faster execution, we need a more multithreading-friendly memory manager.

Replacing the default memory manager

While writing a new memory manager is a hard job, installing it in Delphi—once it is completed—is very simple. The *System* unit implements functions `GetMemoryManager` and `SetMemoryManager` that help with that:

```
type
  TMemoryManagerEx = record
    {The basic (required) memory manager functionality}
    GetMem: function(Size: NativeInt): Pointer;
    FreeMem: function(P: Pointer): Integer;
    ReallocMem: function(P: Pointer; Size: NativeInt): Pointer;
    {Extended (optional) functionality.}
    AllocMem: function(Size: NativeInt): Pointer;
    RegisterExpectedMemoryLeak: function(P: Pointer): Boolean;
    UnregisterExpectedMemoryLeak: function(P: Pointer): Boolean;
```

```
  end;

procedure GetMemoryManager(var MemMgrEx: TMemoryManagerEx); overload;
procedure SetMemoryManager(const MemMgrEx: TMemoryManagerEx); overload;
```

A proper way to install a new memory manager is to call `GetMemoryManager` and store the result in some global variable. Then, the code should populate the new `TMemoryManagerEx` record with pointers to its own replacement methods and call `SetMemoryManager`. Typically, you would do this in the `initialization` block of the unit implementing the memory manager.

The new memory manager **must** implement functions `GetMem`, `FreeMem`, and `ReallocMem`. It **may** implement the other three functions (or only some of them). Delphi is smart enough to implement `AllocMem` internally, if it is not implemented by the memory manager, and the other two will just be ignored if you call them from the code.

When memory manager is uninstalled (usually from the `finalization` block of the memory manager unit), it has to call `SetMemoryManager` and pass to it the original memory manager configuration stored in the global variable.

The nice thing with memory managers is that you can call functions from the previous memory manager in your code. That allows you to just add some small part of functionality which may be useful when you are debugging some hard problem or researching how Delphi works.

To demonstrate this approach, I have written a small logging memory manager. After it is installed, it will log all memory calls (except the two related to memory leaks) to a file. It has no idea how to handle memory allocation, though, so it forwards all calls to the existing memory manager.

The demonstration program, `LoggingMemoryManager`, shows how to use this logging functionality. When you click the **Test** button, the code installs it by calling the `InstallMM` function. In the current implementation, it logs information info the file, `<projectName>_memory.log` which is saved to the `<projectName>.exe` folder.

Then the code creates a `TList<integer>` object, writes 1,024 integers into it and destroys the list.

At the end, the memory manager is uninstalled by calling `UninstallMM` and the contents of the log file are loaded into the listbox:

```
procedure TfrmLoggingMM.Button1Click(Sender: TObject);
var
  list: TList<integer>;
```

```
    i: Integer;
    mmLog: String;
  begin
    mmLog := ChangeFileExt(ParamStr(0), '_memory.log');
    if not InstallMM(mmLog) then
      ListBox1.Items.Add('Failed to install memory manager');

    list := TList<integer>.Create;
    for i := 1 to 1024 do
      list.Add(i);
    FreeAndNil(list);

    if not UninstallMM then
      ListBox1.Items.Add('Failed to uninstall memory manager');

    LoadLog(mmLog);
  end;
```

The memory manager itself is implemented in the unit *LoggingMM*. It uses three global variables. `MMIsInstalled` contains the current installed/not installed status, `OldMM` stores the configuration of the existing state, and `LoggingFile` stores a handle of the logging file:

```
  var
    MMIsInstalled: boolean;
    OldMM: TMemoryManagerEx;
    LoggingFile: THandle;
```

The installation function firstly opens a logging file with a call to the Windows API `CreateFile`. After that, it retrieves the existing memory manager state, sets a new configuration with pointers to the logging code, and exits. Memory leak functions are not used so corresponding pointers are set to `nil`:

```
  function InstallMM(const fileName: string): boolean;
  var
    myMM: TMemoryManagerEx;
  begin
    if MMIsInstalled then
      Exit(False);

    LoggingFile := CreateFile(PChar(fileName), GENERIC_WRITE, 0, nil,
      CREATE_ALWAYS, FILE_ATTRIBUTE_NORMAL, 0);
    if LoggingFile = INVALID_HANDLE_VALUE then
      Exit(False);

    GetMemoryManager(OldMM);

    myMM.GetMem := @LoggingGetMem;
```

```
    myMM.FreeMem := @LoggingFreeMem;
    myMM.ReallocMem := @LoggingReallocMem;
    myMM.AllocMem := @LoggingAllocMem;
    myMM.RegisterExpectedMemoryLeak := nil;
    myMM.UnregisterExpectedMemoryLeak := nil;
    SetMemoryManager(myMM);

    MMIsInstalled := True;
    Result := True;
  end;
```

Using Windows API makes my logging memory manager bound to the operating system so why don't I simply use a `TStream` for logging?

Well, you have to remember that the purpose of this exercise is to log all memory requests. Using any built-in Delphi functionality may cause hidden memory manager operations. If I'm not careful, an object may get created somewhere or a string could get allocated. That's why the code stays on the safe side and uses Windows API to work with the logging file.

Uninstalling memory manager is simpler. We just have to close the logging file and restore the original configuration:

```
  function UninstallMM: boolean;
  begin
    if not MMIsInstalled then
      Exit(False);

    SetMemoryManager(OldMM);

    if LoggingFile <> INVALID_HANDLE_VALUE then begin
      CloseHandle(LoggingFile);
      LoggingFile := INVALID_HANDLE_VALUE;
    end;

    MMIsInstalled := False;
    Result := True;
  end;
```

Logging itself is again tricky. The logging code is called from the memory manager itself, so it can't use any functionality that would use the memory manager. Most important of all, we cannot use any `UnicodeString` or `AnsiString` variable. The logging code therefore pieces the log output together from small parts:

```
function LoggingGetMem(Size: NativeInt): Pointer;
begin
  Result := OldMM.GetMem(Size);
  Write('GetMem(');
  Write(Size);
  Write(') = ');
  Write(NativeUInt(Result));
  Writeln;
end;
```

Logging a string is actually pretty easy as Delphi already provides a terminating `Chr(0)` character at the end of a string. A `Write` method just passes correct parameters to the `WriteFile` Windows API:

```
procedure Write(const s: PAnsiChar); overload;
var
  written: DWORD;
begin
  WriteFile(LoggingFile, s^, StrLen(s), written, nil);
end;

procedure Writeln;
begin
  Write(#13#10);
end;
```

Logging a number is tricky, as we can't call `IntToStr` or `Format`. Both are using dynamic strings which means that memory manager would be used to manage strings, but as we are already inside the memory manager we cannot use memory management functions.

The logging function for numbers therefore implements its own conversion from `NativeUInt` to a buffer containing a hexadecimal representation of that unit. It uses the knowledge that `NativeUInt` is never more than 8 bytes long, which generates, at max, 16 hexadecimal numbers:

```
procedure Write(n: NativeUInt); overload;
var
  buf: array [1..18] of AnsiChar;
  i: Integer;
  digit: Integer;
begin
```

```
    buf[18] := #0;
    for i := 17 downto 2 do
    begin
      digit := n mod 16;
      n := n div 16;
      if digit < 10 then
        buf[i] := AnsiChar(digit + Ord('0'))
      else
        buf[i] := AnsiChar(digit - 10 + Ord('A'));
    end;
    buf[1] := '$';
    Write(@buf);
  end;
```

Even with these complications, the code is far from perfect. The big problem with the current implementation is that it won't work correctly in a multithreaded code. A real-life implementation would need to add locking around all the `Logging*` methods.

Another problem with the code is that logging is really slow because of the frequent `WriteFile` calls. A better implementation would collect log data in a larger buffer and only write it out when the buffer becomes full. An improvement in that direction is left as an exercise for the reader.

The following image shows the demonstration program, `LoggingMemoryManager` in action. The first `GetMem` call creates the `TList<Integer>` object. The second creates a `TArray<Integer>` used internally inside the `TList<Integer>` to store the list data. After that, `ReallocMem` is called from time to time to enlarge this `TArray`. We can see that it is not called for every element that the code adds to the list, but in larger and larger steps. Memory is firstly enlarged to $10 bytes, then to $18, $28, $48, and so on to $1,008 bytes. This is a result of the optimization inside the `TList<T>` that I mentioned at the beginning of this chapter.

Furthermore, we can see that the built-in memory manager doesn't always move the memory around. When a memory is enlarged to $10 bytes, the memory manager returns a new pointer (original value was $2E98B20, new value is $2ED3990). After the next two allocations, this pointer stays the same.

Only when the memory is enlarged to $48 bytes, does the memory manager have to allocate a new block and move the data:

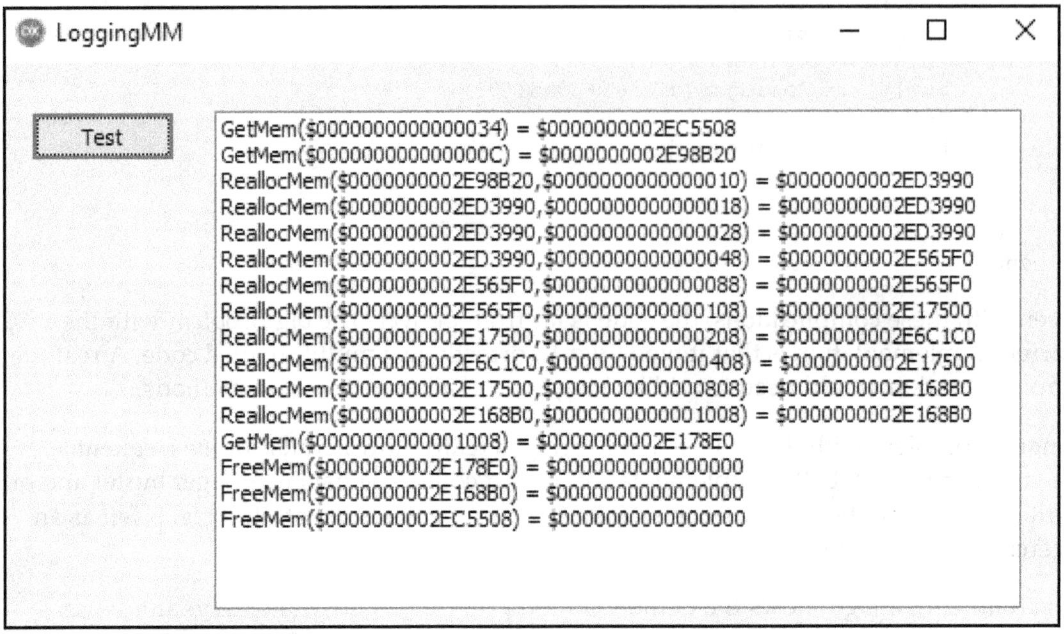

An interesting call happens after all the reallocations. Another copy of the list data is allocated with a call to `GetMem($1008)`. A little digging shows that this happens when list capacity is set to `0` inside the destructor:

```
destructor TList<T>.Destroy;
begin
  Capacity := 0;
  inherited;
end;
```

This allocation is caused by the notification mechanism which allows `TObjectList<T>` to destroy owned objects. Data needs to be stored temporary before it is passed to the notification event and that is done with a temporary array.

I'm pretty sure you will not be writing a new memory manager just to improve speed of multithreaded programs. I'm sure I won't do it. Luckily, there are crazier and smarter people out there who put their work out as open source.

ScaleMM

First such memory manager is *ScaleMM*. It is the work of André Mussche and can be downloaded from `https://github.com/andremussche/scalemm`. You can use it in practically any application, as it is released under a tri-license MPL 1.1/GPL 2.0/LGPL 2.1. It only supports the Windows platform.

ScaleMM is written in Delphi and assembler. To use ScaleMM, you just have to download it, store it somewhere on the disk and add the *ScaleMM2* unit as a first unit in the program.

ScaleMM was created as a faster replacement for FastMM. It is not as loaded with debugging features as FastMM but implements just a base memory manager functionality. Because of that, it makes sense to run FastMM while debugging, and ScaleMM while testing and in production.

The older version of Delphi didn't like it if you put the `{$IFDEF}` directive inside the main program's uses list. Delphi will remove this directive when you add a new form to the program. The easiest way to fix this is to create a new unit and add it as a first unit in the main program's uses list. In this new unit, you can then put `{$IFDEF}` in the used memory manager however you wish.

An example of the uses list in such a main program is shown here:

```
program ParallelAllocation;

uses
  ParallelAllocationMM,
  Vcl.Forms,
  ParallelAllocationMain in 'ParallelAllocationMain.pas'
{frmParallelAllocation};
```

Unit `ParallelAllocationMM` can then be implemented as shown here:

```
unit ParallelAllocationMM;

interface

uses
  {$IFDEF DEBUG}
  FastMM4 in 'FastMM\FastMM4.pas';
  {$ELSE}
  ScaleMM2 in 'ScaleMM\ScaleMM2.pas';
  {$ENDIF}
```

```
implementation

end.
```

Replacing FastMM with ScaleMM in the test program, `ParallelAllocation` shows a noticeable improvement. With FastMM and `{$DEFINE UseReleaseStack}`, the parallel version is at best 6.3x faster than the serial one. With ScaleMM it is up to 6.7x faster:

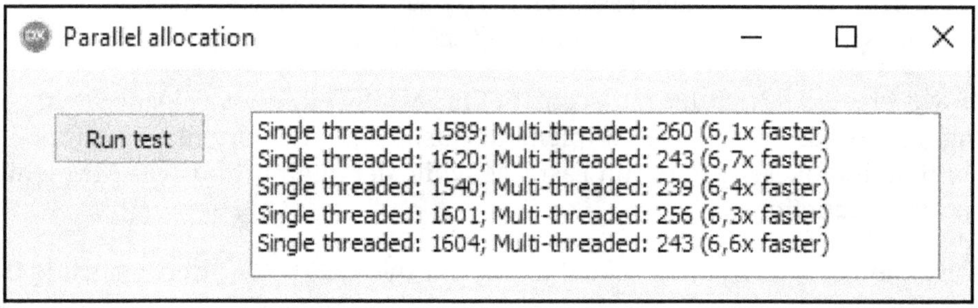

TBBMalloc

Another good alternative for a memory manager is Intel's *TBBMalloc*, part of their *Thread Building Blocks* library. It is released under the Apache 2.0 license which allows usage in open source and commercial applications. You can also buy a commercial license, if the Apache 2.0 license doesn't suite you. As ScaleMM, this memory manager only supports the Windows platform.

Intel's library was designed for C and C++ users. While you can go and download it from `https://www.threadingbuildingblocks.org`, you will still need a Delphi unit that will connect Delphi's memory management interface with the functions exported from Intel's *tbbmalloc* DLL.

Alternatively, you can download the *Intel TBBMalloc Interfaces* project from `https://sites.google.com/site/aminer68/intel-tbbmalloc-interfaces-for-delphi-and-delphi-xe-versions-and-freepascal`. The package you'll get there contains both compiled `tbbmalloc.dll` and a unit *cmem* which links this DLL into your application.

> TIP: In order to be able to run the application, you'll have to make sure that it will find `tbbmalloc.dll`. The simplest way to do that is to put the DLL in the `exe` folder. For 32-bit applications, you should use the DLL from the `tbbmalloc32` subfolder and for 64-bit applications, you should use the DLL from the `tbbmalloc64` subfolder.

Intel TBBMalloc Interfaces actually implements three different interface units, all named *cmem*. A version in subfolder `cmem_delphi` can be used with Delphis up to 2010, subfolder `cmem_xe` contains a version designed for Delphi XE and newer, and there's also a version for FreePascal in subfolder `cmem_fps`.

Creating an interface unit to a DLL is actually pretty simple. The *cmem* unit firstly imports functions from the `tbbmalloc.dll`:

```
function scalable_getmem(Size: nativeUInt): Pointer; cdecl;
  external 'tbbmalloc' name 'scalable_malloc';

procedure scalable_freemem(P: Pointer); cdecl;
  external 'tbbmalloc' name 'scalable_free';

function scalable_realloc(P: Pointer; Size: nativeUInt): Pointer; cdecl;
  external 'tbbmalloc' name 'scalable_realloc';
```

After that, writing memory management functions is a breeze. You just have to redirect calls to the DLL functions:

```
function CGetMem(Size: NativeInt): Pointer;
begin
  Result := scalable_getmem(Size);
end;

function CFreeMem(P: Pointer): integer;
begin
  scalable_freemem(P);
  Result := 0;
end;

function CReAllocMem(P: Pointer; Size: NativeInt): Pointer;
begin
  Result := scalable_realloc(P, Size);
end;
```

The `AllocMem` function is implemented by calling the `scallable_getmem` DLL function and filling the memory with zeroes afterwards:

```
function CAllocMem(Size : NativeInt) : Pointer;
begin
  Result := scalable_getmem(Size);
  if Assigned(Result) then
    FillChar(Result^, Size, 0);
end;
```

The `ParallelAllocation` demo is all set for testing with *TBBMalloc*. You only have to copy `tbbmalloc.dll` from the `tbbmalloc32` folder to `Win32\Debug` and change the `ParallelAllocation.dpr` so that it will load *cmem* instead of *FastMM* or *ScaleMM*:

```
program ParallelAllocation;

uses
  cmem in 'tbbmalloc\cmem_xe\cmem.pas',
  Vcl.Forms,
  ParallelAllocationMain in 'ParallelAllocationMain.pas'
{frmParallelAllocation};
```

What about the speed? Unbeatable! Running the `ParallelAllocation` demo with *TBBMalloc* shows parallel code being up to 8.6x faster than the serial code:

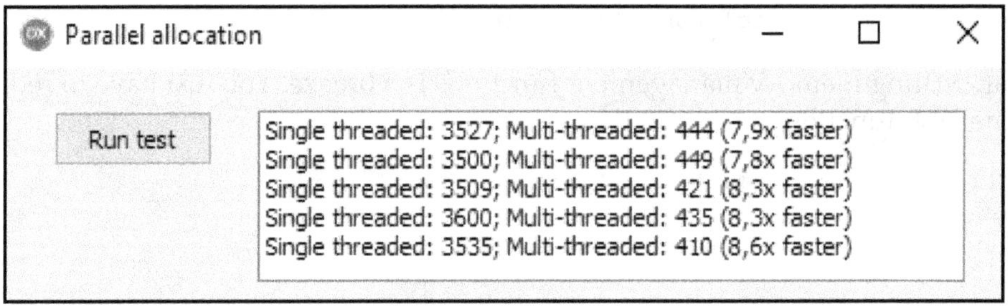

Fine-tuning SlowCode

We are near the end of the chapter. Let's step back a little and take a breath.

This chapter is packed with information, but if I would have to pick the most important lesson, it would be: don't enlarge strings (arrays, lists) element by element. If you know how much space some data will take, allocate the space at the beginning.

As all recommendations go, this too must be taken with a grain of salt. Most of the time such optimizations will not matter. You should always have the following checklist in mind:

1. Measure. Find where the problem actually is.
2. See if you can improve the algorithm. This will give the best results.
3. Fine-tune the code.

In the previous chapter, we have optimized the heart out of our old friend, `SlowCode`. Just to remind you, the latest version `SlowCode_Sieve_v2_opt` processes 10 million elements in a mere 529 ms. Still, there is a little room for improvement that I've neglected so far.

The problem lies in the function, `Filter` which expands the `Result` array, element by element:

```
function Filter(list: TList<Integer>): TArray<Integer>;
var
  i: Integer;
  reversed: Integer;
begin
  SetLength(Result, 0);
  for i in list do
  begin
    reversed := ReverseInt(i);
    if not ElementInDataDivides(list, reversed) then
    begin
      SetLength(Result, Length(Result) + 1);
      Result[High(Result)] := i;
    end;
  end;
end;
```

A much better approach would be to create a "just right" result array at the beginning. But how big is "just right"? We don't know how many elements the resulting array will have to store.

That's true, but we know one thing—it will not be larger than the `list`. All elements that are inserted into `Result` come from this list so `Result` can only contain the same amount or less elements, not more.

If we don't know how big the resulting array will be, we'll do the next best thing. At the beginning, we'll set it to the maximum possible value. Then we'll add elements to it. At the end, we'll truncate it to the correct size.

This method is implemented in the function `Filter` in the program, `SlowCode_Sieve_v3`:

```
function Filter(list: TList<Integer>): TArray<Integer>;
var
  i: Integer;
  reversed: Integer;
  outIdx: Integer;
begin
  SetLength(Result, list.Count);
  outIdx := 0;
```

```
    for i in list do
    begin
      reversed := ReverseInt(i);
      if not ElementInDataDivides(list, reversed) then
      begin
        Result[outIdx] := i;
        Inc(outIdx);
      end;
    end;
    SetLength(Result, outIdx);
  end;
```

How fast is this "improved and optimized" version? Sadly, not very much. The time to process 10 million numbers went from 529 to 512 ms.

So, what does this prove? Exactly what I was telling you before. Most of the time you don't gain much by fiddling with small details. That, and—oh my, is FastMM fast!

Don't forget though that in a multithreaded world the overhead from the memory manager is automatically higher (as I have shown earlier). When you write multithreaded programs such small optimizations can give you a bigger improvement than in the single-threaded world.

Just to be sure I'm not missing something, I've enlarged the test set from 10 to 100 million numbers. `SlowCode_Sieve_v2_opt` needed 7,524 ms and `SlowCode_Sieve_v3` needed 7,512 ms. The difference is miniscule. It is quite obvious that the biggest problem is not memory reallocations but other processing. Maybe a parallel approach will be able to help? We'll see.

Summary

This chapter dove deep into the murky waters of memory managers. We started on the light side with a discussion of strings, arrays and how memory for them is managed.

After that, I enumerated all memory management functions exposed by Delphi. We saw how we can allocate memory blocks, change their size, and free them again. We also learned about memory management functions designed to allocate and release managed data—strings, interfaces, dynamic arrays, and so on.

The next part of the chapter was dedicated to records. We saw how to allocate them, how to initialize them, and even how to make dynamically allocated records function together with generic types. We also saw that records are not just faster to create than objects, but also uses less memory.

Then we went really deep into the complicated world of memory manager implementation. I explained—from a very distant viewpoint—how FastMM is organized internally and what tricks it uses to speed up frequently encountered situations.

After that, I proved that even FastMM is not perfect. It offers great performance in single-threaded applications but can cause slowdowns in a multithreaded scenario. I have shown a way to detect such bottlenecks in a multithreaded program and also how to improve the FastMM speed in such situations.

Sometimes, this is still not enough but Delphi offers a solution. You can swap the memory manager for another. To show this approach, I developed a small memory manager wrapper which logs all memory manager calls to a file. After that, I showed how you can replace FastMM with two alternative memory managers, ScaleMM and TBBMalloc.

The question may arise whether to always replace FastMM with an alternative. After all, alternatives are faster. The answer to that question is a resounding - **no**! I believe that the program should be—if at all possible—deployed with the same memory manager that it was tested with. FastMM offers such great capabilities for debugging (which I sadly didn't have space to discuss here) that I simply refuse to use anything else during development. I would create a release version of a program with a non-default memory manager only under very specific circumstances and only after extensive testing.

At the end, we have returned to the `SlowCode` program. Although it contained excessive memory reallocations, it turned out that they didn't slow down the program in a significant way. Still, fixing that was an interesting exercise.

In the next chapter, I'll return to the bigger picture. We'll forget all about the optimizations at the level of memory allocations and object creation, and we'll again start fiddling with the algorithms. This time we'll look in a completely new direction. We'll force our programs to do multiple things at once! In other words, we'll learn to multithread.

5
Getting Started with the Parallel World

If you are reading this book from start to finish, without skipping chapters, you've been through quite a lot. I've discussed algorithms, optimization techniques, memory management, and more, but I've quite pointedly stayed away from parallel programming (or *multithreading*, as it is also called).

I had a very good reason for that. Parallel programming is hard. It doesn't matter if you are an excellent programmer. It doesn't matter how good the supporting tools are. Parallel programming gives you plenty of opportunities to introduce weird errors into the program: errors that are hard to repeat and even harder to find. That's why I wanted you to explore other options first.

If you can make your program fast enough without going the parallel way, then make it so! Classical non-parallel (*single-threaded*) code will always contain less bugs and hidden traps than parallel code.

Sometimes this is not possible, and you have to introduce parallel programming techniques into the code. To do it successfully, it's not enough to know how to **do** parallel programming. Much more important is that you know what you should absolutely **never** do in parallel code.

To set you in the right mood, this chapter will cover the following topics:

- What is parallel programming and multithreading?
- What are the most common causes of program errors in parallel code?
- How should we handle the user interface in a parallel world?

- What is synchronization, and why is it both good and bad?
- What is interlocking, and when is it better than synchronization?
- How can we remove the synchronization from the picture?
- What communication tools does Delphi offer to a programmer?
- What other libraries are there to help you?

Processes and threads

As a programmer, you probably have already some understanding about what a process is. As operating systems look at it, a process is a rough equivalent of an application. When a user starts an application, an operating system creates and starts a new process. The process owns the application code and all the resources that this code uses—memory, file handles, device handles, sockets, windows, and so on.

When the program is executing, the system must also keep track of the current execution address, state of the CPU registers, and state of the program's stack. This information, however, is not part of the process, but of a **thread** belonging to this process. Even the simplest program uses one thread.

In other words, the process represents the program's *static* data while the thread represents the *dynamic* part. During the program's lifetime, the thread describes its line of execution. If we know the state of the thread at every moment, we can fully reconstruct the execution in all its details.

All operating systems support one thread per process (the main thread) but some go further and support multiple threads in one process. Actually, most modern operating systems support **multithreading,** as this approach is called. With multithreading, the operating system manages multiple execution paths through the same code. Those paths may execute at the same time (and then again, they may not—but more on that later).

The default thread created when the program starts is called the *main thread*. Other threads that come afterwards are called **worker** or **background** threads.

In most operating systems (including Windows, OS X, iOS, and Android), processes are **heavy**. It takes a long time (at least at the operating system level where everything is measured in microseconds) to create and load a new process. In contrast to that, threads are **light**. New threads can be created almost immediately—all that the operating system has to do is to allocate some memory for the stack and set up some control structures used by the kernel.

Another important point is that processes are **isolated**. The operating system does its best to separate one process from another so that buggy (or malicious) code in one process cannot crash another process (or read private data from it). Threads, however, don't benefit from this protection.

If you're old enough to remember Windows 3, where this was not the case, you can surely appreciate the stability this isolation is bringing to the user. In contrast to that, multiple threads inside a process **share** all process resources—memory, file handles, and so on. Because of that, threading is inherently fragile—it is very simple to bring down one thread with a bug in another.

In the beginning, operating systems were single-tasking. In other words, only one task (that is, a process) could be executing at one time, and only when it completed the job (when the task terminated) could a new task be scheduled (started).

As soon as the hardware was fast enough, **multitasking** was invented. Most computers still had only one processor, but through the operating system magic it looked like this processor was executing multiple programs at the same time.

Each program was given a small amount of time to do its job. After that it was paused and another program took its place. After some indeterminate time (depending on the system load, the number of higher priority tasks, and so on), the program could execute again and the operating system would run it from the position in which it was paused, again only for a small amount of time.

Two very different approaches to multitasking were in use through history. In **cooperative** multitasking, the process itself tells the operating system when it is ready to be paused. This simplifies the operating system but gives a badly written program an opportunity to bring down the whole computer. Remember Windows 3? That was cooperative multitasking at its worst.

A better approach is **pre-emptive** multitasking, where each process is given its allotted time (typically about a few tens of milliseconds in Windows) and is then *pre-empted*; that is, the hardware timer fires and takes control from the process and gives it back to the operating system, which can then schedule next process.

This approach is used in current Windows, OS X, and all other modern desktop and mobile operating systems. That way, a multitasking system can appear to execute multiple processes at once even if it has only one processor core. Things get even better if there are multiple cores inside the computer, as multiple processes can then really execute at the same time.

The same goes for threads. Single-tasking systems were limited to one thread per process by default. Some multitasking systems were single-threaded (that is, they could only execute one thread per process), but all modern operating systems support multithreading—they can execute multiple threads inside one process. Everything I said about multitasking applies to threads too. Actually, it is the threads that are scheduled, not the processes.

When to parallelize the code?

Before you start parallelizing the code, you should understand whether the particular code is a good candidate for parallelization or not. There are some typical examples where parallelization is particularly simple, and there are some where it is really hard to implement.

One of the most common examples is executing long parts of code in the *main thread*. In Delphi, the main thread is the only one responsible for managing the user interface. If it is running some long task and not processing user interface events, then the user interface is blocked. We can solve this problem by moving the long task into a background thread, which will allow the main thread to manage the user interface. A responsive program makes for a happy user, as I like to say.

Another problem that is usually relatively simple to solve is enabling a server application to handle multiple clients at once. Instead of processing client requests one by one, we can create a separate thread for each client (up to some reasonable limit) and process requests from that client in that thread.

As requests from different clients really should not interact directly with one another, we don't have to take care of data sharing or inter-thread communications which are, as you'll see, the biggest source of problems in multithreaded programming. The biggest problem which we usually have is to determine the upper limit for concurrent running threads, as that is affected both by the problem we are solving and the number of processors in the user's computer.

The last class of problems, which is also hardest to implement, is speeding up some algorithm. We must find a way to split an algorithm into parts, and that way will be different in each application. Sometimes we can just process part of the input data in each thread and aggregate partial results later, but that will not always be possible. We'll return to this advanced topic in `Chapter 7`, *Exploring Parallel Practices*.

Most common problems

Before we start writing multithreaded code, I'd like to point out some typical situations that represent the most common sources of problems in multithreaded programs. After that, I'll look into the possible ways of solving such situations.

The biggest problem with the situations I'm about to describe is that they are all completely valid programming approaches if you are writing a single-threaded code. Because of that, they sometimes slip even into (multithreaded) code written by the best programmers.

As we'll see later in the chapter, the best way to work around them is just to stay away from problematic situations. Instead of data sharing, for example, we can use data duplication and communication channels. But I'm getting ahead of myself ...

All of the situations I'm going to describe have something in common. They are a source of problems that can stay well hidden. Lots of times, parallel programs seem to be working during the testing but then randomly fail only at some customers.

> The examples in this chapter are carefully chosen so they **always** cause problems in multithreaded code. In real life, sadly, the situation is quite different.

The only way to detect such problems in multithreaded code is to put a lot of effort into testing. Only automated unit tests running for a long time have any chance of finding them.

You'll notice that I'm skipping ahead a bit here. I did not tell you how to write multithreaded code at all, but I'm already using it in examples. For now, you can just believe me that the code in the examples does what I'm saying. In the next chapter, you'll learn all you need to know to really understand what I'm doing here, and then you can return to the examples from this chapter and re-examine them.

Never access UI from a background thread

Let's start with the biggest source of hidden problems—manipulating a user interface from a background thread. This is, surprisingly, quite a common problem—even more so as all Delphi resources on multithreaded programming will simply say to never do that. Still, it doesn't seem to touch some programmers, and they will always try to find an excuse to manipulate a user interface from a background thread.

Indeed, there *may* be a situation where VCL or FireMonkey may be manipulated from a background thread, but you'll be treading on thin ice if you do that. Even if your code works with the current Delphi, nobody can guarantee that changes in graphical libraries introduced in future Delphis won't break your code. It is **always** best to cleanly decouple background processing from a user interface.

Let's look at an example which nicely demonstrates the problem. The `ParallelPaint` demo has a simple form, with eight `TPaintBox` components and eight threads. Each thread runs the same drawing code and draws a pattern into its own `TPaintBox`. As every thread accesses only its own `Canvas`, and no other user interface components, a naive programmer would therefore assume that drawing into paintboxes directly from background threads would not cause problems. A naive programmer would be very much mistaken.

If you run the program, you will notice that although the code paints constantly into some of the paint boxes, others stop to be updated after some time. You may even get a *Canvas does not allow drawing* exception. It is impossible to tell in advance which threads will continue painting and which will not.

The following image shows an example of an output. The first two paint boxes in the first row, and the last one in the last row, were not updated anymore when I grabbed the image:

The lines are drawn in the `DrawLine` method. It does nothing special, just sets the color for that line and draws it. Still, that is enough to break the user interface when this is called from multiple threads at once, even though each thread uses its own `Canvas`:

```
procedure TfrmParallelPaint.DrawLine(canvas: TCanvas; p1, p2: TPoint;
color: TColor);
begin
  Canvas.Pen.Color := color;
  Canvas.MoveTo(p1.X, p1.Y);
  Canvas.LineTo(p2.X, p2.Y);
end;
```

Is there a way around this problem? Indeed there is. Delphi's `TThread` class implements a method, `Queue`, which executes some code in the main thread. (Actually, `TThread` has multiple methods that can do that; I'll return to this topic later in the chapter.)

`Queue` takes a procedure or anonymous method as a parameter and sends it to the main thread. After some short time, the code is then executed *in the main thread*. It is impossible to tell how much time will pass before the code is executed, but that delay will typically be very short, in the order of milliseconds. As it accepts an anonymous method, we can use the magic of *variable capturing* and write the corrected code, as shown here:

```
procedure TfrmParallelPaint.QueueDrawLine(canvas: TCanvas; p1, p2: TPoint;
color: TColor);
begin
  TThread.Queue(nil,
    procedure
    begin
      Canvas.Pen.Color := color;
      Canvas.MoveTo(p1.X, p1.Y);
      Canvas.LineTo(p2.X, p2.Y);
    end);
end;
```

In older Delphis you don't have such a nice `Queue` method but only a version of `Synchronize` that accepts a normal method. If you have to use this method, you cannot count on anonymous method mechanisms to handle parameters. Rather, you have to copy them to fields and then `Synchronize` a parameterless method operating on these fields. The following code fragment shows how to do that:

```
procedure TfrmParallelPaint.SynchronizedDraw;
begin
  FCanvas.Pen.Color := FColor;
  FCanvas.MoveTo(FP1.X, FP1.Y);
  FCanvas.LineTo(FP2.X, FP2.Y);
end;

procedure TfrmParallelPaint.SyncDrawLine(canvas: TCanvas; p1, p2: TPoint;
color: TColor);
begin
  FCanvas := canvas;
  FP1 := p1;
  FP2 := p2;
  FColor := color;
  TThread.Synchronize(nil, SynchronizedDraw);
end;
```

If you run the corrected program, the final result should always be similar to the following image, with all eight `TPaintBox` components showing a nicely animated image:

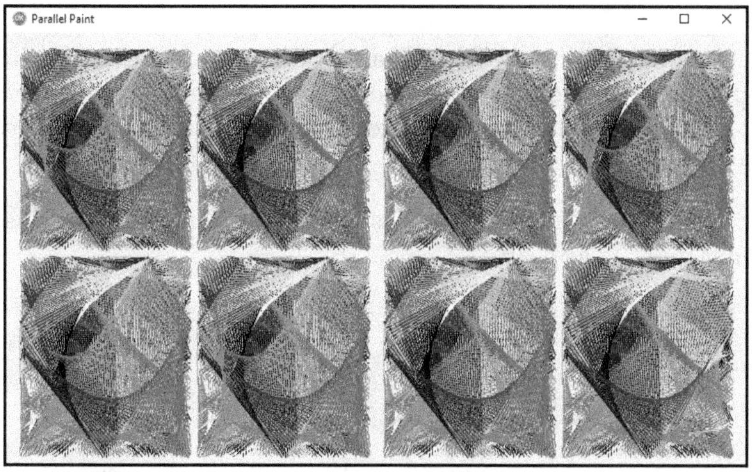

Simultaneous reading and writing

The next situation which I'm regularly seeing while looking at a badly-written parallel code is simultaneous reading and writing from/to a shared data structure, such as a list. The `SharedList` program demonstrates how things can go wrong when you share a data structure between threads. Actually, scrap that, it shows how things **will** go wrong if you do that.

This program creates a shared list, `FList: TList<Integer>`. Then it creates one background thread which runs the method `ListWriter` and multiple background threads, each running the `ListReader` method. Indeed, you can run the same code in multiple threads. This is a perfectly normal behavior and is sometimes extremely useful.

The `ListReader` method is incredibly simple. It just reads all the elements in a list and does that over and over again. As I've mentioned before, the code in my examples makes sure that problems in multithreaded code really **do** occur, but because of that, my demo code most of the time also looks terribly stupid. In this case, the reader just reads and reads the data because that's the best way to expose the problem:

```
procedure TfrmSharedList.ListReader;
var
  i, j, a: Integer;
begin
```

```
    for i := 1 to CNumReads do
      for j := 0 to FList.Count - 1 do
        a := FList[j];
end;
```

The `ListWriter` method is a bit different. It also loops around, but it also sleeps a little inside each loop iteration. It would actually be easier to repeat the problem without this extra `Sleep(1)`, but I'll need it to demonstrate something else later in the chapter. Just ignore it for now.

After the `Sleep`, the code either adds to the list or deletes from it. Again, this is designed so that the problem is quick to appear:

```
procedure TfrmSharedList.ListWriter;
var
  i: Integer;
begin
  for i := 1 to CNumWrites do
  begin
    Sleep(1);
    if FList.Count > 10 then
      FList.Delete(Random(10))
    else
      FList.Add(Random(100));
  end;
end;
```

If you start the program in a debugger, and click on the **Shared lists** button, you'll quickly get an `EArgumentOutOfRangeException` exception. A look at the stack trace will show that it appears in the line `a := FList[j];`.

In retrospect, this is quite obvious. The code in `ListReader` starts the inner `for` loop and reads the `FListCount`. At that time, `FList` has 11 elements so `Count` is 11. At the end of the loop, the code tries to read `FList[10]`, but in the meantime `ListWriter` has deleted one element and the list now only has 10 elements. Accessing element `[10]` therefore raises an exception.

We'll return to this topic later, in the section about *Locking*. For now you should just keep in mind that sharing data structures between threads causes problems.

Sharing a variable

OK, so rule number two is "Shared structures *bad*". What about sharing a simple variable? Nothing can go wrong there, right? Wrong! There are actually multiple ways something can go wrong.

The program `IncDec` demonstrates one of the bad things that can happen. The code contains two methods: `IncValue` and `DecValue`. The former increments a shared `FValue: integer;` some number of times, and the latter decrements it by the same number of times:

```
procedure TfrmIncDec.IncValue;
var
  i: integer;
  value: integer;
begin
  for i := 1 to CNumRepeat do begin
    value := FValue;
    FValue := value + 1;
  end;
end;

procedure TfrmIncDec.DecValue;
var
  i: integer;
  value: integer;
begin
  for i := 1 to CNumRepeat do begin
    value := FValue;
    FValue := value - 1;
  end;
end;
```

A click on the **Inc/Dec** button sets the shared value to *0*, runs `IncValue`, then `DecValue`, and logs the result:

```
procedure TfrmIncDec.btnIncDec1Click(Sender: TObject);
begin
  FValue := 0;
  IncValue;
  DecValue;
  LogValue;
end;
```

I know you can all tell what `FValue` will hold at the end of this program. Zero, of course. But what will happen if we run `IncValue` and `DecValue` in parallel? That is, actually, hard to predict!

A click on the **Multithreaded** button does almost the same, except that it runs `IncValue` and `DecValue` in parallel. How exactly that is done is not important at the moment (but feel free to peek into the code if you're interested):

```
procedure TfrmIncDec.btnIncDec2Click(Sender: TObject);
begin
  FValue := 0;
  RunInParallel(IncValue, DecValue);
  LogValue;
end;
```

Running this version of the code may still sometimes put zero in `FValue`, but that will be extremely rare. You most probably won't be able to see that result unless you are very lucky. Most of the time, you'll just get a seemingly random number from the range *-10,000,000* to *10,000,000* (which is the value of the `CNumRepeat`constant).

In the following image, the first number is a result of the single-threaded code, while all the rest were calculated by the parallel version of the algorithm:

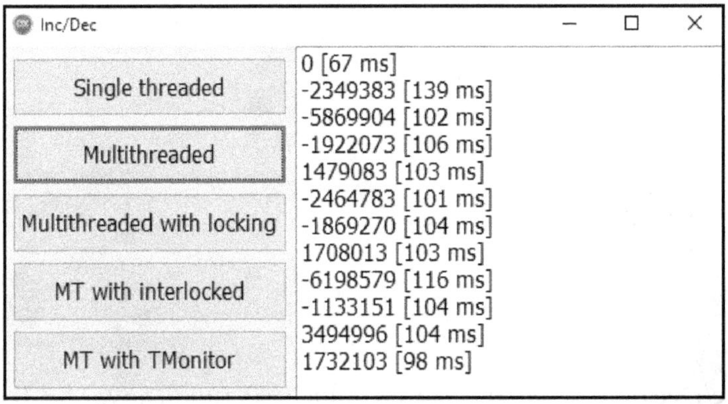

To understand what's going on, you should know that Windows (and all other operating systems) does many things at once. At any given time, there are hundreds of threads running in different programs and they are all fighting for the limited number of CPU cores. As our program is the active one (has focus), its threads will get most of the CPU time, but still they'll sometimes be paused for some amount of time so that other threads can run.

Because of that, it can easily happen that `IncValue` reads the current value of `FValue` into `value` (let's say that the value is *100*) and is then paused. `DecValue` reads the same value and then runs for some time, decrementing `FValue`. Let's say that it gets it down to *-20,000*. (That is just a number without any special meaning.)

After that, the `IncValue` thread is awakened. It should increment the value to *-19,999*, but instead of that it adds *1* to *100* (stored in `value`), gets *101*, and stores **that** into `FValue`. Ka-boom! In each repetition of the program, this will happen at different times and will cause a different result to be calculated.

You may complain that the problem is caused by the two-stage increment and decrement, but you'd be wrong. I dare you—go ahead, change the code so that it will modify `FValue` with `Inc(FValue)` and `Dec(FValue)` and it still won't work correctly.

Well, I hear you say, so I shouldn't even modify one variable from two threads at the same time? I can live with that. But surely, it is OK to write into a variable from one thread and read from another?

The answer, as you can probably guess given the general tendency of this section, is again—no, you may not. There are some situations where this is OK (for example, when a variable is only one byte long) but, in general, even simultaneous reading and writing can be a source of weird problems.

The `ReadWrite` program demonstrates this problem. It has a shared buffer, `FBuf: Int64`, and a pointer variable used to read and modify the data, `FPValue: PInt64`. At the beginning, the buffer is initialized to an easily recognized number and a pointer variable is set to point to the buffer:

```
FPValue := @FBuf;
FPValue^ := $7777777700000000;
```

The program runs two threads. One just reads from the location and stores all the read values into a list. This value is created with `Sorted` and `Duplicates` properties, set in a way that prevents it from storing duplicate values:

```
procedure TfrmReadWrite.Reader;
var
  i: integer;
begin
  for i := 1 to CNumRepeat do
    FValueList.Add(FPValue^);
end;
```

The second thread repeatedly writes two values into the shared location:

```
procedure TfrmReadWrite.Writer;
var
  i: integer;
begin
  for i := 1 to CNumRepeat do begin
    FPValue^ := $7777777700000000;
    FPValue^ := $0000000077777777;
  end;
end;
```

At the end, the contents of the `FValueList` list are logged on the screen. We would expect to see only two values—*$7777777700000000* and *$0000000077777777*. In reality, we see four, as the following screenshot demonstrates:

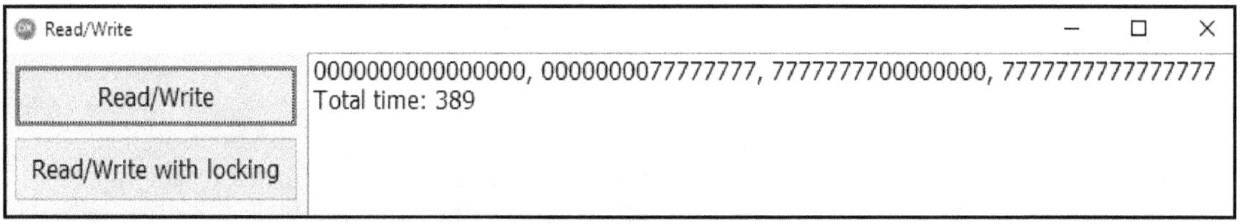

The reason for that strange result is that Intel processors in 32-bit mode can't write a 64-bit number (as `int64` is) in one step. In other words, reading and writing 64-bit numbers in 32-bit code is not *atomic*.

> When multithreading programmers talk about something being *atomic,* they want to say that an operation will execute in one indivisible step. Any other thread will either see a state before the operation or a state after the operation, but never some undefined intermediate state.

How do values *$7777777777777777* and *$0000000000000000* appear in the test application? Let's say that `FValue^` contains *$7777777700000000*. The code then starts writing *$0000000077777777* into `FValue` by firstly storing a $77777777 into the bottom four bytes. After that it starts writing *$00000000* into the upper four bytes of `FValue^`, but in the meantime `Reader` reads the value and gets *$7777777777777777*.

In a similar way, `Reader` will sometimes see *$0000000000000000* in the `FValue^`.

We'll look into a way to solve this situation immediately, but in the meantime, you may wonder—when is it okay to read/write from/to a variable at the same time? Sadly, the answer is—it depends. Not even just on the CPU family (Intel and ARM processors behave completely differently), but also on a specific architecture used in a processor. For example, older and newer Intel processors may not behave the same in that respect.

You can always depend on access to byte-sized data being atomic, but that is that. Access (reads and writes) to larger quantities of data (words, integers) is atomic only if the data is correctly *aligned*. You can access *word* sized data atomically if it is word aligned, and integer data if it is double-word aligned. If the code was compiled in 64-bit mode, you can also atomically access int64 data if it is quad-word aligned.

When you are not using data packing (such as packed records) the compiler will take care of alignment and data access should automatically be atomic. You should, however, still check the alignment in code, if nothing else to prevent stupid programming errors.

If you want to write and read larger amounts of data, modify the data, or if you want to work on shared data structures, correct alignment will not be enough. You will need to introduce *synchronization* into your program.

Synchronization

Whenever you need to access the same data from multiple threads, and at least one thread is modifying the data, you have to *synchronize* access to the data. As we've just seen, this holds for shared data structures and for simple variables.

Synchronization will make sure that one thread cannot see invalid intermediate states that another thread creates temporarily while updating the shared data. In a way this is similar to database transactions at the *read committed* level, when other users cannot see changes applied to the database while a transaction is in progress.

The simplest way to synchronize two (or more) threads is to use *locking*. With locking you can protect a part of the program so that only one thread will be able to access it at any time. If one thread has successfully *acquired* but not yet *released* the lock (we also say that the thread now *owns* the lock), no other threads will be able to acquire that same lock. If any thread tries to acquire a lock, it will be paused until the lock is available (after the original lock owner releases the lock).

We could compare such a lock with a real-world lock. When somebody wants to access a critical resource that must not be shared (for example, a toilet), he will lock the door behind him. Any other potential users of the critical resource will queue in a line. When the first user is finished using the critical resource, he will unlock it and leave, allowing the next user the access.

Synchronization mechanisms are almost always implemented directly by the operating system. It is possible to implement them directly in the code, but that should only be used to solve very specific circumstances. As a general rule, you should not attempt to write your own synchronization mechanism.

If you are writing a multi-platform application, accessing operating system synchronization mechanisms can be a pain. Luckily, Delphi's runtime library provides a very nice platform-independent way to work with them.

The simplest way to implement locking is to use a *critical section*. In Delphi, you should use the `TCriticalSection` wrapper implemented in the `System.SyncObjs` unit instead of accessing the operating system directly.

Critical sections

The easiest way to explain the use of critical sections is with an example. As the `ReadWrite` example is still fresh in your mind, I'll return to it. This program implements—in addition to the unsafe reading/writing approach—a code that reads and writes data with additional protection from a critical section lock.

This critical section is created when a form is created, and destroyed when the form is destroyed. There is only one critical section object shared by both threads:

```
procedure TfrmReadWrite.FormCreate(Sender: TObject);
begin
  FLock := TCriticalSection.Create;
end;

procedure TfrmReadWrite.FormDestroy(Sender: TObject);
begin
  FreeAndNil(FLock);
end;
```

When a reader wants to read from `FPValue^`, it will firstly acquire the critical section by calling `FLock.Acquire`. At that point, the thread will either successfully acquire the ownership of the lock and continue execution or it will block until the lock becomes unowned.

After some finite time, the thread will manage to acquire the lock and continue with the next line, `value := FPValue^`. This will safely read the value into a temporary variable, knowing that nobody can be writing to the value at the same time. After that the critical section is immediately released by calling `FLock.Release`, which also makes the lock unowned:

```
procedure TfrmReadWrite.LockedReader;
var
  i: integer;
  value: int64;
begin
  for i := 1 to CNumRepeat do begin
    FLock.Acquire;
    value := FPValue^;
    FLock.Release;
    FValueList.Add(value);
  end;
end;
```

> `TCriticalSection` also implements the aliases `Enter` and `Leave`, which function exactly the same as `Acquire` and `Release`. Which you use is entirely up to you.

The writer does something similar. Before a `FPValue^` is written to, the lock is acquired and after that the lock is released:

```
procedure TfrmReadWrite.LockedWriter;
var
  i: integer;
begin
  for i := 1 to CNumRepeat do begin
    FLock.Acquire;
    FPValue^ := $7777777700000000;
    FLock.Release;
    FLock.Acquire;
    FPValue^ := $0000000077777777;
    FLock.Release;
  end;
end;
```

Before we look into the result of that change, I'd like to point out something very important. Introducing a lock doesn't automatically solve problems. You also have to use it in the right place (in this example, when reading and writing the shared value), and you have to use it in **all** places where shared data is accessed.

For example, if `LockedReader` would be using a critical section, as it is now, but `LockedWriter` would not, access to the shared value would still be unsynchronized and we would be getting wrong results from the program.

Let's see how introducing a critical section affects our program. The following screenshot shows the result of both versions of the code—unprotected and synchronized:

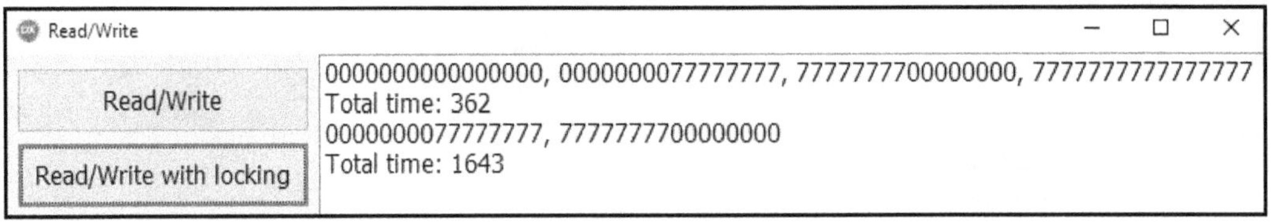

We can see two important consequences of locking here. One, the output from the code is now correct. Two, the program runs much longer with locking.

That is a typical result of synchronizing access with locks. They are slow—at least if you are trying to acquire them many thousand times per second, as my test program does. If you are using them sparingly, they will not affect the program that much.

An interesting thing about critical sections is that they will happily let through a thread that already owns a lock. A thread that already owns a lock can therefore call `Acquire` for the second time and be sure that it will not be blocked. It must then also call `Release` two times to release the critical section.

For example, the following code is perfectly valid:

```
FLock.Acquire;
FLock.Acquire;
value := FPValue^;
FLock.Release;
FLock.Release;
```

This situation sometimes comes up when procedure A locks a critical section and calls procedure B, which also locks a critical section. Instead of refactoring the code so that the critical section is only the acquired one, we can rely on this fact and acquire the critical section in both places. Acquiring an already acquired critical section is very fast.

This behavior is called *re-entrancy*, and a locking mechanism that allows such coding is deemed *re-entrant*.

There are two big problems that critical sections can introduce into your code. One we've already seen—the program runs slower with locking. The second is even worse—if such synchronization is not implemented correctly, it may cause the program to endlessly wait for a lock that will never become free. We call that **deadlocking**.

Deadlocking happens when thread 1 acquires critical section A and then tries to acquire critical section B while in the meantime thread 2 acquires critical section B and then tries to acquire critical section A. Both threads will be blocked as they will wait for a critical section that will never be released.

Deadlocking is not specific to critical sections. It can appear regardless of the locking mechanism used in the code.

This situation is demonstrated in program *Deadlocking*. It contains two threads, both accessing the shared variable, `Counter`, stored in the shared object, `Shared`. To synchronize access to this shared variable, they both acquire and release the critical section, `shared.LockCounter`.

To demonstrate the problem, both threads also acquire the additional critical section, `shared.LockOther`. In this demo, the second critical section is meaningless, but, in a badly designed real-life code, such situations occur a lot. A code may acquire a critical section, then do some processing, and in the middle of the processing access different data, protected with a different critical section.

When multiple critical sections are always acquired in the same order, everything works just fine. But if—because of a programming error or a weird system design—one thread acquires critical sections in a different order than another thread, a deadlock may occur.

The same situation is programmed into the `Deadlocking` program. The `TaskProc1` method acquires `LockCounter` first and `LockOther` second, while the `TaskProc2` method (running in a different thread) acquires `LockOther` first and `LockCounter` second. Both methods are shown here:

```
procedure TaskProc1(const task: ITask; const shared: TSharedData);
begin
  while frmDeadlock.FTask1.Status <> TTaskStatus.Canceled do begin
    shared.LockCounter.Acquire;
    shared.LockOther.Acquire;
    shared.Counter := shared.Counter + 1;
    shared.LockOther.Release;
    shared.LockCounter.Release;
  end;
end;

procedure TaskProc2(const task: ITask; const shared: TSharedData);
begin
  while frmDeadlock.FTask1.Status <> TTaskStatus.Canceled do begin
    shared.LockOther.Acquire;
    shared.LockCounter.Acquire;
    shared.Counter := shared.Counter + 1;
    shared.LockCounter.Release;
    shared.LockOther.Release;
  end;
end;
```

If you start only one thread, everything will work just fine. Thread will continue to acquire both critical sections, increment the shared resource, and release both critical sections. If you start both threads, however, the program will quickly deadlock. `TaskProc1` will acquire `LockCounter` and block on waiting for `LockOther`, while at the same time `TaskProc2` will acquire `LockOther` and block on waiting for `LockCounter`.

Luckily, sources of deadlocking are easy to find if you can repeat the problem in a debugger. When the program blocks, just click the *Pause* icon and go through the threads in the *Thread status* window. Double-click each thread and check if the *Call stack* for the thread is currently inside an *Acquire* call. Any such thread should then be carefully investigated to see if it is part of the problem.

The following screenshot shows the `TaskProc1` method paused during a deadlock:

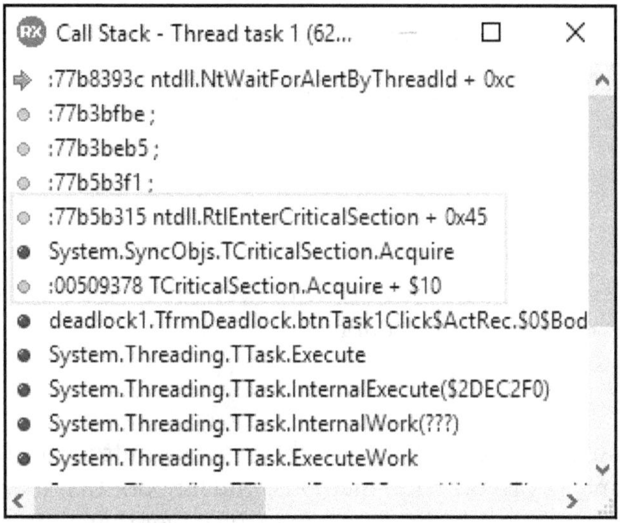

The best solution for such problems is good program design. The part of the code where the critical section is acquired should always be very short and should—if at all possible—never call other code that acquires critical sections. If that could not be prevented, you should design the code so that it always acquires all the needed critical sections first (and always in the same order), and only then call the protected code.

If that is also not possible, the last solution is to not use `Acquire` (or its namesake `Enter`), but the `TryEnter` function. That one tries to acquire the critical section, returns `False` if the critical section is already locked, or acquires the critical section and returns `True`. It will never block. An adapted version of the code is shown here:

```
procedure TryTaskProc1(const task: ITask; const shared: TSharedData);
begin
  while frmDeadlock.FTask1.Status <> TTaskStatus.Canceled do begin
    shared.LockCounter.Acquire;
    if shared.LockOther.TryEnter then
    begin
      shared.Counter := shared.Counter + 1;
      shared.LockOther.Leave;
    end;
    shared.LockCounter.Release;
  end;
end;

procedure TryTaskProc2(const task: ITask; const shared: TSharedData);
```

```
begin
  while frmDeadlock.FTask1.Status <> TTaskStatus.Canceled do begin
    shared.LockOther.Acquire;
    if shared.LockCounter.TryEnter then
    begin
      shared.Counter := shared.Counter + 1;
      shared.LockCounter.Leave;
    end;
    shared.LockOther.Release;
  end;
end;
```

If you enter a critical section with `TryEnter`, you should leave it with a call to `Leave`, just for readability reasons.

If you run the demo and use the `TryTask1` and `TryTask2` buttons to start the `TryTaskProc1` and `TryTaskProc2` methods, you'll notice that the program continues to work but also that it increments the counter much slower than with only one thread running. This happens because both threads are constantly fighting for the second critical section. Most of the time, each thread acquires the first critical section, then tries to acquire the second one, fails, and does nothing.

To learn more about deadlocks and ways to fix them, go to the beautiful *The Deadlock Empire* web site (`http://deadlockempire.4delphi.com/delphi/`), where you can explore this topic through a game.

Other locking mechanisms

Critical sections are not the only mechanism that operating systems expose to applications. There are also other approaches that may be preferable in different situations. In Delphi, most of them are nicely wrapped into system-independent wrappers, implemented in the `System.SyncObjs` unit.

The first such object is a *mutex*. It is very similar to a critical section, as you can use it to protect access to a critical resource. The big difference between a mutex and a critical section is that a critical section can only be shared between the threads of one program. A mutex, on other hand, can have a *name*. Two (or more) programs can create mutexes with the same name and use them to access some shared resource (for example, a file) that may only safely be used by one program at a time.

A mutex is implemented in a `TMutex` class which exposes the same API as a `TCriticalSection`. After you `Create` a mutex, you can call `Acquire` to access and lock the mutex and `Release` to unlock it.

If you create a mutex without a name, it can only be used inside one program and functions exactly as a critical section. Locking with mutexes, however, is *significantly* slower than locking with critical sections. As the `IncDec` demo shows, locking with mutexes (activated with the **MT with mutex** button) can be more than 50 times slower than locking with critical sections (**MT with locking** button). An image with a comparison of the timing for different locking approaches is shown later in this chapter.

Mutexes do provide one advantage over a critical section. You can acquire a mutex by calling a `WaitFor` function, which accepts a timeout value in milliseconds. If the code fails to lock a mutex in that amount of time, it will return `wrTimeout` and continue. This works just the same as `TCriticalSection.TryEnter`, except with an additional timeout. Nevertheless, if you need such functionality, you'll probably be better off by using the `TSpinlock` mechanism described later in this chapter.

The next standard synchronization mechanism is a *semaphore*. A **semaphore** is used to synchronize access to resources which can be used by more than one user (more than one code path) at the same time, but have an upper limit on the number of concurrent users.

For example, if you want to protect a resource which supports up to three concurrent users, you can create a semaphore with a count of *three*. When you *acquire* such a semaphore, you decrement the number of available resources (the semaphore's internal counter) by one. If you try to acquire a semaphore when its internal counter is at zero, you'll be blocked. `Release`, on the other hand, increments the internal counter and allows another thread to enter the critical path.

Semaphores, as mutexes, can have names and can be used to synchronize multiple programs. They are also equally slow, so I won't peruse them in this book. Still, semaphores are an interesting topic as they can be used to solve many difficult problems. For more information on the topic, I'd like to recommend a beautiful (free) book, *The Little Book of Semaphores*, which you can read or download, at `http://greenteapress.com/wp/semaphores/`.

One of the problems with critical sections is that you have to create and manage them in parallel to the data being protected. To solve that, in Delphi 2009, the developers have extended the `TObject` class with an additional pointer field used by the new `TMonitor` record, which was added to the *System* unit.

As the TObject is the base parent of each and every class type in Delphi programs, this caused the size of every object created in your program to increment by 4 bytes (8 if you're compiling for a 64-bit processor). This and the abysmally bad TMonitor implementation have caused some programmers to call this the worst abuse of space in the entire history of Delphi. I must say that I mostly agree with this assessment.

The idea behind TMonitor was completely solid. It was designed to provide a per-object locking capability together with some additional functionality that allowed for the creation of a fast in-process event and fast in-process semaphore (more on that in a moment). In reality, the implementation was so flawed that the only part that you could safely use was the basic locking, implemented with the Enter, TryEnter, and Exit functions. All other implementation was broken for many Delphi versions and was only fixed a few years later.

As far as I know, in recent releases (Tokyo and a few before), TMonitor doesn't have any known bugs. Still, most of programmers who make a living by writing multithreaded code have developed such a deep distrust of it that we simply don't want to use it.

Regardless of my preconceptions, TMonitor can safely be used to function as a critical section. It is faster and simpler (you don't have to create a separate object) than a critical section. It is also sometimes inconvenient, as it can only be used to lock some existing object, and appropriate object may not exist in the code.

The IncDec demo works around that by locking the form object itself. This doesn't affect the normal VCL operations in any way, as VCL doesn't use TMonitor to lock TForm objects. In a larger program, however, that would be frowned upon, as the meaning of the code is hard to grasp. You should use TMonitor only when you really work with a shared **object** so you can put a lock directly on it.

Another small problem with TMonitor is a naming conflict. Delphi VCL already defines a TMonitor class in the Vcl.Forms unit. If your unit includes Vcl.Forms (and every form unit does that), you'll have to type System.TMonitor instead of TMonitor to make the code compile. Alternatively, you can call MonitorEnter and MonitorExit procedures which do the same.

Let's look at the code that protects access to a shared counter with TMonitor. It was taken from the IncDec demo. To synchronize access to the counter, it firstly locks the form object by calling System.TMonitor.Enter(Self). After that it can safely operate on the counter. At the end, it unlocks the form object by calling System.TMonitor.Exit(Self). The other part of the demo, MonitorLockedIncValue (not shown here) does the same:

```
procedure TfrmIncDec.MonitorLockedDecValue;
var
  value: integer;
```

```
    i: Integer;
  begin
    for i := 1 to CNumRepeat do begin
      System.TMonitor.Enter(Self);
      value := FValue;
      FValue := value + 1;
      System.TMonitor.Exit(Self);
    end;
  end;
```

TIP

To acquire and release a `TMonitor` you can also call helper methods `MonitorEnter` and `MonitorExit`.

If you run the demo, you'll notice that the `TMonitor` approach is much faster than working with `TCriticalSection`. On my test computer, it is about four times faster. This is a result of the internal implementation of `TMonitor`, which doesn't use a critical section, but an improved idea called **spinlock**.

The difference between a critical section and a spinlock lies in the implementation of the `Acquire` call. When a thread cannot access a critical section because it is already locked, Windows puts this thread to sleep. (Other operating systems behave mostly the same.) When a critical section becomes available, Windows selects one of the threads waiting for it and wakes it up.

A spinlock, on the other hand, assumes that the code protected with it is very short and that the spinlock will be released quickly. If a spinlock is already acquired from another thread, the code firstly tries to *actively wait* or *spin*. Instead of going to sleep, the code runs in a tight loop and constantly checks if the spinlock has become available. Only if that doesn't happen after some time, the thread goes to sleep.

Delphi implements a spinlock object which you can use directly in your code. It is called `TSpinLock` and can be found in the `System.SyncObjs` unit.

A `TSpinLock` is a record, not an object, so there's no need to free it. You still have to create it though, as some data is initialized in the constructor. The code in the `IncDec` demo does that by calling `FSpinlock := TSpinLock.Create(false)`.

The code then uses `FSpinlock.Enter` to acquire a spinlock and `FSpinlock.Exit` to release it. `TSpinLock` also implements a `TryEnter` method which accepts a *timeout* parameter. If the spinlock cannot be acquired in *timeout* milliseconds, `TryEnter` returns `False`:

```
procedure TfrmIncDec.SpinlockDecValue;
var
  i: integer;
  value: integer;
begin
  for i := 1 to CNumRepeat do begin
    FSpinlock.Enter;
    value := FValue;
    FValue := value - 1;
    FSpinlock.Exit;
  end;
end;
```

The only problem with `TSpinLock` is that it is not *re-entrant*. If a thread which has already acquired a spinlock calls `Enter` for a second time, a code will either raise an exception (if you have passed `True` to the constructor) or block. The implementation, however, provides the `IsLocked` and `IsLockedByCurrentThread` functions, which you can use to write a re-entrant spinlock, using `TSpinLock` as a base.

The `System.SyncObjs` unit also implements a faster implementation of an event, `TLightweightEvent`, and a faster implementation of a semaphore, `TLightweightSemaphore`. They are both based around an idea of actively spinning in a loop (for some short time) if the object cannot be immediately acquired.

The following screenshot shows the execution time comparison for all the locking mechanisms that I've discussed so far. Well, all and one more. The last approach, *Interlocking*, will be discussed in the *Interlocked operations* section later in this chapter.

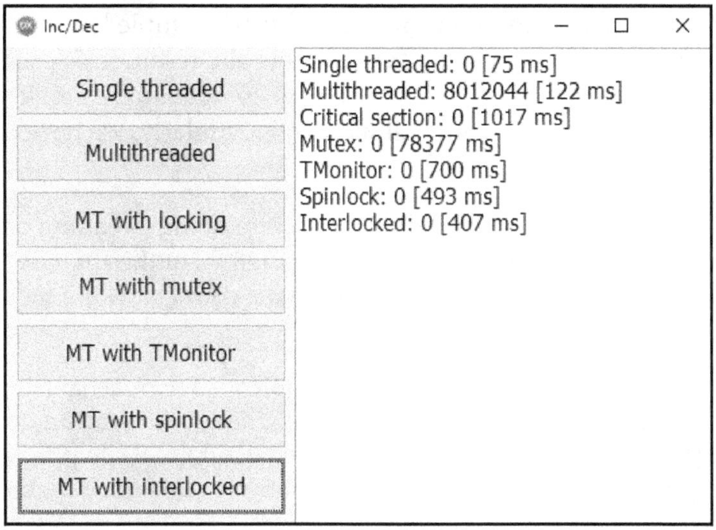

All the mechanisms I've discussed so far are completely symmetrical. They treat all the threads the same. Sometimes, though, this is not what we would like.

Lots of the time, threads in a program have to share access to data that is mostly read from and almost never changed. In this case, it is inefficient if the reader threads block one another. The only time the access must be protected is when a thread has to modify the shared data.

In such cases, we can use a synchronization mechanism that allows multiple simultaneous readers to access a shared resource, but at the same time allows only one writer. In addition, a writer must block out all the readers, as they should not read from a shared resource while it is being modified. We've seen before in the `SharedList` example that this is not going to work.

In Delphi, such a mechanism is called `TMultiReadExclusiveWriteSynchronizer`, and is defined in `System.SysUtils` unit. As this name is terribly impractical to type, Delphi also provides a shorter alias, `TMREWSync`.

In the literature and in alternative implementations, you'll also see such a mechanism called *single writer, multiple readers,* or *SWMR*.

With a `TMREWSync` and similar mechanisms that provide multiple levels of access to a resource, we cannot just call `Acquire` or `Enter` to lock the resource. We also have to state our intentions in advance. With `TMREWSync`, we have to call `BeginRead` if we want to read from a resource and `BeginWrite` if we will write to it. Similarly, we have to call `EndRead` or `EndWrite` to release a resource.

Keep in mind that the compiler cannot tell what you are doing—reading or writing—with a shared resource. Actually, the compiler cannot event tell what the shared resource is. It is entirely your responsibility as a programmer to use the correct locking methods in appropriate places of the code.

The Delphi implementation of a single writer, multiple readers mechanism is quite complicated and that shows with the speed. I actually had to fine-tune a demo program a bit to make it perform faster than a simple critical section. In real-life programs, you should always test whether a `TCriticalSection` or `TMREWSync` make for a better performance.

A short note on coding style

In all the examples so far, I used a simple coding style:

```
// acquire access
// work with shared resource
// release access
```

For example, the `IncDec` demo from this chapter contains the following code:

```
FSpinlock.Enter;
value := FValue;
FValue := value - 1;
FSpinlock.Exit;
```

In reality, I don't code resource locking in that way. I'm a strong proponent of the thought that all resource management pairs, such as create/destroy, acquire/release, beginupdate/endupdate, and so on should, if at all possible, be written in a `try..finally` block. I would therefore write the previous example as follows:

```
FSpinlock.Enter;
try
  value := FValue;
  FValue := value - 1;
finally
  FSpinlock.Exit;
end;
```

This approach has two big advantages. One is that acquiring and releasing a resource are now visibly connected with a `try..finally` construct. When you browse through the code, this pair of operations will immediately jump out at you.

The other advantage is that the resource will be released if your code crashes while the resource is allocated. This is important when the code that reacts to the exception also tries to access the shared resource. Or maybe the program tries to shut down cleanly and during the cleanup accesses the shared resource. Without a `try..finally`, the resource would stay acquired forever and that second part of code would just deadlock.

Saying all that, it may seem weird that I didn't insert `try..finally` blocks everywhere in the test code. Well, I had a reason for that. Two, actually.

Firstly, I wanted to keep code examples short. I don't like to read books that have long code examples spanning multiple pages and so I kept all code examples in this book very short.

Secondly, I wanted to write this note on coding style and that was a good excuse for it.

Shared data with built-in locking

Sometimes you don't need to implement an additional locking mechanism because Delphi already does that for you. The runtime library contains three such data structures—`TThreadList`, `TThreadList<T>`, and `TThreadedQueue<T>`. The first one can be found in the `System.Classes` unit, while the other two live in `System.Generics.Collections`.

Both variants of `TThreadList` work the same. They don't expose the normal list-management functions (such as `Add`, `Remove`, `Items[]`, and so on). Instead of that, they implement the `LockList` function, which uses `TMonitor` to acquire access to an internal `TList` (or `TList<T>`) object and returns that object. To release access to this list, the program has to call the `UnlockList` function.

The following example from the `SharedList` demo shows how to use `TThreadList<Integer>` to represent the shared storage. To access the shared list, the code calls `FThreadList.LockList`. This function returns a `TList<Integer>` object, which can be then used in the code. To release the shared list, the code calls `FThreadList.UnlockList`:

```
procedure TfrmSharedList.ThreadListReader;
var
  i, j, a: Integer;
  list: TList<Integer>;
```

```
begin
  for i := 1 to CNumReads do
  begin
    list := FThreadList.LockList;
    for j := 0 to FList.Count - 1 do
      a := FList[j];
    FThreadList.UnlockList;
  end;
end;
```

Using the list returned from the `LockList` after `UnlockList` was called is a programming error that cannot be caught by the compiler. Be careful!

Comparing the various approaches in the `SharedList` demo gives interesting results. As expected, the critical section-based locking is the slowest. More interestingly, the `TMonitor` locking used in the `TThreadList` is faster than the `TMREWSync` implementation. The following screenshot shows a comparison of execution times measured on the test computer:

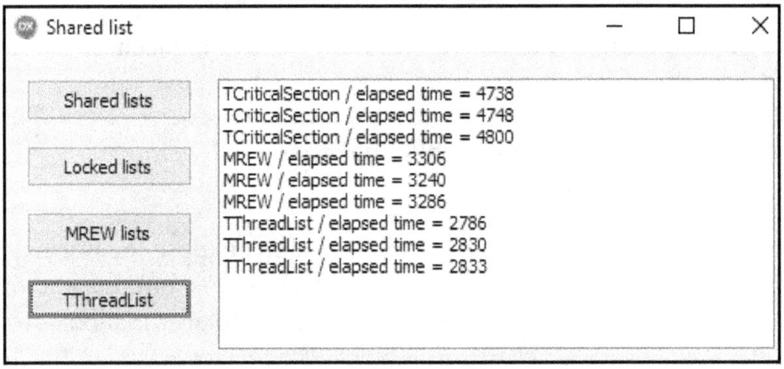

I've said it before and I'll say it again—Delphi's multiple readers, exclusive writer implementation is really not very fast. You should always compare it to a normal locking, implemented with either a `TMonitor` or a `TSpinLock`.

The third data structure, `TThreadedQueue<T>`, implements a standard first in, first out fixed-size queue. All operations on the queue are protected with a `TMonitor`. I will use this data structure in practical examples near the end of this chapter and all through `Chapter 6`, *Working with Parallel Tools*.

Interlocked operations

When a shared data is small enough and you only need to increment it or swap two values, there's an option to do that without locking. All modern processors implement instructions that can do simple operations on memory locations in such a way that another processor can not interrupt the operation in progress.

Such instructions are sometimes called *interlocked operations,* while the whole idea of programming with them is called *lock-free* programming or, sometimes, *microlocking*. The latter term is actually more appropriate, as the CPU indeed does some locking. This locking happens on an assembler instruction level, and is therefore much faster than the operating system-based locking, such as critical sections.

As these operations are implemented on an assembler level, you have to adapt the code to the specific CPU target. Or, and this is very much advised, you just use the `TInterlocked` class from the `System.SyncObjs` unit.

Functions in the `TInterlocked` class are mostly just simple wrappers for the `Atomic*` family of the CPU-dependent function from the *System* unit. For example, `TInterlocked.Add` is implemented as a simple call to `AtomicIncrement`:

```
class function TInterlocked.Add(var Target: Integer; Increment: Integer):
Integer;
begin
  Result := AtomicIncrement(Target, Increment);
end;
```

Interlocked functions are declared as `inline`, so you won't lose any cycles if you call `TInterlocked.Add` instead of `AtomicIncrement` directly.

Windows implements more interlocked functions than are exposed in the `TInterlocked` class. If you want to call them directly, you can find them in the `Winapi.Windows` unit. All their names start with `Interlocked`.

We can split interlocked functions into two big families. One set of functions modifies a shared value. You can use them to increment or decrement a shared value by some amount. Typical representatives of this family are `Increment`, `Decrement`, and `Add`.

The other set of functions is designed to exchange two values. It contains only two functions with multiple overloads that support different types of data, `Exchange` and `CompareExchange`.

The functions from the first family are easy to use. They take a value, increment or decrement it by some amount, and return the new value. All that is done *atomically*, so any other thread in the system will always see the old value or the new value but not some intermediate value.

The only exception to that pattern are the `BitTestAndSet` and `BitTestAndClear` functions. They both test if some bit in a value is set and return that as a `boolean` function result. After that they either set or clear the same bit, depending on the function. Of course, all that is again done atomically.

We can use `TInterlocked.Increment` and `TInterlocked.Decrement` to manipulate the shared value in the `IncDec` demo. Although `TInterlocked` is a class, it is composed purely from class functions. As such, we never create an instance of the `TInterlocked` class, but just use its class methods directly on our code, as shown in the following example:

```
procedure TfrmIncDec.InterlockedIncValue;
var
  i: integer;
begin
  for i := 1 to CNumRepeat do
    TInterlocked.Increment(FValue);
end;

procedure TfrmIncDec.InterlockedDecValue;
var
  i: integer;
begin
  for i := 1 to CNumRepeat do
    TInterlocked.Decrement(FValue);
end;
```

As we've seen in the previous section, this approach beats even the spinlocks, which were the fastest locking mechanism so far.

Functions in the second family are a bit harder to use. `Exchange` takes two parameters: shared data and a new value. It returns the original value of the shared data and sets it to the new value.

In essence, the `Exchange` function implements the steps outlined in the following function, except that they are done in a safe, atomic way:

```
class function TInterlocked.Exchange(var Target: Integer; Value: Integer):
Integer;
begin
```

```
  Result := Target;
  Target := Value;
end;
```

The second set of data exchanging functions, `CompareExchange`, are a bit more complicated. `CompareExchange` takes three parameters—shared data, new value, and test value. It compares shared data to the test value and, if the values are equal, sets the shared data to the new value. In all cases, the function returns the original value of the shared data.

he following code exactly represents the `CompareExchange` behavior, except that the real function implements all the steps as one atomic operation:

```
class function CompareExchange(var Target: Integer; Value: Integer;
Comparand: Integer): Integer;
begin
  Result := Target;
  if Target = Comparand then
    Target := Value;
end;
```

How can we know whether the shared data was replaced with the new value? We can check the function result. If it is equal to the test value, `Comparand`, then the value was replaced, otherwise it was not.

A helper function, `TInterlocked.Read`, can be used to atomically read from the shared data. It is implemented as such:

```
class function TInterlocked.Read(var Target: Int64): Int64;
begin
  Result := CompareExchange(Target, 0, 0);
end;
```

If the original value is equal to 0, it will be replaced with *0*. In other words, it will not be changed. If it is not equal to *0*, it also won't be changed because `CompareExchange` guarantees that. In both cases, `CompareExchange` will return the original value, which is exactly what the function needs.

We can use `TInterlocked.Read` and `TInterlocked.Exchange` to re-implement the `ReadWrite` demo without locking:

```
procedure TfrmReadWrite.InterlockedReader;
var
  i: integer;
  value: int64;
begin
  for i := 1 to CNumRepeat do begin
```

```
      value := TInterlocked.Read(FPValue^);
      FValueList.Add(value);
    end;
  end;

  procedure TfrmReadWrite.InterlockedWriter;
  var
    i: integer;
  begin
    for i := 1 to CNumRepeat do begin
      TInterlocked.Exchange(FPValue^, $7777777700000000);
      TInterlocked.Exchange(FPValue^, $0000000077777777);
    end;
  end;
```

If you run the code, you'll see that it is indeed faster than the locking approach. On the test computer it executes about 20% faster, as you can verify in the following screenshot:

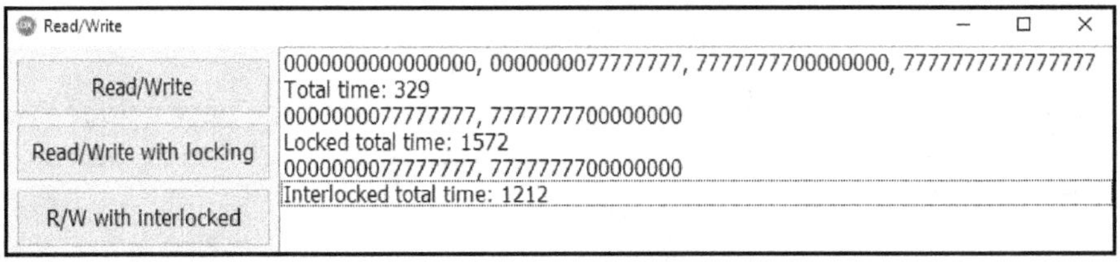

Similar to locking, interlocking is not a magic bullet. You have to use it correctly and you have to use it in all the relevant places. If you modify shared data with interlocked instructions but read that same data with a normal read, the code will not work correctly.

You can verify that by changing the `value := TInterlocked.Read(FPValue^);` line in the `InterlockedReader` method to `value := FPValue^;`. If you rerun the test, it will give the same (wrong) results as the original, fully unsafe version.

Object life cycle

Special care should be given to the way objects are created and destroyed in a multithreaded environment. Not every approach is safe, and it is quite simple to make a mistake that would cause occasional crashes.

The simplest way is to lock all access to an object. If you create it from a critical section, use it from a critical section and destroy it in a critical section, everything will work. This way, however, is very slow and error-prone, as it is quite simple to forget to lock something.

If you create the object before the background tasks are created, and destroy it after the background tasks are destroyed, everything would work, too. If this is a normal object on a non-ARC platform, you are just sharing a pointer and that is never a problem. If you are sharing an interface-implementing object or if you are compiling for an ARC platform, the reference counting mechanism kicks into action. As the reference counting is threadsafe, that is again not a problem. Of course, all methods of that object that are called from the parallel code must work correctly if they are called from two or more threads at the same time.

Problems appear if you would like to create or destroy the shared object when the parallel tasks using that object are already running. Creation is possible—with some care. Destruction, you should stay away from.

Let's discuss the latter first. If you have a normal object in non-ARC environment, then it is obvious that you cannot destroy it in one thread while another thread is using it. With interfaces or ARC that is not very obvious. You may think that it is safe to assign nil to a shared interface in one thread (`FShared := nil;`) while another thread copies it into a different interface and uses that copy (`tmp := FShared; tmp.DoSomething;`). Trust me, that will not work. One thread will try to clear the object by calling `_IntfClear` while another will try to copy the object by calling `_IntfCopy`. Depending on luck, this will either work or the second thread will own invalid reference to a destroyed object and will crash when trying to use it.

Contrary to that, creating an object from a thread is indeed possible. (As you dig deeper and deeper into parallel code, you'll start to notice that the biggest problem in the parallel world is not how to set up parallel computation, but how to clean it up when the task is done.) Let's assume that we have a shared object of type `TSharedObject`, which for some reason cannot be initialized before the worker threads are started. At some time, a thread will need this object and will try to create it. But, hey, we're living in a parallel world, so it's entirely possible that some other thread will try to do that at the same time too!

One way to approach the problem is with locking. We have to establish a shared lock that will be used just for the purpose of initializing an object and use it to synchronize access to the object creation. The following code fragment shows an idea of how that could be implemented:

```
//In main thread
FInitializationLock := TCriticalSection.Create;

//In a thread
FInitializationLock.Acquire;
if not assigned(FSharedObject) then
  FSharedObject := TSharedObject.Create;
```

```
FInitializationLock.Release;
```

The important part of this approach is that we need to test whether the shared object is assigned from within the acquired critical section (or a spinlock or `TMonitor`). If we do the test before acquiring the critical section, the code would sometimes fail. It would be entirely possible for two threads to test whether the object is assigned, then both acquire the critical section (one after another, of course) and both store a newly created `TSharedObject` into the shared variable. After that, one instance of the shared object would be lost forever.

Instead of locking, we can use interlocked operation to create an object. The following example code shows how:

```
procedure CreateSharedObject;
var
  value: TSharedObject;
begin
  if not assigned(FSharedObject) then
  begin
    value := TSharedObject.Create;
    if TInterlocked.CompareExchange(pointer(FSharedObject), pointer(value),
nil) <> nil then
      value.Free;
  end;
end;
```

The code firstly checks whether the `FSharedObject` is already created. If not, it will create a new instance of `TSharedObject` and store it in a temporary value. After that, it will use `CompareExchange` to store the temporary value in the shared variable, but only if `FSharedObject` still contains `nil`.

`CompareExchange` can return a value that is not `nil`. That will happen if another thread has tested whether `FSharedObject` is assigned at the same time as the first thread. It also created a new `TSharedObject` but managed to execute `CompareExchange` just before the first thread. If that happens, the code keeps the value in `FSharedObject` and throws the `TSharedObject` stored in a temporary variable away.

This approach is also called *optimistic* initialization, because the thread optimistically creates an object and expects that it will be able to store it in the shared value. As in most cases a conflict between threads rarely occurs; this is, in general, a fast and useful way to create shared objects. It also doesn't require a separate synchronization primitive, which may in some occasions be a big advantage.

Communication

Seeing all that, you may now agree with me when I say that data sharing is hard. It is hard to do it safely as there are so many opportunities to make a mistake in the code. It is also hard to do it fast, because locking approaches don't *scale* well. In other words, locking will prevent the code from working two times faster when you run the code on twice the CPU cores.

Luckily, there's a better way. Better, but way harder. Instead of sharing, we can do what I've been advocating since the beginning of this book, and change the algorithm. And to do that, we'll need some *communication* techniques. In my parallel projects, I always prefer communication to synchronization, and I strongly suggest that you try to do the same.

You may find it strange that I've dedicated that much space to data sharing and synchronization techniques if I don't recommend using them. Well, sometimes you just have to bite the bullet and share data because nothing else makes sense. In such cases, you also have to intimately know everything that can go wrong and ways to fix it.

The best way to remove data sharing from the equation is to replace it with *data duplication* and *aggregation*. Before creating the threads, we make a copy of the original data, one for each thread. A thread can then do its work in peace as it is not sharing data with anybody. At the end, the thread sends its result back to the main thread (here the *communication* comes in to play) so that the main thread can then combine (aggregate) partial results together.

Sending data from one thread to another is simpler if you don't have to care about the object ownership. It is best to always use just simple data types (such as integers) and managed data types (strings and interfaces). As this data is never simultaneously used in two threads, the rules from the section *Object life cycle* don't apply. We can create and destroy such objects in completely normal ways.

Sending data from main thread to the worker thread and sending data in the opposite direction are two completely different problems, and we have to approach them in a different way. The way we choose to send data always depends on the implementation of the receiving thread. Before we learn how to send data to worker threads, we have to learn how to create and manage them. I'll therefore cover this in the latter chapters.

Sending data from worker threads to the main thread depends only on the implementation of the main thread, and that is something we are familiar with. In the rest of the chapter, we'll look into four techniques for communicating with the main thread—sending Windows messages, `Synchronize`, `Queue`, and polling.

To demonstrate the technique, I have re-implemented the code from the `IncDemo` in new program, `IncDecComm`. All background tasks in that program are started in the same way. A click on a button calls the `RunInParallel` method and passes, as parameters, names of two methods, one to increment and one to decrement the initial value.

`RunInParallel` creates a new background task for each worker method and passes to it the initial value, 0. In this program, passing the same value to both worker methods represents the most basic implementation of *data copying:*

```
procedure TfrmIncDecComm.RunInParallel(task1, task2: TProc<integer>);
begin
  FNumDone := 0;
  FTasks[0] := TTask.Run(procedure begin task1(0); end);
  FTasks[1] := TTask.Run(procedure begin task2(0); end);
end;
```

Result *aggregation* depends on the communication method and will be evaluated separately for each approach.

Windows messages

The first method works by sending Windows messages to the main thread. As the name suggests, it is limited to the Windows operating system. I'll show two ways to achieve the same result. The first works only in VCL applications, while the second also works with FireMonkey.

Before the tasks are started, the code initializes the result `FValue` to zero so that partial results can be aggregated correctly. It also sets the variable `FNumDone` to zero. This variable counts the tasks that have completed their work:

```
procedure TfrmIncDecComm.btnMessageClick(Sender: TObject);
begin
  FValue := 0;
  FNumDone := 0;
  RunInParallel(IncMessage, DecMessage);
end;
```

Both tasks are implemented in the same way, so I'll only show one method here. `IncMessage` increments the starting value `CNumRepeat` times. At the end, it posts a `MSG_TASK_DONE` message back to the main form and passes the resulting `value` as a parameter. `DecMessage` looks the same except that the value is decremented inside the `for` loop:

```
procedure TfrmIncDecComm.IncMessage(startValue: integer);
var
  i: integer;
  value: integer;
begin
  value := startValue;
  for i := 1 to CNumRepeat do
    value := value + 1;
  PostMessage(Handle, MSG_TASK_DONE, value, 0);
end;
```

Message parameters `wParam` and `lParam` can be used to pass data alongside the message. They have the same size as a pointer, which allows us to use an object or an interface as data storage. I'll show an example of such code near the end of this section.

To process this message in the main form, we have to declare the `MSG_TASK_DONE` variable (`WM_USER` indicates the start of the message range reserved for custom use) and add a message-handling method `MsgTaskDone` to the form:

```
const
  MSG_TASK_DONE = WM_USER;

procedure MsgTaskDone(var msg: TMessage); message MSG_TASK_DONE;
```

This method is called every time the main form receives the message, `MSG_TASK_DONE`. Inside, we firstly increment the `FValue` value by the partial result, passed in the `msg.WParam` field (*aggregation* step). After that, we increment the `FNumDone` counter. We know that we will receive exactly two messages, so we can call the cleanup method, `Done`, when `FNumDone` is equal to `2`:

```
procedure TfrmIncDecComm.MsgTaskDone(var msg: TMessage);
begin
  Inc(FValue, msg.WParam);
  Inc(FNumDone);
  if FNumDone = 2 then
    Done('Windows message');
end;
```

In the `Done` method, we only have to clean the worker task interfaces:

```
procedure TfrmIncDecComm.Done(const name: string);
begin
  FTasks[0] := nil;
  FTasks[1] := nil;
end;
```

This seems like a lot of work, but it is worth it. I'll show the actual results after I finish discussing all four methods, but I can already tell you that this approach is finally faster than the single-threaded code.

This method of declaring a message handler is specific to VCL. On FireMonkey, you have to invest a bit more work and create a hidden window which will receive and process messages.

When you click on a **Message + AllocateHwnd** button, the following code executes. It initializes `FValue` and `FNumDone`, as in the previous example, and then creates a hidden window by calling `AllocateHwnd`:

```
procedure TfrmIncDecComm.btnAllocateHwndClick(Sender: TObject);
begin
  FValue := 0;
  FNumDone := 0;
  FMsgWnd := AllocateHwnd(MsgWndProc);
  Assert(FMsgWnd <> 0);
  RunInParallel(IncMsgHwnd, DecMsgHwnd);
end;
```

The task method, `IncMsgHwnd`, looks the same as `IncMethod`, except the last line which must now post the message to the handle `FMsgWnd`:

```
PostMessage(FMsgWnd, MSG_TASK_DONE, value, 0);
```

The `MsgWndProc` method processes all messages sent to this hidden window. We are only interested in `MSG_TASK_DONE`. Any other messages are passed to the Windows function, `DefWindowProc`. The code that handles `MSG_TASK_DONE` is identical to code in the `MsgTaskDone` method:

```
procedure TfrmIncDecComm.MsgWndProc(var msg: TMessage);
begin
  if Msg.Msg = MSG_TASK_DONE then
  begin
    Inc(FValue, msg.WParam);
    Inc(FNumDone);
    if FNumDone = 2 then
      Done('Windows message');
  end
  else
    DefWindowProc(FMsgWnd, msg.Msg, msg.wParam, msg.lParam);
end;
```

To clean up this hidden window, we have to call the `DeallocateHwnd` method:

```
if FMsgWnd <> 0 then
begin
  DeallocateHwnd(FMsgWnd);
  FMsgWnd := 0;
end;
```

I promised before to show how you can send an object or an interface as message parameters, so here's a short example. To send an object, we simply have to cast it to the appropriate type. In Delphi 10.2 Tokyo that is `NativeUInt` for `wParam` and `NativeInt` for `lParam`.

If we did the same with an interface, it would be destroyed on exit from `btnObjIntClick`. To prevent that, we have to increase its reference count by calling `_AddRef`:

```
procedure TfrmIncDecComm.btnObjIntClick(Sender: TObject);
var
  tobj: TObject;
  iint: IInterface;
begin
  tobj := TObject.Create;
  iint := TInterfacedObject.Create;
  iint._AddRef;
  PostMessage(Handle, MSG_OBJ_INT, NativeUInt(tobj), NativeInt(iint));
end;
```

On the receiving side, we can simply cast the object back to the appropriate object type (`TObject` in this example). We also have to remember to destroy it when we're done with it.

An interface can also be cast to the appropriate interface type (`IInterface` in this example) but then we also have to remove the reference added in `btnObjIntClick` by calling `_Release`. We can then use this interface as we need, and it will be destroyed once it is no longer in use and its reference count drops to zero. The following code demonstrates this:

```
procedure TfrmIncDecComm.MsgObjInt(var msg: TMessage);
var
  tobj: TObject;
  iint: IInterface;
begin
  tobj := TObject(msg.WParam);
  tobj.Free;
  iint := IInterface(msg.LParam);
  iint._Release;
end;
```

Synchronize and Queue

The second and third approaches are so similar that I've condensed them into one section.

The setup for this approach is the same as with the first shown in the Windows message method—we only have to initialize `FValue` and `FNumTasks`. The code in increment and decrement tasks also starts the same, with a `for` loop that increments or decrements the value but then uses a different approach to pass the value back to the main thread.

The following code uses `TThread.Synchronize` to execute an anonymous method in the target thread. `Synchronize` accepts a `TThread` object as a first parameter and an anonymous method in the second. It will execute the second parameter in the main thread. In the first parameter, we can pass either the current `TThread` object or, as the following code does, a `nil` value. In the next chapter, I will discuss this parameter in more detail.

```
procedure TfrmIncDecComm.IncSynchronize(startValue: integer);
var
  i: integer;
  value: integer;
begin
  value := startValue;
  for i := 1 to CNumRepeat do
    value := value + 1;

  TThread.Synchronize(nil,
    procedure
    begin
      PartialResult(value);
    end);
end;
```

`Synchronize` **pauses** the execution in the worker thread, then somehow (the implementation depends on the graphical library in use) passes the second parameter to the main thread, waits for the main thread to execute that code, and only then resumes the worker thread. Let me explain this again as it is important. While the `TThread.Synchronize` call executes in the **worker** thread, the anonymous method passed as the second parameter—and by extension the `PartialResult` method—executes in the **main** thread.

The fast that `Synchronize` pauses the execution of a worker thread is not important in our case, as the worker had already finished the job. However, sometimes this slows down the background task. A typical example would be sending notifications about the progress to the main thread. Each time `Synchronize` is called, the worker thread pauses for some time, which makes the CPUs underutilized.

In such cases, it is better to use `TThread.Queue` instead of `Synchronize`. This method accepts the same parameters as `Synchronize` and works almost completely the same, with one exception. It does not wait for the main thread to execute the anonymous method. Instead of that, it returns immediately, which allows the background task to continue processing data.

Result processing in the `PartialResult` method is completely the same as in `MsgTaskDone`. I'm just using different methods in different approaches so that each implementation is separated from the others. It also allows me to log appropriate method names in the log:

```
procedure TfrmIncDecComm.PartialResult(value: integer);
begin
  Inc(FValue, value);
  Inc(FNumDone);
  if FNumDone = 2 then
    Done('Synchronize');
end;
```

Polling

Instead of reacting to notifications from the thread, we can also periodically check the status of background calculation from the main thread. In other words, we *poll* their status.

If we want to send some data from a background worker, we can simply insert it into a `TLockedList<T>` or, for a faster operation, into `TThreadedQueue<T>`. In the main thread, we must then periodically check if something has appeared in this queue and process the data.

As the `TThreadedQueue<T>` has quite an unwieldy user interface which doesn't allow us to check whether the queue is empty, we have to take care while creating it. The following code initializes the queue with two parameters (queue size—we know that we'll only put two values in the queue), *0* (push timeout), and *0* (pop timeout). The last parameter is the most important because it allows our polling code to work correctly. I'll return to that shortly.

The polling is done from a `TimerCheckQueue` timer, which is set to trigger every *10* milliseconds but is disabled when the program starts. The following code also starts this timer:

```
procedure TfrmIncDecComm.btnThQueueAndTImerClick(Sender: TObject);
begin
  FValue := 0;
  FNumDone := 0;
  FResultQueue := TThreadedQueue<integer>.Create(2, 0, 0);
  RunInParallel(IncThQueue, DecThQueue);
  TimerCheckQueue.Enabled := true;
end;
```

The worker task starts with a now standard `for` loop. After that, it stores the partial result in the queue by calling `PushItem`:

```
procedure TfrmIncDecComm.IncThQueue(startValue: integer);
var
  i: integer;
  value: integer;
begin
  value := startValue;
  for i := 1 to CNumRepeat do
    value := value + 1;
  Assert(FResultQueue.PushItem(value) = wrSignaled);
end;
```

If the queue is full, `PushItem` waits for some user-configurable timeout before it returns. If a free space appears in the queue in that time, the item is pushed to the queue and the call returns `wrSignaled`. If, after the timeout, the queue is still full, the call returns `wrTimeout`. It would be great if we could specify the timeout as a parameter to `PushItem` but, sadly, this is not implemented. We have to pass it to the constructor and it defaults to infinite waiting (constant `INFINITE`).

The timer method triggers every *10* milliseconds and tries to fetch a value from the queue. If the queue is empty, `PopItem` waits up to a configurable timeout before it returns `wrTimeout`. If there's data in the queue, the method returns `wrSignaled`. As with the `PushItem`, we can only configure the timeout in the constructor. The default value for timeout is again `INFINITE`.

When the timer manages to retrieve partial data from the queue, it aggregates it to the result, increments the number of tasks, and terminates the operation when both tasks are completed. After that it breaks out of the `while` loop because the `Done` method destroys the queue, so we can't read from it anymore:

```
procedure TfrmIncDecComm.TimerCheckQueueTimer(Sender: TObject);
var
  qsize: integer;
  value: integer;
begin
  while FResultQueue.PopItem(qsize, value) = wrSignaled do begin
    FValue := FValue + value;
    Inc(FNumDone);
    if FNumDone = 2 then begin
      Done('TThreadedQueue + TTimer');
      break; //while
    end;
  end;
end;
```

In the `Done` method, we have to stop the timer and destroy the thread in addition to stopping the worker tasks:

```
TimerCheckQueue.Enabled := false;
FreeAndNil(FResultQueue);
```

The `TThreadedQueue<T>` is also useful in combination with the *push* notifications. We can, for example, store some complex data type in a queue and then send a simple Windows message to notify the main thread that it should read from the queue.

Performance

Let's complete this section by examining the execution times of different communication approaches. Even more importantly, let's compare them with the original single-threaded implementation and with locking methods.

The original single-threaded code needed *75* ms to increment and decrement values. Critical section based synchronization needed *1017* ms, `TMonitor` implementation took *700* ms, spinlock needed *493* ms, and the fastest parallel implementation so far, `TInterlocked`, used 407 ms.

In comparison, communication-based approaches are blindingly fast. Both message-based mechanisms needed only *23-24* milliseconds, `Synchronize` and `Queue` are even faster with *17* milliseconds, and even the slowest timer- based code needed *36* milliseconds at worst:

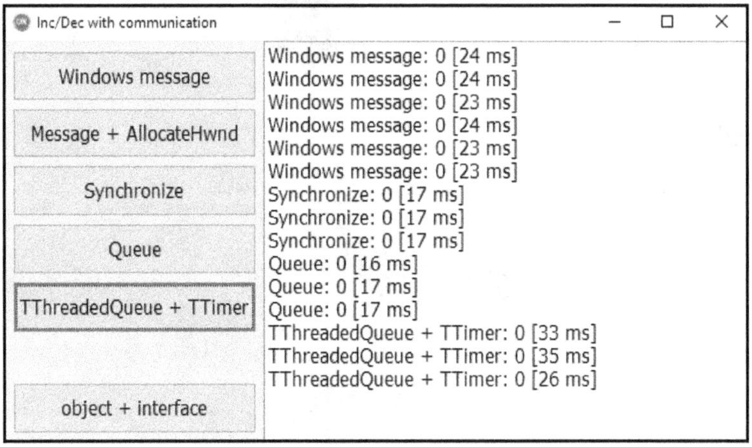

It is obvious why the timer-based code is the slowest in the pack. After the last value is calculated, we may have to wait up to *10* ms for the timer to trigger.

What is interesting is that other approaches are more than twice as fast as the single-threaded code. The main reason for that is the incrementation and decrementation of a value, which is in the new code done in one line (`value := value + 1`), while in the old code it needed two assignments:

```
value := FValue;
 FValue := value + 1;
```

If we correct the original code, then it needs around *34* ms to do the job. In other words, the `Synchronize` and `Queue`-based approaches are exactly twice as fast as the original code, which is the best possible result we can get from running parallel code on two cores.

Third-party libraries

While this book focuses almost exclusively on the out-of-the-box Delphi experience, sometimes I do point to external libraries that can simplify your programming experience. In the context of this chapter, such libraries are Spring4D (`www.spring4d.org`) and OmniThreadLibrary (`www.omnithreadlibrary.com`).

Spring4D is a multipurpose library with very limited support for parallel programming. It is, however, widely used in the Delphi community. If you are already using it, you may find the following notes helpful.

I've said before that creating and destroying `TCriticalSection` objects is a pain. To fix that, Spring4D introduces a `Lock` record which doesn't require initialization. You just declare a variable of that type and then use its `Enter` and `Leave` methods.

Another useful Spring4D addition is the optimistic initializer, `TLazyInitializer`. In the section *Object life cycle*, I've shown how to safely initialize the `FSharedObject: TSharedObject` variable and it was not very simple. With `TLazyInitializer` we can do it in one line:

```
TLazyInitializer.EnsureInitialized<TSharedObject>(FSharedObject);
```

As opposed to Spring4D, **OmniThreadLibrary** has everything to do with parallel programming. Similar to Spring4D, it contains an easy-to-use critical section, `TOmniCS`, with the `Acquire` and `Release` methods. It also implements an optimistic initializer, `Atomic<T>`, which can be used as in the next example:

```
Atomic<TSharedObject>.Initialize(FSharedObject);
```

OmniThreadLibrary also implements very fast multiple readers, and an exclusive writer synchronization mechanism called `TOmniMREW`. It should only be used to lock very short parts of code because access methods never sleep when access is locked. They always use the spinning mechanism, which can use lots of CPU time when waiting for a longer time. This mechanism is also not re-entrant and should be used with care.

At the end, I would like to mention OmniThreadLibrary lock-free data structures. There's a fixed-size stack, `TOmniBoundedStack`, fixed-size queue, `TOmniBoundedQueue`, and a very fast dynamically-allocated queue, `TOmniBaseQueue`. All of them can easily be used with standard Delphi multithreading code.

Summary

In this chapter, we finally started learning to write parallel code. I started with a short introduction about processes and threads, single and multithreading, single-tasking, and multitasking. I also explained the most important differences between processes and threads.

After that, we started learning what **not** to do when writing multithreaded code. Firstly, I brought up the most important dogma—"Never access the user interface from a background thread". Such strong words deserve proof and I gave you one.

In the next, largest part of the chapter, I slowly explained why you should be extremely careful if you want to access shared data from multiple threads. While simultaneous reading is OK, you should always use protection when reading and writing at the same time.

In the context of parallel programming and data sharing, this protection is implemented by the introduction of one of the synchronization mechanisms. I spent quite some time introducing critical sections, mutexes, semaphors, TMonitor, spinlocks, and the terribly named TMultiReadExclusiveWriteSynchronizer. Using synchronization inevitably brings in new problems, and so I also spent some time discussing deadlocks. I also mentioned three data structures that implement locking internally—TThreadList, TThreadList<T>, and TThreadedQueue<T>.

After that I introduced a less powerful but faster way of locking—interlocked operations. We examined the TInterlocked class and all the interlocked operations it implements. As interlocked operations are frequently used in optimistic initialization, we also dealt with the object life cycle in the parallel world.

Towards the end, I introduced a much faster replacement for synchronization—communication. We saw how a parallel program can use data duplication and aggregation to achieve the highest possible speed. I went over four communication techniques, namely Windows messages, Synchronize, Queue, and polling. We also saw how TThreadedQueue<T> can be used in practice.

To wrap things up, I introduced two libraries that contain helpful parallel programming helpers—Spring4D and OmniThreadLibrary.

In the next chapter, we'll finally start writing parallel code. I'll talk about threads, tasks, and writing parallel code with TThread and with the Parallel Programming Library, which has been part of Delphi since release XE7.

6
Working with Parallel Tools

After using one whole chapter to warn you about the traps of parallel programming, it is now finally time to write some code! Although I always prefer using modern multithreading approaches—and we'll spend all of the next chapter learning them—it is also good to know the basics. Because of that, I have dedicated this chapter to the good old `TThread` class.

In this chapter, we will cover the following topics:

- How can you use `TThread` to write multithreading code?
- What different approaches to thread management does `TThread` support?
- How can exceptions in threads be handled?
- Which additional functions does `TThread` implement?
- How can we implement a communication channel sending messages to a thread?
- How can we centralize thread-message handling in the owner form?
- How can we simplify thread writing to the max by implementing a specific framework for one usage pattern?

TThread

Multithreading support has been built into Delphi since its inception.

The very first 32-bit version, Delphi 2, introduced a `TThread` class. At that time, `TThread` was a very simple wrapper around the Windows `CreateThread` function. In later Delphi releases, `TThread` was extended with multiple functions and with support for other operating systems, but it still remained a pretty basic tool.

The biggest problem with `TThread` is that it doesn't enforce the use of any programming patterns. Because of that, you can use it to create parallel programs that are hard to understand, hard to debug, and which work purely by luck. I should know—I shudder every time I have to maintain my old `TThread`-based code.

Still, the `TThread` approach can be very effective and completely readable, provided that you use it correctly. On the next pages, I'll firstly show the basic `TThread` usage patterns and then improve the basic approach by introducing the *communication* techniques into the old framework.

A `TThread` class is declared in the `System.Classes` unit. You cannot use it directly, as it contains an abstract method, `Execute`, which you have to override in a derived class:

```
TMyThread = class(TThread)
protected
  procedure Execute; override;
end;
```

When you create an instance of this class, Delphi uses operating system functions to create a new thread and then runs the `Execute` method in that thread. When that method exits, the thread is terminated.

The **TThread** and **Stop** button in the `Threads` demo one way of using `TThread` to create a thread. The former creates the thread descendant and starts the thread. It also sets up an event handler, which gets triggered when the thread is terminated:

```
procedure TfrmThreads.btnThreadClick(Sender: TObject);
begin
  FThread := TMyThread.Create;
  FThread.OnTerminate := ReportThreadTerminated;
end;
```

By default, `TThread.Create` creates and **starts** the thread. It is also possible to create a thread in a **suspended** (paused) state by providing `True` as an argument to the constructor. In that case, you have to call `TThread.Start` at some time, to actually start the thread.

The following code fragment is functionally equivalent to the previous code, except that it initially creates a thread in a suspended state. This approach is safer if we are doing additional initialization on the thread object, (`FThread`), as it makes sure that the thread did not start up before it was fully initialized:

```
procedure TfrmThreads.btnThreadClick(Sender: TObject);
begin
  FThread := TMyThread.Create(True);
  FThread.OnTerminate := ReportThreadTerminated;
```

```
  FThread.Start;
end;
```

In our case, the thread will only stop when we tell it to. It is therefore safe to assign the `OnTerminate` handler to a running (not suspended) thread, as we did in the initial version.

> **TIP:** Although the `TThread` object implements the methods `Suspend` and `Resume`, which pause and start the thread, you should never use them in your code! Unless they are used with great care, you cannot know exactly in what state the thread is when you suspend it. Using these two functions will only bring you great pain and weird, hard-to-repeat problems.

The traditional way to stop a thread is to firstly call a `Terminate` method, which sets a `Terminated` flag. The `Execute` method should check this flag periodically and exit when it is set. (I'll show you an example of that in a moment). Next, we should call the `WaitFor` method, which waits on a thread to finish execution. After that, we can destroy the thread object. The following code is executed when you click the **Stop** button:

```
procedure TfrmThreads.btnStopThreadClick(Sender: TObject);
begin
  FThread.Terminate;
  FThread.WaitFor;
  FreeAndNil(FThread);
end;
```

A simpler way is to just destroy the thread object, as it will internally call `Terminate` and `WaitFor` itself. Sometimes, though, it is good to know that we can do this in three separate steps:

```
procedure TfrmThreads.btnStopThreadClick(Sender: TObject);
begin
  FreeAndNil(FThread);
end;
```

Let's now move away from the thread management to actual code running in the thread. It is implemented in the `TMyThread.Execute` method. In the `Threads` demo, this code just checks the `Terminated` flag to see whether it should terminate, posts a message to the main window, and sleeps for a second. As we learned in the previous chapter, we could also use the `Synchronize` or `Queue` methods to do the same:

```
procedure TMyThread.Execute;
begin
  while not Terminated do
  begin
```

```
      PostMessage(frmThreads.Handle, WM_PING, ThreadID, 0);
      Sleep(1000);
    end;
  end;
```

Every thread in a system has a unique integer ID, which we can access through the `ThreadID` property.

Terminating a thread is always a cooperative process. The main program sets a flag that tells the thread to terminate, and the thread must cooperate by checking this flag as frequently as possible. Later in this chapter, we'll also see how to do thread termination without constant checking (without *polling*).

The form implements a simple `MsgPing` method, which handles the `WM_PING` message handler. Inside the method, the code logs the thread ID passed in the `wParam` message parameter:

```
procedure TfrmThreads.MsgPing(var msg: TMessage);
begin
  ListBox1.Items.Add('Ping from thread ' + msg.WParam.ToString);
end;
```

When we terminate the thread, the `OnTerminated` event handler is called. The thread object being destroyed is passed in the `Sender` parameter. The code just logs the thread ID of the thread being destroyed:

```
procedure TfrmThreads.ReportThreadTerminated(Sender: TObject);
begin
  Assert(Sender is TThread);
  ListBox1.Items.Add('Terminating thread ' +
    TThread(Sender).ThreadID.ToString);
end;
```

This concludes the first example. As you can see, managing a thread is not that hard. The problems appear when we want to do some useful work in the `Execute` method and especially when we want to communicate with the thread. Before I deal with that, however, I'd like to show you some simplifications that `TThread` supports.

The thread management that I've shown is most appropriate when we have a long-running thread providing some service. The main program starts the thread when it needs that service and stops it when the service is no longer needed. Lots of times, though, the background thread runs some operations and then stops. At times, it is simpler to allow the thread to terminate itself.

We can do that by making one simple change—by setting the `FreeOnTerminate` property to `True`. The demo program does that when you click on the **Free on terminate** button. Although not strictly required in this case, the code creates the thread in a suspended state so it can be safely initialized:

```
procedure TfrmThreads.btnFreeOnTermClick(Sender: TObject);
begin
  FThreadFoT := TFreeThread.Create(True);
  FThreadFoT.FreeOnTerminate := true;
  FThreadFoT.OnTerminate := ReportThreadTerminated;
  FThreadFoT.Start;
end;
```

The `TFreeThread` class—just as the `TMyThread`—overrides only the `Execute` method:

```
procedure TFreeThread.Execute;
var
  i: Integer;
begin
  for i := 1 to 5 do
  begin
    PostMessage(frmThreads.Handle, WM_PING, GetCurrentThreadID, 0);
    Sleep(1000);
    if Terminated then
      Exit;
  end;
end;
```

There's no need to destroy the `FThreadFoT` object, as Delphi will do that for us. We should, however, still clear the field when the thread is destroyed so that we don't keep a reference to the destroyed object in the code. The simplest way to do that is with the `OnTerminated` event handler:

```
procedure TfrmThreads.ReportThreadTerminated(Sender: TObject);
begin
  Assert(Sender is TThread);
  ListBox1.Items.Add('Terminating thread ' +
    TThread(Sender).ThreadID.ToString);
  FThreadFoT := nil;
end;
```

If you need to run a shorter operation, but you still want to be able to abort it, both approaches can be combined. The thread can check the `Terminated` flag even when it is run in `FreeOnTerminate` mode. The main program can then just call `Terminate` to terminate the thread, and the thread will terminate itself.

The demo program uses this approach to destroy both threads when the form is closed:

```
procedure TfrmThreads.FormDestroy(Sender: TObject);
begin
  FreeAndNil(FThread);
  if assigned(FThreadFoT) then
    FThreadFoT.Terminate;
end;
```

Sometimes, we don't care much about thread management because we know that the thread will only run for a short time. In such a cases, we can forego the creation of a derived class and simply call the `CreateAnonymousThread` method, which creates a slightly misnamed *anonymous thread*.

This method takes an anonymous method (`TProc`) as a parameter. Internally, it creates an instance of a `TAnonymousThread` class (found in `System.Classes`) and returns it as a function result. When the `Execute` method of that class runs, it executes your anonymous method.

An anonymous thread is always created in the suspended state and has the `FreeOnTerminate` flag set. In the simplest form, you can create and start such a thread and ignore any returned value:

```
TThread.CreateAnonymousThread(PingMe).Start;
```

The code in the demo assigns the result to a temporary `thread` variable, so that it can set the termination handler:

```
procedure TfrmThreads.btnAnonymousClick(Sender: TObject);
var
  thread: TThread;
begin
  thread := TThread.CreateAnonymousThread(PingMe);
  thread.OnTerminate := ReportThreadTerminated;
  thread.Start;
end;
```

The background code is now implemented as a normal method of the `TfrmThreads` form object. This makes such an approach inherently dangerous, as it blurs the boundaries between the user interface (accessible through the form methods) and the background thread, which has full access to the form object. When you work with anonymous threads, you should always be careful and respect the separation between objects used in the main and background threads. (And never, *never!* access user interface from the background thread!)

As the `PingMe` method isn't implemented in a class derived from `TThread`, it cannot access the `ThreadID` property directly. It can, however, access the `TThread.Current` property, which returns the `TThread` instance of the current thread:

```
procedure TfrmThreads.PingMe;
var
  i: Integer;
begin
  for i := 1 to 5 do
  begin
    PostMessage(Handle, WM_PING, TThread.Current.ThreadID, 0);
    Sleep(1000);
  end;
end;
```

Advanced TThread

The `TThread` class offers the programmer a collection of various properties and methods. In this section, I'll take you through the most useful ones.

The `FatalException` property deals with exceptions. If an exception arises inside your `Execute` method and is not caught, it will be handled inside the system code:

```
if not Thread.Terminated then
try
  Thread.Execute;
except
  Thread.FFatalException := AcquireExceptionObject;
end;
```

The best place to check whether this property is assigned is the `OnTerminate` handler. If the `FatalException` is not `nil`, we can log the exception and call `ReleaseExceptionObject` to destroy the exception object or we can reraise the exception. The following code from the `Threads` demo shows how to implement such logging:

```
procedure TfrmThreads.ReportThreadTerminated(Sender: TObject);
var
  thread: TThread;
begin
  thread := Sender as TThread;
  if assigned(thread.FatalException) then
  begin
    ListBox1.Items.Add(Format('Thread raised exception: [%s] %s',
      [thread.FatalException.ClassName,
       Exception(thread.FatalException).Message]));
    ReleaseExceptionObject;
  end;
end;
```

The demo contains a `TExceptThread` class, which just raises an exception so we can test the exception-handling mechanism. To run a thread of this class, click on the **Exception in a thread** button:

```
procedure TExceptThread.Execute;
begin
  Sleep(1000);
  raise Exception.Create('Thread exception');
end;
```

A thread can return an integer value by setting its `ReturnValue` property. This property is, however, protected and hard to access from the main thread. Delphi offers better implementation of such functionality with a `Future<T>` pattern, which we'll explore in the next chapter.

Next come the communication methods `Synchronize`, `Queue` and `ForceQueue`. The first two I've mentioned already in the previous chapter, while the `ForceQueue` is a special version of `Queue`. If you call `Queue` from the main thread, the code detects that and executes your anonymous method immediately (without queuing). In contrast to that, `ForceQueue` always queues the anonymous method, even when called from the main thread.

All communication methods accept a `TThread` parameter, which in all the previous examples we passed simply as `nil`. This parameter, when set, connects the anonymous method with a thread. We can use that to remove all queued but unhandled events by calling the `TThread.RemoveQueueEvents` function. For example, we can call this method from a thread's `OnTerminate` handler to prevent any queued events for that thread from being executed, after the thread was destroyed.

At the end, I'd like to mention methods that are useful when you are tuning the multithreading performance. A class property, the `ProcessorCount`, will give you the total number of processing cores in the system. This includes all hyper-threading cores, so in a system with 4 cores where each of them is hyper-threaded, the `ProcessorCount` would be *8*.

> Running a system with multiple processing cores doesn't necessarily mean that all of them are available for your program. In Windows, it is possible to limit the number of cores that a program can see. To get a real number of available cores on Windows, call the `GetProcessAffinityMask` function declared in the `Winapi.Windows` unit.

The property, `Priority` can be used to read and set the thread's *priority*. A priority represents how important that thread is in the system. In Windows, this property can have the following values:

```
TThreadPriority = (tpIdle, tpLowest, tpLower, tpNormal, tpHigher,
tpHighest, tpTimeCritical);
```

`tpIdle` represents a very low-priority thread, which only runs when the system is idle. `tpTimeCritical`, on the other hand, represents a thread which must always be running, if at all possible. In reality, a high-priority thread cannot completely stop a low-priority thread from running, as Windows dynamically adjusts the thread priorities to allow all of them at least a small chance of executing.

I would strongly recommend that you never set the priority to `tpTimeCritical`. If you run multiple CPU intensive threads with this priority, this can really cripple your system.

Thread priority should always be left at the default value of `tpNormal`. Windows is extremely good at scheduling threads and tuning thread priorities. Only in very special situations should it be necessary to raise or lower a thread priority, but even then you should not go above `tpHighest`.

On non-Windows systems the `Priority` property has the type `integer`. A range of allowed values may differ from platform to platform but at least on POSIX compliant systems (OS X, Linux) you can assume that the allowed range is from *0* to *31* with *0* representing the lowest priority.

A thread that is running in a loop may want to give some slice of its CPU time to other threads, from time to time. One way to do it is to call `Sleep(0)`, which signals to the operating system that a thread has finished its job at the moment but that it would like to continue executing soon, please. The code can also call `TThread.Yield`, instead. This also pauses the thread and allows the execution of another thread that is ready to run on the *current processor*. Calling `Yield` instead of `Sleep` generally means that your thread will be woken again a bit sooner.

Setting up a communication channel

The biggest problem of `TThread` is that it only allows communication to flow from the background thread to the owner. As you've seen in the previous chapter, we can use different mechanisms for that—Windows messages, `Synchronize`, `Queue`, and polling. There is, however, no built-in way to send messages in a different direction, so you have to build such a mechanism yourself. This is not entirely trivial.

Another problem with built-in mechanisms is that they make for unreadable code. `Synchronize` and `Queue` are both inherently messy because they wrap a code that executes in one thread inside a code executing in a different thread. Messages and polling have a different problem. They decouple code through many different methods, which sometimes makes it hard to understand the system.

To fix all these problems (and undoubtedly introduce some new ones as, sadly, no code is perfect), I have built a better base class `TCommThread`. You can find it in unit `DHPThreads`, which is part of this book's code archive. The demonstration program for the new class is called `ThreadsComm`. You can use this unit without any limitations in your projects.

This thread contains two parts. Firstly, there is communication channel running from the owner to the thread. Secondly, there's a channel running in a different direction, from the thread to the owner. I'll explain them one by one.

The code needs some container mechanism that will store messages sent from the owner, but not yet processed by the thread. Although it is hard to use, I've decided to go with the `TThreadedQueue`, which doesn't need a separate synchronization mechanism. As I have no idea what kind of data you'll be storing in the queue, I've implemented the queue as `TThreadedQueue<T>`. This type from the `System.Rtti` unit can store any Delphi data structure inside, so it's very appropriate for such task.

It is true that the flexibility of `TValue` means that it is a bit slower then using a specific data type directly. On the other hand—as I always say—if your code depends on millions of messages to be processed each second, then the problem lies not in the implementation but in your architecture. For all normal usage patterns, `TValue` is more than fast enough.

The code also needs a way to tell the thread that something has happened when a message is sent. I've chosen to use a `TEvent`, as it allows the thread to completely sleep while nothing is going on. This removes the need for constant *polling*, which would use a bit of CPU time.

The following code fragment shows how the two are declared in the `TCommThread` object. The `Event` field is declared `protected`, as it was designed to be used directly from the derived class:

```
strict private
  FQueueToThread : TThreadedQueue<TValue>;
protected
  Event: TEvent;
```

Both fields are initialized in the constructor, which, in addition to the standard `CreateSuspended` parameter, accepts a queue size. It is set to 1,024 elements by default, but you can make this value larger or smaller, if that's required. In the actual unit the constructor is a bit more complicated, as it also initializes the second communication channel. I've removed that part in the code shown here, to make it clearer:

```
constructor TCommThread.Create(CreateSuspended: boolean = False;
  ToThreadQueueSize: integer = 1024);
begin
  inherited Create(CreateSuspended);
  FQueueToThread := TThreadedQueue<TValue>.Create(ToThreadQueueSize, 0, 0);
  Event := TEvent.Create;
end;
```

> **TIP**
> The constructor creates both fields *after* the inherited constructor was called, even when `CreateSuspended` is `False`. This doesn't cause problems because the thread is actually not started in the `TThread` constructor. It is only started in the `TThread.AfterConstruction` method, which is executed *after* `TCommThread.Create` finishes its job.

To send a message to the thread, the code has to call the `SendToThread` public function. This very simple method pushes an item into the queue and sets the event, if the push was successful. If the queue is full, the function returns `False`:

```
function TCommThread.SendToThread(const value: TValue): boolean;
begin
  Result := (FQueueToThread.PushItem(value) = wrSignaled);
  if Result then
    Event.SetEvent;
end;
```

To process these messages, the code in the `Execute` method must be written in a specific manner. It must periodically check the `Event`, or it can even spend all of the time waiting on the `Event` to get set. The `TMyThread` from the `ThreadCommMain` unit of the example program can serve as a good starting point for your code.

This method calls `Event.WaitFor(5000)` to wait for a new message. `WaitFor` will either return `wrSignaled`, if a message has been received; `wrTimeout`, if nothing happened in five seconds; and something else, if something unexpected happened. In the latter case, the code exits the thread, as there's nothing better that can be done at the moment.

If `wrSignaled` or `wrTimeout` is received, the code enters the loop. Firstly, it resets the event by calling `Event.ResetEvent`. This is mandatory and allows for proper functioning of the code. Without that call, the event would stay *signalled* (set), and the next time around, `WaitFor` would immediately return `wrSignaled`, even though no new messages would be received.

After that, the code calls `GetMessage` to fetch messages from the queue. You should always empty the entire queue, otherwise there's a possibility that messages could get stuck inside for an unknown time (until next message is sent). The code also exits when the `Terminated` flag is set.

At the end, the code sends a message back to the owner. This part is omitted in the code shown here, as I haven't discussed that part of the mechanism yet:

```
procedure TMyThread.Execute;
var
  pingMsg: integer;
  value: TValue;
begin
  while Event.WaitFor(5000) in [wrSignaled, wrTimeout] do
  begin
    Event.ResetEvent;
    // message processing
    while (not Terminated) and GetMessage(value) do
      pingMsg := value.AsInteger;
    // termination
    if Terminated then
      break;
    // send message to the owner ...
  end;
end;
```

A careful reader may have started thinking about the thread termination now. Doesn't this implementation mean that when we request the thread to terminate, we will have to wait for up to five seconds for the thread to do so? After all, `WaitFor` may just have been called, and we have to wait until it reports a timeout. Even worse—what if the thread is completely message-driven and does no other processing? In that case, we can wait with `Event.WaitFor(INFINITE)`, but wouldn't that prevent the thread from exiting?

Indeed, careful reader, these are all valid worries. Do not fear, though, as there's a simple solution already built into the `TCommThread`! Besides the message-handling code, it also overrides the `TerminatedSet` virtual method, which `TThread` calls when the `Terminated` flag is set. Inside this overridden method, the code signals the `Event` event, and this causes the `WaitFor` to immediately exit:

```
procedure TCommThread.TerminatedSet;
 begin
 Event.SetEvent;
 inherited;
 end;
```

The only missing part of this half of the puzzle is the `GetMessage` method. That one is again trivial and just reads from the queue:

```
function TCommThread.GetMessage(var value: TValue): boolean;
begin
  Result := (FQueueToThread.PopItem(value) = wrSignaled);
end;
```

Sending messages from a thread

The second part of the solution deals with sending messages back to the parent. As I've mentioned before, you already have several possibilities to do the same with built-in Delphi functions. They all work well in combination with the previously described method for sending messages to a thread. This second part is therefore purely optional, but I believe it is a good solution, because it centralizes the message-handling for each thread.

Again, the code starts by creating a `TThreadedQueue<TValue>` to store sent values. We cannot use an event to signal new messages, though. Delphi forms interact with the operating system and with the user by constantly processing messages, and we cannot block this message processing by waiting on an event, or the whole user interface will freeze. Instead of that, `TCommThread` uses `Queue` to call a method of your own choosing to process messages. You pass this method to the constructor as a parameter.

The following code fragment shows relevant types and fields, together with (now complete) constructor. Besides the user-provided `MessageReceiver` method that will process messages, you can also set the queue size:

```
public type
  TMessageReceiver = TProc<TValue>;
strict private
  FQueueToMain : TThreadedQueue<TValue>;
  FMessageReceiver: TMessageReceiver;

constructor TCommThread.Create(MessageReceiver: TMessageReceiver;
  CreateSuspended: boolean = False;
  ToThreadQueueSize: integer = 1024; ToMainQueueSize: integer = 1024);
begin
  inherited Create(CreateSuspended);
  FQueueToThread := TThreadedQueue<TValue>.Create(ToThreadQueueSize, 0, 0);
  Event := TEvent.Create;
  FMessageReceiver := MessageReceiver;
  if assigned(MessageReceiver) then
    FQueueToMain := TThreadedQueue<TValue>.Create(ToMainQueueSize, 0, 0);
end;
```

The message-receiver parameter is optional. If you set it to `nil`, the channel for sending messages back to the owner won't be created, and this part of the functionality will be disabled.

The code also overrides the standard `TThread` constructor to create a `TCommThread` with only one communication channel—the one towards the thread:

```
constructor TCommThread.Create(CreateSuspended: Boolean);
begin
  Create(nil, CreateSuspended);
end;
```

The code can use the protected method, `SendToMain`, to send messages back to the owner. It checks whether the necessary queue was created, posts a message to the queue, and, if that was successful, queues a `PushMessagesToReceiver` method. If the queue is full, this method returns `False`:

```
function TCommThread.SendToMain(const value: TValue): boolean;
begin
  if not assigned(FQueueToMain) then
    raise Exception.Create('MessageReceiver method was not set in
constructor!');
  Result := (FQueueToMain.PushItem(value) = wrSignaled);
  if Result then
    TThread.Queue(nil, PushMessagesToReceiver);
end;
```

The `PushMessagesToReceiver` method is implemented in the `TCommThread` object. It reads messages from the queue, and, for each message, calls the user-provided `FMessageReceiver` method:

```
procedure TCommThread.PushMessagesToReceiver;
var
  value: TValue;
begin
  // This method executes from the main thread!
  while FQueueToMain.PopItem(value) = wrSignaled do
    FMessageReceiver(value);
end;
```

The value of this approach is twofold. Firstly, all message processing for a thread is concentrated in one method. Secondly, you can pass different types of data through this channel—from basic types to objects, interfaces, and even records.

> **TIP:** A word of caution is necessary. Never destroy the thread object from inside the message receiver. Instead, use the `ForceQueue` method to queue a code to destroy the thread object. That will cause that code to execute *after* the message receiver does its job.

In the `ThreadCommMain` unit, all this comes together. The **Start thread** button creates a new thread and immediately sends a number 42 to it. It only sets the message receiver method (`ProcessThreadMessages`) and leaves other parameters at default:

```
procedure TfrmThreadComm.btnStartClick(Sender: TObject);
begin
  FThread := TMyThread.Create(ProcessThreadMessages);
  FThread.SendToThread(42);
end;
```

The **Change** button sends the current value of a spin edit to the thread via the communication mechanism:

```
procedure TfrmThreadComm.btnChangePingClick(Sender: TObject);
begin
  FThread.SendToThread(inpPing.Value);
end;
```

The **Stop thread** button just destroys the thread object:

```
procedure TfrmThreadComm.btnStopClick(Sender: TObject);
begin
  FreeAndNil(FThread);
end;
```

The `TMyThread` object overrides the `Execute` method. We've seen a part of that method before. The full implementation is shown here.

The code immediately sends a message of a `TPingMsg` type back to the owner. This message carries the current value of the local variable, `pingMsg`, and the current thread ID. The message is sent over the built-in communication mechanism.

Next, the code starts the `while` loop, which I have already described. The only new part here appears under the `// workload` comment, when the code again sends the current `pingMsg` and thread ID to the owner:

```
type
  TPingMsg = TPair<integer,cardinal>;

procedure TMyThread.Execute;
var
```

```
    pingMsg: integer;
    value: TValue;
  begin
    pingMsg := 0;
    if not SendToMain(TValue.From<TPingMsg>(
             TPingMsg.Create(pingMsg, ThreadID)))
    then
      raise Exception.Create('Queue full!');
    while Event.WaitFor(5000) in [wrSignaled, wrTimeout] do
    begin
      Event.ResetEvent;
      // message processing
      while (not Terminated) and GetMessage(value) do
        pingMsg := value.AsInteger;
      // termination
      if Terminated then
        break;
      // workload
      if not SendToMain(TValue.From<TPingMsg>(
               TPingMsg.Create(pingMsg, ThreadID)))
      then
        raise Exception.Create('Queue full!');
    end;
  end;
```

The behavior of this method can be described in a few words. It sends `pingMsg` back to the owner every five seconds. When it receives a message, it assumes that it contains an integer and stores that integer in the `pingMsg` variable. The code terminates when the `Terminated` flag is set.

The only part I haven't shown yet is the `ProcessThreadMessages` method, which simply shows the data stored inside the `TPingMsg`:

```
procedure TfrmThreadComm.ProcessThreadMessages(value: TValue);
var
  pingMsg: TPingMsg;
begin
  pingMsg := value.AsType<TPingMsg>;
  ListBox1.Items.Add(Format('%s: %d from thread %d',
    [FormatDateTime('hh:nn:ss.zzz', Now), pingMsg.Key, pingMsg.Value]));
end;
```

And there you have it—a thread with two communication channels!

Implementing a timer

If you play with the demo application, you'll soon find that it works fine, just not exactly as I described before. I stated that "(the code) sends `pingMsg` back to the owner every five seconds." As the following image shows, that isn't exactly so.

This image shows one short testing session. During the testing, I started the thread. That caused two messages to be logged. The initial value of *0* is sent from the thread immediately when the thread is started. After that, the main thread sent a new value *42* to the worker thread, and that resulted in an immediate *ping* response.

After that, I didn't click anything for 11 seconds, which generated two *ping* messages, each sent 5 seconds after the previous message. Next, I clicked **Change** twice, which resulted in two *ping* messages. After that, I changed the value to *8*, *9*, and *0*, and each time a *ping* was immediately received:

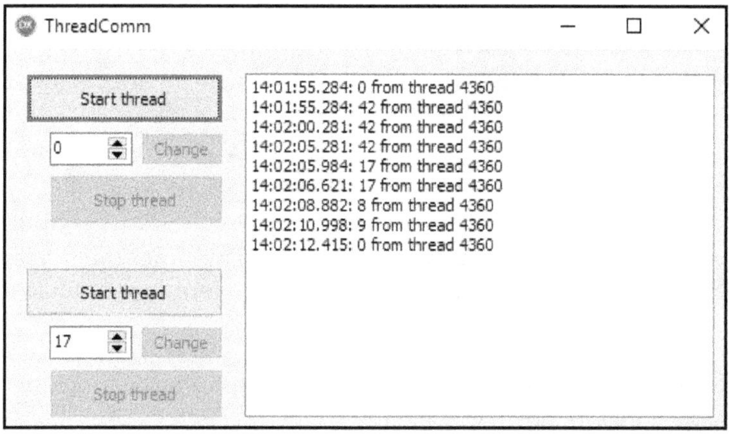

A proper description of the worker thread would therefore be this: It sends a message every 5 seconds, unless a new message is received, in which case it sends it back immediately.

If that's OK with you, fine! Feel free to use this framework. But sometimes you need a better timer. I could fix that in the `TMyThread` with a better calculation of the timeout parameter passed to the `WaitFor`. I would also have to fix the code, which now works the same, regardless of the `WaitFor` result (`wrSignaled` or `wrTimeout`). I could do that, but then you would have to repeat my steps each time you needed a thread with a built-in timer. Instead of that, I did something better and implemented a generic parent for all such tasks, a `TCommTimerThread`.

This time my implementation is closer to the approach used in all modern parallel libraries. It is not a multipurpose tool, such as `TThread` or `TCommThread`, but a specific solution that satisfies one *usage pattern*. Because of that, you don't have to implement any of the nasty multithreading plumbing to use it—such as when we had to implement a very specific `Execute` method in the previous example. Using a `TCommTimerThread` is more akin to using the VCL. You just plug in a few methods, and the framework does the rest. We'll see this approach a lot in the next chapter.

This approach has numerous advantages over the classical `TThread`. Firstly, it is easier to write the code, as all the hard stuff has already been taken care of. Secondly, the code will have less bugs, as you don't have to write error-prone multithreading plumbing. As many people are using the same framework, any potential bugs in the framework can be found quickly.

The usage pattern my implementation covers is "a background task that can send and receive messages and process timer-based events". While this looks simple, and even primitive, it can be used to solve many different kinds of problems, especially as you can ignore the message-processing part or the timer event part, if you don't need them.

Let us look at the implementation now. `TCommTimerThread` is derived from the `TCommThread` class so that it can reuse its communication mechanism. It exposes a public property `Interval`, which you can use to set the timer interval, in milliseconds. Setting `Interval` to a value equal to or smaller than zero disables the timer. In addition to that, the code uses a `FTimer: TStopwatch` record to determine the time to the next timer event.

Instead of overriding the `Execute` function, you override four methods (or just some of them). `Initialize` is called immediately after the thread is created, and `Cleanup` is called just before it is destroyed. You can do your own initialization and cleanup inside them. `ProcessTimer` is called each time a timer event occurs, and `ProcessMessage` is called for each received message. The code fragment here shows all the important parts of the `TCommTimerThread`:

```
TCommTimerThread = class(TCommThread)
strict private
  FInterval: integer;
  FTimer: TStopwatch;
protected
  procedure Cleanup; virtual;
  procedure Execute; override;
  procedure Initialize; virtual;
  procedure ProcessMessage(const msg: TValue); virtual;
  procedure ProcessTimer; virtual;
```

```
public
  property Interval: integer read GetInterval write SetInterval;
end;
```

All important parts of the functionality are implemented in the overridden `Execute` method. It is very similar to `TMyThread.Execute`, except that the `WaitFor` timeout is calculated dynamically and that processing depends on the value returned from the `WaitFor`. If it returns `wrSignaled`, the code checks the `Terminated` flag and fetches waiting messages. If it returns `wrTimeout`, the timer is restarted, and the timer-handling function is called:

```
procedure TCommTimerThread.Execute;
var
  awaited: TWaitResult;
  timeout: Cardinal;
  value: TValue;
begin
  Initialize;
  try
    repeat
      awaited := Event.WaitFor(CalculateTimeout);
      event.ResetEvent;
      case awaited of
        wrSignaled:
          begin
            while (not Terminated) and GetMessage(value) do
              ProcessMessage(value);
            if Terminated then
              break;
          end;
        wrTimeout:
          begin
            FTimer.Reset;
            FTimer.Start;
            ProcessTimer;
          end
        else
          break; //Terminate thread
      end;
    until false;
  finally
    Cleanup;
  end;
end;
```

The demonstration program implements `TMyTimerThread`, which uses this approach to implement the same functionality as the `TMyThread`. Instead of using a monolithic `Execute`, the code implements three very small overridden methods. Another change is that the local variable `pingMsg` is now a field, as it must be shared between different methods:

```
TMyTimerThread = class(TCommTimerThread)
strict private
  FPingMsg: integer;
protected
  procedure Initialize; override;
  procedure ProcessMessage(const msg: TValue); override;
  procedure ProcessTimer; override;
end;
```

The code to create this thread looks almost the same as the code that creates `TMyThread`, except that it also sets the interval between messages:

```
procedure TfrmThreadComm.btnStartTimerClick(Sender: TObject);
begin
  FTimerThread := TMyTimerThread.Create(ProcessThreadMessages);
  FTimerThread.Interval := 5000;
  FTimerThread.SendToThread(42);
end;
```

Sending a message to the thread and stopping the thread looks completely the same as before. This thread also uses the same *message receiver* function in the main form, `ProcessThreadMessage`.

When a thread is initialized, the code sends a *ping* message to the owner. There's no need to initialize `FPingMsg`, as all of the object fields are initialized to zero when an object is created. The timer event handler, `ProcessTimer`, just calls the same helper function, `SendPing`, to send a message to the owner. And the message processing is trivial—it just sets the shared field:

```
procedure TMyTimerThread.Initialize;
begin
  SendPing;
end;

procedure TMyTimerThread.ProcessMessage(const msg: TValue);
begin
  FPingMsg := msg.AsInteger;
end;

procedure TMyTimerThread.ProcessTimer;
```

```
begin
  SendPing;
end;

procedure TMyTimerThread.SendPing;
begin
  if not SendToMain(TValue.From<TPingMsg>(
           TPingMsg.Create(FPingMsg, ThreadID)))
  then
    raise Exception.Create('Queue full!');
end;
```

When the code is written in such way, it becomes clear why I prefer using patterns and communication over standard `TThread` code. There is no data sharing, no weird communication calls and, best of all, no mess.

Summary

While this chapter focused on a single topic, it was still quite diverse. You've learned everything about the `TThread` class, which is a basis for all multithreading code in Delphi. Even the task-based approach that we'll explore in the next chapter uses `TThread` as a basic building block.

I have shown three different ways of creating a `TThread`-based, multithreading solution. A program can take complete ownership of a thread so that it is created and destroyed by the owner. This approach is best used when a thread implements a *service,* as in such cases the main program knows best when the service is needed.

Another way, more appropriate for *background calculations,* is `FreeOnTerminate` mode. With this approach, a thread object is immediately destroyed when a thread's `Execute` function exits. The thread owner can set up an `OnTerminate` event to catch this condition and process the result of the calculation.

Instead of writing a separate class for each background operation, we can also create a thread that executes an *anonymous method.* This approach is most appropriate for short-lived tasks that don't require any interaction with the thread's owner.

After that, we looked into exception handling inside a thread. I've also discussed a few other important `TThread` methods and properties.

The second half of the chapter focused on writing better threading tools. Firstly, I have extended a `TThread` with two communication channels. The result, `TCommThread`, can be used as a base class for your own threads, which can use these channels to communicate with the thread owner.

For the finishing touch, I have implemented a specific solution for one usage pattern—a background task that can send and receive messages and react to timer events. I have then shown how you can produce very clean and understandable code, by using such threading implementation.

In the next chapter, we'll focus even more on a usage-pattern approach. We'll dig deeply into Delphi's **Parallel Programming Library** (**PPL**), which is all about usage patterns. For good measure, I'll also implement a few patterns that PPL doesn't cover.

7
Exploring Parallel Practices

You made it! I admit that the previous two chapters were not much fun and that they mostly tried to scare you away from multithreaded code. Now it's time for something completely different.

In this chapter, I'll cover the fun parts of multithreaded programming by moving to high-level concepts—tasks and patterns. We will not create any threads in the code, no we won't. Instead, we'll just tell the code what we need, and it will handle all the nitty-gritty details.

When you have read this chapter to its conclusion, you'll know all about the following topics:

- What are tasks, and how are they different from threads?
- How do we create and destroy tasks?
- What are our options for managing tasks?
- How should we handle exceptions in tasks?
- What is thread pooling, and why is it useful?
- What are patterns, and why are they better than tasks?
- How can we use the Async/Await pattern to execute operations in a thread?
- How can we use Join pattern to execute multiple parts of code in parallel?
- What is a Future, and how can it help when calculating functions?
- How can we convert a normal loop into a parallel loop with Parallel For?
- How can a pipeline help us parallelize many different problems?

Tasks and patterns

Traditionally, parallel programming was always implemented with a focus on threads and data sharing. The only support we programmers got from the operating system and the language runtime libraries were thread—and synchronization—related functions. We were able to create a thread, maybe set some thread parameters (like thread priority), and kill a thread. We were also able to create some synchronization mechanisms—a critical section, mutex, or a semaphore. But that was all.

As you are not skipping ahead and you read the previous two chapters, you already know that being able to start a new thread and do the locking is not nearly enough. Writing parallel code that way is a slow, error-prone process. That's why in the last decade the focus in parallel code has shifted from threads to *tasks* and *patterns*. Everyone is doing it—Microsoft with the .NET Task Parallel Library, Intel with Thread Building Blocks, Embarcadero with the Parallel Programming Library and third-party extensions such as OmniThreadLibrary, and so on.

The difference between threads and tasks is simple. A **thread** is an operating system concept that allows executing multiple parts of a process simultaneously. A **task** is merely a part of the code that we want to execute in that way. Or, to put it in different words—when you focus on threads, you tell the system *how* to do the work. When you work with tasks you tell the library *what* you want to be done. You don't lose time with *plumbing*, with setting up threads, communication mechanisms, and so on. Everything is already ready and waiting for you.

As it turns out, working with tasks is usually still too low level. For example, if you want the program to iterate over some loop with multiple tasks in parallel, you would not want to do that by using basic tasks. I'll create such an example in this chapter and you'll see that it still takes some work. A much simpler approach is to use a specific usage *pattern* —a *parallel for* in this example.

Many such patterns exist in modern parallel libraries. Delphi's Parallel Programming Library offers *join, future,* and *parallel for*. .NET has *async* and *await*. Thread Building Blocks offers an incredibly powerful *flow graph*. OmniThreadLibrary gives you *background worker, pipeline, timed task,* and more.

In this chapter, I'll cover all the patterns implemented by the Parallel Programming Library, and then some. I'll extend the set with patterns that you can freely use in your code. Before that, however, we have to cover the basics and deal with *tasks*.

Variable capturing

Before I start writing parallel code, I have to cover something completely different. As you'll see in this chapter, the big part of the incredible usefulness of tasks and patterns is the ability to use them in combination with anonymous methods and variable capturing. As powerful as that combination is, however, it also brings in some problems.

The code in this chapter will frequently run into the problem of capturing a *loop variable*. Instead of trying to explain this problem at the same time as dealing with the already hard concepts of parallel code, I decided to write a simple program that demonstrates the problem and does nothing more.

The code in the `AnonMethod` project tries to write out the numbers from *1* to *20* in a convoluted way. For each value of `i`, the code calls `TThread.ForceQueue` and passes in an anonymous method that calls `Log(i)` to write the value into a `ListBox`.

The problem with the following code lies in the programmer's assumptions. When you write code like this, you should not forget that by writing an anonymous method you are creating a completely separate part of the code that will be executed at some other time. In this example, `Log` will be called *after* `btnAnonProblemClick` finishes the execution:

```
procedure TfrmAnonMthod.btnAnonProblemClick(Sender: TObject);
var
  i: Integer;
begin
  ListBox1.Items.Add('');
  for i := 1 to 20 do
    TThread.ForceQueue(nil,
      procedure
      begin
        Log(i);
      end);
end;

procedure TfrmAnonMthod.Log(i: integer);
begin
  ListBox1.Items[ListBox1.Items.Count - 1] :=
  ListBox1.Items[ListBox1.Items.Count - 1] + i.ToString + ' ';
end;
```

To support this, the compiler must somehow make the value of `i` available to our anonymous method when it is executed. This is done through the magic of *variable capturing*. I'm not going to go into specifics here, as this is a book about high performance computing and not about Delphi implementation details. The only important part you have to know is that the compiler doesn't capture the current *value* of `i` (as the author of the preceding code fragment assumed) but a *reference* to the value (a pointer to `i`).

Because of that, all `Log` calls will receive the same parameter—a value that some pointer points to. It will contain whatever was left inside `i` after the `for` loop completed, namely `21`. That is just how Delphi works. After a `for` loop, a loop variable will contain upper bound plus *1*. (Or *minus 1*, if the loop is counting downwards.)

A trick that solves the problem of capturing a loop variable is to write an intermediate function that creates an anonymous method. If we pass our loop variable (`i`) to such a function, the compiler captures the parameter to the function and not the loop variable, and everything works as expected.

Don't worry if you did not understand any of the mumbo-jumbo from the previous paragraph. Writing about anonymous methods is hard, but luckily they are easily explained through the code. The following example shows how we can fix the code in `AnonMethod`. The `MakeLog` function creates an anonymous method that logs the value of parameter `i`. In the loop, we then call `MakeLog` for each value of `i` and pass the output of this function to the `ForceQueue` call:

```
function TfrmAnonMthod.MakeLog(i: integer): TThreadProcedure;
begin
  Result :=
    procedure
    begin
      Log(i);
    end;
end;

procedure TfrmAnonMthod.btnAnonFixClick(Sender: TObject);
var
  i: Integer;
begin
  ListBox1.Items.Add('');
  for i := 1 to 20 do
    TThread.ForceQueue(nil, MakeLog(i));
end;
```

The following screenshot shows both the unexpected output from the original code and good output from the fixed code:

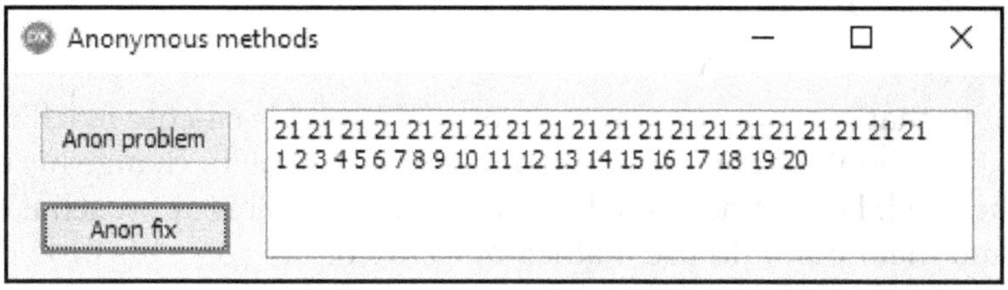

Tasks

Let's get back to business, and in this chapter business means tasks. I don't want to spend all the time talking about the theory and classes and interfaces, so I will start by introducing some code. Actually, it is not my code—I got it from our good friend, Mr. Smith.

For the past few chapters, he was quite busy, working on things botanical, so I let him be. (He gave me a comprehensive overview of his activities, but I'm just a programmer, and I didn't really understand him.) Now he has more spare time, and he returned to his great love—prime numbers. He is no longer trying to improve `SlowCode`. Now he studies how the probability of finding a prime number changes when numbers become larger. To do so, he wrote two simple functions (shown as follows) that check a range of numbers and count how many prime numbers are in this range:

```
function IsPrime(value: integer): boolean;
var
  i: Integer;
begin
  Result := (value > 1);
  if Result then
    for i := 2 to Round(Sqrt(value)) do
      if (value mod i) = 0 then
        Exit(False);
end;

function FindPrimes(lowBound, highBound: integer): integer;
var
  i: Integer;
begin
```

```
    Result := 0;
    for i := lowBound to highBound do
      if IsPrime(i) then
        Inc(Result);
  end;
```

He soon found out that his code is using only one CPU on his 64-core machine. As he found out that I'm writing about parallel programming, he asked me to change his code so that all the CPUs will be used. I didn't have the heart to tell him that his approach is flawed from the beginning and that he should use mathematical theory to solve his problem. Rather, I took his code and used it as a starting point for this chapter. There are different ways to parallelize such code. It probably won't surprise you that I'll start with the most basic one, *tasks*.

In Delphi's Parallel Programming Library, tasks are objects that implement the `ITask` interface. They are created through methods of the `TTask` class. Both the class and the interface are implemented in the `System.Threading` unit.

The code in the `ParallelTasks` demo shows basic operations on the tasks. The following method is executed if you click on the **Run tasks** button.

The first task is created by calling the `TTask.Run` method. This method creates a new task and immediately starts it. The task will be started in a thread, run the `SleepProc` code, and terminate. `Run` returns an `ITask` interface, which we can use to query and manipulate the task.

The second task is created by calling the `TTask.Create` method. This method creates a new task but does not start it. It returns an `ITask` interface, just as `Run` does. In this second example, the task payload is a simple anonymous method. As we want it to start running immediately, the code then calls the `ITask.Start` method, which starts the task. `Start` returns the task's `ITask` interface, which the code saves in the `tasks` array.

The code then waits for both tasks to complete by calling the `TTask.WaitForAll` method. It will wait until both the anonymous method and `SleepProc` exit. The program will be blocked for about 2.5 seconds in `WaitForAll`, which is not optimal. Later we'll look into different techniques to work around the problem:

```
procedure SleepProc;
begin
  Sleep(2500);
end;

procedure TfrmParallelTasks.btnRunTasksClick(Sender: TObject);
var
```

```
  tasks: array [1..2] of ITask;
begin
  tasks[1] := TTask.Run(SleepProc);
  tasks[2] := TTask.Create(procedure begin Sleep(2000) end).Start;
  TTask.WaitForAll(tasks);
end;
```

If we don't want to block the main program, we have to use a different technique to find out when the task has finished its work. We can apply any of the notification methods from the previous chapter—Windows messages, `Synchronize`, `Queue`, or polling. In this example, I used the `Queue`.

When you click the **Async TTask** button in the `ParallelTasks` demo, the `btnAsyncTaskClick` method (shown as follows) is executed. This method creates a task by calling `TTask.Run` and stores the task interface into the form field `FTask: ITask`. The code also disables the button to give a visual indication that the task is running.

The task then executes the `LongTask` method in its own thread. After the hard work (`Sleep`) is done, it queues the notification method, `LongTaskCompleted`, to the main thread. This method cleans up after the finished task by setting the `FTask` field to `nil` and reactivates the `btnAsyncTask` button:

```
procedure TfrmParallelTasks.LongTask;
begin
  Sleep(2000);
  TThread.Queue(nil, LongTaskCompleted);
end;

procedure TfrmParallelTasks.LongTaskCompleted;
begin
  FTask := nil;
  btnAsyncTask.Enabled := True;
end;

procedure TfrmParallelTasks.btnAsyncTaskClick(Sender: TObject);
begin
  FTask := TTask.Run(LongTask);
  btnAsyncTask.Enabled := False;
end;
```

When you have to wait for multiple tasks to complete, the code becomes a bit more complicated. You have to keep count of running tasks and only trigger the notification when the last task completes. You'll have to wait a bit for the practical example. Later in this chapter, I'll implement a custom `join` pattern, and I'll return to the notification problem then.

Exceptions in tasks

Handling exceptions in tasks is a tricky business. The best approach is to handle exceptions explicitly by wrapping the task code in a `try..except` block.

The following code shows how exceptions are handled in the `ExplicitExceptionTask` task. This task is executed when the user clicks on the **Exception 1** button in the `ParallelTasks` demo.

The code always raises an exception, so `LongTaskCompleted` is never called. Instead of that, the code always executes the `except` block, which queues `LongTaskError` to be executed in the main thread.

As the queued code is not executed immediately, we have to *grab* the exception object by calling the `AcquireExceptionObject` method. Variable capturing will take care of the rest. If we did not call the `AcquireExceptionObject` method, the exception object would be already destroyed by the time the queued anonymous method was called:

```
procedure TfrmParallelTasks.ExplicitExceptionTask;
var
  exc: TObject;
begin
  try
    raise Exception.Create('Task exception');
    TThread.Queue(nil, LongTaskCompleted);
  except
    on E: Exception do
    begin
      exc := AcquireExceptionObject;
      TThread.Queue(nil,
        procedure
        begin
          LongTaskError(exc);
        end);
    end;
  end;
end;
```

The `LongTaskError` just logs the details about the exception and calls `ReleaseExceptionObject` to release exception acquired with the `AcquireExceptionObject`.

```
procedure TfrmParallelTasks.LongTaskError(exc: Exception);
begin
  ListBox1.Items.Add(Format('Task raised exception %s %s', [exc.ClassName,
exc.Message]));
  ReleaseExceptionObject;
end;
```

Another option is to not use the `try..except` block in the task but to periodically check the `ITask.Status` property. If a task raises an unhandled exception, `TTask` implementation will catch it, store the exception object away, and set the status to `TTaskStatus.Exception`.

A click on the **Exception 2** button in the demo program calls the `btnException2Click` method, which starts such a task. At the same time, the code enables a timer, which periodically checks the status of the `FTask` task:

```
procedure TfrmParallelTasks.btnException2Click(Sender: TObject);
begin
  FTask := TTask.Run(ExceptionTask);
  TimerCheckTask.Enabled := true;
end;

procedure TfrmParallelTasks.ExceptionTask;
begin
  Sleep(1000);
  raise Exception.Create('Task exception');
end;
```

The code in the timer event handler jumps through lots of hoops to get the exception information from the task. It looks like the designer of the `ITask` decided that you ought to always explicitly handle task exceptions, and he made this second approach needlessly complicated.

The full code for the timer method is shown as follows. Firstly, it checks the task's status. If it is one of `Completed`, `Canceled`, or `Exception` then the task has finished its work. `Completed` is used to indicate a normal task completion. `Canceled` means that somebody called the `ITask.Cancel` method of that task. `Expection` tells us that an unhandled exception was raised by the task.

In all three cases, the code clears the `FTask` field and disables the timer. If the status was `Exception`, it goes through more steps to log that exception.

Unfortunately, there's no clean way to access the exception object raised by the task. We can only see its contents by calling the `ITask.Wait` method. This method waits for a specified time on a task to complete (in our code, the time is set to *0* milliseconds). It returns `True` if the task has completed, `False` if timeout was reached and the task is still running, or it raises an exception if the task was cancelled or an exception was caught.

> The `Deadlock` demo from `Chapter 5`, *Getting Started with the Parallel World,* shows how to cancel a task.

We must wrap the `Wait` call in a `try..except` block to catch that exception. It will not be a simple exception object but an instance of the `EAggregateException` class, which can contain multiple *inner* exceptions. The code then uses a loop to log all caught exceptions:

```
procedure TfrmParallelTasks.TimerCheckTaskTimer(Sender: TObject);
var
  i: integer;
begin
  if assigned(FTask) then
  begin
    if FTask.Status in [TTaskStatus.Completed, TTaskStatus.Canceled,
TTaskStatus.Exception] then
    begin
      if FTask.Status = TTaskStatus.Exception then
      try
        FTask.Wait(0);
      except
        on E: EAggregateException do
          for i := 0 to E.Count - 1 do
            ListBox1.Items.Add(Format('Task raised exception %s %s',
              [E[i].ClassName, E[i].Message]));
      end;
      FTask := nil;
      TimerCheckTask.Enabled := true;
    end;
  end;
end;
```

All in all, this is terribly complicated, which is why I strongly support explicit exception handling in task code.

Parallelizing a loop

Let us now return to Mr. Smith's problem. He is calling the `FindPrimes` method, which checks the primality of natural numbers in a `for` loop. I've shown that code at the beginning of the chapter, but for convenience I'll reprint it here:

```
function FindPrimes(lowBound, highBound: integer): integer;
var
  i: Integer;
begin
  Result := 0;
  for i := lowBound to highBound do
    if IsPrime(i) then
      Inc(Result);
end;
```

When he calls, for example, `FindPrimes(1,10000000)`, the computer spends a long time doing the calculation during which time only one CPU is busy. That is not surprising given that in any Delphi program only one thread is running by default. If we want to make other CPUs busy too, we have to run multiple threads.

In his case, it is quite simple to split the job between multiple tasks. Let's say we want to check numbers from 1 to 100,000 with four tasks. We'll let the first task scan the numbers from 1 to 25,000, the second from 25,001 to 50,000, and so on. The tricky part is collecting partial results back together. Each thread will count the number of primes in its subrange, and we have to collect and aggregate (add together) all the partial results. I'll show two different ways to do that.

The first approach is implemented in the `btnCheckPrimes1Click` method, which is activated by clicking the **Check primes 1** button. The number of tasks created is dictated by the `inpNumTasks` spin edit so the code allocates a `tasks: TArray<ITask>` array of that length. It also allocates a `results: TArray<Integer>` array, which will be used to collect partial results.

After that, the code creates and starts all the tasks. Some simple mathematics makes sure that each task gets the subrange of approximately the same size. The actual anonymous method that is run in the task is returned by the `PrepareTask` function to circumvent the problem of capturing a `for` variable. Each task receives three parameters—lower and upper bound for the search range (`lowBound` and `highBound`) and a pointer to the slot, which will receive the partial result (`@results[i-1]`).

When all tasks are created and started, the code waits for all of them to complete. After that a simple `for` loop aggregates the partial results:

```
function TfrmParallelTasks.PrepareTask(lowBound, highBound: integer;
taskResult: PInteger): TProc;
begin
  Result :=
    procedure
    begin
      taskResult^ := FindPrimes(lowBound, highBound);
    end;
end;

procedure TfrmParallelTasks.btnCheckPrimes1Click(Sender: TObject);
var
  aggregate: Integer;
  i: Integer;
  highBound: Integer;
  lowBound: Integer;
  numTasks: Integer;
  results: TArray<Integer>;
  sw: TStopwatch;
  tasks: TArray<ITask>;
begin
  sw := TStopwatch.StartNew;
  numTasks := inpNumTasks.Value;
  SetLength(tasks, numTasks);
  SetLength(results, numTasks);

  lowBound := 0;
  for i := 1 to numTasks do
  begin
    highBound := Round(CHighestNumber / numTasks * i);
    tasks[i-1] := TTask.Run(PrepareTask(lowBound, highBound,
      @results[i-1]));
    lowBound := highBound + 1;
  end;
  TTask.WaitForAll(tasks);

  aggregate := 0;
```

```
    for i in results do
      Inc(aggregate, i);

    sw.Stop;
    ListBox1.Items.Add(Format(
      '%d prime numbers from 1 to %d found in %d ms with %d tasks',
      [aggregate, CHighestNumber, sw.ElapsedMilliseconds, numTasks]));
  end;
```

The second approach uses a variable, shared between tasks (`aggregate`), to store the number of found prime numbers. To ensure a proper operation, it is updated with a call to `TInterlocked.Add`. The code in `btnCheckPrimes2Click` implements that. As it looks mostly the same as the preceding code, I'll show here just the worker function that creates the task method:

```
  function TfrmParallelTasks.PrepareTask2(lowBound, highBound: integer;
  taskResult: PInteger): TProc;
  begin
    Result :=
      procedure
      begin
        TInterlocked.Add(taskResult^, FindPrimes(lowBound, highBound));
      end;
  end;
```

If you start the program and test the code with different numbers of tasks, you may be in for a surprise. I said "may be" because the behavior depends on the way you test the code and on the Delphi version you are using.

There's a nasty bug in the `System.Threading` code that was introduced in Delphi 10.2 Tokyo. I certainly hope that it will be fixed in the next release, as it makes the Parallel Programming Library hard to use. It sometimes causes new threads *not* to be created when you start a task. That forces your tasks to execute one by one, not in parallel.

To demonstrate this, I have enhanced the code executed when you click the **Check primes 2** button. It counts the number of tasks that are executing in parallel and reports that at the end.

If you compile the demo with Tokyo and then start it with four tasks, then two tasks, and finally one task, you'll get the expected result. In my case, calculations run for 2.5, 4.2, and 6.6 seconds, respectively, which is exactly what we would expect. The log window also shows that four, two, and one tasks were running in parallel during the tests, which is again what we wanted.

On the other hand, if you first run the code with one task, then with two, and finally with four, you'll see that each operation takes about the same time and that they all run only one operation in parallel. This is caused by the aforementioned bug. The following screenshot shows both test runs on my test computer:

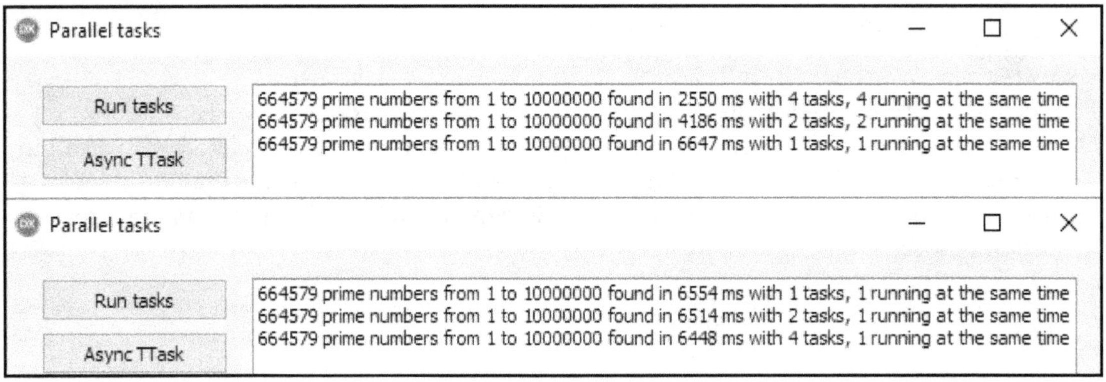

As far as I know, there are two ways around the problem. One is to insert a little delay after each `TTask.Run`. The `btnCheckPrimes2Click` method contains a commented-out `Sleep(1)` call. If you uncomment it, everything will work as expected. (By the way, `Sleep(0)` is not enough to fix the problem.)

Another workaround is to create a new *thread pool* and limit the minimum number of running threads in that pool. (I know I haven't yet mentioned thread pools, but I'll fix that in a moment.) We can then tell the task to run in that thread pool.

The demo program has a method called `btnCustomThreadPoolClick`, which does exactly that. It is almost completely equal to `btnCheckPrimes2Click`, except in four places.

Firstly, it declares an internal thread pool variable, `tp: TThreadPool`. Secondly, it creates this thread pool and limits the minimum number of threads it will run. This will prevent the thread pool from starting too few worker threads. Thirdly, the `tp` variable is passed as an additional parameter to `TTask.Run`. That tells `TTask` to start the task in our thread pool and not in the default one. Lastly, the `tp` threadpool is destroyed after all tasks are done with their job.

The following code fragment shows only the central part of that method, enough to see how the thread pool is put to use:

```
tp := TThreadPool.Create;
if not tp.SetMinWorkerThreads(numTasks) then
  ListBox1.Items.Add('Failed to set minimum number of worker threads');

lowBound := 0;
for i := 1 to numTasks do
begin
  highBound := Round(CHighestNumber / numTasks * i);
  tasks[i-1] := TTask.Run(PrepareTask2(lowBound, highBound, @aggregate),
tp);
  lowBound := highBound + 1;
end;
TTask.WaitForAll(tasks);

FreeAndNil(tp);
```

Thread pooling

While starting a thread is much faster than creating a new process, it is still a relatively slow operation. It may easily take few milliseconds to create a new thread. Because in high-performance applications every millisecond counts, most task- and pattern-based libraries use a concept of a *thread pool*.

A thread pool is just a storage that manages unused threads. For example, let's say that your application—which was working in a single thread until now—has just created (and started) its first task. The Parallel Programming Library will then ask a thread pool to run that task. Unless you pass a custom thread pool parameter to `TTask.Create` or `TTask.Run`, a default thread pool will be used.

The thread pool will then create a new thread to run your task in. After the task completes its job, the thread will not die, but will be stored in the list of inactive threads.

If the program now starts another task, the thread pool will not create a new thread, but will reuse the previous one. If a new task is started while the previous one is still active, a new thread will be created.

This creation and storage of inactive threads can be controlled by changing the properties of the `TThreadPool` object, which implements a thread pool. The following code fragment shows the public interface exposed by a thread pool:

```
function SetMaxWorkerThreads(Value: Integer): Boolean;
function SetMinWorkerThreads(Value: Integer): Boolean;

property MaxWorkerThreads: Integer read GetMaxWorkerThreads;
property MinWorkerThreads: Integer read GetMinWorkerThreads;
```

Calling `SetMinWorkerThreads` limits the minimum number of worker threads—except that it does not. The comment inside the code states that *"The actual number of pool threads could be less than this value depending on actual demand"*. So this call is actually just a hint to the library. The `MinWorkerThreads` property gives you a read access to that value. By default, this value is initialized to the number of CPU cores in the system.

Calling `SetMaxWorkerThreads` limits the maximum number of worker threads. If that number of threads is active and you start a new task, it will have to wait for another task to complete its work. The `MaxWorkerThreads` property gives you a read access to that value. By default, this value is initialized to the number of CPU cores in the system **times 25,** which is a pretty high value—much too high if your tasks are CPU-intensive.

Async/Await

Tasks are powerful but clumsy. The real power of modern multithreading libraries comes not from them, but from specialized code designed to solve specific usage patterns (*pattern* or a *parallel pattern* for short). Although I intend to cover all of the patterns implemented in the Parallel Programming Library, I'll start with a pattern you won't find there.

The *Async/Await* pattern comes from .NET. It allows you to start a background task (*async*) and execute some code in the main thread after the task completes its work (*await*). In Delphi, we cannot repeat the incredible usefulness of the .NET syntax, as it requires support from the compiler, but we can approximate it with something that is useful enough. Such an implementation can be found in my OmniThreadLibrary. For the purpose of this book, I have re-implemented it in the unit `DHPThreading`, which you can freely use in your code.

The `AsyncAwait` demo shows when this pattern can be useful and how to use it. The **Long task** button calls a method that simulates a typical old-school Delphi code.

Firstly, the user interface (the button) is disabled. Then, some time-consuming operation is executed. For example, a program could fetch data from a database, generate a report, export a long XML file, and so on. In this demo program, the `LongTask` method simply executes `Sleep(5000)`. At the end, the user interface is enabled again:

```
procedure TfrmAsyncAwait.btnLongTaskClick(Sender: TObject);
begin
  btnLongTask.Enabled := false;
  btnLongTask.Update;
  LongTask;
  btnLongTask.Enabled := true;
end;
```

This typical pattern has one big problem. It blocks the user interface. While the code is running, the user cannot click into the program, move the window around, and so on. Sometimes the long operation can easily be adapted to run in a background thread, and in such cases a pattern, such as *Async/Await* (or, as we'll later see, a *Future*), can be really helpful.

Async/Await allows you to rewrite the code, shown as follows. The code still disables the user interface but does not call `btnLongTask.Update`. This method will exit almost immediately, and the normal Delphi message loop will take over, redrawing the controls as required.

The code then calls `Async(LongTask)` to start the long task in a background thread. The second part of the command, `.Await`, specifies a *termination event*, a code that is called after the `LongTask` method exits. This event will execute in a main thread, and so it is a good place to update the user interface:

```
TfrmAsyncAwait.btnLongTaskAsyncClick(Sender: TObject);
begin
  btnLongTaskAsync.Enabled := false;
  Async(LongTask)
  .Await(
    procedure
    begin
      btnLongTaskAsync.Enabled := true;
    end
  );
end;
```

If you click the **Long task async** button in the demo program, it will call this method. The time-consuming task will start, but the program will still be responsive. After 5 seconds, the button will be re-enabled, and you'll be able to start the task again.

Actually, the program has three buttons, which all start the same code. If you click all three, three background threads will be created, and `LongTask` will be started in each of them. The following screenshot shows what happens inside the program if you do that. The screenshot proves that the long tasks are started in three threads (*Long task started ...*) and that *await* handlers are executed in the main thread (*Await in thread ...*):

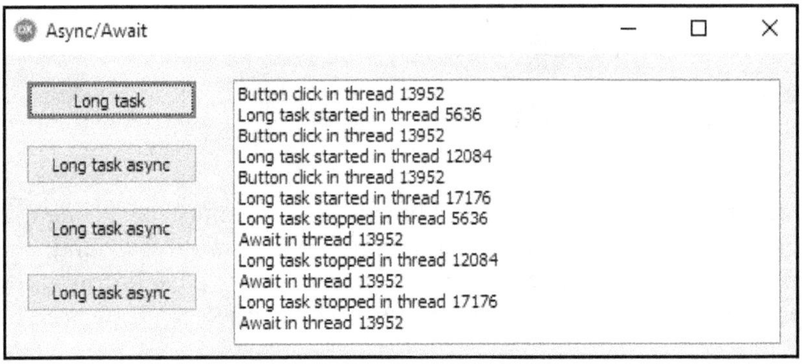

The `DHPThreads` unit implements `Async` as a method returning an `IAsync` interface, which implements the `Await` method:

```
type
  IAsync = interface ['{190C1975-FFCF-47AD-B075-79BC8F4157DA}']
    procedure Await(const awaitProc: TProc);
  end;

function Async(const asyncProc: TProc): IAsync;
```

The implementation of `Async` creates an instance of the `TAsync` class and returns it. The `TAsync` constructor is also trivial; it just stores the `asyncProc` parameter in an internal field:

```
function Async(const asyncProc: TProc): IAsync;
begin
  Result := TAsync.Create(asyncProc);
end;

constructor TAsync.Create(const asyncProc: TProc);
begin
  inherited Create;
  FAsyncProc := asyncProc;
end;
```

Everything else happens inside the `Await` call. It stores the `awaitProc` parameter in an internal field and starts the `Run` method in a task.

The tricky part is hidden in assignment `FSelf := Self`. In the main program, `Async` creates a new `IAsync` interface but doesn't store it away in a form field. Because of that, this interface would be destroyed on exit from the `btnLongTaskAsyncClick` method. To prevent that, `Await` stores a reference to itself in a `FSelf` field. This increases the reference count and prevents the interface from being destroyed:

```
procedure TAsync.Await(const awaitProc: TProc);
begin
  FSelf := Self;
  FAwaitProc := awaitProc;
  TTask.Run(Run);
end;
```

The `Run` method simply runs `FAsyncProc` and then queues an anonymous method to the main thread. This method firstly calls `FAwaitProc` in the main thread and then clears the `FSelf` field. This decrements the reference count and destroys the `ITask` interface:

```
procedure TAsync.Run;
begin
  FAsyncProc();

  TThread.Queue(nil,
    procedure
    begin
      FAwaitProc();
      FSelf := nil;
    end
  );
end;
```

The *Async/Await* pattern is intentionally simple. It offers no capability for processing exceptions, no communication channel to return a value, no interface to stop the running task, and so on. Later we'll see more complicated patterns that offer better control, but sometimes simplicity is exactly what you need.

Join

The next pattern I want to present is *Join*. This is a very simple pattern that starts multiple tasks in parallel. In the Parallel Programming Library, *Join* is implemented as a class method of the `TParallel` class. To execute three methods, `Task1`, `Task2`, and `Task3`, in parallel, you simply call `TParallel.Join` with parameters collected in an array:

```
TParallel.Join([Task1, Task2, Task3]);
```

This is equivalent to the following implementation, which uses tasks:

```
var
  tasks: array [1..3] of ITask;

tasks[1] := TTask.Run(Task1);
tasks[2] := TTask.Run(Task2);
tasks[3] := TTask.Run(Task3);
```

Although the approaches work the same, that doesn't mean that `Join` is implemented in this way. Rather than that, it uses a pattern that I haven't yet covered, a *parallel for* to run tasks in parallel.

The `Join` starts tasks but doesn't wait for them to complete. It returns an `ITask` interface representing a new, composite task, which only exits when all of its subtasks finish execution. You can do with this task anything you can with a *normal* instance of `TTask`. For example, if you want to wait for the tasks to finish, you can simply call `Wait` on the resulting interface.

The following line of code starts two tasks in parallel and waits on both of them to finish. An overload of the `Join` function allows you to pass in two `TProc` parameters without the array notation:

```
TParallel.Join(Task1, Task2).Wait;
```

There's not much to say about `Join`, except that in current Delphi it doesn't work correctly. A bug in the 10.1 Berlin and 10.2 Tokyo implementations causes `Join` to not start enough threads. For example, if you pass in two tasks, it will only create one thread and execute tasks one after another. If you pass in three tasks, it will create two threads and execute two tasks in one and one in another.

The `ParallelJoin` program demonstrates this problem. You can use it to check whether the version of Delphi you are using is affected.

A **Join 2 tasks** button executes the following code:

```
procedure TfrmParallelJoin.btnJoin2Click(Sender: TObject);
begin
  ListBox1.Items.Add('Starting tasks');
  TParallel.Join(Task1, Task2);
end;
```

Both tasks look the same. They log a message, wait a little, log another message, and exit:

```
procedure TfrmParallelJoin.QueueLog(const msg: string);
begin
  TThread.Queue(nil,
    procedure
    begin
      ListBox1.Items.Add(msg);
    end);
end;

procedure TfrmParallelJoin.Task1;
begin
  QueueLog('Task1 started in thread ' + TThread.Current.ThreadID.ToString);
  Sleep(1000);
  QueueLog('Task1 stopped in thread ' + TThread.Current.ThreadID.ToString);
end;

procedure TfrmParallelJoin.Task2;
begin
  QueueLog('Task2 started in thread ' + TThread.Current.ThreadID.ToString);
  Sleep(1000);
  QueueLog('Task2 stopped in thread ' + TThread.Current.ThreadID.ToString);
end;
```

The **Join 3 tasks** button starts a similar code that executes three tasks all working in the same fashion as the preceding two tasks.

If you start the program and click **Join 2 tasks,** you'll see that both tasks are executed in the same thread. Because of that—as a thread can only do one thing at a time—the second task is only started when the first task finishes execution. Of course, this only happens if the `Join` implementation is buggy. With good implementation, the tasks will be started at the same time in two different threads.

If you click the **Join 3 tasks** button, two tasks will be started immediately, each in their own thread. After the first of them exits, its thread will be reused to run the third task. Again, a good implementation will start three tasks in three threads at (almost) the same time.

The following screenshot shows the behavior with the buggy implementation of `Join`:

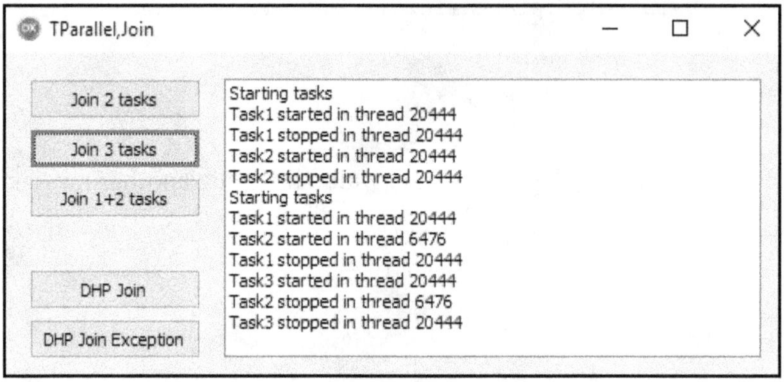

A simple workaround for this problem is to start one task too many. The extra task should not do anything and should be executed first. When it exits (which will be almost immediately), a new, real task will be started in the same thread.

The `ParallelJoin` program has the **Join 1+2 tasks** button, which demonstrates this behavior. Clicking on a button starts tasks `NullTask`, `Task1`, and `Task2`. A bad implementation will start `NullTask` and `Task1` in two threads. As `NullTask` immediately exits, its thread is reused to start `Task2`:

```
procedure NullTask;
begin
end;

procedure TfrmParallelJoin.btnJoin1p2Click(Sender: TObject);
begin
  ListBox1.Items.Add('Starting tasks');
  TParallel.Join([NullTask, Task1, Task2]);
end;
```

The following screenshot shows this workaround in action:

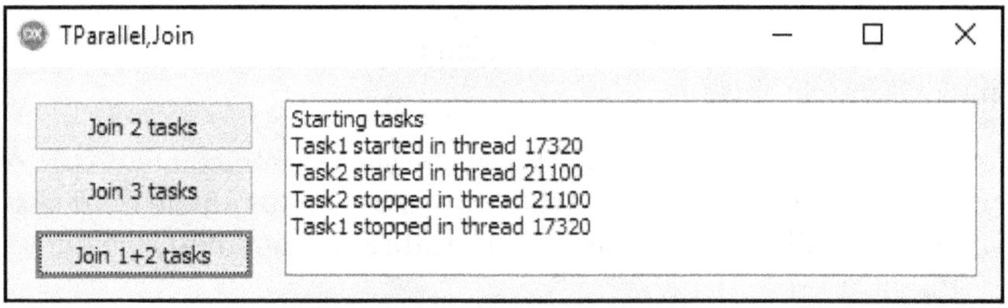

Join/Await

Another way to work around the `TParallel.Join` problem is to create a different implementation of the same pattern. As with the *Async/Await* pattern, I've created a version that supports the *Join/Await* pattern.

As with the `TParallel` version, `Join` accepts multiple `TProc` parameters. It, however, doesn't return an `ITask` interface but `IJoin`. This interface is similar to the `IAsync` interface used for the *Async/Await* pattern. It implements two versions of the `Await` method. One is the same as in the `IAsync` version, while the other can be used to catch exceptions raised in tasks:

```
type
  IJoin = interface ['{ED4B4531-B233-4A02-A09A-13EE488FCCA3}']
    procedure Await(const awaitProc: TProc); overload;
    procedure Await(const awaitProc: TProc<Exception>); overload;
  end;

function Join(const async: array of TProc): IJoin;
```

Full implementation of the *Join/Await* pattern can be found in the `DHPThreading` unit. In this book, I'll only show the interesting parts.

A trivial function `Join` creates and returns an instance of a `TJoin` class. The `TJoin` constructor makes a copy of Join's `async` parameter and nothing more.

The interesting things start happening in `Await`. It stores `FAwaitProc` away, initializes a counter of running tasks, `FNumRunning`, makes sure that it cannot be destroyed by using the `FSelf := nil` trick, and starts all tasks. The helper function, `GetAsyncProc`, is used to work around the problem of capturing a `for` loop variable.

If compiled with Delphi 10.2 Tokyo, the code also inserts a short `Sleep` after `TTask.Run` to work around the problem I mentioned previously in this chapter. I certainly hope this bug will be fixed in the next release.

```
function TJoin.GetAsyncProc(i: integer): TProc;
begin
  Result :=
    procedure
    begin
      Run(FAsyncProc[i]);
    end;
end;

procedure TJoin.Await(const awaitProc: TProc<Exception>);
```

```
var
  i: integer;
begin
  FAwaitProc := awaitProc;
  FNumRunning := Length(FAsyncProc);
  FSelf := Self;
  for i := Low(FAsyncProc) to High(FAsyncProc) do begin
    TTask.Run(GetAsyncProc(i));
    {$IF CompilerVersion = 32}Sleep(1);{$IFEND}
  end;
end;
```

The main part of the *Join/Await* implementation is the `Run` method, which is started once for each task passed to the `Join` call. First it calls the `asyncProc` parameter (executing your task in the process) and catches all exceptions. Any exception will be passed to the `AppendException` function, which I'll cover in a moment.

After that, the code decrements the number of running tasks in a thread-safe manner. If the counter has dropped to *0* (as `TInterlocked` is used, this can only happen in one task), the code queues an anonymous method that calls the *Await* handler and drops the reference to itself so that the `TJoin` object can be destroyed.
The `CreateAggregateException` function will be shown in a moment.

```
procedure TJoin.Run(const asyncProc: TProc);
begin
  try
    asyncProc();
  except
    on E: Exception do
      AppendException(AcquireExceptionObject as Exception);
  end;

 if TInterlocked.Decrement(FNumRunning) = 0 then
   TThread.Queue(nil,
     procedure
     begin
       FAwaitProc(CreateAggregateException);
       FSelf := nil;
     end);
end;
```

The `AppendException` function adds the caught exception object to an `FExceptions` array. As it may be called from multiple threads at once (if more than one task fails simultaneously), locking is used to synchronize access to `FExceptions`:

```
procedure TJoin.AppendException(E: Exception);
begin
  TMonitor.Enter(Self);
  try
    SetLength(FExceptions, Length(FExceptions) + 1);
    FExceptions[High(FExceptions)] := e;
  finally
    TMonitor.Exit(Self);
  end;
end;
```

The `CreateAggregateException` exception is only called when all tasks have finished execution and so doesn't need any locking. If the `FExceptions` array is empty, the function returns nil. Otherwise, it creates an `EAggregateException` object containing all caught exceptions:

```
function TJoin.CreateAggregateException: Exception;
begin
  if Length(FExceptions) = 0 then
    Result := nil
  else
    Result := EAggregateException.Create(FExceptions);
end;
```

What about the second `Await` overload? It simply calls the `Await` that we've already seen. If any of the tasks raises an exception, it will be reraised inside the `Await` code. Otherwise, your `awaitProc` will be called:

```
procedure TJoin.Await(const awaitProc: TProc);
begin
  Await(
    procedure (E: Exception)
    begin
      if assigned(E) then
        raise E;
      awaitProc();
    end);
end;
```

The **DHP Join Exception** button on the `ParallelJoin` demo shows how to use the exception-handling mechanism. The code starts three tasks. One works as in the previous `Join` examples, while the other two tasks raise exceptions (only one of those tasks is shown as follows):

```
procedure TfrmParallelJoin.Task2E;
begin
  QueueLog('Task2E started in thread ' +
    TThread.Current.ThreadID.ToString);
  Sleep(1000);
  QueueLog('Task2E raising exception in thread ' +
    TThread.Current.ThreadID.ToString);
  raise Exception.Create('Task2 exception');
end;

procedure TfrmParallelJoin.btnDHPJoinExcClick(Sender: TObject);
begin
  ListBox1.Items.Add('Starting tasks');
  Join([Task1, Task2E, Task3E]).Await(TasksStopped);
end;
```

The termination handler, `TasksStopped`, is called in the main thread after all tasks have finished their job. If the `E` parameter is nil, there was no exception—but we already know that in the demo program this is not so.

When at least one exception is raised (and not handled) in a task, the `E` parameter will contain an `EAggregateException` object. The code in `TaskStopped` iterates over all inner exceptions stored in that object and logs them on the screen:

```
procedure TfrmParallelJoin.TasksStopped(E: Exception);
var
  i: Integer;
begin
  ListBox1.Items.Add('Tasks stopped');
  if assigned(E) then
    for i := 0 to EAggregateException(E).Count - 1 do
      ListBox1.Items.Add('Task raised exception: ' +
        EAggregateException(E)[i].Message);
end;
```

The demo program also contains a **DHP Join** button, which starts the same three tasks that we used to test the `TParallel.Join` implementation. In addition to the `TParallel` demo, the code logs the moment when all tasks are completed:

```
procedure TfrmParallelJoin.btnDHPJoinClick(Sender: TObject);
begin
```

```
    ListBox1.Items.Add('Starting tasks');
    Join([Task1, Task2, Task3]).Await(
      procedure
      begin
        ListBox1.Items.Add('Tasks stopped');
      end);
  end;
```

In the following screenshot, we can see how with this implementation all three tasks start in each in their own thread. The screenshot also shows an output of the exception-handling code:

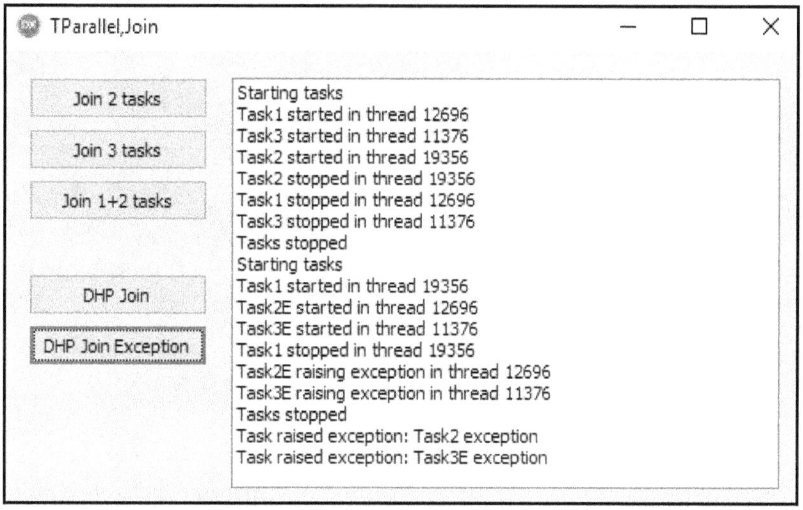

Future

A big category of operations that we would like to execute in a background thread can be summarized with the words "do something and return a result". Such operations are represented by a pattern called *Future*.

A *Future* always wraps some function. In Delphi's Parallel Programming Library, a Future is represented by an `IFuture<T>` interface, where `T` is the data type returned from the function. This interface is created by calling the `TTask.Future<T>` function. `IFuture<T>` is derived from `ITask`, so it supports all `ITask` methods and properties, such as `Status`, `Cancel`, `Wait`, and so on.

The `ParallelFuture` demo shows two ways of using an `IFuture<T>`. In the first scenario, the code creates a Future, does some other work, and then asks the Future about the result of the calculation. If the background calculation is not yet finished, the code waits until the result is ready. That could block the user interface, so this approach should only be used if you know that the Future will be calculated relatively quickly.

In the demo, the **Create Future** button starts the calculation, while the **Get value** button reads the result of the calculation. The calculation is performed by the `CountPrimes` function, which counts prime numbers from 2 to *5,000,000*:

```
function CountPrimes: integer;
var
  i: Integer;
begin
  Result := 0;
  for i := 2 to 5000000 do
    if IsPrime(i) then
      Inc(Result);
end;
```

A Future is created simply by calling `TTask.Future<integer>`, passing in `CountPrimes` as a parameter:

```
procedure TfrmFuture.btnFutureClick(Sender: TObject);
begin
  FFuture := TTask.Future<integer>(CountPrimes);
end;
```

Getting a result of a Future—if you don't mind waiting until the result is calculated—is as simple as accessing its `Value` property. After that, the code destroys the Future interface by assigning it a `nil` value:

```
procedure TfrmFuture.btnGetValueClick(Sender: TObject);
begin
  ListBox1.Items.Add('Result = ' + FFuture.Value.ToString);
  FFuture := nil;
end;
```

The second approach is more appropriate for general use. First, it calculates the resulting value and then notifies the main thread that the value was calculated. We can use any notification mechanism to do that—Windows messages, `TThread.Queue`, polling, and so on.

A click on the **Create Future 2** button in the demo program starts the `btnFuture2Click` method, which uses this approach. As before, the code begins by calling the `TTask.Future<integer>` function, but this time its argument is an anonymous function returning an `Integer`. When a background thread executes this anonymous function, it first calls our real calculation—`CountPrimes`—and then queues a method, `ReportFuture`, to be executed in the main thread:

```
procedure TfrmFuture.btnFuture2Click(Sender: TObject);
begin
  FFuture := TTask.Future<integer>(
    function: Integer
    begin
      Result := CountPrimes;
      TThread.Queue(nil, ReportFuture);
    end);
end;
```

The `ReportFuture` reads the `Value` property to access the result of the calculation:

```
procedure TfrmFuture.ReportFuture;
begin
  ListBox1.Items.Add('Result = ' + FFuture.Value.ToString);
  FFuture := nil;
end;
```

The big difference between the two approaches is that, in the first case, reading from `FFuture.Value` may block until the result is calculated. In the second case, the result is guaranteed to be ready at that point, and the value is returned immediately.

If a Future calculation raises an exception, this exception is caught by the `TTask` and will be reraised when main thread accesses the `Value` property. You can use the technique described in the section *Exceptions in tasks* or—what I would wholeheartedly recommend—catch and handle all exceptions in the background task itself.

Parallel for

The Parallel Programming Library implements only one pattern that I haven't talked about yet—*Parallel for*, a multithreaded version of a `for` loop. This pattern allows for very simple parallelization of loops, but this simplicity can also get you into trouble. When you use *Parallel for*, you should always be very careful that you don't run into some data sharing trap.

For comparison reasons, the `ParallelFor` demo implements a normal `for` loop (shown as follows), which goes from 2 to 10 million, counts all prime numbers in that range, and logs the result:

```
const
  CHighestNumber = 10000000;

procedure TbtnParallelFor.btnForClick(Sender: TObject);
var
  count: Integer;
  i: Integer;
  sw: TStopwatch;
begin
  sw := TStopwatch.StartNew;
  count := 0;

  for i := 2 to CHighestNumber do
    if IsPrime(i) then
      Inc(count);

  sw.Stop;
  ListBox1.Items.Add('For: ' + count.ToString + ' primes. ' +
    'Total time: ' + sw.ElapsedMilliseconds.ToString);
end;
```

To change this `for` loop into a Parallel for, we just have to call `TParallel.For`, instead of using `for`, and pass in both range boundaries and workloads as parameters. A **Parallel for - bad** button in the demo program activates the `btnParallelForBadClick` method, which implements this approach—with a small (intentional) mistake.

The three parameters passed to `TParallel.For` in the following code are lower bound for the iteration (`2`), higher bound (`CHighestNumber`), and a worker method (an anonymous method). A worker method must accept one parameter of type `integer`. This parameter represents the loop variable (`i`) of a standard `for` statement:

```
procedure TbtnParallelFor.btnParalleForBadClick(Sender: TObject);
var
  count: Integer;
  i: Integer;
  sw: TStopwatch;
begin
  sw := TStopwatch.StartNew;
  count := 0;

  TParallel.For(2, CHighestNumber,
    procedure (i: integer)
```

```
      begin
        if IsPrime(i) then
          Inc(count);
      end);

    sw.Stop;
    ListBox1.Items.Add('Parallel for - bad: ' + count.ToString +
      ' primes. ' + 'Total time: ' + sw.ElapsedMilliseconds.ToString);
  end;
```

This code demonstrates the classical data-sharing problem. It is so easy to replace `for` with `TParallel.For` that sometimes you forget that the body of this iteration executes in multiple parallel copies and that all access to shared variables (`count` in this example) must be protected.

We could use locking to solve that problem, but we've already seen that interlocked operations are faster. The code activated by the **Parallel for - good** button therefore uses `TInterlocked.Increment` instead of `Inc` to fix the problem.

The following code fragment shows the Parallel for loop from the `btnParallelForClick` method. All other parts of the method are the same as in the preceding code fragment.

```
  TParallel.For(2, CHighestNumber,
    procedure (i: integer)
    begin
      if IsPrime(i) then
        TInterlocked.Increment(count);
    end);
```

The following screenshot compares all three versions. We can clearly see that the parallel version is about four times faster than the single-threaded code. The test machine had four physical cores, so this is not surprising. We can also see that the "bad" code produces a different value each time. The code runs without any other problems, and that's why such errors are usually hard to detect:

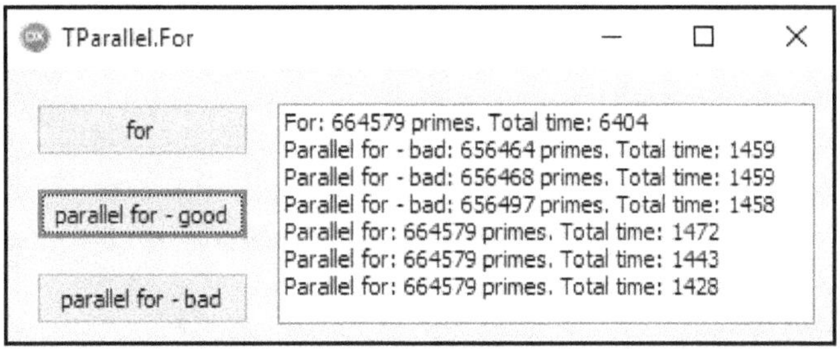

What the screenshot doesn't show is that `TParallel.For` stops the main thread until all the work is done. This is completely understandable. A Parallel for is meant as an in-place replacement for a `for` loop, and with this approach you can sometimes speed up a program with very little work.

If this behavior blocks the user interface for too long, you can still wrap a *Parallel for* pattern inside a *Future* pattern. A Future will take care of a non-blocking execution, while the Parallel for will speed up the program.

TIP

Alternatively, you can wrap a *Parallel for* in an *Async/Await* pattern.

The **Async Parallel for** button in the demo program does exactly that. When you click it, a code starts a computation function, `ParallelCountPrime` in a Future. This function will return a number of primes in the tested range:

```
procedure TbtnParallelFor.btnAsyncParallelForClick(Sender: TObject);
begin
  FStopWatch := TStopwatch.StartNew;
  FParallelFuture := TTask.Future<Integer>(ParallelCountPrimes);
end;
```

The `ParallelCountPrimes` function is executed in a background thread by the Future pattern. It uses `TParallel.For` and `TInterlocked.Increment` to quickly and correctly count prime numbers. After that it assigns the `count` variable to the `Result` function so that the main thread will be able to read it via the `Value` property. At the end, the code queues an anonymous function that will log the result in the main thread and destroy the Future interface:

```
function TbtnParallelFor.ParallelCountPrimes: integer;
var
  count: Integer;
begin
  count := 0;
  TParallel.For(2, CHighestNumber,
    procedure (i: integer)
    begin
      if IsPrime(i) then
        TInterlocked.Increment(count);
    end);
  Result := count;

  TThread.Queue(nil,
```

```
    procedure
    begin
      FStopwatch.Stop;
      ListBox1.Items.Add('Async parallel for: ' +
        FParallelFuture.Value.ToString +
        ' primes. Total time: ' + FStopwatch.ElapsedMilliseconds.ToString);
      FParallelFuture := nil;
    end);
end;
```

If your parallel iteration code raises an exception, it will be caught and reraised in the main thread. In theory, you should be able to wrap `TParallel.For` with a `try` .. `except` block and process the exception there. In practice, however, the implementation of exception catching is buggy (as are many parts of the Parallel Programming Library), and you are likely to run into trouble that way.

A click on the **Parallel for exception** button runs a code, shown as follows, which demonstrates the exception-catching technique. It starts multiple background tasks to process a small range of integers (from 1 to 10) and raises an exception in each task. When Parallel for catches an exception, it tries to shut down the background operation, but during that time a different thread may have already raised the exception too. As the multithreading is unpredictable by nature, a different number of exceptions will be raised each time.

The Parallel for pattern collects all exceptions and joins them in an `EAggregateException`. The following code iterates over all exceptions in this object and logs them on screen:

```
procedure TbtnParallelFor.btnParallelForExceptionClick(Sender: TObject);
var
  i: Integer;
begin
  ListBox1.Items.Add('---');
  try
    TParallel.For(1, 10,
      procedure (i: integer)
      begin
        Sleep(100);
        raise Exception.Create('Exception in thread ' +
          TThread.Current.ThreadID.ToString);
      end);
  except
    on E: EAggregateException do
      for i := 0 to E.Count - 1 do
        if not assigned(E) then
          ListBox1.Items.Add(i.ToString + ': nil')
        else
```

```
          ListBox1.Items.Add(i.ToString + ': ' + E[i].ClassName + ': ' +
            E[i].Message);
      on E: Exception do
        ListBox1.Items.Add(E.ClassName + ': ' + E.Message);
    end;
  end;
```

If you try to run this code, you should do it without the debugger. I was not able to successfully run the program inside the debugger, as, after a few exceptions, the debugger stopped responding.

Even if you run the program without the debugger, it may report weird results from time to time. The preceding code has a special `if` clause that checks whether an inner exception, `E[i]`, is assigned at all. As you can see from the following screenshot, this is necessary, because sometimes an inner exception is not correctly captured. In such cases, `E[i]` contains `nil`:

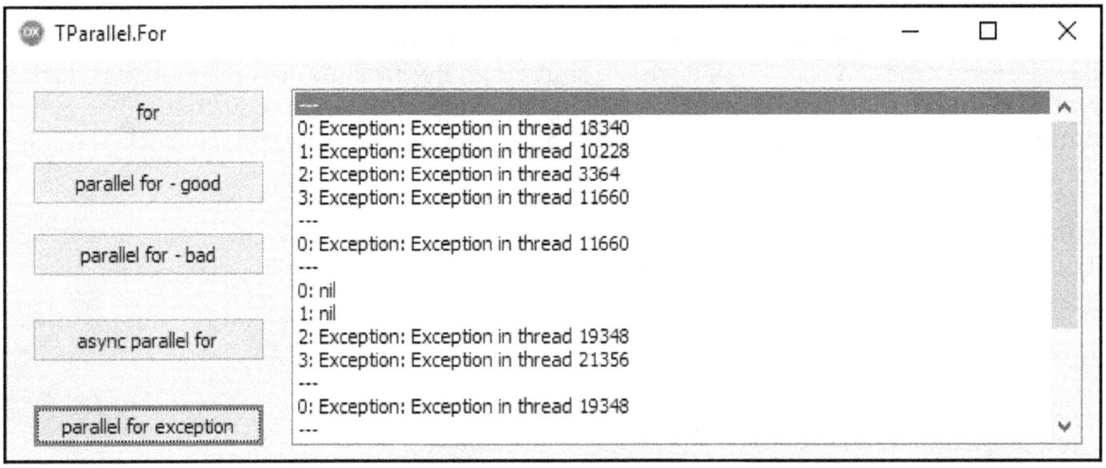

I did some debugging and found out that this is caused by an improperly designed code in the Parallel Programming Library, which sometimes tries to access fields from a destroyed object. As we can have no idea what additional problems that may cause, it is best that the parallel iteration code doesn't raise any exceptions.

Pipelines

So far, I have discussed two different categories of problems that can be solved using patterns. In the first category, there are long operations that we just want to push into the background. We are happy with the execution time, but we would like to keep the user interface responsive, and so we need to execute them in a background thread. *Async/Await* and *Future* are tools for this occasion.

In the second category, there are problems that can be split into parts that are independent or mostly independent of each other. We can use *Join*, *Join/Await*, or *Parallel for* to parallelize them and implement the "mostly" part with locking or interlocked operations.

This, however, doesn't even nearly cover all the use cases. There's at least one big category left that is hard to parallelize with the Parallel Programming Library tools. I'm talking about problems that are hard to split into parts but where operations executed on a given data item (an atomic part of the input data) can be split into stages.

To work on such problems, we need a pattern that can transfer data from one stage to another. In Thread Building Blocks, such a pattern is called the *Flow graph*, while OmniThreadLibrary implements the less powerful *Pipeline*. As OmniThreadLibrary is much easier to use with Delphi, I'll focus on the latter.

> **TIP:** OmniThreadLibrary is simple to set up. You can use Delphi's GetIt Package Manager, or you can surf to `www.omnithreadlibrary.com` and follow the instructions on the *Download* page.

Explaining the *pipeline* concept is easiest with a concrete example. And describing an example is much less confusing if it is backed with code. I'll therefore focus on the `ParallelPipeline` demo, which is included with the book. The code archive also contains a copy of OmniThreadLibrary, so you can just open the demo, press *F9*, and the code will compile.

The `ParallelPipeline` demo implements a very simple source code analyzer. It runs on all files with the extension `.pas` in some folder (including subfolders), for each file counts the number of lines, words, and characters in a file, and displays cumulative statistics for all found files.

From the implementation view, the program must enumerate over the folders and for each file do the following:

- Read the file from the disk into the buffer
- Count the number of lines, words, and characters in that buffer
- Update cumulative statistics with information about that file

We can parallelize this operation by first finding all files in the folder, storing their names in a string list, and using *Parallel for* to process that list. If we do so, however, we have to wait until the initial file list is built, and that can take some time, especially if there's lots of files and they are stored on a network server. We would rather start working immediately after the first filename is known, and a pipeline is designed exactly for that.

To create a pipeline, we must think about the problem in a different way: as a series of work stages, connected with communication channels. In a way, we are implementing my favorite technique of speeding up programs—*changing the algorithm*.

In our problem, the first stage is just enumerating files. Its input is the name of the folder that is to be scanned, and its output is a list of files with extension `.pas` files found in that folder and its subfolders. Instead of storing the names of found files in some list, the stage is writing them into a communication channel.

The second stage is a simple file reader. It is connected to the first stage by using a shared communication channel—the first stage is writing into the channel, and the second stage is reading from it. This stage reads the next filename from the channel, opens the file, reads its content into some buffer, and writes that buffer into its own output channel.

This pattern of stage - channel - stage - channel ... then continues. The third stage reads data buffers from its input (which is at the same time the output of the second stage), performs analysis on the data, and writes the result of the analysis into its own output.

The last, fourth stage collects all of the partial analysis results and generates the summary report, which the main program accesses after the job is done.

In that way, we can create a sequence of small workers, connected with communication channels. The nice part about this approach is that the workers are completely independent and because of that simple to parallelize. None of them are accessing any shared data at all. The only shared parts are communication channels, but they are implemented and managed by the pattern, and so your code doesn't have to care about them.

This independence of stages also means that we can execute more than one instance of some stage if we think that the stage will be executing slower than other stages in the chain. To support this, the communication channel used to connect stages must support multiple simultaneous readers and writers. This can be achieved either by locking (as in Delphi's `TThreadedQueue<T>`) or by using interlocked operations (in OmniThreadLibrary's `TOmniQueue` and `IOmniBlockingCollection`).

The pipeline built by the demo program uses that extensively. It implements only one instance of the first and last stage, two instances of the statistics analysis stage, and multiple instances (depending on the number of cores in the system) of the file-reading stage. Accessing files is a relatively slow operation that doesn't use much CPU, and it makes sense to run it in parallel.

The following diagram shows the pipeline created by the `ParallelPipeline` demo. You will notice that there are two additional communication channels that I only hinted at. The first stage also has a communication channel on the input, and the last stage on the output. They will be typically used by the main program to provide initial data (the starting folder in our example) and to read the result (cumulative statistics). In OmniThreadLibrary, they are accessed through the pipeline's `Input` and `Output` properties:

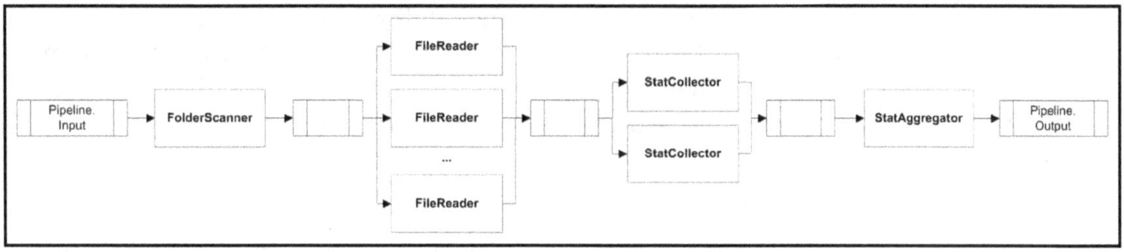

Creating the pipeline

Let's look at the code now. The user interface has one button that can both start and stop the parallel operation. It's `OnClick` event is shown as follows. When starting the process, it calls the `CreatePipeline` method. To stop the process, it just calls the pipeline's `Cancel` method. The pipeline object will be destroyed later, through a termination event. I'll return to that part later.

```
procedure TfrmPipeline.btnStartClick(Sender: TObject);
begin
  if btnStart.Tag = 0 then begin
    ListBox1.Items.Add(inpStartFolder.Text);
```

```
      CreatePipeline;
      btnStart.Caption := 'Stop';
      btnStart.Tag := 1;
      TimerUpdateProcessing.Enabled := true;
    end
    else
      if assigned(FPipeline) then
        FPipeline.Cancel;
  end;
```

The `CreatePipeline` method (shown as follows) creates, configures, and starts the pipeline. First, `FPipeline: IOmniPipeline` (a form field) is created by calling the `Parallel.Pipeline` method. In OmniThreadLibrary, the `Parallel` class functions as a factory for all patterns, similar to Delphi's own `TParallel` class.

Next, the code creates all four stages by calling the `Stage` function for each of them. Some stages require additional configuration to set the number of instances, to specify message handlers, and to limit the size of the output queue. For example, the first stage (`FolderScanner`) and the last stage (`StatAggregator`) are created without any additional configuration, while the code specifies that there should be two instances of the third stage (`StatCollector`) by calling `NumTasks(2)` after specifying the stage method.

> TIP
>
> In OmniThreadLibrary, functions usually follow the *fluent* programming style. Almost every `IOmniPipeline` method is implemented as a function that returns `Self`. That allows you to chain method calls. In the following code, this behavior is used when configuring the second stage (`Stage().NumTasks().Throttle()`) and the third stage (`Stage().NumTasks()`).

The configuration of the second stage (`FileReader`) is the most complex. Besides setting the number of parallel tasks for this stage to the number of CPUs that are available to the process, we also limit the size of the output queue to 1,000 items (`Throttle(1000)`) and specify the function that will process messages sent from the stage to the main thread (`Parallel.TaskConfig.OnMessage`).

The code also sets up an event handler, which will be called (in the main thread) after all the pipeline tasks complete their execution (`OnStopInvoke`). This event handler is also called when the process is cancelled by the user.

After all the configuration is done, the code calls `Run` to start the pipeline. Tasks for all stages will be created, and each will try to read from its own communication channel. As there is no data present in the channels yet, they will all simply go to sleep until some data appears. At this point, the pipeline doesn't use any CPU.

To kickstart the process, the code writes the starting folder into the pipeline's input (`FPipeline.Input.Add`). This will wake the `FolderScanner` stage, which will scan the folder, send all found files to the output channel, and so on. After that, it will try to read the next starting folder from the input, and, as there will be no data present, the stage will again go to sleep.

As the code knows that there's only one input element to be processed, we want to prevent that. After the first stage is done with its input, it should exit and not try to read the next element. We can enforce that by calling the `CompleteAdding` method on the input channel. This puts the channel into *completed* mode, which indicates that no more data can be written into the channel, thus allowing the first stage to stop:

```
procedure TfrmPipeline.CreatePipeline;
begin
  FPipeline := Parallel.Pipeline;
  FPipeline.Stage(FolderScanner);
  FPipeline.Stage(FileReader,
                  Parallel.TaskConfig.OnMessage(HandleFileReaderMessage))
    .NumTasks(Environment.Process.Affinity.Count)
    .Throttle(1000);
  FPipeline.Stage(StatCollector)
    .NumTasks(2);
  FPipeline.Stage(StatAggregator);

  FPipeline.OnStopInvoke(ShowResult);

  FPipeline.Run;

  FPipeline.Input.Add(inpStartFolder.Text);
  FPipeline.Input.CompleteAdding;
end;
```

When the first stage is done processing the data, it will put its output channel into *completed* mode, which will allow the second stage to stop. In that way, the indication that the pipeline is finished with its work trickles down the communication channels. A similar mechanism is used by the `Cancel` method, which is used to cancel currently running operations.

A note on communication channel size and throttling is in order at this point. By default, each communication channel can store up to 10,240 elements. After that number is reached, the *producer* (the task writing into the channel) will go to sleep when it tries to write a new data item to the channel. Only when the channel becomes partially empty (by default that happens when it is under 75% full), will the producer awaken.

This mechanism was implemented so that one very fast task cannot produce so much data that it fills up the computer's memory. The default value sometimes needs manual adjustment, though. That's why the second stage limits its output to 1,000 data buffers. A content of a file can be relatively big, especially compared with other outputs (a filename outputted from stage one and statistics data outputted from stage three).

I must admit that the number of tasks I specified for stages two and three was not determined scientifically, but by guesswork. In a real-life application, it would be prudent to test such a program with different configuration parameters (different number of tasks and different communication channel sizes) on local and network folders. A true *flow graph* implementation should do such tuning automatically, but `IOmniPipeline` was never designed to do that but to be a simple and powerful pattern that can be easily controlled.

Stages

Let us now see how the stages are implemented. The first stage, `FolderScanner`, scans a folder and writes all found Pascal files to the output. Its implementation is shown as follows.

The stage method receives two parameters of type `IOmniBlockingCollection`, which represent its input and output communication channel, and an optional parameter that allows access to the task that runs the stage code (`task: IOmniTask`).

An `IOmniBlockingCollection` channel contains items of type `TOmniValue`, which is a fast variation of Delphi's `Variant` or `TValue`. This type can store any other Delphi data type inside.

A typical stage would run a `for value in input` loop to read all the data from the input. This `for` doesn't exit if there is no data on the input but simply enters a *wait* state, which uses no CPU power. Only when the `input` is put into *completed* mode *and* there is no data inside will the `for` exit.

TIP

We know that the input will only contain one item, so we could also just call the `input.TryTake` function to read that value. The approach implemented in the `FolderScanner` method is more flexible, though.

The code then uses the helper function, `DSiEnumFilesEx`, from the `DSiWin32` library, which is included with the OmniThreadLibrary. This function scans folders and their subfolders and calls an anonymous method for each found file.

This anonymous method first checks whether the operation should be aborted by calling `task.CancellationToken.IsSignalled`. If so, it will set the `stopEnum` flag, which tells `DSIEnumFilesEx` to stop enumerating files and to exit. If everything is OK, however, it concatenates the folder and filename parts and writes them to the output. A `TryAdd` method is used instead of `Add`, as this call may fail when the pipeline is cancelled (when the code calls `IOmniPipeline.Cancel`):

```
procedure TfrmPipeline.FolderScanner(
  const input, output: IOmniBlockingCollection;
  const task: IOmniTask);
var
  value: TOmniValue;
begin
  for value in input do begin
    DSiEnumFilesEx(
      IncludeTrailingPathDelimiter(value) + '*.pas', 0, true,
      procedure (const folder: string; S: TSearchRec;
                 isAFolder: boolean; var stopEnum: boolean)
      begin
        stopEnum := task.CancellationToken.IsSignalled;
        if (not stopEnum) and (not isAFolder) then
          output.TryAdd(IncludeTrailingPathDelimiter(folder) + S.Name);
      end);
  end;
end;
```

The second stage, `FileReader`, is implemented with a similar loop. It also checks the cancellation token and exits if it is signaled. Without that check, the stage would always process all data waiting in its input queue before exiting, even if the pipeline was cancelled.

Inside the loop, the code loads the contents of a file to a string list. An implicit operator converts `value` into a string parameter, needed in the `LoadFromFile` method. After that, the `TStringList` is sent to the output queue. To assure that somebody will always destroy this object, even if the list is canceled, it is best to store it as an *owned object*. It will then be reference-counted and destroyed when appropriate:

```
procedure TfrmPipeline.FileReader(
  const input, output: IOmniBlockingCollection;
  const task: IOmniTask);
var
  sl: TStringList;
  value: TOmniValue;
  outValue: TOmniValue;
begin
  for value in input do begin
    if task.CancellationToken.IsSignalled then
```

```
        break;

      sl := TStringList.Create;
      try
        sl.LoadFromFile(value);
        outValue.AsOwnedObject := sl;
        sl := nil;
        output.TryAdd(outValue);
        task.Comm.Send(MSG_OK, value);
      except
        task.Comm.Send(MSG_ERROR, value);
        FreeAndNil(sl);
      end;
    end;
  end;
```

The preceding code sends a message to the main thread when a file is read or when an exception is raised when accessing a file. This message is sent via OmniThreadLibrary's built-in message channel (`task.Comm`) and is dispatched to the `HandleFileReaderMessage` method, which was specified as a message handler while building the pipeline.

This following method displays all errors on the screen but only stores the currently processed file in a global field. It would be useless to overflow the user interface with information on all processed files, and so the code is using a timer (not shown in the book), which every quarter of a second displays the current `FLastProcessed` on screen:

```
procedure TfrmPipeline.HandleFileReaderMessage(
  const task: IOmniTaskControl;
  const msg: TOmniMessage);
begin
  if msg.MsgID = MSG_ERROR then
    ListBox1.ItemIndex := ListBox1.Items.Add('*** ' + msg.MsgData)
  else
    FLastProcessed := msg.MsgData;
end;
```

Let's move to the third stage, `StatCollector`, which analyzes one file. It is implemented as a *simple stage*, meaning that the `for .. in` loop is implemented in the pipeline pattern itself. The pattern also handles the cancellation.

This approach is ideal when each input value produces zero or one output value. The stage method is called once for each item read from the input channel. If the stage writes anything into its `output` parameter, that value is written to the stage's output channel. If the stage leaves `output` untouched, nothing is written out.

The third stage calls the `GenerateStatistics` function to generate the statistics. I decided not to show it in the book, as the implementation is not relevant for the pipeline pattern. The resulting record is assigned to the `output` parameter via a special `FromRecord<T>` function, which can store a record inside `TOmniValue`.

There's no need to destroy the `TStringList` that is contained in each input `TOmniValue`. Because it was assigned to the `AsOwnedObject` property, it will be destroyed automatically:

```
type
  TStatistics = record
    Files: Int64;
    Lines: int64;
    Words: int64;
    Chars: int64;
  end;

procedure TfrmPipeline.StatCollector(const input: TOmniValue;
  var output: TOmniValue);
var
  stat: TStatistics;
begin
  stat := GenerateStatistics(input.ToObject<TStringList>);
  output := TOmniValue.FromRecord<TStatistics>(stat);
end;
```

The last stage, `StatAggregator`, reads all `TStatistics` records from the input queue. The `ToRecord<T>` function is used to extract record from a `TOmniValue` item. The `Merge` function, which is not shown in the book, merges current aggregate and new partial statistics data together.

Only after all the data is processed (when the `for` loop exits), will the resulting aggregate value be written to the pipeline's output:

```
procedure TfrmPipeline.StatAggregator(const input,
  output: IOmniBlockingCollection; const task: IOmniTask);
var
  aggregate: TStatistics;
  stat: TStatistics;
  value: TOmniValue;
begin
```

```
    aggregate := Default(TStatistics);

    for value in input do begin
      if task.CancellationToken.IsSignalled then
        break;

      stat := value.ToRecord<TStatistics>;
      Merge(aggregate, stat);
    end;

    output.TryAdd(TOmniValue.FromRecord<TStatistics>(aggregate));
  end;
```

If we wanted to implement the parallelization in some other way (for example, with a *Parallel for* pattern), then this part would need to implement locking to access the shared aggregate state. As the pipeline pattern gently guides you to use the data duplication and communication instead, there is no need for sharing, locking, and other complications.

Displaying the result and shutting down

When all tasks have finished execution, the `ShowResult` method is called. It tries to read the result of the computation from the pipeline's output channel by calling `FPipeline.Output.TryTake`. This function will return `false` if the pipeline was cancelled, so no result will be displayed in that case:

```
procedure TfrmPipeline.ShowResult;
var
  value: TOmniValue;
  stat: TStatistics;
begin
  if FPipeline.Output.TryTake(value) then begin
    stat := value.ToRecord<TStatistics>;
    ListBox1.Items.Add(Format(
      'Files: %d, Lines: %d, Words: %d, Characters: %d',
      [stat.Files, stat.Lines, stat.Words, stat.Chars]));
  end;
  Cleanup;
end;
```

At the end, `ShowResult` calls the `Cleanup` method, which destroys the pipeline interface by setting it to `nil`. It also clears and resets the user interface and prepares it for a new operation:

```
procedure TfrmPipeline.Cleanup;
begin
  FPipeline := nil;
  TimerUpdateProcessing.Enabled := false;
  lblProcessing.Visible := false;
  btnStart.Caption := 'Start';
  btnStart.Tag := 0;
end;
```

Pipelines are a very interesting concept that implements the *data duplication* and *communication* paradigms to the max. It allows for the parallelization of many different problems that don't fit into other patterns.

Summary

This was the final chapter, dedicated to multithreading, which put a finishing touch on a story line that started in `Chapter 5`, *Getting Started with the Parallel World*. I started by describing all the bad things that can happen when writing parallel code, then spent one chapter showing the cumbersome `TThread`, which makes multithreaded code such an unnecessary pain, and then in this chapter I finally moved on to the nice parts of the puzzle—tasks and patterns.

The chapter opened with a discussion of tasks and patterns—what they are and how they can be used to simplify multithreaded programming. For a bonus, I threw in a short treatise about variable capturing, which focused only on one problematic part—the capturing of a loop variable.

Then we looked at how we can use tasks to split a loop into multiple parallel loops. We saw that there's quite some work involved, particularly around task creation and setup. On the way, we also learned about the thread-pooling concept.

The last part of the very long section on tasks discussed the exception handling. We learned that it is quite hard to correctly capture in the main thread exceptions that were raised inside a task and that it is better to catch all task exceptions explicitly in the code.

After that, we finally moved from the (merely acceptable) tasks to (fun and simple) patterns. For starters, I've shown how to implement a very simple *Async/Await* pattern, something that is missing from the Parallel Programming Library.

Next on the list was the *Join* pattern. This very simple tool sometimes allows for very efficient parallelization of completely independent pieces of code. Sadly, I also had to demonstrate a failing in the current Delphi implementation, and I provided two workarounds. I also implemented a more powerful and simpler *Join/Await*, which allows you to capture exceptions raised in tasks.

After that, we looked into the *Future* (with a capital F). This interesting and powerful pattern allows you to execute a function in a task, while it simplifies accessing the function result in the main thread. The Delphi implementation of this pattern is quite flexible and can be used in different ways.

As the last Parallel Programming Library pattern, I covered *Parallel For*. This pattern allows for a very simple parallelization of a standard `for` loop. I cautioned you about the problems that can sprout from its use, and I added a short trick that demonstrated how to create a non-blocking Parallel for.

At the end of the chapter, I moved to my own OmniThreadLibrary. From all the patterns it implements, I picked the one that is, in my opinion, the most powerful—the *Pipeline*. I used it to implement a small utility: a filesystem scanner that generates simple file statistics. If you are interested in knowing more about OmniThreadLibrary, you should read the book that focuses on this topic, *Parallel Programming with OmniThreadLibrary* (`www.omnithreadlibrary.com/tutorials.htm`).

I could spend a lot longer discussing parallel programming and parallel patterns. I could fill up a whole book, without doubt. As this is not a book on parallel programming, but a book about high-performance practices, I have to move on to the last topic. In the next chapter, we'll see what we can do if Delphi can't handle something and we have to bring in another compiler.

8
Using External Libraries

We've seen many different ways of improving program speed in this book. We've changed algorithms, reduced the number of memory allocations, fine-tuned the code, made parts of programs parallel, and more. Sometimes, however, all of this is not enough. Maybe the problem is too hard and we give up, or maybe the fault lies in Delphi; more specifically, in the compiler.

In such cases, we will look outside the boundary of a local computer or company, and search the internet for a solution. Maybe, somebody has already solved the problem and created a nicely wrapped solution for it. Sometimes, we'll be able to find it. Most of the time, it will **not** be written with Delphi in mind.

Face it, Delphi programmers (even though there are millions of us) are still a minority in a world of C, Java, and Python. It is much simpler to find a C or C++ solution for hard problems than a Delphi one. This is, however, not a reason to give up. It is always possible—with a bit of hard work—to use such a solution in a Delphi program, even if it is pre-packaged for C or C++ users.

In this chapter, we'll answer the following questions:

- What are the types of C and C++ files that you can use in your projects?
- What are the most frequently used object file formats?
- Which object formats can be used in Delphi projects?
- What traps await you when you try to link object files to Delphi?
- How can you use C++ libraries in Delphi projects?

Using object files

Before I jump into the complicated world of interfacing with C and C++, I'll introduce a simpler example—a library written in Delphi. The motivation for its use comes not from a bad algorithm that Mr. Smith wrote, but from a badly performing 64-bit compiler. This is not something that I am claiming without proof. Multiple Delphi programmers have pointed out that the 64-bit Windows compiler (dcc64) generates pretty bad floating point code that is 2-3 times slower than the floating point generated from an equivalent source by a C compiler.

When you have already explored all the standard approaches of speeding up the program, and the compiler is the only source of the problem, you cannot do much. You can only rewrite parts of the program in the assembler, or use an external library that works faster than the native code. Such a library will either use lots of assembler code or—most of the time—contain a bunch of object files compiled with an optimizing C compiler.

Sometimes, such an external library will only cover your basic needs. For example, the `FastMath` library, which is written in Delphi (`https://github.com/neslib/FastMath`) contains floating-point functions that operate on vectors and matrices. Others, such as *Intel's Math Kernel Library* (`https://software.intel.com/en-us/mkl/`) also add more complicated mathematical algorithms, such as Fast Fourier Transform.

For a short example, let's look into `FastMath` and how it implements a `Radians` function that converts a vector of four floating-point numbers (`TVector4`) from degrees to radians. For your convenience, the copy of the `FastMath` repository is included in the code archive for this chapter, in the `FastMath-master` folder.

As a fallback, the library implements a pure Pascal `Radians` function in the `Neslib.FastMath.Pascal.inc` file. The trivial implementation shown in the following, only calls the `Radians` function for a single-precision argument four times:

```
function Radians(const ADegrees: Single): Single;
begin
  Result := ADegrees * (Pi / 180);
end;

function Radians(const ADegrees: TVector4): TVector4;
begin
  Result.Init(Radians(ADegrees.X), Radians(ADegrees.Y),
    Radians(ADegrees.Z), Radians(ADegrees.W));
end;
```

A different implementation in unit `Neslib.FastMath.Sse2_32.inc` (shown in the following) implements the same method with much faster Intel SSE2 assembler instructions. A similar code in `Neslib.FastMath.Sse2_64.inc` (which is not shown in the book but can be found in the `FastMath` folder in the code archive) does the same for a 64-bit Intel target:

```
function Radians(const ADegrees: TVector4): TVector4; assembler;
asm
  movups xmm0, [ADegrees]
  movups xmm1, [SSE_PI_OVER_180]
  mulps xmm0, xmm1
  movups [Result], xmm0
end;
```

For ARM platforms (Android and iOS) the same code is implemented in `trig_32.S` (and `trig_64.S` for 64-bit platforms). A fragment of that file showing 32-bit implementation is reproduced in the following:

```
_radians_vector4: // (const ADegrees: TVector4; out Result: TVector4);
  adr r2, PI_OVER_180
  vld1.32 {q0}, [r0]
  vld1.32 {q1}, [r2]
  vmul.f32 q0, q0, q1
  vst1.32 {q0}, [r1]
  bx lr
```

The batch files in `fastmath-android` and `fastmath-ios` folders use native development tools, made by Google and Apple, to compile assembler sources into the object libraries, `libfastmath-android.a` and `libfastmath-ios.a`. Functions are then linked to this library in the `Neslib.FastMath.Internal.inc` unit with a mechanism that we'll explore in the continuation of this chapter.

A simple series of `$IF`/`$INCLUDE` statements then links those include files in one unit, `Neslib.FastMath.pas`:

```
{$IF Defined(FM_PASCAL)}
// Pascal implementations
{$INCLUDE 'Neslib.FastMath.Pascal.inc'}
{$ELSEIF Defined(FM_X86)}
// 32-bit SSE2 implementations
{$INCLUDE 'Neslib.FastMath.Sse2_32.inc'}
{$ELSEIF Defined(FM_X64)}
// 64-bit SSE2 implementations
{$INCLUDE 'Neslib.FastMath.Sse2_64.inc'}
{$ELSEIF Defined(FM_ARM)}
// Arm NEON/Arm64 implementations
```

```
{$INCLUDE 'Neslib.FastMath.Arm.inc'}
{$ENDIF}
```

This design allows the library to present a unified application interface that uses the best implementation for each platform to your Delphi application.

In this case, the implementation is linked against a static library (`.a`). This will not be the case when trying to include a C-specific solution in a Delphi project. You'll have a bunch of object files (`.obj`, `.o`) instead.

Object files are a complicated topic, as there is not a single standard governing them, but a bunch of competing specifications. Before we start using them in Delphi, we should therefore have at least some understanding of what is encountered in the wild.

Object file formats

Object files come in different formats and not all are useful for linking with Delphi. The three most common file formats that you'll encounter are *OMF*, *COFF*, and *ELF*.

The **Relocatable Object Module Format** (**OMF**) is a format developed by Intel. It was extensively used in DOS times. Support for linking OMF object files was already included in Turbo Pascal DOS compilers and is still present in modern Delphi.

> This format can be linked with Delphi's Win32 and compilers. It is generated by the C++Builder's Win32 compiler (bcc32).

To analyze an OMF file you can use the `tdump` utility (part of the Delphi and C++Builder standard installation) with the `-d` switch. A command such as `tdump -d object_file.obj` will output a bunch of information about the OMF file. It is best if you *redirect* this output into a file by using the command-line redirect functionality. For example, you can type `tdump -d object_file.obj > object_file.txt` to redirect the output to `object_file.txt`.

Once you have the file, search for entries with labels `PUBDEF` or `PUBD32` to find names of exported functions. You can also use the command-line parameter `-oiPUBDEF` (or `-oiPUBD32`) to limit output to `PUBDEF (PUBD32)` records.

The following output shows the results of the command `tdump -d -oiPUBDeF LzmaDec.obj`. The file, `LzmaDec.obj` is part of the code archive for this chapter and will be used as an example in the next section. We can see that this object file contains the functions, `LzmaDec_InitDicAndState`, `LzmaDec_Init`, and so on. These functions can, with some work, be used from a Delphi program:

```
Turbo Dump Version 6.5.4.0 Copyright (c) 1988-2016 Embarcadero
Technologies, Inc.
Display of File lzmadec.obj
002394 PUBDEF 'LzmaDec_InitDicAndState' Segment: _TEXT:172E
0023B5 PUBDEF 'LzmaDec_Init' Segment: _TEXT:176B
0023CB PUBDEF 'LzmaDec_DecodeToDic' Segment: _TEXT:17D2
0023E8 PUBDEF 'LzmaDec_DecodeToBuf' Segment: _TEXT:1A6E
002405 PUBDEF 'LzmaDec_FreeProbs' Segment: _TEXT:1B40
002420 PUBDEF 'LzmaDec_Free' Segment: _TEXT:1B78
002436 PUBDEF 'LzmaProps_Decode' Segment: _TEXT:1B9B
002450 PUBDEF 'LzmaDec_AllocateProbs' Segment: _TEXT:1C9A
00246F PUBDEF 'LzmaDec_Allocate' Segment: _TEXT:1CE5
002489 PUBDEF 'LzmaDecode' Segment: _TEXT:1D6D
```

The second file format that you'll frequently encounter is **Common Object File Format** (**COFF**). It was introduced in *Unix System V* and is generated by Microsoft's Visual C++ compilers. Delphi Win32 and Win64 compilers can link to it.

To dump this file, use Embarcadero's `tdump` with the `-E` switch, or Microsoft's `dumpbin` utility, which is part of Visual Studio.

The third most popular object format is **Executable and Linkable Format** (**ELF**). It is mostly used on Unix platforms. This format is used in the *LLVM* compiler infrastructure and as such, is supported by some Delphi and C++Builder compilers—namely the ones that use the LLVM toolchain. This file format is not supported by the `tdump` utility.

ELF format is not supported by current Win32 and Win64 Delphi compilers. Usually, that would not present a big problem, except that the Win64 C++Builder compiler (bcc64) uses the LLVM infrastructure and therefore generates object files in ELF format. As far as I can tell, there's currently no way to use the C++Builder to generate 64-bit object files that can be linked to Delphi.

Object file linking in practice

To demonstrate some typical problems that you may run into when trying to link object files to Delphi, I picked two simple examples from the *Abbrevia* open source library. Abbrevia was originally a commercial compression library developed by TurboPower. They were selling multiple libraries—AsyncPro, Orpheus, and SysTools, which were later donated to the open source community. Their current home is at `https://github.com/TurboPack`.

For simplicity, I have included the complete Abbrevia repository in the code archive. All demos are already configured so you can just press *F9* in Delphi and enjoy.

The first demo is called `LzmaDecTest` and it links in a single object file—`LzmaDec.obj`. That file is stored in the `Abbrevia\source\Win32` folder (or `Win64` if you are compiling for 64-bit Windows). This demo is a standard Windows console application with one additional line linking the object file:

```
{$L LzmaDec.obj}
```

If you try to compile the test project, you'll notice that compilation fails with the following error message:

```
[dcc32 Error] LzmaDecTest.dpr(22): E2065 Unsatisfied forward or external
declaration: 'memcpy'
```

This happens a lot when linking object files created with C compilers. An object file can contain references to functions that are not implemented inside the object file. The same situation happens with Delphi—a `.dcu` file can (and most probably will) contain references to methods implemented in different units.

An experienced programmer will try to minimize these dependencies when writing a library, simply because that helps with portability, but there are always some basic functions that are necessary in almost all C programs. Think of the Delphi's *System unit*—all units in your program implicitly depend on it and most of the time you are not aware of that (and you don't have to be). Most of the object files that you'll have to link to will be compiled with Microsoft's C compiler, and typically they will depend on a `msvcrt` library.

There are two ways out of this problem. Firstly, you can write the missing functions yourself. They are implemented by the `MSVCRT.DLL` dynamic library and you only have to link to them.

For example, in our case we would need the missing memcpy function. We can simply import it from the appropriate DLL by adding the following line to the program. We would also have to add the Windows unit to the uses list as the size_t type is defined in it:

```
function memcpy(dest, src: Pointer; count: size_t): Pointer; cdecl;
  external 'msvcrt.dll';
```

Alternatively, we can just add the System.Win.Crtl unit to the uses list. It links to all functions from the MSVCRT.DLL dynamic library.

Be aware though, MSVCRT.DLL is not part of the operating system. If you want to distribute an application that links to this DLL, you should also include the *Microsoft Visual C++ Redistributable* package, which you can download from the Microsoft web server.

For the second demo, I wanted to link to the decompress.obj file, which is also part of Abbrevia and is stored in the same folder as LzmaDec.obj. This demo is named DecompressTest.

Again, I started with an empty console application to which I added {$LINK decompress.obj}. ({$L} and ${LINK} are synonyms.) The compiler reported four errors:

```
[dcc32 Error] DecompressTest.dpr(45): E2065 Unsatisfied forward or external
declaration: 'BZ2_rNums'
[dcc32 Error] DecompressTest.dpr(45): E2065 Unsatisfied forward or external
declaration: 'BZ2_hbCreateDecodeTables'
[dcc32 Error] DecompressTest.dpr(45): E2065 Unsatisfied forward or external
declaration: 'BZ2_indexIntoF'
[dcc32 Error] DecompressTest.dpr(45): E2065 Unsatisfied forward or external
declaration: 'bz_internal_error'
```

To fix such problems, you'll always have to use the documentation that comes with the object files. There's no way to know what those symbols represent simply by looking at the object file. In this case, I found out that the first is an initialization table (so the symbol is actually a name of a global variable). The second and third functions are implemented in other object files, and the last one is an error handling function that we have to implement in the code. Adding the following code fragment to the file left me with two errors:

```
var
  BZ2_rNums: array[0..511] of Longint;

procedure bz_internal_error(errcode: Integer); cdecl;
begin
  raise Exception.CreateFmt('Compression Error %d', [errcode]);
end;
```

Take note of the calling convention used here. C object files will almost invariably use the `cdecl` convention.

To find the object files with missing functions, you can use a full-text search tool that handles binary files, and searche for missing names. This will give you false positives as it will also return object files that are *using* those functions. You can then use the `tdump` utility to examine potential candidates and find the true source of those units.

Or, you can look into the documentation. But who does that?

I found `BZ2_hbCreateDecodeTables` in `huffman.obj` and `BZ2_indexIntoF` in `bzlib.obj`. Only two lines are needed to add them to the project:

```
{$LINK huffman.obj}
{$LINK bzlib.obj}
```

That fixes the two errors about missing symbols but introduces three new errors:

```
[dcc32 Error] DecompressTest.dpr(40): E2065 Unsatisfied forward or external
declaration: 'BZ2_crc32Table'
 [dcc32 Error] DecompressTest.dpr(40): E2065 Unsatisfied forward or
external declaration: 'BZ2_compressBlock'
 [dcc32 Error] DecompressTest.dpr(40): E2065 Unsatisfied forward or
external declaration: 'BZ2_decompress'
```

`BZ2_crc32Table` is an initialization table (says the documentation) so we need another variable:

```
var
  BZ2_crc32Table: array[0..255] of Longint;
```

Further detective work found `BZ2_compressBlock` in the file `compress.obj`, so let's add this to the project. We only have to add one line:

```
{$LINK compress.obj}
```

The second error is trickier. Research showed that this function is actually implemented in the `decompress.obj` unit, which is already linked to the project! Why is the error reported then? Simply because that's how the single-pass Delphi compiler works.

As it turns out, the compiler will happily resolve symbols used by object file *A* if they are defined in object file *B*, which is loaded **after** file *A*. It will, however, **not** resolve symbols used by object file *B* if they are defined in object file *A*.

In our case, the `compress.obj` file needs the `BZ2_decompress` symbol, which is defined in `decompress.obj`, but as the latter is linked **before** the former, we get the error. You could try rearranging the units but then some other symbol will not be found.

Luckily, this problem is very simple to fix. We just have to tell the compiler that `BZ2_decompress` exists. The compiler is happy with that and produces workable code. When all units are compiled, *linker* kicks in to collect them in the EXE file. Linker is smarter than the compiler and finds the correct implementation, regardless of the include order.

If we add the following line to the code, the error about *unsatisfied* `BZ2_decompress` *declaration* goes away. I also like putting in a comment that marks the source of the function:

```
procedure BZ2_decompress; external; //decompress.obj
```

Linking `compress.obj` causes three new errors to appear:

```
[dcc32 Error] DecompressTest.dpr(45): E2065 Unsatisfied forward or external
declaration: 'BZ2_hbMakeCodeLengths'
[dcc32 Error] DecompressTest.dpr(45): E2065 Unsatisfied forward or external
declaration: 'BZ2_hbAssignCodes'
[dcc32 Error] DecompressTest.dpr(45): E2065 Unsatisfied forward or external
declaration: 'BZ2_blockSort'
```

The first two are defined in `huffman.obj`, which is already linked, so we have to add the following two lines to the code:

```
procedure BZ2_hbMakeCodeLengths; external; //huffman.obj
procedure BZ2_hbAssignCodes; external;     //huffman.obj
```

The last one comes from `blocksort.obj`, which we have yet to link in. After that, the code finally compiles:

```
{$LINK blocksort.obj}
```

This is, of course, just the first step toward a working program. Now we have to check how functions exported from these object files are actually defined. Then, we have to add appropriate `external` declarations to the Delphi source.

If we look at the previous example, `LzmaDecTest`, we can implement functions to initialize and free the decoder by adding the following two lines:

```
procedure LzmaDec_Init(var state); cdecl; external;
procedure LzmaDec_Free(var state; alloc: pointer); cdecl; external;
```

This declaration is actually incomplete, as the first parameter to both functions should be a complicated record, which I didn't want to try to decipher just for this simple demo. Rather than do that (and a whole lotta additional work), I would use the already-prepared Abbrevia library.

By now, you've probably noticed that linking in object files is hard work. If at all possible, you should try to find a Delphi (or at least a Free Pascal) wrapper. Even if it covers only a part of the functionality you need, it will spare you hours and hours of work.

Using C++ libraries

Using C object files in Delphi is hard but possible. Linking to C++ object files is, however, nearly impossible. The problem does not lie within the object files themselves, but in C++.

While C is hardly more than an assembler with improved syntax, C++ represents a sophisticated high-level language with runtime support for strings, objects, exceptions, and more. All these features are part of almost any C++ program and are as such compiled into (almost) any object file produced by C++.

The problem here is that Delphi has no idea how to deal with any of that. A C++ object is not equal to a Delphi object. Delphi has no idea how to call functions of a C++ object, how to deal with its inheritance chain, how to create and destroy such objects, and so on. The same holds for strings, exceptions, streams, and other C++ concepts.

If you can compile the C++ source with C++Builder then you can create a package (`.bpl`) that can be used from a Delphi program. Most of the time, however, you will not be dealing with a source project. Instead, you'll want to use a commercial library that only gives you a bunch of C++ header files (`.h`) and one or more static libraries (`.lib`). Most of the time, the only Windows version of that library will be compiled with Microsoft's Visual Studio.

A more general approach to this problem is to introduce a *proxy* DLL created in C++. You will have to create it in the same development environment as was used to create the library you are trying to link into the project. On Windows, that will in most cases be Visual Studio. That will enable us to include the library without any problems.

To allow Delphi to use this DLL (and as such use the library), the DLL should expose a simple interface in the Windows API style. Instead of exposing C++ objects, the API must expose methods implemented by the objects as normal (non-object) functions and procedures. As the objects cannot cross the API boundary we must find some other way to represent them on the Delphi side.

Instead of showing how to write a DLL wrapper for an existing (and probably quite complicated) C++ library, I have decided to write a very simple C++ library that exposes a single class, implementing only two methods. As compiling this library requires Microsoft's Visual Studio, which not all of you have installed, I have also included the compiled version (`DllLib1.dll`) in the code archive.

The Visual Studio solution is stored in the `StaticLib1` folder and contains two projects. `StaticLib1` is the project used to create the library while the `Dll1` project implements the proxy DLL.

The static library implements the `CppClass` class, which is defined in the header file, `CppClass.h`. Whenever you are dealing with a C++ library, the distribution will also contain one or more header files. They are needed if you want to use a library in a C++ project—such as in the proxy DLL `Dll1`.

The header file for the demo library `StaticLib1` is shown in the following. We can see that the code implements a single `CppClass` class, which implements a constructor (`CppClass()`), destructor (`~CppClass()`), a method accepting an integer parameter (`void setData(int)`), and a function returning an integer (`int getSquare()`). The class also contains one integer private field, `data`:

```
#pragma once
class CppClass
{
  int data;
public:
  CppClass();
  ~CppClass();
  void setData(int);
  int getSquare();
};
```

The implementation of the `CppClass` class is stored in the `CppClass.cpp` file. You don't need this file when implementing the proxy DLL. When we are using a C++ library, we are strictly coding to the interface—and the interface is stored in the header file.

In our case, we have the full source so we can look inside the implementation too. The constructor and destructor don't do anything and so I'm not showing them here. The other two methods are as follows. The `setData` method stores its parameter in the internal field and the `getSquare` function returns the squared value of the internal field:

```
void CppClass::setData(int value)
{
  data = value;
```

```
}

int CppClass::getSquare()
{
  return data * data;
}
```

This code doesn't contain anything that we couldn't write in 60 seconds in Delphi. It does, however, serve as a perfect simple example for writing a proxy DLL.

Creating such a DLL in Visual Studio is easy. You just have to select **File** | **New** | **Project**, and select the **Dynamic-Link Library (DLL)** project type from the **Visual C++** | **Windows Desktop** branch.

The `Dll1` project from the code archive has only two source files. The file, `dllmain.cpp` was created automatically by Visual Studio and contains the standard `DllMain` method. You can change this file if you have to run project-specific code when a program and/or a thread attaches to, or detaches from, the DLL. In my example, this file was left just as the Visual Studio created it.

The second file, `StaticLibWrapper.cpp` fully implements the proxy DLL. It starts with two `include` lines (shown in the following) which bring in the required RTL header `stdafx.h` and the header definition for our C++ class, `CppClass.h`:

```
#include "stdafx.h"
#include "CppClass.h"
```

The proxy has to be able to find our header file. There are two ways to do that. We could simply copy it to the folder containing the source files for the DLL project, or we can add it to the project's search path. The second approach can be configured in **Project** | **Properties** | **Configuration Properties** | **C/C++** | **General** | **Additional Include Directories**. This is also the approach used by the demonstration program.

The DLL project must be able to find the static library that implements the `CppClass` object. The path to the library file should be set in project options, in the **Configuration Properties** | **Linker** | **General** | **Additional Library Directories** settings. You should put the name of the library (`StaticLib1.lib`) in the **Linker** | **Input** | **Additional Dependencies** settings.

The next line in the source file defines a macro called EXPORT, which will be used later in the program to mark a function as *exported*. We have to do that for every DLL function that we want to use from the Delphi code. Later, we'll see how this macro is used:

```
#define EXPORT comment(linker, "/EXPORT:" __FUNCTION__ "=" __FUNCDNAME__)
```

The next part of the StaticLibWrapper.cpp file implements an IndexAllocator class, which is used internally to cache C++ objects. It associates C++ objects with simple integer identifiers, which are then used outside the DLL to represent the object. I will not show this class in the book as the implementation is not that important. You only have to know how to use it.

This class is implemented as a simple static array of pointers and contains at most MAXOBJECTS objects. The constant MAXOBJECTS is set to 100 in the current code, which limits the number of C++ objects created by the Delphi code to *100*. Feel free to modify the code if you need to create more objects.

The following code fragment shows three public functions implemented by the IndexAllocator class. The Allocate function takes a pointer obj, stores it in the cache, and returns its index in the deviceIndex parameter. The result of the function is FALSE if the cache is full and TRUE otherwise.

The Release function accepts an index (which was previously returned from Allocate) and marks the cache slot at that index as empty. This function returns FALSE if the index is invalid (does not represent a value returned from Allocate) or if the cache slot for that index is already empty.

The last function, Get, also accepts an index and returns the pointer associated with that index. It returns NULL if the index is invalid or if the cache slot for that index is empty:

```
bool Allocate(int& deviceIndex, void* obj)
bool Release(int deviceIndex)
void* Get(int deviceIndex)
```

Let's move now to functions that are exported from the DLL. The first two—Initialize and Finalize—are used to initialize internal structures, namely the GAllocator of type IndexAllocator and to clean up before the DLL is unloaded. Instead of looking into them, I'd rather show you the more interesting stuff, namely functions that deal with CppClass.

The CreateCppClass function creates an instance of CppClass, stores it in the cache, and returns its index. The important three parts of the declaration are: extern "C", WINAPI, and #pragma EXPORT.

extern "C" is there to guarantee that CreateCppClass name will not be changed when it is stored in the library. The C++ compiler tends to *mangle* (change) function names to support method overloading (the same thing happens in Delphi) and this declaration prevents that.

WINAPI changes the *calling convention* from cdecl, which is standard for C programs, to stdcall, which is commonly used in DLLs. Later, we'll see that we also have to specify the correct calling convention on the Delphi side.

The last important part, #pragma EXPORT, uses the previously defined EXPORT macro to mark this function as *exported.*

The CreateCppClass returns *0* if the operation was successful and -1 if it failed. The same approach is used in all functions exported from the demo DLL:

```
extern "C" int WINAPI CreateCppClass (int& index)
{
#pragma EXPORT
  CppClass* instance = new CppClass;
  if (!GAllocator->Allocate(index, (void*)instance)) {
    delete instance;
    return -1;
  }
  else
    return 0;
}
```

Similarly, the DestroyCppClass function (not shown here) accepts an index parameter, fetches the object from the cache, and destroys it.

The DLL also exports two functions that allow the DLL user to operate on an object. The first one, CppClass_setValue, accepts an index of the object and a value. It fetches the CppClass instance from the cache (given the index) and calls its setData method, passing it the value:

```
extern "C" int WINAPI CppClass_setValue(int index, int value)
{
#pragma EXPORT
  CppClass* instance = (CppClass*)GAllocator->Get(index);
  if (instance == NULL)
    return -1;
  else {
    instance->setData(value);
    return 0;
  }
}
```

The second function, `CppClass_getSquare` also accepts an object index and uses it to access the `CppClass` object. After that, it calls the object's `getSquare` function and stores the result in the output parameter, `value`:

```
extern "C" int WINAPI CppClass_getSquare(int index, int& value)
{
#pragma EXPORT
  CppClass* instance = (CppClass*)GAllocator->Get(index);
  if (instance == NULL)
    return -1;
  else {
    value = instance->getSquare();
    return 0;
  }
}
```

A proxy DLL that uses a mapping table is a bit complicated and requires some work. We could also approach the problem in a much simpler manner—by treating an address of an object as its external identifier. In other words, the `CreateCppClass` function would create an object and then return its address as an untyped pointer type. A `CppClass_getSquare`, for example, would accept this pointer, cast it to a `CppClass` instance, and execute an operation on it. An alternative version of these two methods is shown in the following:

```
extern "C" int WINAPI CreateCppClass2(void*& ptr)
{
#pragma EXPORT
  ptr = new CppClass;
  return 0;
}

extern "C" int WINAPI CppClass_getSquare2(void* index, int& value)
{
#pragma EXPORT
  value = ((CppClass*)index)->getSquare();
  return 0;
}
```

This approach is simpler but offers far less security in the form of error checking. The table-based approach can check whether the index represents a valid value, while the latter version cannot know if the pointer parameter is valid or not. If we make a mistake on the Delphi side and pass in an invalid pointer, the code would treat it as an instance of a class, do some operations on it, possibly corrupt some memory, and maybe crash.

Finding the source of such errors is very hard. That's why I prefer to write more verbose code that implements some safety checks on the code that returns pointers.

Using a proxy DLL in Delphi

To use any DLL from a Delphi program, we must firstly import functions from the DLL. There are different ways to do this—we could use *static* linking, *dynamic* linking, and static linking with *delayed loading*. There's plenty of information on the internet about the art of DLL writing in Delphi so I won't dig into this topic. I'll just stick with the most modern approach—delay loading.

The code archive for this book includes two demo programs, which demonstrate how to use the `DllLib1.dll` library. The simpler one, `CppClassImportDemo` uses the DLL functions directly, while `CppClassWrapperDemo` wraps them in an easy-to-use class.

Both projects use the `CppClassImport` unit to import the DLL functions into the Delphi program. The following code fragment shows the `interface` part of that unit which tells the Delphi compiler which functions from the DLL should be imported, and what parameters they have.

As with the C++ part, there are three important parts to each declaration. Firstly, the `stdcall` specifies that the function call should use the `stdcall` (or what is known in C as `WINAPI`) calling convention. Secondly, the name after the `name` specifier should match the exported function name from the C++ source. And thirdly, the `delayed` keyword specifies that the program should not try to find this function in the DLL when it is started but only when the code calls the function. This allows us to check whether the DLL is present at all before we call any of the functions:

```
const
  CPP_CLASS_LIB = 'DllLib1.dll';

function Initialize: integer;
  stdcall; external CPP_CLASS_LIB name 'Initialize' delayed;
function Finalize: integer;
  stdcall; external CPP_CLASS_LIB name 'Finalize' delayed;
function CreateCppClass(var index: integer): integer;
  stdcall; external CPP_CLASS_LIB name 'CreateCppClass' delayed;
function DestroyCppClass(index: integer): integer;
  stdcall; external CPP_CLASS_LIB name 'DestroyCppClass' delayed;
function CppClass_setValue(index: integer; value: integer): integer;
  stdcall; external CPP_CLASS_LIB name 'CppClass_setValue' delayed;
function CppClass_getSquare(index: integer; var value: integer): integer;
  stdcall; external CPP_CLASS_LIB name 'CppClass_getSquare' delayed;
```

The implementation part of this unit (not shown here) shows how to catch errors that occur during *delayed loading*—that is, when the code that calls any of the imported functions tries to find that function in the DLL.

> If you get an External exception C06D007F exception when you try to call a delay-loaded function, you have probably mistyped a name—either in C++ or in Delphi. You can use the tdump utility that comes with Delphi to check which names are exported from the DLL. The syntax is tdump -d <dll_name.dll>.
>
> If the code crashes when you call a DLL function, check whether both sides correctly define the calling convention. Also check if all the parameters have correct types on both sides and if the var parameters are marked as such on both sides.

To use the DLL, the code in the CppClassMain unit firstly calls the exported Initialize function from the form's OnCreate handler to initialize the DLL. The cleanup function, Finalize is called from the OnDestroy handler to clean up the DLL. All parts of the code check whether the DLL functions return the OK status (value 0):

```
procedure TfrmCppClassDemo.FormCreate(Sender: TObject);
begin
  if Initialize <> 0 then
    ListBox1.Items.Add('Initialize failed')
end;

procedure TfrmCppClassDemo.FormDestroy(Sender: TObject);
begin
  if Finalize <> 0 then
    ListBox1.Items.Add('Finalize failed');
end;
```

When you click on the **Use import library** button, the following code executes. It uses the DLL to create a CppClass object by calling the CreateCppClass function. This function puts an integer value into the idxClass value. This value is used as an identifier that identifies a CppClass object when calling other functions.

The code then calls CppClass_setValue to set the internal field of the CppClass object and CppClass_getSquare to call the getSquare method and to return the calculated value. At the end, DestroyCppClass destroys the CppClass object:

```
procedure TfrmCppClassDemo.btnImportLibClick(Sender: TObject);
var
  idxClass: Integer;
```

```
    value: Integer;
  begin
    if CreateCppClass(idxClass) <> 0 then
      ListBox1.Items.Add('CreateCppClass failed')
    else if CppClass_setValue(idxClass, SpinEdit1.Value) <> 0 then
      ListBox1.Items.Add('CppClass_setValue failed')
    else if CppClass_getSquare(idxClass, value) <> 0 then
      ListBox1.Items.Add('CppClass_getSquare failed')
    else begin
      ListBox1.Items.Add(Format('square(%d) = %d',
        [SpinEdit1.Value, value]));
      if DestroyCppClass(idxClass) <> 0 then
        ListBox1.Items.Add('DestroyCppClass failed')
    end;
  end;
```

This approach is relatively simple but long-winded and error-prone. A better way is to write a wrapper Delphi class that implements the same public interface as the corresponding C++ class. The second demo, `CppClassWrapperDemo` contains a unit `CppClassWrapper` which does just that.

This unit implements a `TCppClass` class, which maps to its C++ counterpart. It only has one internal field, which stores the index of the C++ object as returned from the `CreateCppClass` function:

```
type
  TCppClass = class
  strict private
    FIndex: integer;
  public
    class procedure InitializeWrapper;
    class procedure FinalizeWrapper;
    constructor Create;
    destructor Destroy; override;
    procedure SetValue(value: integer);
    function GetSquare: integer;
end;
```

I won't show all of the functions here as they are all equally simple. One—or maybe two—will suffice.

The constructor just calls the `CreateCppClass` function, checks the result, and stores the resulting index in the internal field:

```
constructor TCppClass.Create;
begin
  inherited Create;
  if CreateCppClass(FIndex) <> 0 then
    raise Exception.Create('CreateCppClass failed');
end;
```

Similarly, `GetSquare` just forwards its job to the `CppClass_getSquare` function:

```
function TCppClass.GetSquare: integer;
begin
  if CppClass_getSquare(FIndex, Result) <> 0 then
    raise Exception.Create('CppClass_getSquare failed');
end;
```

When we have this wrapper, the code in the main unit becomes very simple—and very Delphi-like. Once the initialization in the `OnCreate` event handler is done, we can just create an instance of the `TCppClass` and work with it:

```
procedure TfrmCppClassDemo.FormCreate(Sender: TObject);
begin
  TCppClass.InitializeWrapper;
end;

procedure TfrmCppClassDemo.FormDestroy(Sender: TObject);
begin
  TCppClass.FinalizeWrapper;
end;

procedure TfrmCppClassDemo.btnWrapClick(Sender: TObject);
var
  cpp: TCppClass;
begin
  cpp := TCppClass.Create;
  try
    cpp.SetValue(SpinEdit1.Value);
    ListBox1.Items.Add(Format('square(%d) = %d',
      [SpinEdit1.Value, cpp.GetSquare]));
  finally
    FreeAndNil(cpp);
  end;
end;
```

Summary

I would be the first to admit that this chapter presents only sketches of ideas rather than fully reusable solutions. That is a direct consequence of the topic, which is too open to give definite answers. Rather than that, I have tried to give you enough information to do your own research on the topic.

The chapter started with a discussion of the possible reasons for including external libraries in your application. They may cover a topic you are unfamiliar with, or they may implement some specific algorithm faster than you are able to—or faster than the Delphi compiler can do it.

That brought us to the `FastMath` Delphi library, which implements fast functions for working with vectors (series of numbers) and matrices (two-dimensional arrays of numbers). This library uses an assembler intermixed with Pascal to give you the best performance in each case. We saw how assembler code is sometimes included internally and sometimes as an external file, and how a unified front is built on top of that.

After that, I took a short detour and inspected most of the popular types of object files that you'll encounter in your work. Object files are frequently used when linking C code with Delphi and it is good to know what you can run into.

I followed up with a longer example on how to link C object files with Delphi, and what problems you can encounter. We saw how to replace the standard Microsoft C library, `msvcrt` with a Delphi equivalent, how to write Delphi functions that plug a hole expected by the object file, and how to include multiple files that use each other in a circular fashion.

Then I moved from C to C++. This is currently the most popular Windows development tool and you'll find it used in most open source and commercial libraries. I explained why we cannot use C++ directly in Delphi applications and how to work around that.

The chapter ended with a practical demonstration that linked a very simple C++ library through a proxy DLL written in C++ to a Delphi application. I looked into two different ways of implementing a proxy DLL and into two ways of using this DLL in a Delphi application.

Linking to C and C++ code is hard and certainly not for everyone, but in critical situations, it can save your skin.

9
Introduction to Patterns

Patterns are everywhere! In architecture, patterns help architects plan buildings and discuss their projects. In programming, they help programmers organize programs and think about the code. They also help to create beautiful knitwear, and help people navigate safely through traffic—in short, they affect your everyday life.

The human brain is a pattern—finding analog computer, so it is not surprising that we humans like to base our life around patterns. We programmers are especially fond of organized, pattern—based thinking.

There are different areas of programming where patterns can be applied, from organizational aspects to coding. This book deals mostly with a subset of programming patterns, namely design patterns. Before we start describing and implementing different design patterns, however, I'd like to talk to you a bit about the history of patterns, their best points, and how they are often misused in practice.

This chapter will cover the following topics:

- What design patterns are
- Why patterns are useful
- The difference between patterns and idioms
- The origins of design patterns
- The classification of common patterns
- Pattern misuse and anti-patterns

Patterns in programming

The concept of a pattern is simple to define. A pattern is something that you did in the past, was successful, and can be applied to multiple situations. Patterns capture experiences in software development that have been proven to work again and again, and thus provide a solution to specific problems. They are not invented: they arise from practical experience.

When many programmers are trying to solve similar problems, they arrive again and again at a solution that works best. Such a solution is later distilled into a solution template, something that we programmers then use to approach similar problems in the future. Such solution templates are often called **patterns**.

Good patterns are problem and language agnostic. In other words, they apply to C++ and Delphi, and to Haskell and Smalltalk. In practice, as it turns out, lots of patterns are at least partially specific to a particular environment. Lots of them, for example, work best with **object-oriented programming** (**OOP**) languages and do not work with functional languages.

In programming, patterns serve a dual role. Besides being a template for problem solving, they also provide a common vocabulary that programmers around the world can use to discuss problems. It is much simpler to say, for example, that we will use an observer pattern to notify subsystems of state changes than it is to talk at length about how that part will be implemented. Using patterns as a base for discussion therefore forces us to talk about implementation concepts, and not about the detailed implementation specifics.

It is important to note that patterns provide only a template for a solution and not a detailed recipe. You will still have to take care of the code and make sure that the pattern implementation makes sense and works well with the rest of the program.

Programming patterns can be split into three groups that cover different abstraction levels. At the very top, we talk about architectural patterns. They deal with program organization as a whole, with a wide, top-down view, but they do not deal with implementation. For example, the famous Model-View-ViewModel approach is an architectural pattern that deals with a user interface-business logic split.

A bit lower down the abstraction scale are design patterns. They describe the run—time behavior of a program. When we use design patterns, we are trying to solve a specific problem in code, but we don't want to go fully to the code level. Design patterns will be the topic of the first ten chapters.

Patterns that work fully on the code level are called **idioms**. Idioms are usually language specific and provide templates for commonly encountered coding problems. For example, a standard way of creating/destroying objects in Delphi is an idiom, as is iterating over an enumerable container with the `for..in` construct.

Idioms are not the topic of this book. I will, however, mention the most important Delphi idioms, while talking about their specific implementation for some of the patterns.

Patterns are useful

This is not a book about the theory behind patterns; rather, this book focuses on the aspects of their implementation. Before I scare you all off with all this talk about design patterns, their history, modern advances, anti-patterns, and so on, I have decided to present a very simple pattern using an example. A few lines of code should explain why a pattern—based approach to problem solving can be a good thing.

In the code archive for this chapter, you'll find a simple console application called `DesignPatternExample`. Inside, you'll find an implementation of a sparse array, as shown in the following code fragment:

```
type
  TSparseRec = record
  IsEmpty: boolean;
  Value : integer;
end;

TSparseArray = TArray<TSparseRec>;
```

Each array index can either be empty (in which case `IsEmpty` will be set to `True`), or it can contain a value (in which case `IsEmpty` will be set to `False` and `Value` contains the value).

If we have a variable of the data: `TSparseArray` type, we can iterate over it with the following code:

```
for i := Low(data) to High(data) do
  if not data[i].IsEmpty then
    Process(data[i].Value);
```

When you need a similar iteration in some other part of the program, you have to type this short fragment again. Of course, you could also be smart and just copy and paste the first two lines (`for` and `if`). This is simple but problematic, because it leads to the copy and paste anti-pattern, which I'll discuss later in this chapter.

For now, let's imagine the following hypothetical scenario. Let's say that at some point, you start introducing nullable types into this code. We already have ready to use nullable types available in the Spring4D library (`https://bitbucket.org/sglienke/spring4d`), and it was suggested that they will appear in the next major Delphi release after 10.2 Tokyo, so this is definitely something that could happen.

In Spring4D, nullable types are implemented as a `Nullable<T>` record, which is partially shown in the following code:

```
type
  Nullable<T> = record
    ...
    property HasValue: Boolean read GetHasValue;
    property Value: T read GetValue;
 end;
```

As far as we know, Delphi's implementation will expose the same properties: `HasValue` and `Value`.

You can then redefine `TSparseArray` as an array of `Nullable<integer>`, as the following code:

```
type
  TSparseArray = TArray<Nullable<integer>>;
```

This is all well and good, but we now have to fix all the places in the code where `IsEmpty` is called and replace it with `HasValue`. We also have to change the program logic in all of these places. If the code was testing the result of `IsEmpty`, we would have to use `not HasValue` and vice versa. This is all very tedious and error prone. When making such a change in a big program, you can easily forget to insert or remove the not, and that breaks the program.

Wouldn't it be much better if there were only one place in the program when that `for/if` iteration construct was implemented? We would only have to correct code at that one location and— voila!—the program would be working again. Welcome to the Iterator pattern!

We'll discuss this pattern at length in `Chapter 14`, *Iterator, Visitor, Observer, and Memento*. For now, I will just give you a practical example.

The simplest way to add an iterator pattern to `TSparseArray` is to use a method that accepts such an array and an iteration method, that is, a piece of code that is executed for each non empty element of the array. As the next code example shows, this is simple to achieve with Delphi's anonymous methods:

```
procedure Iterate(const data: TSparseArray; const iterator:
TProc<integer>);
var
  i: Integer;
begin
  for i := Low(data) to High(data) do
```

```
    if not data[i].IsEmpty then
      iterator(data[i].Value);
  end;
```

In this example, data is the sparse array that we want to array over, and iterator represents the anonymous method that will be executed for each non null element. The TProc<integer> notation specifies a procedure accepting one integer argument (TProc<T> is a type declared in System.SysUtils).

> **TIP:** As we don't want to make a full copy of the array data each time Iterate is called, the data parameter is marked with a const qualifier. This can make a big difference in the execution speed. The const on the iterator parameter is just a minor optimization that stops the iterator's reference count being incremented while the Iterate is executing. Anonymous methods are internally implemented as interfaces in Delphi, and they are managed in the same way.

In the following code, we call Iterate and pass it the array to be iterated upon (data), and an anonymous method will be executed for each non empty element:

```
Iterate(data,
  procedure (value: integer)
  begin
    Process(value);
  end);
```

If we had to adapt this code to a nullable-based implementation, we would just edit the Iterate method and change not data[i].IsEmpty into data[i].HasValue—simple, effective, and, most importantly, foolproof!

Delphi also offers us a nice idiom that we can implement in an iterator pattern: enumerators and the for..in language construct. Using this idiom we can iterate over our sparse array with the following elegant code:

```
for value in data.Iterator do
  Process(value);
```

I will leave the implementation details for Chapter 14, *Iterator, Visitor, Observer, and Memento*. You are, of course, welcome to examine the demonstration project DesignPatternExample to see how data.Iterator is implemented (hint: start at TSparseArrayHelper).

Delphi idioms – Creating and destroying an object

Patterns are mostly language independent. We could have written an equivalent of the `Iterate` method from the previous sections in most languages, even in old Turbo Pascal for DOS or in an assembler. The `for..in` construct, however, is specific to Delphi. We call such a low-level pattern an idiom.

Idioms are not that useful when we are thinking about or discussing the program design. The knowledge of a language's is, however, necessary for you to become fluent in a language. Idioms teach us about the best ways of performing common operations in a particular environment.

The most important Delphi idiom concerns how object creation and destruction should be handled in code. It is used whenever we require a common three-step operation: create an object, do something with it, destroy the object.

> It must be said that this idiom applies only to Windows and OS X development. Compilers for Android, iOS, and Linux support **Automatic Reference Counting** (**ARC**), which means that objects are handled the same way as interfaces.

This idiom also shows how we can run into problems if we stray from the path and try to manage objects in a different manner. But first, I'd like to show you the recommended ways of handling objects in code. All examples can be found in the demonstration project `ObjectLifecycle`.

For simplicity's sake, we'll be using two objects: `obj1` and `obj2` of type `TObject`, as shown in the following code:

```
var
  obj1, obj2: TObject;
```

In practice, you'll be using a different class, as there's not much that a `TObject` could be used for. But all other details (that is, the idiom) will remain the same.

The first idiomatic way of handling objects is shown in the following code. Let's call it Variant A:

```
obj1 := TObject.Create;
try
  // some code
finally
  FreeAndNil(obj1);
end;
```

Firstly, we create the object. Then we enter a `try..finally` construct and execute some code on object `obj1`. In the end, the object is destroyed in the `finally` part. If the `// some code` part raises an exception, it is caught, and the object is safely destroyed in the `finally` section.

> **TIP:** Is it better to use `obj1.Free` or `FreeAndNil(obj1)`? There is a big debate regarding this in the Delphi community, and verdict is inconclusive. I prefer `FreeAndNil` because it doesn't leave dangling references to uninitialized memory.

Variant A is short and concise, but it becomes unwieldy when you need more than one object. To create two objects, do something with them, and then destroy them, we have to nest the `try..finally` constructs, as shown in the following code fragment:

```
obj1 := TObject.Create;
try
  obj2 := TObject.Create;
  try
    // some code
  finally
    FreeAndNil(obj2);
  end;
finally
  FreeAndNil(obj1);
end;
```

This approach correctly handles the `obj1` destruction when an exception is raised inside any code dealing with `obj2`, including its creation.

The long-windedness of Variant A makes many programmers adopt the following designed approach:

```
try
  obj1 := TObject.Create;
  obj2 := TObject.Create;
  // some code
finally
  FreeAndNil(obj1);
  FreeAndNil(obj2);
end;
```

Let me say it loud and clear: this technique does not work correctly! If you are using such an approach in your code, you should fix the code!

The problem here is that creating `obj2` may fail. The `TObject.Create` phrase will succeed for sure (unless you run out of memory), but in a real-life example, a different object may raise an exception inside the constructor. If that happens, the code will firstly destroy `obj1` and then it will proceed with destroying `obj2`.

This variable, however, is not initialized, and so the code will try to destroy some random part of memory, which will in most cases lead to access violation—that is, if you're lucky. If you're not, it will just corrupt a part of another object and cause a random and potentially very wrong behavior of the program.

For the same reason, the following simplified version also doesn't work:

```
try
  obj1 := TObject.Create;
  // some code
finally
  FreeAndNil(obj1);
end;
```

If an `obj1` constructor fails, the code will try to free the object by referencing the uninitialized `obj1`, and that will again cause problems.

In such situations, we can use Variant B of the idiom as follows:

```
obj1 := nil;
try
  obj1 := TObject.Create;
  // some code
finally
  FreeAndNil(obj1);
end;
```

Now, we can be sure that `obj1` will either contain `nil` or a reference to a valid object. The code will work because `TObject.Free`, which is called from `FreeAndNil`, disposes of an object in the following manner:

```
procedure TObject.Free;
begin
  if Self <> nil then
    Destroy;
end;
```

If the object (`Self` in this code) is already `nil`, then calling `Free` does nothing.

Variant B also nicely expands to multiple objects, as shown in the following code:

```
obj1 := nil;
obj2 := nil;
try
  obj1 := TObject.Create;
  obj2 := TObject.Create;
  // some code
finally
  FreeAndNil(obj1);
  FreeAndNil(obj2);
end;
```

Again, all object variables are always correctly initialized and the destruction works properly.

The only problem with Variant B is that `obj2` doesn't get destroyed if the destructor for `obj1` raises an exception. Raising an exception in a destructor is, however, something that you should definitely not do, as that may also cause the object to be only partially destroyed.

Gang of Four started it all

The design pattern movement (as it applies to programming) was started by the **Gang of Four**. By Gang of Four, we don't mean the Chinese Cultural Revolution leaders from the seventies or a post-punk group from Leeds, but four authors of a prominent book: *Design Patterns: Elements of Reusable Object-Oriented Software*. This book, written by *Erich Gamma, Richard Helm, Ralph Johson*, and *John Vlissides*, was published in 1994, and thoroughly shook the programming community.

Back in 1994, when C++ was becoming more and more prominent, object orientation was all the rage, and people were programming in Smalltalk. Programmers were simply not thinking in terms of patterns. Every good programmer, of course, had their own book of recipes that work, but they were not sharing them or trying to describe them in a formal way. The *GoF* book, as it is mostly called in informal speech, changed all that.

The majority of the book is dedicated to 23 (now classic) software design patterns. The authors started with a rationale for each one, providing a formal description of the pattern and examples in Smalltalk and C++. These patterns now provide the very core of a programmer's toolset, although later, more patterns were discovered and formalized. Notably missing from the book are design patterns that relate to parallel programming (multi-threading).

In the first two chapters of their book, the authors explored the power and the pitfalls of OOP. They drew two important conclusions: you should program to an interface, not an implementation, and favor object composition over class inheritance.

The former rule corresponds to the **dependency inversion principle** (the **D** part of the **SOLID** principle, which I'll cover in more detail later in this chapter).

The latter contradicts the whole object-oriented movement, which preached class hierarchy and inheritance. As the distinction between the two approaches is not well known in the Delphi world, I have prepared a short example in the next section.

Don't inherit – compose!

If you are a programmer of a certain age, it will be hard for you, as it was for me, to accept the don't inherit—compose philosophy. After all, we were taught that OOP is the key to everything and that it will fix all our problems.

That was indeed the dream behind the OOP movement. The practice, however, dared to disagree. In most real-life scenarios, the OOP approach leads only to mess and ugly code. The following short example will succinctly demonstrate why this happens.

Let's say we would like to write a class that implements a list of only three operations. We'd like to add integer numbers (`Add`), get the size of the list (`Count`), and read each element (`Items`). Our application will use this list to simulate a data structure from which elements can never be removed and where data, once added, can never be modified. We would therefore like to prevent every user of this class, from calling methods that will break those assumptions.

We can approach this problem in three different ways. Firstly, we can write the code from scratch. We are, however, lazy, and we want Delphi's `TList` to do the actual work. Secondly, we can inherit from `TList` and write a derived class `TInheritedLimitedList` that supports only the three operations we need. Thirdly, we can create a new base class `TCompositedLimitedList` that uses `TList` for data storage. The second and third approach are both shown in the project called `CompositionVsInheritance`, which you can find in the code archive for this chapter.

When we start to implement the inherited version of `TList`, we immediately run into problems. The first one is that `TList` simply implements lots of functionality that we don't want in our class. An example of such methods would be `Insert`, `Move`, `Clear`, and so on.

The second problem is that inheriting from `TList` was simply not a factor when that class was designed. Almost all of its methods are static, not virtual, and as such cannot really be overridden. We can only `reintroduce` them, and that, as we'll see very soon, can cause unforeseen problems.

Another problematic part is the `Clear` method. We don't want to allow the users of our class to call it, but, still, it is implicitly called from `TList.Destroy`, and so we cannot fully disable it.

We would also like to access the elements as `integer` and not as `Pointer` data. To do this, we also have to reintroduce the `Items` property.

A full declaration of the `TInheritedLimitedList` class is shown next. You will notice that we have to reintroduce a whole bunch of methods:

```
type
  TInheritedLimitedList = class(TList)
  strict private
    FAllowClear: boolean;
  protected
    function Get(Index: Integer): Integer;
    procedure Put(Index: Integer; const Value: Integer);
  public
   destructor Destroy; override;
   function Add(Item: Integer): Integer; inline;
```

```
    procedure Clear; override;
    procedure Delete(Index: Integer); reintroduce;
    procedure Exchange(Index1, Index2: Integer); reintroduce;
    function Expand: TList; reintroduce;
    function Extract(Item: Pointer): Pointer; reintroduce;
    function First: Pointer; reintroduce;
    function GetEnumerator: TListEnumerator; reintroduce;
    procedure Insert(Index: Integer; Item: Pointer); reintroduce;
    function Last: Pointer; reintroduce;
    procedure Move(CurIndex, NewIndex: Integer); reintroduce;
    function Remove(Item: Pointer): Integer; reintroduce;
    function RemoveItem(Item: Pointer;
      Direction: TList.TDirection): Integer; reintroduce;
    property Items[Index: Integer]: Integer read Get write Put; default;
  end;
```

Some parts of the implementation are trivial. The next code fragment shows how `Delete` and `Exchange` are disabled:

```
procedure TInheritedLimitedList.Delete(Index: Integer);
begin
  raise Exception.Create('Not supported');
end;

procedure TInheritedLimitedList.Exchange(Index1, Index2: Integer);
begin
  raise Exception.Create('Not supported');
end;
```

Most of the implementation is equally dull, so I won't show it here. The demo project contains a fully implemented class that you can peruse in peace. Still, I'd like to point out two implementation details.

The first is the `Items` property. We had to reintroduce it, as we'd like to work with integers, not pointers. It is also implemented in a way that allows read-only access:

```
function TInheritedLimitedList.Get(Index: Integer): Integer;
begin
  Result := Integer(inherited Get(Index));
end;

procedure TInheritedLimitedList.Put(Index: Integer; const Value: Integer);
begin
  raise Exception.Create('Not supported');
end;
```

The second interesting detail is the implementation of the `Clear` method. It is normally disabled (because calling `Clear` would result in an exception). The `Destroy` destructor, however, sets an internal flag that allows `Clear` to be called from the inherited destructor, as shown in the following code:

```
destructor TInheritedLimitedList.Destroy;
begin
  FAllowClear := true;
  inherited;
end;

procedure TInheritedLimitedList.Clear;
begin
  if FAllowClear then
    inherited
  else
    raise Exception.Create('Not supported');
end;
```

There are numerous problems with this approach. We had to introduce some weird hacks, and write a bunch of code to disable functions that should not be used. This is partially caused by the bad `TList` design (bad from an object-oriented viewpoint), which does not allow us to override virtual methods. But worst of all is the fact that our inheritance based list still doesn't work correctly!

Looking at the following code fragment, everything seems OK. If we run it, we get an exception in the `list[1] := 42` statement:

```
var
  list: TInheritedLimitedList;

list.Add(1);
list.Add(2);
list.Add(3);
list[1] := 42;
```

If, however, we pass this list to another method that expects to get a `TList`, that method would be able to modify our list! The following code fragment changes the list to contain elements `1`, `42`, and `3`:

```
procedure ChangeList(list: TList);
begin
  list[1] := pointer(42);
end;

var
```

```
 list: TInheritedLimitedList;

list.Add(1);
list.Add(2);
list.Add(3);
ChangeList(list);
```

This happens because `Get` and `Put` in the original `TList` are not `virtual`. Because of this, the compiler has no idea that a derived class can override them and just blindly calls the `TList` version. Assigning to `list[1]` in `ChangeList` therefore uses `TList.Put`, which doesn't raise an exception.

> TIP: Raising exceptions to report coding errors is another problem with this approach. When working with strongly typed languages, such as Delphi, we would like such coding problems to be caught by the compiler, not during testing.

Compared to inheritance, implementing a list by using composition is totally trivial. We just have to declare a class that exposes the required functionality and write a few methods that use an internal `FList: TList` object to implement this functionality. All our public methods are very simple and only map to methods of the internal object. By declaring them `inline`, the compiler will actually create almost identical code to the one we would get if we are use `TList` instead of `TCompositedLimitedList` in our code. As the implementation is so simple, as you can see from the following code it can be fully included in the book:

```
type
  TCompositedLimitedList = class
  strict private
    FList: TList;
  strict protected
    function Get(Index: Integer): Pointer; inline;
    function GetCount: Integer; inline;
  public
    constructor Create;
    destructor Destroy; override;
    function Add(Item: Pointer): Integer; inline;
    property Count: Integer read GetCount;
    property Items[Index: Integer]: Pointer read Get; default;
  end;

constructor TCompositedLimitedList.Create;
begin
  inherited Create;
  FList := TList.Create;
end;
```

```
destructor TCompositedLimitedList.Destroy;
begin
  FList.Free;
  inherited;
end;

function TCompositedLimitedList.Add(Item: Pointer): Integer;
begin
  Result := FList.Add(Item);
end;

function TCompositedLimitedList.Get(Index: Integer): Pointer;
begin
  Result := FList[Index];
end;

function TCompositedLimitedList.GetCount: Integer;
begin
  Result := FList.Count;
end;
```

By using composition instead of inheritance, we get all the benefits fast code, small and testable implementation, and error checking in the compiler.

Pattern taxonomy

The original *Gang of Four* book separated patterns into three categories: creational, structural, and behavioral. To these three, another large category was added in recent years, concurrency patterns. Some concurrency patterns were covered in another classic book: *Pattern-Oriented Software Architecture: Patterns for Concurrent and Networked Objects, Volume* 2, by *Douglas C Schmidt, Michael Stal, Hans Rohnert,* and *Frank Buschmann.*

Creational patterns deal with delegation. They are focused on creating new objects and groups of related objects. These patterns will create objects for you, meaning that you don't have to create them directly.

The focus of structural patterns is aggregation. They define ways to compose objects in a way that creates new functionality from the constituent parts. They help us create software components.

Behavioral patterns are big on consultation they talk about responsibilities between objects. Unlike structural patterns, which only specify a structure, behavioral patterns define communication paths and messages.

Concurrency patterns deal with cooperation. They make a system composed of multiple components, running in parallel, work together. The main concerns of concurrency patterns are resource protection and messaging.

The next few pages will give an overview of the most important design patterns, organized by category and sorted by name.

Creational patterns

The patterns in the first group of patterns, creational patterns, are used when simple and composite objects are created. The following patterns belong to this group:

- **Abstract factory pattern**: You can use this pattern to create entire families of related objects but without the need to specify their classes. This pattern is described in `Chapter 11`, *Factory Method, Abstract Factory, Prototype, and Builder.*
- **Builder pattern**: This pattern abstracts the construction of a complex object, and allows the same process to create different representations. It is described in `Chapter 10`, *Singleton, Dependency Injection, Lazy Initialization, and Object Pool.*
- **Dependency injection pattern**: This is used to send specific instances of depended objects into a class (injecting them), instead of the class creating them directly. This pattern is described in `Chapter 11`, *Factory Method, Abstract Factory, Prototype, and Builder.*
- **Factory method pattern**: This pattern defines an interface for creating a single object. Subclasses can then decide which class to instantiate. This is described in `Chapter 11`, *Factory Method, Abstract Factory, Prototype, and Builder.*
- **Lazy initialization pattern**: This delays the creation of an object or the calculation of a value until it is actually needed. In the *GoF* book, it appeared as a *virtual proxy*. This pattern is described in `Chapter 11`, *Factory Method, Abstract Factory, Prototype, and Builder.*
- **Multiton pattern**: This pattern similar to singleton. It allows multiple named instances, while serving as the only way of accessing them. It is not covered in this book.
- **Object pool pattern**: This pattern recycles objects to avoid the expensive acquisition and creation of resources. A special case, connection pool, is well-known to all database programmers. This pattern is described in Chapter 10, *Singleton, Dependency Injection, Lazy Initialization, and Object Pool.*
- **Prototype pattern**: This specifies how to create objects based on a template object that is cloned to produce new objects. This pattern is described in `Chapter 10`, *Singleton, Dependency Injection, Lazy Initialization, and Object Pool.*

- **Resource acquisition is initialization pattern (RAII)**: This pattern ensures that resources are properly released by tying them to the lifespan of an object. In Delphi, we implement this pattern by using an interface as a resource owner. It is not covered in this book.
- **Singleton pattern**: This pattern ensures that a class has only one instance. It also provides a common point of access to that instance. This pattern is described in `Chapter 10`, *Singleton, Dependency Injection, Lazy Initialization, and Object Pool.*

Structural patterns

The second group of patterns, structural patterns, handles the way objects are composed into new objects. The following patterns belong to this group:

- **Adapter pattern**: This pattern, which is also known as a wrapper or a translator pattern, converts the interface of a class into another interface expected by a client. It is described in `Chapter 5`, *Adapter, Decorator, Facade, and Proxy.*
- **Bridge pattern**: This decouples an abstraction from its implementation, which allows the two to vary independently. This pattern is described in `Chapter 4`, *Composite, Flyweight, Marker Interface, and Bridge.*
- **Composite pattern**: This composes from the hierarchies of more basic objects. This pattern is described in `Chapter 12`, *Composite, Flyweight, Marker Interface, and Bridge.*
- **Decorator pattern**: This pattern allows an object to take additional responsibilities, in addition to its original interface. Decorators are an alternative to subclassing for an extending functionality. This pattern is described in `Chapter 13`, *Adapter, Proxy, Decorator, and Facade.*
- **Extension object pattern**: This pattern allows you to adding of a functionality to a hierarchy without changing that hierarchy. This is not covered in this book.
- **Facade pattern**: This pattern combines a set of interfaces exposed by subsystems into a simpler interface that is easier to use. This pattern is described in `Chapter 13`, *Adapter, Proxy, Decorator, and Facade.*
- **Flyweight pattern**: This pattern uses data-sharing to efficiently support large numbers of similar objects. It is described in `Chapter 13`, *Adapter, Proxy, Decorator, and Facade.*
- **Front controller pattern**: This pattern is used when designing web applications and provides a centralized entry point for request handling. It is not covered in this book.

- **Marker pattern**: This allows us to associate metadata with a class. This pattern is described in `Chapter 12`, *Composite, Flyweight, Marker Interface, and Bridge.*
- **Module pattern**: This pattern groups several related elements into one conceptual entity. It is not covered in this book.
- **Proxy pattern**: It provides a replacement for another object so it can control access to it. This pattern is described in `Chapter 13`, *Adapter, Proxy, Decorator, and Facade.*
- **Twin pattern**: This pattern helps simulating multiple inheritance in programming languages that don't support this feature. It is not covered in this book.

Behavioral patterns

The third group of patterns, behavioral patterns, deals with communication between objects and with the distribution of responsibilities. The following patterns belong to this group:

- **Blackboard pattern**: This is an **artificial intelligence** (**AI**) pattern for combining different data sources. It is not covered in this book.
- **Chain of responsibility pattern**: This is an object-oriented version of an `if` ladder idiom (`if ... else if ... else if ... else`). It works by constructing a chain of processing objects. It is not covered in this book.
- **Command pattern**: This pattern encapsulates a request as an object. It is especially useful for building user interfaces where it allows for the support of undoable operations. This pattern is described in `Chapter 14`, *Nullable Value, Template Method, Command, and State.*
- **Interpreter pattern**: This pattern defines a representation of a language grammar and gives an interpreter for that grammar. It is not covered in this book.
- **Iterator pattern**: This provides a way to access elements of an aggregate object (list, array, symbol table, tree, and so on) sequentially, without exposing the underlying implementation of that object. This pattern is described in `Chapter 15`, *Iterator, Visitor, Observer, and Memento.*
- **Mediator pattern**: This defines an object that handles interaction between other objects. This pattern supports loose coupling by preventing objects from referring to one another explicitly. It is not covered in this book.
- **Memento pattern**: This specifies how to store and restore an object's internal state without violating encapsulation. This pattern is described in `Chapter 15`, *Iterator, Visitor, Observer, and Memento.*

- **Null object pattern**: This removes the reason for using a `nil` pointer, by providing a special, default value for a class. This pattern is described in `Chapter 14`, *Nullable Value, Template Method, Command, and State.*
- **Observer pattern**: This pattern is also known as a publish/subscribe pattern. It provides another way to prevent tight coupling in a system, by setting up a system where a change of objects results in all of its dependents being notified about the change. This pattern is described in `Chapter 15`, *Iterator, Visitor, Observer, and Memento.*
- **Servant pattern**: This pattern defines an object that implements a common functionality for a group of classes. It is not covered in this book.
- **Specification pattern**: This pattern provides support for business logic that can be recombined by chaining the rules together with boolean operations. It is not covered in this book.
- **State pattern**: This allows an object to change its behavior when there is a change to its internal state. It is described in `Chapter 14`, *Nullable Value, Template Method, Command, and State.*
- **Strategy pattern**: This pattern defines a family of algorithms that can be used interchangeably. It is not covered in this book.
- **Template method pattern**: This defines a skeleton of on operation and defers some steps to subclasses. This pattern is described in `Chapter 14`, *Nullable Value, Template Method, Command, and State.*
- **Visitor pattern**: This pattern specifies an operation that is performed on all elements of an object's internal structure. It is described in `Chapter 15`, *Iterator, Visitor, Observer, and Memento.*

Concurrency patterns

The last group, concurrency patterns, contains patterns that are needed in the world of parallel programming. The following patterns belong to this group:

- **Active object pattern**: This pattern hides the concurrency by implementing asynchronous method inside an object, which serves as a scheduler for handling requests. It is not covered in this book.
- **Binding properties pattern**: This pattern combines multiple observers to force synchronization on properties in different objects. It is not covered in this book.
- **Blockchain pattern**: This provides a decentralized way for storing data in a linked list protected with cryptographic means. It is not covered in this book.

- **Compute kernel pattern**: This pattern executes the same calculation many times in parallel, differing only on integer input parameters. It is frequently related to GPU calculation. It is not covered in this book.
- **Double-checked locking pattern**: This reduces the overhead of acquiring a lock in a safe manner. This pattern is described in `Chapter 16`, *Locking patterns*.
- **Event-based asynchronous pattern**: This pattern defines a way of executing parallel operations where a caller is notified when a worker finishes the execution. It is not explicitly described in this book, although it is used as a basis for concrete implementations in `Chapter 17`, *Thread pool, Messaging, Future and Pipeline*.
- **Future pattern**: This pattern pushes a calculation into a background and replaces it with a promise that a result will be available in the future. It is described in `Chapter 17`, *Thread pool, Messaging, Future and Pipeline*.
- **Guarded suspension pattern**: This pattern manages operations that depend on a two-part condition: a precondition that must be satisfied and a lock that must be acquired. It is not covered in this book.
- **Join pattern**: This pattern provides a way to write distributed and parallel systems, by message passing. It is not covered in this book.
- **Lock pattern**: This protects shared resources by implementing a locking mechanism. This pattern is described in `Chapter 16`, *Locking patterns*.
- **Lock striping pattern**: This pattern optimizes locking, by replacing a single global lock with a set of specialized locks. It is described in `Chapter 16`, *Locking patterns*.
- **Messaging design pattern (MDP):** This is based on the interchange of information between components in the system. This pattern is described in `Chapter 17`, *Thread Pool, Messaging, Future, and Pipeline*.
- **Monitor object pattern**: This pattern combines locking with a mechanism for signalling other threads that their condition was met. It is not covered in this book.
- **Optimistic initialization pattern**: This reduces the cost of locking by replacing it with the small probability of extraneous objects being created and thrown away. This pattern is described in `Chapter 16`, *Locking patterns*.
- **Pipeline pattern**: This pattern specifies a way of decoupling thread dependencies by passing small subsets of data from one worker thread to another through a message-passing pipeline. It is described in `Chapter 17`, *Thread Pool, Messaging, Future, and Pipeline*.
- **Reactor pattern**: This is a reactor object that provides an asynchronous interface to resources that must be handled synchronously. It is not covered in this book.

- **Read-write lock pattern**: This allows multiple objects to simultaneously read a shared resource, but forces exclusive access for write operations. This pattern is described in `Chapter 16`, *Locking patterns*.
- **Scheduler pattern**: This pattern controls when threads may execute single-threaded code. It is not covered in this book.
- **Thread pool pattern**: This is a parallel version of an object pool creational pattern that provides a pool of worker threads that execute numerous tasks. It is described in `Chapter 17`, *Thread Pool, Messaging, Future, and Pipeline*.
- **Thread-specific storage pattern**: This allows us to use global memory that is local to a thread. In Delphi, we implement this by declaring a variable with the `threadvar` directive. It is not covered in this book.

Criticism

While design patterns are undoubtedly a useful tool, many prominent computer scientists have expressed criticism directed both at the *Design Patterns: Elements of Reusable Object-Oriented Software* book and at the general way patterns are used in practice.

Over the years, programmers have learned that the patterns in the *GoF* book really aren't as widely applicable as the authors thought. Lots of them only apply to the object-oriented world. If we try to use them with a functional language, they are largely useless. They can also be greatly simplified when used in aspect-oriented languages.

Delphi, however, is an object-oriented language, so we can reuse most of the Gang of Four observations. Still, it is important to keep in mind how patterns should be used in practice.

As a main rule, you should never use design patterns to architect the software. Design patterns tell you how to write code to solve a specific problem while software design should be done on a higher abstraction level, without referring to implementation details. Rather, you should use them to approach specific problems that you run into while programming.

The second idea that should be present in your mind at all times is that patterns are not the goal: they are just a tool. Design patterns formalize only some aspects of programming, not all of it. You should also never follow a design pattern blindly. Think about what it says, think about how it applies to your problem, and then use it wisely. Programming is a craft, not a paint by numbers book, and patterns are not a silver bullet.

If you look at the code and the pattern stands out to you, it was not implemented correctly. A good pattern will hide in the code, and only a careful observer will be able to say: Oh! I see you used a visitor pattern here. Nice. It is important to understand the concepts behind the design patterns, and not the exact names of the methods and properties that were used in an implementation you found somewhere (even if that was in the *Design Patterns* book).

Design patterns *are* a great tool for refactoring and communication. Hey, gals and guys, this part of our system is completely messed up, and we should use a publish/subscribe pattern instead, is a type of a statement that should appear more frequently in our discussions!

Anti-patterns

Every yin has its yang, and every hero has their dark side, and so the very existence of patterns suggest that there exists the opposite. We could simply call it a mess, but programmers try to find an order to everything, even in chaos, and so they cataloged the mess and described the many kinds of anti-patterns. I will only briefly touch on this topic, as the goal of this book is to teach you about order, not disorder, but there is always something to learn from bad examples.

Design patterns are nicely classified, and most programmers agree on how they should be named and defined. Anti-patterns, on the other hand, are messier. They hide behind different names and they provide mere sketches of behavior, not fully defined templates.

The nastiest of the anti-patterns is sometimes called a **big ball of mud**. A typical sign of this anti-pattern is that the code is a mess, no matter how you look at it. It is unreadable: the data is global; every class uses every other class, except for the code that no one uses at all; and so on and so on. If you are ever hired to work on such a project, find a better job (just some friendly advice).

Another anti-pattern is the **blob**. It occurs when the problem was not correctly decomposed. One class is doing most of the work, while others represent just small fragments that don't do anything significant. In Delphi, we can find this anti-pattern in badly organized projects where most of the functionality is implemented in the main form of class. Such a project can usually be saved by applying SOLID design principles, which I'll discuss in the next section.

The golden hammer anti-pattern happens when a programmer uses one technology to solve everything. I've seen projects where every data structure was a `TStringList` and others where all data structures were implemented with in-memory datasets. The best way of rescuing such projects is to put them in the hands of programmers with a wide knowledge of programming, data structures, and available tools.

Everyone who programmed in old-school BASIC has an intimate knowledge of a spaghetti code pattern: the code jumps here and there, doesn't follow any logic, and definitely does not use standard flow-control constructs, such as `while`. It is usually too difficult to decode and fix such an implementation. A better approach is to write a decent set of unit tests and then rewrite the problematic part from scratch.

The last anti-pattern I want to mention is called **copy and paste programming**. A typical sign of this anti-pattern is longer sequences of code that are frequently repeated in the source. There are almost no shared methods; everything is copied all over the place. This is a direct violation of the DRY design principle, which will be described in the next section and can be more-or-less simply solved by applying the same principle.

Design principles

Patterns are not the only way of formalizing metaprogramming concepts. Patterns address specific problems, but sometimes we would like to express ideas that are not problem specific. Such formalizations are called **principles**. If they are related to program design, we call them, quite obviously, design principles.

Principles provide a view of a problem that is complementary to patterns. They don't give specific instructions on how to solve problems but rather instruct us how to write good code. A good programmer should, therefore, know both design patterns and design principles by heart. An excellent programmer, of course, also knows when to use patterns and principles and when to ignore them, but that's another story. You can only get such a level of knowledge by practicing programming for a long time.

Still, everyone has to start somewhere, and at the beginning, it is advantageous to know well-known and commonly appreciated principles. I'll finish this chapter with a short review of the most important design principles.

SOLID

The most important principle of OOP is undoubtedly SOLID. It covers five ideas that are a subset of many principles promoted by software engineer and author Robert C Martin (you may know him as *Uncle Bob*). SOLID is an acronym in which each letter represents one of the following principles:

- **Single responsibility principle**: This principle states that a class should only have one responsibility. It goes hand-in-hand with software decomposition. If we cannot nicely decompose software implementation into components, it will also be hard to implement classes with only one responsibility. Taking care of the single responsibility principle helps prevent the blob anti-pattern.
- **Open/closed principle:** This principle states that software entities should be open for extensions but closed for modification. In other words, a module (class) should be extensible (open for extensions) without having to modify its source code (closed for modification). This extensibility is usually achieved either with the careful use of object-oriented principles (inheritance, virtual functions) or delegation (for example, providing a custom comparison function to a sorting method).
- **Liskov substitution principle:** Introduced in 1987 by *Barbara Liskov*, this tells us that the program should continue to work correctly if we substitute one object with its sub-type (a derived class, for example). This principle requires that a derived class cannot have more strict requirements than its base class (the preconditions cannot be stronger in a derived class) and that it cannot give weaker guarantees about output data (post-conditions cannot be weaker).
- **Interface segregation principle:** This principle merely states that multiple interfaces with a specific functionality are better than one general-purpose interface. An interface segregation principle makes the system more decoupled and easier to refactor.
- **Dependency inversion principle:** The last SOLID principle states that you should depend on abstraction and not on the concrete implementation. When you use a class, you should only depend on the interface that is exposed and not on the specific implementation. This principle is frequently used to refer to programming for an interface, not for an implementation.

We could jokingly say that the SOLID principle doesn't respect its own rules. By the interface segregation principle, we would expect to read about five different principles and not one larger set. Other design principles in this chapter are simpler and cover only one idea.

Don't repeat yourself

The **don't repeat yourself** principle (**DRY**), states that every piece of knowledge should have a single representation within a system. In other words, you should implement each small part of functionality as one method, and not use copy and paste.

In practice, such detailed decomposition will also cause problems. We will usually use a function from multiple places in the code. If that shared function changes behavior, we have to explicitly check all call sites (all places that use it) to see whether the new functionality is indeed required and desired at that place. Still, this is much better than the mess introduced by copy and paste programming.

KISS and YAGNI

The **KISS** principle came into programming from the US Navy. It states that systems are more reliable when they are kept simple. Although many sources say that KISS stands for keep it simple, stupid, the original author described it as keep it simple stupid. In other words, it is not that the engineer is stupid, but that the implementation should be simple stupid, or as trivial as possible.

This principle goes hand in hand with another idea taken from the extreme programming world—**YAGNI**. Meaning *you ain't gonna need it,* this acronym teaches us to only implement parts of code that are actually needed. If you try to foresee what will be needed in the future and write it in advance, you will, in many cases, just lose time, as either you'll be mistaken or the software specification will change.

Both KISS and YAGNI require frequent refactoring when software specification is updated, so it is helpful if you know the refactoring tools in Delphi or use a software add-on, such as MMX Code Explorer.

Summary

This chapter provided a brief overview of a topic that will be discussed in the rest of the book: design patterns. We took a look at the broader picture and found that patterns are everywhere and that design patterns are only part of a larger group of programming patterns. We also learned about architectural patterns, which function on a higher level, and idioms, which are very low-level patterns. Delphi idioms are introduced throughout this book, starting with this chapter.)

We then learned about at the history of patterns, and were introduced to Gang of Four and their *Design Patterns* book. We learned that patterns are not fixed in time, but are evolving, and that many patterns, especially ones dealing with parallel programming, were documented after that book was published.

After this, I gave an overview of design pattern classification, where we saw how patterns can be split into four big groups, and we learned what the most important patterns in each group are. This will help you research patterns that are not covered in this book.

The chapter ended with a short section on design principles, which represent more generic ideas than patterns. Design principles represent a foundation of a programmer's knowledge, and it is recommended that you know them, even before you start studying design patterns.

In the next chapter, we'll start discovering design patterns. I'll start with the first group (creational patterns) and give detailed examples of four design patterns: singleton, dependency injection, lazy initialization, and object pool.

10
Singleton, Dependency Injection, Lazy Initialization, and Object Pool

In **Object-Oriented Programming** (**OOP**), everything starts with an object, and if we want to use one, we have to create it first. In most cases, that simply means calling `TSomeClass.Create`, but in a more complex scenario, a specialized design pattern that creates an object for us can be quite handy.

In this chapter, we'll look into four patterns from the creational group. At the end of the chapter, you'll know the following:

- A singleton pattern, which makes sure that a class has only one instance
- A dependency injection pattern, which makes program architecture more flexible and suitable for test-driven development
- A lazy initialization pattern, which makes sure that we don't spend time and resources creating objects that we don't really need
- An object pool pattern, which speeds up the creation of objects that take a long time to create

Singleton

The **singleton** pattern was part of the original Design Patterns collection. It makes sure that a class, which we call a `singleton` class, has only one instance. In other words, only one object of that class may ever be created during the program's life. Such a class must also provide global access to this instance.

> Let me give a real-life example to clarify this definition. You probably live in a country that allows one, and only one, president (or monarch, head of state, and so on.) to exist at the same time. So, that person is a singleton.

You will notice that the pattern tells us nothing about how that one singleton instance should be destroyed. It also doesn't specify when the singleton instance should be created.

Whenever you need to create a singleton, you should first answer the following questions:

- Does the singleton have to be initialized on demand, or will it be created on first use?
- Can the singleton be destroyed when the program ends, or should it disappear when nobody is using it?
- And, most importantly, do you really need to use a singleton?

I believe the use of singletons should be kept to an absolute minimum. After all, a singleton is just a glorified global variable, and inherits all of its problems. It will, for example, cause problems with test-driven development and unit testing. It will also, unless it is created when the program starts, be hard to configure.

In most cases, you simply need an instance of a class and you don't need to bother with preventing this class from creating other instances (other objects). For example, Delphi VCL has a global variable, `Application` of the `TApplication` type, which is effectively a singleton. In a normal program, one and only one `Application` will exist. As the programmers are not idiots, they will not create new instances of `TApplication`, and the program will work just fine.

The code archive for this chapter contains the `Singleton` folder with the project, `SingletonPattern`. Inside this project, you'll find the `Singleton_GlobalVar` unit, which shows how such a singleton-like implementation could look. As it is short and simple, it is fully reproduced here:

```
unit Singleton_GlobalVar;

interface

uses
  Vcl.StdCtrls;

type
  TSingletonGV = class
  public
    procedure Log(logTarget: TListBox; const msg: string);
  end;

var
  SingletonGV: TSingletonGV;

implementation

procedure TSingletonGV.Log(logTarget: TListBox; const msg: string);
begin
  logTarget.ItemIndex := logTarget.Items.Add(
    Format('[%p] %s %s',
           [pointer(Self), FormatDateTime('hh:mm:ss', Now), msg]));
end;

initialization
  SingletonGV := TSingletonGV.Create;
finalization
  FreeAndNil(SingletonGV);
end.
```

In this example, the singleton instance is stored in the global variable, `SingletonGV`, which is created when an application is starting up and is destroyed when an application is shutting down. It implements the `Log` function which is used in the demo.

As the singleton is created when the program starts, we are quite limited in customizing it. We cannot, for example, pass the logging target (the `TListBox` parameter) to the singleton's constructor, as this listbox doesn't yet exist when the singleton is created. We are forced to accept this inflexibility and pass the `logTarget` parameter each time `Log` is called.

> In Delphi, the code in all `initialization` blocks is executed before the first statement of the `.dpr` program. Similarly, all `finalization` blocks are executed after the last statement of the program. You could say that initialization blocks are executed in the program's `begin` statement and that finalization blocks are executed in the program's `end` statement.

Still, sometimes, we really need a true singleton. How can we implement it? Maybe we could start by copying an implementation from a different language. So, how do other languages do it?

In C++, C#, and Java, the recommended solution is to make a constructor private. Access to that constructor is then limited to the method from the singleton class and we can implement a single-point access function. A naive Delphi implementation could try a similar approach, but, as we'll soon see, that wouldn't work.

Still, the `SingletonPattern` project contains the `Singleton_HiddenCreate` unit that implements a singleton class in that manner. I will soon tear this implementation apart, but first let's take a look at the full source code for that unit:

```
unit Singleton_HiddenCreate;

interface

uses
  Vcl.StdCtrls;

type
  TSingletonHC = class
  strict protected
    constructor Create;
  public
    class function Instance: TSingletonHC;
    procedure Log(logTarget: TListBox; const msg: string);
  end;

implementation

uses
  SysUtils;
```

```
var
  GSingleton: TSingletonHC;

constructor TSingletonHC.Create;
begin
  inherited Create;
end;

class function TSingletonHC.Instance: TSingletonHC;
begin
  if not assigned(GSingleton) then
    GSingleton := TSingletonHC.Create;
  Result := GSingleton;
end;

procedure TSingletonHC.Log(logTarget: TListBox; const msg: string);
begin
  logTarget.ItemIndex := logTarget.Items.Add(
    Format('[%p] %s %s',
           [pointer(Self), FormatDateTime('hh:mm:ss', Now), msg]));
end;

initialization
finalization
  FreeAndNil(GSingleton);
end.
```

This code tries to implement a singleton by hiding the constructor. This works in C++, C#, and Java, but Delphi implements constructors in a different way. If a code calls `TSingletonHC.Create`, the first visible constructor in the object hierarchy will be called and will happily create the object. In this instance, `TObject.Create` will be called and will construct a new object for us. This attempt therefore immediately fails.

The `Instance` function tries to make sure that there is one (and only one) instance of the `TSingletonHC` class created. The constructor problem, however, completely thwarts its work.

I should mention here that the code idiom used to create a global instance in the instance method (test whether the singleton exists, create the singleton, and use the singleton) works correctly only in a single-threaded code. If you are using a thread, you need better ways of creating the global instance. For more information, see the *Double-checked locking* and *Optimistic initialization* patterns in `Chapter 16`, *Locking Patterns*.

The singleton is destroyed when the program shuts down. This is completely acceptable, and I can say nothing bad about this part of the implementation.

> Delphi requires the `initialization` section to be present if we want to use the `finalization` section. The `initialization` section may be empty, as is in this example, but it must be present.

Besides being able to create multiple instances of `TSingletonHC`, this implementation suffers from another nasty problem. Any part of the code is capable of destroying the singleton object, but the implementation will think that the object is still alive.

Let's examine the following simple code sequence:

```
TSingletonHC.Instance.Log(listBox, 'A message');
TSingletonHC.Instance.Free;
TSingletonHC.Instance.Log(listBox, 'Another message');
```

Let's assume that the singleton was not created before. The first instance call creates a new `TSingletonHC` object and stores it in the `GSingletonHC` variable. This instance is then returned and its `Log` method is executed.

The second instance call retrieves the existing object. The code then executes `Free` on that object and destroys the singleton instance. The `GSingletonHC` variable, however, still contains a pointer to the memory location! (In Delphi, an object variable is nothing more than a simple pointer to the memory location where the object lies.)

The third instance call then retrieves the existing value of `GSingletonHC`. This value points to the object that was just destroyed! In real life, the third line would most probably execute correctly, as the program was not yet able to reuse this memory for a different purpose, and that makes the problem even bigger. We cannot even be sure that it will be noticed immediately after the singleton object has been destroyed. The program will just start throwing out weird errors some undefined time after that!

The following code from the `SingletonPattern` project demonstrates both problems. You can execute it by clicking on the `TestHiddenCreate` button:

```
procedure TfrmSingleton.btnTestHiddenCreateClick(Sender: TObject);
var
  Singleton1: TSingletonHC;
  Singleton2: TSingletonHC;
  Singleton3: TSingletonHC;
begin
  Singleton1 := TSingletonHC.Instance;
  Singleton2 := TSingletonHC.Instance;
```

```
  // It is still possible to create a new instance of this "singleton"
  Singleton3 := TSingletonHC.Create;

  Singleton1.Log(ListBox1, 'TSingletonHC[1]');
  Singleton2.Log(ListBox1, 'TSingletonHC[2]');
  Singleton3.Log(ListBox1, 'TSingletonHC[3]');
  if Singleton1 <> Singleton2 then
   Singleton2.Log(ListBox1, 'TSingletonHC: Singleton1 <> Singleton2');
  if Singleton2 <> Singleton3 then
   Singleton3.Log(ListBox1, 'TSingletonHC: Singleton2 <> Singleton3');

  Singleton3.Free; // no problem, this is a separate instance
  // Uncommenting the next line will actually free Singleton1,
  // too, as they are the same object
  // Singleton1.Log call below may still work,
  // but program may raise access violations on exit
  // Singleton2.Free;

  Singleton1.Log(ListBox1, 'TSingletonHC alive');
end;
```

At the beginning of this method, the singleton is accessed twice via the `Instance` method. This works correctly and stores the same object (the same pointer) into both the `Singleton1` and `Singleton2` variables. Immediately after that, however, `TSingletonHC.Create` creates a new object, which destroys the whole singleton idea.

Logging code in the middle of the method checks whether all singleton instances are the same. If you run the program and execute this code, you'll notice that the message **TSingletonHC: Singleton2 <> Singleton3** is displayed. The following screenshot shows the output from the program:

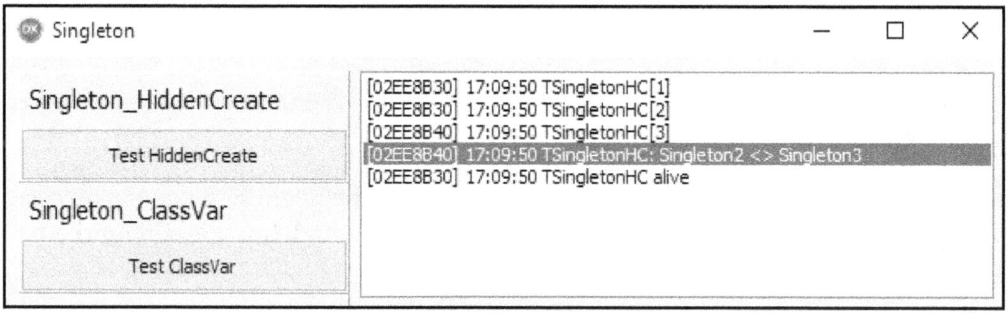

Proof that Singleton_HiddenCreate doesn't work correctly

At the end of the method, the code destroys the `Singleton3` object. This doesn't represent a problem, because this singleton is actually a separate instance of the `TSingletonHC` class. If you uncomment a call to `Singleton2.Free`, however, you'll run into problems. This statement will also destroy `Singleton1`. Also, all future calls to `TSingletonHC.Instance` will return a destroyed object!

As a workaround, we could make the constructor public and throw an exception from it if a global singleton variable is not nil. That would more-or-less work, but it is an ugly solution that just masks a bad approach. As we'll see in a moment, Delphi offers a better way to prevent the creation of multiple instances.

As a bonus, the sample project also includes the `Singleton_ClassVar` unit. This unit stores the singleton in a class variable and not in a global variable. It suffers from the same problems as the hidden constructor variation. I have included this implementation, because you can find some similar solutions on the web, and I don't want them to mislead you.

NewInstance

The proper way to create a singleton in Delphi is not to mess with constructors, but to override the `NewInstance` and `FreeInstance` methods.

When an object is created, the compiler firstly calls the `NewInstance` class method of that object and only then executes the constructor. The `NewInstance` method is `virtual`, and so we can easily override it in our singleton class.

The default implementation in `TObject.NewInstance` calls the `InstanceSize` method to get the number of bytes that are needed to store the new object, then calls `GetMem` to allocate that number of bytes, and in the end, it calls `InitInstance` to fill this memory with zeros.

Instead of all of that, we can change our overridden `NewInstance` method to always return the same memory—our singleton object.

Similarly, the `FreeInstance` method is called to release the memory when the object is destroyed. This method is a normal method, not a class method, but it is still marked as virtual, and we can easily change its implementation in the singleton class.

Both techniques are combined in the `Singleton_NewInstance` unit. The full content of that unit is shown here:

```
unit Singleton_NewInstance;

interface

uses
  Vcl.StdCtrls;

type
  TSingletonNI = class
  strict private
  class var
    FSingleton : TSingletonNI;
    FShuttingDown: boolean;
  strict protected
    class function GetInstance: TSingletonNI; static;
  public
    class destructor Destroy;
    class function NewInstance: TObject; override;
    class property Instance: TSingletonNI read GetInstance;
    procedure FreeInstance; override;
    procedure Log(logTarget: TListBox; const msg: string);
  end;

implementation

class destructor TSingletonNI.Destroy;
begin
  FShuttingDown := true;
  FreeAndNil(FSingleton);
  inherited;
end;

procedure TSingletonNI.FreeInstance;
begin
  if FShuttingDown then
    inherited;
end;

class function TSingletonNI.GetInstance: TSingletonNI;
begin
 Result := TSingletonNI.Create;
end;

class function TSingletonNI.NewInstance: TObject;
begin
```

```
    if not assigned(FSingleton) then
      FSingleton := TSingletonNI(inherited NewInstance);
    Result := FSingleton;
  end;

  procedure TSingletonNI.Log(logTarget: TListBox; const msg: string);
  begin
    logTarget.ItemIndex := logTarget.Items.Add(
      Format('[%p] %s %s',
             [pointer(Self), FormatDateTime('hh:mm:ss', Now), msg]));
  end;

  end.
```

In this implementation, `NewInstance` is overridden to create only the singleton instance, `FSingleton` the first time it is called. That takes care of the instances that are created by calling `TSingletonNI.Create`. To provide a nicer global access to this instance, the class implements an `Instance` property. Reading that property calls the `GetInstance` class function, which simply creates a new object and returns it. That way, the singleton is always accessed through the constructor.

On the other hand, `FreeInstance` simply refuses to do anything unless the `FShuttingDown` flag is set. This can only happen when a class destructor is called, and this can only happen when the program is shutting down.

Class destructors are called after all `finalization` sections have been executed.

The `SingletonPattern` project demonstrates that this implementation really always returns the same object. Click on the `Test NewInstance` button and see for yourself!

This implementation still suffers from a design problem. It offers two ways of accessing the singleton instance. You can either call the `Create` constructor or access the `Instance` property. We could fix this by removing the `Instance` function, and that's exactly what the next example will do. This, however, is not as practical, as using `Instance` in code is simpler than using `Create`. A forthcoming demonstration will prove that.

But, first, let's examine a different problem. Can we change the singleton implementation so that the singleton instance will still be created on demand but also be destroyed when nobody is using it? Well, to do that, we must always know how many users of the singleton are out there, and to do that we must somehow count them. The implementation in `Singleton_NewInstanceCounted` does that by removing the access via the `Instance` property. You can only access the singleton by calling `TSingletonNIC.Create`, and you must release it by calling `TSingletonNIC.Free`. The following code shows this implementation:

```
unit Singleton_NewInstanceCounted;

interface

uses
  Vcl.StdCtrls;

type
  TSingletonNIC = class
  strict private
  class var
    FInstanceCount: integer;
    FSingleton    : TSingletonNIC;
  public
    class destructor Destroy;
    procedure FreeInstance; override;
    class function NewInstance: TObject; override;
    procedure Log(logTarget: TListBox; const msg: string);
  end;

implementation

class destructor TSingletonNIC.Destroy;
begin
  FreeAndNil(FSingleton);
  inherited;
end;

procedure TSingletonNIC.FreeInstance;
begin
  Dec(FInstanceCount);
  if FInstanceCount = 0 then begin
    inherited;
    FSingleton := nil;
  end;
end;

class function TSingletonNIC.NewInstance: TObject;
```

```
begin
  if not assigned(FSingleton) then
    FSingleton := TSingletonNIC(inherited NewInstance);
  Result := FSingleton;
  Inc(FInstanceCount);
end;

procedure TSingletonNIC.Log(logTarget: TListBox; const msg: string);
begin
  logTarget.ItemIndex := logTarget.Items.Add(
    Format('[%p] %s %s',
          [pointer(Self), FormatDateTime('hh:mm:ss', Now), msg]));
end;

end.
```

This implementation works, but using the `TSingletonNIC` singleton is very clumsy. As the secondary form, `TfrmSecondary`, of the `SingletonPattern` demo shows, most singleton implementation can be used through the `Instance` property. The following code fragment shows how some of the implementations can be used:

```
SingletonGV.Log(frmSingleton.ListBox1, 'SingletonGV');
TSingletonHC.Instance.Log(frmSingleton.ListBox1, 'TSingletonHC');
TSingletonNI.Instance.Log(frmSingleton.ListBox1, 'TSingletonNI');
```

The counted implementation, however, requires the following clumsy approach:

```
var
  logger: TSingletonNIC;

logger := TSingletonNIC.Create;
logger.Log(frmSingleton.ListBox1, 'TSingletonNIC');
logger.Free;
```

This approach is required because we have to manually count the instances in use. Wouldn't it be nice if there existed a mechanism that would do that for us? Oh, but there is one! Delphi interfaces do exactly what we need!

Lateral thinking

Delphi gives us a very nice way to implement something that is, for all practical purposes, a singleton—an interface. An interface-based singleton doesn't strictly confront to the singleton design pattern, but we'll see later that the same property that makes it an almost singleton also gives it additional powers.

As I said before, a singleton pattern is not really a practical solution for (almost) anything. It is better to use a practical solution that is not a full singleton but can be used as one.

The singleton implementation in the `Singleton_Factory` unit borrows from the design patterns book and implements a `Factory` method design pattern. As shown next, this allows us to replace the singleton class with an interface and a method that returns the one and only instance of that class:

```
unit Singleton_Factory;

interface

uses
  Vcl.StdCtrls;

type
  ISingletonF = interface ['{5182E010-121F-4CD9-85EB-4F31D34354F2}']
    procedure Log(logTarget: TListBox; const msg: string);
  end;

function SingletonF: ISingletonF;

implementation

uses
  System.SysUtils;

type
  TSingletonF = class(TInterfacedObject, ISingletonF)
  public
    destructor Destroy; override;
    procedure Log(logTarget: TListBox; const msg: string);
  end;

var
  GSingletonF: TSingletonF;

function SingletonF: ISingletonF;
begin
  if not assigned(GSingletonF) then
    GSingletonF := TSingletonF.Create;
  Result := GSingletonF;
end;

destructor TSingletonF.Destroy;
begin
  GSingletonF := nil;
```

```
  inherited;
end;

procedure TSingletonF.Log(logTarget: TListBox; const msg: string);
begin
  logTarget.ItemIndex := logTarget.Items.Add(
    Format('[%p] %s %s',
           [pointer(Self), FormatDateTime('hh:mm:ss', Now), msg]));
end;

end.
```

This almost-trivial implementation stores the singleton instance inside the global variable, `GSingletonF`. The factory function, `SingletonF`, uses the standard test, and use idiom to create the global instance. I would like to stress again that this idiom works only in a single-threaded code and that you should check `Chapter 16`, *Locking Patterns*, for approaches that work in the parallel world.

> This tests, creates, uses idiom is actually an example of a lazy initialization pattern. We will cover it later in this chapter.

The singleton instance is automatically destroyed when all references to it (all interfaces created by the `SingletonF` factory and all copies of these interfaces) are no longer in use. A standard destructor makes sure that the global reference, `GSingletonF`, is also cleared.

If you don't want the singleton to be automatically destroyed when nobody is using it, you just have to change `GSingletonF: TSingletonF` to `GSingletonF: ISingletonF`. This will store an additional reference to the interface in `GSingletonF`, and the singleton will be destroyed only when the program exits.

What about the almost-singleton part I mentioned before? Well, nobody can stop a programmer from creating another class that implements the same `ISingletonF` interface and then passes the instance of that interface around. In real life, this doesn't represent any problem. If anything, it makes the code more flexible and simplifies testing.

At the end of this long discussion, I'd like to present another singleton implementation where Delphi will do everything for us. Its only limitation is that the singleton instance is always created when the program starts and is destroyed when the program ends.

The trick lies in Delphi's concept of class constructors, class methods, and class variables. In essence, every definition inside a class that is prefixed by the class directive can be thought of as a method/variable of another meta class that always has only one instance. This hidden class is created when the code starts up and is destroyed when the program terminates. We therefore don't have to take any care managing the instance and so on.

The following code shows the full implementation of such a singleton, stored in the `Singleton_Class` unit:

```
unit Singleton_Class;

interface

uses
  Vcl.StdCtrls;

type
  SingletonCl = class
  public
    class procedure Log(logTarget: TListBox; const msg: string);
  end;

implementation

uses
  System.SysUtils;

class procedure SingletonCl.Log(logTarget: TListBox; const msg: string);
begin
  logTarget.ItemIndex := logTarget.Items.Add(
    Format('[%p] %s %s',
           [pointer(Self), FormatDateTime('hh:mm:ss', Now), msg]));
end;

end.
```

This brings us to the end of the singleton story. As I mentioned a few times, singletons cause problems with unit testing. Mostly, that happens because they are hard to be replaced with a different implementation (they are hard to mock).

Another problem with singletons is that it is hard to configure them. If the singleton instance is created automatically when the program starts, there's no way to provide any configuration. If, however, the singleton is created on first use, we must pass this configuration each time we access the singleton. That is a) not practical and b) fragile, as one part of the code can pass in a different configuration than the others.

There's a hacky way out of this conundrum. We can push the configuration into some global state that is then used by the singleton class when the singleton instance is created. Still, this is bad from the design view.

There's a much better way to solve this problem. We can simply move away from the singleton pattern and replace it with a dependency injection.

Dependency injection

The **Dependency injection** (**DI**) pattern is the first of many design patterns in this book that were not described in the Gang of Four book. There's a good reason for that. The DI pattern has sprung from the unit-testing movement, and in 1994, unit testing was not yet a thing. In that era, applications were treated as monolithic blocks of code, and not as collections of loosely connected units.

DI works by changing responsibility for object creation. In classical OOP, each object creates new objects that it needs for functioning. This makes the program very rigid and hard to test. DI turns this on its head. If an object needs other objects to functions, the owner (the code which creates the first objects) should also create these other objects and pass them to the first one. In short, a dependency injection says this: Don't create things yourself; your owner should provide them. This decouples objects (makes interconnections between them less tight) and simplifies testing.

For a real-life example, imagine a remote-controlled model car with a fixed rechargeable battery. Do whatever you want, but you are not able to exchange this battery for a better model. This is how coding was approached in a classical object-oriented style.

The same car, built according to dependency injection principles, uses an interchangeable battery pack. When you want to play with the car, you insert (inject) a fresh battery pack and start driving. You can also do long-term tests of the motor by replacing the battery pack with an adapter plugged into the A/C power.

Dependency injection gives you flexibility in exchange for slightly increased complexity. (A car with an interchangeable battery pack has more parts and is harder to make.)

Some programmers argue that DI is actually a case of a strategy design pattern from the design patterns book. (A strategy pattern is not covered in this book.) Indeed, they look very similar, but the difference is, at least in my opinion, in the way they are used. Strategy helps us to write code where different implementations are part of solving a problem. DI, on the other hand, is used when different implementations are parts of testing. A strategy pattern introduces true implementations, while a dependency injection introduces fake implementations, used only for testing.

We could argue that DI is much more than a pattern, and, in a way, this is true. This pattern is so comprehensive that we can easily treat it as a design principle. (Design principles are covered in `Chapter 9`, *Introduction to patterns*).

To simplify the topic, I decided to cover only the basics of dependency injection. This book will therefore abstain from discussing the **Inversion Of Control** (**IOC**) approach, which really is more a design principle than a pattern. If you want to know more about DI, I would strongly recommend a great book by *Nick Hodges, Dependency Injection in Delphi* (`https://leanpub.com/dependencyinjectionindelphi`).

The simplest way to explain DI is through an example. I will start with an old-school object-oriented code and, in a few steps, introduce the dependency injection pattern. At the end, I'll add unit tests to prove that the code has become more testable and maintainable. The main project used in this section is stored in the `Dependency Injection` folder in the `DependencyInjectionPattern` project. You can also start by opening a `DependencyInjection` project group that contains both a demo project and a `DUnit` test project.

The demonstration project is a trivial VCL application with four buttons, each executing a different implementation of the code that we want to convert. The first button, `No Dependency Injection`, executes the following code, which runs the `TDataProcessor.ProcessData` method from the `DataProcessing.NoDI` unit:

```
procedure TfrmDI.btnNoDIClick(Sender: TObject);
var
  processor: DataProcessing.NoDI.TDataProcessor;
begin
  processor := DataProcessing.NoDI.TDataProcessor.Create;
  try
    processor.ProcessData;
  finally
    FreeAndNil(processor);
  end;
end;
```

The `ProcessData` method is shown next:

```
procedure TDataProcessor.ProcessData;
var
  count: integer;
  reader: TReader;
  sum: int64;
  value: integer;
  writer: TWriter;
begin
  reader := TReader.Create('..\..\data.txt');
  try
    sum := 0;
    count := 0;
    while reader.GetNext(value) do
    begin
      Inc(sum, value);
      Inc(count);
    end;
    writer := TWriter.Create('..\..\data.csv');
    try
      writer.WriteOut(count, sum, sum/count);
    finally
      FreeAndNil(writer);
    end;
  finally
    FreeAndNil(reader);
  end;
end;
```

The code firstly creates a data reader, `TReader`. It is implemented in the `DataProcessing.Reader` unit. This is a very simple text file reader class that, on each call of the `GetNext` method, reads the next line from the file, converts it into the integer value, and returns it in the `value` parameter. When there's no more data in the file, the function returns `False`.

The code then calls this `GetNext` method, adds all numbers together, and maintains a count of read numbers.

In the last step, the code creates a `TWriter` class and writes three values into a **Comma Separated Values** (**CSV**) text file. The first value contains a number of read values, the second a sum of all numbers, and the last one the average value of all data.

The statistical part of that code is really hard to test. We have to create an input text file in an expected format, run the code, and then open and parse the output file. That means lots of work, and, besides that, this defeats the whole idea of unit testing, because we are actually testing an integration of three units: reader, data processor, and writer.

The dependency injection pattern states that it is the owner who should pass the required dependency to the worker class. This approach is implemented in the `DataProcessing.InjectedParam` unit and is activated by the `Injected parameters` button. A click on this button executes the following code:

```
procedure TfrmDI.btnInjectedParamsClick(Sender: TObject);
var
  processor: DataProcessing.InjectedParam.TDataProcessor;
  reader: TReader;
  writer: TWriter;
begin
  reader := TReader.Create('..\..\data.txt');
  try
    writer := TWriter.Create('..\..\data.csv');
    try
      processor := DataProcessing.InjectedParam.TDataProcessor.Create;
      try
        processor.ProcessData(reader, writer);
      finally
        FreeAndNil(processor);
      end;
    finally
      FreeAndNil(writer);
    end;
  finally
    FreeAndNil(reader);
  end;
end;
```

An implementation of `TDataProcessor.ProcessData` is now much simpler:

```
procedure TDataProcessor.ProcessData(AReader: TReader; AWriter: TWriter);
var
  count: integer;
  sum: int64;
  value: integer;
begin
  sum := 0;
  count := 0;
  while AReader.GetNext(value) do begin
    Inc(sum, value);
    Inc(count);
```

```
    end;
    AWriter.WriteOut(count, sum, sum/count);
  end;
```

This version already looks much better. The reader and writer are created in the part of code that would also set the correct file names in a real application. The `ProcessData` method does not need to know where the data lies anymore.

From classes to interfaces

Such an approach, while more maintainable, still isn't good for unit testing. We cannot simply create a replacement for `TReader`, as `GetNext` is not a virtual method. (The same goes for `TWriter` and `WriteOut`.) Even if we fix that, the fact remains that creating mock classes (classes used only for testing other classes) by deriving from real implementation is a recipe for trouble. Doing it that way just brings in lots of dependencies and interconnectedness.

A better way is to extract the public interface of a class to an interface and change the code to depend on an interface, not on a class. In this example, both interfaces are intentionally simple, as the following code fragment shows:

```
type
  IReader = interface ['{9B32E26A-456F-45D1-A494-B331C7131020}']
    function GetNext(var value: integer): boolean;
  end;

  IWriter = interface ['{ED6D0678-5FCE-41BA-A161-BE691FCB6B7B}']
    procedure WriteOut(count: integer; sum: int64; average: real);
  end;
```

This approach is implemented in the `DataProcessing.InjectedProperties` unit and is activated with a click on the `Injected properties` button. The following method shows how to create appropriate interfaces and pass them to `ProcessData`:

```
procedure TfrmDI.btnInjectedPropsClick(Sender: TObject);
var
  processor: DataProcessing.InjectedProperties.TDataProcessor;
  reader: IReader;
  writer: IWriter;
begin
  reader := TReader.Create('..\..\data.txt');
  writer := TWriter.Create('..\..\data.csv');
  processor := DataProcessing.InjectedProperties.TDataProcessor.Create;
  try
```

```
    processor.Reader := reader;
    processor.Writer := writer;
    processor.ProcessData;
  finally
    FreeAndNil(processor);
  end;
end;
```

In this example, I' have changed the way dependent implementations are injected into the worker method. Instead of passing them as parameters to `ProcessData`, they are injected into `TDataProcessor` properties. This was done for demonstration purposes and is not connected to the change from object-based to interface-based implementation. I just wanted to show that there are other options on how dependencies are injected. At the very end of this section, I will enumerate and evaluate them all.

The new `TDataProcessor` implementation is shown next:

```
type
  TDataProcessor = class
  strict private
    FReader: IReader;
    FWriter: IWriter;
  public
    procedure ProcessData;
    property Reader: IReader read FReader write FReader;
    property Writer: IWriter read FWriter write FWriter;
  end;

procedure TDataProcessor.ProcessData;
var
  count: integer;
  sum: int64;
  value: integer;
begin
  sum := 0;
  count := 0;
  while FReader.GetNext(value) do begin
    Inc(sum, value);
    Inc(count);
  end;
  FWriter.WriteOut(count, sum, sum/count);
end;
```

Now we have a fully testable implementation. A `UnitTestDependencyInjection` project shows how unit tests can be done in practice. This project is implemented with the `DUnit` framework because it is included in standard Delphi installation, but it could be implemented equally well with `DUnit2`, `DUnitX`, or any other testing framework. Let's take a look at one test taken from the `DataProcesing.DUnit` unit:

```
procedure TestTDataProcessor.TestSequence;
var
  writer: ITestWriter;
begin
  writer := TTestWriter.Create;
  FDataProcessor.Reader := TTestReader.Create([1, 1, 2, 2]);
  FDataProcessor.Writer := writer as IWriter;
  FDataProcessor.ProcessData;
  CheckEquals(4, writer.Count);
  CheckEquals(6, writer.Sum);
  CheckEquals(double(1.5), double(writer.Average));
end;
```

The `TTestReader` and `TTestWriter` classes are now true mock classes and have no connection to the actual `TReader` and `TWriter` implementations. `TTestReader` (implemented in the `DataProcessing.Reader.DUnit` unit) is a simple class that enumerates over an array and returns one value in each `GetNext` call. Although simple, the implementation is quite interesting, and I urge you to explore this code.

The `TTestWriter` class is a bit more complicated. It must implement the `WriteOut` method and allow us to check the values that we passed to that call. To do that, it implements two interfaces: the original `IWriter` and a test interface `ITestWriter`. This class is implemented in the `DataProcessing.Writer.DUnit` unit.

I' have implemented several tests, and one of them pointed to a deficiency in the `ProcessData` implementation. The next method tests what happens when `GetNext` returns no data (`False` is returned from the first call):

```
procedure TestTDataProcessor.TestZero;
var
  writer: ITestWriter;
begin
  writer := TTestWriter.Create;
  FDataProcessor.Reader := TTestReader.Create([]);
  FDataProcessor.Writer := writer as IWriter;
  FDataProcessor.ProcessData;
  CheckEquals(0, writer.Count);
  CheckEquals(0, writer.Sum);
```

```
    CheckEquals(double(0), double(writer.Average));
  end;
```

Instead of working as expected, `ProcessData` raises a floating point invalid operation exception.

The reason is not hard to find. `ProcessData` executes the following line:

```
FWriter.WriteOut(count, sum, sum/count);
```

As the `count` is zero in this test, the code tries to divide by zero and raises an exception.

Using a factory method

One way to fix this problem would be to add a simple test to the `ProcessData` method and write out three zeros (or some other value). This solution is simple but provides no educational value, so I decided to do something different. My solution is to simply not create an output file if the input data is empty.

Once we do that, the code doesn't always need the `IWriter` interface. It is therefore wasteful to create this interface before we call the `ProcessData` method. We can instead use a lazy initialization pattern, which I already mentioned while discussing different singleton implementations.

The lazy initialization will be covered in the next section, but it is so simple and intuitive that I won't confuse you if I use it in the dependency injection example. After all, I already used it to implement singletons, and you didn't think twice about it, I'm sure.

The simplest possible way to introduce lazy initialization to a dependency injection is to use yet another design pattern, `factory method`. (This pattern will be covered in depth in `Chapter 11`, *Factory Method, Abstract Factory, Prototype, and Builder*.) Instead of injecting an interface, we will inject an anonymous method that creates this interface. The worker code will only call this anonymous method when an interface is actually required.

The fourth button in the demo application, `Injected factory`, executes the following code, which calls the new and improved implementation:

```
procedure TfrmDI.btnInjectedFactoryClick(Sender: TObject);
var
  processor: DataProcessing.Factory.TDataProcessor;
begin
  processor := DataProcessing.Factory.TDataProcessor.Create;
  try
    processor.Reader := TReader.Create('..\..\data.txt');
```

```
      processor.WriterFactory :=
        function: IWriter
        begin
          Result := TWriter.Create('..\..\data.csv');
        end;
      processor.ProcessData;
    finally
      FreeAndNil(processor);
    end;
  end;
```

The new `TDataProcessor` is stored in the `DataProcessing.Factory` unit. Its implementation is shown here:

```
type
  TDataProcessor = class
  strict private
    FReader: IReader;
    FWriterFactory: TFunc<IWriter>;
  public
    procedure ProcessData;
    property Reader: IReader read FReader write FReader;
    property WriterFactory: TFunc<IWriter> read FWriterFactory
      write FWriterFactory;
  end;

procedure TDataProcessor.ProcessData;
var
  count: integer;
  sum: int64;
  value: integer;
begin
  sum := 0;
  count := 0;
  while FReader.GetNext(value) do begin
    Inc(sum, value);
    Inc(count);
  end;

  if count > 0 then
    FWriterFactory.WriteOut(count, sum, sum/count);
end;
```

This version of `ProcessData` creates the `IWriter` interface (by calling the `FWriterFactory` anonymous method) only if a number of values read from the source is greater than zero.

TIP: Delphi allows us to use the `FWriterFactory.WriteOut` or the `FWriterFactory().WriteOut` syntax to call the anonymous method. In such cases, a method stored in the `FWriterFactory` parameter is implicitly executed. Some still like to write parentheses after it so that the intent of the code is more explicit.

This revised implementation is tested with the `TestZeroFixed` and `TestSequenceFixed` in the `DataProcessing.DUnit` unit.

Wrapping up

The examples in this section have demonstrated two of three common ways to inject dependencies:

- **Constructor injection**: When concrete implementations are used for proper functioning of the entire class, we can inject them as parameters to the constructor. This approach was not used in examples from this section, but I did implement a version of `TDataProcessor` that uses a constructor injection. You can explore the `DataProcessing.ClassParams` unit yourself to see how the constructor injection could be used in practice.
- **Property injection**: Sometimes, concrete implementations are used only under specific circumstances. In such cases, we can inject them as properties. Implementations in `DataProcessing.InjectedProperties` and `DataProcessing.Factory` are using this approach.
- **Method injection**: If concrete implementations are only used inside one method, we can inject them as parameters to that method. An implementation in the `DataProcessing.InjectedParam` unit uses this approach.

At the end of this lengthy introduction to dependency injection, I would like to return to the `SingletonPattern` project from the previous section. The secondary form, `SingletonPatternSecondary` implements (in addition to all singleton examples), logging via the injected `InjectedLogger` property.

A proper way to introduce this logger would be the constructor injection (because the logger may be used each time the form is displayed), but that's hard to do with forms that are automatically created, and so the example uses the next best approach: property injection.

Lazy initialization

After two lengthy discussions, a section about a lazy initialization pattern should present a comfortable change. This pattern appeared in the *Gang of Four* book under the name of virtual proxy, which virtually nobody is using today. Lazy initialization, on the other hand, has become a common household name.

Lazy initialization is a very simple pattern that merely states whether an object is not always required, creating it only when it is needed. We would use this pattern on two occasions: when the creation of an object or its initialization is a slow process, or when the very existence of the object signifies something.

> Whenever I go somewhere with a car, I have to take into account the small possibility that the car will not start. If that happens, I call my mechanic. That's lazy initialization.
>
> Doing it in a classical object-oriented way would be entirely stupid. Just imagine, I want to go out, and so I call my mechanic and say: Please come here; I intend to start the car, and maybe I'll need you... probably not, but still...

Implementing lazy initialization is trivial, so we usually don't even think about it. Instead of initializing an object when the program starts or when the owner object is created, we use the `test`, `create`, `use` idiom, as shown here:

```
if not assigned(lazyObject) then
  lazyObject := TLazyObject.Create;
Use(lazyObject);
```

The problem with lazy initialization is that the programmer may forget to code the initialization part. For example, we could by mistake call `Use(lazyObject)` directly before firstly checking whether `lazyObject` had been created. A good implementation of a lazy object therefore makes sure that the object can never be accessed directly.

Let's say that this lazily created object (let's call it a `lazy` object) is part of another object (`parent` object). If the parent object never uses the lazy object directly, we can simply hide the lazy object behind a property getter. This getter will take care of a lazy initialization when the lazy object is accessed for the first time.

The example project `LazyInitializationPattern` contains the class `TLazyOwner` in the `Lazy` unit. Inside this class, you'll find a `FLazyObject: TLazyObject` field. This field is not used inside the `TLazyOwner` class. From the viewpoint of the external code, it can only be accessed through the `LazyObject` property. The following code fragment shows the relevant parts of the `TLazyOwner` class:

```
type
  TLazyOwner = class
  strict private
    FLazyObject: TLazyObject;
  strict protected
    function GetLazyObject: TLazyObject;
    property LazyInternal: TLazyInternal read GetLazyInternal;
  public
    destructor Destroy; override;
    property LazyObject: TLazyObject read GetLazyObject;
  end;

destructor TLazyOwner.Destroy;
begin
  FreeAndNil(FLazyObject);
  inherited;
end;

function TLazyOwner.GetLazyObject: TLazyObject;
begin
  if not assigned(FLazyObject) then
    FLazyObject := TLazyObject.Create;
  Result := FLazyObject;
end;
```

This code shows how an object can be lazily initialized in a single-threaded program. On the other hand, it is completely broken in a multi-threaded code! To see how a project should be properly initialized in a multithreaded program, check the patterns *Double-Checked Locking* and *Optimistic initialization* in `Chapter 16`, *Locking Patterns*.

The example program contains some logging code that I removed from the previous code sample. If you run the program and click on the **Create/destroy owner** button, followed by a click on the **Access lazy object** button, you should get the same result, as shown in the next screenshot:

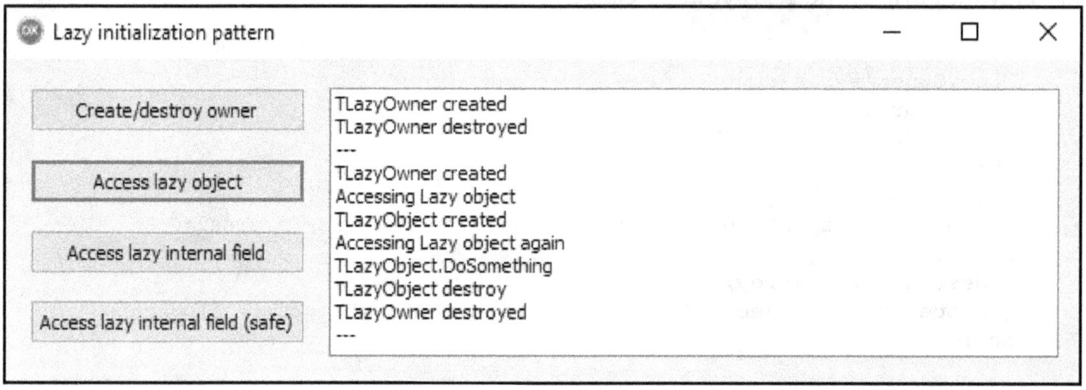

The lazy object is only created when the LazyObject property is accessed.

We can see from this screenshot that the lazy object is not created if the parent object is created and then immediately destroyed. Only if the code accesses the `LazyObject` property is the underlying object created.

Safe programming is not so easily enforced if the parent object itself is using the lazy object. The `TLazyOwner` class also implements a `FLazyInternal` object that's used inside the `TLazyOwner.ProcessUsingLazy` method. In this case, we can easily make a mistake and use `FLazyInternal` directly, instead of accessing it through the `LazyInternal` property.

If we want to protect ourselves from such mistakes, we have to make it impossible to access the lazy object directly. One of the possible solutions is to hide it inside a nested class. If we put it inside a `strict private` section, even the parent object won't have access to it! The declaration is shown in the next code fragment:

```
type
  TLazyOwner = class
  strict private
  type
    THiddenLazyInternal = class
    strict private
      FLazyInternalSafe: TLazyInternal;
    public
      constructor Create;
```

```
      destructor Destroy; override;
      property LazyInternal: TLazyInternal read FLazyInternalSafe;
    end;
  var
    FLazyInternalSafe: THiddenLazyInternal;
  strict protected
    function LazyInternalSafe: TLazyInternal;
  public
    constructor Create;
    destructor Destroy; override;
 end;
```

The real lazy object is stored inside the `FLazyInternalSafe` field of the `THiddenLazyInternal` class. Because it is marked as `strict private`, the code in the `TLazyOwner` class cannot access it directly. It can, however, be accessed through the `LazyInternalSafe` function, which creates the internal `THiddenLazyInternal` object and returns its `LazyInternal` property, as shown:

```
constructor TLazyOwner.THiddenLazyInternal.Create;
begin
  inherited Create;
  FLazyInternalSafe := TLazyInternal.Create;
end;

destructor TLazyOwner.THiddenLazyInternal.Destroy;
begin
  FreeAndNil(FLazyInternalSafe);
  inherited;
end;

function TLazyOwner.LazyInternalSafe: TLazyInternal;
begin
  if not assigned(FLazyInternalSafe) then
    FLazyInternalSafe := THiddenLazyInternal.Create;
  Result := FLazyInternalSafe.LazyInternal;
end;
```

This code exposes lazy object through a function, not through a property as the previous example did. Both approaches are equally valid.

Using Spring

If you intend to use a large number of lazily created objects, you will soon get fed up of writing all of the management code. A simpler solution is to use a pre-made lazy initialization wrapper, such as Lazy<T> from the Spring4D library (https://bitbucket.org/sglienke/spring4d).

I have prepared an example, LazyInitializationSpring4D that uses Lazy<T> to do the hard work. It requires the Spring4D library to function. To run the example program, you'll have to install this library and then add its Source and Source\Base folders to Delphi's Library path or to the project's Search path. If you unpack the library into the Chapter10\Spring4D folder, the project's search path will already be correctly configured.

> TIP: If you have git installed, you can execute the following command in the folder Chapter 10 folder to install Spring4D: git clone https://bitbucket.org/sglienke/spring4d.

The following code fragment shows how to lazily initialize an object using this method. This implementation can be found in the LazySpring4D.Lazy unit:

```
type
  TLazyOwner = class
  strict private
    FLazyObj: Lazy<TLazyObj>;
  strict protected
    function GetLazy: TLazyObj;
  public
    constructor Create;
    destructor Destroy; override;
    property Lazy: TLazyObj read GetLazy;
  end;

constructor TLazyOwner.Create;
begin
  inherited Create;
  FLazyObj := Lazy<TLazyObj>.Create;
end;

destructor TLazyOwner.Destroy;
begin
  FLazyObj.Value.Free;
  inherited;
end;
```

```
function TLazyOwner.GetLazy: TLazyObj;
begin
  Result := FLazyObj;
end;
```

In the constructor, we have to make sure that Lazy<TLazyObj> is correctly initialized. The call to Lazy<TLazyObj>.Create will not create the TLazyObj object; it will just set up everything so that the lazy wrapper can be properly used.

The code in the destructor destroys the lazy object if it was created before. As Free works correctly when executed on a nil object, we can call it freely without firstly checking whether the lazy object was indeed initialized.

The GetLazy function retrieves the lazy object. At the first use of this function, the object will be initialized. All ugly plumbing code is hidden inside the Spring4D library.

> TIP: This approach to lazy initialization is also thread-safe, so you can use it without any reservations in a multi-threaded program.

The same project also shows how we can lazily initialize an interface. In this case, we don't have to take care about destruction. We must, however, provide an additional piece of code, a factory method that will create the interface. The factory method pattern will be discussed in the next chapter. Relevant parts of the TLazyOwner class are shown in the next code fragment:

```
type
  TLazyOwner = class
  strict private
    FLazyInt: Lazy<ILazyInt>;
  strict protected
    function GetLazyInt: ILazyInt;
  public
    constructor Create;
    property LazyInt: ILazyInt read GetLazyInt;
  end;

constructor TLazyOwner.Create;
begin
  inherited Create;
  FLazyInt := Lazy<ILazyInt>.Create(
    function: ILazyInt
    begin
      Result := TLazyInt.Create;
    end);
```

```
end;

function TLazyOwner.GetLazyInt: ILazyInt;
begin
  Result := FLazyInt;
end;
```

The factory method that creates an object implementing the `ILazyInt` interface is passed as an anonymous method parameter to the `Lazy<ILazyInt>.Create` constructor. All other pieces of the solution are the same as in the previous example.

As you can see, the lazy initialization pattern really isn't complicated, as long as you know whether it will be used in a single-threaded or a multi-threaded environment and uses an appropriate implementation.

Object pool

The last pattern in this chapter, object pool, is again not part of the original design patterns book. Object pools as a concept appeared early in the history of OOP, but somehow the Gang of Four didn't see them as a design pattern.

Object pool functions as storage for objects. When we have an object that takes a long time to create and initialize, we sometimes don't want to spend time doing it all over again. Instead of destroying such an object, we can simply put it away in a special container: an object pool. Later, we can just ask the object pool to return the already-created object, an operation that's much faster than creating a new object.

> If you have to write a letter (yes, a physical one, on paper!), you need a pen. If there is no pen in the house, you will go to the shop and buy one. Acquiring a new pen is therefore a costly operation. Because of that, you don't throw a pen away once you've finished the letter. Instead, you store it in a drawer.
>
> The next time you have to write a letter, you just take a pen from a drawer, bypassing all of the costly creation of a new pen. You can also have multiple pens in the drawer, hence easily satisfying the writing urges of other family members.

A standard example of an object pool is a database-connection pool. Connecting to a database is a relatively slow operation, and if you want fast response times, you'll store already-open but unused connections in a pool.

Another typical example comes from a parallel world. Creating a new thread is a costly operation. It can easily take ten milliseconds and more. Sometimes, for example when you are debugging a program in Delphi IDE, it can take up to half a second to create a new thread. A well-designed framework for multithreaded computing therefore stores inactive threads in a thread pool.

An object pool is less important in Delphi than in garbage-collected environments (Java and .NET). In the latter, object pools are also used to fight memory fragmentation. That represented a problem in early Delphi versions, too, but since the 2006 release, the FastMM memory manager takes care of the fragmentation problem.

An object pool needs a storage mechanism to store our objects when they are not used. We can use any data container for this storage: an array, a list, or something else. In most cases, we will set the maximum size for an object pool at the time it is created. Sometimes, though, we will want the object pool to grow as required. Both approaches are perfectly valid. You will use the one that fits your problem better.

The life cycle of objects stored inside a pool (pooled objects) is managed by the pool itself. If a pool cannot retrieve a pooled object and there is still room to grow (or size is not limited), then it will create a new instance of a pooled object and will return it. When a pool is destroyed, it will destroy the pooled objects too.

When a pool is empty (all objects are in use) and the maximum size has been reached, a caller cannot retrieve a new object from the pool. A pool can in such a case either return a failure (by returning a `nil` object or failure status or raising an exception), or it can block and wait until an object is available. The last approach is especially useful in a multithreaded application. One thread can wait for a pooled object (can block) until another thread has finished with it.

To create a new pooled object, a pool can call the default constructor `Create`. Alternatively, we can provide a `factory` method that will create a new pooled object when required. The `factory` method design pattern is described in the next chapter.

Sometimes, an object pool can implement a timeout mechanism. If an object has not been used for a configured time period, the pool will destroy the object, and with that release some resources. You will see such behavior in most thread pool implementations.

You must be careful not to leave any secret information stored inside a pooled object when it is not in use. If you are implementing an object pool in a server application where multiple clients can use objects created from a pool, it would be especially bad if information put there by one client somehow leaked to the next one. Make sure that you always clear such parts of an object before it is put back into use.

It is quite hard to find a problem where an object pool is really necessary in Delphi, apart from the standard candidates, connection, and thread pool. As the thread pool pattern will be described in `Chapter 17`, *Thread pool, Messaging, Future and Pipeline*, this chapter focuses on a connection pool, not one that's connecting to databases, though, but a pool that stores https connections.

> TIP: Object pools can be very useful in multithreaded applications. When multiple threads are allocating and releasing objects at the same time, access to the memory manager can become very slow.

If you think that you need an object pool in your code, measure execution times first. Many times, you'll find that the slow part of the program lies somewhere else, not in object creation and initialization.

Stock quote connection pool

As a short example, I've created an application that reads data about stock symbols (**AAPL** (**Apple**), IBM, and **MSFT** (**Microsoft**)) and returns some basic information about the symbol, such as the latest stock value. This information is retrieved from a public server provided by the company IEX (`https://iextrading.com/developer/docs/#attribution`).

The demonstration program, `ObjectPoolPattern` allows you to enter the name of a stock symbol and then query the server for this symbol's data by clicking the `Get data` button. This will generate a request in the `https://api.iextrading.com/1.0/stock/SYMB/quote` form, where SYMB will be replaced with the actual symbol (for example, MSFT).

As connecting to a https server is a relatively lengthy operation, it makes sense to store currently unused connections in an object pool.

The actual https query is implemented by using Delphi's standard `TNetHTTPClient` component. This component supports asynchronous operation. We can start a query and provide a callback (similar to an event handler) that will be called when the operation completes. Our program is still responsive during that time, and the user can request data for another stock, even when the first query didn't return the result.

This connection mechanism is implemented in the class `TStockQuoteConnection` in the unit `ObjectPool.StockQuotePool`. Besides the constructor and destructor, which you can look up in the code, this class implements the method `Query`, which is called from the main program to fetch the data for a stock symbol. When the https query returns, the function `HandleHttpRequestCompleted` is called. Both functions are shown next:

```
type
  TStockQuoteResponse = reference to procedure (const symbol, content:
string);

procedure TStockQuoteConnection.HandleHttpRequestCompleted(
  const Sender: TObject; const AResponse: IHTTPResponse);
begin
  if assigned(AResponse) then
    FResponseProc(FSymbol, AResponse.ContentAsString)
  else
    FResponseProc(FSymbol, '');
end;

procedure TStockQuoteConnection.Query(const symbol: string;
  const responseProc: TStockQuoteResponse);
begin
  FSymbol := symbol;
  FResponseProc := responseProc;
  FHttpClient.Get('https://api.iextrading.com/1.0/stock/'
    + symbol + '/quote');
end;
```

A caller will call the `Query` method with two parameters: a name of the stock symbol and a callback method. This callback is implemented as an anonymous method because that, as we'll see later, simplifies the code in the main program.

The `Query` method simply stores both parameters in class fields and then composes and executes a `GET` request to a `https://` address. The `Get` method soon returns, and the program can continue with execution.

Some time later, depending on how quickly the web server responds, the `HandleHttpRequestCompleted` is called from the `TNetHTTPClient` code. This method simply uses previously stored callback (`FResponseProc`) and a stock symbol (`FSymbol`) and executes the callback.

Let's now see how this is used in the program. The main form uses an object pool, `FStockQuotePool: TStockQuotePool` to manage the connection. (We will see soon how this pool is implemented.) To retrieve a new connection, the code must call the `GetConnection` method. When a connection is not needed anymore, it must be returned to the pool with a call to the `ReleaseConnection` method. The following code fragment shows how the pool is used in the main program:

```
procedure TfrmObjectPool.QuerySymbol(const symbol: string);
var
  connection: TStockQuoteConnection;
begin
  connection := FStockQuotePool.GetConnection;
  if not assigned(connection) then
    Log(symbol + ': All connections are busy!'#13#10)
  else
    connection.Query(symbol,
      procedure (const symbol, response: string)
      begin
        Log(Format('%s [%p]', [symbol, pointer(connection)])
            + #13#10 + response + #13#10);
        FStockQuotePool.ReleaseConnection(connection);
      end);
 end;
```

The code firstly requests a new connection. As the connection pool is limited in size (we will see soon how this is done), `GetConnection` may fail and return `nil`. In such a case, the code will log `All connections are busy!`

When a connection object is successfully acquired, the code calls its `Query` method and passes in a stock symbol name `symbol` and an anonymous method that is constructed in its place. This anonymous method will be called from the `HandleHttpRequestCompleted` method.

In the anonymous method, we simply log the response and release the connection back to the pool by calling `ReleaseConnection`. Through the magic of anonymous methods and variable capturing, we can simply reuse the `connection` variable in the anonymous method.

This is the afore-mentioned part, when using an anonymous method simplifies the code. If we were using a standard event handler (`procedure ... of object`), we would have to store `connection` into a form field so that the event handler would be able to access it later. We would also have to manage multiple connections, as the user can execute multiple simultaneous requests. By using the anonymous methods and variable capturing, the code gets simplified a lot.

For testing purposes, the object pool is limited to two objects. You can easily change this by editing the `FormCreate` method, shown next:

```
procedure TfrmObjectPool.FormCreate(Sender: TObject);
begin
  FStockQuotePool := TStockQuotePool.Create(2);
end;
```

If you click the **Get all 3** button, three simultaneous queries will be activated, one for each stock symbol. As the pool can only provide two connections, the third query will immediately fail. Moments later, results from other two queries will appear. The next screenshot shows a screenshot of the demo program in that state:

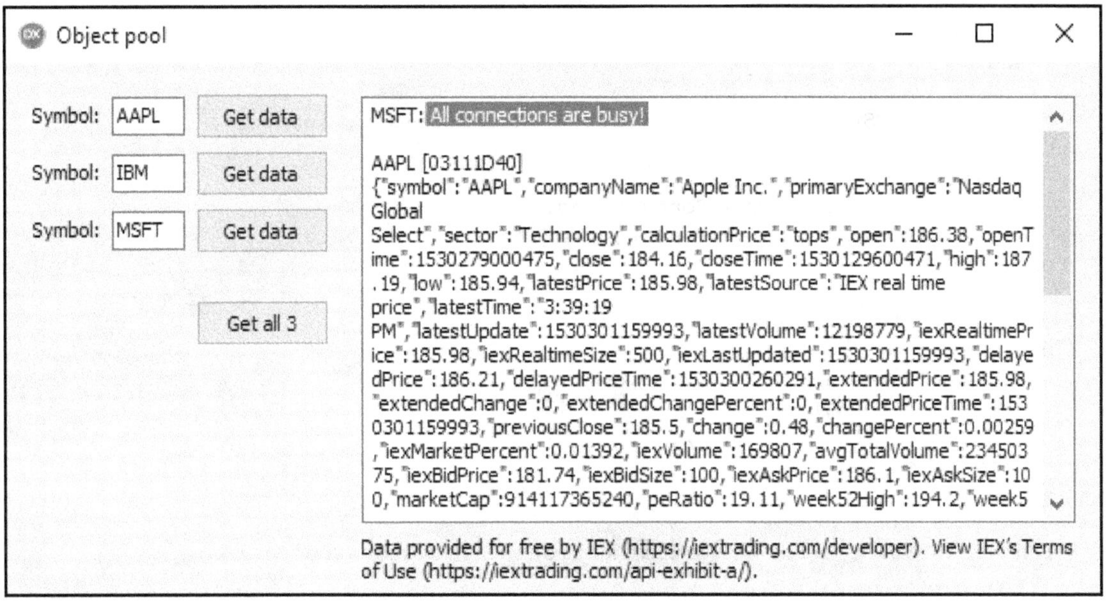

Stock quote connection pool in action.

The two succeeding requests will both have `[somenumber]` displayed next to the stock symbol. In the previous screenshot, for example, a line, **AAPL [03111D40],** contains that number. This number is the address of the connection object used to query the server. If you continue clicking on the *Get data* buttons, you'll notice that only two addresses are used. They correspond to two connection objects stored in the object pool.

Let's now look at the object pool implementation. `Object pool` is implemented in class `TStockQuotePool`, stored in unit `ObjectPool.StockQuotePool`. Its implementation is as follows:

```
type
  TStockQuotePool = class(TInterfacedObject)
  strict private
    FMaxConnections: integer;
    FNumConnections: integer;
    FConnections : TStack<TStockQuoteConnection>;
  public
    constructor Create(AMaxConnections: integer);
    destructor Destroy; override;
    function GetConnection: TStockQuoteConnection;
    procedure ReleaseConnection(connection: TStockQuoteConnection);
  end;

constructor TStockQuotePool.Create(AMaxConnections: integer);
begin
  inherited Create;
  FMaxConnections := AMaxConnections;
  FConnections := TStack<TStockQuoteConnection>.Create;
end;

destructor TStockQuotePool.Destroy;
begin
  while FConnections.Count > 0 do
    FConnections.Pop.Free;
  FreeAndNil(FConnections);
  inherited;
end;

function TStockQuotePool.GetConnection: TStockQuoteConnection;
begin
  if FConnections.Count > 0 then
    Exit(FConnections.Pop);
  if (FMaxConnections > 0) and (FNumConnections >= FMaxConnections) then
    Exit(nil);
  Result := TStockQuoteConnection.Create;
  Inc(FNumConnections);
end;

procedure TStockQuotePool.ReleaseConnection(connection:
TStockQuoteConnection);
begin
  FConnections.Push(connection);
end;
```

The stock connection pool stores pooled objects in a TStack structure. I selected this structure because it is simple and fast. We can only store data on a stack (Push) and retrieve data from the top of the stack (Pop), but that is enough for our purposes.

The constructor creates a background storage and sets the field FMaxConnections, which limits the maximum pool size. You can set it to 0, and that will allow the pool to grow without any limits.

The destructor takes all the connections from the stack and destroys each one. In the end, it destroys the stack storage.

Getting a connection from the pool is the most complicated part. Firstly, a connection is taken from the stack if it is not empty. If that fails and the pool can still grow, a new connection is created and the total number of managed connections is updated.

To release a connection back to the pool, the code simply pushes it on to the stack.

> As we are only using the connection pool from the main thread, it was not designed to function correctly in a multithreaded environment!
>
> If you need the object pool to function in a multi-threaded code, you should implement locking. See the DPObjectPool unit (discussed next) for an example of this.

The code in the archive for this chapter also contains the unit DPObjectPool that implements a generic object pool class TObjectPool<T>. You can use it freely in your applications whenever you need an object pool. This pool implements an interface that is very similar to TStockQuotePool. The next code fragment shows relevant parts of the class definition:

```
type
  TObjectPool<T:class,constructor> = class
  public
    constructor Create(maxSize: integer = 0;
      const factory: TFunc<T> = nil); overload;
    constructor Create(const factory: TFunc<T>); overload;
    destructor Destroy; override;
    function Allocate: T;
    procedure Release(const obj: T);
  end;
```

This pool will be limited in size if you set the `maxSize` to a positive number. If the `factory` parameter is provided, it will be used to create new pooled objects. You can, for example, create the pool as in the following code fragment to pass some additional information to the object's constructor:

```
pool := TObjectPool<TPoolObject>.Create(
  function: TPoolObject
  begin
    Result := TPoolObject.Create(42);
  end);
```

The `Allocate` method retrieves an object from the pool (possibly creating it in the process). The `Release` method releases a pooled object back to the pool.

The implementation closely matches stock connection pool implementation, so I will not show it in the book. I would only like to point out that the `TObjectPool<T>` implementation uses *locking* to protect the critical code, so this pool can be safely used in a multithreaded environment. For a longer discussion on locking, see `Chapter 8`, *Locking patterns*. A full implementation of the `Release` method is shown here:

```
procedure TObjectPool<T>.Release(const obj: T);
begin
  MonitorEnter(Self); // lock
  try
    FPool.Push(obj);
  finally
    MonitorExit(Self); // unlock
  end;
end;
```

Summary

In this chapter, I have explored four basic creational patterns.

The first one was singleton, a pattern used when we need exactly one instance of a class. The chapter looked at a few bad and a few good implementations and explored alternatives.

After that, I switched to the DI pattern, which can sometimes be used to replace a singleton. As DI is incredibly large area, the chapter has focused on basics and explored different injection mechanisms.

The third pattern in this chapter was lazy initialization. The mechanism behind the lazy initialization (the test, create, use idiom) is so simple that most of the time we don't think about this concept as a pattern. It can still be tricky to implement this pattern correctly, and I have pointed to few potential problems and offered a way to overcome them.

For the last pattern in this chapter, I have looked into the object pool. This pattern is used when creating and initializing new object is a costly operation. The object pool represents a storage for objects that are not currently in use. For this demonstration, I have built a connection pool that caches https connections to a stock quote service.

In the next chapter, we'll look into four more complex creational patterns: Factory method, Abstract Factory, Prototype, and Builder.

11
Factory Method, Abstract Factory, Prototype, and Builder

Creating an object can sometimes be a complicated operation, especially if we are dealing with a complicated hierarchy of interdependent objects. Patterns can introduce order into chaos in such situations.

In this chapter, we'll look into four more patterns from the creational group. You will learn about the following:

- A factory method pattern that simplifies the creation of dependent objects
- An abstract factory pattern that functions as a factory for factories and creates whole families of objects
- A prototype pattern that produces perfect copies of objects
- A builder pattern that separates instructions for creating an object from its representation

Factory method

The factory method pattern specifies how an object can defer creation of some internal data and leave the actual task of creation for the derived class. It is part of the original *Gang of Four* book.

Imagine a kid making cookies out of dough. They can do nothing until they invoke the `factory` method and say, Give me a cutter. So, you provide them with a cookie cutter (the result of the `factory` method), and they can finally start making cookies.

By implementing this approach, you can be flexible and select the appropriate cookie shape for the occasion. Output from the factory method therefore changes the final result.

The functionality of this pattern, as described in the original Design Patterns publication, looks very similar to the dependency injection approach, but implemented with pure object-oriented tools. This section will mostly focus on the original approach, but at the end, I will spend some time modernizing this technique.

The pure GoF example is stored in the folder of the `Factory` method in the project example. It implements the base class `TBaseClass`, which uses the factory method `MakeSomething` to create an instance of the `TSomething` class. As we'll soon see, this instance is used for further calculations.

Both classes are defined as follows:

```
type
  TSomething = class
  public
    function Value: integer; virtual; abstract;
  end;

  TBaseClass = class
  strict protected
    FSomething: TSomething;
  protected
    function MakeSomething: TSomething; virtual; abstract;
  public
    constructor Create;
    destructor Destroy; override;
    function Value: integer;
  end;
```

As you can see, `TBaseClass` is not directly usable, because the declaration of `MakeSomething` is marked as `abstract`. This tells the Delphi compiler that we are intentionally skipping the declaration part of this method and that we know that the resulting class will be incomplete. If you still try to create `TBaseClass` in the code by calling `TBaseClass.Create`, you will get the compiler warning `W1020`. If you insist on running such a program, `TBaseClass.Create` will raise an exception: `EAbstractError`. The following diagram shows this warning, exception, and code that caused both:

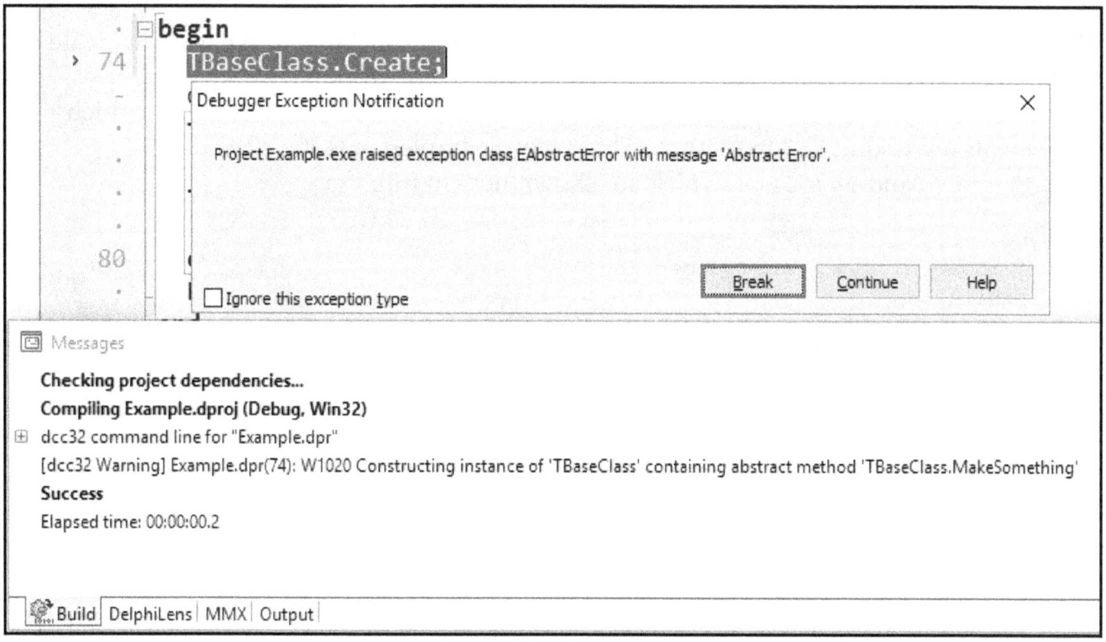

Delphi does not allow you to create an instance of a class containing abstract methods

For a similar reason, you cannot create an instance of the `TSomething` class. This class actually functions just like an interface in modern languages: it provides method declaration but no implementation.

The `something` object is created inside `TBaseClass.Create` and is used in `TBaseClass.Value`. The following code fragment shows both methods:

```
constructor TBaseClass.Create;
begin
  inherited;
  FSomething := MakeSomething;
end;
```

```
function TBaseClass.Value: integer;
begin
  Result := FSomething.Value * 2;
end;
```

At this moment, we have two classes. One calls a method that does not exist (`MakeSomething`) to create an object. The other exposes the `Value` method, which also doesn't exist. It looks as if we have produced a bunch of useless code. How can we make it do anything useful?

The answer, as is usual with pure object-oriented code, is subclassing. We have to create a new class, derived from `TBaseClass`, which implements a working `MakeSomething` method. We also need a new class, derived from `TSomething`, which implements a working `Value` method. This example implements the classes `T21Something` and `T42Class`, which are shown here in full:

```
type
  T21Something = class(TSomething)
  public
    function Value: integer; override;
  end;

  T42Class = class(TBaseClass)
  protected
    function MakeSomething: TSomething; override;
  end;

  function T21Something.Value: integer;
  begin
    Result := 21;
  end;

  function T42Class.MakeSomething: TSomething;
  begin
    Result := T21Something.Create;
  end;
```

As you can see, there is really not much to these two classes. All basic functionality already exists in the `TBaseClass` class, and we are merely plugging the holes.

To use this class, we have to create not the `TBaseClass` but an instance of a derived class: `T42Class`. The following code fragment, taken from the preceding example, shows how:

```
var
  data: TBaseClass;
```

```
begin
  data := T42Class.Create;
  try
    Writeln(data.Value);
  finally
    FreeAndNil(data);
  end;
end.
```

Let's go through the steps the code is taking to return a value from the `Value` method:

1. The code calls `T42Class.Create` to create an instance of this class.
2. As there is no constructor defined in the `T42Class`, the compiler calls the constructor from the parent class, `TBaseClass`.
3. During `TBaseClass.Create`, the `MakeSomething` method is called.
4. As this method is marked as `virtual`, the program tries to find the overridden version of this method in the `T42Class`.
5. This search succeeds and `T42Class.MakeSomething` is called.
6. `MakeSomething` creates and returns the `T21Something` object. As `T21Something` is derived from `TSomething`, we can return such an object, even though the function returns a `TSomething`.
7. The result of `MakeSomething` is stored in the field `FSomething`. Although the field is declared as `TSomething`, it actually contains a `T21Something` object.
8. The object is fully constructed, and `Value` is called.
9. There is no `T42Class.Value`, so `TBaseClass.Value` is executed.
10. `TBaseClass.Value` calls `FSomething.Value`.
11. As the `Value` method is declared `virtual` in the `TSomething` class, the code searches for this method in the actual `T21Something` object once more.
12. `T21Something.Value` is found and called. It returns the value 21.
13. `TBaseClass.Value` multiples that 21 by 2 and returns 42.

Wow! What a convoluted trip! Don't worry; this is something that is happening all the time when you are using derived objects (also known as subclassing) and virtual methods, and you don't need to spend much time thinking about it.

Painter

I have also prepared a more useful example of a simple painting application. As shown in the following image, the Painter project allows you to draw with two tools: one drawing squares and another drawing circles:

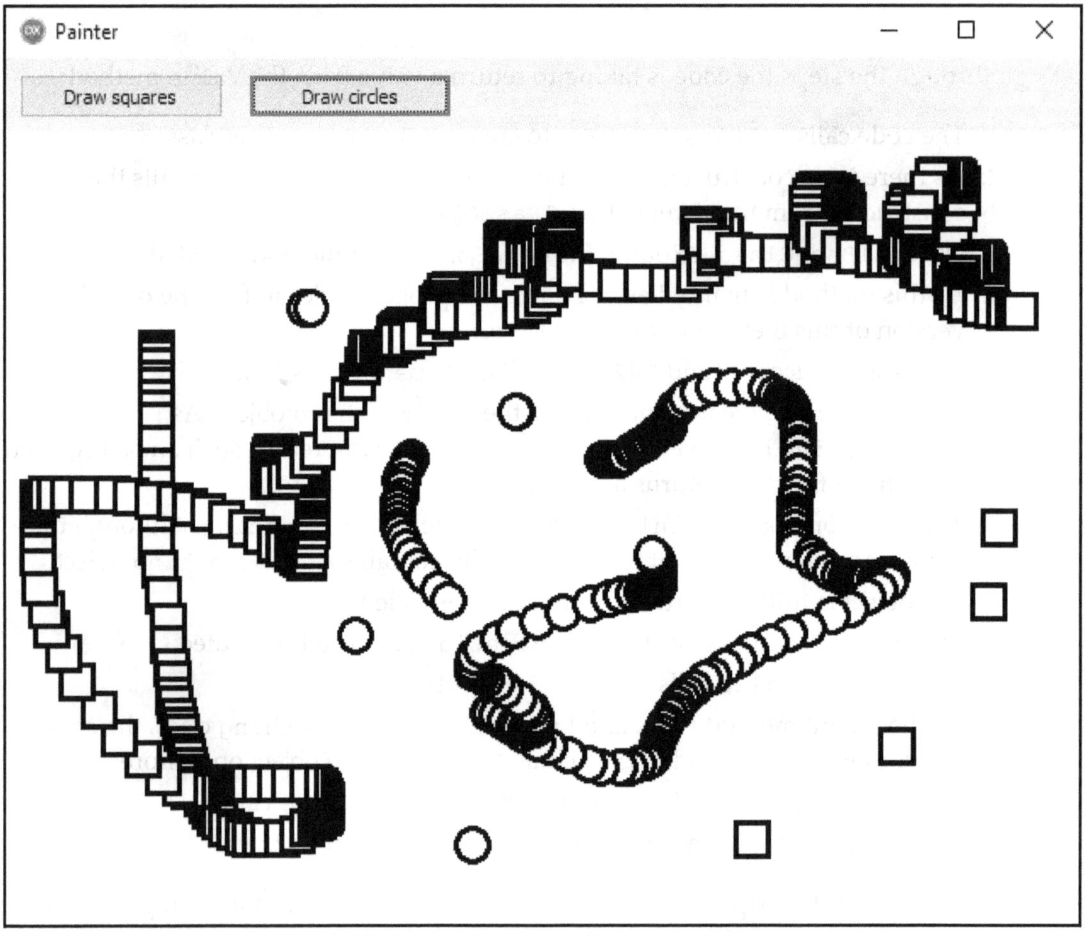

Painter project in action.

The painting tools are implemented in the `Painter.Tools` unit. As in the first example, they are implemented in a true GoF manner by deriving from the base abstract class. The following code fragment shows tool definitions:

```
type
  TPaintStamp = class
  public
    procedure Apply(canvas: TCanvas; x, y: integer); virtual; abstract;
  end;

  TSquareStamp = class(TPaintStamp)
  public
    procedure Apply(canvas: TCanvas; x, y: integer); override;
  end;

  TCircleStamp = class(TPaintStamp)
  public
    procedure Apply(canvas: TCanvas; x, y: integer); override;
  end;

  TPaintTool = class
  protected
    function MakeStamp: TPaintStamp; virtual; abstract;
  public
    constructor Create(canvas: TCanvas);
    procedure PaintStampAt(x, y: integer);
  end;

  TPaintSquare = class(TPaintTool)
  protected
    function MakeStamp: TPaintStamp; override;
  end;

  TPaintCircle = class(TPaintTool)
  protected
    function MakeStamp: TPaintStamp; override;
  end;
```

As in the original example, we have one base class, `TPaintTool`, that provides basic painting functionality but is missing the `MakeStamp` method. This method creates an object that can actually do some painting. The two derived classes, `TPaintSquare` and `TPaintCircle` override this method to create an appropriate instance, as shown in the following code:

```
function TPaintSquare.MakeStamp: TPaintStamp;
begin
  Result := TSquareStamp.Create;
```

```
end;

function TPaintCircle.MakeStamp: TPaintStamp;
begin
  Result := TCircleStamp.Create;
end;
```

In the main unit, `PatternMain`, the code merely creates an appropriate tool when a button is clicked:

```
procedure TfrmPainter.btnSquareClick(Sender: TObject);
begin
  FreeAndNil(FTool);
  FTool := TPaintSquare.Create(PaintImage.Canvas);
end;

procedure TfrmPainter.btnCirclesClick(Sender: TObject);
begin
  FreeAndNil(FTool);
  FTool := TPaintCircle.Create(PaintImage.Canvas);
end;
```

An actual drawing is performed in the `OnMouseDown` and `OnMouseMove` handlers. As the following code fragment shows, they merely call the `PaintStampAt` method, which then calls the `Apply` method of the `TPaintStamp` descendant to do the painting:

```
procedure TfrmPainter.PaintImageMouseDown(Sender: TObject;
  Button: TMouseButton; Shift: TShiftState; X, Y: Integer);
begin
  if assigned(FTool) then
    FTool.PaintStampAt(X, Y);
  FMouseDown := true;
end;

procedure TfrmPainter.PaintImageMouseMove(Sender: TObject;
  Shift: TShiftState; X, Y: Integer);
begin
  if assigned(FTool) and FMouseDown then
    FTool.PaintStampAt(X, Y);
end;
```

Modernizing the factory method pattern

The factory method, as specified originally, is almost useless in current times. It is not very flexible and requires a complicated hierarchy of classes. Nowadays, we still use the general idea, providing a method that creates something, but we wrap it into modern concepts. Usually, we use some form of dependency injection. An example of such a modification can be found in the project ExampleDI. For more information on dependency injection, see `Chapter 10`, *Singleton, Dependency Injection, Lazy Initialization, and Object Pool.*

As I have mentioned before, the whole reason for the `TSomething` class is to specify an interface. We can therefore replace it with a pure interface `ISomething` as shown in the following code:

```
type
  ISomething = interface
    function Value: integer;
  end;
```

There is also no need to create classes that are derived from the `TBaseClass`. We can simply pass in the correct implementation of `ISomething` to the constructor, as the following code fragment shows:

```
type
  TBaseClass = class
  strict protected
    FSomething: ISomething;
  public
    constructor Create(const something: ISomething);
    function Value: integer;
  end;

  constructor TBaseClass.Create(const something: ISomething);
  begin
    inherited Create;
    FSomething := something
  end;
```

An actual implementation of `ISomething`, `T21Something` is very similar to the implementation from the previous example. We just have to derive from `TInterfacedObject`, not `TSomething` (the latter doesn't exist in this approach) and implement `ISomething`. The following code fragment shows the full declaration and implementation of `T21Something`:

```
type
  T21Something = class(TInterfacedObject, ISomething)
  public
    function Value: integer;
  end;

  function T21Something.Value: integer;
  begin
    Result := 21;
  end;
```

To use a concrete implementation, we can just pass an instance of the `T21Something` class to the `TBaseClass` constructor, as shown here:

```
data := TBaseClass.Create(T21Something.Create);
```

The compiler will take care of the `T21Something` life cycle (because it is managed as an interface) and will destroy it at an appropriate time (when the `TBaseClass` instance `data` is destroyed).

Alternatively, we can define a simple derived class, `T42Class` and use it in our code. We only have to re-implement the constructor, which takes care of passing the appropriate `ISomething` implementation to the base class, as shown here:

```
type
  T42Class = class(TBaseClass)
  public
    constructor Create;
  end;

constructor T42Class.Create;
begin
  inherited Create(T21Something.Create);
end;
```

Abstract factory

The abstract factory pattern is closely related to the factory method pattern. Sometimes, the problem requires the creation of multiple distinct objects that are somehow related. In such a case, we could introduce multiple factory methods, but then we have to manage them separately, which increases the possibility of implementations becoming out of sync. This approach also makes it hard to share common logic and state between those factory methods. A better way is to introduce an abstract factory, which functions as a factory for factories.

If a factory method is a kid with a cookie cutter, an abstract factory is a kitchen chef. Give them a set of cooking tools and they'll make you a great dish. Give them access to a baking set and they'll make you a perfect pie.

We can implement abstract factory in the same object-oriented way that was used in the factory method pattern. We have to create a base abstract factory class that defines factory methods and a base class for the object that uses this factory. Then, we derive from the abstract factory to create specific implementations. We also have to create an overridden class to instantiate the concrete factory. The following code fragment sketches this approach:

```
type
  TBaseTool1 = class
    procedure UseTool; virtual;
  end;

  TBaseTool2 = class
    procedure UseTool; virtual;
  end;

  TBaseFactory = class
    function MakeTool1: TBaseTool1; virtual; abstract;
    function MakeTool2: TBaseTool2; virtual; abstract;
  end;

  TBaseClass = class
    function MakeFactory: TBaseFactory;
  end;

  TRealTool1 = class(TBaseTool1)
    procedure UseTool; override;
  end;

  TRealTool2 = class(TBaseTool2)
```

```
    procedure UseTool; override;
  end;

  TRealFactory = class(TBaseFactory)
   function MakeTool1: TBaseTool1; override;
   function MakeTool2: TBaseTool2; override;
  end;

  TRealClass = class(TBaseClass)
    function MakeFactory: TBaseFactory;
  end;

procedure TRealTool1.UseTool;
begin
  // do the work
end;

procedure TRealTool2.UseTool;
begin
  // do the work
end;

function TRealFactory.MakeTool1: TBaseTool1;
begin
  Result := TRealTool1.Create;
end;

function TRealFactory.MakeTool2: TBaseTool2;
begin
  Result := TRealTool2.Create;
end;

function TRealClass.MakeFactory: TBaseFactory;
begin
  Result := TRealFactory.Create;
end;
```

This approach works, but exhibits all the problems of the classical object-oriented factory method implementation. It is cumbersome, requires us to define and implement a bunch of classes, and restricts us in many ways. A much better way, which I'll explore in this section, is to use modern tools, such as **interfaces** and **injection**.

Finding a good topic to demonstrate abstract factories is not simple. A typical example in literature uses this pattern to dynamically create a user interface. This topic was important in the time when the Gang of Four book was created. A typical application with a graphical user interface in that time was running on Unix using X Windows Server with some specific toolkit to create the UI. An abstract factory provided a way to create multiple interface implementations that used multiple toolkits in one application.

In modern times, we approach such problems in a different way. A typical way would be to extract all business functionality into a model and then build a separate Model-View-Whatever application for each user interface. Still, writing a generic UI interface provides a good example, so I built a demonstration of the abstract factory pattern around that concept.

In the `Abstract factory` folder, you'll find the `AbstractUI` project group which contains two projects: `UIHostVCL` and `UIHostFMX`. Both create a minimal main form with one button. Clicking that button creates a secondary form by using a generic form-creation class and two factories: one to create a VCL form and another to create a FireMonkey form. Both applications are shown side-by-side in the following screenshot:

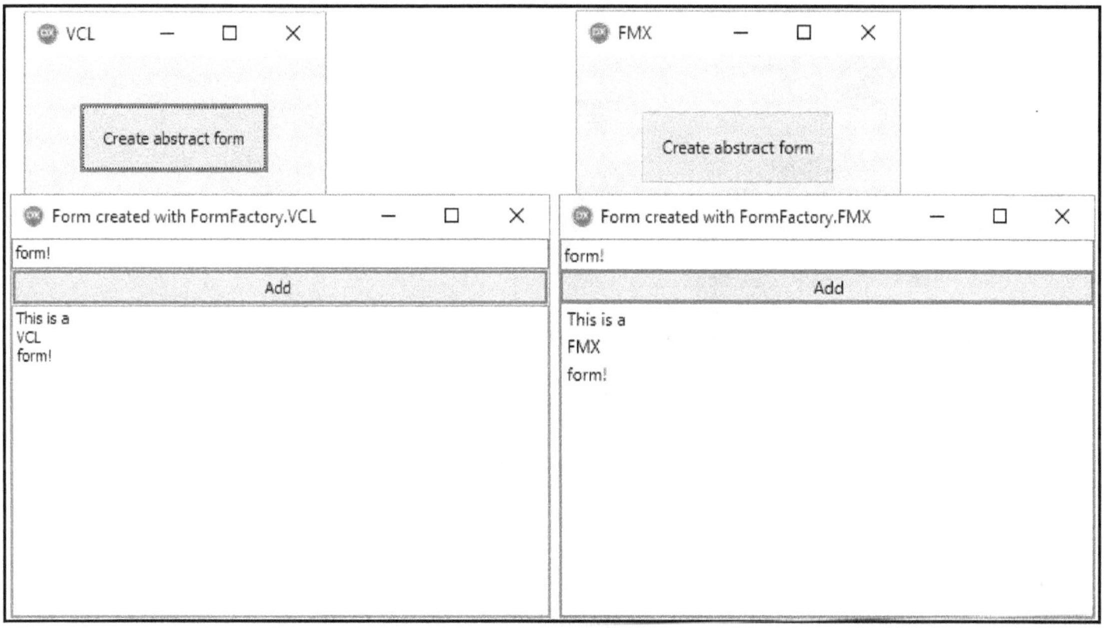

VLC and FMX forms, created with an abstract factory.

The form in this example is created and managed by the `TAbstractEBLForm` class, which is stored in the `AbstractEBLForm` unit. This class knows nothing about VCL or FMX; it creates the form through an abstract factory interface `IFormFactory`. The implementation of this class is shown here in full:

```
uses
  FormFactory.Intf;

type
  TAbstractEBLForm = class
  strict private
    FFactory: IFormFactory;
    FForm: IForm;
    FButton: IButton;
    FEdit: IEdit;
    FListbox: IListBox;
  public
    constructor Create(const factory: IFormFactory);
    procedure Make;
    procedure Show;
  end;

constructor TAbstractEBLForm.Create(const factory: IFormFactory);
begin
  inherited Create;
  FFactory := factory;
end;

procedure TAbstractEBLForm.Make;
begin
  FForm := FFactory.CreateForm;
  FEdit := FFactory.CreateEdit(FForm);
  FButton := FFactory.CreateButton(FForm);
  FButton.Caption := 'Add';
  FListbox := FFactory.CreateListbox(FForm);
  FButton.OnClick :=
    procedure
    begin
      FListbox.Add(FEdit.GetText);
    end;
end;

procedure TAbstractEBLForm.Show;
begin
  FForm.Show;
end;
```

The abstract factory is injected into the constructor from the code that creates the `TAbstractEBLForm` object. This way, we don't have to create a `TAbstractEBLForm` descendants that implements just a factory-creating function and nothing more. We will see soon how this constructor is called.

The `Make` method uses the abstract factory to create form, create and configure edit, button, and listbox components, and to define a button's `OnClick` handler. In short, this form implements the very first public Delphi 1 demo, an application with one `TEdit`, one `TButton`, and one `TListBox`, which appends text from the edit box to the listbox when the button is clicked.

The method `Show` simply calls the `IForm.Show` method to show the form. We will look into the implementation details later.

This code clearly uses no VCL or FMX concepts. It merely refers to interfaces defined in `FormFactory.Intf` without any knowledge about the specific implementation. In a way, this is an extreme implementation of the coding to the interface design principle.

Let's now examine how this abstract form is used. The VCL implementation in unit `UIHostVCLMain` uses concrete implementation of the abstract factory `TVCLFormFactory` from unit `FormFactory.VCL` to create a VCL form as shown next:

```
procedure TfrmVCLHost.Button1Click(Sender: TObject);
var
  form: TAbstractEBLForm;
begin
  form := TAbstractEBLForm.Create(TVCLFormFactory.Create);
  try
    form.Make;
    form.Show;
  finally
    FreeAndNil(form);
  end;
end;
```

A FireMonkey-targeting implementation in unit `UIHostFMXMain` is almost the same, except that it uses the factory `TFMXFormFactory` from the unit `FormFactory.FMX` to create the user interface components:

```
procedure TfrmFMXHost.Button1Click(Sender: TObject);
var
  form: TAbstractEBLForm;
begin
  form := TAbstractEBLForm.Create(TFMXFormFactory.Create);
  try
```

```
      form.Make;
      form.Show;
    finally
      FreeAndNil(form);
    end;
  end;
```

Let me now switch the focus from the top-level parts of the implementation to the platform-specific code. The full implementation is too long for the book, so I will only show selected parts here.

The factory interface `IFormFactory` is defined in the unit `FormFactory.Intf`. The next code fragment shows the factory interface and two of the four component interfaces: `IForm` and `IEdit`. The other two you can check in the source code:

```
type
  IForm = interface ['{EB4D0921-F0FD-4044-80E8-80156C71D0E0}']
    procedure Show;
  end;

  IEdit = interface ['{39D02BD4-582A-4EBD-8119-2D6013E31287}']
    function GetText: string;
  end;

  IFormFactory = interface ['{776122CF-C014-4630-ACBF-8C639BEAE975}']
    function CreateForm: IForm;
    function CreateEdit(const form: IForm): IEdit;
    function CreateButton(const form: IForm): IButton;
    function CreateListbox(const form: IForm): IListbox;
  end;
```

We already saw how this factory is used. `CreateForm` creates a form, `CreateEdit` an edit box, and so on.

More interesting than that is the factory implementation. Let's start with the VCL factory, implemented in unit `FormFactory.VCL`. Again, I will only show the form and edit box implementations in full.

The factory implementation `TVCLFormFactory` is very simple. It just creates concrete objects that implement interfaces from `FormFactory.Intf`. The next code fragment shows the definition of the class and the implementation of functions that create the `IForm` and `IEdit` interfaces:

```
type
  TVCLFormFactory = class(TInterfacedObject, IFormFactory)
  public
```

```
    function CreateForm: IForm;
    function CreateEdit(const form: IForm): IEdit;
    function CreateButton(const form: IForm): IButton;
    function CreateListbox(const form: IForm): IListbox;
  end;

function TVCLFormFactory.CreateForm: IForm;
begin
  Result := TVCLForm.Create;
end;

function TVCLFormFactory.CreateEdit(const form: IForm): IEdit;
begin
  Result := TVCLEdit.Create(form as IVCLForm);
end;
```

As the VCL implementation of virtual components needs access to the `TForm` object, the `TVCLForm` class implements a special interface `IVCLForm`. As shown next, this interface defines the method `AsForm`, which returns the base `TForm` object:

```
type
  IVCLForm = interface ['{8EC67205-31FD-4A40-B076-F572EF76CF0A}']
    function AsForm: TForm;
  end;

  TVCLForm = class(TInterfacedObject, IForm, IVCLForm)
  strict private
    FForm: TForm;
  public
    constructor Create;
    destructor Destroy; override;
    function AsForm: TForm;
    procedure Show;
  end;

constructor TVCLForm.Create;
begin
  inherited Create;
  FForm := TForm.CreateNew(nil);
  FForm.Position := poScreenCenter;
  FForm.Caption := 'Form created with FormFactory.VCL';
  FForm.Width := 400;
  FForm.Height := 300;
end;

destructor TVCLForm.Destroy;
begin
  FreeAndNil(FForm);
```

```
  inherited;
end;

function TVCLForm.AsForm: TForm;
begin
  Result := FForm;
end;

procedure TVCLForm.Show;
begin
  FForm.ShowModal;
end;
```

Form creation is simplified as much as possible to reduce the size of the example. Form size and position are hardcoded, and so is the caption. In a real-world GUI factory, such properties would have to be exposed through the `IForm` interface.

The edit box implementation `TVCLEdit` uses the `TForm` object so that it can correctly set the ownership and parenting of the `TEdit` component. The implementation of this class is shown next:

```
type
  TVCLEdit = class(TInterfacedObject, IEdit)
  strict private
    FEdit: TEdit;
  public
   constructor Create(owner: IVCLForm);
   function GetText: string;
  end;

constructor TVCLEdit.Create(owner: IVCLForm);
begin
  inherited Create;
  FEdit := TEdit.Create(owner.AsForm);
  FEdit.Parent := owner.AsForm;
  FEdit.Align := alTop;
end;

function TVCLEdit.GetText: string;
begin
  Result := FEdit.Text;
end;
```

For the implementation of the button and listbox components, you can check the code.

The other factory, `TFMXFormFactory` from unit `FormFactory.FMX` is almost line-for-line the same as the VCL factory. The used units differ, of course (for example, `FMX.StdCtrls` and `FMX.Forms` are used instead of `Vcl.StdCtrls` and `Vcl.Forms`), and some components have different names (`TButton.Text` instead of `TButton.Caption`), but all implementation logic follows the same principles. For example, `TFMXEdit` is defined and implemented as follows:

```
type
  TFMXEdit = class(TInterfacedObject, IEdit)
  strict private
    FEdit: TEdit;
  public
    constructor Create(owner: IFMXForm);
    function GetText: string;
  end;

constructor TFMXEdit.Create(owner: IFMXForm);
begin
  inherited Create;
  FEdit := TEdit.Create(owner.AsForm);
  FEdit.Parent := owner.AsForm;
  FEdit.Align := TAlignLayout.Top;
end;

function TFMXEdit.GetText: string;
begin
  Result := FEdit.Text;
end;
```

If you want to implement the user interface in this manner, be warned! You will have to write large amounts of code to implement all the needed components and their properties. The task, however, is not incredibly complicated, just tedious.

Prototype

The prototype pattern is very simple in concept. It describes a way for an object to make a copy of itself. In other words, we start with one object (prototype) and end with two indistinguishable copies.

We don't have to look far to find a real-life example of the prototype pattern. Life, as we know it, is based on cellular division, a process in which one cell divides into two identical copies of itself.

Every implementation of this pattern is very specific to the target environment. In Delphi, we can implement a prototype pattern by creating a new object and copying old contents to the new instance in some way. Creating a new object is simple, but copying data may not be. In this section, we'll mostly deal with the copy mechanism.

By implementing the prototype pattern (or cloning, as we also call this process), we bypass object initialization, which may be a lengthy operation. Sometimes, we even don't have access to the original data from which the object was initialized and the only possible way to create a copy of an object is to implement this pattern.

Although I am using the word object in this introduction, a prototype pattern equally applies to records. It's just that technical problems that we have to solve are different. As it turns out, cloning a Delphi record can be simpler than cloning an object.

Cloning records

Making copy of a record is simple, because records are value types in Delphi, similar to integers, floating-point numbers, and booleans. We can just assign one variable of a record type to another and the compiler will make a copy:

```
var
  a, b: TSomeRecord;

begin
  a.Initialize;
  b := a;
  // b now contains same data as a
end;
```

There are limitations to this approach, and they are best explained with an example. In the `Prototype` folder of this chapter's code, you'll find the project `PrototypeRecord`, which demonstrates simplicity, and problems, with record cloning.

In the unit `Prototype.Rec`, you'll find the definition of a record type `TCloneableRec` that contains fields of different types: string, integer, two kinds of arrays, interface, object, and nested record. The following code fragment shows all important parts of the record definition (internal fields, getters, and setters were removed for clarity):

```
type
  TNestedRecord = record
    ValueI: integer;
    ValueS: string;
  end;

IInteger = interface ['{722BD9CC-BF41-4CDC-95C1-7EF17A28BF7B}']
  property Value: integer read GetValue write SetValue;
end;

TInteger = class(TInterfacedObject, IInteger)
  property Value: integer read GetValue write SetValue;
end;

TStaticArray = array [1..10] of integer;
TDynamicArray = TArray<integer>;

TCharacter = class
  property Value: char read FValue write FValue;
end;

TCloneableRec = record
  Str: string;
  Int: integer;
  Intf: IInteger;
  ArrS: TStaticArray;
  ArrD: TDynamicArray;
  Rec: TNestedRecord;
  Obj: TCharacter;
end;
```

The code in the main unit `PrototypeRecordMain` creates and initializes a master record and logs its contents. Then it creates a clone and logs the contents of the copy. The code then modifies the original record and logs the clone again. The following screenshot shows the end result of this operation:

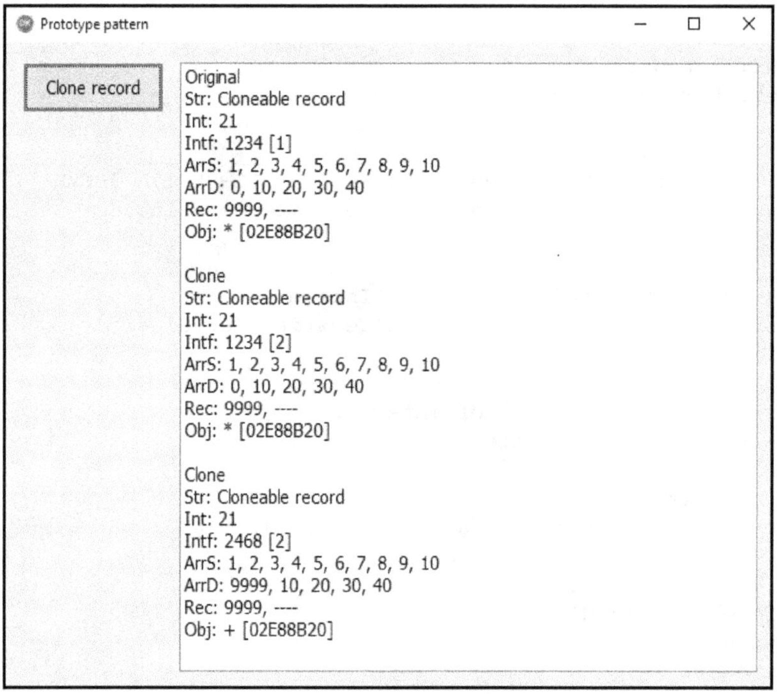

The end result of the PrototypeRecord program.

The first third of the output contains the content of the original record. There are two interesting parts of this output that I would like to point out.

Firstly, the text **Intf: 1234 [1]** means that the `Intf` field contains the value 1234 and that the reference count of this interface is 1. In other words, there is only one place in the code that refers to this interface, namely the `Intf` field.

Secondly, the text **Obj: * [02E88B20]** shows the content of the `Obj` object's value property and the address of the `Obj` object.

The middle part of the output contains the content of the cloned record. Mostly, it is the same as the output of the original record, but again there are two specifics that I'd like to mention.

The content of the `Intf` field now contains text [2]. When the copy of the original record was made, the compiler copied the address of the object implementing the `IInteger` interface from the original record's `Intf` field into the clone record's `Intf` field and incremented the interface's reference count to indicate that. Both records now share the same `IInterface` with a reference count of 2, indicating two owners.

Almost the same thing happens with the `Obj` field. It contains an address of the object, and this address is copied from the original record to the clone. The content of both `Obj` fields therefore contains the same address, and we cannot tell which record owns this object.

> This only holds for classic Delphi platforms where objects are not reference-counted. On ARC-supporting platforms (Android, iOS, Linux), objects behave more-or-less the same as interfaces.

To facilitate this behavior, the example program maintains the `TCharacter` object globally. The main form creates one instance of this class and stores a reference to this instance (its address) in the original record. Making a copy of the record causes no problems, as both records are referring to the same master object, managed by the form. Only at the end, when the program is shutting down, is the object destroyed.

Before logging the last part, the code modifies the original record, as shown in the next fragment. A clone record is then logged:

```
source.Str := 'Changed';
source.Intf.Value := source.Intf.Value * 2;
source.ArrS[Low(source.ArrS)] := 9999;
source.ArrD[Low(source.ArrD)] := 9999;
source.Obj.Value := '+';
LogRecord('Clone', clone);
```

Although the source `Str` field was changed, the contents of the cloned `Str` were not modified. Most frequently used string types in Delphi (namely, `AnsiString` and `UnicodeString`, also known as `string`) are reference-counted, the same as interfaces, but they implement a copy-on- write mechanism that makes sure that changing one string variable doesn't cause any effect on shared copies.

Unlike this, the modified contents of `Intf.Value` (1234 originally, now 2468) in the original records are visible in the cloned record. Both records are just pointing to the same instance of the interface, and so a change in one place is reflected in the other. The same holds for the `Obj.Value` field.

Modifying an array results in two different results. The full content of a static array is stored inside an owner. Modifying a static array in the original therefore makes no change to the clone. A dynamic array, on the other hand, is a reference type, the same as objects, interfaces, and strings. Both records are therefore pointing to the same dynamic array instance, and modifying it in one place (in the original record) also makes it change in the clone.

A full discussion about value and reference types, interface reference counting, and the copy-on-write mechanism is unfortunately too long to be included in this book. You can read more about such topics in my book *Delphi High Performance*, which was published by *Packt Publishing*.

When copying (cloning) records, you should always examine the type of data stored inside the record so that you can prevent unwanted data modification.

Cloning objects

Unlike records, objects in Delphi are reference types. When you create an object, memory is dynamically allocated and stored in the object variable. A variable that stores an object is actually just a pointer, pointing to the memory where the real object is stored.

The following code fragment therefore doesn't create a copy of an object:

```
var
  a, b: TSomeObject;

begin
  a := TSomeObject.Create;
  b := a;
  // a and b are now sharing the same object
  // they are both pointing to the same memory address
end;
```

To create a clone of an object, we have to *create* a new object and copy the content of the object from the original to the new object. There are three idiomatic ways to do that in Delphi and all are demonstrated in the prototype project.

The code in this project works with the class `TCloneable`, which is defined in the unit `Prototype.Cloneable`. The full class definition is shown next:

```
type
  TCloneable = class
  strict private
    FData: TStream;
    FIsBar: boolean;
    FName: string;
  public
    constructor Create;
    constructor CreateFrom(baseObj: TCloneable);
    destructor Destroy; override;
    procedure Assign(baseObj: TCloneable);
    function Clone: TCloneable;
    function FooBar: string;
    property Data: TStream read FData;
    property Name: string read FName write FName;
  end;
```

This class contains three fields: a boolean, a string, and a nested `TStream` class. To create a full clone, we have to copy all three.

The first idiomatic way to do this is to implement the function `Clone`, which creates and returns a new object. It is implemented as follows:

```
function TCloneable.Clone: TCloneable;
var
  dataPos: int64;
begin
  Result := TCloneable.Create;

  // make copy of published data
  Result.Name := Name;

  // clone state of owned objects
  // make sure not to destroy the state of owned objects
  // during the process!
  dataPos := Data.Position;
  Result.Data.CopyFrom(Data, 0);
  Data.Position := dataPos;
  Result.Data.Position := dataPos;

  // clone private state
  Result.FIsBar := FIsBar;
end;
```

We simply use the default constructor `Create` to create a new instance of the `TCloneable` class and then make a full copy of all the data. To create a completely identical object, we have to know how internally used classes (`TStream` in this case) are implemented so that we can correctly copy their properties. In our case, we have to not only copy the contents of the stream but correctly initialize the `Position` property in the clone.

To create a clone `FClone` of the original `FMaster`, we simply call the `Clone` method, as shown next:

```
FClone := FMaster.Clone;
```

Personally, I'm against this approach, as it makes for unreadable code. It differs enough from the standard way of creating Delphi objects that it's easy to ignore the this line creates new instance, meaning when you read it. That's why I prefer to use the second idiomatic approach: cloning with constructor.

A second way of doing the same thing works by implementing a constructor that accepts a `template` object: an object that is used as a master data source. In the example project, this functionality is implemented in `TCloneable.CreateFrom`, as shown next:

```
constructor TCloneable.CreateFrom(baseObj: TCloneable);
begin
  Create;
  Assign(baseObj);
end;

procedure TCloneable.Assign(baseObj: TCloneable);
var
  dataPos: int64;
begin
  // make copy of published data
  Name := baseObj.Name;

  // clone state of owned objects
  dataPos := baseObj.Data.Position;
  Data.CopyFrom(baseObj.Data, 0);
  baseObj.Data.Position := dataPos;
  Data.Position := dataPos;

  // clone private state
  FIsBar := baseObj.FIsBar;
end;
```

The code firstly calls the default constructor `Create`, which initializes the object and creates an internal `TStream` field. Then it calls the helper method `Assign`, which contains exactly the same code to copy the state from one object to another as it was implemented in the `Clone` function.

TIP

I like to call this *cloning* constructor `CreateFrom`, but you can name it anything. It can simply be called `Create`, if that is more to your liking.

To create a clone in this way, you simply call `TCloneable.CreateFrom` as the next code fragment shows:

```
FClone := TCloneable.CreateFrom(FMaster);
```

I do believe that this approach more clearly indicates that an object is created at this point.

The third idiomatic way of cloning an object simply calls the default constructor `Create` and then explicitly calls `Assign` to copy the contents. The next code fragment shows how this can be done:

```
FClone := TCloneable.Create;
FClone.Assign(FMaster);
```

This way of doing things is undoubtedly the most flexible, as you can choose the constructor that will create the object, if there is more than one. It is also useful if you don't like using constructors with arguments.

If you are making the `Assign` method public, however, you should know that Delphi's run-time library overloads this method with a special meaning. When the users of your code see that it implements public `Assign`, they may have certain expectations, and it is proper that you anticipate this and meet them. The next few pages of the book deal with this topic.

Delphi idioms – Assign and AssignTo

The Delphi RTL class `TPersistent`, which is implemented in unit `System.Classes`, defines two methods: `Assign` and `AssignTo`. Relevant parts of this class are shown next:

```
type
  TPersistent = class(TObject)
  protected
    procedure AssignTo(Dest: TPersistent); virtual;
  public
```

```
    procedure Assign(Source: TPersistent); virtual;
  end;

procedure TPersistent.Assign(Source: TPersistent);
begin
  if Source <> nil then Source.AssignTo(Self) else AssignError(nil);
end;

procedure TPersistent.AssignTo(Dest: TPersistent);
begin
  Dest.AssignError(Self);
end;
```

Any descendent of the `TPersistent` class can override any or both of these methods. When you know how to copy data from some type into the object, you override `Assign`. When you know how to copy data from the object into some type, you override `AssignTo`. A typical implementation should follow the following pattern:

```
procedure TMyClass.Assign(Source: TPersistent);
begin
  if {we can handle Source} then
    // copy data from Source
  else
    inherited;
end;

procedure TMyClass.AssignTo(Dest: TPersistent);
begin
  if {we can handle Dest} then
    // copy data to Dest
  else
    inherited;
end;
```

When the program calls `Assign` method on an object, the following happens:

- If the object knows how to handle the source, it assigns the data and exits.
- If it doesn't, `Assign` from the parent class is called.
- This continues until a class is able to handle the source data or `TPersistent` is reached.
- `TPersistent.Assign` checks whether the input data is empty (`nil`) and simply calls `Source.AssignTo(Self)` otherwise. The reasoning behind this is as follows: Nobody in this chain of derived classes knows how to copy data from the source. Maybe somebody in the source's chain of derived classes knows how to copy data into our class.

- `AssignTo` from the `Source` class is called. If it knows how to handle our class, and it copies the data and exits.
- Otherwise, `AssignTo` from the parent class is called.
- This continues until a class is able to handle the destination data or `TPersistent` is reached.
- `TPersistent.AssignTo` simply raises an exception.

TIP

You should always call `Assign` in your code to copy data between two objects. `AssignTo` is `protected`, anyway, and you cannot call it directly.

This chain of events results in a very flexible system for copying data that we can also exploit in creative ways. The example project `PrototypePersisten` shows how cloning can be implemented by using `Assign`.

The unit `Prototype.CloneablePersistent` implements two classes: a base class `TCloneable`, which derives from `TPersistent`, and a derived class `TNewCloneable`. Both implement the `Assign` method to implement the prototype pattern. The relevant parts of both classes are shown in the next code fragment:

```
type
  TCloneablePersistent = class(TPersistent)
  public
    procedure Assign(Source: TPersistent); override;
    function FooBar: string;
    property Data: TStream read FData;
    property Name: string read FName write FName;
  end;

  TNewCloneable = class(TCloneablePersistent)
  public
    procedure Assign(Source: TPersistent); override;
    property Value: integer read FValue write FValue;
  end;

procedure TCloneablePersistent.Assign(Source: TPersistent);
var
  baseObj: TCloneablePersistent;
  dataPos: int64;
begin
  if not (Source is TCloneablePersistent) then
    inherited
  else begin
    baseObj := TCloneablePersistent(Source);
```

```
      // make copy of published data
      Name := baseObj.Name;

      // clone state of owned objects
      dataPos := baseObj.Data.Position;
      Data.CopyFrom(baseObj.Data, 0);
      baseObj.Data.Position := dataPos;
      Data.Position := dataPos;

      // clone private state
      FIsBar := baseObj.FIsBar;
    end;
  end;

  procedure TNewCloneable.Assign(Source: TPersistent);
  begin
    if Source is TNewCloneable then
      Value := TNewCloneable(Source).Value;
    inherited;
  end;
```

The `TCloneablePersistent.Assign` method checks whether the `Source` is of type `TCloneablePersistent`. If so, it executes the already-well-known code to copy state from one object to another. If not, inherited is called so that the expected behavior of `Assign` is not broken.

The `TNewCloneable.Assign` checks whether the `Source` is of type `TNewCloneable` and if so, copies the `Value` property. Then, it always calls the inherited `Assign`. If the source is `TNewCloneable`, the inherited method will copy other data fields. Otherwise, it will pass execution to the parent of `TCloneablePersistent`.

As I said before, these functions (especially `AssignTo`) can be used in creative ways. We can, for example, use `AssignTo` to implement the logging functionality for our classes. Both classes in the example program use `AssignTo` to log their state into a `TStrings` object. The main program can then simply call `AssignTo` to log an object's state into a listbox, as the next code fragment shows:

```
var
  lbLog: TListBox;

lbLog.Items.Assign(FClone);
```

By implementing `AssignTo`, we can extend the functionality of a class that we cannot change. We cannot extend `TStrings.Assign` to handle our class, but we can easily handle `TStrings` in our `AssignTo` and the net result is the same.

You can check the implementation of `TCloneablePersistent.AssignTo` in the source code. `TNewCloneable.AssignTo`, which is simpler (as it only logs one value); it is implemented as follows:

```
procedure TNewCloneable.AssignTo(Dest: TPersistent);
begin
  inherited;

  if Dest is TStrings then
    TStrings(Dest).Add('Value: ' + Value.ToString);
end;
```

In this case, we are calling inherited first so that fields from the base class `TCloneablePersistent` are logged before fields from the derived class `TNewCloneable`.

Serialization

In addition to techniques discussed in this chapter, we can also use the *memento* pattern (also known as serialization) to clone objects. As an example, I have created a project `PrototypeJSON`, which converts an object into a JSON string and then creates a new object from that string. If you examine the project, you'll also notice that I had to remove the `TStream` internal field because it was not correctly handled. We will learn to deal with such problems in `Chapter 15`, *Iterator, Observer, Visitor, and Memento.*

Builder

The last pattern from this chapter, builder, helps with creating complex objects or their representations. The general idea behind the pattern is to separate such a process into two parts: one gives instructions to an abstract builder interface, and another converts the instructions into a concrete representation. This allows us to create multiple representations from the same construction process.

> The builder pattern is similar to an automated coffee/tea machine that always follows the same build process: put a cup on the tray, insert the correct beverage into the system, flow hot water through the system into the cup, and beep at the end. While the build process is always the same, the end result depends on a concrete implementation of step two.

The builder pattern is very similar to the abstract factory pattern. In both cases, the shared class uses an abstract interface to execute a task. The difference is that the builder pattern is focused on step-by-step instructions that the builder object gives to the builder interface. These instructions can be hardcoded into the program, or can be generated according to some input.

There's a thin line between an abstract factory and a builder. For example, we could say that the VCL/FMX user interface generator example from the abstract factory pattern section is actually an example of a builder pattern. You can think of the abstract factory pattern as being a more generic mechanism that can be used to implement a builder pattern.

To demonstrate this, the *Builder* project from the builder folder implements a process that follows the step-by-step instructions paradigm even more closely. The implementation, however, matches the example from the abstract factory section.

The program implements a builder that creates an abstract structured data object that can be converted to an XML or a JSON representation. The builder interface `IDataBuilder` is defined in the unit `DataBuilder.Intf` and main program uses it as follows:

```
type
  IDataBuilder = interface ['{1BA8B314-4968-4209-AF1E-2496C7BEC390}']
    procedure BeginData;
    procedure BeginNode(const name: string);
    procedure AddField(const name, value: string);
    procedure EndNode;
    procedure EndData;
    function Make: string;
  end;

function TfrmBuilder.MakeData(const builder: IDataBuilder): string;
begin
  builder.BeginData;
  builder.BeginNode('Book');
  builder.AddField('Title', 'Hands-on Design Patterns');
  builder.AddField('Topic', 'design patterns, Delphi');
  builder.BeginNode('Author');
  builder.AddField('Name', 'Primoz Gabrijelcic');
  builder.AddField('Blog', 'thedelphigeek.com');
```

```
    builder.EndNode;
    builder.EndNode;
    builder.EndData;

    Result := builder.Make;
  end;
```

The data object is constructed in a purely abstract manner. The `MakeData` method receives an implementation of the `IDataBuilder` interface and uses its methods to create an abstract object. In the last line, this representation is converted into a concrete representation. The result of both conversions, to JSON and to XML, is shown in the next screenshot:

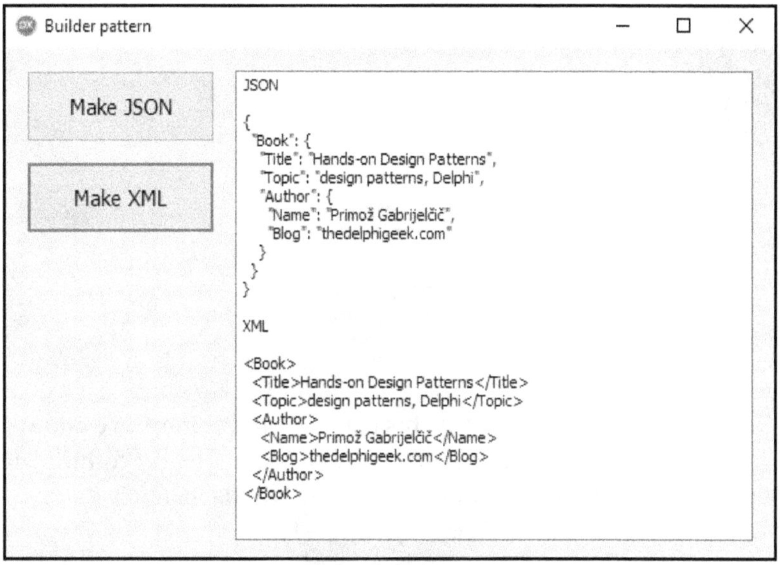

Abstract data structure converted to JSON and XML formats.

The data object from this example has the same internal structure as the following Delphi record:

```
  Book = record
    Title: string;
    Topic: string;
    Author: record
      Name: string;
      Blog: string;
    end;
  end;
```

The actual implementations of the `IDataBuilder` interface are found in units `DataBuilder.JSON` and `DataBuilder.XML`. Both are very similar in nature: representation is created line by line and is appropriately indented. To simplify the code, the shared functionality is implemented within another builder class: `TIndentedBuilder` from the unit `IndentedBuilder`. This class uses an internal field `FData: TStringList` to store data, and implements only four public functions, shown next:

```
procedure TIndentedBuilder.Indent;
begin
  Inc(FIndent, 2);
end;

procedure TIndentedBuilder.IndentLine(const line: string);
begin
  FData.Add(StringOfChar(' ', FIndent) + line);
end;

function TIndentedBuilder.ToString: string;
begin
  Result := FData.Text;
end;

procedure TIndentedBuilder.Unindent;
begin
  Dec(FIndent, 2);
end;
```

The XML builder `TXMLBuilder` then uses this class by *composition*. We could also inherit both builders from the indented builder, but that would needlessly complicate the code and introduce dependencies. Remember what `Chapter 9`, *Introduction to patterns* said: Favor object composition over class inheritance.

Besides the internal `TIndentedBuilder` field, XML builder also uses a stack of open (active) nodes. When we close a node, the builder has to end an element by inserting a `</node>` string. The name of that node has to be remembered somewhere, and so the `BeginNode` puts it on a stack and `EndNode` takes it off the stack.

The following code fragment shows the full implementation of the XML builder class:

```
type
  TXMLBuilder = class(TInterfacedObject, IDataBuilder)
  strict private
    FBuilder: TIndentedBuilder;
    FNodes: TStack<string>;
  public
    procedure AfterConstruction; override;
```

```
    procedure BeforeDestruction; override;
    procedure AddField(const name, value: string);
    procedure BeginNode(const name: string);
    procedure BeginData;
    procedure EndData;
    procedure EndNode;
    function Make: string;
  end;

procedure TXMLBuilder.AddField(const name, value: string);
begin
  FBuilder.IndentLine('<' + name + '>' + value + '</' + name + '>');
end;

procedure TXMLBuilder.AfterConstruction;
begin
  inherited;
  FBuilder := TIndentedBuilder.Create;
  FNodes := TStack<string>.Create;
end;

procedure TXMLBuilder.BeforeDestruction;
begin
  FreeAndNil(FNodes);
  FreeAndNil(FBuilder);
  inherited;
end;

procedure TXMLBuilder.BeginData;
begin
  // do nothing
end;

procedure TXMLBuilder.BeginNode(const name: string);
begin
  FBuilder.IndentLine('<' + name + '>');
  FBuilder.Indent;
  FNodes.Push(name);
end;

procedure TXMLBuilder.EndData;
begin
  // do nothing
end;

procedure TXMLBuilder.EndNode;
begin
  FBuilder.Unindent;
```

```
  FBuilder.IndentLine('</' + FNodes.Pop + '>');
end;

function TXMLBuilder.Make: string;
begin
  Result := FBuilder.ToString;
end;
```

The JSON builder is implemented in a similar manner. For details, see the source code.

I must point out that this implementation is very simple and should not be used in production. Input data is not checked, invalid XML/JSON characters (such as < and `"`) are not converted into appropriate representations, and so on. Both builders should be treated as a demonstration only.

Idioms – Fluent interfaces

A concept of a builder is often used together with a concept of fluent interfaces. When an interface or a class is written in a fluent manner, its every method (or at least most of the methods) returns the implementing object itself. To put this in Delphi terms: each method returns `Self`.

This idiom is not specific to Delphi. Fluent interfaces are programmed in all kinds of languages, from C# to JavaScript.

Fluent interfaces allow us to chain method calls. For example, given an initialized object `sb` of type `TStringBuilder` (from unit `System.SysUtils`), we can create a simple string by using the following four commands:

```
sb.Append('The answer: ');
sb.Append(42);
sb.AppendLine;
ShowMessage(sb.ToString);
```

As both `Append` and `AppendLine` are actually functions returning `TStringBuilder`, we can simplify this code as follows:

```
ShowMessage(sb.Append('The answer: ').Append(42).AppendLine.ToString);
```

TIP

This approach simplifies the code but slightly complicates the debugging. If you use it and the code doesn't work correctly, you should rewrite it in a classical way so it will be simpler to debug.

Another great example of fluent interface are string helpers from the `System.SysUtils` unit. They allow us to write code such as this:

```
data := stringValue.TrimLeft.ToLower.Split([', '],
  TStringSplitOptions.ExcludeEmpty));
```

Or, you can use fluent interfaces to construct SQL statement in code. My open source `GpSQLBuilder` project (`https://github.com/gabr42/GpSQLBuilder`) allows you to construct SQL commands, as shown in the next example:

```
ExecuteQuery(CreateGpSQLBuilder
  .Select
    .Column(['DISTINCT', DBPLY_DBField_ID])
    .&Case
      .When([DBSBF_DBField_CreatedTime, '< ''2010-01-01'''])
        .&Then('*')
      .&Else('')
    .&End
  .From(DBT_PLY)
  .LeftJoin(DBT_SBF)
    .&On([DBSBF_PLY_ID, '=', DBPLY_DBField_ID])
  .OrderBy(DBPLY_DBField_ID)
  .AsString);
```

The last example comes from my multithreading library `OmniThreadLibrary` (`https://github.com/gabr42/OmniThreadLibrary`). It uses a fluent approach to construct parallel tasks. You can, for example, use the following code fragment to create a timed task that periodically executes some code in a background thread:

```
FTimedTask :=
  Parallel.TimedTask
  .Every(1000)
  .TaskConfig(Parallel.TaskConfig.OnMessage(Self))
  .Execute(SendRequest_asy);
```

Let me now return to the example from the beginning of this section. We can rewrite it in a fluent manner by changing interface methods to return the interface itself. We only cannot change the `Make` function, as it already returns a string. The new interface `IDataBuilderFluent` is defined in unit `DataBuilderFluent.Intf` as follows:

```
type
  IDataBuilderFluent = interface ['{1BA8B314-4968-4209-AF1E-2496C7BEC390}']
    function BeginData: IDataBuilderFluent;
    function BeginNode(const name: string): IDataBuilderFluent;
    function AddField(const name, value: string): IDataBuilderFluent;
    function EndNode: IDataBuilderFluent;
    function EndData: IDataBuilderFluent;
    function Make: string;
  end;
```

The project `BuilderFluent` shows how to use the fluent version of the builder interface. All builder functions have had to be modified in the same manner: they must return `Self` at the end, for example: `TXMLBuilder.BeginNode` is now implemented as follows:

```
function TXMLBuilder.BeginNode(const name: string): IDataBuilderFluent;
begin
  FBuilder.IndentLine('<' + name + '>');
  FBuilder.Indent;
  FNodes.Push(name);
  Result := Self;
end;
```

The new builder implementations can be found in units `DataBuilderFluent.JSON` and `DataBuilderFluent.XML`.

To simplify the comparison, I will repeat the original `MakeData` method here:

```
function TfrmBuilder.MakeData(
  const builder: IDataBuilder): string;
begin
  builder.BeginData;
  builder.BeginNode('Book');
  builder.AddField('Title', 'Hands-on Design Patterns');
  builder.AddField('Topic', 'design patterns, Delphi');
  builder.BeginNode('Author');
  builder.AddField('Name', 'Primož Gabrijelčič');
  builder.AddField('Blog', 'thedelphigeek.com');
  builder.EndNode;
  builder.EndNode;
  builder.EndData;
```

```
  Result := builder.Make;
end;
```

In the fluent version, it is implemented as follows:

```
function TfrmBuilderFluent.MakeData(
  const builder: IDataBuilderFluent): string;
begin
  builder
    .BeginData
      .BeginNode('Book')
        .AddField('Title', 'Hands-on Design Patterns')
        .AddField('Topic', 'design patterns, Delphi')
        .BeginNode('Author')
          .AddField('Name', 'Primoz Gabrijelcic')
          .AddField('Blog', 'thedelphigeek.com')
        .EndNode
      .EndNode
    .EndData;

  Result := builder.Make;
end;
```

Besides a bit less typing (we don't have to repeat the builder part all over), this approach allows us to get creative with indentation. The code indentation now resembles the structure of the generated data, which improves readability.

Summary

In this chapter, I have explored four more creational patterns.

The first pattern was a factory method. This pattern simplifies the creation of objects that depend on one another. We can implement it by following the classical object-oriented approach or in a modernized way by using interfaces and dependency injection.

From there, we moved to an abstract factory pattern. Abstract factory is a factory for factories. This pattern defines how abstract interfaces should be used to create collections of dependent objects.

The third pattern, prototype, is about making perfect copies of objects. In Delphi, we have to do this manually, and this section mostly explored the different ways of implementing the data-copying mechanism.

The last pattern in this chapter, builder, is closely related to an abstract factory pattern. It is used to split the creation of complex objects into two parts: one issues instructions to the abstract builder, which then generates a concrete representation.

In the next chapter, we will move to the new pattern group: structural patterns. We will explore the Composite pattern, Flyweight, Marker, and Bridge.

12
Composite, Flyweight, Marker Interface, and Bridge

Managing complex objects and collections of objects can quickly turn into a mess. **Structural patterns** were designed to help you think about object composition and to change disorder into order.

Structural patterns come in different shapes and sizes. Some consume one interface and expose the same or a slightly modified version of that interface to the user. Others consume multiple objects, or enhance their behavior in aspects that are completely unrelated to the functionality of consumed objects.

In this chapter, we'll firstly look into three unrelated structural patterns that cover different use cases. At the end, the bridge pattern will introduce us to the area of patterns that consume only one interface and mostly leave it unchanged, which will be the main topic of the next chapter. In this chapter, you will learn about the following:

- A composite pattern, which allows clients to ignore the difference between simple and complex objects
- A flyweight pattern, which minimizes memory consumption with data sharing
- A marker interface pattern, which introduces metadata programming
- A bridge pattern, which helps us to separate an abstract interface from its implementation

Composite

Sometimes, we have to work with data that is organized into a tree structure. There is an entry point, an object of some class *N*, which owns other objects of the same class *N* or objects of class *L*. We call this entry point a root, class *N*, an inner node, and *L*, a leaf.

When we perform some operation on such compound data, it is helpful if we can treat all objects the same. In other words, we don't want to distinguish between a root, an inner node, and a leaf. The composite pattern allows us to treat all types of components the same.

> Imagine an irrigation system. At some point, it is connected to a water supply. The irrigation system can then split into multiple branches that end in different kinds of water dispensers. We don't care much about that complicated structure, as all components of the system implement the same interface: you put the water in and it flows out the other end.

As specified in the Gang of Four book, a composite pattern works with two types of objects. Compound objects can own other objects, while leaf objects represent endpoints of the structure: they can only hold data but not other compounds or leaf objects.

To make sure that both kinds of objects implement the same interface, we derive both from the abstract class, which specifies these interfaces. For example, the following Delphi code fragment defines a very simple collection of classes implementing the composite pattern:

```
type
  TBaseClass = class
  public
    procedure Operation; virtual; abstract;
  end;

  TCompoundClass = class(TBaseClass)
  public
    procedure Operation; override;
  end;

  TLeafClass = class(TBaseClass)
  public
   procedure Operation; override;
  end;
```

It should be noted that, when we are discussing the composite pattern, the word interface does not mean `interface` as we know it in Delphi. The Gang of Four design patterns are purely object-oriented, and in this context, an interface means just a set of methods that a class exposes publicly.

In modern times, we mostly stay away from the composite pattern. In the case of a tree data structure, for example, we would work with just one data type: node. Each node can have multiple children of the same type. If it doesn't have any children, it represents a leaf node—simple and effective.

In other situations, when we need different classes to expose the same interface, we can do that by using Delphi interfaces. For example, we could easily rewrite the previous example as follows:

```
type
  ICommonInterface = interface
    procedure Operation;
  end;

  TCompoundClass = class(TInterfacedObject, ICommonInterface)
  public
    procedure Operation;
  end;

  TLeafClass = class(TInterfacedObject, ICommonInterface)
  public
    procedure Operation;
  end;
```

Still, this requires us to work with interfaces instead of objects, and sometimes that would require a significant rewrite of the existing code. In such cases, the composite pattern still represents a powerful tool.

Child management

While the composite pattern tries to equalize different kinds of objects in a data structure, there is still a significant difference between compound and leaf nodes, namely that compound nodes own other objects. To use this functionality in the code, compound nodes must implement child management operations. In other words, they must implement operations for adding, removing, and accessing child objects. It is, however, not clear in which place the class hierarchy we should implement these methods.

We can approach this in two different ways. One possibility is to define these operations in the interface class (`TBaseClass` in our example). This is called **design for uniformity** and enables the clients to treat leaf and composite objects completely uniformly. This approach, however, loses type safety, as the code can perform child management operations on leaf objects, and that doesn't make much sense. To prevent such errors, we have to override child management operations in the leaf class (`TLeafClass`) to raise an exception if they are called.

Another possibility is to implement child management operations in the composite class (`TCompoundClass`). This approach is called **design for type safety**. We gain type safety, child management is now simply not implemented for leaf objects, but we lose uniformity.

In my opinion, it is better to design for type safety as, in this case, the compiler can catch most of our errors. Still, it is good to understand both approaches so the next example will demonstrate both techniques.

The composite project in the composite folder implements a simple structure that can be used to define a modular system, for example, a personal computer. Two parallel implementations are made, one designed for uniformity and another for type safety. The designed-for-uniformity version is implemented in the `CompositeUniformity` unit, as shown here:

```
type
  TComponentU = class
  public
    constructor Create(const AName: string; const APrice: real);
    procedure Add(component: TComponentU); virtual;
    function Components: TArray<TComponentU>; virtual;
    function TotalPrice: real; virtual;
    property Name: string read FName;
    property Price: real read FPrice;
  end;

  TConfigurableComponentU = class(TComponentU)
  public
    procedure AfterConstruction; override;
    procedure BeforeDestruction; override;
    procedure Add(component: TComponentU); override;
    function Components: TArray<TComponentU>; override;
    function TotalPrice: real; override;
  end;

  TBasicComponentU = class(TComponentU)
  end;
```

The `TComponentU` class provides a common interface. Each component has a name (`Name`) and price (`Price`), and can return the price for itself and all subcomponents (`TotalPrice`). It also provides access to subcomponents (`Components`) and a method to add a new component (`Add`). To simplify the example, removing components is not supported. This class also provides some basic implementation for handling the name and price.

A composite object, `TConfigurableComponentU` implements child storage and management. It also overrides the `TotalPrice` method to take subcomponents into account. The code is trivial, and you can look it up in the `CompositeUniformity` unit. The most complicated method in the whole unit is the calculation of the total price for a composite object, which is shown next:

```
function TConfigurableComponentU.TotalPrice: real;
var
  comp: TComponentU;
begin
  Result := Price;
  for comp in FComponents do
    Result := Result + comp.TotalPrice;
end;
```

As we can see, this method doesn't care whether each child object is `TConfigurableComponentU` or `TBasicComponentU`. It simply calls the `TotalPrice` method, which is guaranteed to work uniformly in all types of components.

When you click the `Composite [Uniformity]` button, the following code creates a sample computer configuration and displays all components and the total price:

```
procedure TfrmComposite.LogComponentsU(component: TComponentU;
  indent: string);
var
  comp: TComponentU;
begin
  lbLog.Items.Add(Format('%s%s: %.1f',
    [indent, component.Name, component.Price]));
  indent := indent + ' ';
  for comp in component.Components do
    LogComponentsU(comp, indent);
 end;

procedure TfrmComposite.btnCompUniformClick(Sender: TObject);
var
  computer: TComponentU;
  motherboard: TComponentU;
begin
  computer := TConfigurableComponentU.Create('chassis', 37.9);
```

```
    computer.Add(TBasicComponentU.Create('PSU', 34.6));
    motherboard := TConfigurableComponentU.Create('motherboard', 96.5);
    motherboard.Add(TBasicComponentU.Create('CPU', 121.1));
    motherboard.Add(TBasicComponentU.Create('memory', 88.2));
    motherboard.Add(TBasicComponentU.Create('memory', 88.2));
    motherboard.Add(TBasicComponentU.Create('graphics', 179));
    computer.Add(motherboard);

    LogComponentsU(computer, '');
    lbLog.Items.Add('Total cost: ' +
      Format('%.1f', [computer.TotalPrice]));
    lbLog.Items.Add('');

    FreeAndNil(computer);
  end;
```

As in the `TotalPrice` method implementation, `LogComponentsU` treats all components the same. It doesn't matter whether the component parameter is actually a `TConfigurableComponentU` or `TBasicComponentU`, as they all implement the same interface.

The problem with the uniformity approach is that we can compile the following code without a problem:

```
cpu := TBasicComponentU.Create('CPU', 121.1);
cpu.Add(TBasicComponentU.Create('memory', 88.2));
```

As the `cpu` is a basic component, it makes no sense to add another component to it. The code, however, compiles and only reports a problem (by raising an exception) when executed.

An alternative implementation designed for type safety is implemented in the `CompositeSafety` unit. As shown here, it is mostly the same as the uniformity implementation, except that the child management functions appear only in the `TConfigurableComponentS` class:

```
type
  TComponentS = class
  public
    constructor Create(const AName: string; const APrice: real);
    function Components: TArray<TComponentS>; virtual;
    function TotalPrice: real; virtual;
    property Name: string read FName;
    property Price: real read FPrice;
  end;

  TConfigurableComponentS = class(TComponentS)
```

```
  public
    procedure AfterConstruction; override;
    procedure BeforeDestruction; override;
    procedure Add(component: TComponentS);
    function Components: TArray<TComponentS>; override;
    function TotalPrice: real; override;
  end;

  TBasicComponentS = class(TComponentS)
  end;
```

Unlike in the previous example, the following code doesn't even compile:

```
cpu := TBasicComponentS.Create('CPU', 121.1);
cpu.Add(TBasicComponentS.Create('memory', 88.2));
```

Both versions are functionally identical and, as expected, provide the same output when used in the demonstration program. The following screenshot shows the program after each button was clicked once:

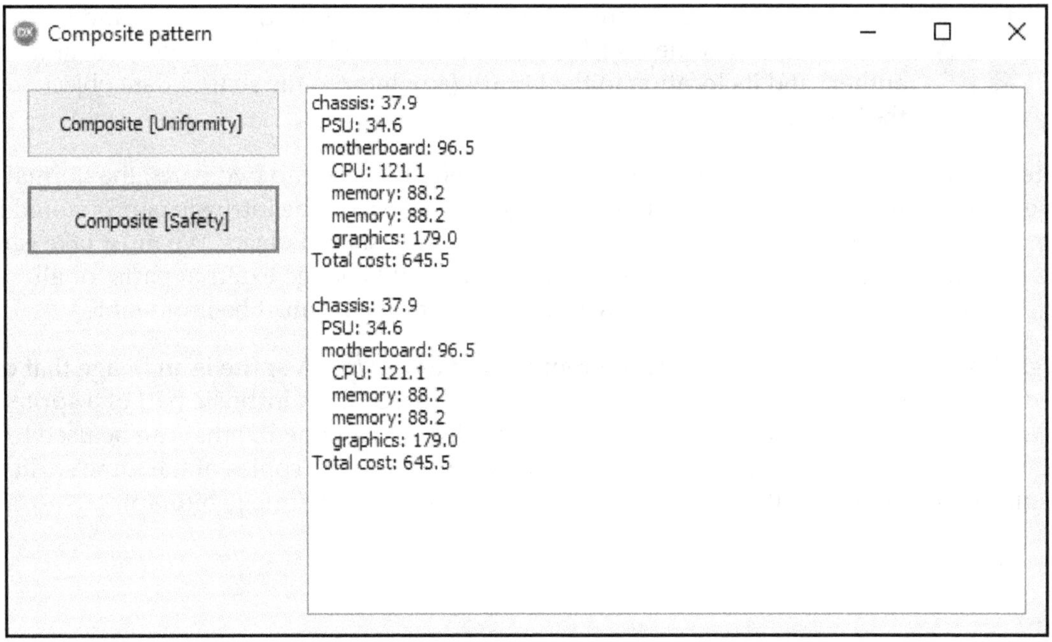

The result of running both uniformity and type safety versions

Flyweight

Structural patterns tell us how to put objects together. Their focus is mostly on organizing software components. They help us to maintain order in our code. That, however, is not true for each and every one of them. A case in point, for example, is the **flyweight pattern**.

The flyweight pattern helps us to reduce memory usage. As such, it is less and less important in modern times, where we are dealing with gigabyte memories. Sometimes, however, we will still significantly decrease memory usage by implementing it. Also, sometimes, it will help speed up the program.

This pattern works best when part of each object contains data that is also used in other objects. Instead of duplicating that data in every object, we can extract shared data into another object. We can then replace original data in an object with a pointer to the shared data. This allows multiple objects to share one copy of the data, hence reducing memory usage.

In the past, libraries stored book indexes on index cards (small pieces of paper). They had different indexes: by title, by author, by topic... and in every index, the index card for a book contained only basic info (title and author) and its location in the library (a pointer to the shared data object: the book).

In terms of flyweight patterns, we divide each flyweight object into two parts: the normal object data (intrinsic part) and the shared data (extrinsic part). The intrinsic part is stored in the object, while the extrinsic part is stored in an external, shared object. We must take care not to accidentally modify the extrinsic part, as that would change external parts for all objects that are referencing it. In other words, the extrinsic part must be immutable.

In games, moving objects are frequently represented as sprites. A sprite is an image that can be displayed multiple times at different locations on a screen. An intrinsic part of a sprite object is its location and some kind of identifier (pointer or unique ID) that can be used to locate a sprite image bitmap (extrinsic part). If we have multiple copies of the same sprite displayed on the screen, they all point to the same extrinsic part (image bitmap).

String interning

If we examine a typical business application, we would frequently find that some string constants are used more than once in the source code. For example, we would probably find the ID, name, and similar strings all around the program.

This doesn't represent a big waste of memory. Compilers, however, sometimes look at that in a different manner and (correctly) notice that we don't really need multiple copies of such strings. Each (distinct) string constant can only be stored once in a complied program, and the code can then reference this shared data. By this, the compiler uses a flyweight design pattern to implement a concept called `string interning`.

We can find this behavior in various programming languages. It is, for example, implemented in Java. A Delphi compiler works in the same way.

A small program, `StringInterning` in the `Flyweight` folder demonstrates this behavior. It is shown in full here:

```
program StringInterning;

{$APPTYPE CONSOLE}

{$R *.res}

var
  a: string;

begin
  a := 'Name';
  Writeln(a);
  Writeln('Name');
  Readln;
end.
```

To actually prove that both name strings are represented by one shared instance, we have to look into the compiled code. The simplest way to do that is to press *F8* to step into debugger and then switch to CPU view with View, Debug Windows, CPU Windows, and Entire CPU. Continue pressing *F8* in the CPU view, until you arrive to a similar code, as shown in the next screenshot:

```
StringInterning.dpr.11: a := 'Name';
0040B10E B888054100         mov eax,$00410588
0040B113 BA88B14000         mov edx,$0040b188
0040B118 E82FBDFFFF         call @UStrAsg
StringInterning.dpr.12: Writeln(a);
0040B11D A130C84000         mov eax,[$0040c830]
0040B122 8B1588054100       mov edx,[$00410588]
0040B128 E8B39DFFFF         call @Write0UString
0040B12D E8AE9EFFFF         call @WriteLn
0040B132 E8F58DFFFF         call @_IOTest
StringInterning.dpr.13: Writeln('Name');
0040B137 A130C84000         mov eax,[$0040c830]
0040B13C BA88B14000         mov edx,$0040b188
0040B141 E89A9DFFFF         call @Write0UString
0040B146 E8959EFFFF         call @WriteLn
0040B14B E8DC8DFFFF         call @_IOTest
StringInterning.dpr.14: Readln;

0040B188 4E 00 61 00 6D 00 65 00 N.a.m.e.
0040B190 00 00 00 00 00 00 00 00 ........
0040B198 00 00 00 00 00 00 00 00 ........
```

Example of string interning in Delphi code.

The address moved into the `edx` register points to the string name. It is possible that in your Delphi this string will be compiled to a different address, but still the same address should be used in both places marked in the screenshot.

If we examine the memory at that address, we'll find the string name. It is a Unicode string, and hence every second byte has a value of 0.

I must point out that the compiler implements string interning only for string constants. If the strings are constructed in code, testing whether a same string is already in use would be entirely too CPU- intensive.

A practical example

To demonstrate the practical aspects of implementing a flyweight pattern, I have put together a simple application that stores and displays information about customers. It is implemented as the `Flyweight` and is stored in the `Flyweight` folder.

A customer is represented by an `ICustomer` interface, defined in the Customer unit as shown here:

```
type
  TPersonalInfo = record
  public
    ID: integer;
    Name: string;
    Address : string;
    constructor Create(const AName, AAddress: string);
  end;

  ICustomer = interface ['{1AE32361-788E-4974-9366-94E62D980234}']
    function GetCompanyInfo: TCompanyInfo;
    function GetPersonalInfo: TPersonalInfo;
    property CompanyInfo: TCompanyInfo read GetCompanyInfo;
    property PersonalInfo: TPersonalInfo read GetPersonalInfo;
  end;
```

The information about a customer is split into two parts. The personal data is stored inside the customer interface as a `TPersonalInfo` record. This represents the intrinsic part of a `Flyweight` object.

The information about the company may be the same for many customers and is therefore stored in an extrinsic record: `TCompanyInfo`. This record is defined in the company unit as follows:

```
type
  TCompanyInfo = record
  public
    ID: integer;
    Name: string;
    Address: string;
    constructor Create(const AName, AAddress: string);
  end;
```

Both `TPersonalInfo` and `TCompanyInfo` store just a name and an address. You can add other fields for an exercise. The `ID` field is not necessary for flyweight implementation. Is is just here to improve logging into the main application.

In the actual implementation of the `ICustomer` interface, `TCustomer`, the intrinsic part is stored directly as a field. The extrinsic part, however, is represented by a field of the `ICompany` type. The following code fragment shows the definition of the `TCustomer` class:

```
type
  TCustomer = class(TInterfacedObject, ICustomer)
  strict private
    FCompanyData: ICompany;
    FPersonalInfo: TPersonalInfo;
  strict protected
    function GetCompanyInfo: TCompanyInfo;
    function GetPersonalInfo: TPersonalInfo;
  public
    constructor Create(const personalInfo: TPersonalInfo;
      const companyInfo: TCompanyInfo;
      companyFactory: TCompanyFactory);
    property CompanyInfo: TCompanyInfo read GetCompanyInfo;
    property PersonalInfo: TPersonalInfo read GetPersonalInfo;
  end;
```

The `ICompany` interface is very simple. It is defined in the `Company` unit and just returns the company info:

```
type
  ICompany = interface ['{36C754FD-2C32-49CA-920E-2FED39121E79}']
    function GetInfo: TCompanyInfo;
    property Info: TCompanyInfo read GetInfo;
  end;
```

To create shared data (`ICustomer`), we have to implement a **factory method** pattern. For more information about this design pattern, see `Chapter 11`, *Factory Method, Abstract Factory, Prototype, and Builder*. In this example, the factory is implemented as the `CreateCompany` method from the `Company` unit. This factory takes the company data record and returns a shared data interface, as shown here:

```
function CreateCompany(const companyInfo: TCompanyInfo): ICompany;
```

We'll look into implementation of this factory method later. For now, let's see how all of these classes, records, and interfaces are used in the code.

When you click **Add customer data** on the main form, the following code creates a new `ICustomer` interface:

```
var
 customer: ICustomer;

customer := CreateCustomer(
  TPersonalInfo.Create(inpPersName.Text, inpPersAddr.Text),
  TCompanyInfo.Create(inpCompName.Text, inpCompAddr.Text),
  Company.CreateCompany);
```

This code uses a **dependency injection** pattern (namely, constructor injection) to inject the factory method, `CreateCompany` into the `TCustomer.Create` constructor. (For more information about the dependency injection, see `Chapter 10`, *Singleton, Dependency Injection, Lazy Initialization, and Object Pool*.) This constructor uses the injected factory function to convert `TCompanyInfo` into `ICompany` as shown next:

```
constructor TCustomer.Create(
  const personalInfo: TPersonalInfo;
  const companyInfo: TCompanyInfo;
  companyFactory: TCompanyFactory);
begin
  inherited Create;
  FPersonalInfo := personalInfo;
  FCompanyData := companyFactory(companyInfo);
end;
```

When the main program needs to access the company info, the code reads from the `ICustomer.CompanyInfo` property. This maps to a call to the `GetCompanyInfo` function, which uses `ICompany.Info` property to map the `ICompany` back into `TCompanyInfo`. `GetCompanyInfo` is shown in the next code fragment:

```
function TCustomer.GetCompanyInfo: TCompanyInfo;
begin
  Result := FCompanyData.Info;
end;
```

The last piece of the puzzle is implemented in the singleton class, `TCompanyStorage` from the unit `Company`. For more information about the singleton pattern, see `Chapter 10`, *Singleton, Dependency Injection, Lazy Initialization, and Object Pool*. The definition of this class is shown next:

```
type
  TCompanyStorage = class // singleton
  strict private
  class var
    FCompanyHash: TDictionary<TCompanyInfo, ICompany>;
    FCompanyComparer: IEqualityComparer<TCompanyInfo>;
    FDefaultComparer: IEqualityComparer<TCompanyInfo>;
  strict protected
    class function CompareInfoNoID(
      const left, right: TCompanyInfo): boolean;
    class function HashInfo(const value: TCompanyInfo): integer;
  public
    class constructor Create;
    class destructor Destroy;
    class function CreateCompany(
      const companyInfo: TCompanyInfo): ICompany;
  end;
```

This singleton implements the mapping function, `CreateCompany`, which is called directly from the factory function `CreateCompany`. It uses a dictionary `FCompanyHash` to store created instances of the `ICompany` interface.

As the next code fragment shows, `CreateCompany` firstly looks into the dictionary to see whether there already exists a shared instance of the company data. If `TryGetValue` fails, such data is not yet stored in the dictionary. In this case, the code creates a new `ICompany` object, sets it as a result, and stores it in the dictionary:

```
class function TCompanyStorage.CreateCompany(
  const companyInfo: TCompanyInfo): ICompany;
begin
  if FCompanyHash.TryGetValue(companyInfo, Result) then
    Exit;

  Result := TCompany.Create(companyInfo);
  FCompanyHash.Add(companyInfo, Result);
end;
```

To test the implementation, we can start the application and enter some data. The following screenshot, for example, shows data for two contacts from Embarcadero, and one from Microsoft:

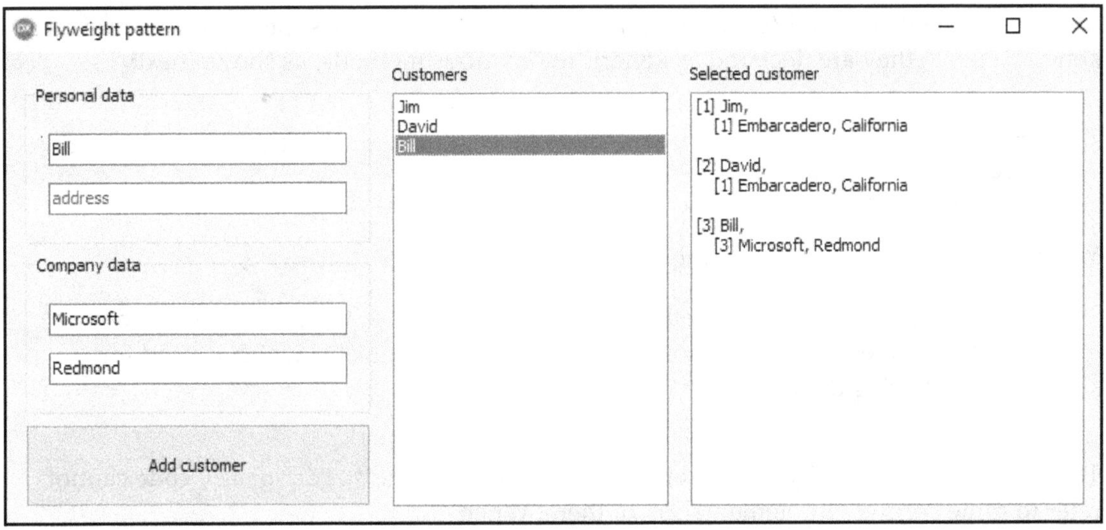

Sample program displaying customer contacts.

We can see from this log that each customer has a unique ID assigned (the number in square brackets before the customer's name). The company info assigned to the first two customers is, however, shared between them; both are referring to the company info record with ID 1.

Delphi idioms – comparers and hashers

The actual implementation of the TCompanyStorage contains some advanced Delphi techniques that come in handy when you are trying to push the most out of the TDictionary.

Delphi's dictionary implementation TDictionary<K,V> is a generic class, operating on two data types (key K and value V) that are specified when we create a concrete instance of that class. For example, in the Flyweight program, the data is stored in the dictionary class TDictionary<TCompanyInfo, ICompany>, so K is TCompanyInfo and V is ICompany.

The algorithm on which TDictionary is based needs two functions that operate on the K type. One takes two values of that type and compares them for equality, returning Boolean. The other takes one value of type K and creates a hash of that value: a smaller integer number calculated from the original value in some way. The former function is called an **equality comparer** and the latter a **hasher**. As they must operate on a generic type, K, they are declared as generic anonymous methods, as shown next:

```
type
  TEqualityComparison<T> = reference to function(const Left, Right: T):
Boolean;
  THasher<T> = reference to function(const Value: T): Integer;
```

You can find these definitions in the unit System.Generics.Defaults.

> Besides these two methods, unit System.Generics.Defaults also defines the comparison function, TComparison<T>, which is used for sorting data.

The problem with equality comparers and hashers is that the TDictionary code cannot refer to some concrete implementation of them. When System.Generics.Collections (the unit containing TDictionary implementation) is compiled, K and V are not yet known. To circumvent this problem, the implementation contains some logic that examines the concrete instances of type K at runtime and then selects the appropriate functions.

This works great in simple cases, but fails when we have more complicated requirements. For example, it fails when K is a record containing a string. Another problematic situation occurs if we don't want to use the full record K for hashing and comparison.

> The problem with hashing records containing strings lies in the implementation of a default record hasher and an equality comparer. They treat strings simply as pointers and not as string data. Two records can contain the same string value that is stored in a different location in memory. In such a case, the default functions won't function correctly. You can see this in action in the DictionaryProblem.

In our example program, we run into both problems at the same time. The TCompanyInfo record contains two string fields. It also has a field ID, which we don't want to use for hashing/comparison.

To fix this problem, we have to write our own IEqualityComparer<K>. We can then pass this interface to the TDictionary constructor. The correct way to construct this interface is to call TEqualityComparer<K>.Construct and pass in two anonymous methods: the equality comparer of type TEqualityComparison<K>, and the hasher of type THasher<K>. In the example program, this is done in the TCompanyStorage constructor, as shown next:

```
class constructor TCompanyStorage.Create;
begin
  FCompanyComparer := TEqualityComparer<TCompanyInfo>.Construct(
    CompareInfoNoID, HashInfo);
  FCompanyHash := TDictionary<TCompanyInfo, ICompany>.Create(
    FCompanyComparer);
 end;
```

The equality comparer, CompareInfoNoID simply compares the name and address part. The code ignores case sensitivity (the words Canada and canada are treated equal), because that is usually what we want in such situations:

```
class function TCompanyStorage.CompareInfoNoID(
  const left, right: TCompanyInfo): boolean;
begin
  Result := SameText(left.Name, right.Name)
            and SameText(left.Address, right.Address);
end;
```

The hashing function HashInfo uses the fast hashing class THashBobJenkins from the System.Hash unit to generate a hash of both the name and the address. As we want to ignore the difference between uppercase and lowercase letters, all data is converted into uppercase before hashing:

```
class function TCompanyStorage.HashInfo(
  const value: TCompanyInfo): integer;
var
  hasher: THashBobJenkins;
begin
  hasher := THashBobJenkins.Create;
  hasher.Update(value.Name.ToUpperInvariant);
  hasher.Update(value.Address.ToUpperInvariant);
  Result := hasher.HashAsInteger;
end;
```

TIP

The System.Hash unit contains implementations of multiple hashing functions. You can use it to calculate MD5 (THashMD5), SHA1 (THashSHA1), and SHA2 (THashSHA2) hashes.

Marker interface

The **marker interface pattern** has its origin in the Java world. It is used to provide metadata capabilities in a language that doesn't have explicit support for that. The marker interface concept was largely replaced with the use of attributes or a similar code annotation tool in modern languages.

In programming, metadata provides a way of adding code-describing tags to the program. Unlike normal data variables and fields, which store information required to run the program and to process user data, metadata provides data about classes (and variables and fields) themselves.

> Metadata is a label attached to a product. It is a note on a car dashboard saying, "*Change oil at 150.000 km,*" or a message on a sandwich in a communal kitchen stating, "*This belongs to me!*"

A marker interface pattern provides a way of adding metadata descriptions to a class without changing its layout. For example, let's say that we have a customer information class, such as `TCustomer`, from the project `Marker` in the folder `Marker` interface. The following code fragment shows the public interface of this class. Private fields and all getters and setters are not shown:

```
type
  ICustomer = interface ['{A736226E-B177-4E3A-9CCD-39AE71FB4E1B}']
    property Address: string read GetAddress write SetAddress;
    property Email: string read GetEmail write SetEmail;
    property Name: string read GetName write SetName;
  end;

  TCustomer = class(TInterfacedObject, ICustomer)
  public
    property Address: string read GetAddress write SetAddress;
    property Email: string read GetEmail write SetEmail;
    property Name: string read GetName write SetName;
  end;
```

For some reason, we want to create a subclass that will contain information about important customers, but we must not add any fields to it. (Both an original and a new class must have the same memory layout.) The only way to do that is to decorate this subclass with metadata information. The unit `Customer.Interfaces` demonstrates how we can do this by using a marker interface pattern:

```
type
  IImportantCustomer = interface ['{E32D6AE5-FB60-4414-B7BF-3E5BDFECDE64}']
```

```
  end;

  TImportantCustomer = class(TCustomer, IImportantCustomer)
  end;
```

Firstly, we define a `marker` interface, `IImportantCustomer`. A marker interface is nothing more than an interface definition that does not contain any methods.

Secondly, we derive a new subclass from `TCustomer`. This derived class implements the marker interface, but it doesn't add any data fields or methods. This, of course, requires that the original class is always used through the interface paradigm. In the demonstration program, for example, the code always uses `ICustomer` and not `TCustomer`.

The main program uses the following code to test the marker interface support:

```
procedure TfrmMarker.btnCustomerCheckIntfClick(Sender: TObject);
var
  cust1: ICustomer;
  cust2: ICustomer;
begin
  cust1 := TCustomer.Create;
  cust1.Name := 'Joe Schmoe';

  cust2 := TImportantCustomer.Create;
  cust2.Name := 'Mr. Big';

  LogCustomerIntf(cust1);
  LogCustomerIntf(cust2);
end;
```

This method simply creates two `ICustomer` interfaces: one implemented by the `TCustomer` object and another by `TImportantCustomer` object. Both interfaces are then passed to a logging function `LogCustomerIntf`, which is shown here:

```
procedure TfrmMarker.LogCustomerIntf(customer: ICustomer);
begin
  lbLog.Items.Add(customer.Name + ' is ' +
    IfThen(Supports(customer, IImportantCustomer),
      'very important client!',
      'just a regular guy'));
end;
```

From the viewpoint of the logging function, the code always passes in a `ICustomer` interface. The logging code then checks for the presence of the marker interface by calling `Supports(customer, IImportantCustomer)`. This function returns `True` if the `customer` interface also supports an `IImportantCustomer` interface.

As the following screenshot shows, the code correctly detects that Joe Schmoe is a regular guy, while Mr. Big is a very important client.

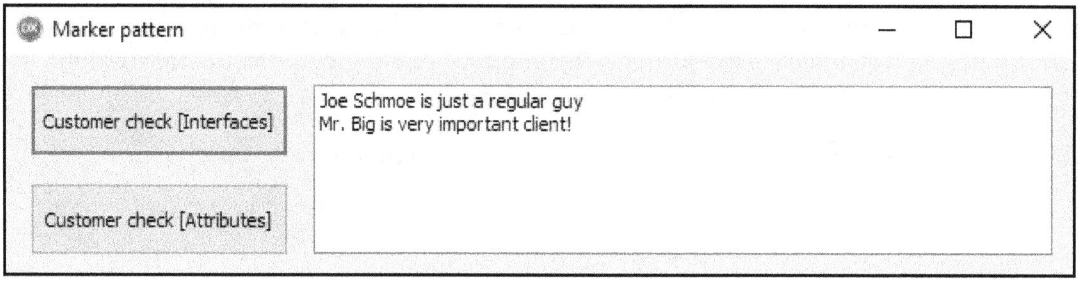

Logging metadata with a marker interface.

The big problem with this approach is that it is very limited. We can only apply marker interfaces to a class. It can also only be used when we are working with interfaces and as such can be hard to apply to a legacy code.

A better way of annotating code with metadata is to use attributes, a concept that was added to Delphi in the 2010 version.

Delphi idioms – attributes

Before we can use an attribute, we have to declare it. To declare an attribute, we have to derive it from a special class, `TCustomAttribute`:

```
type
  SpecialClassAttribute = class(TCustomAttribute)
  end;
```

To use this attribute, we annotate a Delphi entity (for example a class) by enclosing the attribute name in square brackets:

```
type
  [SpecialClassAttribute]
  TThisIsMySpecialClass = class
  end;
```

The Delphi compiler allows us to shorten the attribute name if it ends with `Attribute`:

```
type
  [SpecialClass]
  TThisIsAnotherSpecialClass = class
  end;
```

By a commonly accepted convention, attribute names end with `Attribute` and don't start with a `T` prefix (even though they are technically classes).

A code can only use an attribute if the attribute class is visible at that point. In other words, the attribute must be declared in the same unit before the point of use, or it must be declared in the interface section of another unit that is listed in the `uses` section. If you forget to include the unit declaring the attribute or if you mistype the attribute name, you'll get a rather cryptic warning: `W1025 Unsupported language feature: custom attribute`.

Delphi allows you to annotate all kinds of entities, not just classes. Attributes work equally well on records, interfaces, fields, properties, methods, and even method parameters. The following interface definition (which has no relation to the code examples for this chapter) shows some of the places where attribute annotation is valid:

```
type
  [UriPath('{cardNumber}/{action}')]
  APIAdminHT = interface ['{54E1D5F5-EE4B-4F69-8025-55ED83960C0E}']
    [Accept('json')]
    function Info(cardNumber: integer;
      [Content] out htInfo: THTInfo): TRestResponse;
  end;
```

As this example shows, we can pass arguments to an attribute. To support this, the attribute must accept parameters in a constructor and store it in an internal field. For example, the `UriPath` attribute is declared as follows:

```
type
  URIPathAttribute = class(TCustomAttribute)
  strict private
    FValue: string;
  public
    constructor Create(const apiPath: string);
    property Value: string read FValue write FValue;
  end;
```

To check whether an entity is annotated with an attribute, we must search through the **run-time type information** (**RTTI**). This will be explored in more detail in the next section.

Markers and attributes

Armed with this information, we can now re-implement the marker interface by using attributes.

The `Customer.Attributes` unit defines a normal customer class as shown here in full:

```
type
  TNormalCustomer = class
  strict protected
    FAddress: string;
    FEmail: string;
    FName: string;
  public
    property Address: string read FAddress write FAddress;
    property Email: string read FEmail write FEmail;
    property Name: string read FName write FName;
  end;
```

As we are no longer using interfaces, we can implement a customer as a normal class, and properties can access storage fields directly, without using getters and setters. This allows for much shorter implementation and simplifies compatibility with a legacy code.

The same unit implements an `ImportantCustomer` attribute. While the marker interface is not configurable (we can only test for its presence), an attribute can accept parameters. In our case, we can pass any number of stars to an attribute to indicate the importance of this customer. The `ImportantCustomerAttribute` definition and implementation is shown next:

```
type
  ImportantCustomerAttribute = class(TCustomAttribute)
  strict private
    FStarred: string;
  public
    constructor Create(const AStarred: string);
    property Starred: string read FStarred;
  end;

constructor ImportantCustomerAttribute.Create(
  const AStarred: string);
begin
  inherited Create;
```

```
    FStarred := AStarred;
  end;
```

Now that we have an attribute defined, we can add multiple subclasses, each with its own star factor:

```
type
  [ImportantCustomer('***')]
  TVIPCustomer = class(TNormalCustomer)
  end;

  [ImportantCustomer('*****')]
  TStarCustomer = class(TNormalCustomer)
  end;
```

The same unit also implements a global function `IsImportantCustomer` that checks whether a customer is important and returns the number of stars, as shown next:

```
function IsImportantCustomer(customer: TNormalCustomer;
  var starred: string): boolean;
var
  a: TCustomAttribute;
  ctx: TRttiContext;
  t: TRttiType;
begin
  Result := false;
  starred := '';

  ctx := TRttiContext.Create;
  try
    t := ctx.GetType(customer.ClassType);
    for a in t.GetAttributes do
      if a is ImportantCustomerAttribute then
      begin
        starred := ImportantCustomerAttribute(a).Starred;
        Exit(true);
      end;
  finally
    ctx.Free;
  end;
end;
```

This function firstly accesses the RTTI by calling `TRTTIContext.Create`. Next, it finds the information about the actual type of the `customer` variable by calling `ctx.GetType`. The code then enumerates all attributes of that class by calling the `GetAttribute` function. This function returns `TArray<TCustomAttribute>` so we can use it directly in a `for..in` iterator.

For each attribute `a` the code checks whether it is actually an `ImportantCustomerAttribute`. If so, the code casts `a` to that type so that it can read the number of stars stored in the attribute.

The main program tests this implementation by creating three customers of a different level and passes each to a logging function. As we are no longer working with interfaces, we must also remember to destroy these three customers at the end:

```
procedure TfrmMarker.btnCustomerCheckAttrClick(Sender: TObject);
var
  cust1: TNormalCustomer;
  cust2: TNormalCustomer;
  cust3: TNormalCustomer;
begin
  cust1 := TNormalCustomer.Create;
  cust1.Name := 'Joe Schmoe';

  cust2 := TVIPCustomer.Create;
  cust2.Name := 'Mr. Big';

  cust3 := TStarCustomer.Create;
  cust3.Name := 'Mars ambassador';

  LogCustomerAttr(cust1);
  LogCustomerAttr(cust2);
  LogCustomerAttr(cust3);

  FreeAndNil(cust1);
  FreeAndNil(cust2);
  FreeAndNil(cust3);
end;
```

The logging function `LogCustomerAttr` looks very much the same as the `LogCustomerIntf`. As shown next, a call to `Supports` was replaced with a call to `IsImportantCustomer` and the number of stars is logged:

```
procedure TfrmMarker.LogCustomerAttr(customer: TNormalCustomer);
var
  descr: string;
  stars: string;
```

```
begin
  if IsImportantCustomer(customer, stars) then
    descr := 'very important client with rating ' + stars
  else
    descr := 'just a regular guy';
  lbLog.Items.Add(customer.Name + ' is ' + descr);
end;
```

The next screenshot proves that the status of customers is correctly identified by this code:

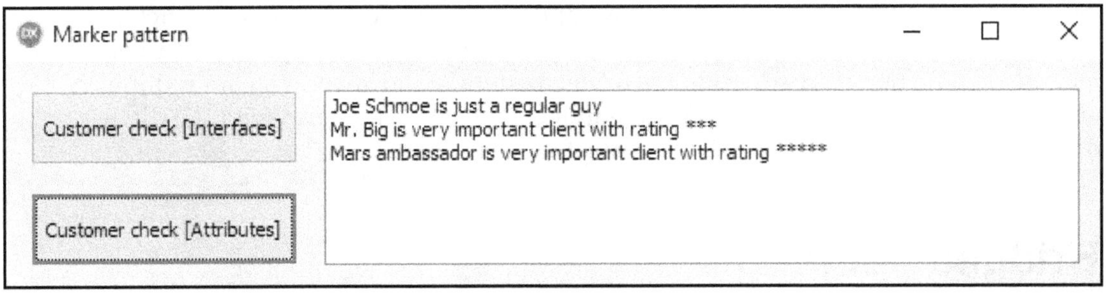

Logging metadata with attributes.

Bridge

An important aspect of a good object-oriented design is strong separation between an abstraction and its implementation. Multiple structural patterns deal specifically with this area. so the next part of the book is dedicated to them. I'll start with the **bridge** pattern and then dedicate the next chapter to other patterns of this kind.

The bridge pattern introduces a strong separation between an interface and its implementation. By this approach, we define the abstraction part as one inheritance hierarchy (a group of derived classes) and the implementation part as another hierarchy. The main point is that the abstraction and implementation hierarchies have nothing in common. The only connection between them is that the abstraction part is using implementation classes through composition.

In modern cars, most controls (steering wheel, throttle, brake...) don't access hardware directly. Instead, signals from controls go to a computer that then controls the electrical motors that drive the actual hardware. With this approach, we can change the implementation (car parts under the hood) without redesigning the interior of the car.

The bridge pattern allows switching different implementations on the fly. It is, however, perfectly valid to only have one implementation. The main idea behind a bridge is separation, not providing support for multiple implementations.

TIP In C++, bridge decomposition with only one implementation frequently surfaces as a **PIMPL** idiom (**pointer to implementation**).

As you'll see in the next chapter, the bridge and adapter patterns look very much the same. The difference between them springs from the use case. If you are writing both abstraction and implementation, you are using the bridge pattern. If, however, you are writing an abstract layer over an existing implementation, you're creating an adapter. I'll discuss these differences in more detail at the beginning of the next chapter.

Bridged painting

For a demonstration of the bridge pattern, let's look at a simple hierarchy of shape objects. The project is called *Bridge* and you'll find it in the folder *Bridge*. The unit `Shapes.Abstraction` contains the following hierarchy of classes:

```
type
  TShape = class
  end;

  TRectangle = class(TShape)
  end;

  TTriangle = class(TShape)
  end;
```

For demonstration purposes, we want to implement support for two very different display types: a **Graphical User Interface** (**GUI**) and a console text mode (ASCII). If we don't use the bridge interface, we need to implement four more classes:

```
type
  TGUIRectangle = class(TRectangle)
  end;

  TASCIIRectangle = class(TRectangle)
  end;

  TGUITriangle = class(TTriangle)
  end;
```

```
  TASCIITriangle = class(TTriangle)
  end;
```

Such exploding hierarchy is usually sign of bad object decomposition. A bridge pattern will greatly improve the situation.

Instead of creating subclasses that are linked to a specific display type, we will move the whole rendering subsystem into the implementation. On the abstraction side, we only need the initial set of three classes. On the implementation side, however, we'll prepare two different implementations (GUI and ASCII) of the rendering subsystem.

To connect implementation to the abstraction, we can use **dependency injection** (for more information see `Chapter 10`, *Singleton, Dependency Injection, Lazy Initialization, and Object Pool*). All concrete rendering subsystems will derive from the abstract class `TPainter`, which is declared in the unit `Shapes.Implementor` as follows:

```
type
  TPainter = class
  public
    procedure DrawRectangle(bounds: TRect); virtual; abstract;
    procedure DrawTriangle(bounds: TRect); virtual; abstract;
  end;
```

A concrete instance of this class is injected into the `TShape` constructor. A full definition and implementation of shape classes is shown next:

```
type
  TShape = class
  strict private
    FPainter: TPainter;
  public
    constructor Create(painter: TPainter);
    destructor Destroy; override;
    property Painter: TPainter read FPainter;
  end;

  TRectangle = class(TShape)
  strict protected
    FBounds: TRect;
  public
    procedure Draw;
    property Bounds: TRect read FBounds write FBounds;
  end;

  TTriangle = class(TShape)
  strict protected
    FBounds: TRect;
```

```
  public
    procedure Draw;
    property Bounds: TRect read FBounds write FBounds;
  end;

constructor TShape.Create(painter: TPainter);
begin
  inherited Create;
  FPainter := painter;
end;

destructor TShape.Destroy;
begin
  FreeAndNil(FPainter);
  inherited;
end;

procedure TRectangle.Draw;
begin
  Painter.DrawRectangle(Bounds);
end;

procedure TTriangle.Draw;
begin
  Painter.DrawTriangle(Bounds);
end;
```

The main program can then use following two functions to draw a GUI and an ASCII rectangle, respectively:

```
procedure TfrmBridge.btnRectGUIClick(Sender: TObject);
var
  rect: TRectangle;
begin
  rect := TRectangle.Create(TPainterGUI.Create(outGUI.Canvas));
  rect.Bounds := TRect.Create(20, 60, 220, 200);
  rect.Draw;
  rect.Free;
end;

procedure TfrmBridge.btnRectASCIIClick(Sender: TObject);
var
  rect: TRectangle;
begin
  rect := TRectangle.Create(TPainterASCII.Create(outASCII.Lines));
  rect.Bounds := TRect.Create(5, 5, 35, 15);
```

```
  rect.Draw;
  rect.Free;
end;
```

All we need now are the GUI and ASCII rendering classes. The GUI version (unit `Shapes.Implementor.GUI`) is very simple, as it only calls appropriate canvas functions. The implementation of `TPainterGUI` is shown here in full:

```
type
 TPainterGUI = class(TPainter)
 strict private
   FCanvas: TCanvas;
 public
   constructor Create(canvas: TCanvas);
   procedure DrawRectangle(bounds: TRect); override;
   procedure DrawTriangle(bounds: TRect); override;
 end;

constructor TPainterGUI.Create(canvas: TCanvas);
begin
  inherited Create;
  FCanvas := canvas;
end;

procedure TPainterGUI.DrawRectangle(bounds: TRect);
begin
  FCanvas.Rectangle(bounds);
end;

procedure TPainterGUI.DrawTriangle(bounds: TRect);
var
  corners: TArray<TPoint>;
begin
  SetLength(corners, 3);
  corners[0] := Point(bounds.Left, bounds.Bottom);
  corners[1] := Point(bounds.Right, bounds.Bottom);
  corners[2] := Point((bounds.Left + bounds.Right) div 2, bounds.Top);
  FCanvas.Polygon(corners);
end;
```

The implementation of the ASCII renderer is much messier. If you'd like to examine it, open the `Shapes.Implementor.ASCII` unit. As a short sample, this is how an ugly triangle is painted:

```
procedure TPainterASCII.InternalDrawTriangle(bounds: TRect);
var
  leftX: integer;
  midX: integer;
```

```
    s: string;
    step: real;
    y: integer;
  begin
    for y := 1 to bounds.Top - 1 do
      FCanvas.Add('');

    midX := (bounds.Left + bounds.Right) div 2;
    step := bounds.Width / bounds.Height / 2;

    for y := bounds.Top + 1 to bounds.Bottom - 1 do
    begin
      s := StringOfChar(' ', bounds.Right);
      s[Round(midX - (y - bounds.Top) * step)] := '/';
      s[Round(midX + (y - bounds.Top) * step)] := '\';
      FCanvas.Add(s);
    end;

    FCanvas.Add(StringOfChar(' ', bounds.Left - 1) + '/' +
    StringOfChar('-', bounds.Width - 2) + '\');
  end;
```

In the following screenshot, you can compare both renderers:

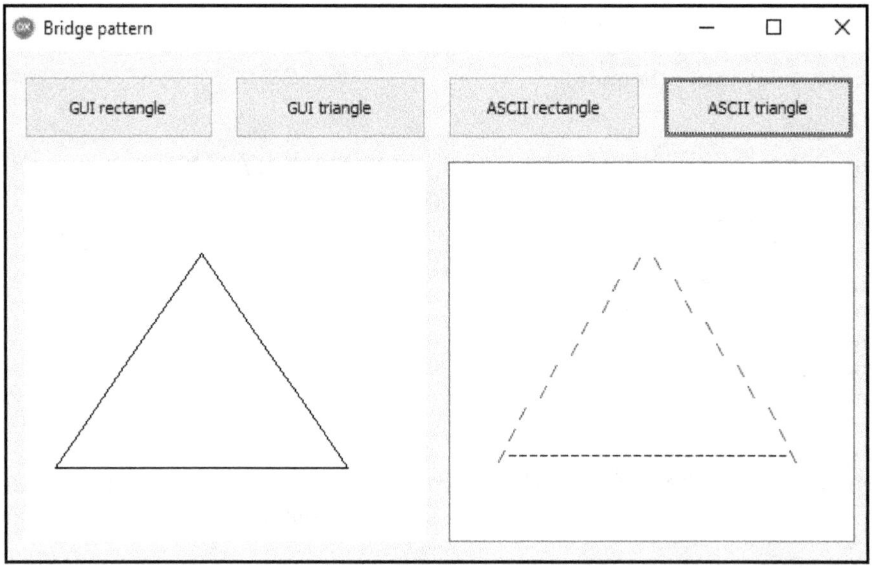

A comparison of the GUI and ASCII rendering of a triangle.

Summary

This chapter provided an overview of structural patterns.

This chapter opened with a composite pattern. This pattern describes how to create an interface that doesn't make a distinction between a basic object and a composite object that is composed of more basic or composite objects. It is especially appropriate when we are operating on tree structures.

The next pattern was flyweight. It is different than other structural patterns because of its focus on memory usage. The flyweight pattern tells us how to share static data between multiple objects to reduce memory usage. This chapter also discussed a practical implementation of this pattern: a string interning, and explored Delphi concepts of equality comparers and hashers.

Next on the list was marker interfaces. This pattern enables metadata annotation in languages that don't provide specific metadata features. In later years, it was mostly replaced with language-specific approaches. In Delphi, we can use attributes to annotate metadata, and so this chapter described this concept in short.

Lastly, we came to the bridge pattern. Its purpose is to put a strong separation between abstraction and implementation layers and enable the switching of different implementations. The bridge pattern is similar to the adapter and other patterns, which I'll explore next.

So, in the next chapter, we'll look into four more structural patterns: Adapter, Decorator, Facade, and Proxy.

13
Adapter, Proxy, Decorator, and Facade

Organizing objects in a clear and easy-to-understand way is an important part of good object design. To facilitate that, structural patterns offer multiple patterns, from composite and bridge, which were discussed in the previous chapter, to four more patterns that are the topic of this chapter.

Finding the correct design pattern to apply to your problem is not always easy. This is even more the case for the four structural patterns from this chapter. To help you find the appropriate solution, this chapter opens with a short discussion on the similarities and distinctions among these four patterns and the bridge pattern from the previous chapter.

This chapter will teach you how to do the following:

- Find out how to recognize a structural pattern that matches your problem
- Learn about the adapter, which helps when adapting old code to new use cases
- Explore the proxy pattern, which wraps an object and provides an identical interface to facilitate remoting, caching, or access control
- See how the decorator pattern allows the expanding functionality of existing objects
- Find out how facade provides a simplified view of a complex system

Selecting an appropriate structural pattern

Distinguishing between the Bridge, adapter, proxy, decorator, and the facade is not always easy. At first glance, both the bridge and the adapter look almost the same, and there is just a small step from a proxy to a decorator, which sometimes looks almost like a facade. To help you select the appropriate pattern, I have put together a few guidelines.

Both the bridge and the adapter design patterns look completely the same. They implement one interface and map it into another. The difference lies in the motivation for using the pattern.

When you define both the abstraction (the public interface) and the implementation (the actual worker object) at the same time, you are creating a bridge. If, however, you already have an existing object that implements an interface and you have to use it in an environment with different expectations, you will write an adapter.

The proxy pattern also looks very similar to both the bridge and the adapter. It, however, exposes the same interface as implemented by the wrapped object. Both the bridge and the adapter wrap an interface and expose a different one.

The decorator is similar to a proxy in the sense that it provides the same interface as a wrapped object. It, however, also defines a new functionality that is available for consumption.

The facade pattern wraps multiple objects and uses them to solve a particular problem. It then exposes a simplified interface that's specific to this problem.

So, bear in mind the following:

- Bridge, adapter, proxy, and decorator wrap one class. Facade wraps multiple classes.
- Bridge and Adapter modify the object's interface. Proxy exposes the same interface. Decorator adds functions to object's interface. Facade exposes a simplified interface.
- With bridge, we define both the abstract interface and the implementation. With adapter, the implementation exists in advance.

Adapter

Reusing existing components (objects, subsystems) is a common part of software development. Usually, it is better to reuse an existing solution than rewriting it from scratch, as the latter will inevitably take longer and introduce new bugs.

Using old components in new code, however, brings its own set of problems. Quite frequently, the newer code works against an abstract interface that does not exactly match the existing functionality. We have to write an intermediate object, a kind of translator from the new interface to the old one. This object is called an **adapter**.

Adapters are used in everyday life. For example, a cable with a USB type A connector on one side and a USB micro connector on the other is an adapter that allows us to plug a mobile phone into a personal computer. Another kind of adapter allows you to plug a device with a German power plug into a UK wall socket, or a device that uses 110 V power into a socket that provides 230 V.

Keep in mind that adapters should not be used when designing code. If parts of the design don't fit together, either change the design or use the bridge pattern. (See `Chapter 12`, *Composite, Flyweight, Marker Interface, and Bridge,* for more information.)

An adapter can do some internal processing. For example, Delphi's VCL library functions mostly as an adapter for existing Windows components. Take a `TCustomListBox` from the `Vcl.StdCtrls` unit as an example; the code mostly sends and processes Windows messages, but still contains some internal fields and does some processing.

An adapter can be implemented by using composition or inheritance. Although composition is usually a better solution, I will show both approaches in the following example. The implementation also differs depending on how the original API is exposed, as a bunch of virtual methods or as an interface.

The `Adapter` project in the `Adapter` folder demonstrates both approaches. The `Adapter.Example` unit defines the `TConsumer` class that implements two functions. The `Process` function uses an interface parameter called `IProducer` to do some processing, while the `FindTheAnswer` function uses an instance of a `TProblemSolver` class. They are declared as follows:

```
type
  IProducer = interface ['{8E4001F9-11EC-4C9C-BAD9-97C9601699FF}']
    function NextData: TValue;
  end;

  TProblemSolver = class
  public
    function SolveProblem(const problem: string): string;
      virtual; abstract;
  end;

  TConsumer = class
  public
    function Process(const intf: IProducer): integer;
    function FindTheAnswer(const solver: TProblemSolver): string;
  end;
```

How the `Process` and `FindTheAnswer` are implemented is not our concern. (If you want to know, check the code.) We are here to deal with a different problem.

Wrapping a class

We have inherited a problem-solver class called `TDeepThough` that we would like to pass to the `FindTheAnswer` function. This class is defined in the `Adapter.Example.Inheritance` unit as follows:

```
type
  TDeepThought = class
  public
    function FindTheAnswer: string;
  end;
```

We cannot use it directly, as it does not descend from the `TProblemSolver` class. Instead, we have to create an adapter. This adapter must inherit from the `TProblemSolver` class (otherwise, we would not be able to pass it to the `FindTheAnswer` function) and must somehow access an instance of a `TDeepThought` class that will do the real work. The following code fragment extracted from the `Adapter.Example.Inheritance` unit shows how this adapter is defined:

```
type
  TProblemAdapter = class(TProblemSolver)
  public
    function SolveProblem(const problem: string): string; override;
  end;
```

We could have created an instance of a `TDeepThough` externally and *injected* it into the `TProblemAdapter` in the constructor. (For more information on dependency injection, see `Chapter 10`, *Singleton, Dependency Injection, Lazy Initialization, and Object Pool.*) This approach will be used in the following example, but for this one, I decided on a simple version. The `TProblemAdapter` creates an instance of `TDeepThought` internally, as shown here:

```
function TProblemAdapter.SolveProblem(const problem: string): string;
var
  dt: TDeepThought;
begin
  dt := TDeepThought.Create;
  try
    Result := dt.FindTheAnswer;
  finally
    FreeAndNil(dt);
```

```
  end;
end;
```

This approach tightly bonds adapter to the implementation. Most of the time, it is better to create such as implementation externally and inject it into the adapter, but sometimes such a simple solution is exactly what you need.

To use the adapter, we have to create an instance of the `TProblemAdapter` class and pass it to the `FindTheAnswer` call. The following code fragment from the main unit `AdapterMain` shows how this is implemented in the example program:

```
procedure TfrmAdapter.btnObjectAdapterClick(Sender: TObject);
var
  answer: string;
  consumer: TConsumer;
  problemAdapter: TProblemAdapter;
begin
  consumer := TConsumer.Create;
  try
    problemAdapter := TProblemAdapter.Create;
    try
      answer := consumer.FindTheAnswer(problemAdapter);
    finally
      FreeAndNil(problemAdapter);
    end;
    lbLog.Items.Add('The answer is: ' + answer);
  finally
    FreeAndNil(consumer);
  end;
end;
```

Wrapping an interface

The second part of the solution creates an adapter that can be used with the `Process` function that expects a `IProducer` interface. The existing code, which can be found in the `Adapter.Example.Composition` unit, however, implements an `IIncompatible` interface. Both the original interface and the adapter are shown here:

```
type
  IIncompatible = interface ['{4422CF75-2CBE-4F7D-9C14-89DC160CD3C7}']
    function NextElement: integer;
  end;

  TIncompatible = class(TInterfacedObject, IIncompatible)
```

```
    function NextElement: integer;
  end;

  TProducerAdapter = class(TInterfacedObject, IProducer)
  strict private
    FWrapped: IIncompatible;
  public
    constructor Create(const wrapped: IIncompatible);
    function NextData: TValue;
  end;
```

In this solution, the adapter must implement the `IProducer` interface so that we are able to pass it to the `Process` function. This adapter is also more flexible than the `TProblemAdapter`, as it does not create the wrapped interface internally. An instance of the `IIncompatible` class is injected into the constructor instead.

> I would like to make clear that the choice of creating an implementation internally versus injecting it has nothing to do with the implementation of the original component (object versus interface). We could equally well inject an existing object or create an interface inside the adapter.

In this case, implementation of the adapter is trivial. The constructor must store the implementation in an internal field and the `NextData` function must forward the call to the old implementation. The full implementation is shown here:

```
constructor TProducerAdapter.Create(const wrapped: IIncompatible);
begin
  inherited Create;
  FWrapped := wrapped;
end;

function TProducerAdapter.NextData: TValue;
begin
  Result := FWrapped.NextElement;
end;
```

To use this adapter, we must first create an instance of the `IIncompatible` class, inject it into the `TProducerAdapter` constructor, and send `IProducer` to the `Process` function. The code for this (from the `AdapterMain` unit) is as follows:

```
procedure TfrmAdapter.btnInterfaceAdapterClick(Sender: TObject);
var
  consumer: TConsumer;
  oldProducer: IIncompatible;
  producerAdapter: IProducer;
  value: integer;
```

```
begin
  consumer := TConsumer.Create;
  try
    oldProducer := TIncompatible.Create;
    producerAdapter := TProducerAdapter.Create(oldProducer);
    value := consumer.Process(producerAdapter);
    lbLog.Items.Add('Result: ' + value.ToString);
  finally
    FreeAndNil(consumer);
  end;
end;
```

Implementing a queue with a list

For a more meaningful example, we can see how we can adapt code that expects to operate on a double-ended queue when we don't have an implementation of such a structure ready.

TIP

A double-ended queue, or **deque**, is a queue that allows you to add and remove elements both at the front and at the back of the queue.

The `AdapterMain` unit implements two methods, `RotateLeft` and `RotateRight`, as follows:

```
procedure TfrmAdapter.RotateLeft(const deque: IDeque<integer>);
begin
  deque.PushBack(deque.PopFront);
end;

procedure TfrmAdapter.RotateRight(const deque: IDeque<integer>);
begin
  deque.PushFront(deque.PopBack);
end;
```

Both are using the following double-ended queue interface from `Deque.Intf`:

```
type
  IDeque<T> = interface
    function IsEmpty: boolean;
    procedure PushBack(const element: T);
    procedure PushFront(const element: T);
    function PopBack: T;
    function PopFront: T;
  end;
```

As we don't have a double-ended queue implementation handy, we would like to use a `TList<T>` for storage, so we have to write an adapter. It is called `TDequeList<T>` and is defined in the `Deque.Adapter` unit as follows:

```
type
  TDequeList<T> = class(TInterfacedObject, IDeque<T>)
  strict private
    FStorage: TList<T>;
  public
    constructor Create(storage: TList<T>);
    function IsEmpty: boolean;
    procedure PushBack(const element: T);
    procedure PushFront(const element: T);
    function PopBack: T;
    function PopFront: T;
  end;
```

The code uses an already-seen approach to wrapping an interface around an injected implementation. The implementation is simple and treats the list element `[0]` as deque's front and the list element `[Count-1]` as deque's back:

```
constructor TDequeList<T>.Create(storage: TList<T>);
begin
  inherited Create;
  FStorage := storage;
end;

function TDequeList<T>.IsEmpty: boolean;
begin
  Result := FStorage.Count = 0;
end;

function TDequeList<T>.PopBack: T;
begin
  if IsEmpty then
    raise Exception.Create('TDequeList<T>.PopBack: List is empty')
  else
  begin
    Result := FStorage[FStorage.Count - 1];
    FStorage.Delete(FStorage.Count - 1);
  end;
end;

function TDequeList<T>.PopFront: T;
begin
  if IsEmpty then
    raise Exception.Create('TDequeList<T>.PopFront: List is empty')
```

```
    else
    begin
      Result := FStorage[0];
      FStorage.Delete(0);
    end;
  end;

  procedure TDequeList<T>.PushBack(const element: T);
  begin
    FStorage.Add(element);
  end;

  procedure TDequeList<T>.PushFront(const element: T);
  begin
    FStorage.Insert(0, element);
  end;
```

The code creates `TList<integer>` storage in the main form's `OnCreate` event and fills it with numbers from `0 to 9`. It then injects this list into the `TDequeList<integer>` adapter and passes the result into `ResultLeft` or `ResultRight`. The relevant parts of the code are shown here:

```
  procedure TfrmAdapter.FormCreate(Sender: TObject);
  var
    i: integer;
  begin
    FData := TList<integer>.Create;
    for i := 0 to 9 do
      FData.Add(i);
  end;

  procedure TfrmAdapter.btnRotateLeftClick(Sender: TObject);
  begin
    RotateLeft(TDequeList<integer>.Create(FData));
    Log(FData);
  end;

  procedure TfrmAdapter.btnRotateRightClick(Sender: TObject);
  begin
    RotateRight(TDequeList<integer>.Create(FData));
    Log(FData);
  end;
```

The output after pressing **Rotate left** nine times followed by pressing **Rotate right** nine times is shown in the following screenshot:

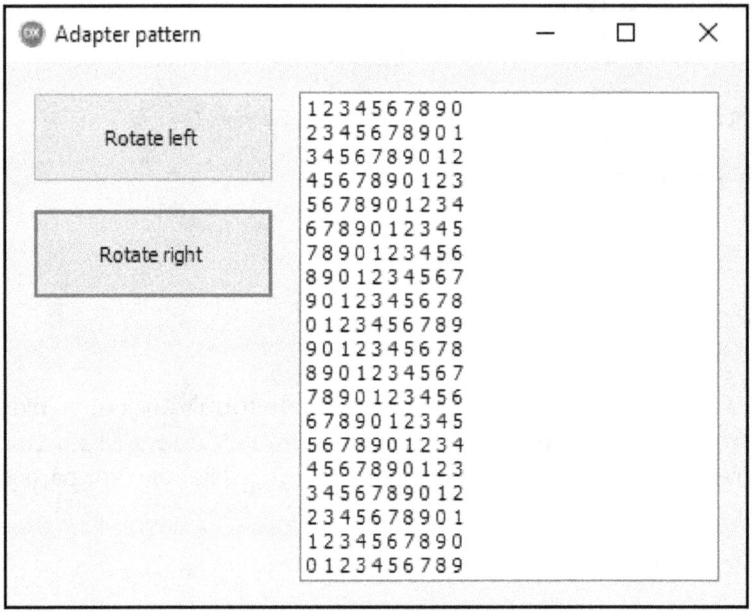

Rotating a list wrapped in an adapter

Proxy

A proxy is a component that wraps another component and exposes the wrapped interface. This definition doesn't make much sense. Why would anyone want to add another layer of indirection (another wrapper) and expose the same wrapped interface? They would do this simply because a proxy doesn't guarantee that each call of that interface will be forwarded to the wrapped object. It is entirely possible that the proxy will generate the result internally or execute something else (introduce a side effect) before or after calling the wrapped interface.

When you are accessing the web from inside a business environment, the traffic usually flows through a http filtering and caching proxy. This software catches all http requests generated in browsers and other applications and then decides whether it will forward a request to the target site, return the result from the cache, or deny the request if the site is on the blocked list.

In that example, an http proxy checks whether the access is allowed and then allows or blocks access to the remote web server. A proxy of that kind, one that checks credentials and acts accordingly, is called a **protection proxy**.

Another kind of proxy, a **remoting proxy**, forwards interface calls over the network to another location, where they are executed. Remote execution frameworks, such as DCOM, RPC, and CORBA, are examples of such a proxy class.

A proxy can delay the creation of a wrapped object until it is required. For example, a remoting proxy may open the connection not when the proxy is created, but when the first wrapped interface function is called. This can save time when a proxy is created by default till the time they are used.

A proxy can work as a caching proxy and return results of some functions from the cache. An extreme example of this kind is a virtual proxy that never creates the wrapped object but rather generates all responses internally. This kind of proxy is especially useful for unit testing, where we call it a **mock object**.

Another interesting possibility is a proxy that logs the parameters and results of wrapped interface functions. This **logging proxy** is especially useful when debugging a hard problem.

Sometimes, we want to use an existing component that was not written with parallel processing in mind in a multithreaded environment. In such a case, we have to protect each call to the existing component's interface with locking. The simplest way to do that is to implement a **locking proxy** that acquires a lock just before the wrapped function is called and releases it immediately after it returns.

In the next part of this chapter, I'll look into three quite different proxy use-cases. I'll implement a logging proxy that logs calls to VCL library, show how smart pointers can simplify object life cycle management, and explore a simple unit-testing scenario.

Delphi idioms – replacing components in runtime

The `LoggingProxy` program from the `Proxy` folder shows how we can catch and log calls to VCL methods, such as `TButton.Click`. It uses an interesting trick that allows our code to insert a proxy class without changing the original code. The only downfall of this method is that it can only replace `virtual` methods, and in the VCL many interesting methods are not marked as such.

The main unit, `LoggingProxyMain`, implements a simple form containing one button and one listbox. When the button is clicked, a message is displayed. The whole form is implemented as follows:

```
type
  TfrmProxy = class(TForm)
    btnLoggingProxy: TButton;
    lbLog: TListBox;
    procedure btnLoggingProxyClick(Sender: TObject);
  public
    procedure Log(const msg: string);
  end;

procedure TfrmProxy.btnLoggingProxyClick(Sender: TObject);
begin
  Log('Click!');
end;

procedure TfrmProxy.Log(const msg: string);
begin
  lbLog.Items.Add(msg);
end;
```

When the Delphi program is started, it loads the form definition from a resource. A binary representation of the `.dfm` form file is stored in the `.exe` file. The code reads this binary representation, walks its structure, and creates controls.

When, for example, the `btnLoggingProxy` definition is found in the resource, a `TButton` object is created, initialized, and placed on the form. We can explore a less-known implementation detail when the `TButton` class is located (so that the object can be created), and the first visible definition of that class is used.

In other words, if we define a `TButton` class inside the `LoggingProxyMain` unit before the `TfrmProxy` is defined, the form-loader will create an instance of *this* class and not of a `TButton` from unit, `Vcl.StdCtrls`.

We can use that fact to insert a proxy for `TButton` into the `LoggingProxyMain` unit. We just have to define a new class with the name `TButton` and derive it from `Vcl.StdCtrls.TButton`. In this class, we can override any `virtual` method to catch its execution.

The demonstration program uses this trick to log every button-click. An injected `TButton` class defines the `Click` method, which overrides the original method. The overridden method writes to the log and calls the `inherited` method (which in turn executes the `OnClick` handler) and writes to the log again. The full implementation of the injected `TButton` is shown here:

```
type
  TButton = class(Vcl.StdCtrls.TButton)
  public
    procedure Click; override;
  end;

  procedure TButton.Click;
  begin
    frmProxy.Log('Button ' + Self.Name + ' will be clicked!');
    inherited;
    frmProxy.Log('Button ' + Self.Name + ' was clicked!');
  end;
```

The following screenshot shows how the execution is logged:

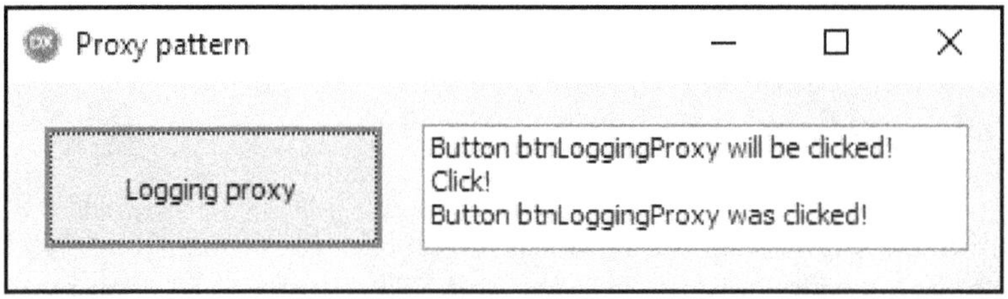

Logging a click on a button control

This component injection method allows for some interesting tricks, as the injected `TButton` could also be defined in a different unit. We only have to make sure that this unit is listed in the `uses` list after the `Vcl.StdCtrls` unit.

Smart pointers

Handling an object's life cycle in Delphi can be a pain. Each object that was created in code must also be destroyed; otherwise, the program will be losing memory. An attempt to solve this was the introduction of **Automatic Reference Counting** (**ARC**), which treats objects the same as interfaces. This experiment, however, is losing tract. It was recently announced that the Linux compiler will stop using ARC and that both mobile compilers (Android and iOS) will also be moved back to normal object implementation in the future.

We can simplify object life cycle management by using smart pointers. As in ARC, a smart pointer is reference counted, so the code knows when it should be destroyed and does that for us.

Delphi doesn't support smart pointers yet. Currently, the best implementation that I know of can be found in the Spring4D library (`https://bitbucket.org/sglienke/spring4d`). The `SpringProxy` demo shows how Spring4D smart pointers are used.

> Why am I talking about smart pointers in the section on the proxy design pattern? Because smart pointers are an implementation of a proxy pattern. A smart pointer wraps certain objects, stores an object in a reference-counted wrapper, and makes sure that we can work with that wrapper, as if it were the original object.

The `SpringProxy` demo requires a Spring4D library to function. To run the program, you'll have to install this library and then add its folders, `Source` and `Source\Base`, to Delphi's Library path or to the project's search path. If you unpack the library into the folder, `Chapter 13\Spring4D` project's search path will already be correctly configured, and you can simply press *F9* to run the program.

> TIP: If you have `git` installed, you can execute the following command in the `Chapter 13` folder to install Spring4D: `git clone https://bitbucket.org/sglienke/spring4d`.

The demonstration program uses the technique from the previous section to inject custom `TButton` and `TListBox` components into the code. The implementation overrides the `Click` method in the `TButton` class and the `DoEnter` and `DoExit` methods in the `TListBox` class, as shown here:

```
type
  TButton = class(Vcl.StdCtrls.TButton)
  public
    procedure Click; override;
  end;

  TListBox = class(Vcl.StdCtrls.TListBox)
  protected
    procedure DoEnter; override;
    procedure DoExit; override;
  end;
```

As in the previous example, these methods will do some logging. This time, however, we would like to log more information. To facilitate that, each method creates an instance of a TLogInfo class, initializes it with the appropriate information, and sends it to the main form so that it can be logged. The implementation of this class is shown here:

```
type
  TLogInfo = class
  strict private
    FClassName: string;
    FComponentName: string;
    FMethodName: string;
  public
    constructor Create(AComponent: TComponent; const AMethod: string);
    property ClassName: string read FClassName write FClassName;
    property ComponentName: string
      read FComponentName write FComponentName;
    property MethodName: string read FMethodName write FMethodName;
  end;

constructor TLogInfo.Create(AComponent: TComponent; const AMethod: string);
begin
  inherited Create;
  ComponentName := AComponent.Name;
  ClassName := AComponent.ClassName;
  MethodName := AMethod;
end;
```

After the main form logs the information, it would have to destroy the TLogInfo instance. This, however, is a good way to introduce problems. If a piece of code implements object creation and destruction at two completely unrelated points, it is just too easy to forget to destroy something. A better way is to use a **reference-counted object** (aka a **smart pointer**), which is destroyed automatically.

> We could also rewrite the code to use an interface approach. TLogInfo would implement ILogInfo, and we would send the interface around. Sometimes, however, we cannot change the object definition and introduce interfaces at will.

In Spring4D, smart pointers are called **shared pointers**. They are created by calling Shared.New<T>, which returns a IShared<T> proxy. I'll return to the implementation in a moment, but first let's take a look at how we can use this in practice.

To create a smart pointer, we have to create the actual `TLogInfo` object and then pass it to the `Shared.New<TLogInfo>` function, which returns `IShared<TLogInfo>`. The following code fragment shows how this is implemented in `TButton.Click`:

```
procedure TButton.Click;
var
  info: TLogInfo;
begin
  inherited;
  info := TLogInfo.Create(Self, 'Click');
  frmProxy.Log(Shared.New<TLogInfo>(info));
end;
```

Delphi allows us to simplify the code, as in this case, the `T` parameter of `New<T>` can be deduced automatically. The code in overridden `TListBox` methods shows this approach:

```
procedure TListBox.DoEnter;
begin
  inherited;
  frmProxy.Log(Shared.New(
  TLogInfo.Create(Self, 'DoEnter')));
end;

procedure TListBox.DoExit;
begin
  inherited;
  frmProxy.Log(Shared.New(
  TLogInfo.Create(Self, 'DoExit')));
end;
```

When we want to treat the data as a smart pointer, we can simply assign this `IShared<TLogInfo>` to another variable (or parameter) of the same type, and it will be managed correctly. When we want to treat it as a `TLogInfo`, we can also do that automatically. For example, the logging function `TfrmProxy.Log` is implemented as follows:

```
procedure TfrmProxy.Log(const logInfo: IShared<TLogInfo>);
begin
  lbLog.Items.Add(Format( 'Executed %s.%s on %s',
    [logInfo.ClassName, logInfo.MethodName, logInfo.ComponentName]));
end;
```

This function accepts a smart pointer, but then accesses the `ClassName`, `MethodName`, and `ComponentName` of the `TLogInfo` class simply by accessing the `logInfo` proxy.

The magic behind the scenes is hidden in the `IShared<T>` implementation (and partially in the Delphi compiler). The relevant parts of the smart pointers implementation are shown here:

```
type
  IShared<T> = reference to function: T;

  Shared = record
  public
    class function New<T>(const value: T): IShared<T>; overload; static;
  end;
```

`Shared.New<T>` creates a `IShared<T>`, but we already know that. The tricky part lies in `IShared<T>` being defined as an anonymous function returning `T`.

In Delphi, anonymous functions are actually interfaces, so they are reference-counted. If we assign one variable of that type to another of the same type, the compiler will treat them as an interface and update reference counts accordingly. In all other cases, the compiler calls the anonymous function that returns the wrapped object. That allows us to call the methods of this object directly. The compiler inserts a call to the anonymous function behind the scenes, but that is not apparent from the code, which merely accesses `logInfo.ClassName` (for example).

That all helps destroy the `IShared<T>` instance when it is no longer in use, but who destroys the original `T` (or `TLogInfo`, in our case)? The answer lies in another implementation trick.

In Delphi, an anonymous function that returns `T` is equivalent to an interface that implements `function Invoke: T`. The `New<T>` function actually creates and returns an instance of an internal `TObjectFinalizer` class that implements `IShared<TObject>`, and is defined as follows:

```
type
  Shared = record
  private type
    TObjectFinalizer = class(TInterfacedObject, IShared<TObject>)
    private
      fValue: TObject;
      function Invoke: TObject;
    public
      constructor Create(typeInfo: PTypeInfo); overload;
      constructor Create(const value: TObject); overload;
      destructor Destroy; override;
    end;
  ...
```

This instance manages the life cyle of the original object. When `IShared<T>` is no longer in use, `TObjectFinalizer` is destroyed, and its destructor destroys the wrapped object.

The smart pointer implementation in Spring also handles records in addition to objects. Records are managed by the `TRecordFinalizer` internal class (not shown here). The `New<T>` function is the final piece of magic that brings all of this together:

```
class function Shared.New<T>(const value: T): IShared<T>;
begin
  case TType.Kind<T> of
    tkClass: IShared<TObject>(Result) :=
      Shared.TObjectFinalizer.Create(PObject(@value)^);
    tkPointer: IShared<Pointer>(Result) :=
      Shared.TRecordFinalizer.Create(PPointer(@value)^, TypeInfo(T));
  end;
end;
```

The only downside of smart pointers is that they require additional memory (used for `TObjectFinalizer` or `TRecordFinalizer`) and that they are slightly slower than accessing the object directly.

Unit testing with mock objects

I mentioned before that proxy objects can be used for unit testing. In unit testing, we frequently encounter a situation when the tested unit uses some interface from another (and therefore not tested) unit and that second interface pulls in whole lots of code, accesses database, runs a lengthy calculation, or in other ways disturbs the testing process. In such cases, we can replace that interface with a mock object that functions as a virtual proxy.

Creating mock objects is a broad topic, and multiple Delphi libraries exist to help with that job. In this example, I will use the Spring4D library (`https://bitbucket.org/sglienke/spring4d`) and its `Mock<T>` record.

A short demonstration of Spring4D mocking, which barely scratches the surface, is given in the `MockingProxy` program. To run the program, you'll have to install the Spring4D library and then add its folders (`Source`, `Source\Base`, `Source\Base\Collections`, `Source\Core\Interception`, and `Source\Core\Mocking`) to Delphi's Library path or to, the project's Search path. If you unpack the library into the folder `Chapter 13\Spring4D` project's Search path will already be correctly configured, and you can simply press *F9* to run the program.

TIP

If you have `git` installed, you can execute the following command in folder `Chapter 13` to install Spring4D: `git clone https://bitbucket.org/sglienke/spring4d`.

The demonstration program doesn't run any real unit tests. For a simple demo, it defines an interface called `ICalculation`, which is used in a form function called `DoSomething`. Both are shown here:

```
type
  {$TYPEINFO ON}
  ICalculation = interface ['{E0040339-325F-4CA8-96D9-12524F58CBAE}']
    function GetTheAnswer: integer;
    function AddTwo(value: integer): integer;
  end;
  {$TYPEINFO OFF}

procedure TfrmMocking.DoSomething(const calc: ICalculation);
begin
  lbLog.Items.Add(Format('ICalculation.GetTheAnswer = %d',
    [calc.GetTheAnswer]));
  lbLog.Items.Add(Format('AddTwo(2) = %d', [calc.AddTwo(2)]));
  lbLog.Items.Add(Format('AddTwo(3) = %d', [calc.AddTwo(3)]));
end;
```

We don't have an implementation of `ICalculation` handy, so we will use mocking to create it. Spring4D's mocking support uses **run-time type information** (**RTTI**) to get information about the wrapped interface, and that requires the interface to be compiled in the `TYPEINFO ON` state.

Another way to force RTTI generation for an interface is to inherit it from `IInvokable` or from another interface that is compiled with the switch `TYPEINFO ON`.

TIP

Instead of `{$TYPEINFO ON}` and `{$TYPEINFO OFF}`, you can also use `{$M+}` and `{$M-}`.

The whole process of setting up the mock object is implemented in the button's `OnClick` handler, as follows:

```
procedure TfrmMocking.btnMockClick(Sender: TObject);
var
  mockCalc: Mock<ICalculation>;
begin
  mockCalc := Mock<ICalculation>.Create(TMockBehavior.Strict);
```

```
  mockCalc.Setup.Returns(42).When.GetTheAnswer;

  mockCalc.Setup.Executes(
    function(const callInfo: TCallInfo): TValue
    begin
      lbLog.Items.Add(Format('%s(%d) is not supported',
        [callInfo.Method.Name, callInfo.Args[0].AsInteger]));
    end).When.AddTwo(TArg.IsAny<integer>);

  mockCalc.Setup.Returns(4).When.AddTwo(2);

  DoSomething(mockCalc);
end;
```

The first line creates our mock object, `Mock<ICalculation>`. It is implemented as a record, but nevertheless I'll use the accepted convention and call it a mock object. This record that functions as a virtual proxy is created in `Strict` mode. In that mode, the code fails if it calls an interface method that is not explicitly set up.

The second line, `mockCalc.Setup.Returns(42).When.GetTheAnswer;`, sets up the proxy so that it returns number 42 whenever the `GetTheAnswer` method is called.

The next block of lines configures the code to log an error whenever the `AddTwo` function is called. The syntax `AddTwo(TArg.IsAny<integer>)` allows us to execute the same code for all possible integer parameters.

Near the end, the line `mockCalc.Setup.Returns(4).When.AddTwo(2);` overrides this behavior and returns 4 if and only if the parameter is 2. You should keep in mind that more generic variations of a call should always be set up first, and more specific variations later.

At the end, the code calls the `DoSomething` method. Although the code expects an `ICalculation` parameter, we can pass in a `Mock<ICalculation>` record. The `Mock<T>.Implicit` operator will convert it into `ICalculation`.

A click on the **Mock** button shows that all the methods are indeed executing as expected. `GetTheAnswer` returns 42, `AddTwo(2)` returns 4, and `AddTwo(3)` logs an error and returns 0, which is the default value for integer results:

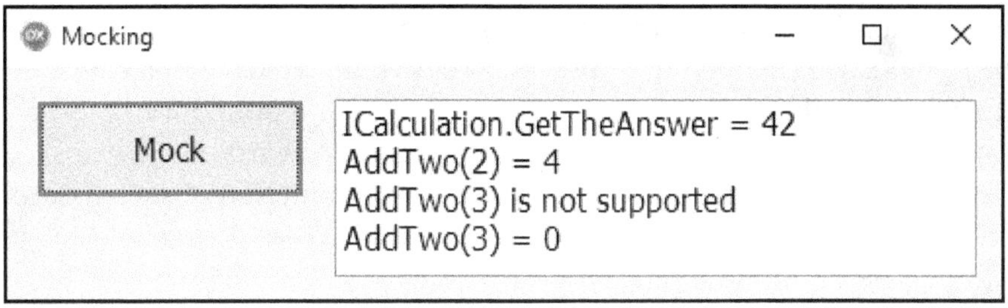

Mock object in action

Decorator

The **decorator** pattern is an incredibly useful tool that helps you enhance existing interfaces with an additional functionality and without changing the original implementation. In addition to that, we can apply this additional functionality to any subclass of the original implementation. As such, the decorator is a useful tool for enhancing existing behavior.

> A Christmas tree by itself doesn't do much. It stands in one place and looks nice. We can, however, enhance its value by adding decorations, such as colorful lights. This decoration doesn't change the original interface of the tree—it just improves it. Furthermore, we can apply the same decoration to many different kinds of trees, not just a specific sort.

Every decorator operates on an existing interface, which is used in two different places. As it has to support original functionality, it must somehow wrap the original interface. Typically, we use an injection to pass the original component to the decorator's constructor. On the other side, the decorator must also expose the original functionality so it either has to implement the original interface, or it must inherit from the original class.

A short example will help clarify that complicated explanation. Let's say we have an original class, `TLegacy`, that exposes an interface, as follows:

```
type
  TLegacy = class
  public
    function Operation: string; virtual;
  end;
```

We want to enhance this functionality with another method, `OperationUC`, that returns the result of the `Operation` changed to uppercase. To do that, we have to create a decorator that both inherits from the `TLegacy` (so that it supports the required interface) and consumes an instance of the `TLegacy` class (so that it can forward `Operation` requests to it). The following code fragment shows a possible implementation of such a decorator:

```
type
  TUCDecorator = class(TLegacy)
  private
    FWrapped: TLegacy;
  public
    constructor Create(wrapped: TLegacy);
    destructor Destroy; override;
    function Operation: string; override;
    function OperationUC: string; virtual;
    property Wrapped: TLegacy read FWrapped;
  end;

constructor TUCDecorator.Create(wrapped: TLegacy);
begin
  inherited Create;
  FWrapped := wrapped;
end;

function TUCDecorator.Operation: string;
begin
  Result := FWrapped.Operation;
end;

function TUCDecorator.OperationUC: string;
begin
  Result := Operation.ToUpper;
end;

destructor TUCDecorator.Destroy;
begin
  FreeAndNil(FWrapped);
  inherited;
end;
```

This code (which can be found in the `Example` in the `Decorator` project folder) demonstrates two important points. Firstly, a decorator typically takes over the ownership of the wrapped object. When a decorator is destroyed, the wrapped object is also destroyed. This simplifies life cycle management in the code that uses the decorator.

> **TIP:** The decorator pattern illustrates the open/closed principle (part *O* of the SOLID principle). It keeps the original implementation closed (the implementation is not modified), yet it makes it open for extensions.

Secondly, operations implemented by the original interface (such as `Operation`) are passed to the wrapped object and not to the `inherited` parent. Always keep in mind that you are wrapping the injected object and not the parent class!

This allows us to decorate any class derived from `TLegacy`. For example, the following code decorates the derived class, `TSubLegacy`:

```
type
  TSubLegacy = class(TLegacy)
  public
    procedure DoSomething(const s: string); virtual;
  end;

var
  decorator: TUCDecorator;

begin
  decorator := TUCDecorator.Create(TSubLegacy.Create);
  TSubLegacy(decorator.Wrapped).DoSomething(decorator.OperationUC);
  decorator.Free;
end;
```

This code fragment shows how we can pass any subclass of `TLegacy` to the decorator. The only problem here is that the decorator loses information about the wrapped object's type, and we have to use casting to access the operations of the `TSubLegacy` class.

One way out of this conundrum is to keep the original reference handy. We could store the `TSubLegacy` object in a separate variable, as shown here:

```
var
  decorator: TUCDecorator;
  subLegacy: TSubLegacy;

begin
  subLegacy := TSubLegacy.Create;
  decorator := TUCDecorator.Create(subLegacy);
  subLegacy.DoSomething(decorator.OperationUC);
  decorator.Free;
  // at this point, subLegacy points to already released memory block
  subLegacy := nil;
end;
```

This approach can cause problems, because now we have two references to the same memory location (the `TSubLegacy` instance), one in the `subLegacy` variable , and another in `decorator.FWrapped`. When we destroy the decorator, the wrapped `TSubLegacy` object is also destroyed and the `subLegacy` variable now points to the memory location that is no longer in use. Other parts of the program may overwrite this memory soon (this holds especially true for multithreaded programs), and in such cases, accessing `subLegacy` after this point may have unexpected consequences. The previous example solves that by setting `subLegacy` to `nil`, but such a step is easy to overlook.

Another solution is to use generics to define the correct type of wrapped objects. The following class definition shows how we could adapt `TUCDecorator` in that direction:

```
type
  TUCDecorator<T: TLegacy> = class(TLegacy)
  private
    FWrapped: T;
  public
    constructor Create(wrapped: T);
    destructor Destroy; override;
    function Operation: string; override;
    function OperationUC: string; virtual;
    property Wrapped: T read FWrapped;
  end;
```

The implementation of `TUCDecorator<T>` looks exactly the same as the implementation of `TUCDecorator` (and you can verify that in the example program). This version, however, allows us to remove casting from the code, as shown here:

```
decoratorT := TUCDecorator<TSubLegacy>.Create(TSubLegacy.Create);
decoratorT.Wrapped.DoSomething(decoratorT.OperationUC);
decoratorT.Free;
```

Decorating streams

To better illustrate the power and problems of writing decorators, the `StreamDecorator` project from the folder folder implements a decorator for the `TStream` class. The `DecoratedStream` unit implements a decorator that extends the `TStream` class (and its subclasses) with eight new functions.

The problem with decorating rich classes such as `TStream` arises from the fact that the decorator must implement complete `TStream` interface. In the case of `TStream`, that means writing lots and lots of functions. Just the declaration of the decorator is a whopping one hundred and eighty-five lines long! The following code fragment shows just a few parts of that declaration:

```
type
  TDecoratedStream = class(TStream)
  strict private
    FWrapped: TStream;
  private
    function GetPosition: Int64;
    procedure SetPosition(const Pos: Int64);
    procedure SetSize64(const NewSize: Int64);
  protected
   function GetSize: Int64; override;
  public
    constructor Create(wrappedStream: TStream);
    destructor Destroy; override;
    // new functionality
    procedure Advance(delta: int64);
    procedure Append(source: TStream);
    function AtEnd: boolean;
    function BytesLeft: int64;
    procedure Clear;
    procedure GoToStart;
    procedure GoToEnd;
    procedure Truncate;

    // TStream
    function Read(var Buffer; Count: Longint): Longint; overload; override;
    function Write(const Buffer; Count: Longint): Longint; overload;
      override;
    // ...
    property Position: Int64 read GetPosition write SetPosition;
    property Size: Int64 read GetSize write SetSize64;
  end;
```

While the implementation of new functions is trivial, the majority of the work lies in writing (equally trivial) implementations for functions from the `TStream` interface. The following code fragment shows the implementation of the new functionality and two examples of how `TStream` methods are implemented:

```
procedure TDecoratedStream.Advance(delta: int64);
begin
  Position := Position + delta;
end;
```

```
procedure TDecoratedStream.Append(source: TStream);
begin
  Position := Size;
  FWrapped.CopyFrom(source, 0);
end;

function TDecoratedStream.AtEnd: boolean;
begin
  Result := (BytesLeft = 0);
end;

function TDecoratedStream.BytesLeft: int64;
begin
  Result := (Size - Position);
end;

procedure TDecoratedStream.Clear;
begin
  Size := 0;
end;

procedure TDecoratedStream.GoToEnd;
begin
  Position := Size;
end;

procedure TDecoratedStream.GoToStart;
begin
  Position := 0;
end;

procedure TDecoratedStream.Truncate;
begin
  Size := Position;
end;

function TDecoratedStream.Read(var Buffer: TBytes; Count: Longint):
Longint;
begin
  Result := FWrapped.Read(Buffer, Count);
end;

procedure TDecoratedStream.ReadBuffer(var Buffer; Count: NativeInt);
begin
  FWrapped.ReadBuffer(Buffer, Count);
end;
```

The main unit uses the new functionality to implement the very simple task of deleting the last 12 characters from a string:

```
procedure TfrmDecorator.btnStreamClick(Sender: TObject);
var
  stream: TDecoratedStream;
begin
  stream := TDecoratedStream.Create(TStringStream.Create(
    'Hands-On Design Patterns with Delphi'));
  try
    stream.GoToStart;
    while stream.BytesLeft > 12 do
      stream.Advance(1);
    stream.Truncate;

    lbLog.Items.Add(TStringStream(stream.Wrapped).DataString);
  finally
    FreeAndNil(stream);
  end;
end;
```

As `TDecoratedStream` doesn't implement typed access to the wrapped object (as was implemented in the `TUCDecorator<T>` example), we have to cast the wrapped object to `TStringStream` if we want to access methods specific to that class.

Delphi idioms – helpers

As you can see, writing decorators can result in lots of very tedious work. If you check the DecoratedStream unit, you'll see more than 900 very boring lines. Is there a better way?

The answer to that is both *yes* and *no*. It's *no* if we want to stick to traditional decorator implementation, but it's *yes* if we are a bit more pragmatic than that and we use a Delphi-specific concept of helpers.

Delphi helpers give us a way to extend existing classes, records, and even simple data types with new methods. They work in the same open/closed way as decorators. The original class, record, or data type stays the same (is closed), but as far as the other parts of code are concerned, it is extended with the new functionality (is open).

The definition of a class helper looks just the same as a normal class definition, except that it is introduced with `class helper for T`, where `T` is the class that we want to extend (or with `record helper for T` if we are extending a record or a simple data type). For example, we could extend the `TLegacy` class with the following helper:

```
type
  TLegacyHelper = class helper for TLegacy
  public
    function UCOperation: string;
  end;

function TLegacyHelper.UCOperation: string;
begin
  Result := Operation.ToUpper;
end;
```

Inside the helper, we can access all parts of the extended class, with the exception of the `strict private` section. We can even refer to the extended class with the identifier `Self` if we have to disambiguate a symbol.

> The `ToUpper` function in `UCOperation` is part of a `TStringHelper` helper that extends the `string` data type. It is defined in the `System.SysUtils` unit.

You should keep in mind that helpers are not decorators. With decorators, we can use an object bare (without any additions), or we can decorate it with a decorator (or even with one of many decorators). We can even do that in runtime, during the execution of the program.

Helpers are more fixed in their ways. Once a helper is visible at some point (either by being declared in the same unit or in an interface section of a used unit), it will be available to the program.

Another problem with helpers is the so-called **Highlander problem**. At any point in the program, there can be only one active helper for a class, record, or data types. If the code declares two helpers for the same type, only the second helper will be active, and the first will be ignored.

Nevertheless, helpers are useful. If nothing else, we can create one with a very small amount of code. The helpers project shows how we can create a `TStream` helper with the same functionality as was implemented in the `TDecoratedStream` decorator. The definition of the helper is shown here, while you can check the `StreamHelper` unit to see the implementation (which is almost the same as the equivalent part of `TDecoratedStream`):

```
type
  TStreamHelper = class helper for TStream
  public
    procedure Advance(delta: int64);
    procedure Append(source: TStream);
    function AtEnd: boolean;
    function BytesLeft: int64;
    procedure Clear;
    procedure GoToStart;
    procedure GoToEnd;
    procedure Truncate;
  end;
```

Helpers extend the class directly. There is no need to access the wrapped instance via the `Wrapped` property in the decorator. This simplifies the code in the demo, which can now directly access the `DataString` property of the `TStringStream`, as shown here:

```
procedure TfrmHelpers.btnStreamClick(Sender: TObject);
var
  stream: TStringStream;
begin
  stream := TStringStream.Create('Hands-On Design Patterns with Delphi');
  try
    stream.GoToStart;
    while stream.BytesLeft > 12 do
      stream.Advance(1);
    stream.Truncate;

    lbLog.Items.Add(stream.DataString);
  finally
    FreeAndNil(stream);
  end;
end;
```

The same example also implements a simple extension for the `string` type that implements the `MixedCase` function, as follows:

```
type
  TStringHelper = record helper for string
    function MixedCase: string;
  end;

function TStringHelper.MixedCase: string;
var
  i: Integer;
begin
  Result := Self;
  for i := 1 to Length(Result) do
    if Odd(i) then
      Result[i] := UpCase(Result[i])
    else if CharInSet(Result[i], ['A'..'Z']) then
      Result[i] := char(Ord(Result[i]) + (Ord('a') - Ord('A')));
end;
```

The code in the main form uses this helper to write out a string converted to the mixed case, as shown here:

```
procedure TfrmHelpers.btnStringClick(Sender: TObject);
begin
  lbLog.Items.Add('Hands-On Design Patterns with Delphi'.MixedCase);
  // Will not work as StringHelper.TStringHelper overrides
  // SysUtils.TStringHelper
  // lbLog.Items.Add('Hands-On Design Patterns with Delphi'.ToUpper);
end;
```

This part of code also demonstrates how the introduction of a string helper disables all functionality of the string helper that's implemented in the `System.SysUtils` unit. If you remove the comment before the last line of the method, the code will not compile, as the compiler will not be able to find the helper function `ToUpper`.

The following screenshot shows both helpers in action:

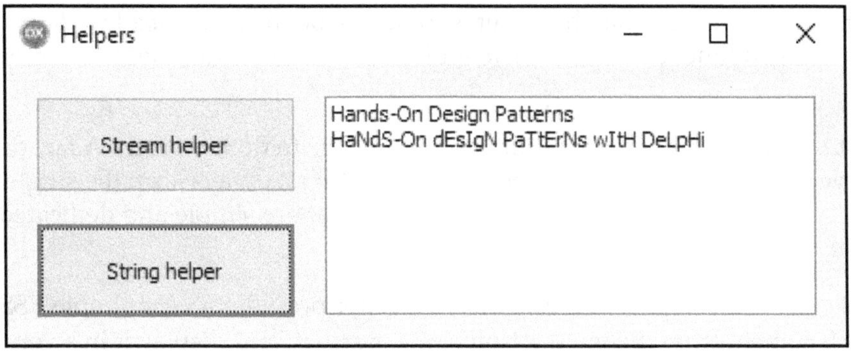

Example implementation of TStream and string helpers

Facade

The last pattern we described in this chapter is a bit different than the three we described before. The previous patterns were all wrapping one and only one component, while the facade pattern wraps multiple components and subsystems. In addition to that, facade is the only pattern from this chapter that provides a reduced interface and not a full feature set of wrapped components.

As such, a facade represents a front for a complex subsystem. Besides connecting subsystems together, it also provides a problem-specific interface. In fact, if we follow the single responsibility principle, we can implement multiple facades for the same set of subsystems, each providing a very specific interface to solve one specific problem.

> When you ask your smart device *OK, <insert name>, will it rain today?*, you are accessing a Facade for an incredibly complex system. Your words are first converted to text, and then another subsystem tries to understand your question. The third one provides information about your location, and the fourth one gives a weather forecast, and at the end a text-to-speech module reads the answer to you. All that complexity is hidden behind very simple user interface.

A facade may provide some additional functionality that is not implemented by the wrapped components. It can also preprocess data before it is sent to wrapped components and postprocess the result. That, however, should not be the focus of a facade. If you need complex additional functionality, implement it in a separate component, and then use it in the facade.

The biggest trap with facades is that sometimes they try to do too much. A facade should not wrap everything, and it must not become a *god object*. Always keep the single responsibility principle in mind and design facades that are simple and dedicated to a specific case.

For example, the `Facade` project in the `Facade` folder provides a very simple RSS reader. It can read RSS content from the web or from a file, parse it, and display it in a very primitive user interface.

RSS is a type of web feed that allows organized access to web resources. It is typically used in news and blog concentrators. The data in an RSS feed is stored in a standarized XML file.

The following screenshot shows the facade project in action:

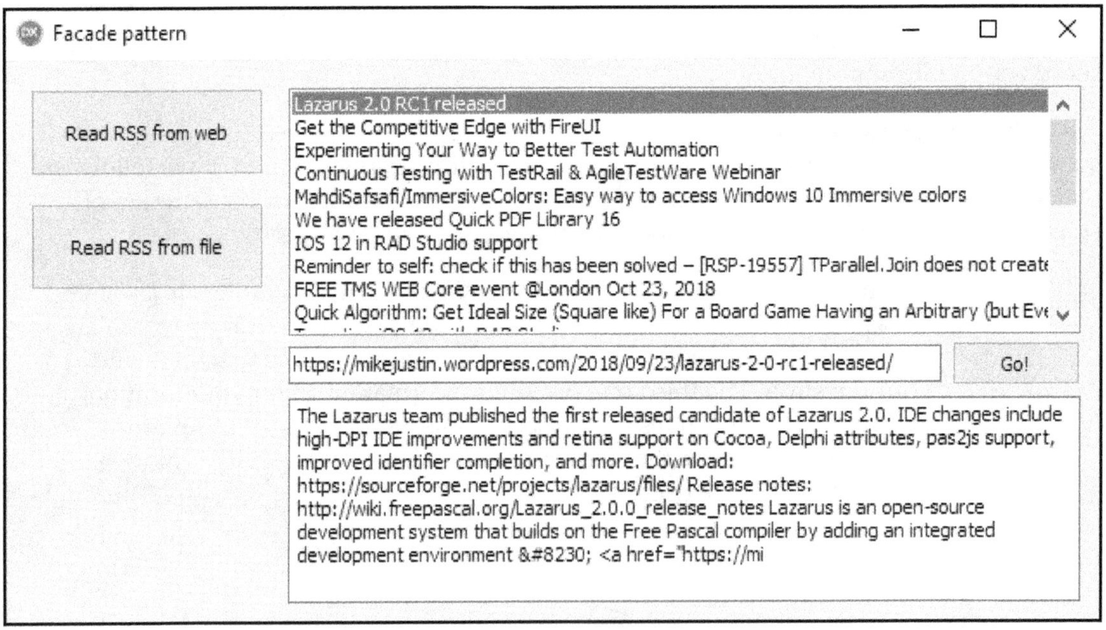

A simple RSS browser

Clicking on the **Read RSS from web** button loads the RSS feed of the popular Delphi blog concentrator site at `http://beginend.net`. A list of posts is displayed at the top. After you click on a post, its URL is shown in the `TEdit` control in the middle, and a short description is shown at the bottom. The description may contain some HTML, as no postprocessing and cleanup is done.

As a side effect, the code asks where to save the downloaded RSS file so you can use it to test the second part of the functionality: loading RSS file from a file. The **Read RSS from file** button does that.

The code behind the web downloader, file reader, and the RSS parser is mildly complicated. It uses the internal class `TRSSParser`, Delphi's classes `THttpClient` and `TStreamReader`, and Delphi's `XML subsystem`.

To simplify the code, and to wrap all multi-purpose classes into a problem-specific interface, the unit RSSReader implements the facade `TRSSReader`. The declaration part of this facade is shown here:

```
type
  TRSSReader = class
  strict private
    FItems: TList<TRSSItem>;
    FRSS: string;
  strict protected
    function Parse(const sRss: string): TRSSError;
  public
    constructor Create;
    destructor Destroy; override;
    function ReadFromURL(const url: string): TRSSError;
    function ReadFromFile(const fileName: string): TRSSError;
    property Items: TList<TRSSItem> read FItems;
    property RSS: string read FRSS;
  end;
```

This gives us enough information to implement the main form. The **Read RSS from web** executes the following code:

```
procedure TfrmFacade.btnReadRSSWebClick(Sender: TObject);
var
  reader: TRSSReader;
begin
  reader := TRSSReader.Create;
  try
    if ShowResult(reader.ReadFromURL(CBeginEndURL), reader) then
      if FileSaveDialog1.Execute then
        SaveToFile(FileSaveDialog1.FileName, reader.RSS);
  finally
    FreeAndNil(reader);
  end;
end;
```

The reader method `ReadFromURL` is called, and its output is passed to the `ShowResult` method, which displays errors and updates the user interface. If the reader was successful, the user is asked for a file name, and the RSS file is saved.

The method activated by clicking the **Read RSS from file** button is equally as simple, as shown here:

```
procedure TfrmFacade.btnReadRSSFileClick(Sender: TObject);
var
  reader: TRSSReader;
begin
  if not FileOpenDialog1.Execute then
    Exit;

  reader := TRSSReader.Create;
  try
    ShowResult(reader.ReadFromFile(FileOpenDialog1.FileName), reader);
  finally
    FreeAndNil(reader);
  end;
end;
```

Firstly, the user is asked for a file name. After that, `ReadFromFile` is called, and the user interface is updated.

The `ShowResult` method clears the UI and then either displays an error or loads the result into the UI controls by calling the `LoadItems` function. Both are shown here:

```
function TfrmFacade.ShowResult(rssResult: TRSSError; reader: TRSSReader):
boolean;
begin
  Result := false;
  lbTitles.Items.Clear;
  inpLink.Clear;
  inpDescription.Clear;
  FItems.Clear;

  case rssResult of
    TRSSerror.OK:
      begin
        FItems.Clear;
        FItems.AddRange(reader.Items);
        LoadItems;
        Result := true;
      end;
    TRSSerror.GetFailed: ShowMessage('GET failed');
    TRSSerror.CantReadFile: ShowMessage('Failed to read from file');
    TRSSerror.InvalidFormat: ShowMessage('Invalid RSS format');
    else raise Exception.Create('Unexpected result!');
  end;
end;

procedure TfrmFacade.LoadItems;
var
  i: integer;
begin
  lbTitles.Items.BeginUpdate;
  try
  for i := 0 to FItems.Count - 1 do
    lbTitles.Items.Add(FItems[i].Title);
  finally
    lbTitles.Items.EndUpdate;
  end;
end;
```

When a user clicks on a post, information is simply updated from the internal `FItems` structure, as shown here:

```
procedure TfrmFacade.lbTitlesClick(Sender: TObject);
begin
  inpLink.Text := FItems[lbTitles.ItemIndex].Link;
  inpDescription.Text := FItems[lbTitles.ItemIndex].Description;
end;
```

This clearly demonstrates how a facade can provide a simple interface over a set of multipurpose classes. Still, we can take a look at how the `ReadFromURL` and `ReadFromFile` are implemented.

The `ReadFromURL` function uses a built-in `THttpClient` to read the contents of the RSS URL for the `BeginEnd` concentrator. As shown here, a helper function called `Parse` is executed on successful read:

```
function TRSSReader.ReadFromURL(const url: string): TRSSError;
var
  httpClient: THttpClient;
  response: IHTTPResponse;
begin
  Result := TRSSError.OK;
  FItems.Clear;

  httpClient := THttpClient.Create;
  try
    response := httpClient.Get(
      'https://www.beginend.net/api/recent.rss.dws');
    if response.StatusCode <> 200 then
      Exit(TRSSError.GetFailed);
    Result := Parse(response.ContentAsString);
  finally
    FreeAndNil(httpClient);
  end;
end;
```

Similarly, `ReadFromFile` reads contents of a file by using Delphi's `TStreamReader`. If the file cannot be read, an exception is converted to a result. Otherwise, the helper `Parse` function is called as in `ReadFromURL`. This function is implemented as follows:

```
function TRSSReader.ReadFromFile(const fileName: string): TRSSError;
var
  reader: TStreamReader;
begin
  Result := TRSSError.OK;
  FItems.Clear;
```

```
    try
      reader := TStreamReader.Create(fileName, true);
    except
      on EFOpenError do begin
        Result := TRSSError.CantReadFile;
        Exit;
      end;
    end;

    try
      Result := Parse(reader.ReadToEnd);
    finally
      FreeAndNil(reader);
    end;
  end;
```

As shown in the following code, the `Parse` function uses the internal `TRSSParser` class from the RSSParser unit to parse the RSS file:

```
function TRSSReader.Parse(const sRss: string): TRSSError;
var
  parser: TRSSParser;
begin
  Result := TRSSError.OK;
  FRSS := sRss;
  parser := TRSSParser.Create;
  try
    if not parser.ParseRSS(FRSS, FItems) then
      Result := TRSSError.InvalidFormat;
  finally
    FreeAndNil(parser);
  end;
end;
```

The `TRSSParser` class uses Delphi's built-in XML processing capabilities to parse the XML file. For details, see the RSSParser unit.

Now, let me restate that a very useful, and often overlooked, use case for facades lies not just in hiding a complex functionality behind the curtain, but to implement a single-purpose interface over a set of multi-purpose tools.

Summary

In this chapter, we have explored four more structural patterns. As they look quite similar to one another, this chapter opened with a discussion about how to select the proper design pattern for your needs.

The first pattern that was described in this chapter was the adapter pattern. Although it is very similar to the bridge pattern from the previous chapters, it occupies a different niche. Bridge is used to connect two parts of a new design, while the adapter helps us reuse old code in a new environment.

After that, I moved to the proxy pattern. It can appear in many different disguises: protection proxy, remoting proxy, virtual proxy, caching proxy, and more. In all cases, the proxy wraps an interface and then exposes the same interface, possibly by changing the operation of some (or even all) methods of that interface.

Next on the list was the decorator pattern. Although similar to the proxy, it works in a completely different way. A decorator wraps an interface and enhances it with a new functionality. As a side effect of the implementation, a decorator can operate on all subclasses of a wrapped class. A similar functionality to decorators is offered by Delphi's helper mechanism, and this chapter explored the similarities and differences between the two.

At the end of this chapter, we covered the facade pattern. It is designed to hide complexities and bind together functionality from multiple classes and subsystems. A very important aspect of this pattern is that it can create a problem-specific interface over a set of multi-purpose classes, which results in code that better conforms to the single responsibility principle (the *S* part in the SOLID principle), which we briefly covered in `Chapter 9`, *Introduction to Patterns*.

In the next chapter, we'll move away from structural patterns and start talking about **behavioral patterns**, a big group of patterns that focuses on defining communications paths and messages among a group of cooperating objects.

14
Nullable Value, Template Method, Command, and State

Every moderately complex program is a collection of many interlocked parts. In Delphi, as in other object—oriented languages, these parts are represented by objects that can cooperate in different ways. They can be tightly connected one object can own others, or they may just cooperate for a short time.

As with every complex system, there's a big chance that it will evolve into a big mess of parts that are connected in random ways without any order and reason. (Sometimes, we affectionately call such a mess a big ball of mud. It is not a pleasant sight.) The patterns in the behavioral group help us to organize objects so that they are tightly coupled where they have to be, can cooperate with each other when the need occurs, and ignore each other in almost all other instances.

In this chapter, you will learn about the following topics:

- The null object pattern, which can reduce the need for frequent if statements in the code
- The Template method pattern, which helps to create adaptable algorithms
- The Command pattern, which treats actions as objects
- The State pattern, which allows an object to change its behavior on demand

Null object

In object-oriented programming, code sometimes refers to an optional object. The absence of an object doesn't represent an error; it is just an obstacle to writing clean code. Sometimes, we can replace such a missing object (a nil value) with a null object. A null object implements the same interface as a real object, but replaces each method with a do nothing implementation.

Most modern operating systems know about the concept of a null device. For example, `NUL` on Windows and `/dev/null` on Unix and similar systems are devices that are empty if we read from them. They will also happily store any file you copy onto them, no matter what the size. You'll never be able to retrieve that file, though, as the null device will stay empty no matter what you do with it.

The null object pattern is a relatively recent addition to the object-oriented programmer's arsenal. It was first introduced in 1996 in a paper by Bobby Woolf, which is still available on the internet at `http://www.cs.oberlin.edu/~jwalker/refs/woolf.ps`.

If you have trouble viewing the PostScript (`.ps`) file, convert it into a PDF file by using any free online converter.

To give a practical example, a null object helps simplify code that looks something like the following:

```
type
  TSomeObject = class
  public
    procedure DoSomething; virtual;
  end;

procedure Process(obj: TSomeObject);
begin
  if assigned(obj) then
    obj.DoSomething;
end;

Process(nil);
```

Instead of testing whether an object is defined and then branching the code, we can introduce a null object that implements the same interface as `TSomeObject`. Instead of passing a `nil` value to the `Process` method, we can use this null object, as demonstrated in the following code fragment:

```
type
  TNullObject = class(TSomeObject)
  public
    procedure DoSomething; override;
  end;

procedure TNullObject.DoSomething;
begin
```

```
end;

procedure Process(obj: TSomeObject);
begin
  obj.DoSomething;
end;

null := TNullObject.Create;
Process(null);
FreeAndNil(null);
```

In a strict object-oriented world, the base object must be ready for an extension its public functions and procedures must be marked as `virtual`. This allows us to derive the null object from the base object and `override` all public methods.

If we are programming with interfaces, there's no need for subclassing. A null object must implement the same interface as the base object, and that's it. The following code fragment shows the previous example, but translated into the language of interfaces:

```
type
  IDoSomething = interface
    procedure DoSomething;
  end;

  TSomeObject = class(TInterfacedObject, IDoSomething)
  public
    procedure DoSomething;
  end;

  TNullObject = class(TInterfacedObject, IDoSomething)
  public
    procedure DoSomething;
  end;

procedure TNullObject.DoSomething;
begin
end;

procedure Process(const something: IDoSomething);
begin
  something.DoSomething;
end;

Process(TNullObject.Create);
```

If the code frequently uses the null object, we can save some memory and CPU cycles and implement it as a singleton. (For more information about singletons, see `Chapter 10`, *Singleton, Dependency Injection, Lazy Initialization, and Object Pool*.)

Writing replacement procedures is simple. As the previous code examples show, the null procedure simply doesn't do anything. When implementing a `null` function, however, we have to return a result. Deciding on what to return is not always easy. We must know how the returned value is used in the algorithm before we can decide what should be returned.

Let's illustrate this with a short example. The following code shows a simple class with two functions and a method that consumes an instance of this class:

```
type
  TBaseClass = class
  public
    function Value1: integer; virtual;
    function Value2: integer; virtual;
  end;

function Process(input: integer; params: TBaseClass): integer;
begin
  if not assigned(params) then
    Result := input
  else
    Result := input * params.Value1 + params.Value2;
end;
```

To write a null object version of `TBaseClass`, we need to return correct the values from `Value1` and `Value2` so that they will not modify the `input` parameter. The following code shows the solution to this:

```
type
  TNullClass = class(TBaseClass)
  public
    function Value1: integer; override;
    function Value2: integer; override;
  end;

function TNullClass.Value1: integer;
begin
  Result := 1;
end;

function TNullClass.Value2: integer;
begin
  Result := 0;
end;
```

```
function Process(input: integer; params: TBaseClass): integer;
begin
  Result := input * params.Value1 + params.Value2;
end;
```

Multiplying by one and adding zero will not change the input, so this code will work.

In some cases, you will not be able write a null version of a function because a single value won't exist that represents a do nothing operation in all places that call the function. If that happens, you still have to use the if..then code in such places.

A null object is functionally equal to a do nothing virtual proxy. (For more information about the proxy pattern, see `Chapter 13`, *Adapter, Proxy, Decorator, and Facade*.) The purpose of both patterns is, however, different. A virtual proxy (a mock object) is used when we need to pass a simple version of an object to a piece of code so that we can test that code. A null object is passed a piece of code so that we can remove conditional statements and simplify the program.

A null object can also be considered a special case of the *strategy* pattern or a special case of the *state* pattern. (For more information on the state pattern, see `Chapter 15`, *Iterator, Observer, Visitor, Memento*. The strategy pattern is not covered in this book.)

> Keep in mind that the `null` and `nullable` objects represent two completely different ideas. The former is a version of the object with a do nothing implementation and the latter is a normal functioning version that can be set to a special, null state (which is not equal to a `nil` value).

To end this section, I have prepared two very simple (but functional) examples. The first implements a null version of a `TStream` class. It is implemented in the `NullStreamPattern` project and is stored in the `Null` object folder.

A null stream should behave the same as the null device that we described at the beginning of this chapter. It should appear empty when the code tries to read from it and it should accept (and throw away) any data that is being written into it.

Interestingly, a `TStream` class itself almost perfectly satisfies these conditions. It is empty and it will throw away any data that's written to it, but it raises an exception if the code queries the current position or size. To fix this, we only have to write one small function, as shown in the following code:

```
type
  TNullStream = class(TStream)
  public
    function Seek(const Offset: Int64;
      Origin: TSeekOrigin): Int64; overload; override;
  end;

function TNullStream.Seek(const Offset: Int64; Origin: TSeekOrigin): Int64;
begin
  if Offset <> 0 then
    raise Exception.Create('Cannot seek in null stream');
  Result := 0;
end;
```

This code that's stored in the `NullStream` unit implements a `Seek` method, which can only move to offset 0. As the code simulates a stream that is always empty, this seems more appropriate than simply returning 0 in all cases.

The second project, `NullLogger`, demonstrates the use of null objects for logging. The `Logger.Intf` unit defines a simple logging interface called `ILogger`, as follows:

```
type
  ILogger = interface ['{738C066A-0777-4BA8-ACB6-2DE68A3968AD}']
    function Initialize: boolean;
    procedure Log(const msg: string); overload;
    procedure Log(const msg: string; const params: array of const);
      overload;
    procedure Close;
  end;
```

The main unit uses the `ILogger` interface in a simple piece of code. Instead of using the if assigned logger then pattern a lot, it depends on the caller providing an initialized `logger` parameter:

```
procedure TfrmNullLogger.Test(const logger: ILogger);
var
  i: Integer;
begin
  logger.Log('Starting test');
  for i := 1 to 10 do
    logger.Log('Step: %d', [i]);
  logger.Log('Test completed');
```

```
end;

procedure TfrmNullLogger.TestWithLogger(const logger: ILogger);
begin
  if not logger.Initialize then
    raise Exception.Create('Failed to initialize logger');
  Test(logger);
  logger.Close;
end;
```

To demonstrate this, the main form provides three buttons. One logs to a file, another logs to a listbox, and the third uses a null object implementation.

Implementations can be found in units, such as `Logger.TextFile` (file logger), `Logger.ListBox` (listbox logger), and `Logger.Null` (null logger). The implementation of the null logger is shown here:

```
uses
  Logger.Intf;

type
  TNullLogger = class(TInterfacedObject, ILogger)
  public
    function Initialize: boolean;
    procedure Log(const msg: string); overload;
    procedure Log(const msg: string; const params: array of const);
      overload;
    procedure Close;
  end;

procedure TNullLogger.Close;
begin
end;

function TNullLogger.Initialize: boolean;
begin
  Result := true;
end;

procedure TNullLogger.Log(const msg: string);
begin
end;

procedure TNullLogger.Log(const msg: string; const params: array of const);
begin
end;
```

In this case, it was not hard to decide what the `Initialize` function should return. The null logger should always be able to initialize itself, so this function must return `True`.

Template method

A template method (sometimes just called a template) is a design pattern that defines a template for an algorithm. Instead of coding a full, working solution, a template method implements just the important parts and leaves some details unfinished. It is up to the derived subclasses to implement the missing parts and through that, provide a working algorithm.

> A recipe in a cookbook represents a template method. It may say something like take three cups of flour (without specifying where exactly you should get this flour from), put into the oven (without specifying exactly which of your baking tins you should use and what specific mark of oven that should be), serve when cold (without providing any detail about serving plates and table setting), and so on.

As defined by the Gang of Four, the template method implements the important part of the algorithm (the business logic) and leaves concrete details unfinished. Usually, they are implemented as a set of abstract methods that are called from the **template** method.

To fully implement an algorithm, you have to implement a derived class that implements these abstract methods (but leaves the template method untouched!). This allows for the development of multiple specialized classes that implement different versions of the algorithm.

Separating important parts of the algorithm from customizable parts and especially writing an algorithm so that it is complete but still open for extensions is not an easy task. It takes some experience to do this correctly, especially if you only have to code one concrete implementation at the moment.

> TIP
>
> Your task will be simpler if you have to write two or more concrete implementations together with the template method. This allows you to better anticipate potential problems when writing future specializations. If you only need one concrete implementation, you can write another one simply for testing purposes.

In a strictly object-oriented approach, the base class implements the template method as a normal method (it is not marked as `virtual`) so that it cannot be changed in a derived class. All customizable parts are implemented as a method that's marked as `virtual; abstract;`. The `virtual` part allows us to `override` (replace) this method in a derived class (a subclass) and the `abstract` specifier tells the compiler that the method is not implemented and that any code that calls this method directly (instead of calling the method from the derived class) will raise an exception.

An example from Delphi's VCL framework shows such a pattern. In the `Vcl.Graphics` unit, the `TCustomCanvas` class defines (besides lots of other methods) two functions, as we can see in the following code:

```
type
  TCustomCanvas = class(TPersistent)
    // lots and lots of definitions
    function TextExtent(const Text: string): TSize; virtual; abstract;
    function TextWidth(const Text: string): Integer;
  end;
```

Out of these two functions, only `TextWidth` is implemented, as shown in the following code:

```
function TCustomCanvas.TextWidth(const Text: string): Integer;
begin
  Result := TextExtent(Text).cX;
end;
```

In this example, `TextWidth` is a template method (a very simple one) and `TextExtent` is the customizable part. It is implemented in two derived classes a normal canvas called `TCanvas` (the `Vcl.Graphics` unit) and a Direct2D canvas called `TDirect2DCanvas` (the `Vcl.Direct2D` unit).

Technically, we could also implement customizable parts through injection. (For more information on dependency injection, see `Chapter 10`, *Singleton, Dependency Injection, Lazy Initialization, and Object Pool*) For example, each customizable part could be injected into the constructor.

TIP

Don't inject customizable parts through property injection. This approach should be used to inject optional code. Inject any required code with constructor injection.

The template method pattern is also useful when working with auto-generated code. A code generator may produce an unfinished template, which is then realized in a derived class. This is, for example, a common approach in lexical parsers and compiler generators.

Calculating the average value

As an example, the `TemplateMethod` project from the `Template method` folder implements two specialized versions of a shared template method. The complete definition of the base object and template method is shown here:

```
type
  TDataAggregatorTemplate = class
  protected
    procedure CloseDataSource; virtual; abstract;
    function GetNextValue(var value: integer): boolean; virtual; abstract;
    function OpenDataSource: boolean; virtual; abstract;
  public
    function CalculateAverage: real;
  end;

function TDataAggregatorTemplate.CalculateAverage: real;
var
  sum: integer;
  total: integer;
  value: integer;
begin
  if not OpenDataSource then
    raise Exception.Create('Failed!');
  try
    total := 0;
    sum := 0;
    while GetNextValue(value) do
    begin
      Inc(total);
      Inc(sum, value);
    end;
    if total = 0 then
      raise Exception.Create(
        'Cannot calculate average of empty data set!');
    Result := sum/total;
  finally
    CloseDataSource;
  end;
end;
```

The template method, `CalculateAverage`, first opens a data source by calling an abstract method called `OpenDataSource`. We don't know what this data source is, and we don't care. It could be a file, an in-memory list, a database, and so on. The template method simply doesn't need to know the specifics.

If the data source cannot be opened, the code simply raises an exception. A better way to handle this error is left as an exercise for the reader.

After initializing a few internal variables, the code starts calling the abstract method, `GetNextValue`, which should return the next value from the data source. If there's no more data, the method must return `False`. The code in the template method adds all of the values together and counts the number of values. This allows it to calculate the average value with a simple division.

At the very end, the code calls the third abstract function, `CloseDataSource`, to close the data source.

A first concrete implementation of our data aggregator works with files. The `TFileDataAggregator` class from the `DataAggregator.TextFile` unit opens a file and reads it line by line. It expects to find exactly one integer number in each line.

An implementation, which is shown in the following code, uses Delphi's `TStreamReader` class from the `System.Classes` unit to read the file line by line:

```
type
  TFileDataAggregator = class(TDataAggregatorTemplate)
  strict private
    FFileName: string;
    FReader: TStreamReader;
  protected
    procedure CloseDataSource; override;
    function GetNextValue(var value: integer): boolean; override;
    function OpenDataSource: boolean; override;
  public
    constructor Create(const fileName: string);
    destructor Destroy; override;
  end;

constructor TFileDataAggregator.Create(const fileName: string);
begin
  inherited Create;
  FFileName := fileName;
end;

destructor TFileDataAggregator.Destroy;
begin
```

```
    CloseDataSource;
    inherited;
  end;

  procedure TFileDataAggregator.CloseDataSource;
  begin
    FreeAndNil(FReader);
  end;

  function TFileDataAggregator.GetNextValue(var value: integer): boolean;
  var
    line: string;
  begin
    while not FReader.EndOfStream do
    begin
      line := FReader.ReadLine;
      if TryStrToInt(line, value) then
        Exit(true);
    end;
    Result := false;
  end;

  function TFileDataAggregator.OpenDataSource: boolean;
  begin
    CloseDataSource;
    try
      FReader := TStreamReader.Create(FFileName);
    except
      on E: EFOpenError do
        Exit(false);
    end;
    Result := true;
  end;
```

Two parts of the code deserve a special mention. First, `OpenDataSource` catches the `EFOpenError` exception, which is raised if the file doesn't exist or cannot be opened and converts it into a `False` result.

Second, the `GetNextValue` function ignores all lines that don't contain an integer value (all lines that cannot be converted from a string to an integer with a call to the `TryStrToInt` function). This is an implementation detail that can be easily changed if it turns out that the customer expects a different behavior.

To calculate an average value with this aggregator, the main unit creates an instance of the `TFileDataAggregator` object and passes in the name of the data file, as shown here:

```
procedure TfrmTemplateMethod.btnFileAggregatorClick(Sender: TObject);
var
  aggregator: TFileDataAggregator;
begin
  aggregator := TFileDataAggregator.Create('..\..\data.txt');
  Log('Average value: %.4f', [aggregator.CalculateAverage]);
  aggregator.Free;
end;
```

The code then calls the `CalculateAverage` function and logs the result. With the data file that comes with the project, the result should be 4.7143 (rounded to four decimal places).

To simplify unit testing, the project also implements a data aggregator that works on dynamic arrays. It is implemented in the `DataAggregator.DynArray` unit as follows:

```
type
  TMockDataAggregator = class(TDataAggregatorTemplate)
  strict private
    FIndex: integer;
    FValues: TArray<integer>;
  protected
    procedure CloseDataSource; override;
    function GetNextValue(var value: integer): boolean; override;
    function OpenDataSource: boolean; override;
  public
    constructor Create(const values: TArray<integer>);
  end;

constructor TMockDataAggregator.Create(const values: TArray<integer>);
begin
  inherited Create;
  FValues := values;
end;

procedure TMockDataAggregator.CloseDataSource;
begin
end;

function TMockDataAggregator.GetNextValue(var value: integer): boolean;
begin
  Result := (FIndex <= High(FValues));
  if Result then
  begin
    value := FValues[FIndex];
    Inc(FIndex);
```

```
    end;
  end;

  function TMockDataAggregator.OpenDataSource: boolean;
  begin
    FIndex := 0;
    Result := true;
  end;
```

The code is even simpler than the one in the file aggregator because it doesn't have to deal with errors. The input can always be opened and the data source cannot contain non-integer data.

To test the template method, the code in the main unit passes an array with the first seven Fibonacci numbers to `TMockDataAggregator` while also displaying a manually calculated result for comparison, as shown here:

```
procedure TfrmTemplateMethod.btnArrayAggregatorClick(Sender: TObject);
var
  aggregator: TMockDataAggregator;
begin
  aggregator := TMockDataAggregator.Create([1, 1, 2, 3, 5, 8, 13]);
  Log('Average value: %.4f, Expected value: %.4f',
    [aggregator.CalculateAverage, (1+1+2+3+5+8+13)/7]);
  aggregator.Free;
end;
```

TIP

This template method is actually an implementation of an Iterator pattern. See `Chapter 15`, *Iterator, Observer, Visitor, Memento*, for more details on how to better approach such problems.

The following screenshot shows both versions of the template method in action:

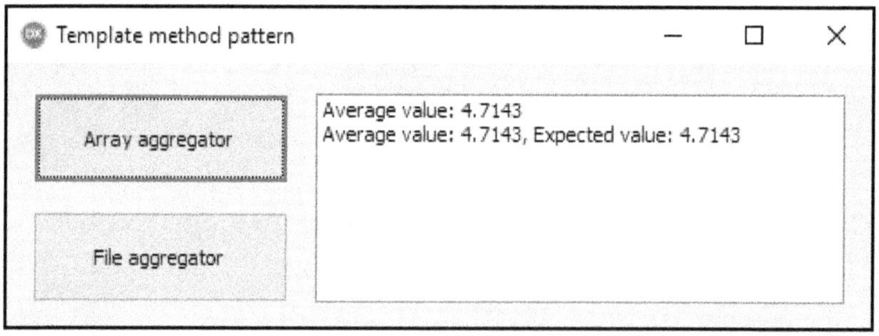

Calculating the average value of file- and memory-based data

Inversion of control

A template method is all well and good, but its use in modern times has greatly declined. This pattern was frequently used to virtualize access to a piece of data (or some other resource) just as in the example from this chapter, that is, the `TemplateMethod` project discussed earlier, but nowadays we know how to approach such problems in a more decoupled and manageable way.

In a way, a template method tells us that the code doesn't follow the single responsibility principle and that it tries to do too much. It wants to be business logic and something else (a data source, in our case).

Instead of writing subclasses that implement missing functionality, we can take a step back, look at the missing functionality as a whole, and try to define what that functionality represents in an abstract sense. Most of the time, we'll find out that it can be represented with one or few simple interfaces that (each by themselves) conform to the single responsibility principle.

In our case, the three missing functions clearly represent a way to access a data source. We can extract them from the `TDataAggregatorTemplate` class into a separate abstract class (a class that contains only an abstract function) or we can use an interface, as shown in the following code fragment:

```
type
  IDataSource = interface ['{63B8C863-E168-4204-9982-3E74D105FFF3}']
    procedure CloseDataSource;
    function GetNextValue(var value: integer): boolean;
    function OpenDataSource: boolean;
  end;
```

This interface, which is defined in the `DataSource.Intf` unit (which is itself part of the `AveragingIoC` project), is then injected into the calculation method. Since the `CalculateAverage` method doesn't depend on any data fields in the `TDataAggregatorTemplate` class, we can remove this class altogether. We only need a single method, implemented in the `DataAggregatorIoC` unit, as follows:

```
function CalculateAverage(const dataSource: IDataSource): real;
var
  sum: integer;
  total: integer;
  value: integer;
begin
  if not dataSource.OpenDataSource then
    raise Exception.Create('Failed!');
  try
```

```
      total := 0;
      sum := 0;
      while dataSource.GetNextValue(value) do
      begin
        Inc(total);
        Inc(sum, value);
      end;
      if total = 0 then
        raise Exception.Create('Cannot calculate average of empty data
set!');
      Result := sum/total;
    finally
      dataSource.CloseDataSource;
    end;
  end;
```

The new version of the code accepts the `IDataSource` interface and uses it to iterate over the data source. There's no need to change this source as all configurable functionality is now encompassed by the `IDataSource` interface.

A program implements two versions of this interface. `TFileDataSource` in the `DataSource.TextFile` unit knows how to iterate over a file. An implementation is line-to-line identical to the implementation in the `TFileDataAggregator` class, so I won't show it here. Another data source, `TArrayDataSource`, from the `DataSource.DynArray` unit, implements the data source working with a dynamic array. Again, the implementation is almost identical to the `TArrayDataAggregator` class, so I will only show the declaration of the `TArrayDataSource` class here:

```
type
  TArrayDataSource = class(TInterfacedObject, IDataSource)
  strict private
    FIndex: integer;
    FValues: TArray<integer>;
  public
    constructor Create(const values: TArray<integer>);
    procedure CloseDataSource;
    function GetNextValue(var value: integer): boolean;
    function OpenDataSource: boolean;
  end;
```

The code in the main unit uses both data sources to calculate the average value of numbers that are stored in an array and in a file. As there's no need to create the data averaging class anymore and as the interfaces are managed by the compiler and destroyed automatically the code is even simpler than before, as follows:

```
procedure TbtnAveraging.btnArrayAggregatorClick(Sender: TObject);
begin
  Log('Average value: %.4f, Expected value: %.4f',
    [CalculateAverage(TArrayDataSource.Create([1, 1, 2, 3, 5, 8, 13])),
    (1+1+2+3+5+8+13)/7]);
end;

procedure TbtnAveraging.btnFileAggregatorClick(Sender: TObject);
begin
  Log('Average value: %.4f',
    [CalculateAverage(TFileDataSource.Create('..\..\data.txt'))] );
end;
```

Command

All interactive programs are organized around actions. The user presses a key, moves or clicks a mouse, touches the screen, and so on, and the program reacts to that by performing an action. This action frequently has parameters attached to it. For example, a keypress action knows which key was pressed, the screen touch knows the coordinates of a person's touch, and so on. At some time at the very moment the action was triggered the action will result in some operation being executed on some object.

The command pattern helps with organizing such a system by converting actions into objects. Instead of treating the action as a bunch of loosely connected data, the code creates a special object (a command) and stores the action parameters inside this command object. A typical system will know about multiple command types, all of which are realized by subclassing the command object. For example, a keypress would create `TKeypressCommand`, a mouse move would create the `TMouseMove` command, and so on.

As defined in the *Design Patterns* book, written by Gang of Four, the command pattern is a complicated mechanism with multiple participants, each performing a specific part of the pattern. To discuss this pattern, we first have to define four important terms: command, client receiver, and invoker.

A command is an action, wrapped inside an object. It is created by the client object, for example, as an response to the user input. When a command is executed, it operates on a target object called a **receiver**. The receiver is determined by the client when the command is created and is stored in the command as a parameter.

The last part, invoker, is responsible for executing commands. A command is not directly executed by the client, but is passed to the invoker instead. The invoker may execute the command immediately, or it can queue the execution or use some other mechanism to execute the command in the appropriate context.

When you send a package through a delivery agency, you are using a command pattern. A package (command) is delivered to the *receiver* by a delivery agency (issuer) and the whole action is triggered by the client (you).

In real-world applications, the invoker and even the receiver may not be represented by an object. A commonly-encountered variation of this pattern implements the invoker as a simple method or an event handler.

A command should be treated as a black box. The client creates the command object and initializes it with parameters, but after that point, the command object is just transferred around and no part of the code changes its content. The command object is also responsible for executing the command action. When the invoker decides that the command has to be executed, it will call the appropriate method inside the command object (typically, this is `Execute`) and the command object will do the rest.

This pattern allows us to do all kinds of interesting things. We can store a command in a list, which enables the creation of an undo/redo mechanism. We can group commands inside other commands and, with that, implement a macro recording mechanism.

We can even store a command in a file or a database to create a log of all executed commands. That enables the application to implement a journaling system that allows the user to start an application and re-apply all of the commands from the previous session (for example, after a program malfunction).

TIP

For more information on preserving objects in external storage, see the *memento* pattern in `Chapter 15`, *Iterator, Visitor, Observer, and Memento.*

We can even implement a scripting system where commands are generated from a script that is executed in an internal interpreter and not as a result of user actions.

Command-based editor

A command pattern has many moving parts, so it is not a surprise that the example for this pattern is one of the more complicated ones in this book.

The `Editor` project in the `Command` folder implements a very simple text editor that internally uses the command pattern. Although it offers only primitive editing capabilities, the example implements both an undo system and a simple macro recorder.

The client part of the pattern is represented by the `TfrmCommand` form in the `EditorMain` unit. The command receiver is a `TMemo` field, which is for reasons of simplicity part of the main form. As we'll see later, the code actually implements two editors, each with its own memo component as a receiver.

The command hierarchy starts with the `TCommand` class. The system also knows what key was pressed via the `TKeyPressCommand` command, what character was deleted via the `TDeleteLeftCommand` command, and what macro was used via the `TMacroCommand` command. There's also a class called `TUndoableCommand` that serves as a basis for all commands that support the undo operation. All of these classes are implemented in the `Editor.Commands` unit.

The invoker is implemented as the `TEditor` class from the `Editor.Editor` unit. It implements both the method execution and the undo stack. As the program contains two memo fields and we want each one to have its own undo stack, the code also creates two invokers.

Creating commands

Instead of writing a full-fledged editor, the `Editor` project simulates just the bare minimum functionality of such a component. The text is displayed in a `TMemo` component with the `Readonly` property set to `True`. This prevents the user from typing directly into the memo field.

> The user can still click inside the memo field and move the caret around with the cursor keys. As an exercise, you can try extending the program so that this functionality will also be implemented with a command pattern.

Key press commands are created in the form's `OnKeyPress` event. To make sure that all of the keys are seen, even when the memo itself has focus, the `KeyPreview` property of the form should be set to `True`. The `OnKeyPress` is only interested in letters, digits, and whitespace, and converts all of these keys into `TKeyPressCommand`. Additionally, a key with code #8 (a backspace key) is converted into `TDeleteLeftCommand`, as shown in the following code:

```
procedure TfrmCommand.FormKeyPress(Sender: TObject; var Key: Char);
begin
  if key.IsLetterOrDigit or key.IsWhiteSpace then
  begin
    Execute(TKeyPressCommand.Create(ActiveMemo, key));
    Key := #0;
  end
  else if key = #8 then
  begin
    Execute(TDeleteLeftCommand.Create(ActiveMemo));
    Key := #0;
  end;
end;
```

In both cases, the resulting command receives the active memo component as a parameter. In the case of the key—pressed command, the key that's pressed is also passed to the command as a parameter.

`ActiveMemo` and `ActiveEditor` are very simple helper functions that return the currently active `TMemo` and `TEditor` components. To find the implementation for this, see the source code.

The `Execute` function passes a command to the invoker. We'll come back to this later.

The creation of the last supported command, `TMacroCommand`, will be explained later in the *Macros* section.

Commands

All commands are subclasses of the `TCommand` class, as shown in the following code:

```
type
  TCommand = class
  strict private
    FReceiver: TMemo;
  public
    constructor Create(receiver: TMemo);
    function Clone: TCommand; virtual;
    procedure Execute; virtual;
    procedure Undo; virtual;
    property Receiver: TMemo read FReceiver write FReceiver;
  end;
```

Each command knows about the intended receiver, which is injected into the constructor. The receiver can also be changed later this functionality is used when replaying macros.

Each command implements the `Execute` (executes the command) and `Undo` (undoes effects of command execution) methods. In the `TCommand` object, both are implemented as empty methods.

Each command also knows how to make a copy of itself. We'll look into the implementation of the `Clone` method later in the *Cloning* section.

The `TCommand` class has only one child class, `TUndoableCommand`. This class is used as a parent for commands that can undo their operations. To support that, its `Execute` method stores the current memo text and position, while the `Undo` method assigns stored text and its position in the memo component. The implementation with the exception of the `Clone` method is shown here:

```
type
  TUndoableCommand = class(TCommand)
  strict private
    FText: string;
    FPosition: Integer;
  strict protected
    procedure StoreState;
  public
    function Clone: TCommand; override;
    procedure Execute; override;
    procedure Undo; override;
  end;

procedure TUndoableCommand.Execute;
```

```
begin
  StoreState;
end;

procedure TUndoableCommand.StoreState;
begin
  FText := Receiver.Text;
  FPosition := Receiver.SelStart;
end;

procedure TUndoableCommand.Undo;
begin
  Receiver.Text := FText;
  Receiver.SelStart := FPosition;
end;
```

All other commands are derived from the `TUndoableCommand` class. They don't override the `Undo` command as the default behavior works fine for all of them. The implementation of `TKeyPressCommand` (again, with the exception of the `Clone` method) is shown here:

```
type
  TKeyPressCommand = class(TUndoableCommand)
  strict private
    FKey: char;
  public
    constructor Create(receiver: TMemo; key: char);
    function Clone: TCommand; override;
    procedure Execaute; override;
  end;

constructor TKeyPressCommand.Create(receiver: TMemo; key: char);
begin
  inherited Create(receiver);
  FKey := key;
end;

procedure TKeyPressCommand.Execute;
var
  pos: Integer;
  s: string;
begin
  inherited;
  s := Receiver.Text;
  pos := Receiver.SelStart;
  Insert(FKey, s, pos+1);
  Receiver.Text := s;
  Receiver.SelStart := pos + 1;
end;
```

For the implementation of `TDeleteLeftCommand`, see the source code. `TMacroCommand` will be examined later in the *Macros* section.

Invoker

The next part of the solution is the invoker, which is stored in the `Editor.Editor` unit. It is defined as a simple class that can execute and undo commands, as shown here:

```
type
  TEditor = class
  strict private
    FUndo: TStack<TCommand>;
  public
    constructor Create;
    destructor Destroy; override;
    procedure Execute(command: TCommand);
    procedure Undo(command: TCommand);
    function IsUndoEmpty: boolean;
    function PopLastCommand: TCommand;
  end;
```

Leaving the boring creation and destruction aside (for more details, see the source code), the interesting methods are implemented as follows:

```
procedure TEditor.Execute(command: TCommand);
begin
  command.Execute;
  FUndo.Push(command);
end;

function TEditor.IsUndoEmpty: boolean;
begin
  Result := FUndo.Count = 0;
end;

function TEditor.PopLastCommand: TCommand;
begin
  Result := FUndo.Pop;
end;

procedure TEditor.Undo(command: TCommand);
begin
  command.Undo;
  command.Free;
end;
```

The `Execute` method executes the command. As noted before, the command is treated as a black box. The invoker has no idea what the `command.Execute` will do. After that, the command object is pushed to the undo stack.

`IsUndoEmpty` and `PopLastCommand` are helper functions that are used by the client to correctly implement the user interface. We'll see them in action in a moment.

At the end, the `Undo` command executes the `Undo` method of the command and destroys the command object.

Client

All of this comes together in the client. Besides creating and dispatching commands, the client also provides a user interface for undoing last action and an interface for recording and playing macros, as shown in the following screenshot:

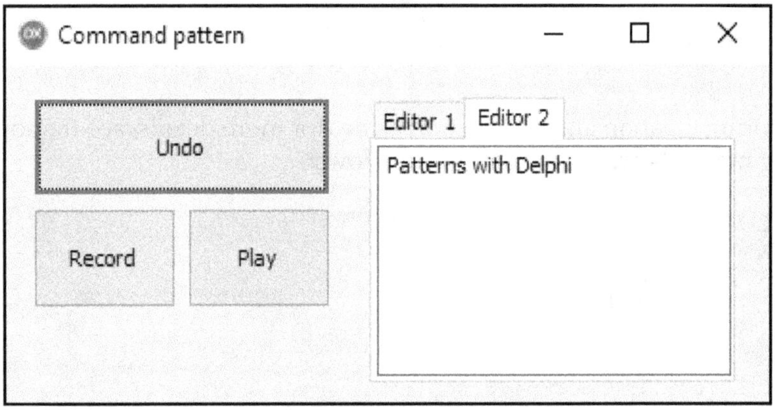

Command-driven editor

All of the user interfaces in this program are action-driven. Every button has a corresponding action with `Update` and `Execute` event handlers attached. This allows the program to enable/disable buttons according to the current program's state.

> Delphi's `TAction` object is in fact, an implementation of the command design pattern!

As we can see in the following code, the `actUndo` action is enabled when the active `TEditor` has at least one command on the undo stack. When executed (when the Undo button is clicked), the action pops the last command from the undo stack and passes it to the `TEditor.Undo` method:

```
procedure TfrmCommand.actUndoExecute(Sender: TObject);
begin
  ActiveEditor.Undo(ActiveEditor.PopLastCommand);
end;

procedure TfrmCommand.actUndoUpdate(Sender: TObject);
begin
  (Sender as TAction).Enabled := (not ActiveEditor.IsUndoEmpty);
end;
```

Macros

For the last part of the puzzle, I have to show you how macro recording is implemented. This is actually the most complicated part of the program.

Let's start with the command object. A macro is just a special kind of command, `TMacroCommand`. As we can see in the following code, it implements an `Add` command, which stores other commands in the internal list:

```
type
  TMacroCommand = class(TUndoableCommand)
  strict private
    FCommands: TObjectList<TCommand>;
  public
    procedure Add(command: TCommand);
    procedure AfterConstruction; override;
    procedure BeforeDestruction; override;
    function Clone: TCommand; override;
    procedure Execute; override;
  end;

procedure TMacroCommand.Add(command: TCommand);
begin
  FCommands.Add(command);
end;
```

When executed, the `Execute` method calls all of the `Execute` methods of all of the commands in the list. As commands can be recorded when one editor is active, and later replayed when the other editors are active, the `Execute` method also forces `Receiver` parameter of all commands in the list to point to the correct receiver, as follows:

```
procedure TMacroCommand.Execute;
var
  cmd: TCommand;
begin
  inherited;
  for cmd in FCommands do begin
    cmd.Receiver := Receiver;
    cmd.Execute;
  end;
end;
```

TIP

The call to `inherited` calls `TUndoableCommand.Execute`, which creates a snapshot of the current state of the `Receiver`, thereby allowing for a later undo operation.

The main program allows for only one macro, which is stored in the form field, `FMacro: TMacroCommand`. This field is (re)created whenever the `actRecord` action is executed. As the following code shows, clicking the `Record` button sets the internal where we are recording flag, sets the button action to `actStop` (so that it will display the text **Stop** instead of **Record**), and recreates the `FMacro` field:

```
procedure TfrmCommand.actRecordExecute(Sender: TObject);
begin
  FRecording := true;
  btnMacro.Action := actStop;
  FreeAndNil(FMacro);
  FMacro := TMacroCommand.Create(nil);
end;
```

The macro command has no dedicated receiver, so the `nil` parameter is passed to the constructor.

When the user clicks the **Stop** button, the internal recording flag is turned off and the action button is set back to `actRecord`, as follows:

```
procedure TfrmCommand.actStopExecute(Sender: TObject);
begin
  FRecording := false;
  btnMacro.Action := actRecord;
end;
```

The actPlay action is enabled only when the FMacro field is assigned and when the program is not recording a macro. When executed, actPlay sets the receiver of the FMacro command to the currently active memo and then calls the invoker's Execute method to execute the macro, as shown in the following code:

```
procedure TfrmCommand.actPlayExecute(Sender: TObject);
begin
  FMacro.Receiver := ActiveMemo;
  ActiveEditor.Execute(FMacro.Clone);
end;

procedure TfrmCommand.actPlayUpdate(Sender: TObject);
begin
  (Sender as TAction).Enabled := (not FRecording) and assigned(FMacro);
end;
```

The macro command is just like every other command stored on the undo stack. If its operation is undone at a later time, the command that's stored on the stack is destroyed. This would also invalidate the FMacro field (it would point to an unallocated area of memory), which could cause all kinds of problems. To prevent that, the code creates a copy of the command by calling its Clone function. I'll return to the cloning implementation in a moment, but first I have to show you one last missing piece of the macro implementation.

You now know how macros are stored and replayed, but nowhere have I shown you how commands are added to the FMacro command. This is done in the Execute method of the main form, which can optionally make a copy of the command being executed and store this copy in the FMacro command, as shown in the following code:

```
procedure TfrmCommand.Execute(command: TCommand);
begin
  if FRecording then
    FMacro.Add(command.Clone);
  ActiveEditor.Execute(command);
end;
```

Again, the cloning mechanism is used to create a copy of the command.

There are three Execute methods inside the TfrmCommand form, the TEditor invoker, and all of the commands based on TCommand. This is slightly confusing, so be careful when you read or modify the program.

Cloning

The last unexplored part of the program is the mechanism for creating copies of command objects (cloning). In this program, I went for a simple solution where each class implements the virtual function known as `Clone`, which knows how to create a perfect copy of the object. The following code fragment shows the implementation of this for four command classes:

```
function TCommand.Clone: TCommand;
begin
  Result := TCommand.Create(Receiver);
end;

function TUndoableCommand.Clone: TCommand;
begin
  Result := TUndoableCommand.Create(Receiver);
end;

function TKeyPressCommand.Clone: TCommand;
begin
  Result := TKeyPressCommand.Create(Receiver, FKey);
end;

function TDeleteLeftCommand.Clone: TCommand;
begin
  Result := TDeleteLeftCommand.Create(Receiver);
end;
```

In each class, the `Clone` function creates an object of the same type and sets its parameters.

Only the more complicated cloning method creates a copy of the `TMacroCommand` object. As we can see in the following code, it must create a copy of the command itself and then fill the command list of the new command with copies of all of the commands that are stored inside the current macro object:

```
function TMacroCommand.Clone: TCommand;
var
  cmd: TCommand;
begin
  Result := TMacroCommand.Create(Receiver);
  for cmd in FCommands do
    TMacroCommand(Result).Add(cmd.Clone);
end;
```

State

The last pattern in this chapter, state, allows an object to change its behavior on demand. This is especially useful when an object implements an algorithm that goes through different execution states. If the object's internal behavior changes when its state is changed, you've got an excellent candidate for a state pattern.

> Any vending machine follows the state pattern. The behavior of a machine when the customer presses the buttons to select a certain product depends on the current state. If the customer has already paid for the product, the machine will deliver the merchandise. Otherwise, it will only display the cost of the product.

This Gang of Four pattern can only be used in rare occasions. A typical candidate for the introduction of this pattern is an object that implements some kind of state machine. Standard examples include TCP socket management, line encryption, text file parsers, and the implementation of painting tools.

> TIP: For more information about state machines, see the Finite-state machine entry in Wikipedia (`https://en.wikipedia.org/wiki/Finite-state_machine`).

The last example is particularly interesting because, at first glance, it doesn't seem to include a changing state. There is, however, a behavior change connected to clicking the mouse buttons. If the user just moves the mouse around, nothing happens (besides the mouse cursor moving around the screen, of course). If, however, the user first clicks and holds the mouse button, the painting application enters a different state and starts drawing on the screen.

To implement a state pattern, we have to move all state-specific functions out of a class into a state object. Then, we implement multiple state objects, one for each possible state of the object. The main object then delegates state-specific functions to the current state object and recreates the state object on each state change.

The main motivation behind the state pattern lies in code organization. Without this pattern, the main object contains all state-specific behavior and uses lots of `case` or `if` statements to execute the appropriate behavior for the current state. After the introduction of this pattern, each state object contains only the code specific to one state and no `case` or `if` statements are needed to select the appropriate behavior.

Unquoting a string

The following example shows two implementations of some code that *unquotes* a string a classical implementation and an implementation with a state pattern.

A quoted string starts and ends with a double-quote character (`"`). Any occurrence of a double-quote character in a string is represented by two occurrences of that character. The following table shows a few examples of strings that have been converted into a quoted form:

String	**Quoted string**
Delphi	"Delphi"
Delphi and patterns	"Delphi and patterns"
Delphi "ROCKS!"	"Delphi ""Rocks!"""

An unquoting algorithm takes the quoted string (for example, `"quoted ""quoted"""`) and converts it into its original form (`quoted "quoted"`). Its behavior can be represented with the following state diagram:

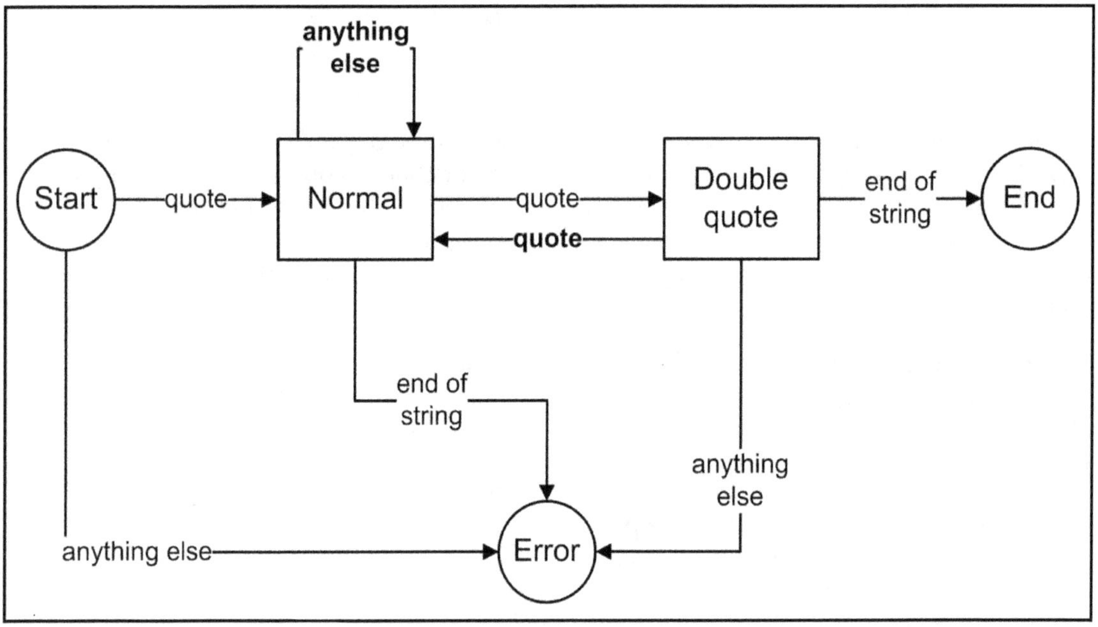

State diagram for unquoting a string

The object always starts in a Start state. A character is then read from the input. If the character is a quote character, the object changes to a Normal state. Otherwise, the input does not represent a quoted string and the converter should report an error.

While in the Normal state, the object reads the next character. If an end of string is encountered, the string is not terminated with a double quote and an error is reported. If the character is not a double quote, the object stays in the same state and copies the character to the output. If the character **is** a double quote, then the code doesn't know what to do. It could have reached the end of the string or a `""` combination in the middle of the string. To resolve this, the state is changed to a double quote.

In the double quote state, the next character is read. If an end of string is reached, the state is changed to End and conversion is completed. If the character is a double quote, the code has found a `""` combination, a single `"` character is written to the output and the state changes back to Normal. In all other cases, the input string is invalid. For example, the `Delphi Pattern` string should cause such an error because the middle `"` character is not duplicated.

The `State` project from the `State` folder implements this algorithm in two different ways. The `UnqoteString.Classical` unit, which I'll explore first, uses a classical parser mess to parse the string. This unit exposes the following public function:

```
function Unquote(const s: string): string;
var
  reader: TStringStream;
  writer: TStringStream;
begin
  reader := TStringStream.Create(s);
  try
    writer := TStringStream.Create('');
    try
      UnquoteStr(reader, writer);
      Result := writer.DataString;
    finally
      FreeAndNil(writer);
    end;
  finally
    FreeAndNil(reader);
  end;
end;
```

The `Unquote` function merely represents a wrapper that allows the parser to treat the input and output string as a stream. The real work is done in the `UnquoteStr` function, as shown in the following code:

```
procedure UnquoteStr(reader, writer: TStringStream);
type
  TState = (stStart, stNormal, stQuote, stEnd);
var
  next : string;
  state: TState;
begin
  state := stStart;
  while state <> stEnd do
  begin
    next := reader.ReadString(1);
    case state of
      stStart:
        begin
          if next = '"' then
            state := stNormal
          else
            InvalidString;
        end;
      stNormal:
        begin
          if next = '"' then
            state := stQuote
          else if next <> '' then
            writer.WriteString(next)
          else
            InvalidString;
        end;
      stQuote:
        begin
          if next = '' then
            state := stEnd
          else if next = '"' then
          begin
            writer.WriteString('"');
            state := stNormal;
          end
          else
            InvalidString;
        end;
      stEnd:
        begin
          raise Exception.Create('UnqouteStr: Internal error');
        end;
```

```
    end; //case state
  end; // while
end;
```

The code works exactly how we described it. It starts in the `stState` state, reads characters, and moves to the appropriate state according to the input. To understand the code, you only have to know that the `ReadString(1)` function returns one character from the input stream or an empty string when the end of the stream is reached.

The helper function, `InvalidString` merely raises an exception.

Even in this simple example, the `UnquoteStr` method looks like a mess. The `If` and `case` statements are all interlocked into unreadable code. Truth be told, we could separate the behavior for each separate state into its own method, but that would only solve one half of the problem. The true order comes from the implementation of the state pattern, as in the `UnquoteString.State` unit.

In this version, the unquoting functionality is implemented in the `TUnquoter` class, which is defined as follows:

```
type
  TUnquoter = class
  strict private
    FState: TUnquoteState;
  strict protected
    function GetState: TState;
    procedure Update(const input: string; var output: string;
      var newState: TState);
    procedure SetState(const value: TState);
    property State: TState read GetState write SetState;
  public
    destructor Destroy; override;
    procedure Unquote(reader, writer: TStringStream);
  end;
```

The input and output streams are again prepared in the `Unquote` function, which you can check in the code.

All state-specific behavior is moved to descendants of the base state class, `TUnquoteState`, which is implemented as follows:

```
type
  TState = (stStart, stNormal, stQuote, stEnd);

  TUnquoteState = class
  strict private
    FState: TState;
  protected
    procedure RaiseInvalidString;
  public
    constructor Create(const state: TState);
    procedure Update(const input: string; var output: string;
      var newState: TState); virtual;
    property State: TState read FState;
  end;

constructor TUnquoteState.Create(const state: TState);
begin
  inherited Create;
  FState := state;
end;

procedure TUnquoteState.RaiseInvalidString;
begin
  raise Exception.Create('Invalid quoted string');
end;

procedure TUnquoteState.Update(const input: string; var output: string;
  var newState: TState);
begin
  output := '';
  newState := State;
end;
```

Each state class knows which state it represents (the `State` property) and can process an input in the `Update` procedure. This procedure also optionally produces `output` (which will be copied to the output stream) and tells the caller what the next state should be (`newState`).

Leaving the implementation of state objects aside for a moment, we can now look into the implementation of the unquoting process in the `TUnquoter` class. As we can see in the following code, the `Unquote` procedure is extremely simple if we compare it to the previously shown `UnquoteStr`:

```
procedure TUnquoter.Unquote(reader, writer: TStringStream);
var
  emit: string;
  newState: TState;
begin
  State := stStart;
  while State <> stEnd do
  begin
    FState.Update(reader.ReadString(1), emit, newState);
    if emit <> '' then
      writer.WriteString(emit);
    State := newState;
  end;
end;
```

The code starts in the `stState` state. Then, for each character from the input stream, it calls the `Update` method on the current state object. If this method produces any data, it is written to the output stream. State is then changed to the new state. Simple, effective, and to the point!

The state-changing magic happens inside the setter for the `State` property. When `State` is written to, the `SetState` setter is called. In this setter, the state object is recreated if the state is changed, as follows:

```
procedure TUnquoter.SetState(const value: TState);
begin
  if assigned(FState) and (FState.State = value) then
    Exit;
  FreeAndNil(FState);
  case value of
    stStart: FState := TStartState.Create(value);
    stNormal: FState := TNormalState.Create(value);
    stQuote: FState := TQuoteState.Create(value);
    stEnd: FState := TEndState.Create(value);
  end;
end;
```

The state-handling logic is now split into four classes. Each handles one possible state. The class definitions are shown in the following code:

```
type
  TStartState = class(TUnquoteState)
  public
    procedure Update(const input: string; var output: string;
      var newState: TState); override;
  end;

  TNormalState = class(TUnquoteState)
  public
    procedure Update(const input: string; var output: string;
      var newState: TState); override;
  end;

  TQuoteState = class(TUnquoteState)
  public
    procedure Update(const input: string; var output: string;
      var newState: TState); override;
  end;

  TEndState = class(TUnquoteState)
  public
    procedure Update(const input: string; var output: string;
      var newState: TState); override;
  end;
```

Implementation of the `Update` method inside each state object is now easy for understand. The `stState` state can only move to the `stNormal` state or raise an error, as shown here:

```
procedure TStartState.Update(const input: string; var output: string;
  var newState: TState);
begin
  inherited;
  if input = '"' then
    newState := stNormal
  else
    RaiseInvalidString;
end;
```

The call to `inherited` initializes `output` to an empty string and `newState` to the current state.

A `stNormal` state can either move to the `stQuote` state, output a character, or raise an exception, as follows:

```
procedure TNormalState.Update(const input: string; var output: string;
  var newState: TState);
begin
  inherited;
  if input = '"' then
    newState := stQuote
  else if input <> '' then
    output := input
  else
    RaiseInvalidString;
end;
```

The `stQuote` state can either move to the `stEnd` state, output a double quote **and** move to the `stNormal` state, or raise an exception, as shown in the following code:

```
procedure TQuoteState.Update(const input: string; var output: string;
  var newState: TState);
begin
  inherited;
  if input = '' then
    newState := stEnd
  else if input = '"' then
  begin
    output := '"';
    newState := stNormal;
  end
  else
    RaiseInvalidString;
end;
```

The `Update` method of the `stEnd` state should never be called. Any activation of this method indicates a programming error and the code reflects that, as shown in the following code:

```
procedure TEndState.Update(const input: string; var output: string;
  var newState: TState);
begin
  raise Exception.Create('TEndState.Update: Internal error');
end;
```

This results in a program that is easy to understand and simple to maintain.

Summary

This chapter provided an overview of four behavioral patterns. All of the patterns in this group help you to organize complex systems into well-behaved maintainable structures.

We opened up with a null object pattern. This simple pattern allows us to remove `if assigned(object)` tests from the code and replace them with a special do-nothing null version of the object. Although the concept behind this pattern is simple, the pattern itself can be very useful.

Next, we looked at the template method pattern. This pattern explains how to use object-oriented programming to design extensible and adaptable algorithms. We also demonstrated how we can solve such problems by using the concepts that were developed after the Gang of Four times.

The command pattern helps with organizing action-based programming. It tells us how to systematically convert actions into objects and how to separate the client code from the code that executes the action object. This flexible approach can be a base for the undo/redo mechanism, macro recording, scripting, and more.

Finally, we described the state pattern. This pattern explains how to organize objects that can change functionality according to an internal state. If your object implements a state machine, this is the pattern that you should use.

In the next chapter, we will stay on topic and look into four more behavioral patterns, which are Iterator, Visitor, Observer, and Memento.

15
Iterator, Visitor, Observer, and Memento

When your task is writing code that is simple to maintain and test, you strive away from tightly connected parts that know too much about each other. The four patterns that will be described in this chapter will help you write complex code that interacts in different ways but is not interconnected in all possible—and impossible—ways in an unmanageable mess.

Two patterns from this chapter, iterator and observer, are, in my opinion, the two most important patterns from the Gang of Four collection. If you incorporate only two patterns into your code, let them be these two! They both help with decoupling parts of code and programming to the interface, not the implementation; two guidelines that will help you write maintainable code.

That doesn't mean that you should ignore other patterns from this chapter, or from this book! All patterns can be important—you just have to know when and how they should be used. Visitor and Memento are certainly no exception.

In this chapter, you will learn about the following:

- How to effectively access all data structures and how to write generic, structure-independent algorithms with the iterator pattern
- How to extend classes in accordance with the Open/Closed principle with the visitor pattern
- How to use the observer pattern to write loosely-coupled programs that react to changes in the business model
- How to store a state of a complex object in a separate container with the memento pattern

Iterator

An iterator pattern is used to traverse a container and access its elements. The power of this pattern is that it decouples algorithms from the container implementation. We can then write an algorithm that is coded to the iterator interface and not to the actual implementation of the container.

Let's say we have two completely different data structures, an array and a linked *list*. If we need to implement the same algorithm operating on both structures, we have to write two versions of the code. You would access an array with direct addressing and the other would walk the linked list.

On the other hand, if both the array and linked list implement the same interface that allows the algorithm to walk over the data and access all elements, we can write only one version of the algorithm. Instead of working with data structures directly, the algorithm would work with that interface.

An *interface* in this context means any public interface (a set of methods). It doesn't have to be implemented with a Delphi interface mechanism.

Even if the code has no such needs and it always works with only one kind of a data structure, using an iterator pattern has its advantages. Using this pattern instead of accessing data elements directly leads to a cleaner code. A code that uses an iterator has no need to hardcode implementation details. A typical example in Delphi is code that iterates over some list, which usually starts as follows:

```
for i := 0 to list.Count - 1 do
```

This `for` loop depends on the fact that the first element in the list has index 0. Of course, that will never change in future Delphi versions, but it still seems wrong that we have to iterate *from* zero to count minus one instead of over all elements. As we'll see in this chapter, an iterator pattern helps with that.

If you browse through TV channels by clicking the next channel button on a remote, you are using an iterator pattern.

An iterator can be external to the object or it can be implemented internally, inside the object. When we are creating a new data structure and we know what iteration interface we want to expose, it is best to implement it inside the data structure object. On the other hand, when adapting existing code, we typically write an interface as an external piece of code.

Special kinds of iterators, called **robust iterators**, allow the underlying data structure to change while an iterator is in use. As a rule of thumb, a typical iterator doesn't support such behavior and it is safer simply not to change the data structure while using an iterator. As far as I know, none of Delphi's built-in iterators are robust.

A special kind of iterator always returns no elements. It is called a **null iterator** and can, in some circumstances, be used to simplify the code.

> Besides being an *iterator*, a null iterator is also an example of a *null object* pattern, as covered in `Chapter 14`, *Nullable Object, Template Method, Command, State.*

Implementing an iterator pattern in code is not complicated. The example project `HandMadeIterators` in the Iterator folder shows two possible approaches, while the last section of this chapter, *Memento,* explores a third option.

The `HandMadeIterators` project defines the `TDataContainer` class, which is just a wrapper around a dynamic array of integers. This class, which is shown as follows, implements two different ways to enumerate its pattern:

```
type
  TDataContainer = class
  public type
    TIterateAction = reference to procedure (value: integer);
  strict private
    FData: TArray<integer>;
    FIndex: integer;
  public
    constructor Create(const data: TArray<integer>);
    procedure Iterate(action: TIterateAction);
    function GetFirst(var value: integer): boolean;
    function GetNext(var value: integer): boolean;
  end;
```

The first iterator is implemented as a method called `Iterate`, which accepts an anonymous method parameter. This anonymous method is called for each element in the data container, as shown here:

```
procedure TDataContainer.Iterate(action: TIterateAction);
var
  i: integer;
begin
  for i := Low(FData) to High(FData) do
    action(FData[i]);
end;
```

The caller of the Iterate method can actually work inside this anonymous method. The following code shows such an example:

```
procedure TfrmHandMade.btnIterateClick(Sender: TObject);
var
  data: TDataContainer;
begin
  data := TDataContainer.Create([1, 2, 3, 4, 5]);
  try
    data.Iterate(
      procedure (value: integer)
      begin
        lbLog.Items.Add(value.ToString);
      end);
  finally
    FreeAndNil(data);
  end;
end;
```

The second implementation uses two functions: `GetFirst` and `GetNext`. Both functions return `False` if there's no more data in the container and `True` (plus an element from the container) otherwise. The difference between them is that `GetFirst` starts iteration from the beginning and `GetNext` resumes from the last element. They are implemented as follows:

```
function TDataContainer.GetFirst(var value: integer): boolean;
begin
  FIndex := 0;
  Result := GetNext(value);
end;

function TDataContainer.GetNext(var value: integer): boolean;
begin
  Result := FIndex <= High(FData);
  if Result then begin
```

```
      value := FData[FIndex];
      Inc(FIndex);
    end;
  end;
```

The `HandMadeMain` unit contains an example of how such code can be used, as follows:

```
procedure TfrmHandMade.btnGetFirstClick(Sender: TObject);
var
  data: TDataContainer;
  element: Integer;
begin
  data := TDataContainer.Create([6, 7, 8, 9, 10]);
  try
    if data.GetFirst(element) then
      repeat
        lbLog.Items.Add(element.ToString)
      until not data.GetNext(element);
  finally
    FreeAndNil(data);
  end;
end;
```

Before using homegrown approaches, you should explore the idiomatic way that's built into Delphi—the `for..in` statement.

Delphi idioms – iterating with for..in

Since version 2005, Delphi supports a concept of iteration over containers. In this version, a classical `for..to` statement was extended with a `for..in` counterpart. It allows us to iterate over arrays, strings, sets, and any other data structure without referring to the implementation details. For example, the `for i := 0 to list.Count - 1 do` statement from the beginning of this chapter can be rewritten as follows:

```
for el in list do
  Process(el);
```

This code will execute the body of the `for` loop once for each element in the `list`. In each iteration, the `el` variable will be set to that element. This `for..in` loop is functionally equivalent to the following code:

```
for i := 0 to list.Count - 1 do
begin
  el := list[i];
  Process(el);
end;
```

The built-in Delphi iterators will always iterate from the lowest to highest index (such as in the previous example). This, however, doesn't need to be the case. An iterator could implement a different traversal order. For example, we could have an iterator that returns elements in order from the last to the first (although such an iterator is not part of Delphi RTL). It would be functionally equivalent to the following code:

```
for i := list.Count - 1 downto 0 do
begin
  el := list[i];
  Process(el);
end;
```

TIP

When iterating over a binary tree data structure, we can usually select from (at least) three possible traversal orders: inorder (left subtree of a node is visited first, followed by the node itself and then the right subtree), preorder (parent node is visited first, left subtree next, and right subtree last), and postorder (left subtree is visited first, followed by the right subtree, and the parent node).

The `BuiltInIterators` project from the `Iterator` folder shows how we can use iterator patterns on some built-in data structures, namely arrays, strings, and sets.

This project shows two ways to iterate over an array. We can either use the implementation-specific knowledge and know that we can get the lowest and highest index of a dynamic array with a call to built-in `Low` and `High` functions, or we can use the `for..in` iteration, as in the following code:

```
procedure TfrmIterator.btnArrayClick(Sender: TObject);
var
  el: Integer;
  fib: TArray<Integer>;
  i: Integer;
begin
  fib := TArray<integer>.Create(1, 1, 2, 3, 5, 8, 13);

  Log('"Standard" array access');
```

```
    for i := Low(fib) to High(fib) do
      Log(fib[i].ToString);

    Log('Iterating over an array');
    for el in fib do
      Log(el.ToString);
  end;
```

We can use this approach to iterate over static and dynamic arrays. The syntax is the same in both cases.

Similarly, we can iterate over all characters in a string. The following code shows how to do that with a standard `for` statement and with a `for..in` version:

```
  procedure TfrmIterator.btnStringClick(Sender: TObject);
  var
    ch: Char;
    s: string;
    i: Integer;
  begin
    s := 'Delphi!';

    Log('"Standard" string access');
    for i := 1 to Length(s) do
      Log(s[i]);

    Log('Iterating over a string');
    for ch in s do
      Log(ch);
  end;
```

In this case, using a standard `for` statement is even more bound to the implementation as strings in Delphi can start from 1 or from 0! (This weird design choice is controlled with the `{$ZEROBASEDSTRINGS}` compiler directive.)

The previous example shows how to iterate over a set. In this case, the `for..in` statement again simplifies the code a lot. As shown in the following, the standard `for` statement has to iterate over all elements in the `TAlign` enumeration and only display ones that are also present in the set. The `for..in` construct does all that internally, as follows:

```
  procedure TfrmIterator.btnSetClick(Sender: TObject);
  var
    align: TAlign;
    alignSet: TAlignSet;
  begin
    alignSet := [alLeft, alRight, alTop, alBottom];
```

```
    Log('"Standard" set access');
    for align := Low(TAlign) to High(TAlign) do
      if align in alignSet then
        Log(AlignName(align));

    Log('Iteration over a set');
    for align in alignSet do
      Log(AlignName(align));
  end;
```

The enumeration over the three types of built-in data that I have just shown are implemented by the compiler. We can, however, add iterator support to any data structure. We only have to implement a few simple functions.

Implementing custom enumerators

If we want to add iterator support to a data structure, we have to implement a **public** method called `GetEnumerator`. This method must return either a class, interface, or a record. Let's call this returned value an enumerator.

The enumerator must implement one function and one property. Both must be declared **public**. The function must be named `MoveNext` and it must return a `boolean` result. The `for..in` loop uses this method to move to the next element in the container and to check whether there are more elements in the container.

The enumerator property must be called `Current` and it must return the current element in the container (however, the enumerator defines what current is). Usually it is implemented by calling the `GetCurrent` method (which you also have to write), but that is not a requirement.

All iterators for Delphi RTL data structures (except the three we have already shown) are implemented in this way.

With this infrastructure in place, the compiler converts the `for..in` statement into a simple while loop. If we have data structure called `collection`, which contains an element of type `T`, the compiler-generated code will be equivalent to the following code fragment:

```
var
  element: T;

enumerator := collection.GetEnumerator;
try
  while enumerator.MoveNext do
  begin
    element := enumerator.Current;
    // process 'element' in the body of the for..in loop
  end
finally
  enumerator.Free;
end
```

The last part, `enumerator.Free`, is only generated if the enumerator is implemented as a class.

An important point that we can derive from this template, and which determines how an enumerator is implemented, is that `MoveNext` is called once before the first data element is accessed. In the following examples, we'll see how this affects the implementation.

TIP

There is also another, even simpler way to add iterator support to a data container. Implement a function (`ToArray`, for example) that returns a dynamic array containing all elements from the data container. As Delphi knows how to iterate over arrays, you can then use a fragment like this to iterate over your container: `for el in container.ToArray do`. This is a perfectly valid solution if the container always stores only a small number of elements.

Using an iterator interface

If we want to write a generic version of an algorithm, one that is not bound to a data structure but to an iterator pattern, we have to somehow pass the iterator pattern to the algorithm.

In the 2005 release, Delphi defined interfaces `IEnumerable` and `IEnumerator`. They can be found in the System unit and are defined as follows:

```
type
  IEnumerator = interface(IInterface)
    function GetCurrent: TObject;
    function MoveNext: Boolean;
    procedure Reset;
    property Current: TObject read GetCurrent;
  end;

  IEnumerable = interface(IInterface)
    function GetEnumerator: IEnumerator;
  end;
```

We can write an algorithm that uses either `IEnumerable` or `IEnumerator`, but then we always have to convert the `Current` property to appropriate data type. This is clumsy, so with the introduction of generics, we also got the generic versions of these interfaces, which are shown as follows:

```
type
  IEnumerator<T> = interface(IEnumerator)
    function GetCurrent: T;
    property Current: T read GetCurrent;
  end;

  IEnumerable<T> = interface(IEnumerable)
    function GetEnumerator: IEnumerator<T>;
  end;
```

At first glance this looks perfect, but as soon as we try to implement `IEnumerator<T>`, we also have to implement `IEnumerator`. To do that, we have to write two `GetCurrent` functions and we cannot use the overloading mechanism (the `overload` keyword) for that because they both have same parameters (none). So, what can we do to resolve this conundrum?

The `CustomIterators.TextFile.IEnumerable` unit from the `CustomIterators` project shows one possible solution. This unit implements an iterator that walks over a text file and returns lines of text, one by one. The only public part of that unit, function `TextFileContentI`, takes a file name and returns an `IEnumerable<string>`, as follows:

```
function TextFileContentI(const fileName: string): IEnumerable<string>;
```

As `IEnumerable<string>` implements a `GetEnumerator` function, we can use this result in a `for..in` loop. The main unit executes the following code if you click the `File IEnumerable` button:

```
procedure TfrmIterator.btnFileInterfaceClick(Sender: TObject);
var
  line: string;
begin
  Log('Content of "CustomIterators.dpr":');
  for line in TextFileContentI('..\..\CustomIterators.dpr') do
    Log(line);
end;
```

The `IEnumerable<string>` interface is implemented in the `TTextFileEnumerator` class, which is defined as follows:

```
type
  TTextFileEnumeratorBase = class(TInterfacedObject, IEnumerable,
                                                     IEnumerator)
  public
    function GetEnumerator: IEnumerator; virtual; abstract;
    function GetCurrent: TObject; virtual; abstract;
    function MoveNext: Boolean; virtual; abstract;
    procedure Reset; virtual; abstract;
    property Current: TObject read GetCurrent;
  end;

  TTextFileEnumerator = class(TTextFileEnumeratorBase, IEnumerable<string>,
                                                       IEnumerator<string>)
  strict private
    FReader: TStreamReader;
    FLine: string;
  public
    constructor Create(const fileName: string);
    destructor Destroy; override;
    function GetEnumerator: IEnumerator<string>;
    function GetCurrent: string; reintroduce;
    function MoveNext: boolean; override;
    procedure Reset; override;
    property Current: string read GetCurrent;
  end;
```

The implementations of the `IEnumerator` and `IEnumerable` methods and properties (we'll see soon why we need both) were put into the `TTextFileEnumeratorBase` class. As they are actually never used, they are marked as `virtual; abstract;` so that we don't have to implement them. All actual code is implemented in the `TTextFileEnumerator` class, which is derived from `TTextFileEnumeratorBase`.

Let's start with the `GetEnumerator` function. It simply returns `Self`, as shown here:

```
function TTextFileEnumerator.GetEnumerator: IEnumerator<string>;
begin
  Result := Self;
end;
```

In this example, one class implements both parts of iterator support: the `GetEnumerator` function and actual enumerator. We can do that because both are implemented as an interface. If we were to implement the iterator support with classes (as we will in the following example), this trick would not work.

The actual enumeration work is done in the `MoveNext` method. It uses an internal `TStreamReader` class to read data from the input line by line and stores each line read in the internal `FLine` field. The `GetCurrent` method then simply returns the contents of the `FLine` field. The important parts of the code are shown as follows:

```
constructor TTextFileEnumerator.Create(const fileName: string);
begin
  inherited Create;
  FReader := TStreamReader.Create(fileName, true);
end;

function TTextFileEnumerator.GetCurrent: string;
begin
  Result := FLine;
end;

function TTextFileEnumerator.MoveNext: boolean;
begin
  Result := not FReader.EndOfStream;
  if Result then
    FLine := FReader.ReadLine;
end;
```

As we have seen before, the compiler guarantees that `MoveNext` will be called once before the `Current` property is accessed so that we always have the correct initial state in the `FLine` field.

Keep in mind that the code can access the Current property multiple times for one element, so GetCurrent should never change the internal state of the enumerator. The safe way is to always do all the work in the MoveNext method and just read data from the internal field in the GetCurrent function.

Since Delphi 2009, when generics were introduced, we got a better and simpler way of working with generic iterators. The TEnumerable<T> and TEnumerator<T> classes are defined in the System.Generics.Collections unit as follows:

```
type
  TEnumerator<T> = class abstract
  protected
    function DoGetCurrent: T; virtual; abstract;
    function DoMoveNext: Boolean; virtual; abstract;
  public
    property Current: T read DoGetCurrent;
    function MoveNext: Boolean;
  end;

  TEnumerable<T> = class abstract
  private
    function ToArrayImpl(Count: Integer): TArray<T>; // used by descendants
  protected
    function DoGetEnumerator: TEnumerator<T>; virtual; abstract;
  public
    destructor Destroy; override;
    function GetEnumerator: TEnumerator<T>;
    function ToArray: TArray<T>; virtual;
  end;
```

The implementation in CustomIterators.TextFile.TEnumerable allows us to iterate over text file lines with the following code:

```
procedure TfrmIterator.btnFileObjectClick(Sender: TObject);
var
  line: string;
begin
  Log('Content of "CustomIterators.dpr":');
  for line in TextFileContentO('..\..\CustomIterators.dpr') do
    Log(line);
end;
```

As you can see, it is completely the same as the previous example, which used the `TextFileContentI` function. The implementation is, however, quite different. As the following code fragment shows, `TextFileContentO` returns a record that implements a `GetEnumerator` function:

```
type
  TTextFileContentO = record
  private
    FFileName: string;
  public
    constructor Create(fileName: string);
    function GetEnumerator: TEnumerator<string>;
  end;

function TextFileContentO(fileName: string): TTextFileContentO;
```

The `for line in TextFileContentO(...)` statement works like this:

1. The `TextFileContentO` function is evaluated. It returns a record. Records are a static data type (they are stored on the stack) and therefore we don't have to care about their life cycle (we don't have to explicitly destroy them).
2. The compiler sees the returned `TTextFileContentO` record and implements a `GetEnumerator` function, so it calls that function and uses the resulting object for enumeration.
3. At the end of enumeration, the object is destroyed.

Instead of showing the rest of the code here, which would be pretty much uninteresting as the code is almost the same as in the `IEnumerator<T>` example, I'll instead show you how to construct an iterator over a built-in data type.

If we want to use a built-in data type (for example, an array) in a generic algorithm, we have to write our own iterator. The array itself doesn't implement either an `IEnumerable` interface or a `TEnumerable` class. (The code that is generated by the compiler when we use `for..in` with an array does not follow the enumeration template that I showed previously.) We have to implement such an iterator ourselves.

The demonstration program shows how to add `TEnumerator<T>` support to a dynamic array, `TArray<T>`. We can then use this enumerator (instead of the built-in version) with the following code:

```
procedure TfrmIterator.btnArrayClick(Sender: TObject);
var
  dynArray: TArray<integer>;
  el: Integer;
```

```
begin
  dynArray := [1, 1, 2, 3, 5, 8, 13];

  Log('Content of a dynamic array:');
  for el in ArrayEnum.Enum<integer>(dynArray) do
    Log(el.ToString);
end;
```

This doesn't make sense by itself, of course, as we could simply write `for el in dynArray do`, but it will be useful later when we pass an array to a generic algorithm.

To implement this support, the `CustomIterators.DynArray` unit implements a record called `ArrayEnum` with one function, `Enum<T>`, as follows:

```
type
  ArrayEnum = record
  public
    class function Enum<T>(const data: TArray<T>): TArrayEnumerable<T>;
      static;
  end;
```

This complication is required because Delphi doesn't allow us to write a generic global function. The `Enum<T>` function simply creates a `TArrayEnumerable<T>` record, as follows:

```
type
  TArrayEnumerable<T> = record
  private
    FData: TArray<T>;
  public
    constructor Create(const data: TArray<T>);
    function GetEnumerator: TEnumerator<T>;
  end;

  class function ArrayEnum.Enum<T>(const data: TArray<T>):
    TArrayEnumerable<T>;
  begin
    Result := TArrayEnumerable<T>.Create(data);
  end;
```

The `TArrayEnumerable<T>` record simply stores away the input data in the constructor and creates an instance of the `TArrayEnumerator<T>` object in `GetEnumerator`, as follows:

```
type
  TArrayEnumerator<T> = class(TEnumerator<T>)
  private
    FData: TArray<T>;
    FCurrent: integer;
  protected
    function DoGetCurrent: T; override;
    function DoMoveNext: Boolean; override;
  public
    constructor Create(const data: TArray<T>);
  end;

constructor TArrayEnumerable<T>.Create(const data: TArray<T>);
begin
  FData := data;
end;

function TArrayEnumerable<T>.GetEnumerator: TEnumerator<T>;
begin
  Result := TArrayEnumerator<T>.Create(FData);
end;
```

The actual enumeration support is implemented partially in the built-in `TEnumerator<T>` and partially in the derived class, `TArrayEnumerable<T>`, as shown here:

```
constructor TArrayEnumerator<T>.Create(const data: TArray<T>);
begin
  inherited Create;
  FData := data;
  FCurrent := -1;
end;

function TArrayEnumerator<T>.DoGetCurrent: T;
begin
  Result := FData[FCurrent];
end;

function TArrayEnumerator<T>.DoMoveNext: Boolean;
begin
  Result := FCurrent < High(FData);
  if Result then
    Inc(FCurrent);
end;
```

We don't have to implement a `Current` property and a `MoveNext` function as they are already defined in the `TEnumerator<T>` class. Instead of that, we have to implement `DoGetCurrent` and `DoMoveNext`, which are called from `TEnumerator<T>`, as shown here:

```
type
  TEnumerator<T> = class abstract
  protected
    function DoGetCurrent: T; virtual; abstract;
    function DoMoveNext: Boolean; virtual; abstract;
  public
    property Current: T read DoGetCurrent;
    function MoveNext: Boolean;
  end;

function TEnumerator<T>.MoveNext: Boolean;
begin
  Result := DoMoveNext;
end;
```

Again, we took into account that `DoMoveNext` (called from `TEnumerator<T>.MoveNext`) is called once before the first element is accessed. That's why `FCurrent` is initialized to -1.

When we want to use this enumerator in code, we can accept `TEnumerable<T>` or `TEnumerator<T>`. The choice in this example was simple, as the code in `CustomIterators.DynArray` doesn't implement `TEnumerable<T>`, just `TEnumerator<T>`.

The main unit `CustomIteratorsMain` implements a method, `GenericEnum`, that walks over a `TEnumerator<string>` supporting data structure. This method skips every second element and logs the rest to the screen, as follows:

```
procedure TfrmIterator.GenericEnum(enumerator: TEnumerator<string>);
begin
  while enumerator.MoveNext do
  begin
    Log(enumerator.Current);

    // skip every second line
    if not enumerator.MoveNext then
      break; //while
  end;
end;
```

When you click the `Generic TEnumerable` button, this code is called twice. The first time it iterates over a file and the second time over a dynamic array. The code is shown here:

```
procedure TfrmIterator.btnGenericClick(Sender: TObject);
var
  dynArray: TArray<string>;
  enumerator: TEnumerator<string>;
begin
  enumerator := TextFileContentO('..\..\CustomIterators.dpr')
                  .GetEnumerator;
  try
    GenericEnum(enumerator);
  finally
    FreeAndNil(enumerator);
  end;

  dynArray := ['D', 'e', 'l', 'p', 'h', 'i', '!'];
  enumerator := ArrayEnum.Enum<string>(dynArray).GetEnumerator;
  try
    GenericEnum(enumerator);
  finally
    FreeAndNil(enumerator);
  end;
end;
```

The result of executing this code is shown in the following screenshot:

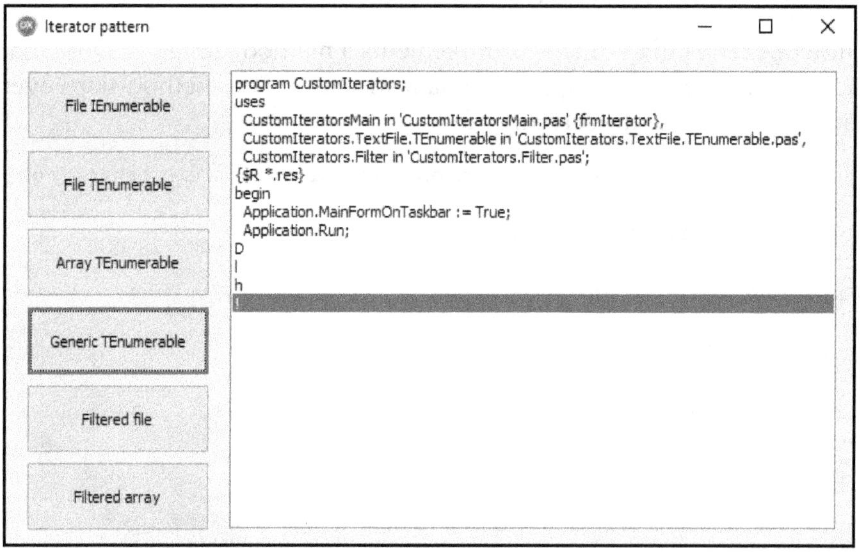

Logging every second line of a file and every second element of an array

This example program also implements a filter enumerator. This type of enumerator wraps around another enumerator (a source) and only returns some elements from the source enumerator. In other words, it acts as a filter.

A `Filter` record in the `CustomIterators.Filter` unit accepts any enumerator and a filtering function, and returns a `TEnumerable<T>` that only returns elements for which the `filter` function returns `True`, as follows:

```
type
  Filter = record
    class function Process<T>(source: TEnumerator<T>;
      const filter: TFilterFunc<T>): TFilterEnumerable<T>; static;
  end;
```

The main program demonstrates how to use this enumerator to display every second line from a file, as follows:

```
procedure TfrmIterator.btnFilterFileClick(Sender: TObject);
var
  line: string;
  enumerator: TEnumerator<string>;
  oddFilter: TFilterFunc<string>;
begin
  // allow even-indexed elements; first element has index = 0
  oddFilter :=
    function (index: integer; const item: string): boolean
    begin
      Result := not Odd(index);
    end;

  enumerator := TextFileContentO('..\..\CustomIterators.dpr')
                  .GetEnumerator;
  try
    Log('Filtered content of a file:');
    for line in Filter.Process<string>(enumerator, oddFilter) do
      Log(line);
  finally
    FreeAndNil(enumerator);
  end;
end;
```

The code uses the already familiar function `TextFileContentO` to create an enumerable record and then calls its `GetEnumerator` function to create the actual enumerator. As the enumerator is implemented as a normal Delphi class, we also have to destroy it later, in the `finally` statement. This enumerator is then passed to the `Filter.Process<string>` function together with an anonymous method that filters out odd-numbered lines.

The implementation of the filter enumerator closely follows the pattern from CustomFilters.DynArray, so it is not included in this book. I will only point out one method, namely DoMoveNext, which is shown here:

```
function TFilterEnumerator<T>.DoMoveNext: Boolean;
begin
  repeat
    Result := FSource.MoveNext;
    if not Result then
      break;
    Inc(FIndex);
  until FFilter(FIndex, Current);
end;
```

In this example, DoMoveNext calls the MoveNext function of the enumerator that was passed to the Filter.Process<T> function (for example, FSource). As we don't want to return all elements, the code must loop until there is no more data in the source enumerator or until the FFilter filtering function returns True.

Visitor

The iterator pattern shows us how to separate the internal structure of a data container from the code that operates on it. A visitor pattern is similar in topic, but applies not so much to composite data as to composite objects. It shows how to implement an algorithm/object separation, which allows us to add new operations to existing objects without modifying their structure. As such, it represents a good example of the Open/Closed principle in practice.

In classical object-oriented code, a part of code (an algorithm) would take an object, inspect its internal structure, and operate on its parts. If we use the visitor pattern, this approach is turned on its head. The algorithm merely passes a method to the object and kindly asks it to execute that method on its constituent parts.

After you enter a city sightseeing bus, you have no longer control over your transportation. The bus driver drives you from one attraction to another and on each stop allows you to perform an action (take some photos).

To implement this pattern, the composite object implements a method (typically called `Accept`), which accepts a visitor object. The code then calls a special method of the visitor object (typically called `Visit`) on each part of the composite object.

While the visitor pattern doesn't work without the proper implementation of the `Accept` method, we only have to implement it once. If we need to add new functionality, we just create a new visitor class and put new functionality there. We only have to update the `Accept` method if internal implementation of the composite model is changed.

If the composite object contains only a list of child objects, the visitor pattern functions pretty much as an iterator in disguise. With an iterator, we would write code like so:

```
for element in DataStructure do
  Process(element);
```

With the visitor pattern, we create a new visitor, which implements a `Visit` method, similar to the following code fragment:

```
procedure TVisitor.Visit(element: T);
begin
  Process(element);
end;
```

Next, we pass this visitor to the composite object, as shown here:

```
var
  visitor: TVisitor;

visitor := TVisitor.Create;
DataStructure.Accept(visitor);
```

This looks like a complicated way to traverse a data structure—and in a way it is. The visitor pattern was designed to iterate over composite objects that contain children objects of many different types. When traversing such hierarchies with a classical iterator, we would have to write code similar to the following:

```
for element in DataStructure do
  if element is ChildType1 then
    DoSomething(ChildType1(element))
  else if element is ChildType2 then
    DoSomethingElse(ChildType2(element))
  else
    ...
```

As we've seen in the section on the *command* pattern in `Chapter 14`, *Nullable Object, Template Method, Command, State*, such if ladders are hard to understand and maintain. A visitor pattern simplifies such code in a manner similar to the command pattern. We only have write a specific `Visit` method for each data type and the `Accept` method does the rest. If we reimplement the previous example with a visitor, the result would look like this:

```
procedure TVisitor.Visit(element: ChildType1);
begin
  DoSomething(element);
end;

procedure TVisitor.Visit(element: ChildType2);
begin
  DoSomethingElse(element);
end;
```

This makes the visitor pattern the perfect tool when we work with a complex model. A typical example of such a pattern is implementing an export of internal rich text representation into multiple formats, for example, HTML, RTF, plain text, and so on. Another use can be found in drawing programs, which can use this pattern to export the drawing into any of supported file formats.

To demonstrate the use of the visitor pattern, I have revisited the *Composite* project from `Chapter 12`, *Composite, Flyweight, Marker Interface, Bridge*. In this example program, I have implemented a simple object model that handles configurable computer configuration. We used it to build a model of a computer with chassis, motherboard, CPU, memory, and a few other parts.

From that model, I borrowed the `CompositeSafety` unit, renamed it to `ComponentModel`, and improved it with a visitor pattern support. The demonstration project is named `Visitor` and is stored in the `Visitor` folder.

The `ComponentModel` unit implements a model for a configurable configuration. Each hardware component is represented with a subclass of the base class `TComponent`. The base class is never created. Instead, the code creates objects of the `TBasicComponent` and `TConfigurableComponent` classes.

The former represents a fixed component that cannot be configured with subcomponents, while the latter represents a configurable component that can contain any number of subcomponents of the `TComponent` type. The full declaration of all three classes is shown as follows:

```
type
  IVisitor = interface;

  TComponent = class
  strict private
    FName: string;
    FPrice: real;
  public
    constructor Create(const AName: string; const APrice: real);
    procedure Accept(const visitor: IVisitor); virtual; abstract;
    function Components: TArray<TComponent>; virtual;
    function TotalPrice: real; virtual;
    property Name: string read FName write FName;
    property Price: real read FPrice write FPrice;
  end;

  TConfigurableComponent = class(TComponent)
  strict private
    FComponents: TObjectList<TComponent>;
  public
    procedure Accept(const visitor: IVisitor); override;
    procedure AfterConstruction; override;
    procedure BeforeDestruction; override;
    procedure Add(component: TComponent);
    function Components: TArray<TComponent>; override;
    function TotalPrice: real; override;
  end;

  TBasicComponent = class(TComponent)
  public
    procedure Accept(const visitor: IVisitor); override;
  end;
```

The base class implements properties that allow the naming of the component (`Name`) and the setting of a price for the component (`Price`). We can also get the total price for the component with all subcomponents (`TotalPrice`) and access all subcomponents (`Components`). In addition, `TConfigurableComponent` allows for the addtion of new subcomponents (`Add`).

All of this allows us to create a computer configuration in code, as in the following example:

```
procedure TfrmVisitor.FormCreate(Sender: TObject);
var
  motherboard: TConfigurableComponent;
begin
  FComputer := TConfigurableComponent.Create('chassis', 37.9);
  FComputer.Add(TBasicComponent.Create('PSU', 34.6));

  motherboard := TConfigurableComponent.Create('motherboard', 96.5);
  motherboard.Add(TBasicComponent.Create('CPU', 121.1));
  motherboard.Add(TBasicComponent.Create('memory', 88.2));
  motherboard.Add(TBasicComponent.Create('memory', 88.2));
  motherboard.Add(TBasicComponent.Create('graphics', 179));

  FComputer.Add(motherboard);
end;
```

To support the visitor pattern, all three classes implement the `Accept` method. As the instances of the base class are never created, `TComponent.Accept` is marked as `abstract`. That saves us from writing a method that is never used and also helps to catch programming errors. If the code somehow manages to call `TComponent.Accept`, an `EAbstractError` exception is raised.

The `Accept` method accepts a visitor parameter of type `IVisitor`. As this visitor has to be able to work with two different subclasses, it needs two overridden `Visit`, methods as shown here:

```
type
  IVisitor = interface ['{147411D4-2555-4174-9923-5AD6B0D91F5D}']
    procedure Visit(component: TConfigurableComponent); overload;
    procedure Visit(component: TBasicComponent); overload;
  end;
```

As I have said before, we don't have to follow Gang of Four definitions to the letter. Although the original visitor pattern specifies that a visitor is an object, a Delphi implementation will frequently be simpler if we implement it as an interface.

The implementation of both `Accept` methods is very simple. The `TBasicComponent` cannot contain any subcomponents and therefore just calls the `visitor` parameter, providing itself as an object, as follows:

```
procedure TBasicComponent.Accept(const visitor: IVisitor);
begin
  visitor.Visit(Self);
end;
```

The `TConfigurableComponent` has a more complex job. Firstly, it visits itself and then recursively calls the `Accept` method on all subcomponents, passing the same visitor as a parameter. The code is shown here:

```
procedure TConfigurableComponent.Accept(const visitor: IVisitor);
var
  component: TComponent;
begin
  visitor.Visit(Self);
  for component in Components do
    component.Accept(visitor);
end;
```

With this implementation, `Accept` recursively walks over the object structure and calls `visitor.Visit` for each object.

The demonstration program contains two buttons. The `Apply discount` button applies 5% discount to basic components and 10% to configurable components, while the Raise prices button raises all prices by 10 units. As shown in the following code, both buttons also log the updated configuration:

```
procedure TfrmVisitor.btnDiscountClick(Sender: TObject);
begin
  FComputer.Accept(TDiscountVisitor.Create(5, 10));

  lbLog.Items.Add(
    'Applied 5% discount to basic and 10% to configurable components');
  LogConfiguration;
end;

procedure TfrmVisitor.btnRaiseClick(Sender: TObject);
begin
  FComputer.Accept(TRaiseVisitor.Create(10));

  lbLog.Items.Add(
    'Raising prices of components by 10 units');
  LogConfiguration;
end;
```

The real job is done in both visitors, `TDiscountVisitor` and `TRaiseVisitor`. As the `Accept` method expects an `IVisitor` parameter, we can just create a visitor object on the fly and pass it to the method. Delphi will treat it as an interface and destroy it when the `OnClick` event handler exits.

Both visitors are implemented in a similar manner. The constructor stores the configuration parameters while the `Visit` methods operate on the composite object. The implementation for `TDiscountVisitor` is as follows:

```
type
  TDiscountVisitor = class(TInterfacedObject, IVisitor)
  strict private
    FDiscountBasic: integer;
    FDiscountConfig: integer;
  public
    constructor Create(discountBasic, discountConfigurable: integer);
    procedure Visit(component: TConfigurableComponent); overload;
    procedure Visit(component: TBasicComponent); overload;
  end;

constructor TDiscountVisitor.Create(discountBasic,
  discountConfigurable: integer);
begin
  inherited Create;
  FDiscountBasic := discountBasic;
  FDiscountConfig := discountConfigurable;
end;

procedure TDiscountVisitor.Visit(component: TBasicComponent);
begin
  component.Price := component.Price * (1 - FDiscountBasic/100);
end;

procedure TDiscountVisitor.Visit(component: TConfigurableComponent);
begin
  component.Price := component.Price * (1 - FDiscountConfig/100);
end;
```

The `TRaiseVisitor` is implemented in the same way, except that it applies different changes to the composite model. As you can see in the following code, both `Visit` methods raise the price, while the visitor for `TConfigurableComponent` also prefixes the component name with the string `NEW` to justify the raised price:

```
type
  TRaiseVisitor = class(TInterfacedObject, IVisitor)
  strict private
    FRaiseBy: real;
  public
    constructor Create(raiseBy: real);
    procedure Visit(component: TConfigurableComponent); overload;
    procedure Visit(component: TBasicComponent); overload;
  end;

constructor TRaiseVisitor.Create(raiseBy: real);
begin
  inherited Create;
  FRaiseBy := raiseBy;
end;

procedure TRaiseVisitor.Visit(component: TConfigurableComponent);
begin
  component.Price := component.Price + FRaiseBy;
  component.Name := 'NEW ' + component.Name;
end;

procedure TRaiseVisitor.Visit(component: TBasicComponent);
begin
  component.Price := component.Price + FRaiseBy;
end;
```

The following screenshot shows the result of applying the discount and then raising the prices:

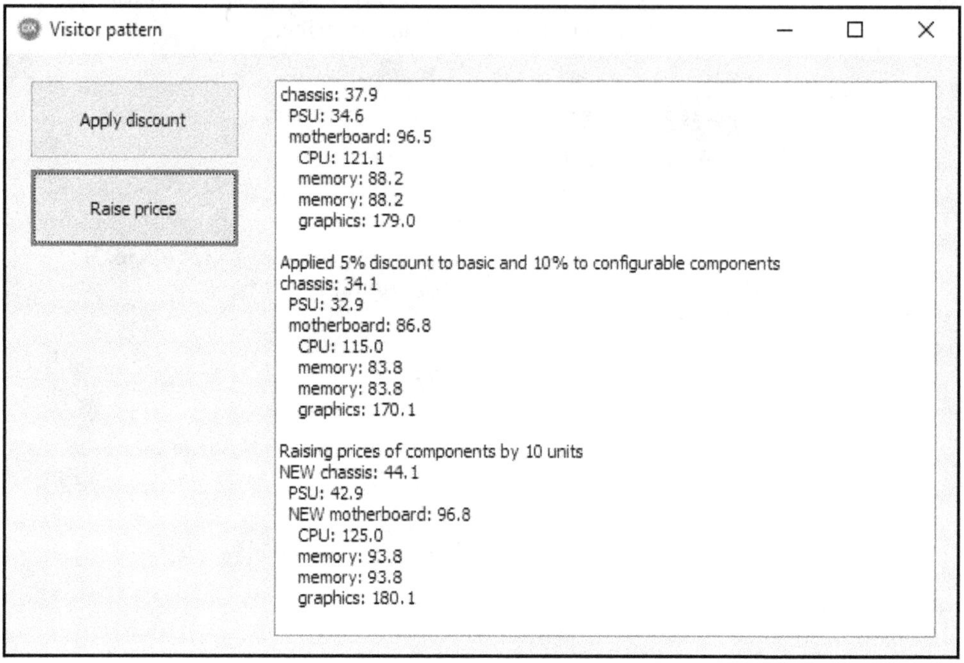

A discount followed by a price raise

Observer

The observer pattern regulates communication between an object (called a **subject**) and other objects (**observers**) that want to react to changes in the subject. Instead of checking periodically for changes, observers register their interest with the subject and are notified about the changes with some callback or messaging mechanism.

> If you subscribe to a magazine, you don't go to the publisher every day to check if a new edition is ready. Rather, you wait until the publisher sends you each issue.

This Gang of Four pattern is a basic part in distributed event handling systems. For example, a Model-View-Controller architectural pattern is always implemented with some application of the observer pattern.

The Live Binding mechanism that's in Delphi is also based on the observer model. It uses the observer mechanism built into the component library (the `TComponent.Observers` property).

Any implementation of the observer pattern follows the following steps:

1. The observer registers its interest with the subject
2. Whenever the subject is modified, it calls a callback method in all registered observers
3. The observer unregisters its interest from the subject

This results in a very tight coupling between the subject and the observers. A variation of the observer pattern called *publish-subscribe* introduces a small change in the notification mechanism, which results in more loose coupling, as follows:

1. The subscriber registers its interest with the publisher
2. Whenever the publisher is modified, it sends a message to all registered subscribers
3. The subscriber unregisters its interest from the publisher

This approach to the observer pattern allows us to split an application into multiple processes, which can (with proper implementation) even run on multiple computers.

The biggest problem with the observer pattern is that it can result in large amounts of updates. If a code modifies multiple properties of the subject, each modification ends in notifying all observers that something has changed. For this reason, the subject sometimes implements a mechanism that temporarily prevents updates to be triggered. We'll see later in this chapter how such functionality can be implemented.

Another problem is that observers have no idea which part of the subject was changed. We can extend the callback mechanism so that the notification method also provides information about the changed parts. We can also change the registration mechanism so that observers specify their area of interest during registration. The subject then notifies only observers that have specified interest in the changed area.

Instead of implementing such modifications, however, you should inspect the actual subject. In many cases, a need for a more granular notification mechanism simply tells us that the subject is too complex and is trying to do too many things. Maybe it is best to split it into multiple subcomponents, where each implements its own observer pattern.

To demonstrate the implementation of observer support from scratch, I have prepared a demonstration project, `Observer`, which is stored in the `Observer` folder.

The subject implements an interface, `ISubject`. This interface allows observers to register (`Attach`) and unregister (`Detach`) their interest with the observer. Each observer must implement the `IObserver` interface containing one method, `Update`. The subject will call this method whenever its content is modified. Both interfaces are defined in the `ObserverModel` unit and are shown as follows:

```
type
  IObserver = interface ['{966246BE-5DE8-431E-BB95-BEB5A1A9C1B8}']
    procedure Update(Subject: TObject);
  end;

  ISubject = interface ['{C9D55859-6009-4AA4-8E8F-B94DE5009D56}']
    procedure Attach(Observer: IObserver);
    procedure Detach(Observer: IObserver);
  end;
```

The subject class, `TObservableModel`, is defined in the same unit. To separate responsibilities, observer functionality was moved to a class called `TObservable`, while the business code is implemented in the `TObservableModel` class. This class also implements the mechanism that can temporarily pause notifications, namely pair of methods called `BeginUpdate`/`EndUpdate`. The following code fragment shows the definition of both classes:

```
type
  TObservable = class(TInterfacedObject, ISubject)
  strict private
    FObservers: TList<IObserver>;
  strict protected
    procedure Notify;
  public
    constructor Create;
    destructor Destroy; override;
    procedure Attach(Observer: IObserver);
    procedure Detach(Observer: IObserver);
  end;

  TObservableModel = class(TObservable, ISubject)
  strict private
    FBasePrice: real;
    FDiscount: integer;
    FUpdateCount: integer;
    FModified: boolean;
  strict protected
    function GetEndPrice: real;
    procedure Notify;
    procedure SetBasePrice(const value: real);
```

```
    procedure SetDiscount(const value: integer);
  public
    procedure BeginUpdate;
    procedure EndUpdate;
    property BasePrice: real read FBasePrice write SetBasePrice;
    property Discount: integer read FDiscount write SetDiscount;
    property EndPrice: real read GetEndPrice;
  end;
```

TIP: Alternatively, we could use composition instead of inheritance, and use `TObservable` as a component inside the `TObservableModel` class.

This approach enables us to reuse code that handles observers (`TObservable`). Later in this chapter, we'll see how we can use observer support implemented in the Spring library instead of writing our own `TObservable`.

The `TObserver` class is just a very basic wrapper around a list of `IObserver` interfaces. The only interesting part, which is shown in the following code, is the `Notify` method:

```
procedure TObservable.Notify;
var
  observer: IObserver;
begin
  for observer in FObservers do
    observer.Update(Self);
end;
```

This method walks the list of registered observers and calls the `Update` method on each of them. The subject (`Self`) is passed as a parameter. The `Notify` method is declared in the `strict protected` section as it should only be called from the `TObservableModel` code.

The `TObservableModel` contains three properties. External code can set the `BasePrice` (price for a product) and `Discount` (applied discount), and then read the `EndPrice` property to get the discounted price. Both `BasePrice` and `Discount` implement setters that change the value and then trigger the notification mechanism, as follows:

```
procedure TObservableModel.SetBasePrice(const value: real);
begin
  FBasePrice := value;
  Notify;
end;

procedure TObservableModel.SetDiscount(const value: integer);
begin
```

```
  Assert((value >= 0) and (value <= 100), 'Discount must be between 0 and
100 percent.');
  FDiscount := value;
  Notify;
end;
```

The `BeginUpdate`, `EndUpdate`, and `Notify` methods work together. They are implemented as follows:

```
procedure TObservableModel.BeginUpdate;
begin
  Inc(FUpdateCount);
end;

procedure TObservableModel.EndUpdate;
begin
  Assert(FUpdateCount > 0);
  Dec(FUpdateCount);
  if (FUpdateCount = 0) and FModified then
  begin
    Notify;
    FModified := false;
  end;
end;

procedure TObservableModel.Notify;
begin
  if FUpdateCount = 0 then
    inherited Notify
  else
    FModified := true;
end;
```

The `Notify` method checks whether the `BeginUpdate` has been called. If not (`FUpdateCount = 0`), it will simply forward the call to the base implementation in `TObserver.Notify`, which will notify all observers. Otherwise, an internal flag called `FModified` is set to `True`.

The `BeginUpdate` method simply increments the `FUpdateCount` count. This counter is decremented in the `EndUpdate` method. If the new value is 0, the code has matched every `BeginUpdate` with an `EndUpdate`, and notifications are no longer suspended. If the `FModified` flag is set (meaning that `Notify` was called after `BeginUpdate`), `Notify` is called again so that it can notify all observers.

This implementation allows us to nest `BeginUpdate/EndUpdate` calls inside other `BeginUpdate/EndUpdate` calls, which can greatly simplify the main program. Delphi RTL implements such `BeginUpdate/EndUpdate` functionality in many places.

The main form contains two spinedit inputs. `inpPrice` specifies the price for the product and `inpDiscount` specifies the applied discount. The subject is stored in the `FModel` field, which is created in the `OnCreate` handler, as follows:

```
procedure TfrmObserver.FormCreate(Sender: TObject);
begin
  FModel := TObservableModel.Create;
  FModel.BasePrice := inpPrice.Value;
  FModel.Discount := inpDiscount.Value;

  FEditObserver := TModelObserver.Create(
    procedure (model: TObservableModel)
    begin
      inpEndPrice.Text := Format('%.1f', [model.EndPrice]);
    end);
  FModel.Attach(FEditObserver);

  FListBoxObserver := TModelObserver.Create(
    procedure (model: TObservableModel)
    begin
      lbLog.ItemIndex := lbLog.Items.Add(
        Format('New price: %.1f (%.1f * %d%%)',
          [model.EndPrice, model.BasePrice, 100 - model.Discount]));
    end);
  FModel.Attach(FListBoxObserver);
end;
```

This event also attaches two observers to the subject. The helper class `TModelObserver` implements the `IObserver` interface and the `Update` method calls an anonymous function, which was passed to the constructor as parameter. This allows for the simple creation of customized observers.

The `OnCreate` handler creates two observers. The `FEditObserver` displays every change in a `TEdit` field and the `FListBoxObserver` logs changes to a listbox.

The full implementation of `TModelObserver` is shown here:

```
type
  TModelObserver = class(TInterfacedObject, IObserver)
  strict private
    FNotifier: TProc<TObservableModel>;
  public
    constructor Create(notifier: TProc<TObservableModel>);
    procedure Update(Subject: TObject);
  end;

constructor TModelObserver.Create(notifier: TProc<TObservableModel>);
begin
  inherited Create;
  FNotifier := notifier;
end;

procedure TModelObserver.Update(Subject: TObject);
begin
  FNotifier(Subject as TObservableModel);
end;
```

The `OnDestroy` event handler unregisters both observers and destroys the subject, as shown here:

```
procedure TfrmObserver.FormDestroy(Sender: TObject);
begin
  FModel.Detach(FEditObserver);
  FModel.Detach(FListBoxObserver);
  FreeAndNil(FModel);
end;
```

To finish the implementation, `OnChange` handlers for both input fields such as `inpDiscount` and `inpPrice` change `FModel` properties, as shown here:

```
procedure TfrmObserver.inpDiscountChange(Sender: TObject);
begin
  FModel.Discount := inpDiscount.Value;
end;

procedure TfrmObserver.inpPriceChange(Sender: TObject);
begin
  FModel.BasePrice := inpPrice.Value;
end;
```

Each change causes the `Update` method in both observers to be triggered and that executes both anonymous methods, which results in both editbox and listbox being updated.

The user interface also contains the **BeginUpdate** and **EndUpdate** buttons, which call the `BeginUpdate` and `EndUpdate` methods of the `FModel`, respectively(not shown here).

If you play with the program, you'll see that each change of the input fields results in the output being updated, that is unless the **BeginUpdate** button was clicked more times than the **EndUpdate** button. In such cases, updates are suspended until **EndUpdate** is clicked enough times. The following screenshot shows one such interaction:

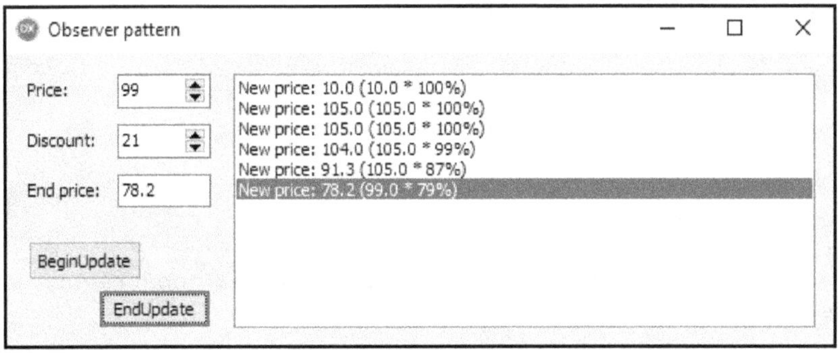

Interacting with an observed business model

Observing with Spring

The next two examples show how we can simplify our code by using support for the observer pattern that is built into the wonderful Spring4D library (`https://bitbucket.org/sglienke/spring4d`).

Both programs that I'll present—SpringObserver and SpringMulticast—require the Spring4D library to function. To run any of them, you'll have to install this library and then add its folders, `Source` and `Source\Base`, to Delphi's Library path or to the project's Search path. If you unpack the library into the `Chapter 15\Spring4D` folder, the project's Search path will already be correctly configured and you can simply press *F9* to run the program.

> TIP: If you have `git` installed, you can execute the following command in the `Chapter 15` folder to install Spring4D: `git clone https://bitbucket.org/sglienke/spring4d`.

Spring4D implements observer support in the `Spring.DesignPatterns` unit. The `IObservable<T>` interface defines support for managing and notifying observers of type `T`. This interface is implemented in `TObservable<T>`, which we can use as a base class for our subject. The following code fragment shows both the interface and the class definition:

```
type
  IObservable<T> = interface(IInvokable)
    procedure Attach(const observer: T);
    procedure Detach(const observer: T);
    procedure Notify;
  end;

  TObservable<T> = class(TInterfacedObject, IObservable<T>)
  private
    fLock: TMREWSync;
    fObservers: IList<T>;
  protected
    procedure DoNotify(const observer: T); virtual; abstract;
    property Observers: IList<T> read fObservers;
  public
    constructor Create;
    destructor Destroy; override;

    procedure Attach(const observer: T);
    procedure Detach(const observer: T);
    procedure Notify;
  end;
```

How `TObservable<T>` is implemented is not really our concern. We just want to use it. Still, if you look into the code, you'll see that the implementation is very similar to `TObservable` from the previous example, with the additional bonus of support for multithreaded programs.

There is, in fact, a small implementation detail that we should be aware of. `TObservable<T>.Notify` doesn't directly call the observers' `Update` method. This class doesn't know in advance what `T` will represent and which methods it will implement. Instead of that, `Notify` calls the virtual `DoNotify` method for each observer. Our subject must override this method and use it to call the appropriate notification mechanism.

The subject implementation in SpringObserverModel (part of the SpringObserver project) is similar to previous implementations of TObservableModel, except that this time it is derived from the TObservable<IObserver> class. As shown in the following code, this version doesn't support BeginUpdate/EndUpdate functionality:

```
type
  IObserver = interface ['{966246BE-5DE8-431E-BB95-BEB5A1A9C1B8}']
    procedure Update(Subject: TObject);
  end;

  TObservableModel = class(TObservable<IObserver>)
  strict private
    FBasePrice: real;
    FDiscount: integer;
  strict protected
   procedure DoNotify(const observer: IObserver); override;
    function GetEndPrice: real;
    procedure SetBasePrice(const value: real);
    procedure SetDiscount(const value: integer);
  public
    property BasePrice: real read FBasePrice write SetBasePrice;
    property Discount: integer read FDiscount write SetDiscount;
    property EndPrice: real read GetEndPrice;
  end;
```

You can add BeginUpdate/EndUpdate support to this implementation as an exercise.

The implementation of TObservableModel in this program is almost the same as the one we have already seen. The biggest difference lies in the DoNotify method, which serves as a mapper from a purely abstract implementation in TObservable<T> into our custom IObserver, as follows:

```
procedure TObservableModel.DoNotify(const observer: IObserver);
begin
  observer.Update(Self);
end;
```

The main program is almost the same as in the previous example. You can try it out on your own.

Another approach that we can use to implement observer support is *multicast events.*

An event handler in Delphi is similar to an observer callback (the `Update` method in our observers), except that it only supports one observer at a time. This limitation can be bypassed with a different event implementation. Each multicast event must be backed by a list of currently attached (registered) event handlers (observers). We can implement such support ourselves or use the already made `Event<T>` record from Spring.

This feature is demonstrated in the `SpringMulticast` project. The `SpringMulticastModel` unit reimplements the already well-known observable model, as follows:

```
type
  TObservableModel = class
  strict private
    FBasePrice: real;
    FDiscount: integer;
    FEndPriceChanged: Event<TNotifyEvent>;
  strict protected
    function GetEndPrice: real;
    procedure SetBasePrice(const value: real);
    procedure SetDiscount(const value: integer);
  public
    property BasePrice: real read FBasePrice write SetBasePrice;
    property Discount: integer read FDiscount write SetDiscount;
    property EndPrice: real read GetEndPrice;
    property EndPriceChanged: Event<TNotifyEvent> read FEndPriceChanged;
  end;
```

Instead of adding support for multiple observers, `TObservableModel` implements the multicast event `EndPriceChanged`. As this event is backed by a record type, `Event<T>`, no special creation or destruction of `FEndPriceChanged` is required.

The code calls `EndPriceChanged.Invoke(Self)` to invoke all event handlers that are currently attached, as shown here:

```
procedure TObservableModel.SetBasePrice(const value: real);
begin
  FBasePrice := value;
  EndPriceChanged.Invoke(Self);
end;

procedure TObservableModel.SetDiscount(const value: integer);
```

```
begin
  Assert((value >= 0) and (value <= 100), 'Discount must be between 0 and
100 percent.');
  FDiscount := value;
  EndPriceChanged.Invoke(Self);
end;
```

The `Self` parameter will be passed to all event handlers as the `Sender` parameter. In other words, all `TNotifyEvent` handlers will be triggered as we expect them to be in Delphi.

The main unit defines two methods with the `TNotifyEvent` signature. As shown in the following code, these two methods are added to the event handler inside the `OnCreate` event and removed in the `OnDestroy` event:

```
type
  TfrmSpringMulticast = class(TForm)
    ...
    procedure PriceChangedEdit(Sender: TObject);
    procedure PriceChangedListBox(Sender: TObject);
  end;

procedure TfrmSpringMulticast.FormCreate(Sender: TObject);
begin
  FModel := TObservableModel.Create;
  FModel.BasePrice := inpPrice.Value;
  FModel.Discount := inpDiscount.Value;

  FModel.EndPriceChanged.Add(PriceChangedEdit);
  FModel.EndPriceChanged.Add(PriceChangedListBox);
end;

procedure TfrmSpringMulticast.FormDestroy(Sender: TObject);
begin
  FModel.EndPriceChanged.Remove(PriceChangedEdit);
  FModel.EndPriceChanged.Remove(PriceChangedListBox);
  FreeAndNil(FModel);
end;
```

The implementation of these two event handlers is the same as the code in the two anonymous methods that were used for the observer action in the previous example. The following fragment shows both event handlers:

```
procedure TfrmSpringMulticast.PriceChangedEdit(Sender: TObject);
begin
  inpEndPrice.Text := Format('%.1f', [(Sender as
TObservableModel).EndPrice]);
end;

procedure TfrmSpringMulticast.PriceChangedListBox(Sender: TObject);
var
  model: TObservableModel;
begin
  model := Sender as TObservableModel;
  lbLog.ItemIndex := lbLog.Items.Add(
    Format('New price: %.1f (%.1f * %d%%)',
      [model.EndPrice, model.BasePrice, 100 - model.Discount]));
end;
```

If you play with the program, you'll see that it behaves exactly the same as the previous example.

It may be tempting to always implement observers, as in the previous example. It required the least amount of code and was the simplest to write. There is, however, a big difference between multicast events and proper observer mechanisms. The client in both observer-based implementations was coded strictly to an interface and was therefore not dependent on an implementation. The multicast event approach forces a client that is fixed to a specific implementation and is therefore harder to test and maintain.

Memento

The last pattern in this chapter, memento, helps us save and restore a state of a complex object. It was originally introduced by the Gang of Four.

When you want to store and restore a current state of a complex object, you can easily run into problems with encapsulation. There may, for example, exist an internal state that is important for the correct functioning of the object, but is not accessible to the public. In such a case, we may not be able to access this state from the code that is not part of the object.

Even if all internal fields are accessible by the public, accessing internal state from external code is a bad practice. The internal representation of an object may change unexpectedly (for example, with a software update), and if a maintainer of such external code is not aware of that, the program would break.

The memento pattern prescribes how a complex object (called originator) saves its internal state into a simpler object (memento). An external object (caretaker) can manage memento objects but cannot inspect their internal structure. In other words, memento objects are opaque to the code outside of the originator and memento objects.

> A memento behaves the same as a save point in a computer game. When you save your state in a game, a representation of your current progress is saved. Later, you can restore the game from this representation to the previous state.

The memento pattern is often used to implement an undo capability in a program. Whenever a new state is stored, a new memento object is created and pushed to the undo stack. When an operation is undone, a memento object is taken from the stack and the state of the program is reloaded from that memento.

Another use of a memento pattern is to implement an iteration mechanism. In this context, a memento object is frequently called a **bookmark**. For example, the following code fragment shows a class called `TDataCollection<T>`, which implements some kind of data storage mechanism for class `T`:

```
type
  TBookmark = record
    //...
  end;

  TDataCollection<T> = class
  //...
  public
    function First: TBookmark;
    function Current(const bookmark: TBookmark): T;
    procedure Next(var bookmark: TBookmark);
    function AtEnd(const bookmark: TBookmark): boolean;
  end;
```

To allow external code to travel this data collection, a memento called `TBookmark` is created in the `First` method. The `Current` method returns a value of type `T`, corresponding to the given bookmark. The `Next` method takes a bookmark, moves to the next value, and updates the bookmark. The last method, `AtEnd`, returns `True` if the current bookmark lies after the last element in the collection.

Together, these methods allows external code to travel the collection, as shown here:

```
var
  data: TDataCollection;
  state: TBookmark;
begin
  state := data.First;
  while not data.AtEnd(state) do
  begin
    Process(data.Current);
    data.Next(bookmark);
  end;
end;
```

As the iteration state is not internal to the `TDataCollection` but external (stored in the caller code), this approach allows multiple iterations to occur in parallel. Of course, if concurrent iterations occur in multiple threads, you have to take special care to protect simultaneous access to `TDataCollection` internals. We'll talk about that in detail in the next chapter, `Chapter 16`, *Locking Patterns*.

TIP

A memento can also be used to implement a `for..in` iteration internally.

Let's take a look at a short example, taken from the *MementoEditor* project in the *Memento* folder. The *MementoExample* unit implements a very simple originator object, `TComplexObject`, as follows:

```
type
  TComplexObject = class
  private
    FValue: integer;
  public
    procedure Increment;
    function CreateMemento: TMemento;
    procedure RestoreMemento(const memento: TMemento);
    property Value: integer read FValue;
  end;
```

This object contains an internal state field, `FValue`, which can be read from external code via the `Value` property. There is, however, no functionality exposed by the `TComplexObject` to set `FValue` to a specific value. This prevents us from implementing a save/restore mechanism by accessing FValue directly.

To fix that, `TComplexObject` implements a function called `CreateMemento`, which creates a *memento* object called `TMemento`, and a procedure called `RestoreMemento`, which takes a memento object and restores its internal state from it.

TIP: In this case, a memento object is actually a record. This simplifies life cycle management of memento objects in the caretaker code. It is, of course, perfectly valid to implement a memento as an object or as an interface.

The following code shows how a memento record is created and consumed in the `TComplexObject` code:

```
function TComplexObject.CreateMemento: TMemento;
begin
  Result.FValue := FValue;
end;

procedure TComplexObject.RestoreMemento(const memento: TMemento);
begin
  FValue := memento.FValue;
end;
```

A memento object can also be used for serialization/deserialization of a complex problem, although that at least partially breaks the pattern. We have to either allow (de)serialization code to access the internal state of the memento object, (which breaks the memento is opaque assumption), or implement the (de)serialization code inside the memento code (which breaks the single responsibility principle).

For a more complex example, I have revisited the *command* pattern demo from `Chapter 14`, *Nullable Object, Template Method, Command, State*. In that chapter, I implemented a simple editor with an undo capability.

The undo mechanism in the Editor demo from that chapter manages a state of a `TMemo` editor inside the `TUndoableCommand` object as a set of fields (`FText` and `FPosition`), as follows:

```
type
  TUndoableCommand = class(TCommand)
  strict private
    FText: string;
    FPosition: Integer;
  strict protected
    procedure StoreState;
  public
```

```
    function Clone: TCommand; override;
    procedure Execute; override;
    procedure Undo; override;
  end;
```

The MementoEditor project in the Memento folder contains an improved version of the Editor demo from the previous chapter.

Instead of accessing the `TMemo` object directly and storing state as a set of fields, the new `TUndoableCommand` uses a memento called `TMemoMemento`, as shown in the following code (the implementation of the `Clone` and `Execute` methods is not shown as it is not relevant for the memento pattern):

```
type
  TUndoableCommand = class(TCommand)
  strict private
    FMemoMemento: TMemoMemento;
  strict protected
    procedure StoreState;
  public
    function Clone: TCommand; override;
    procedure Execute; override;
    procedure Undo; override;
  end;

procedure TUndoableCommand.StoreState;
begin
  FMemoMemento := Receiver.CreateMemento;
end;

procedure TUndoableCommand.Undo;
begin
  Receiver.RestoreMemento(FMemoMemento);
end;
```

This code fully follows the memento opaque approach. The `TUndoableCommand` only creates, stores, and uses a memento. It doesn't access its internal implementation.

The memento itself is implemented in `Memo.Memento` unit. `TMemoMemento` is a memento object (although implemented as a record) for a `TMemo` object. It only stores four `TMemo` properties that interest us, as shown here:

```
type
  TMemoMemento = record
  private
    FCaretPos: TPoint;
    FSelLength: Integer;
```

```
    FSelStart: Integer;
    FText: string;
  end;
```

> **TIP:** A memento doesn't have to store the full internal state of an originator object. It may only store a partial state, as shown in this example.

As we cannot implement methods to create and restore a memento inside the originator object, they are implemented as a class helper. This allows the code in the `TUndoableCommand` (as shown before) to directly call `CreateMemento` and `RestoreMemento` on the `TMemo` object. The following code fragment shows the definition and implementation of the memo helper `TMemoHelper`:

```
type
  TMemoHelper = class helper for TMemo
  public
    function CreateMemento: TMemoMemento;
    procedure RestoreMemento(const memento: TMemoMemento);
  end;

function TMemoHelper.CreateMemento: TMemoMemento;
begin
  Result.FCaretPos := CaretPos;
  Result.FSelStart := SelStart;
  Result.FSelLength := SelLength;
  Result.FText := Text;
end;

procedure TMemoHelper.RestoreMemento(const memento: TMemoMemento);
begin
  CaretPos := memento.FCaretPos;
  SelStart := memento.FSelStart;
  SelLength := memento.FSelLength;
  Text := memento.FText;
end;
```

The rest of the example project is left unchanged from the previous chapter.

Summary

In this chapter, we have examined four more behavioral patterns. They are a bit more complex than the patterns from the previous chapter, but they also help a lot with organizing the code and are well worth your consideration.

The iterator pattern is well-known to Delphi programmers. Most of you know how to write a `for..in` loop, even though the implementation details hiding behind this construct may not be your biggest concern. In this chapter, we have also explored the other part of iterators, namely, how to use them as a tool for writing generic algorithms.

This chapter continued with the *visitor* pattern, which is in some aspects iterator's counterpart. Unlike the iterator, this pattern wasn't designed to walk over data structures, but to iterate over complex object structures. With a proper implementation, it allows us to open a small window into object internals and use it to write extensions that enhance existing objects.

The observer pattern, also know as publish-subscribe, is a basic tool behind event-driven systems, such as the Model-View-Controller architecture or Delphi's own LiveBindings. In this chapter, I looked into multiple implementations based on custom code and on the popular open source Spring4D library.

The last behavioral pattern covered in this book, memento, is one of the simplest ones. In fact, it looks so trivial that it's easy to overlook and ignore. Nevertheless, the concept of memento is something that you should have in mind when you work with systems that need to capture and restore the state of complex objects.

In the next chapter, we'll move away from Gang of Four patterns and step into the modern world of multithreaded programming, where even the simplest tasks require special care and consideration.

16
Locking Patterns

Very modern programmer should know something about parallel programming, and we Delphi programmers are no exception. The programs we write and maintain are getting more and more complex, while our customers expect them to keep performing swiftly and without blocking the user interface. A lot of times, we can only satisfy such requirements by introducing parallelism into our software.

Getting parallel, however, is far from simple. When we introduce multiple threads of execution into our programs, we also introduce a big source of potential problems. Writing good parallel code means writing very ordered code that follows established patterns—even more so than that in a standard, single-threaded application.

The most important concept of multithreaded programs is data sharing. After all, no thread is an island and we must somehow make sure that all code in the program is cooperating instead of fighting with each other. That is why this chapter is dedicated to different variations of a locking pattern, which regulates access to shared resources.

In this chapter, you will do the following:

- Learn the basics of multithreaded programming with Delphi
- Find out everything about the locking pattern
- Explore lock striping to see how locking can be even more granular
- Learn how to optimize the creation of shared resources with double-checked locking
- Make resource initialization even faster with optimistic locking
- Learn how to make data readers and data writers work in perfect harmony with readers-writer lock

Delphi idioms – parallel programming

Delphi offers many tools to write multithreaded programs. As this is a book about patterns, not about parallel programming, I will not be able to go into much detail on that topic. Still, it is good to know which tools you have available so that you can do additional research in your own time.

In this introductory section, I will walk you through the Delphi tools that facilitate the writing of multithreaded applications. The `DelphiThreading` project from the `Parallel programming in Delphi` folder provides a simple example for every one of them.

A standard platform-independent way to create a new thread in Delphi is to create a descendant of a `TThread` class (implemented in the `System.Classes` unit) and override its `Execute` method. Delphi will use operating system functions to create a new thread and start the `Execute` method inside that thread. This functionality has been available since Delphi 2, which was the first Delphi version to support 32-bit Windows (16-bit Windows did not support threaded programming at all).

The demonstration project implements a `TStandardThread` object, which posts a message to the main window every second until the thread is destroyed. It is implemented as follows:

```
type
  TStandardThread = class(TThread)
  protected
    procedure Execute; override;
  end;

procedure TStandardThread.Execute;
begin
  while not Terminated do
  begin
    PostMessage(frmDelphiThreading.Handle, WM_LOG, ThreadID, 0);
    Sleep(1000);
  end;
end;
```

To create this thread, the code simply creates a new `TStandardThread` object. The code also sets an `OnTerminate` event, which is called once the thread has terminated, as shown here:

```
procedure TfrmDelphiThreading.btnThreadClick(Sender: TObject);
begin
  FThread := TStandardThread.Create;
  FThread.OnTerminate := ReportThreadTerminated;
  btnThread.OnClick := btnStopThreadClick;
  btnThread.Caption := 'Stop';
end;
```

To destroy the thread, the code calls its `Terminate` method, which sets the `Terminated` property of the `TThread` class. A thread will sooner or later (at most, in one second) see that `Terminated` has been set and will exit. The `WaitFor` call waits for the thread to exit from the `Execute` method. After that, the code can destroy the thread object. The whole process is shown here:

```
procedure TfrmDelphiThreading.btnStopThreadClick(Sender: TObject);
begin
  FThread.Terminate;
  FThread.WaitFor;
  FreeAndNil(FThread);
  btnThread.OnClick := btnThreadClick;
  btnThread.Caption := 'TThread';
end;
```

The code can also create a thread that automatically destroys its object when it is no longer used by setting the `FreeOnTerminate` property, as shown here:

```
procedure TfrmDelphiThreading.btnFreeOnTermClick(Sender: TObject);
begin
  FThreadFoT := TFreeOnTerminateThread.Create(True);
  FThreadFoT.FreeOnTerminate := true;
  FThreadFoT.OnTerminate := ReportThreadTerminated;
  FThreadFoT.Start;
end;
```

When a thread object requires some configuration (as in this case), it is good practice to create it in a suspended (non-running) state by passing `True` to the constructor. After that, you can configure everything, knowing that the thread is not running yet. At the end, you must call `Start` to actually start the thread.

The first approach of manually stopping the thread is more appropriate when we have a long-running thread providing some service. The main program starts the thread when it needs that service and stops it when the service is no longer needed. If, however, the background thread just runs some operation and then stops, it is simpler to allow the thread to terminate itself.

Delphi also allows us to use an anonymous method instead of a `TThread` descendant for code that is to be run in a thread. This approach is suitable for small tasks that require just a few lines of code.

In Delphi XE7, a new unit, `System.Threading`, was introduced, which moved multi-threaded programming from the thread-based approach to modern task-based code. Instead of having to deal with threads (starting, stopping, and managing them), the new approach automates all of these processes. We merely create a task (for example, a piece of code that we want to run in a thread) and the infrastructure from `System.Threading` will do the rest.

The following code example creates a new task interface, `FTask: ITask`, that executes the `Asy_TaskWorker` method in a new thread:

```
procedure TfrmDelphiThreading.btnITaskClick(Sender: TObject);
begin
  FTask := TTask.Create(Asy_TaskWorker);
  FTask.Start;
end;
```

Instead of calling `Create` followed by `Start`, you can also call the helper `Run` function, as follows:

```
procedure TfrmDelphiThreading.btnITaskClick(Sender: TObject);
begin
  FTask := TTask.Run(Asy_TaskWorker);
end;
```

The `Asy_TaskWorker` method does some work (simulated with a `Sleep` function) and then uses `TThread.Queue` to execute an anonymous method in a main thread. This anonymous method logs the status to the listbox and destroys the `FTask` interface, as follows:

```
procedure TfrmDelphiThreading.Asy_TaskWorker;
var
  i: Integer;
  threadID: TThreadID;
begin
  threadID := GetCurrentThreadID;
```

```
    Sleep(5000);

    TThread.Queue(nil,
      procedure
      begin
        lbLog.Items.Add('Task in thread ' + threadID.ToString +
          ' has stopped');
        FTask := nil;
      end);
end;
```

TIP: When writing multithreaded code in Delphi, always keep in mind that you should only access VCL from the main thread!

This code is equivalent to the `FreeOnTerminate` version of `TThread` based code. We could also write the task in a service-like way, so that it runs in a loop until the main thread stops it. In both cases, we can use the `Wait` method of the `ITask` interface to wait until the task finishes execution.

The approach of using tasks in combination with explicit waiting is used in all examples in this chapter.

The task approach is used to create wrappers that operate on an even higher level of abstraction. Delphi XE7 introduced three such abstractions: join, future, and parallel for.

Join allows us to start any number of tasks in parallel. The following call creates two tasks, each running the same method, `Asy_TaskWorker`:

```
TParallel.Join(Asy_TaskWorker, Asy_TaskWorker);
```

`TParallel.Join` returns an `ITask` interface that we can use to control execution. We can, for example, call its `Wait` method to wait on all parallel tasks to complete their work.

`Join` should use multiple threads to execute the tasks, but this doesn't work correctly in all Delphi versions. Delphi 10.1 Berlin introduced a bug that was only fixed in Delphi 10.3 Rio, which caused the `Join` method to sometimes execute the first two tasks in the same thread.

If you start the DelphiThreading program and click on the `Join` button, you'll see messages from two threads if you are using Delphi without this bug, and messages that come only from one thread if you are using Delphi 10.1 or 10.2.

As a workaround, you can insert a null task as a first parameter to the `Join` call, as in the following example:

```
TParallel.Join([procedure begin end, Asy_TaskWorker, Asy_TaskWorker]);
```

The second abstraction, future, creates a function that executes in a thread and returns a result. This kind of execution is initialized by calling the `ITask.Future<T>` function, which returns a future interface called `IFuture<T>`. The `Future` button in the demonstration program creates such a background calculation, as follows:

```
procedure TfrmDelphiThreading.btnFutureClick(Sender: TObject);
begin
  FFuture := TTask.Future<integer>(
    function: Integer
    begin
      Sleep(2000);
      Result := 42;
      TThread.Queue(nil, ReportFuture);
    end);
end;

procedure TfrmDelphiThreading.ReportFuture;
begin
  lbLog.Items.Add('Result = ' + FFuture.Value.ToString);
  FFuture := nil;
end;
```

The last high-level abstraction included with Delphi is a parallel for. It allows us to very simply replace a normal `for` loop with a parallel version. Unlike join and future, parallel for stops the main thread until the loop is completed. This simplifies the programming while still allowing you to run a parallel loop inside a task if you don't want to block the main thread.

The following code shows how to implement a parallel for loop:

```
procedure TfrmDelphiThreading.btnParallelForClick(Sender: TObject);
begin
  TParallel.For(1, 16,
    procedure (i: integer)
    begin
      PostMessage(frmDelphiThreading.Handle, WM_LOG,
        TThread.Current.ThreadID, i);
      Sleep(100);
    end);
end;
```

If you are only programming for Windows and you are not using the FireMonkey framework, you can also use my parallel programming library, OmniThreadLibrary (`www.omnithreadlibrary.com`). It offers superior support for communication between threads and many other high-level abstractions, such as pipeline, timed task, background worker, and more.

Lock

The big power of multithreaded programming lies in the fact that all threads can access all the memory in the program. When we create a new thread that will process some program data, we don't need any special preparations. We just create the thread and that data will be available to it.

This, however, is also the biggest weakness of multithreaded programming. If multiple threads are accessing the same data, they can easily interfere with each other. One thread can overwrite the data of another thread or it can modify the structure that another thread is using. This results in all kinds of problems, including random crashes at unexpected locations.

As an example, imagine this situation. A first thread is walking some list and processing elements with the following code:

```
for i := 0 to FList.Count - 1 do
  DoSomethingWith(FList[i]);
```

`FList` is a global object and while this `for` loop is running, the second thread deletes an element from the list with `FList.Delete(0)`.

Let's say that the `FList` initially contains 1,000 elements with indices from 0 to 999. Before the `for` loop starts, the Delphi compiler calculates `FList.Count - 1` and stores the result (999) in a temporary variable. This expression is only calculated on the beginning and not on each repetition of the `for` loop!

While the `for` loop is executing, the second thread deletes the first element from the list, which now contains only 999 elements with indices from 0 to 998. The first thread has no knowledge of that and at the end of the `for` loop, it tries to access element 999, which results in a range check exception.

This problem can potentially occur every time multiple threads are operating on the same data and at least one thread modifies that data. As we will soon see, we don't need a complicated structure, such as a list, to exhibit the problem. It can occur even when threads are accessing one simple `integer` field.

> **TIP:** Such problems will also appear if you try to work with the user interface (manipulate VCL controls) from a background thread. All Delphi programmers that want to use multithreaded code should always keep the prime directive in mind: never access VCL from a background thread!

We can fix such a situation in two ways. One is to re-architect the application so that multiple threads never share the data. This is hard to do and in some situations almost impossible. I will discuss potential approaches for changing the code that way in the next chapter.

The other approach is to introduce the lock pattern. For this pattern to function, we must wrap each access to shared data in this pattern. That can again be hard work, especially if we are adapting existing code that uses the shared data object all over the place. The pattern is effective only if all code that accesses the data uses the pattern! Miss one place and the code can still run into problems.

The lock pattern protects the shared resource in the same way as a normal lock does. Before the program uses the shared resource, it must acquire the lock. This locks the door for any other thread. If another thread tries to acquire the same lock, it will have to stop and wait for the resource to be unlocked (we also say that the thread is blocked).

When the first thread doesn't need the shared resource anymore, it *releases* the lock. This unlocks the resource and allows another thread to acquire the lock. If a thread is already waiting for the lock, the operating system will automatically re-lock the resource and allow that thread to continue execution.

Of course, there are cases when multiple threads may be waiting on the same lock. In such cases, the operating system will wake only one of the threads at a time and keep the others waiting.

> **Info:** In real life, a lock corresponds to a latch on the inner side of a changing room door. While locked, it prevents other users from accessing the changing room that is already in use.

Before we look into the different ways we can implement this pattern, let us write some pseudocode. If we are using some fictional `lock` object with the `Acquire` and `Release` methods we can rewrite the previous example as follows:

```
procedure Thread1;
begin
  lock.Acquire;
  try
    for i := 0 to FList.Count - 1 do
      DoSomethingWith(FList[i]);
  finally
    lock.Release;
  end;
end;

procedure Thread2;
begin
  lock.Acquire;
  try
    FList.Delete(0);
  finally
    lock.Release;
  end;
end;
```

In this example, one thread is executing the `Thread1` procedure and another is executing `Thread2`. As access to the `FList` is now protected, its contents cannot be modified while the `for` loop is being executed and the problems cannot occur.

If, however, we forget to fix just one place in code and `FList.Delete(0)` is called there without being wrapped in a lock, the program can still crash! That one piece of code is enough to corrupt the data while another thread is thinking that it can safely iterate over the list.

Locks should be inserted so that they wrap the smallest amount of code that uses the shared resource. We could, for example, acquire the lock when a thread is created, and release it when it is destroyed, but that would completely negate the purpose of multithreaded programming, as we would only be able to run one thread at a time.

It is also possible to lock too small an area of code. For example, the following code would not operate properly:

```
lock.Acquire;
try
  count := FList.Count;
finally
  lock.Release;
end;

for i := 0 to count - 1 do
begin
  lock.Acquire;
  try
    DoSomethingWith(FList[i]);
  finally
    lock.Release;
  end;
end;
```

This implementation still locks every access to the shared resource but does so on a too-local level. With this implementation, the content of the list can still be modified while the `for` loop is running.

You may have noticed that I am using the `try..finally` statement to ensure that the lock is always released in case of an exception. This is important, as some other part of the program (for example, code that tries to save data to disk in case of an exception) may need to use the same lock. If we didn't unlock at the place of exception, that other part would get stuck in its *acquire* call and the whole program would lock up.

Another decision that awaits you, as a programmer in the multithreaded world, is how many locks to introduce into code. Technically, we can fix everything with only one lock, but then one part of the code would wait for object A while another thread would work on object B, even when they are completely unrelated. Introducing a master lock is a great way to make multithreaded program slow down to a crawl.

Usually, you will want to protect each shared resource with a separate lock. Sometimes, however, this is not the best idea and we need to introduce locks that protect multiple objects. Unfortunately, there is no solution that will apply to all cases. You will have to think about what your program is doing and then protect the appropriate areas.

Before I show you how the lock pattern can be implemented in Delphi code, I would like to show another example of bad code: two threads fighting to access the same integer-sized data. The example project, `Lock`, in the `Lock` folder, contains all the code that will be used in the continuation of this chapter.

The Unsafe data access button starts very simple code that uses two threads. The `btnUnsafeClick` method initializes the shared data field `FSharedData: integer` to 0, starts two threads, waits on both to finish work, and logs the execution time and final value of `FSharedData`, as follows:

```
procedure TfrmLock.btnUnsafeClick(Sender: TObject);
var
  decTask: ITask;
  incTask: ITask;
  timer: TStopwatch;
begin
  FSharedData := 0;
  timer := TStopwatch.StartNew;
  incTask := TTask.Run(IncrementValue);
  decTask := TTask.Run(DecrementValue);
  incTask.Wait;
  decTask.Wait;
  timer.Stop;
  Log('Unsafe value: %d; time: %d ms',
    [FSharedData, timer.ElapsedMilliseconds]);
end;
```

The first thread runs the `IncrementValue` method, as follows:

```
const
  CNumRepeats = 1000000;

procedure TfrmLock.IncrementValue;
var
  i: integer;
begin
  for i := 1 to CNumRepeats do
    Inc(FSharedData);
end;
```

This code simply increments the shared value by a million times.

The other thread runs the `DecrementValue` method, which decrements the shared value by a million times, as follows:

```
procedure TfrmLock.DecrementValue;
var
  i: integer;
begin
  for i := 1 to CNumRepeats do
    Dec(FSharedData);
end;
```

If we execute one method after another, the result would be obvious. The shared value would be incremented a million times and then decremented a million times, so at the end it would reach the starting value of zero. Running both operations in parallel, though, has unexpected consequences. We can never know what the end value will be, and the following screenshot proves that:

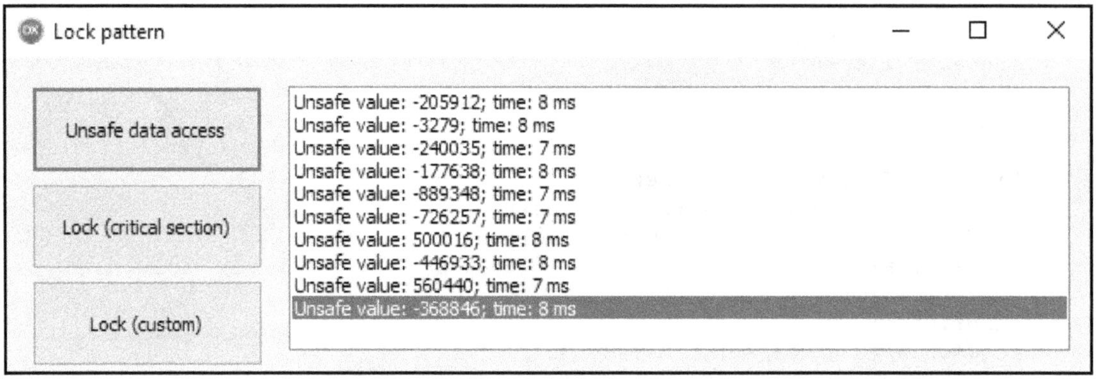

Modifying the shared value from multiple threads ends in an unpredictable result

The problem here is that the `Inc` and `Dec` instructions are not atomic (they don't execute in one indivisible step). Rather, `Inc` is implemented on the CPU as the following sequence of operations:

1. Load the data from memory.
2. Increment the value.
3. Store the data back to memory.

`Dec` is very similar, except that it decrements the value.

Because of that, the following can happen. Let's assume that `FSharedValue` contains the value 42. The two threads (let's call them I and D) then execute the following operations:

- Thread I loads value 42 from `FSharedValue`.
- Thread D loads value 42 from `FSharedValue`.
- Thread I increments the value and gets 43.
- Thread D decrements the value and gets 41.
- Thread I saves value 43 to `FSharedValue`.
- Thread D saves value 41 to `FSharedValue`.

The starting value, 42, was incremented and decremented once, so ideally it should stay the same. However, the value is now 41. As this will happen many times during the execution of a program, we will get a completely unpredictable result.

To fix the code, we have to introduce locking, and a common approach to that is to use a concept called a critical section. This concept is implemented on all major operating systems and it will work equally well on all platforms that Delphi can compile for. As the implementation is different on each operating system, Delphi nicely hides the specifics from us in a platform-independent class called `TCriticalSection`. It is implemented in the `System.SyncObjs` unit.

As it is a class, we have to create it before its first use and destroy it when we don't need it anymore. The `Lock` program does that in the `OnClick` handler for the **Lock** *(critical section)* button, as shown here:

```
procedure TfrmLock.btnCriticalSectionClick(Sender: TObject);
var
  decTask: ITask;
  incTask: ITask;
  timer: TStopwatch;
begin
  FLock := TCriticalSection.Create;
  try
    FSharedData := 0;
    timer := TStopwatch.StartNew;
    incTask := TTask.Run(LockIncrementValue);
    decTask := TTask.Run(LockDecrementValue);
    incTask.Wait;
    decTask.Wait;
    timer.Stop;
    Log('Lock value: %d; time: %d ms',
      [FSharedData, timer.ElapsedMilliseconds]);
  finally
    FreeAndNil(FLock);
  end;
end;
```

The rest of the code is very similar to that of the previously seen `btnUnsafeClick`, except that now, the following two methods are executed in separate threads:

```
procedure TfrmLock.LockDecrementValue;
var
  i: integer;
begin
  for i := 1 to CNumRepeats do
  begin
```

```
      FLock.Acquire;
      try
        Dec(FSharedData);
      finally
        FLock.Release;
      end;
    end;
  end;

  procedure TfrmLock.LockIncrementValue;
  var
    i: integer;
  begin
    for i := 1 to CNumRepeats do
    begin
      FLock.Acquire;
      try
        Inc(FSharedData);
      finally
        FLock.Release;
      end;
    end;
  end;
```

Each `Inc` and `Dec` is now protected with a critical section so that both `Inc` and `Dec` can never be executed at the same time. As the `for` loop doesn't depend on the `FSharedData` value, we are locking each increment/decrement. That allows the threads to run in parallel. The following screenshot shows the result of the fixed code:

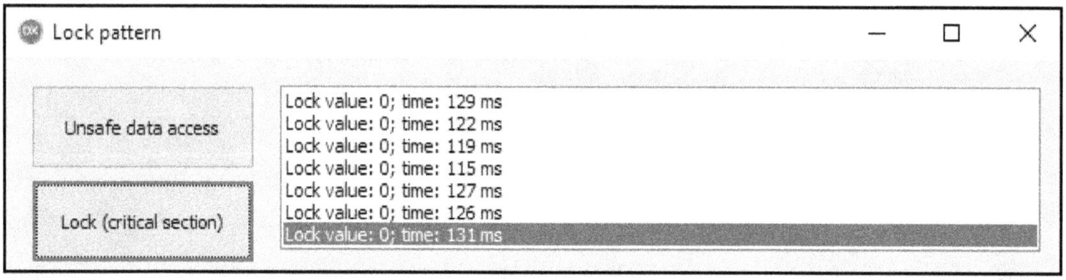

Locking with a critical section

We can immediately notice two things. First, the result is always correct! Second, the code now needs around 120 milliseconds to execute. Before the change, it needed only 8! Using critical sections will fix your program, but it will also make it run slower.

TIP One way to improve the code is to use interlocked instructions, namely `TInterlocked.Increment` and `TInterlocked.Decrement`. They implement locking at the CPU level. As they can only be used in very specific circumstances, I will not discuss them in this book.

We are, however, not limited to using `TCriticalSection`. Operating systems support other synchronization concepts, such as mutexes and semaphores, which I will not explore in this book. I will instead show how to use the `TMonitor` class, which was introduced in Delphi 2009.

The `TMonitor` class is implemented in *System* and allows us (besides other functionality) to lock any Delphi object without the need to maintain a separate lock. This represents a big improvement over a critical section where we have to maintain a separate lock object.

To lock an object, `obj`, we simply call `TMonitor.Enter(obj)` and to unlock, we call `TMonitor.Exit(obj)`. As the name `TMonitor` (unfortunately) conflicts with the `TMonitor` class from the `Vcl.Forms` unit, we can also use the helper functions `MonitorEnter` and `MonitorExit`.

The **Lock (monitor)** button starts the `MonitorIncrementValue` and `MonitorDecrementValue` methods, which it uses to protect access to the shared `FSharedData`. They are implemented as follows:

```
procedure TfrmLock.MonitorIncrementValue;
var
  i: integer;
begin
  for i := 1 to CNumRepeats do
  begin
    System.TMonitor.Enter(Self);
    try
      Inc(FSharedData);
    finally
      System.TMonitor.Exit(Self);
    end;
  end;
end;

procedure TfrmLock.MonitorDecrementValue;
var
  i: integer;
begin
  for i := 1 to CNumRepeats do
  begin
    MonitorEnter(Self);
```

```
        try
          Dec(FSharedData);
        finally
          MonitorExit(Self);
        end;
      end;
    end;
```

To demonstrate two possible ways of locking/unlocking an object, each method uses one approach. In practice, of course, you will decide on one. I'm always using `MonitorEnter`/`MonitorExit` as it requires less typing.

The code also uses a non-obvious trick. `TMonitor` can only be used to lock objects and our shared data is not an object. To simplify the code, the program simply locks the form object itself (Self). This would be a bad habit in a complex program and should be reserved for testing and trivial examples.

Let's see how `TMonitor` fares in practice. The following screenshot shows the results of a few consecutive runs:

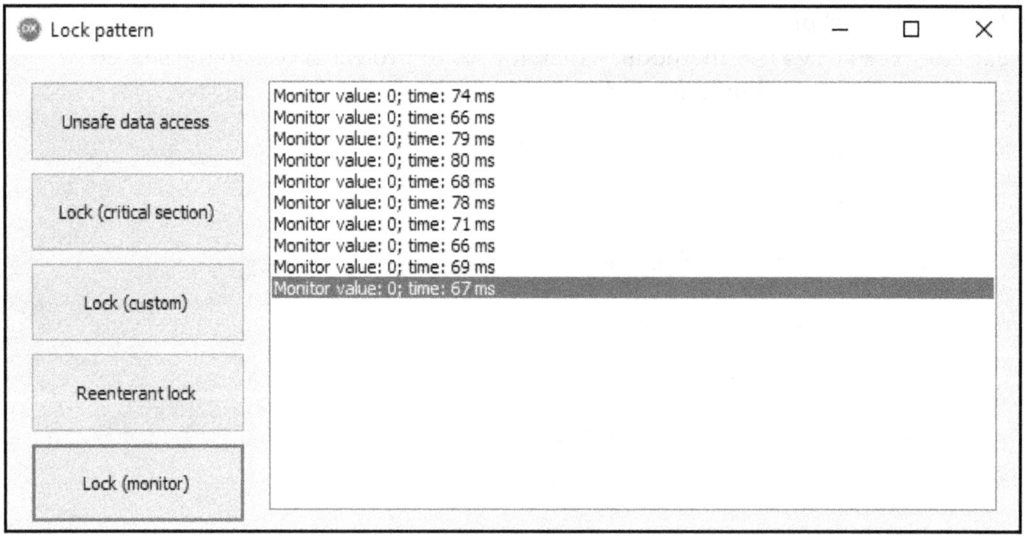

Locking with TMonitor

Not only is the result correct, but the code is now much faster! This gives us another good reason (besides not requiring a separate lock object) to use it for locking.

Custom locking mechanism

It is actually not that hard to implement a lock pattern in our code without using any external implementation. We only need a little help in the form of the `TInterlocked` class that I mentioned previously. The **Lock (custom)** button on the demonstration program activates two methods that use this approach.

The code uses an integer field called `FCustomLock: integer` as a lock. The logic is very simple; when this field contains a value of 0, access is granted. If the value is 1, access is locked.

The main program creates two threads, one executing `CustomLockIncrementValue` and another executing `CustomLockDecrementingValue`. The former is shown here:

```
procedure TfrmLock.CustomLockIncrementValue;
var
  i: integer;
begin
  for i := 1 to CNumRepeats do
  begin
    CustomAcquire(FCustomLock);
    try
      Inc(FSharedData);
    finally
      CustomRelease(FCustomLock);
    end;
  end;
end;
```

As with the previous examples, the pattern is lock-use-unlock. The `CustomRelease` method is very simple. It just stores a zero into the lock field, as shown here:

```
procedure TfrmLock.CustomRelease(var lock: integer);
begin
  lock := 0;
end;
```

The `CustomAcquire` method, however, is not so simple. It executes code that functions like this:

```
procedure CustomAcquireBad(var lock: integer);
begin
  while lock <> 0 do
    ;
  lock := 1;
end;
```

This code waits for the lock to become unlocked and then sets it to 1 to lock the access. This implementation, however, would fail in a multithreaded environment. Imagine the following scenario:

- The lock is unlocked
- Thread A reaches the `while` statement. As the lock is unlocked, `while` does not execute
- Thread B reaches the `while` statement. The lock is still unlocked, so `while` does not execute
- Thread A locks the lock
- Thread B locks the lock

The lock is now locked, but both threads think that they own the lock and both threads continue operation.

We need to execute this loop *and* set operation atomically, that is, in one indivisible step, and the correct way to do that is to use the appropriate CPU instructions. Instead of supporting each platform separately, however, it is better to use the platform-independent class `TInterlocked` from the `System.SyncObjs` unit. We can then rewrite the code as follows:

```
procedure TfrmLock.CustomAcquire(var lock: integer);
begin
  while TInterlocked.CompareExchange(lock, 1, 0) <> 0 do
    ;
end;
```

This code uses the very helpful `CompareExchange` method, which works as follows:

- It compares the first parameter (lock) with the third parameter (`0`)
- If both are the same, it sets the first parameter to the second parameter (`1`)
- In both cases, the code returns the original value of the first parameter

All three steps are executed as one indivisible unit.

The `CustomAcquire` method calls `CompareExchange`. If the old value of `lock` is `0`, it will set it to `1` and return `0`. The `while` loop will then exit. If the old value of `lock` is `1`, `CompareExchange` will not change it and will return `1` (old value). The `while` loop will then repeat the `CompareExchange` call.

If two threads call this code at the same time, only one `CompareExchange` will win. It will see the `lock` value as `0` and will set it to `1` and exit. The other one will see it as `1` and will wait until it is set to `0`.

If you run the code and test this lock, you will see that it a) works and b) runs slower than a critical section, which brings forth the question: why would we want to use such a custom solution if it is slower and more complicated?

In most cases, the answer is simple—we wouldn't. It is better and much safer to use an existing solution. In some cases, however, we could use such tricks to conserve memory usage. The *Lock striping pattern* section, later in this chapter will extend this approach to a more meaningful solution.

This custom lock also demonstrates one aspect of locks that I have not yet mentioned. Locks can be reentrant or non-reentrant. A reentrant lock can be acquired again in the same thread (after which we also need an additional release call to unlock it). Simply put, a reentrant lock allows us to run the following code:

```
lock.Acquire;
lock.Acquire;
ModifySharedValue;
lock.Release;
// lock is still owned by this thread
lock.Release
// lock is now unlocked
```

A non-reentrant lock does not support such usage. The previous example would stop forever in the second `Acquire` call if the `lock` is a non-reentrant lock.

This code looks stupid, but in practice, and especially when adapting legacy code, this second lock may be hidden in some other code that is called from `ModifySharedValue`. The Reentrant lock button on the demonstration program shows how such a situation may be reached. One thread, for example, executes the `LockReenterIncrementValue` method, which is shown here:

```
procedure TfrmLock.ChangeValue(var value: integer; delta: integer);
begin
  FLock.Acquire;
  try
    value := value + delta;
```

```
    finally
      FLock.Release;
    end;
  end;

  procedure TfrmLock.LockReenterIncrementValue;
  var
    i: integer;
  begin
    for i := 1 to CNumRepeats do
    begin
      FLock.Acquire;
      try
        ChangeValue(FSharedData, +1);
      finally
        FLock.Release;
      end;
    end;
  end;
```

This method locks access to `FSharedData` and then calls `ChangeValue`, which locks/unlocks access again. This is only possible because a `TCriticalSection` implements a reentrant lock.

TIP: `TMonitor` also implements a reentrant lock. Our custom solution, however, is non-reentrant.

Before I end this discussion on locking, I must mention another problem that locks introduce (besides slowing the program down). If we want to put together multiple parts of code that use locking, we must understand how locks are used in the original code if we want to write a correct program.

Imagine the following situation. A banking system uses the `Deposit` method that uses locking to guarantee that an account is not modified by anyone else while the method is operating. It also uses a `Withdraw` method that locks the account for the same reason. Let's say that they are implemented with the following pseudocode:

```
procedure Deposit(money, account);
begin
  lock(account);
  put money into account;
  unlock(account);
end;
```

```
procedure Withdraw(money, account);
begin
  lock(account);
  take money from account;
  unlock(account);
end;
```

This locking, however, doesn't help us when we want to transfer money from one account to another. So, the following approach doesn't work:

```
procedure Transfer(money, from, to);
begin
  Withdraw(money, from);
  Deposit(money, to);
end;
```

After `Withdraw` has executed but before `Deposit` starts, both accounts are unlocked and in a consistent state, but money cannot be found in any of them!

This is not acceptable, and to fix it we need to know how both `Deposit` and `Withdraw` are implemented internally and how they use locks. We can then write the fixed implementation, as follows:

```
procedure Transfer(money, from, to);
begin
  lock(from); lock(to);
  Withdraw(money, from);
  Deposit(money, to);
  unlock(to); unlock(from);
end;
```

We, therefore, cannot just put operations that use locking together to create more complicated operations. We can also say that locks don't compose.

Such an approach of locking multiple locks before executing the critical code can also bring the program into deadlock. Let's say that the following two calls are executed at exactly the same time in two threads:

```
Transfer(100, accA, accB);
Transfer(100, accB, accA);
```

In other words, we want to transfer the same amount of money from one account to another and back, at exactly the same time. The code will then run like so:

- The first thread locks the accA account (`lock(from)`).
- The second thread locks the accB account (`lock(from)`).
- The first thread tries to lock the accB account (`lock(to)`). As it is already locked, the thread starts waiting.
- The second thread tries to lock the accA account (`lock(to)`). As it is already locked, the thread starts waiting.
- The threads wait until the heat death of the universe or until someone kills the program.

In practice, this occurs when the code uses multiple locks but doesn't always lock them in the same order. For example, the demonstration program uses the following two methods to demonstrate a deadlock:

```
procedure TfrmLock.Lock12;
var
  i: integer;
begin
  for i := 1 to CNumRepeats do
  begin
    FLock.Acquire;
    FLock2.Acquire;

    FLock2.Release;
    FLock.Release;
  end;
end;

procedure TfrmLock.Lock21;
var
  i: integer;
begin
  for i := 1 to CNumRepeats do
  begin
    FLock2.Acquire;
    FLock.Acquire;

    FLock.Release;
    FLock2.Release;
  end;
end;
```

The first method locks `FLock` first and `FLock2` second. The second method has this order reversed.

If you click the Deadlock button, nothing will happen because both threads will block. If you click the pause button in the IDE (or select Run, Program Pause from the menu), the program will break into the debugger. At that moment, the Thread Status window will tell you that our two worker threads are waiting for each other, as shown in the following screenshot:

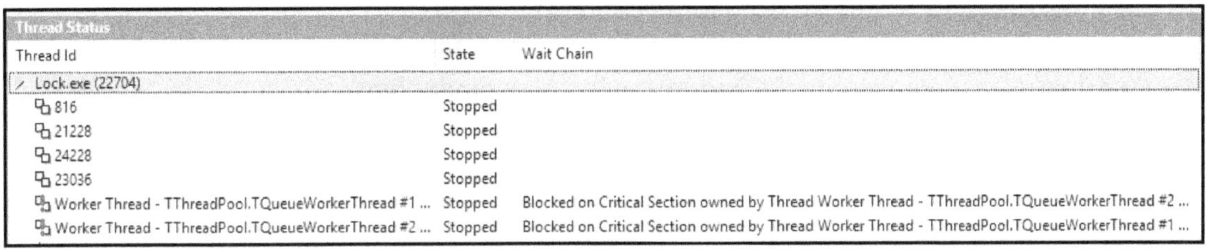
Thread Status
Thread Id
State
Wait Chain
Lock.exe (22704)
816
Stopped
21228
Stopped
24228
Stopped
23036
Stopped
Worker Thread - TThreadPool.TQueueWorkerThread #1 ...
Stopped
Blocked on Critical Section owned by Thread Worker Thread - TThreadPool.TQueueWorkerThread #2 ...
Worker Thread - TThreadPool.TQueueWorkerThread #2 ...
Stopped
Blocked on Critical Section owned by Thread Worker Thread - TThreadPool.TQueueWorkerThread #1 ...

Two deadlocked threads

The solution is to always lock in the same order. If you, for example, change `Lock21` to acquire `FLock` first and `FLock2` second, the code will work correctly.

> TIP: The order of `Release` calls is not important.

In practice, this situation is frequently hard to find because both `Acquire` calls will not appear next to each other, but will be scattered around the code. The simplest solution is to use a helper function that locks all required locks and calls that function when entering any area of code that requires these locks. If you are using a reentrant lock, the original code can then acquire locks again in any order. That will work because all locks will already be acquired.

Lock striping

In the previous section, I recommended using one lock per shared resource. We also saw that sometimes we cannot do such fine-grained locking and that we have to implement locks that protect more than one resource at the same time.

The lock striping pattern covers the opposite case. Sometimes, one lock per resource is not enough. On some occasions, we may want to implement multiple locks for one shared resource. We could, for example, add a lock to each element in an array or list.

> Imagine the fitting rooms in a clothing store. They are not protected with one master lock as that would prevent multiple customers from trying out clothes at the same time. Rather, each room has its own lock.

This pattern can only be applied when the size of the shared resource is not modified during the execution. It does not help us if we lock two elements in an array and then another thread ignores these locks and removes one element between them, shifting the data around.

It can also be expensive (in terms of time and memory usage) to maintain all these additional locks. Later in this section, I'll show you how we can implement a custom locking mechanism that only uses one additional bit. If we can find one bit of data that is not used in the program, we can use it as a lock. Such an implementation needs no additional memory and doesn't have to manage additional locks.

To demonstrate the lock striping pattern, the LockStriping program in the Lock striping folder shuffles a deck of cards with four parallel threads.

For simplicity, the cards are represented by a number from 0 to 51. They are stored in a dynamic integer array called TArray<integer> and are generated with the following method:

```
function TfrmLockStriping.GenerateData: TArray<integer>;
var
  i: integer;
begin
  SetLength(Result, 52);
  for i := 0 to 51 do
    Result[i] := i + 1;
end;
```

> The program ignores the actual names of the cards. You can write your own function that maps from the integer range 0–51 to card names for practice. For example, numbers from 0 to 12 could represent one suite, numbers from 13 to 25 another, and so on.

To shuffle the deck, the program starts four parallel threads, which all repeat the following two steps 100,000 times:

- Select two cards
- Exchange these two cards

The following code is used to select two cards. It simply calculates two random numbers from 0 to 51 and returns them in two `var` parameters, as follows:

```
procedure TfrmLockStriping.PickTwo(dataLen: integer; var idx1, idx2:
integer);
var
  temp: integer;
begin
  idx1 := Random(dataLen);
  idx2 := Random(dataLen);
  if idx1 > idx2 then
  begin
    temp := idx1;
    idx1 := idx2;
    idx2 := temp;
  end;
end;
```

The code guarantees that `idx2` is always equal to or greater than `idx1`. This will become important once we implement the lock striping pattern.

The selection algorithm doesn't access any shared resource (the process just creates two random numbers). That is not true for the code that exchanges two cards as it must modify the shared resource—the deck of cards. One possible solution is to simply use a lock pattern to get exclusive access to the deck before two cards are switched.

The following method generates a deck, starts shuffling threads, waits for them to finish, and logs the state of the shuffled deck, all with a master lock we'll call, well, `lock`:

```
procedure TfrmLockStriping.btnMasterLockClick(Sender: TObject);
var
  data: TArray<integer>;
  lock: TCriticalSection;
  time_ms: int64;
begin
  data := GenerateData;
  lock := TCriticalSection.Create;
  try
    time_ms := RunTasks(
      procedure
```

```
      var
        iShuffle: integer;
      begin
        for iShuffle := 1 to CNumShuffles do
          ExchangeTwoMaster(lock, data);
      end);
    LogData('Master lock', time_ms, data);
    VerifyData(data);
  finally
    FreeAndNil(lock);
  end;
end;
```

Threads are started in the `RunTasks` method, which is not important for this discussion. You can look it up in the source code.

The actual shuffling is implemented in the `ExchangeTwoMaster` method, which takes two parameters, a master lock and a dynamic array that is to be shuffled. The code selects two cards, locks the master lock, exchanges the cards, and unlocks the master lock, as follows:

```
procedure TfrmLockStriping.ExchangeTwoMaster(lock: TCriticalSection;
  const data: TArray<integer>);
var
  idx1: Integer;
  idx2: Integer;
  temp: Integer;
begin
  PickTwo(Length(data), idx1, idx2);
  if idx1 = idx2 then
    Exit;

  lock.Acquire;
  try
    temp := data[idx1];
    data[idx1] := data[idx2];
    data[idx2] := temp;
  finally
    lock.Release;
  end;
end;
```

As an optimization step, the code also immediately exits (without locking) if the `PickTwo` method has picked the same card twice.

TIP

To verify that locking is indeed required in this case, just comment out the `Acquire` and `Release` calls and run the program. You will see that shuffling now generates an invalid deck in which some numbers (some cards) are repeating.

This code works and you can immediately test it by running the demonstration program and clicking on the Master lock button. But we can do better than that. Let's look at the card switching code again:

```
temp := data[idx1];
data[idx1] := data[idx2];
data[idx2] := temp;
```

This code actually doesn't have to protect the whole deck of cards. It only requires access to elements with indices `idx1` and `idx2`, so we only need to protect access to these two elements. Other threads can do whatever they want with the rest of the deck while this exchange is in progress.

Instead of using a master lock, we can implement the lock striping pattern by generating 52 critical sections. Each critical section protects one element of the card deck array.

The `btnSeparateLocksClick` method generates such an array of locks, then runs the testing code, and at the end, cleans up all additional locks. The rest of the code is mostly the same as before, except that an `ExchangeTwoSeparate` method is called to exchange two cards, as follows:

```
procedure TfrmLockStriping.btnSeparateLocksClick(Sender: TObject);
var
  data: TArray<integer>;
  locks: TArray<TCriticalSection>;
  time_ms: int64;
  i: Integer;
begin
  data := GenerateData;
  SetLength(locks, Length(data));
  for i := Low(locks) to High(locks) do
    locks[i] := TCriticalSection.Create;
  try
    time_ms := RunTasks(
      procedure
      var
        iShuffle: integer;
      begin
      for iShuffle := 1 to CNumShuffles do
        ExchangeTwoSeparate(locks, data);
      end);
```

```
    LogData('Separate locks', time_ms, data);
    VerifyData(data);
  finally
    for i := Low(locks) to High(locks) do
    locks[i].Free;
  end;
end;
```

The card-exchanging method again receives two parameters, but this time the first parameter represents the whole array of additional locks. As shown in the following code, the code selects two cards, locks both cards, exchanges them, unlocks, and exits:

```
procedure TfrmLockStriping.ExchangeTwoSeparate(
  const locks: TArray<TCriticalSection>; const data: TArray<integer>);
var
  idx1: Integer;
  idx2: Integer;
  temp: Integer;
begin
  PickTwo(Length(data), idx1, idx2);
  if idx1 = idx2 then
    Exit;

  locks[idx1].Acquire;
  try
    locks[idx2].Acquire;
    try
      temp := data[idx1];
      data[idx1] := data[idx2];
      data[idx2] := temp;
    finally
      locks[idx2].Release;
    end;
  finally
    locks[idx1].Release;
  end;
end;
```

We can now see why `PickTwo` returns an ordered pair of cards. As we are locking two critical sections, we must always lock them in the same order, otherwise the code can deadlock. The simplest way to enforce the order is to always lock the critical section with smaller index first.

The following screenshot shows the program after the cards were shuffled five times with a **Master lock** algorithm and five times with a lock striping algorithm:

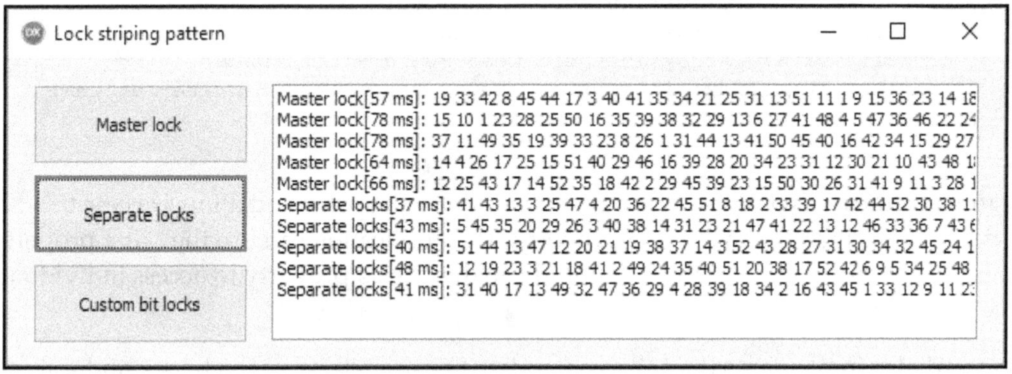

Comparing master lock with lock striping

We can see that both algorithms shuffle the deck (no surprise here) and that a lock striping approach is indeed faster. The pattern, therefore, works at least in this case, but it is quite awkward to implement with all the additional locks that we have to maintain. We can fix this problem by implementing a custom locking method that reuses one bit of data for locking purposes.

Single bit locks

Getting one bit of data is not as hard as you may think. In our case, for example, most of the `integer` data type that's used to store a card number is unused. We only need 6 bits to represent numbers from 0 to 51, which means that the other 24 bits are unused. In most cases, you'll be able to find one such spare bit in existing data (if not, you can still implement lock striping by introducing additional locks).

To make the code clearer, I have extracted the logic that maintains the lock-striped array of cards into a separate record of type `TLockStripingArray`. It is defined in the `LockStripingArray` unit, as follows:

```
type
  TLockStripingArray = record
  private const
    CMaskBit = 31;
    CBitMask = 1 SHL CMaskBit;
  var
    FData: TArray<integer>;
```

```
    function GetItem(idx: integer): integer; inline;
    procedure SetItem(idx: integer; const value: integer); inline;
  public
    procedure Acquire(idx: integer); inline;
    procedure Release(idx: integer); inline;
    property Data: TArray<integer> read FData write FData;
    property Items[idx: integer]: integer read GetItem write SetItem;
      default;
  end;
```

This record stores a dynamic integer array in its `Data` property and allows access to individual items through the `Items` property. The application can use the `Data` property to initialize the record, but after that, it should use the `Items` property to access individual items.

The record also implements the `Acquire` and `Release` methods, which lock and unlock a specific item. All of this is used in the main program, as follows:

```
procedure TfrmLockStriping.btnCustomLocksClick(Sender: TObject);
var
  data: TLockStripingArray;
  time_ms: int64;
begin
  data.Data := GenerateData;
  time_ms := RunTasks(
    procedure
    var
      iShuffle: integer;
    begin
      for iShuffle := 1 to CNumShuffles do
        ExchangeTwoCustom(data);
    end);
  LogData('Custom bit lock', time_ms, data.Data);
  VerifyData(data.Data);
end;
```

This code is the simplest of all three approaches as it doesn't have to maintain any locks at all. The item exchanging method `ExchangeTwoCustom`, shown in the following code, still has to lock and unlock array elements and is almost identical to the lock striping implementation `ExchangeTwoSeparate`:

```
procedure TfrmLockStriping.ExchangeTwoCustom(
  const data: TLockStripingArray);
var
  idx1: Integer;
  idx2: Integer;
  temp: Integer;
```

```
begin
  PickTwo(Length(data.Data), idx1, idx2);
  if idx1 = idx2 then
    Exit;

  data.Acquire(idx1);
  try
    data.Acquire(idx2);
    try
      temp := data.Data[idx1];
      data.Data[idx1] := data.Data[idx2];
      data.Data[idx2] := temp;
    finally
      data.Release(idx2);
    end;
  finally
    data.Release(idx1);
  end;
end;
```

The locking implementation is very similar to the custom solution from the section on the lock pattern from the *Lock* section.It uses the highest integer bit- bit 31-to represent a lock. If the bit is 0, the integer is not locked. Setting the bit to 1 acquires a lock.

As with the previous custom implementation, releasing a lock is simple. We merely have to clear bit 31, as follows:

```
procedure TLockStripingArray.Release(idx: integer);
begin
  FData[idx] := FData[idx] AND NOT CBitMask;
end;
```

If you are not familiar with Delphi bitwise operations (`AND NOT CBitMask`), don't worry. I will explain this concept later in this chapter.

To acquire a lock, we must again implement an atomic compare and set operation. If bit 31 is zero, we would like to set it to 1 and exit. If bit 31 is 1, we would like to wait until it becomes zero. The `Acquire` method implements this logic, as shown here:

```
procedure TLockStripingArray.Acquire(idx: integer);
var
  el: Integer;
begin
  while TInterlocked.BitTestAndSet(FData[idx], 31) do
    ;
end;
```

The `BitTestAndSet` method of the `TInterlocked` class does the heavy work. Similar to `CompareExchange`, which we have used before, it returns the previous state of the bit (`False` or `True` for 0 and 1) and sets the bit to 1. The `Acquire` method works as follows:

- If the bit 31 is 0, it is set to 1 and `False` is returned. The `While` loop then exits.
- If the bit 31 is 1, it is not changed and `True` is returned. The `While` loop then repeats.

As this is done atomically, the code works correctly in a multithreaded environment.

This covers the locking, but we must still do some additional work to correctly implement the `Items` properly. If, for example, we lock an element containing value 42, the bit 31 of that value gets set, turning 42 (or $2A) into $8000002A, or -2147483606. If we read the value at that time, we would get an invalid result (this is the reason why the `Data` property must not be used directly while the program is running). The `GetItem` function, therefore, strips bit 31 away and returns bits from 0 to 30, as follows:

```
function TLockStripingArray.GetItem(idx: integer): integer;
begin
  Result := FData[idx] AND NOT CBitMask;
end;
```

A reverse operation happens when the code is assigned to the `Items` property. The original bit 31 of the `FData` array must be preserved (as it indicates the lock state), and only other value bits must be modified. The `SetItem` implements this logic as follows:

```
procedure TLockStripingArray.SetItem(idx: integer; const value: integer);
begin
  FData[idx] := (value AND NOT CBitMask) OR (FData[idx] AND CBitMask);
end;
```

The following screenshot shows a comparison between an implementation with a critical section and a custom implementation with a lock bit:

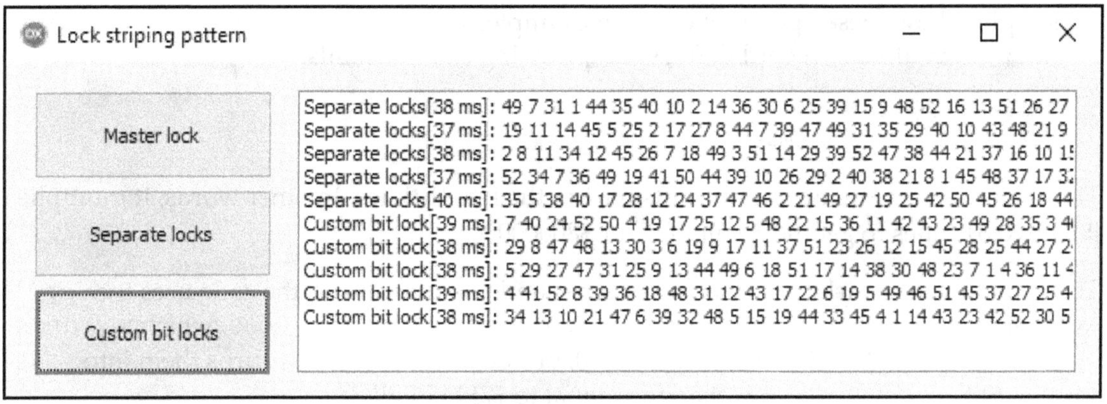

Comparing critical sections with custom bit locks

We can see that neither outperforms the other. The final choice, that is, using separate locks or stealing a data bit somewhere, is yours. Use whatever fits best into the architecture of your program.

Delphi idioms – bitwise operators

The standard logical operators `and`, `or`, `xor`, and `not` have an additional hidden side in Delphi. We can also use them to perform operations on individual bits of a number. Besides being logical operators, they also function as bitwise (bit by bit) operators.

The meaning of an operator, for example, `and`, is automatically detected from the context. When the compiler encounters a code like `a and b` and both `a` and `b` are Boolean variables (or expressions), `and` is compiled to a logical operator. If `a` and `b` are both an `integer` (or `word` or `NativeUInt`, or any other integer type), `and` is compiled to a bitwise operator. If `a` is an `integer` and `b` is a `boolean`, the compiler reports an error.

> To improve readability of code, I write logical operators in lower case (`and`, `or`, ...) and bitwise operators in upper case (`AND`, `OR`, ...).

Bitwise operators work exactly the same as logical operators, except that the operation is performed on each bit pair (taking into account that 0 is the same as `False` and 1 is the same as `True`). The operator combines bit 0 of both operands into bit 0 of the result, bit 1 of both operands into bit 0 of the result, and so on.

Let's explore how these operators work on examples from the custom bit locking code. The `TLockStripingArray` record defines the following two constants:

```
CMaskBit = 31;
 CBitMask = 1 SHL CMaskBit;
```

The `1 SHL CMaskBit` operation shifts bit 1 to the left 31 times. In other words, it multiplies it by two 31 times to get the result of 2^{31} or $80000000.

To get the reverse mask (where zeros are ones and ones are zeros), the code uses the expression `NOT CBitMask`. The `CBitMask` starts with binary `1000 0000`, which `NOT` turns into `0111 1111` or $7F. Other bytes are all 0, or `0000 0000`, and `NOT` turns them into `1111 1111` or $FF. `NOT CBitMask` is therefore equal to $7FFFFFFF.

To remove the lock bit from value, the code uses `AND NOT CBitMask`, which is the same as `AND $7FFFFFFF`. If, for example, the original value has a lock bit set, it must be in the form of $800000xy (the last two places are enough to represent all values from 0 to 51). The initial byte is calculated as `1000 0000 AND 0111 1111 = 0000 0000` (as with Boolean values, `0 AND 1 = 0` and `1 AND 1 = 1`). The highest bit is therefore removed. All middle bytes stay at zero because `0000 0000 AND 1111 1111 = 0000 0000`.

The last byte, which holds the actual card number, can be written as `00ab cdef`, where each letter represents one bit. When we `AND` it with `1111 1111`, we get the original value back. If `a` (or any other bit) is 0, `0 AND 1 = 0` and the result is 0. If `a` is 1, `1 AND 1 = 1` and the result is 1. `AND 1`, therefore, leaves the original bit unchanged.

To merge a value and the lock bit, the code executes the following expression:

```
(value AND NOT CBitMask) OR (FData[idx] AND CBitMask)
```

As we are using bit 31 to represent a lock, it must not be used for data; therefore, we must remove it with `value AND NOT CBitMask` (we have already seen how that works). The code then extracts the state of the current lock bit with `FData[idx] AND CBitMask`. This will give us either $00000000 (if the value is not locked) or $80000000 (if it is).

Both values are then combined with `OR`. When we `OR` with 0, the result will be the same as the original bit (`0 OR 0 = 0`, `1 OR 0 = 1`). All `value` bits (from 0 to 30) will, therefore, be left unchanged. The highest bit, which is 0 in `value AND NOT CBitMask`, is OR-ed with the current lock bit (0 or 1). That leaves the lock bit unchanged (`0 OR 0 = 0`, `0 OR 1 = 1`).

The result, therefore, takes the highest bit from `FData[idx]` and all other bits from `value`, which is exactly what we need.

The following table will help you write such bitwise expressions:

Expression	Result
NOT 0	1
NOT 1	0
x OR 0	x
x OR 1	1
x OR y	y OR x
x AND 0	0
x AND 1	x
x AND y	y AND x

Double-checked locking

When we are writing code that sometimes requires some object to be created, and sometimes not, we can save some execution time by only creating this object when it is needed. This process-lazy initialization is explained in `Chapter 10`, *Singleton, Dependency Injection, Lazy Initialization, and Object Pool*. That chapter, however, only covered single-threaded applications.

To do lazy initialization properly in a multithreaded world, we need locking. And to do it correctly and fast, we need a double-checked locking pattern. This pattern can speed up any lock that is only acquired if some condition is met. It is also called *test, lock, and test again*.

For instance, when you are changing lanes in a car, you check the traffic around you first, then turn on your indicator, check the traffic again, and then change lane.

In the demonstration program `DoubleCheckedLocking` from the `Double-checked locking` folder, the `TLazyOwner` class functions as an owner that can create a field called `FLazy: TLazyObject` on demand. Both classes are defined as follows:

```
type
  TLazyObject = class
  public
    constructor Create;
    destructor Destroy; override;
```

```
  end;

  TLazyOwner = class
  strict private
    FLazy: TLazyObject;
    FLock: TCriticalSection;
  public
    function DoubleChecked: TLazyObject;
    function LazySingleThreaded: TLazyObject;
    function LockAndCheck: TLazyObject;
    function TestAndLock: TLazyObject;
    constructor Create;
    destructor Destroy; override;
  end;
```

The code uses a standard test and create pattern to create the `FLazy` object in single-threaded code, as shown here:

```
function TLazyOwner.LazySingleThreaded: TLazyObject;
begin
  if not assigned(FLazy) then
    FLazy := TLazyObject.Create;
  Result := FLazy;
end;
```

The demonstration program then creates a `TLazyOwner` object, logs some information, accesses the lazily created objects, logs some more, and exits, as follows:

```
procedure TfrmDoubleChecked.btnLazyInitClick(Sender: TObject);
var
  lazy: TLazyObject;
  owner: TLazyOwner;
begin
  owner := TLazyOwner.Create;
  try
    Log('Execute some code ...');
    Log('Access lazy object...');
    lazy := owner.LazySingleThreaded;
    Log('Use lazy object ...');
    Log('Destroy lazy object ...');
  finally FreeAndNil(owner); end;
end;
```

If you run the program and click on the Lazy initialization button, you'll see in the log when the `TLazyObject` object is created and destroyed.

The problems occur when we want to lazily create a shared object in a multithreaded application. Multiple threads cannot just use a simple test and create algorithm, as it can result in lost objects, as shown here:

```
if not assigned(FLazy) then
  FLazy := TLazyObject.Create;
```

If two threads execute this at the same time, they would both decide that `FLazy` doesn't exist yet, they would both create a new `TLazyObject`, and they would both store it in the `FLazy` property. One would do that slightly before the other and its `FLazy` object will be lost because `FLazy` will be overwritten with the value generated in the second thread. The first object will stay lost in memory until the program is closed.

The simplest solution to this problem is to use a *lock* pattern. A lock and test algorithm in the function `LockAndCheck` enters a critical section, tests whether the object has already been created, and creates it if required. It is shown here:

```
function TLazyOwner.LockAndCheck: TLazyObject;
begin
  FLock.Acquire;
  try
    if not assigned(FLazy) then
      FLazy := TLazyObject.Create;
  finally
    FLock.Release;
  end;
  Result := FLazy;
end;
```

You already know that any introduction of locking slows down the program. Programmers that don't yet know the double-checked locking pattern frequently try to speed up the code by introducing a test and lock anti-pattern. The `TestAndLock` function shows how lazy creation should never be performed in the multithreaded environment, as follows:

```
function TLazyOwner.TestAndLock: TLazyObject;
begin
  // Bad implementation, do not use!
  if not assigned(FLazy) then
  begin
    FLock.Acquire;
    try
      FLazy := TLazyObject.Create;
    finally
```

```
        FLock.Release;
      end;
    end;
    Result := FLazy;
  end;
```

The code tests whether `FLazy` exists. If not, it enters a critical section, creates the object, and exits the critical section. This, however, doesn't fix anything. It is quite possible that `FLazy` was created in another thread after the `if` test passed and before the critical section was acquired which, again, results in a lost object!

A proper solution is to implement double-checked locking, or the test, lock, and test again pattern. The following `DoubleChecked` function shows how the test should be performed:

```
function TLazyOwner.DoubleChecked: TLazyObject;
begin
  if not assigned(FLazy) then
  begin
    FLock.Acquire;
    try
      if not assigned(FLazy) then
        FLazy := TLazyObject.Create;
    finally
      FLock.Release;
    end;
  end;
  Result := FLazy;
end;
```

The code first tests whether `FLazy` is assigned. If not, it enters the critical section and performs the same test again. In a way, the whole initialization is still executed inside the critical section. The initial `if` statement is just an optimization step that prevents the critical section from being unnecessarily acquired once the object is created.

We could rewrite the function as follows and it would perform the same action:

```
function TLazyOwner.DoubleChecked: TLazyObject;
begin
  if not assigned(FLazy) then
    Result := LockAndCheck;
end;
```

It can still happen that two threads execute the `if` statement at the same time and both enter the `LockAndCheck` method, but as this method does both (test and create) in one atomic step, only one object would be created.

The test code runs two threads and inside each calls the object creation method one million times. The following screenshot shows a comparison of the three initialization methods:

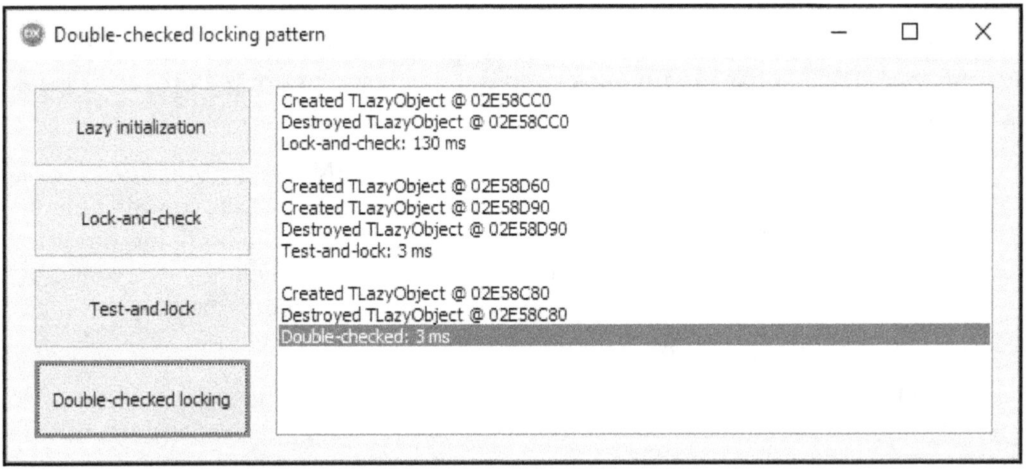

Comparing the "lock and test", "test and lock", and "test, lock, and test again" algorithms

The initial approach of locking and testing does the job in 130 milliseconds. Bad test and lock implementation is much faster. It runs in 3 milliseconds, but it creates two `TLazyObject` objects. The double-checked locking approach takes the best aspects from both, and as a result, the code is correct and fast.

Optimistic locking

We saw before that locks can sometimes be replaced with interlocked operations and we also used such operations to implement custom-made locking. Interlocked operations are also the basis for the optimistic locking pattern, which can be used to implement changes in shared data without using a classical locking mechanism.

Optimistic locking works when a chance of conflict between threads is very low. Like a database transaction mechanism, optimistic locking assumes that there will be no problem and applies required modifications on its own copy of the data (creates a new object, for example). In the second step, optimistic locking tries to commit the change. With one atomic step (usually implemented with an interlocked instruction), the current state is replaced with a new value.

This atomic replacement can, however, fail (if the state was modified by another thread in the meantime). In such a case, optimistic locking must revert the change (roll back a transaction). As such, this locking may result in duplicate work.

Even though it may sometimes do something twice, optimistic locking can work faster than a classical approach because modifying shared data with an interlocked operation is faster than acquiring and releasing a lock.

> In modern version control systems, such as SVN and git, you don't lock a file that you want to change. Instead, you modify the file, commit a new version to the version control system, and hope that nobody has modified the same lines of the same file in the meantime. In the unlikely event of a conflict, you have to spend some additional time fixing the problem (merging the changes).

We can use optimistic locking to implement lazy initialization without any additional lock. We already know how to do it with the double-checked locking pattern, as demonstrated in the following pseudocode:

```
if object is not yet created then
begin
  acquire lock;
  if object is not yet created then
    shared object := create object;
  release lock;
  return shared object;
end;
```

With optimistic locking, this algorithm changes to the following:

```
if object is not yet created then
begin
  temp object := create object;
  if not atomically store temp object into shared object then
    destroy temp object;
  return shared object;
end;
```

The `OptimisticLocking` project from the `Optimistic locking` folder implements this pattern to lazily initialize an object. The program has the same structure as the `DoubleCheckedLocking` program from the previous section and implements the same double-checked locking algorithm. This allows us to compare the results of both techniques.

Optimistic lazy initialization is implemented in the `Optimistic` method, as follows:

```
function TLazyOwner.Optimistic: TLazyObject;
var
  tempLazy: TLazyObject;
begin
  if not assigned(FLazy) then
  begin
    tempLazy := TLazyObject.Create;
    if TInterlocked.CompareExchange(pointer(FLazy), tempLazy, nil) <> nil
then
      FreeAndNil(tempLazy);
  end;
  Result := FLazy;
end;
```

The code first checks whether the `FLazy` field has already been created. If not, it assumes that there will be no problems and creates a new `TLazyObject`. As we cannot write into the shared `FLazy` field without special care, we have to store the newly-created object in a temporary variable.

After that, the code uses the interlocked `CompareExchange` instruction to store a new object in the `FLazy` field if `FLazy` is still nil. If `FLazy` has been modified between the `if` and `CompareExchange`, the latter will return a non-nil value (an object that was created in another thread), which is a signal for the `Optimistic` method to throw the temporary object away.

If you run the program, you'll see that both approaches, double-checked locking and optimistic locking, need the same time to execute the code. This is not surprising as both methods create the object only once. Most of the time, they just test the `if not assigned(FLazy)` condition and then do nothing. The following screenshot proves that:

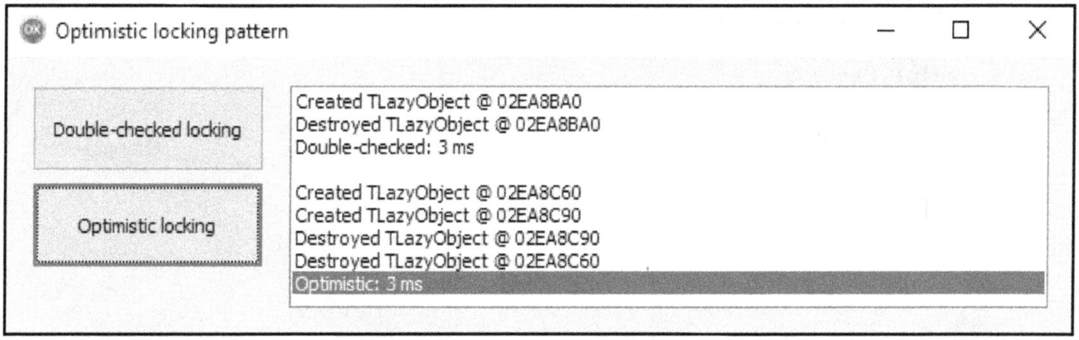

Comparing double-checked locking and optimistic locking

This screenshot also shows that in optimistic locking, one object too many was created and thrown away.

To really compare the execution speed, I had to create a version of the program that repeats the test 100,000 times (you can find it in the `OptimisticLockingSpeedTest` project). This results in the lazy object also being created 100,000 times, and that gives us a measurable result. The following screenshot shows the result of this modified program:

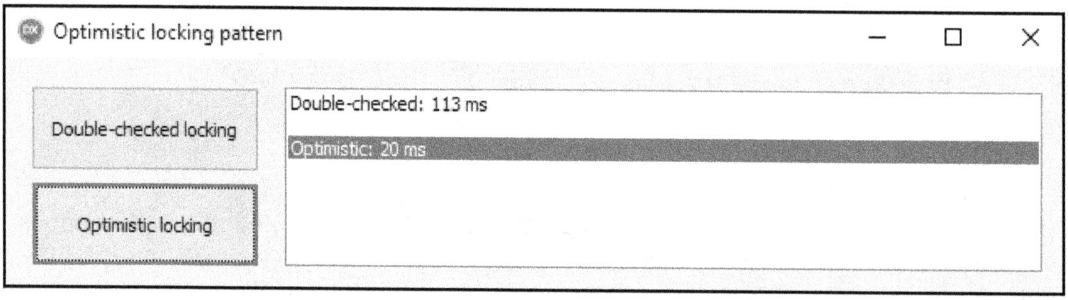

Comparing 100,000 executions of double-checked and optimistic locking

As I mentioned in `Chapter 10`, *Singleton, Dependency Injection, Lazy Initialization, and Object Pool,* we can use the Spring4D library to lazily initialize objects. As Spring4D implementation supports multithreading, let's take a look at the technique used in the library. The following method can be found in the Spring unit:

```
class function TLazyInitializer.EnsureInitialized<T>(var target: T): T;
var
  value: T;
begin
  if target = nil then
  begin
    value := T.Create;
    if AtomicCmpExchange(PPointer(@target)^, PPointer(@value)^, nil) <> nil
then
      value.Free;
  end;
  Result := target;
end;
```

As we can see, it is almost the same as the `Optimistic` method except that it uses `AtomicCmpExchange` and not `TInterlocked.CompareExchange`. The latter (which lives in the `System.SyncObjs` unit) is actually implemented as an `inline` function, which directly calls the `AtomicCmpExchange` function (from the *System* unit) as follows:

```
class function TInterlocked.CompareExchange(var Target: Pointer;
  Value: Pointer; Comparand: Pointer): Pointer;
begin
  Result := AtomicCmpExchange(Target, Value, Comparand);
end;
```

In most cases, both will compile to the same code because of the `inline` directive. The difference between the two is that `AtomicCmpExchange` doesn't require us to list the SyncObjs unit in the `uses` clause. You can use whichever you want.

Readers-writer lock

All the locking mechanisms that I have discussed so far were designed for *symmetric* scenarios. In all examples, they were synchronizing multiple threads that were all doing (more or less) the same work. This is, however, not the only type of shared data access we can encounter.

Another frequent situation that occurs in multithreaded applications is when multiple threads are just reading from the shared data without doing any modifications. That by itself would not require any locking at all, except that from time to time, the data has to be modified. To do that, we somehow have to stop the reading threads. We must also, as before, prevent two writers from working on the data at the same time.

In such a situation, we need a synchronization mechanism that allows multiple *readers* to *share* the resource while also allowing one *writer* to acquire *exclusive* access to the resource when necessary. We call such a synchronization mechanism a *readers-writer* or *shared-exclusive* lock (other names are also used in the literature and on the internet, including **multiple readers, single writer** *(***MRSW***)*, **multiple readers, exclusive writer** *(***MREW***)*, **single writer, multiple readers** *(***SWMR***)*, and more).

This design allows readers who are the most frequent users of the resource to work at the same time. Where there's a need to modify the resource, the writer requests exclusive access, which blocks all readers, modifies the resource, and unlocks it.

A road is a resource that was designed for sharing. Multiple cars are using it at the same time. When there's a need to modify the road (paint new road marks, fix the pavement, and so on), they have to close down the traffic so that the road is exclusively available to the maintenance crew.

Readers-writer lock is a complicated mechanism that can be implemented in many different ways. As with normal locks, it can be reentrant or non-reentrant. A reentrant lock can be acquired again for the same level of access after it has been acquired once.

A reentrant lock allows a read (shared) lock to be acquired again for the read (shared) access but not for a write (exclusive) access. Turning a reader into a writer without dropping the lock in the meantime is only possible if the locking mechanism supports that. A lock that enables such a promotion is called **upgradeable** or **promotable**. A lock may also allow a writer to be changed into a reader, in which case we call it **downgradeable**.

Readers-writer lock implementations also differ in how they handle requests for write access. If at least one reader is active, a writer cannot get access immediately. It has to wait for that reader to release the lock. If in the meantime, another thread requests read access, the lock can respond in two ways.

A read-biased or read-preferring lock will immediately grant read access to the new thread. Such an implementation is faster, but can lead to writer starvation. If at least one reader exists at all times, a writer can never get access to the resource.

An alternative approach implemented by a writer-biased or write-preferring lock would, in such an event, block the new reader. With such an implementation, a reader can never get access to the shared resource while at least one writer is waiting its turn. This prevents writer starvation, but requires a more complicated implementation, which makes the lock perform slower.

The name *readers-writer* may suggest that you can only have one writer thread. That is not true. You most certainly *can* have more than one, but they can only get write access one at a time.

Delphi comes with a custom implementation of a readers-writer lock in the form of a `TMultiReadExclusiveWriteSynchronizer` class, which can be found in the `System.SysUtils` unit. As typing that long name is not good for your fingers, the same unit also defines a shorter alias: `TMREWSync`.

This synchronize is only available on Windows. On other supported platforms, `TMultiReadExclusiveWriteSynchronizer` is just an alias for the `TSimpleRWSync` class. They both implement the same interface, `IReadWriteSync`, which exposes readers-writer functionality. The following code fragment will help you understand the relationship between these classes on different platforms:

```
type
  IReadWriteSync = interface ['{7B108C52-1D8F-4CDB-9CDF-57E071193D3F}']
    procedure BeginRead;
    procedure EndRead;
    function BeginWrite: Boolean;
    procedure EndWrite;
  end;

  TSimpleRWSync = class(TInterfacedObject, IReadWriteSync)
    ...
  end;

{$IFDEF MSWINDOWS}
  TMultiReadExclusiveWriteSynchronizer = class(TInterfacedObject,
IReadWriteSync)
    ...
  end;
{$ELSE}
  TMultiReadExclusiveWriteSynchronizer = TSimpleRWSync;
{$ENDIF}

  TMREWSync = TMultiReadExclusiveWriteSynchronizer;
```

The big difference between `TSimpleRWSync` and Windows-only `TMultiReadExclusiveWriteSynchronizer` is that the latter is a true readers-writer lock, while the former simply functions as a wrapper around a `TMonitor` lock. By using `TSimpleRWSync`, the code will only support one simultaneous reader.

This approach allows multiplatform programs to use `TMREWSync` on all platforms. On Windows, the code will benefit from multiple readers working in parallel, while on other platforms it will not work as fast, but at least it will still work.

Another possibility is to use the Slim Reader/Writer synchronisation mechanism, which has been part of the Windows operating system since Windows Vista. To help you use this implementation, I have written a simple class called `TSlimReaderWriter`, which wraps the Windows API and exposes it through the `IReadWriteSync` interface. It is implemented in the `SlimReaderWriter` unit and is defined as follows:

```
type
  IReadWriteSyncEx = interface ['{21BDDB51-29B4-44A4-B80A-1E5D72FB43DA}']
    function TryBeginRead: Boolean;
    function TryBeginWrite: Boolean;
  end;

  TSlimReaderWriter = class(TInterfacedObject, IReadWriteSync,
IReadWriteSyncEx)
  public
    constructor Create;
    procedure BeginRead;
    function BeginWrite: Boolean;
    procedure EndRead;
    procedure EndWrite;
    function TryBeginRead: Boolean;
    function TryBeginWrite: Boolean;
  end;
```

Comparing reader-writer implementations

To compare different implementations, I have prepared a test program called `ReadersWriterLock` stored in the `Readers-writer lock` folder. This program starts six reader threads that process a shared list and one writer thread that modifies this list ten times per second.

A method, `RunTests`, which you can look up in the code, accepts a `IReadWriteSync` interface and runs the tests on it. The form contains three buttons, each one to run tests on a specific implementation, as follows:

```
procedure TfrmReadersWriter.btnMREWClick(Sender: TObject);
begin
  RunTests('TMREWSync', TMREWSync.Create);
end;

procedure TfrmReadersWriter.btnSimpleRWClick(Sender: TObject);
begin
  RunTests('TSimpleRWSync', TSimpleRWSync.Create);
end;
```

```
procedure TfrmReadersWriter.btnSRWClick(Sender: TObject);
begin
  RunTests('TSlimReaderWriter', TSlimReaderWriter.Create);
end;
```

The reader thread runs the `TestReader` method, which accepts a shared resource called `list` and a readers-writer lock called `mrew`, as follows:

```
function TfrmReadersWriter.TestReader(list: TList<integer>;
  const mrew: IReadWriteSync): integer;
var
  a: real;
  el: Integer;
  timer: TStopwatch;
  i: Integer;
begin
  Result := 0;
  timer := TStopwatch.StartNew;
  while timer.ElapsedMilliseconds < (CTestDuration_sec * 1000) do
  begin
    mrew.BeginRead;
    try
      for el in list do
      begin
        a := 1/el;
        // simulate workload
        for i := 1 to 1000 do
          a := Cos(a);
      end;
    finally
      mrew.EndRead;
    end;
    Inc(Result);
    Sleep(1);
  end;
end;
```

The code runs for 3 seconds and tries to process the list as many times as possible. To prevent a total starvation of the writer thread, the code sleeps for 1 millisecond after each processing cycle.

The writer thread `TestWriter` adds 1,000 elements to the shared list, waits for 100 milliseconds, and repeats, as follows:

```
function TfrmReadersWriter.TestWriter(list: TList<integer>;
  const mrew: IReadWriteSync): Integer;
var
  nextEl: Integer;
```

```
    timer: TStopwatch;
    i: Integer;
  begin
    Result := 0;
    timer := TStopwatch.StartNew;
    nextEl := 1;
    while timer.ElapsedMilliseconds < (CTestDuration_sec * 1000) do
    begin
      mrew.BeginWrite;
      try
        for i := 1 to 1000 do
        begin
          list.Add(nextEl);
          Inc(nextEl);
        end;
      finally
        mrew.EndWrite;
      end;
      Inc(Result);
      Sleep(100);
    end;
  end;
```

The testing code displays how many times the writer was able to update the data in 3 seconds and how many times each reader thread did the same. The following screenshot shows the comparison of three locking implementations:

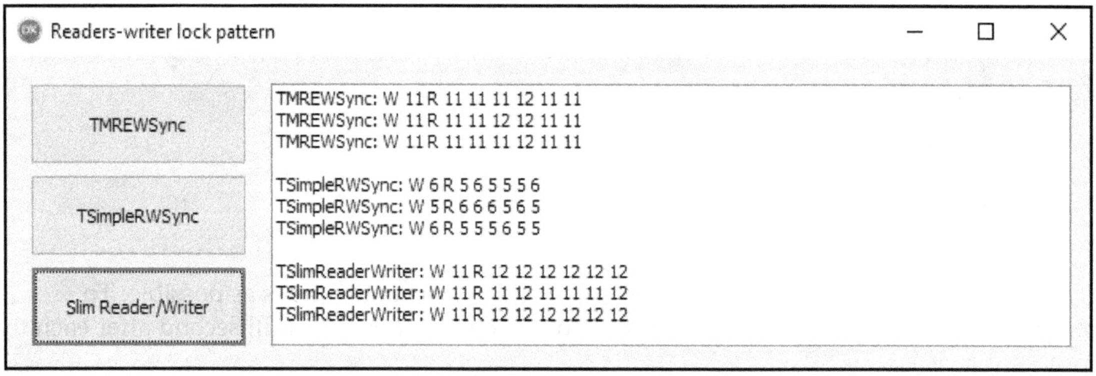

Comparing TMREWSync, TSimpleRWSync, and TSlimReaderWriter

As expected, the lock-based `TSimpleRWSync` is the slowest of the three. As it doesn't allow multiple readers to execute in parallel, the program runs only at about 50% speed.

The other two implementations run at approximately the same speed. A writer did 11 updates in both cases, while each reader managed to do between 11 and 12 cycles. The Windows implementation seems just a tad faster, though.

This is not surprising given the fact that the Delphi and Windows implementations are very different in design. The `TMREWSync` is reentrant, upgradeable, and write-biased. The Slim Reader/Writer, on the other hand, is non-reentrant, non-upgradeable, and read-biased.

In this program, the raw speed of the Delphi and Windows implementation doesn't matter much because the program doesn't access the locks that much. If we were locking smaller parts of code with greater frequency, however, the speed of particular implementation would come into play.

To measure the raw speed of each readers-writer implementation, the `ReadersWriterLock` program uses another test, `SpeedTest`, which measures the time required to get a read lock 1 million times, and then does the same for the write lock. It is implemented as follows:

```
procedure TfrmReadersWriter.SpeedTest(const name: string;
  const mrew: IReadWriteSync);
var
  i: Integer;
  readTime: int64;
  timer: TStopwatch;
begin
  timer := TStopwatch.StartNew;
  for i := 1 to CSpeedTestRepeats do
  begin
    mrew.BeginRead;
    mrew.EndRead;
  end;
  readTime := timer.ElapsedMilliseconds;
  timer := TStopwatch.StartNew;
  for i := 1 to CSpeedTestRepeats do
  begin
    mrew.BeginWrite;
    mrew.EndWrite;
  end;
  timer.Stop;
  lbLog.Items.Add(Format('%s: W %d R %d',
    [name, timer.ElapsedMilliseconds, readtime]));
 end;
```

This method gives us an entirely different view of the three implementations. The following screenshot shows the execution speed being measured on my test computer:

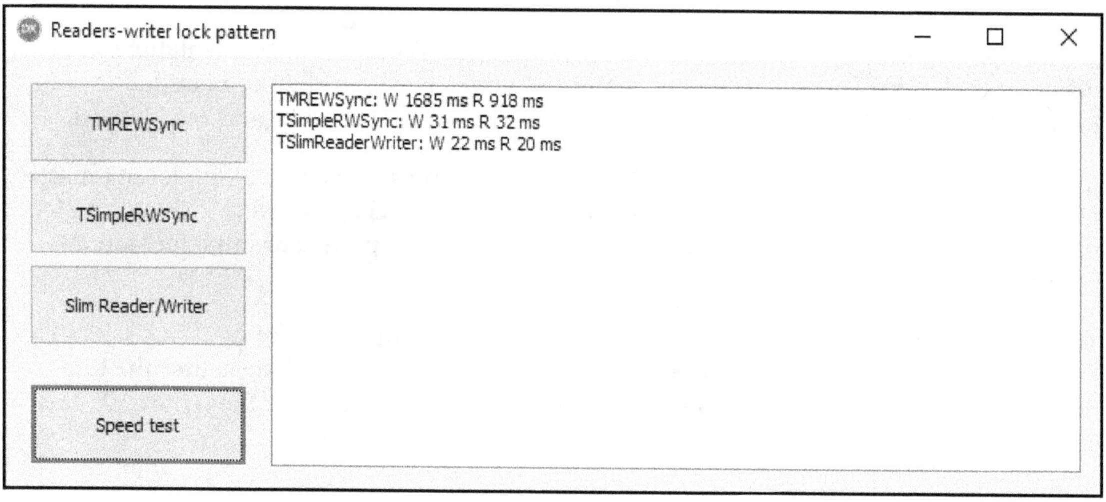

Comparing the raw speed of TMREWSync, TSimpleRWSync, and TSlimReaderWriter

We can see that the `TMREWSync` implementation is really, really slow. While the `TMonitor` implementation needs 30 milliseconds to execute 1 million readers or writers and the Windows implementation is even faster than that, `TMREWSync` needs 18x more time to acquire a read lock and 37x more time to get a write lock!

If you need a readers-writer lock in your program, you should not use the Delphi implementation, but the Windows one instead. If, however, you are writing a multiplatform program, you should code against the `IReadWriteSync` interface and then use a `TSlimReaderWriter` implementation on Windows and a `TSimpleRWSync` implementation on other operating systems.

Summary

This chapter opened with the topic of *Concurrency* patterns by exploring five different patterns related to managing access to shared data from multiple threads.

We learned that the lock pattern ensures that two threads are not trying to modify shared data or an object at the same time. It is also useful when one thread is reading from a shared object while another wants to modify it. We explored three different implementations of this pattern and compared their advantages and disadvantages.

We also learned that the lock pattern can be improved by introducing lock striping—a pattern that further fragments data inside one object and protects it with multiple locks instead of one. This approach is useful when we manipulate data in a list or array and don't add or remove existing elements. We explored two use possibilities, adding an array of locks or using one unused bit of existing data in combination with a custom locking solution.

After that, we spent some time exploring the lazy creation of objects in a multithreaded environment. As we always want programs to run as fast as possible, we cannot use the normal locking approach for this. Rather, we must introduce a specialized pattern of double-checked locking. Under some conditions, we can replace it with an even faster optimistic locking, which we covered as well.

Finally, we ended this chapter with a discussion of asymmetric data access. When we have multiple reader threads working on data that is only rarely modified, standard locking doesn't give us good enough performance. Instead, we should use a *readers-writer lock*. We discussed two implementations: a built-in Delphi version and the Slim Reader/Writer synchronization mechanism, which is part of the Windows operating system.

In the next chapter, we will explore four more concurrency patterns: thread pools, messaging, future, and pipeline.

17
Thread pool, Messaging, Future and Pipeline

Multithreaded programming is complicated. I hope that the previous chapter has sufficiently demonstrated how hard it is to coordinate multiple threads that work on shared data. There are just so many possibilities for writing code that doesn't always work correctly or to implement a fix that slows a program down so much that the new and improved parallel solution is actually slower than the original single-threaded code.

In this chapter, I will continue exploring design patterns (with a bit of architectural thinking thrown in) in a completely different direction. Instead of working on shared data, the patterns from this chapter will be used to write parallel tasks that are independent of each other. To achieve that, they use multiple copies of data and communicate with messages.

Introducing such patterns, however, often requires a redesign of the program architecture, which may be an impossible task in some situations. To help with such situations, this chapter also introduces two patterns that can be simply plugged into existing code – thread pool and future.

In this chapter, you will do the following:

- See how to speed up thread creation by introducing a thread pool pattern
- Learn how the locking architecture can be replaced with messaging
- Find out about different messaging solutions that can be used in your programs
- Learn how to speed up programs with minimal complications by introducing the future pattern into your code
- Learn about pipelines and how they can be used to speed up complicated tasks

Thread pool

A thread pool pattern can be simply described as a collection of threads. Some of them may be doing useful work, while others are sitting idle, waiting for you to run any job in them.

To the careful reader of this book, the thread pool pattern would seem like an old acquaintance. After all, it is nothing more than a variation on a object pool pattern, which was discussed in `Chapter 10`, *Singleton, Dependency Injection, Lazy Initialization, and Object Pool.*

> A thread pool is like a taxi service. When you need to travel somewhere, you call the dispatch and as soon as they have a taxi ready, they will send it to pick you up.

Using a thread pool minimizes the time a background task needs to start up. Creating a thread can take some time (up to ten milliseconds and more on older hardware), which can be a problem in highly optimized, heavily multi-threaded programs, for example, in a server handling many concurrent clients. Starting a job in a thread from a thread pool (provided that at least one thread is sitting idle), however, is a much faster operation.

A thread pool can also regulate your program thread consumption. Starting too many threads at the same time will just slow you down as the system will then spend too much time on thread switching and not enough on executing the program. A good thread pool will therefore limit the maximum number of concurrently running threads. When a thread pool is full (all threads are busy working), new jobs will enter a waiting queue. As the threads finish their current work, they take jobs from the waiting queue and process them.

Another advantage of thread pools is their capability of initializing some shared resource when a thread is created and freeing it up when the thread is destroyed. We can, for example, initialize a database connection when a thread is created and then reuse this connection for all operations that are executed in the context of this thread. This enables us to create a connection pool – a pool of threads that are connected to the database. Each time a database request has to be made, a thread from the connection pool can execute it without the overhead of connecting to the database.

Although you can write your own thread pool, this is a cumbersome and error-prone process. There were some attempts at providing Delphi programmers with a generic thread pool, but none were widespread. The first really useful thread pool appeared with the introduction of the OmniThreadLibrary open source library (`www.omnithreadlibrary.com`) in Delphi 2007, while we had to wait for the first built-in solution until Delphi XE7 when the `System.Threading` unit was introduced.

Traditionally, we used the `TThread` object to create new threads in Delphi. Calling `TThread.Create` creates a new thread and then executes your workload inside that thread. Using tasks, on the other hand, automatically uses a thread pool for server management. Calling `TTask.Run`, for example, runs your task in a thread that comes from the internal thread pool `TThreadPool.Default`.

> **TIP:** For more information on starting and managing threads. see the *Delphi idioms – parallel programming* section in `Chapter 16`, *Locking Patterns*.

The demonstration program `ThreadPool` from the `Thread pool` folder proves that allocating threads from a thread pool is indeed a faster operation than creating new threads. The program creates a number of threads or tasks (the number is settable in the user interface) and measures how long it takes until all threads are started up.

The thread example uses a worker thread called `TWorkerThread`. This simple object sets up an internal is started flag as soon as the thread's `Execute` method is invoked. Then, the code sleeps for two seconds (simulating hard work) and exits. The thread definition and implementation, which is part of the program's main unit, is shown here:

```
type
  TWorkerThread = class(TThread)
  strict private
    FIsStarted: boolean;
  public
    procedure Execute; override;
    property IsStarted: boolean read FIsStarted;
  end;

procedure TWorkerThread.Execute;
begin
  FIsStarted := true;
  Sleep(2000);
end;
```

A bit more work is needed to manage the threads. Clicking on the **Start threads** button calls the `btnThreadsClick` method which implements the test as follows:

```
procedure TfrmThreadPool.btnThreadsClick(Sender: TObject);
var
  i: Integer;
  sw: TStopwatch;
  threads: TArray<TWorkerThread>;
begin
```

```
    SetLength(threads, inpWorkers.Value);
    sw := TStopwatch.StartNew;
    for i := Low(threads) to High(threads) do
      threads[i] := TWorkerThread.Create;
    for i := Low(threads) to High(threads) do
      while not threads[i].IsStarted do
        ;
    sw.Stop;

    for i := Low(threads) to High(threads) do
    begin
      threads[i].WaitFor;
      lbLog.Items.Add('Thread ID: ' + threads[i].ThreadID.ToString);
      threads[i].Free;
    end;

    lbLog.ItemIndex := lbLog.Items.Add('Threads were created in ' +
    sw.ElapsedMilliseconds.ToString + ' ms');
  end;
```

The code stores all running threads in the internal `threads` array. The measurement part starts a stopwatch, creates all the threads (stores them in the array), and waits until all threads have set the `IsStarted` flag. Then, the code stops the stopwatch. The number of running threads is set by changing the Number of workers input field in the user interface.

After that, the code waits for each thread to finish execution by calling the `WaitFor` method, logs the unique ID of the executing thread (`ThreadID`), and destroys the thread. At the end, the time that's required to start the thread is reported.

TIP

You should always run such code without the Delphi debugger. (Instead of *F9*, you should press *Ctrl-Shift-F9*.) The Delphi debugger interferes with thread creation and drastically slows it down. You can run this program with and without the debugger to see the difference the debugger makes.

If you run the program and start a larger amount of threads (sixty, for example), you'll notice that it takes a few milliseconds to start them up. Next time you click this button, the code will take approximately the same time to start the threads.

If you limit the number of running threads to a lower number (for example, four) and click the **Start threads** button a few times, you'll see that different thread IDs are displayed for each execution. This proves that new threads are created each time. (The operating system assigns each new thread a random thread ID.)

Testing with tasks is a bit trickier. The following example shows some slightly simplified code from the demonstration program:

```
procedure TfrmThreadPool.btnTasksClick(Sender: TObject);
var
  i: Integer;
  sw: TStopwatch;
  tasks: TArray<ITask>;
  taskID: TArray<TThreadID>;
  taskStarted: TArray<boolean>;

  function MakeTask(num: integer): TProc;
  begin
    Result :=
      procedure
      begin
        taskStarted[num] := true;
        taskID[num] := TThread.Current.ThreadID;
        Sleep(2000);
      end;
  end;

begin
  SetLength(tasks, inpWorkers.Value);
  SetLength(taskID, Length(tasks));
  SetLength(taskStarted, Length(tasks));

  sw := TStopwatch.StartNew;
  for i := Low(tasks) to High(tasks) do
    tasks[i] := TTask.Run(MakeTask(i));
  for i := Low(tasks) to High(tasks) do
    while not taskStarted[i] do
      ;
  sw.Stop;

  TTask.WaitForAll(tasks);
  for i := Low(tasks) to High(tasks) do
    lbLog.Items.Add('Thread ID: ' + taskID[i].ToString);

  lbLog.ItemIndex := lbLog.Items.Add('Tasks were created in ' +
    sw.ElapsedMilliseconds.ToString + ' ms');
end;
```

The worker tasks have been created as anonymous functions. This was done by calling the `MakeTask` function. The task stores its running flag in the internal array `taskStarted` and the thread ID of the executing thread in the internal array `taskID`. The logic of measuring the startup time and logging the information stays the same.

Before you click the **Start tasks** button, make sure that the **Min threads in pool** value is at least as large as the **Number of workers** and that the **Max threads in pool** value is larger than the **Min threads in pool**. The reasons for that will become clear soon.

If you run the test on sixty tasks, you'll notice that the program needs about the same time to run the tasks as it needed to start the threads. When you click this button for the second time, however, you'll see that the startup time drops to less than one millisecond.

If you repeat the test with four tasks, you'll also notice that the same thread IDs are displayed when you run the test multiple times. This proves that threads are not destroyed but reused.

The following screenshot shows four threads being created twice, followed by four tasks being also created twice. There's no significant difference in speed, but you can see that the second run of the four tasks uses the same thread IDs as the first run:

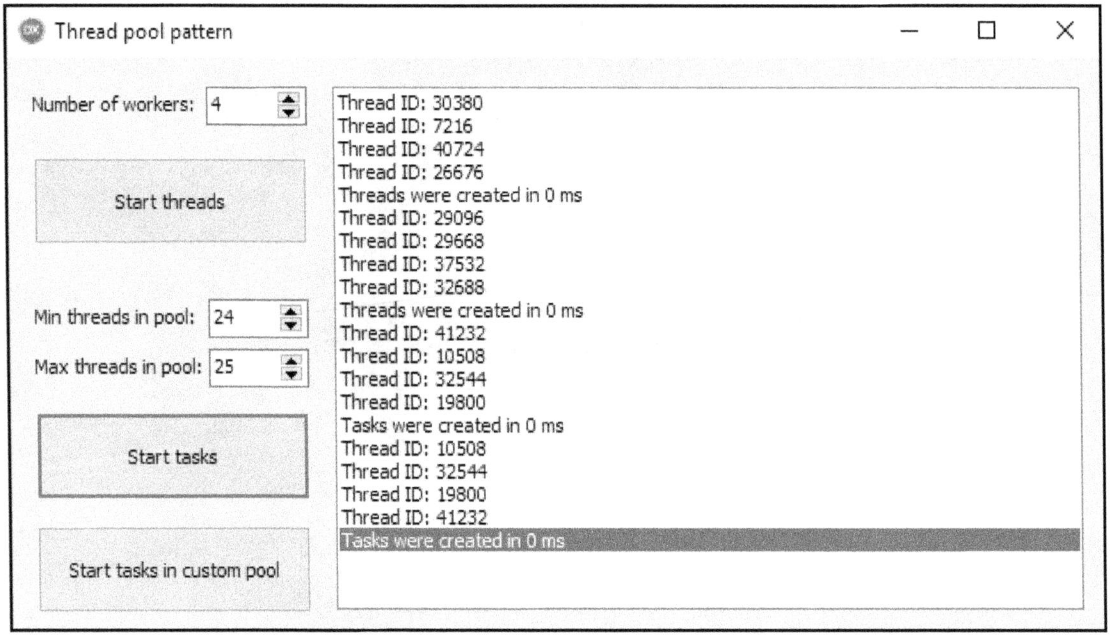

Comparing thread and task creation

Idiosyncrasies of Delphi's TThreadPool

As expected of a good thread pool, Delphi's implementation allows you to set the minimum and maximum number of executing threads. The maximum number of executing threads represents a hard limit of the maximum number of concurrently executing tasks. If you create more tasks than that, some of them will wait until the threads in the pool finish executing previous tasks.

The minimum number of executing threads sets the number of threads that are always waiting for new tasks. Setting this number to a high value preallocates a large number of threads, which allows a large number of tasks to quickly start when needed.

At least, that is the theory. The implementation, however, can be best described as weird.

The number of maximum threads is set by calling the `SetMaxWorkerThreads` method, while the number of minimum threads is set by calling the `SetMinWorkerThreads` method. The demonstration program contains the following two lines, which were not shown in the previous code example, and are used to adjust the thread pool limits before tasks are started:

```
TThreadPool.Default.SetMaxWorkerThreads(inpMaxThreads.Value);
TThreadPool.Default.SetMinWorkerThreads(inpMinThreads.Value);
```

The default values for these limits are initialized to very high numbers. The `TThreadPool.Create` constructor sets the defaults, as follows:

```
FMinLimitWorkerThreadCount := TThread.ProcessorCount;
FMaxLimitWorkerThreadCount := TThread.ProcessorCount * MaxThreadsPerCPU;
```

The `MaxThreadsPerCPU` constant is equal to twenty-five, so on a computer with six cores, the limits would be set to six and one-hundred and fifty, respectively. On a better workstation with twenty-four cores, the limits would be twenty-four and six-hundred. The value for the upper limit is, let me say, extremely high, and should only be used if your tasks spend most of their time waiting for something to happen. If, on the other hand, the tasks are CPU intensive, starting that many concurrent threads is a sure way to bring the system to a crawl.

If your process starts multiple CPU intensive tasks and uses a thread pool to limit them in number, make sure that you always call the `SetMaxWorkerThreads` method with a lower number (`TThread.ProcessorCount`, for example). Interestingly, you cannot set the maximum number of threads to a number lower than the number of CPU cores in the system as the `SetMaxWorkerThreads` implementation prevents that!

The second weird part comes from `SetMinWorkerThreads`, which makes sure that the minimum number of threads is always strictly smaller than the maximum number of threads. That's why I recommended that you test the program with **Max threads in pool** set to a higher value than **Min threads in pool**. You cannot have a thread pool where all of the threads are pre-allocated and cannot be created or destroyed. Or, again, that is the theory.

As it turns out, the minimum number of threads doesn't actually mean what you would assume. If you call `SetMinWorkerThreads(8)`, for example, the thread pool will not create eight threads. This is only documented in the source code, where a comment states the following:

> *"The actual number of pool threads could be less than this value depending on actual demand."*

Even after taking all of that in account, the implementation has its quirks. For example, set the **Number of workers** to four, **Min threads in pool** to four, and **Max threads in pool** to nine. Start the tasks once.

Now, change both the **Number of workers** and **Min threads in pool** to eight. Click the **Start tasks** button. As we are now starting 8 tasks in a thread pool with at least eight threads (and at most nine or the number of cores in the system, whichever's larger), we would expect all of the tasks to be started in parallel – but no! As the following screenshot proves, only four threads are used and starting the tasks takes two seconds as the first set of four tasks must finish their job before the next set of four tasks is started:

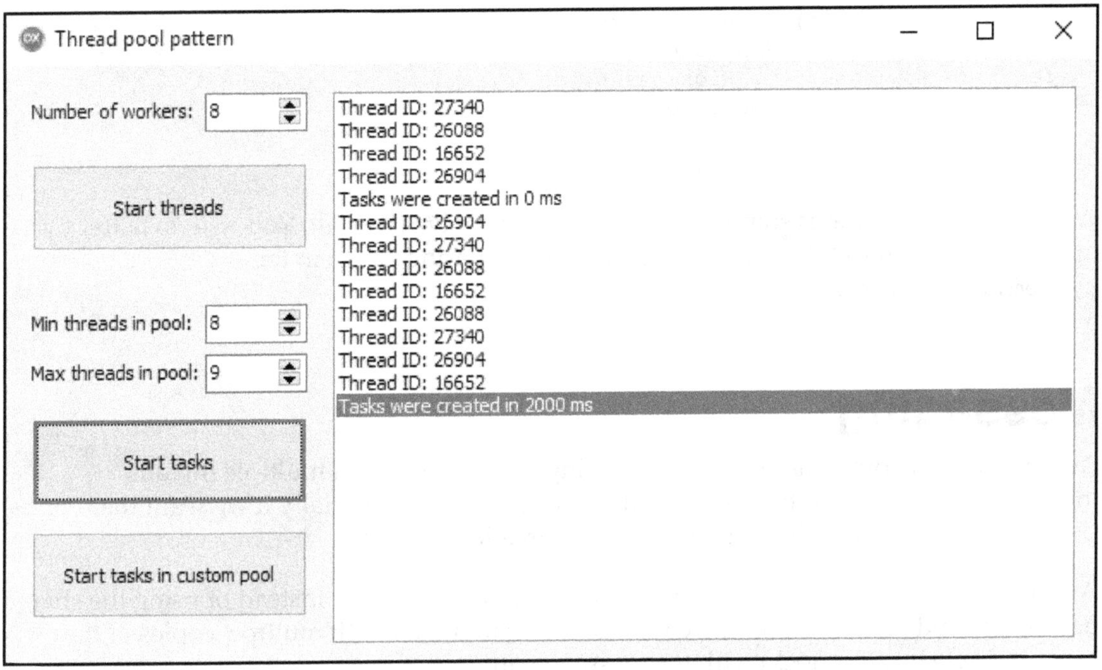

Running 8 tasks after running 4 tasks in Delphi's thread pool

This problem has only been fixed in Delphi 10.3 Rio, which was released during the production of this book. To prevent such problems in Delphi 10.2 and below, you can use the following workaround.

The `TTask.Create` and `TTask.Run` methods accept a `TThreadPool` parameter, which represents a thread pool that will be used to run the task. Instead of using the default thread pool, you can create a new one in the code by calling `ThreadPool.Create`. When a required minimum number of threads in the pool changes, the current thread pool can be destroyed (provided that no threads are running in it, of course) and recreated. The event handler `btnTasksCustomClick`, which is called by clicking the **Start tasks in custom pool** button, uses the following code to (re)create a custom pool and start a task in that pool:

```
TThreadPool.Default.SetMaxWorkerThreads(inpMaxThreads.Value);
if (not assigned(FCustomPool)) or (FCustomPool.MinWorkerThreads <>
inpMinThreads.Value) then begin
  FreeAndNil(FCustomPool);
  FCustomPool := TThreadPool.Create;
  FCustomPool.SetMinWorkerThreads(inpMinThreads.Value);
end;

sw := TStopwatch.StartNew;
```

```
for i := Low(tasks) to High(tasks) do
  tasks[i] := TTask.Run(MakeTask(i), FCustomPool);
for i := Low(tasks) to High(tasks) do
  while not taskStarted[i] do
    ;
sw.Stop;
```

While this hack alleviates some problems, it doesn't solve them all. You will do better by upgrading to fresh Delphi, which fixes some other glaring errors in the `System.Threading` unit.

Messaging

As we saw in the previous chapter, processing shared data from multiple threads introduces all sorts of problems that cannot be easily fixed especially if we want the program to executed faster than in a single—threaded version.

A common solution for this problem is to redesign the program. Instead of using the shared data access and locking pattern, we replace the shared data with multiple copies of the same and synchronize (lock) with the message pattern.

> If you play chess on the internet, you are not sharing a chessboard with your partner. Instead, each of you have your own copy of the chessboard and figures, and you synchronize the state between the two copies by sending messages (representing the piece moves) to each other.

Messaging is not a design but an architectural pattern. The implementation of messaging is, however, usually specific to a platform or a language and can be considered almost an idiom. As the messaging pattern is extremely important if you want to write parallel programs that are fast and relatively easy to debug, I decided to cover it in this book.

Messaging frequently takes an active role in the implementation of other patterns. It can, for example, be used to implement a publish-subscribe pattern (see the discussion of the Observer pattern in `Chapter 15`, *Iterator, Visitor, Observer, and Memento*). I will also use it later in this chapter to enhance the future pattern and to implement the pipeline pattern.

In the messaging pattern, one side (sender) creates a message and sends it to the other side (receiver). The message typically consists of an ID and data (although this is not a requirement, as we'll see later). The message ID tells the receiver what to do with the message data.

A message is delivered with help from some mechanism that is, in most cases, implemented in our code externally. It can be part of an operating system or a runtime library. We can also use custom messaging solutions, but that should be reserved for special cases where none of the pre-made messaging solutions fit.

The important point of the messaging pattern is that the message can easily travel from one thread to another. Support for that is usually built into the implementation of the message transfer mechanism. It can use normal queues combined with locking or some form of thread-safe queues, which typically use interlocked operations internally to deliver thread-safety.

To demonstrate different ways of messaging, I have built a `Messaging` project that's stored in the `Messaging` folder. This program shows four different ways that messages can be sent from a background thread to a main thread. (For sending messages from any thread to a background thread, see the implementation of the pipeline pattern later in this chapter.)

The `Messaging` project implements a simple thread called `TFooBarThread`, which plays the well-known FooBar game. The thread generates numbers from 1 to 100 but replaces each number that is divisible by three with a Foo, each number divisible by five with a Bar, and each number divisible by both three and five with a FooBar.

The implementation of this thread, which can be found in the `ThreadedFooBar` unit, is not complete. It implements the kernel of the algorithm that uses the `abstract` method `SendMessage` to send the current element (either a number, a Foo, Bar, or FooBar) to the main thread. This method is implemented in derived classes, which we'll explore later.

The implementation of the base thread `TFooBarThread` is as follows:

```
type
  TFooBarThread = class(TThread)
  strict protected
    procedure SendMessage(const msg: string); virtual; abstract;
  public
    procedure Execute; override;
  end;

procedure TFooBarThread.Execute;
var
  number: Integer;
begin
  for number := 1 to 100 do begin
    case number mod 15 of
      0: SendMessage('FooBar');
      3,6,9,12: SendMessage('Foo');
```

```
        5,10: SendMessage('Bar');
        else SendMessage(number.ToString);
      end;
      Sleep(100);
    end;
    SendMessage(#13#10);
  end;
```

Messages are sent with a slight delay (hundred milliseconds) so that we can better see how they are processed and displayed in the form.

Windows messages

The first option we have available is to use the Windows messaging system to send messages to the main thread. (This messaging system can also be used to send messages to a background thread, which is a more complicated topic that I will not pursue in this book.)

One limitation of this approach is obvious. We can only use it if we compile our program for Windows. If you are targeting other operating systems, you must use one of the other available solutions.

Another limitation is that a Windows message consists of a message ID and two integer parameters that represent message data. We cannot attach an object or a string as message data – at least not directly. We'll see how to circumvent this limitation later.

The `ThreadedFooBar.WindowsMsg` unit contains an implementation of a `TWindowsMsgFooBarThread`, a descendant of `TFooBarThread` that uses windows messaging to send messages. This thread class is defined as follows:

```
type
  TWindowsMsgFooBarThread = class(TFoobarThread)
  strict private
    FMessage: cardinal;
    FReceiver: THandle;
  strict protected
    procedure SendMessage(const msg: string); override;
  public
    constructor Create(receiver: THandle; message: cardinal;
      createSuspended: boolean);
  end;
```

The constructor takes two additional parameters. `Receiver` specifies the window (form) that will receive the messages, while `message` contains the message ID that will be used for communication. As our thread has no idea how it will be integrated into the application and which messages will be sent to the receiving form from other components, it is best that the form injects this message ID into the thread.

As we cannot send string messages over the Windows messaging subsystem, the code in the `SendMessage` method wraps each message into an instance of the `TFooBarMessage` class. Each Delphi object is internally represented with a pointer to the memory block where the object resides. We can treat this pointer as an integer and send it as message data. The receiving side must then make sure to destroy the object when it is no longer needed. The following code fragment shows the string wrapper class and the `SendMessage` implementation:

```
type
  TFooBarMessage = class
  strict protected
    FValue: string;
  public
    constructor Create(const AValue: string);
    property Value: string read FValue write FValue;
  end;

constructor TFooBarMessage.Create(const AValue: string);
begin
  inherited Create;
  FValue := AValue;
end;

procedure TWindowsMsgFooBarThread.SendMessage(const msg: string);
begin
  PostMessage(FReceiver, FMessage, WParam(TFooBarMessage.Create(msg)), 0);
end;
```

In the main thread, we must define a custom message (`WM_FOOBAR_MSG`). Windows allows us to use values that are greater or equal to `WM_USER` (a constant defined in the `Winapi.Messages` unit) as custom messages. Next, we declare a message handler, `MsgFooBar`, which will be automatically called whenever the form receives this message. The following code shows relevant parts of form implementation:

```
const
  WM_FOOBAR_MSG = WM_USER;

type
  TfrmMessaging = class(TForm)
```

```
    ...
    procedure MsgFooBar(var msg: TMessage); message WM_FOOBAR_MSG;
  end;

procedure TfrmMessaging.MsgFooBar(var msg: TMessage);
var
  oMsg: TFooBarMessage;
begin
  oMsg := TFooBarMessage(msg.WParam);
  memoLog.Text := memoLog.Text + oMsg.Value + ' ';
  oMsg.Free;
end;
```

On the receiving side, the integer parameter is again treated as a `TFooBarMessage` object. The contents of that object are then logged and the object is destroyed.

To create the thread, the `btnWindowsMsgClick` event handler creates the `TWindowsMsgFooBarThread` object and passes it to the constructor of the `Handle` of the main form and the `WM_FOOBAR_MSG` message ID. The form is set to automatically destruct whenever the `Execute` method completes its job (`FreeOnTerminate := true`), as shown in the following code:

```
procedure TfrmMessaging.btnWindowsMsgClick(Sender: TObject);
var
  fooBar: TWindowsMsgFooBarThread;
begin
  fooBar := TWindowsMsgFooBarThread.Create(Handle, WM_FOOBAR_MSG, true);
  fooBar.FreeOnTerminate := true;
  fooBar.Start;
end;
```

If you run the program and click on the **Windows messages** button, you'll see that messages from the worker thread are displayed as they arrive.

Queue and Synchronize

The second (and third) messaging option provided by Delphi is to use `TThread.Queue` or `TThread.Synchronize`. As they are just variations of the same concept, I'll describe them together.

Unlike Windows messages, which can be sent from the main thread to a background thread if you write the background thread in an appropriate way, `Queue` and `Synchronize` don't provide any support for that. You can only use them to send messages to the main thread.

The beauty of `Queue` and `Synchronize` is that they are completely platform independent. Delphi's RTL makes sure that you can use them with VCL or FireMonkey on any of their supported platforms.

TIP

If you want to use `Queue` or `Synchronize` in a console application, your application must periodically call the `CheckSynchronize` method, which is defined in the `System.Classes` unit.

The `Queue` and `Synchronize` methods don't use the message ID/message data concept. Instead, you pass in an anonymous method that's captured on the sending side and executed in the main thread. To pass any data along the "message", you just use it in the anonymous method and Delphi's capturing mechanism will take care of the rest.

The `ThreadedFooBar.Queue` unit implements a `TQueueFooBarThread` that's derived from `TFooBarThread` and implements a Queue-based messaging mechanism. The following code fragment shows the definition and implementation of this thread in full:

```
type
  TQueueFooBarThread = class(TFooBarThread)
  strict private
    FOnNewValue: TProc<string>;
    FOnTerminated: TProc;
  strict protected
    procedure SendMessage(const msg: string); override;
  public
    procedure Execute; override;
    property OnNewValue: TProc<string> read FOnNewValue write FOnNewValue;
    property OnTerminated: TProc read FOnTerminated write FOnTerminated;
  end;

procedure TQueueFooBarThread.Execute;
begin
  inherited;
  OnTerminated();
end;

procedure TQueueFooBarThread.SendMessage(const msg: string);
begin
  TThread.Queue(nil,
    procedure
    begin
      OnNewValue(msg);
    end);
end;
```

As with the Windows message approach, the worker thread doesn't know what method of the main form it should execute when `SendMessage` is called. Instead of introducing hard-coded dependencies, the implementation defines the `OnNewValue` event, which is called from `SendMessage`. The application must take care of correctly initializing this event handler before the thread is started.

The `TThread.Queue` call takes two parameters – a `TThread` (which is `nil` in this example) and an anonymous method. `Queue` then inserts these two parameters in an internal queue and immediately exits. The thread can then continue with its execution.

At some later time, the main thread calls the `CheckSynchronize` method from `System.Classes` (this typically happens when the application is idle). `CheckSynchronize` checks the internal queue, fetches the anonymous method(s) from it, and executes them one by one.

The first parameter of the `TThread` type tells the system which thread produced the message. You can set it to `nil`, as in this code example. Alternatively, you can set it to `TThread.Current` – a function that returns the current `TThread` object.

If you use the second approach, you will be able to remove specific messages from the queue before they are executed by calling the `TThread.RemoveQueuedEvents` method. As this functionality is rarely required, you'll see that most examples simply use `nil` for the first parameter, which is a tad faster than calling `TThread.Current`.

If you use `TThread.Queue` with a thread that automatically destroys itself when `Execute` exits (`FreeOnTerminate := True`), you have to be very careful. Let's think about what can happen if `TQueueFooBarThread` were to automatically destroy itself:

- The thread calls `SendMessage`, which calls `TThread.Queue`.
- An anonymous method that refers the `OnNewValue` handler is inserted in the queue.
- The thread exits. As its `FreeOnTerminate` property is set to `True`, the thread object is destroyed. The `OnNewValue` handler does not exist anymore.
- The main form takes the anonymous method from the message queue and tries to execute it. With some luck, this ends in access violation when the anonymous method tries to call `OnNewValue`. If you are unlucky, some random code may execute and do something undefined.

This is a serious problem, but luckily Delphi RTL offers a way out of this trap. You just have to be aware of it and write your code accordingly. There are two ways to fix this problem, so you have to pick the one that applies to your specific situation.

If you are using a `FreeOnTerminate` thread, then you should never pass `nil` to `TThread.Queue`. Just before the thread is destroyed, the `TThread` destructor calls `RemoveQueuedEvents(Self)`, which removes all unprocessed messages that are sent by this thread from the queue.

If you want all messages to be received and processed in the main thread, however, you should never use the `FreeOnTerminate` approach. Instead of that, the code should signal the main thread to say that execution was completed, as in this example. As that will be the last message that's sent by the thread, all previous messages will be already processed when this last method is executed and so the thread can be safely destroyed.

Your thread may also work for a long time, in which case the main program will be the one that tells the thread to stop. In that case, the code should always use the idiomatic approach to stop the thread, as follows:

```
thread.Terminate;
thread.WaitFor;
FreeAndNil(thread);
```

The important step is a call to `WaitFor`. Inside this method, `CheckSynchronize` is called to clean the message queue. When `WaitFor` exits, you can be sure that there are no messages from that thread waiting in the queue, and you can safely destroy the thread object.

The following code shows how `TQueueFooBarThread` is created and destroyed in the main program:

```
procedure TfrmMessaging.btnQueueClick(Sender: TObject);
var
  fooBar: TQueueFooBarThread;
begin
  fooBar := TQueueFooBarThread.Create(true);
  fooBar.OnNewValue :=
    procedure (value: string)
    begin
      memoLog.Text := memoLog.Text + value + ' ';
    end;
  fooBar.OnTerminated :=
    procedure
    begin
      fooBar.Free;
    end;
  fooBar.Start;
end;
```

We must make sure that the thread doesn't run before event handlers are set so that the thread object is created in a suspended state (the `true` parameter of the constructor enforces that). After that, both event handlers are set and the thread is started. `btnQueueClick` then exits.

When a new message is posted via `SendMessage`, `OnNewValue` is eventually called. The code looks like it's part of `btnQueueClick`, but in reality `procedure (value: string) ...` is an independent entity that exists as long as the `OnNewValue` handler refers to it. (An anonymous method is implemented as an interfaced object that exists as long as some other part of the code is referring to it.)

To destroy the thread, we must keep the thread object (`fooBar`) active until the `OnTerminated` event handler is called. In traditional Delphi programming, we would have to define a form field, such as `FFooBar: TQueueFooBarThread`, and store the thread object in it.

If we use anonymous methods, as in this example, the local variable `fooBar` is captured by the compiler and exists somewhere (we don't really care where) while the `OnTerminated` anonymous method is alive. The anonymous method can therefore safely refer to the local variable (which is now not really a local variable, but we don't care about that) and destroy it by calling `fooBar.Free`.

> TIP: If you call `TThread.Queue` from a main thread, the anonymous method is executed directly from the `Queue` method and is not inserted in the internal queue. To put an anonymous method in an internal queue from a main thread, you should use the `ForceQueue` method, which is only available in Delphi 10.2 Tokyo and later.

The `Synchronize` method is used in exactly the same way as `Queue`. The differences only show up when the program is running.

While the `Queue` pushes the message into a queue and immediately exits so that the thread can do further work, `Synchronize` waits until the main thread **receives** and **processes** the message. Only after that will the code inside the thread continue execution. `Synchronize` therefore **blocks** the thread's execution, which slows the thread down. You should use it only when absolutely necessary, for example, when a background thread needs the main thread to provide a certain value. (Even then, using `Synchronize` indicates bad program architecture that should be rethought.)

The demonstration program implements `TSynchronizeFooBarThread` in the `ThreadedFooBar.Synchronize` unit. Both the implementation of the thread and thread management in the main form are almost the same as in the `Queue` example.

Polling

For the last approach, I will show a solution that doesn't require any support from an operating system or runtime library. You can implement it with standard tools, for example, with a timer, list, and critical section.

Unlike the previous solutions, which followed a push model (a message triggers some code in the main thread that can't do much to prevent that), this approach requires cooperation from code running in a main thread. This code will periodically check (poll) whether a message has arrived.

To implement this kind of messaging system, both the main thread and the background thread must share some structure that can store a list of messages and which is *thread-safe* (can be safely used in a multi-threaded environment). We can, for example, use a standard `TList` in combination with a *critical section* or `TMonitor` for locking or, as in the following example, a thread-safe queue, `TThreadedQueue<T>`. (For more information on locking with critical sections and `TMonitor`, see `Chapter 16`, *Locking Patterns*).

A thread sends a message by storing information in this shared structure. As we have the shared structure under our own control, we don't run into the same problem as with Windows messages where we could only send integer data.

The receiving thread must check the shared queue from time to time. This process is known as **polling**. If there's a message in the queue, the receiving thread removes the message from the queue and processes it.

The beauty of this approach is that we don't really care which thread is a background thread and which is the main thread. We can post messages (put them into the shared queue) from any thread. We can also poll the queue from a main thread (with a `TTimer` or in the `OnIdle` event) or from a background thread (with a simple loop). In this section, I will show you how to read from such a queue in a main thread. To see how you can receive messages in a background thread, check the discussion of the pipeline pattern later in this chapter.

This solution is also useful when you have multiple senders or even multiple receivers. This capability will also be used in the pipeline pattern.

The downside of the polling approach is that is typically uses a bit more CPU time than other solutions and messages are not processed as promptly as with other approaches. As we'll see later, we can make the polling more responsive, but for the price of a larger CPU usage.

A polling approach is implemented in `TPollingFooBarThread`, which is implemented in the `ThreadedFooBar.Polling` unit, as follows:

```
type
  TPollingFooBarThread = class(TFooBarThread)
  strict private
    FQueue: TThreadedQueue<string>;
  strict protected
    procedure SendMessage(const msg: string); override;
  public
    procedure AfterConstruction; override;
    procedure BeforeDestruction; override;
    property MessageQueue: TThreadedQueue<string> read FQueue;
  end;

procedure TPollingFooBarThread.AfterConstruction;
begin
  inherited;
  FQueue := TThreadedQueue<string>.Create(100);
end;

procedure TPollingFooBarThread.BeforeDestruction;
begin
  FreeAndNil(FQueue);
  inherited;
end;

procedure TPollingFooBarThread.SendMessage(const msg: string);
begin
  FQueue.PushItem(msg);
end;
```

As the thread is only sending `string` data, the shared message queue is implemented as a `TThreadedQueue<string>` object, which is managed by the thread. This class requires us to set the maximum number of stored entities (strings, in this example) when it is created. The code sets this value to 100, thus assuming that the main thread will have no problems reading messages from the queue.

To send a message, the code simply calls `FQueue.PushItem`. This will add a message to the queue in a thread-safe way. In other words, we don't care what the other threads are doing with this `TThreadedQueue` as the implementation of `PushItem` guarantees correctness in the multi-threaded world.

In the unlikely event of a queue being full, `PushItem` will simply wait until the main thread removes one message from the queue. Then, it will write the message into the queue and exit. In such a situation the execution of the background thread can be temporarily blocked. If that is a problem, you can increase the queue size or decrease the push timeout (which can be set by providing additional parameters to the `TThreadedQueue` constructor).

A bit more work than usual has to be done in the main thread. The code in `btnPollingClick` sets up the thread and event handlers, as follows:

```
procedure TfrmMessaging.btnPollingClick(Sender: TObject);
begin
  FPollingFooBar := TPollingFooBarThread.Create(true);
  FPollingFooBar.OnTerminate := PollingFooBarTerminated;
  FPollingFooBar.Start;
  btnPolling.Enabled := false;
  tmrPollThread.Enabled := true;
end;
```

This code also enables the timer that will read and process the messages and disables the button that created the polling thread. Unlike the previous approaches, where the implementation allowed us to create multiple worker threads, the simple polling implementation in the demonstration program allows for only one worker.

The timer method `tmrPollThreadTimer` checks whether there are messages in the shared queue and reads them one by one with `PopItem`, as shown here:

```
procedure TfrmMessaging.tmrPollThreadTimer(Sender: TObject);
begin
  while FPollingFooBar.MessageQueue.QueueSize > 0 do
    memoLog.Text := memoLog.Text + FPollingFooBar.MessageQueue.PopItem + '
';
end;
```

The thread termination handler `PollingFooBarTerminated` is called when `TPollingFooBarThread` terminates. It disables the timer and calls the timer message method `tmrPollThreadTimer` for the last time. That cleans potential unprocessed messages from the queue. After that, it destroys the thread and re-enables the button. This method is shown in the following code:

```
procedure TfrmMessaging.PollingFooBarTerminated(Sender: TObject);
begin
  tmrPollThread.Enabled := false;
  tmrPollThreadTimer(nil);
  FPollingFooBar.Terminate;
  FPollingFooBar := nil;
  btnPolling.Enabled := true;
end;
```

If you run the program, you'll notice that the messages from the polling thread appear in chunks, a few at a time. This happens because the timer interval is set to two hundred and fifty milliseconds, while the messages are produced one every one hundred milliseconds. You can improve the responsiveness of the program by decreasing the timer interval. This will, of course, increase the number of times the timer method is called, which will slightly increase the CPU usage. It is up to you to find a polling interval that works well in your situation.

Future

The future pattern, also known as a promise, can be simply described as a function that runs in the background thread. The basic usage pattern is intentionally very simple:

- The main thread creates a future (starts a calculation in another thread).
- The main thread does some other work.
- The main thread reads the result of the future (reads the result of the calculation). If the calculation is not finished yet, the main thread blocks until the result is available.

The future pattern allows the program to execute multiple tasks in parallel while it neatly encapsulates the background calculation in a separate function. It also provides a simple way of re-synchronization between two threads when the result of calculation is required.

> In a kitchen, the chef asks their assistant to cut up a few onions. While the assistant peels, cuts, and cries, the chef continues preparing other meals. At a later time, when they need to use the onion, it will hopefully be already prepared and waiting.

This simple pattern is also equally simple to use in Delphi programs. We only have to call `TTask.Future<T>` to create a future, returning `T`, which is represented by a `IFuture<T>` interface. This automatically creates a new task that starts calculating the result.

When the program needs to use this result, the code accesses the `Value` property of the `IFuture<T>` interface. This returns the result of the calculation. If the calculation is not finished yet, the code will wait (block) inside the `Value` getter until the calculation is done and the result can be returned.

The `Future` program from the `Future` folder demonstrates this approach. The **Create Future** button executes the following code, which creates and starts the future:

```
procedure TfrmFuture.btnFutureClick(Sender: TObject);
begin
  FFuture := TTask.Future<integer>(CountPrimes);
end;
```

The `FFuture` is a form field of the `IFuture<integer>` type.

The `CountPrimes` function counts all prime numbers that are smaller than 5,000,000. On a typical personal computer, the code returns the results in a few seconds.

To read the result, the **Get value** button reads the `FFuture.Value` property. After the result is displayed, the code destroys the future interface by setting the `FFuture` field to `nil`, as shown in the following code:

```
procedure TfrmFuture.btnGetValueClick(Sender: TObject);
begin
  if not assigned(FFuture) then
    Exit;

  lbLog.Items.Add('Result = ' + FFuture.Value.ToString);
  FFuture := nil;
end;
```

If you run the program, click the **Create Future** button, wait a few seconds and click the **Get value** button, you'll immediately get the result. If, however, you click the **Get value** button immediately after clicking the **Create Future** button, the main thread will block for a few seconds inside the `FFuture.Value` getter. During that time, the program will be unresponsive. You will not, for example, be able to move the program window around the screen.

If this potential blocking is not acceptable, we can sometimes redesign the program to function asynchronously. We can start the future like we did previously, but instead of reading the result directly, we delay that until we know that the future has finished its job (has calculated the result). The simplest way to achieve this is to use the messaging pattern to send a message from the future back to the main thread when the result is ready.

The **Create Future 2** button in the demonstration program starts a future that notifies the main program when the result is ready. The code is as follows:

```
procedure TfrmFuture.btnFuture2Click(Sender: TObject);
begin
  FFuture := TTask.Future<integer>(
    function: Integer
    begin
      Result := CountPrimes;
      TThread.Queue(nil, ReportFuture);
    end);
end;
```

The `ReportFuture` method simply reads the result of the calculation and destroys the `FFuture` interface. As the result is guaranteed to exist at this point, accessing the `Value` property will never block. The code for this is as follows:

```
procedure TfrmFuture.ReportFuture;
begin
  lbLog.Items.Add('Result = ' + FFuture.Value.ToString);
  FFuture := nil;
end;
```

Although with this approach the user interface can never block, we have to redesign the program, and sometimes this is not feasible. In such cases, we can still use the original pattern, which doesn't give perfect results but still speeds up the execution of the program.

Pipeline

To wrap up our discussion of concurrency patterns, I will present a very important concept – the pipeline pattern. This pattern, which is sometimes also called **staged processing**, is not strictly a design pattern, but more of an architectural one. It is, nevertheless, one of the most important patterns you can use in parallel programming, which is why it is covered in this book.

If we are to be able to apply the pipeline pattern to a process, two conditions must be applied. First, the process must be able to process parts of the input one by one. In other words, we must be able to split the input into smaller blocks (processing units), which are processed sequentially. Second, the process itself must be doing the processing in separate steps (stages) that are executed one after another.

The pipeline works by passing the first processing unit to the first stage. After the stage finishes its work, it passes the partially processed unit to the second stage. While the second stage does its work, the first stage can already work on the second processing unit. This process continues with as many stages as we need – the longer the processing pipeline, the more stages can be working at the same time and the better results we'll achieve.

A robotized assembly line builds a product in stages. Each robot takes a partially finished product, makes some modifications, and passes the product to the next robot. This allows multiple robots to work at the same time, which speeds up production.

The following simple example will help you understand the process of creating a pipeline from a normal, sequential process. Let's say we have a file encryption process, which works like so:

1. A file is read into memory.
2. Data is encrypted.
3. The encrypted data is written into another file.

Since we may be working with huge files that may not fit into our available memory, we have coded this algorithm like so:

```
while not EndOfSource do
begin
  ReadFromSource(buffer);
  Encrypt(buffer);
  WriteToDestination(buffer);
end;
```

This pseudocode reads data from input one buffer at a time. Each buffer is encrypted and then written to a destination file.

We can see that this process satisfies the conditions I stated previously. Data is processed in smaller units (`buffer`) and the process itself runs in three separate stages.

To show you how we can create a pipeline out of such a process, let's complicate this process a little and put a message queue between stages. The code would still execute at approximately the same speed, except the data would (seemingly without any reason) pass through a queue before it is used in the next stage. The pseudocode would look as follows:

```
while not EndOfSource do
begin
  ReadFromSource(buffer1);
  queue1.Write(buffer1);

  queue1.Read(buffer2);
  Encrypt(buffer2);
  queue2.Write(buffer2);

  queue2.Read(buffer3);
  WriteToDestination(buffer3);
end;
```

Now, the stages don't use the same `buffer` (shared data), but each work with their own copy of the data. We can now simply split up each process into a thread (or a task), as the following pseudocode shows:

```
// thread 1
while not EndOfSource do
begin
  ReadFromSource(buffer1);
  queue1.Write(buffer1);
end;
queue1.Close;

// thread 2
while not queue1.Closed do
begin
  queue1.Read(buffer2);
  Encrypt(buffer2);
  queue2.Write(buffer2);
end;
queue2.Close;

// thread 3
while not queue2.Closed do
begin
  queue2.Read(buffer3);
  WriteToDestination(buffer3);
end;
```

The only data shared between the threads are message queues, which are by nature designed with this application in mind. The data itself is never shared, so we don't need to implement any locking.

This example also shows how to stop a pipeline. Each stage must be able to somehow signal to the next stage that the work was done. We can implement this by sending a special message over the message queue or we can use support that's built into a messaging subsystem, as in this example.

In practice, we usually implement the pipeline so that all of the stages use two message queues; one for input and one for output. The first stage can then receive initial data (if any) from the main thread over the input queue and the last stage can return results (if any) to the main thread over its output queue.

> TIP: If we don't care about the order in which the output is produced, we can run some stages in multiple parallel threads. By doing that, we add more workers to the slowest part of the problem. To do that, the messaging subsystem must support multiple simultaneous readers and writers.

The beauty of a pipeline is that it can be easily implemented with standard Delphi functionality. Each stage runs as a separate `TThread` or `ITask`, while the `TThreadedQueue` is used for interconnecting message queues.

The following template can be used for each stage in a pipeline:

```
procedure Stage(
  inQueue: TThreadedQueue<T1>;
  outQueue: TThreadedQueue<T2>);
var
  data: T1;
begin
  // initialize per-thread data
  try
    while inQueue.PopItem(url) = wrSignaled do
    begin
      if inQueue.ShutDown then
        break; //while

      outQueue.PushItem(ProcessInput(data));
    end;
    outQueue.DoShutDown;
  finally
    // cleanup per-thread data
  end;
end;
```

Each stage runs as a separate task, which receives data of type T1 over the TThreadedQueue<T1> queue and outputs data of type T2 into the TThreadedQueue<T2> queue. Both queues are *injected* as parameters.

Data structures that are used for the entire process can be initialized at the beginning and cleaned up at the end. There's no need to recreate them each time a processing unit is received. At the beginning, for example, we could open a database connection, which is typically a relatively slow process.

The task runs until the input queue is not closed. If we use TThreadedQueue for messaging, we can close it by calling its DoShutDown method and check whether it is closed by testing the ShutDown property.

If the input queue is correctly initialized, the PopItem call will wait forever. It will only return if there's new data in the input queue or if the input queue was shut down. If the return value is wrSignaled, all is well and we can continue. Any other result indicates an unexpected error and the only thing the stage can do is shut down.

> TIP: This code also assumes that ProcessInput cannot throw any exceptions. If that is a possibility, data processing should be wrapped in a try..except handler and errors should be appropriately handled.

This sample code generates one processing unit on the output for each received processing unit. This is not a requirement, and in practical applications, this will most often not be a case you need to worry about. As you will see later in this chapter, one input processing unit can result in multiple or no processing units being sent to the output queue.

Web spider

To show a more complex example that you can take and adapt to your own needs, the Pipeline demo from the Pipeline folder implements a simple web spider. This code accepts a URL and retrieves all of the pages on that website.

> This project is not meant to be a fully functional web spider application, but a relatively simple demo. It may not work correctly on all sites. It may also cause you to be temporarily locked out of accessing the site that you are trying to crawl as it can generate a big amount of http requests, which may trigger security measures on the website.

This example is significantly more complicated than the pipeline concept I have discussed so far. It extracts data (URLs) from the retrieved pages and feeds them back into the pipeline so that new URLs can be processed. As we'll see later, this makes it hard for the pipeline to determine when the work has finished. Still, a self-feeding pipeline is a useful architecture and you should know how to write one.

The web spider pipeline is fully implemented in the `WebSpider` unit, which provides a very simple interface, as shown here:

```
type
  TWebSpider = class
  public
    procedure Start(const baseUrl: string);
    procedure Stop;
    property OnPageProcessed: TProc<string>
      read FOnPageProcessed write FOnPageProcessed;
    property OnFinished: TProc read FOnFinished write FOnFinished;
  end;
```

We can only start and stop the pipeline, nothing more. The pipeline triggers the `OnPageProcessed` event each time one web page has been processed. It also calls the `OnFinished` event when the work is done. (We can, of course, always stop the process by calling the `Stop` method, even if the website hasn't been fully crawled yet.)

The main form uses this class in a fairly straightforward manner, as we can see in the following code:

```
procedure TfrmPipeline.btnStartClick(Sender: TObject);
begin
  if not assigned(FWebSpider) then begin
    FWebSpider := TWebSpider.Create;
    FWebSpider.OnPageProcessed :=
      procedure (url: string)
      begin
        lbLog.Items.Add(url);
      end;
    FWebSpider.OnFinished := StopSpider;
    FWebSpider.Start(inpUrl.Text);
    inpUrl.Enabled := false;
    btnStart.Caption := 'Stop';
  end
  else
    StopSpider;
end;

procedure TfrmPipeline.StopSpider;
```

```
begin
  FWebSpider.Stop;
  FreeAndNil(FWebSpider);
  inpUrl.Enabled := true;
  btnStart.Caption := 'Start';
end;
```

To start the process, the code creates a `TWebSpider` object, sets up event handlers, and calls the `Start` method, passing in the initial URL. If the user later clicks the same button, the web spider will be stopped and destroyed – as it will be if the `OnFinished` handler is called.

The process works in three stages:

1. The first stage receives a URL. It checks whether this URL has already been processed. If not, it passes the URL to the second stage. The first stage functions as a filter.
2. The second stage receives a URL and retrieves its contents. If the operation is successful, both the URL and returned HTML are passed to the third stage. The second stage is a downloader.
3. The third stage parses the HTML, extracts all URLs that are referenced by that page, and sends them back to the first stage. (The first stage then makes sure that the process doesn't cycle indefinitely.) The third stage functions as a parser.

The whole process is set up in the `Start` method, as follows:

```
procedure TWebSpider.Start(const baseUrl: string);
var
  i: integer;
begin
  FPipelineInput := TThreadedQueue<string>.Create(100);
  FHttpGetInput := TThreadedQueue<string>.Create;
  FHtmlParseInput := TThreadedQueue<THttpPage>.Create;

  FPageCount := 1;
  FPipelineInput.PushItem('');

  FThreadPool := TThreadPool.Create;
  FThreadPool.SetMaxWorkerThreads(TThread.ProcessorCount + 3);
  FThreadPool.SetMinWorkerThreads(TThread.ProcessorCount + 2);
  FTasks := TList<ITask>.Create;
  FTasks.Add(TTask.Run(
    procedure
    begin
      Asy_UniqueFilter(baseUrl, FPipelineInput, FHttpGetInput);
    end,
```

```
    FThreadPool));

  for i := 1 to TThread.ProcessorCount do
    FTasks.Add(TTask.Run(
      procedure
      begin
        Asy_HttpGet(FHttpGetInput, FHtmlParseInput);
      end,
      FThreadPool));

  FTasks.Add(TTask.Run(
    procedure
    begin
      Asy_HtmlParse(FHtmlParseInput, FPipelineInput);
    end,
    FThreadPool));
end;
```

First, the code creates three message queues. `FPipelineInput` functions as an input to the filter stage; the downloader reads data from `FHttpGetInput` and the parser reads from `FHtmlParseInput`.

Then, the code sets the number of unprocessed work items in the pipeline to one and pushes the initial item (an empty string indicating the starting `baseUrl`) to the input of the first stage. We'll see how `FPageCount` is used to stop the pipeline when all the work is done later.

The code then creates its own thread pool and makes sure that we'll have enough threads at our disposal.

Finally, the code sets up all the tasks and passes the appropriate message queues to the workers. Since we don't care about the order in which the pages are crawled, the code creates multiple copies of the slowest stage, downloader. The web download doesn't use much CPU when it performs this process, so we can start lots of downloader threads. They will be mainly waiting for data anyway.

To shut down the pipeline, the `Stop` method merely shuts down the first message queue and waits for all tasks to finish their work, as follows:

```
procedure TWebSpider.Stop;
begin
  FPipelineInput.DoShutDown;
  TTask.WaitForAll(FTasks.ToArray);
  FreeAndNil(FTasks);
  FreeAndNil(FThreadPool);
end;
```

Filter stage

The filter stage creates a `TStringList` object, which holds the names of all the URLs that have already been processed. For each URL received on the input, it checks whether the URL is already in the list. If so, the URL is thrown away. The code also checks if the URL belongs to the site we are crawling. If not, it is also thrown away. (We certainly don't want to crawl the entire internet!) If all of the tests pass, the URL is added to the list of already processed links and is sent to the output queue.

The `Asy_UniqueFilter` method implements the filter stage, as follows:

```
procedure TWebSpider.Asy_UniqueFilter(baseUrl: string;
  inQueue, outQueue: TThreadedQueue<string>);
var
  baseUrl2: string;
  url: string;
  visitedPages: TStringList;
begin
  TThread.NameThreadForDebugging('Unique filter');

  visitedPages := TStringList.Create;
  try
    visitedPages.Sorted := true;
    if not (baseUrl.StartsWith('https://')
            or baseUrl.StartsWith('http://'))
    then
      baseUrl := 'http://' + baseUrl;
    if baseUrl.StartsWith('http://') then
      baseUrl2 := baseUrl.Replace('http://', 'https://')
    else
      baseUrl2 := baseUrl.Replace('https://', 'http://');

    while inQueue.PopItem(url) = wrSignaled do
    begin
      if inQueue.ShutDown then
        break; //while

      if url.IndexOf(':') < 0 then
        url := baseUrl + url;
      if (url.StartsWith(baseUrl) or url.StartsWith(baseUrl2))
         and (visitedPages.IndexOf(url) < 0) then
      begin
        visitedPages.Add(url);
        outQueue.PushItem(url);
      end
      else if TInterlocked.Decrement(FPageCount) = 0 then
        NotifyFinished;
```

```
      end;
      outQueue.DoShutDown;
    finally
      FreeAndNil(visitedPages);
    end;
  end;
```

In addition to the standard `while inQueue.PopItem` loop that we described previously, the code also sets the name for this thread (`TThread.NameThreadForDebugging`). This enables us to quickly locate this thread in the debugger's Thread Status window.

Additional complication in the code comes from the fact that many websites nowadays quietly redirect you from a `http://` address to a `https://` address. I want such URLs to be treated as part of the website that is crawled. The code sets up two strings, `baseUrl` and `baseUrl2`, that are later used for testing whether an URL belongs to the website we are crawling.

The most important part of this stage are the following lines:

```
if (url.StartsWith(baseUrl) or url.StartsWith(baseUrl2))
   and (visitedPages.IndexOf(url) < 0) then
begin
  visitedPages.Add(url);
  outQueue.PushItem(url);
end
else if TInterlocked.Decrement(FPageCount) = 0 then
  NotifyFinished;
```

If the URL belongs to the website (`StartsWith`) and was not processed before (`IndexOf`), it is passed to the output stage. Otherwise, we are done processing this URL and it can be thrown away. As we do so, however, we must decrement the shared `FPageCount` counter, which holds the number of processing units in the pipeline. If it falls to zero, the pipeline is now empty and can be stopped. The code calls `NotifyFinished` to signal this, as shown here:

```
procedure TWebSpider.NotifyFinished;
begin
  TThread.Queue(nil,
    procedure
    begin
      if assigned(OnFinished) then
        OnFinished();
    end);
end;
```

This code uses the messaging approach we explored previously in this chapter to execute the `OnFinished` handler in the main thread.

This approach of queuing the event handlers to the main thread is also the reason why we must use a custom thread pool in the web spider code.

I have mentioned before that the RTL makes sure that all queued anonymous methods are executed in the `TThread.WaitFor` call. In the web spider implementation, however, we are using tasks and not threads. If we were using the common thread pool, the worker thread would not be destroyed after a task has completed its job. Although the `TWebSpider` would be then destroyed, the worker `TThread` would be not and the queued message would still be delivered, which could cause all kinds of problems.

As we are using a custom thread pool, however, all of the threads are destroyed when the thread pool is destroyed (in the `Stop` method), which makes sure that all the queued anonymous methods are processed before the `TWebSpider` is destroyed.

Downloader stage

The downloader stage uses a `THTTPClient` object to download the web page. This task is implemented in the `Asy_HttpGet` method, as follows:

```
procedure TWebSpider.Asy_HttpGet(
  inQueue: TThreadedQueue<string>;
  outQueue: TThreadedQueue<THttpPage>);
var
  httpClient: THTTPClient;
  response: IHTTPResponse;
  url: string;
begin
  TThread.NameThreadForDebugging('Http get');

  httpClient := THTTPClient.Create;
  try
    while inQueue.PopItem(url) = wrSignaled do
    begin
      if inQueue.ShutDown then
        break; //while

    try
      response := httpClient.Get(url);
    except
      if TInterlocked.Decrement(FPageCount) = 0 then
        NotifyFinished;
    end;
```

```
    if (response.StatusCode div 100) = 2 then
      outQueue.PushItem(THttpPage.Create(url, response))
    else if TInterlocked.Decrement(FPageCount) = 0 then
      NotifyFinished;
    end;
    outQueue.DoShutDown;
  finally
    FreeAndNil(httpClient);
  end;
end;
```

As the `Start` method creates multiple tasks, there are multiple `Asy_HttpGet` methods being executed in parallel. This is OK, as each uses its own local variables and there is no conflict between them.

If the web download fails (raises an exception or the response code is not 2xx), the code throws the input URL away. As before, the code then decrements the shared `FPageCount` counter in a thread-safe manner and notifies the owner about job completion if the counter drops to zero.

If everything is OK, the code pushes a `THttpPage` record to the output queue. This record is defined as follows:

```
THttpPage = TPair<string,IHTTPResponse>;
```

Parser stage

The parser stage parses the returned HTML and extracts all hyperlinks (`<a>` tags). Delphi does not contain a HTML parser in a standard distribution and as I wanted to remove any dependencies on third-party HTML parsers, I cheated a bit and used regular expressions to detect `<a href="..."` in the page.

The parser doesn't check whether the returned content is actually in HTML format or not. It merely scans the result for a simple regular expression.

> In production code, you should never parse HTML with a regular expression. This doesn't work. Regular expressions are too limited to parse HTML.

The parser stage sets up the regular expression parser and then loops through all the data in the input queue. Each input is parsed and all detected URLs are sent back to the first stage for filtering. This task is implemented in the `Asy_HtmlParse` method, as follows:

```
procedure TWebSpider.Asy_HtmlParse(
  inQueue: TThreadedQueue<THttpPage>;
  outQueue: TThreadedQueue<string>);
var
  hrefMatch: TRegEx;
  match: TMatch;
  page: THttpPage;
begin
  TThread.NameThreadForDebugging('Html parse');

  hrefMatch := TRegEx.Create('<a href="(.*?)"\s.*?>', [roIgnoreCase,
roMultiLine]);
  while inQueue.PopItem(page) = wrSignaled do
  begin
    if inQueue.ShutDown then
      break; //while

    try
      match := hrefMatch.Match(page.Value.ContentAsString);
      while match.Success do
      begin
        if outQueue.ShutDown then
          break; //while;
        TInterlocked.Increment(FPageCount);
        outQueue.PushItem(match.Groups[1].Value);
        match := match.NextMatch;
      end;
    except
    end;

    NotifyPageProcessed(page.Key);
    if TInterlocked.Decrement(FPageCount) = 0 then
      NotifyFinished;
  end;
end;
```

Each detected `a href` hyperlink represents a new work unit. For each hyperlink, the code increments the number of work units in the pipeline (`FPageCount`) and then pushes the hyperlink into the output queue.

After the input is parsed, the processing of this URL is done. The code therefore decrements the number of processing units and calls the `OnFinished` event handler if necessary.

The need to always maintain the correct state in the shared `FPageCount` counter is what makes writing self-feeding pipelines a complicated process. You must absolutely make sure that you increment the counter for each addition to the pipeline and decrement the counter when the processing unit is not needed anymore.

TIP

Always increment the shared counter before pushing data to the output queue.

Always add data to the output queue before dropping the current processing unit.

This code also triggers the `OnPageProcessed` event, which notifies the main thread that a page was processed, as shown here:

```
procedure TWebSpider.NotifyPageProcessed(const url: string);
begin
  if assigned(OnPageProcessed) then
    TThread.Queue(TThread.Current,
      procedure
      begin
        if assigned(OnPageProcessed)
          OnPageProcessed(url);
      end);
end;
```

The test, queue, and test again pattern is used here for optimization. The second `if assigned(OnPageProcessed)` (inside the anonymous method) test is required, while the initial `if assigned(OnPageProcessed)` test is only used as an optimization step. After all, there is no need to spend time in the `Queue` call if the event handler is not set.

The following screenshot shows the web spider in action:

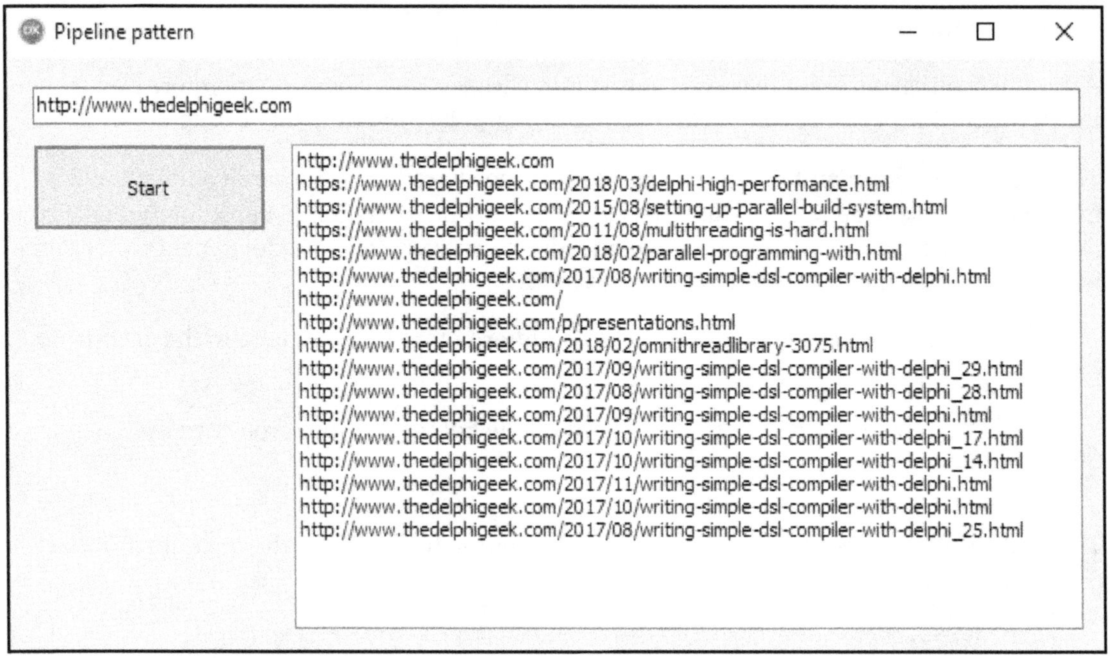

Web spider browsing my blog

Admittedly, the current web spider doesn't do any useful work (except providing a complete example of a complicated pipeline). To convert it into a more useful application, however, you only need to add one stage, which will either save received HTML pages to a disk or store them in a database. This part is left as an exercise for the reader.

Summary

In this chapter, we have explored four more concurrency patterns, in which two of them have been designed as simple drop-in replacements for the original code and two are required for rearchitecting parts of the code.

The thread pool pattern is a variation of an object pool pattern, and is designed to store threads. Instead of creating a new thread each time we need to execute some code in the background, we can take the already created thread from a thread pool and ask it to run our code. This speeds up the performance of the program and allows for some other interesting tricks.

After that, we were introduced to the concept of messaging. Although it belongs to architectural patterns, a proper use of this concept requires detailed knowledge of the tools that are offered by the operating system and the programming environment. This chapter explored three implementations of a messaging subsystem – the first used the Windows messaging infrastructure, the second was based on messaging support that's built into Delphi, and the third was based on being fully built with custom code.

The next section introduced the future pattern. We saw how this pattern allows us to easily push function calculations into the background and do something else while the result is being calculated. Although the future pattern is intentionally very simple, we can make it more powerful by combining it with the messaging pattern.

The last pattern in this chapter, pipeline, is more architectural than a design pattern because it requires a program redesign from standard code to a solution based on messaging. Still, it allows us to parallelize code that cannot be put into multiple threads with other approaches and because of that it's a powerful tool for any programmer's toolbox.This brings our journey of standard design patterns to an end.

Other Books You May Enjoy

If you enjoyed this book, you may be interested in these other books by Packt:

Expert Delphi
Paweł Głowacki

ISBN: 978-1-78646-016-5

- Understand the basics of Delphi and the FireMonkey application platform as well as the specifics of Android and iOS platforms
- Complete complex apps quickly with access to platform features and APIs using a single, easy-to-maintain code base
- Work with local data sources, including embedded SQL databases, REST servers, and Backend-as-a-Service providers
- Take full advantage of mobile hardware capabilities by working with sensors and Internet of Things gadgets and devices
- Integrate with cloud services and data using REST APIs and scalable multi-tier frameworks for outstanding multi-user and social experience
- Architect and deploy powerful mobile back-end services and get super-productive by leveraging Delphi IDE agile functionality
- Get to know the best practices for writing a high-quality, reliable, and maintainable codebase in the Delphi Object Pascal language

Leave a review - let other readers know what you think

Please share your thoughts on this book with others by leaving a review on the site that you bought it from. If you purchased the book from Amazon, please leave us an honest review on this book's Amazon page. This is vital so that other potential readers can see and use your unbiased opinion to make purchasing decisions, we can understand what our customers think about our products, and our authors can see your feedback on the title that they have worked with Packt to create. It will only take a few minutes of your time, but is valuable to other potential customers, our authors, and Packt. Thank you!

Index

A

B

O

P

Q

T

V

W

Y

www.ingramcontent.com/pod-product-compliance
Lightning Source LLC
Chambersburg PA
CBHW060633060326
40690CB00020B/4392
* 9 7 8 1 8 3 8 9 8 9 1 1 8 *